A-Z MOTORISTS' LONDON

C000072148

London Main Routes at 1" to 1 mile

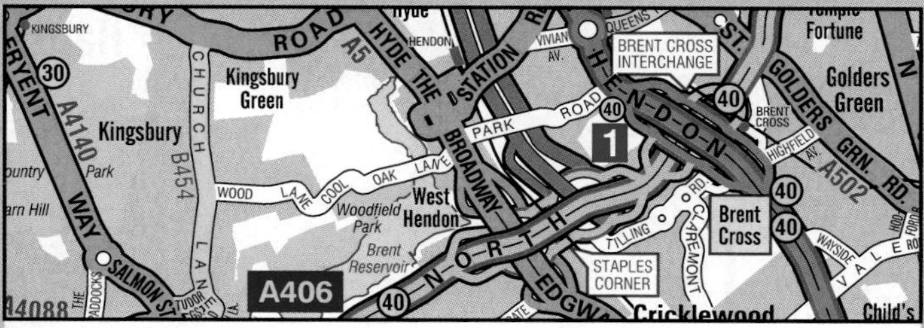

Kingsbury Green
Kingsbury
Fortune
Golders Green
BRENT CROSS INTERCHANGE
Brent Cross
West Hendon
Woodfield Park
Brent Reservoir
STAPLES CORNER
A406
Cricklewood
NORTH CIRCULAR
HYDE
A5
A502
A4140
B454

Key Page .... 2 - 3
Map Pages .... 4 - 35
Index to Streets, Places and Areas, Named Junctions and Selected Tourist Information .... 36 - 52

- Motorway — M3
- Motorway Junction Number
  - Unlimited Interchange — 18
  - Limited Interchange — 19
- Motorway Service Area — S HESTON
- Mileage between Motorway Junctions — 6
- Primary Route — A2
- North & South Circular Roads and Inner Ring Road R
- Primary Route Junction Number — 12
- Primary Route Destination — ROMFORD
- A Road — A320
- B Road — B466
- Dual Carriageway
- Transport for London Road Network (Red Route)
  - Primary Route
  - North & South Circular Roads and Inner Ring Road R
  - A Road
- One Way Road (Motorway, Primary Route & A Road only - Traffic flow indicated by heavy line on driver's left)
- Tunnel
- Major Road Under Construction
- Major Road Proposed
- Selected Other Road
- Junction Name — ELEPHANT & CASTLE
- Toll — TOLL
- Safety Cameras with Speed Limits
  - Single — 30
  - Multiple — 50
  - Variable Speed Limit — V
  - The position of the camera symbol does not indicate the direction of the camera
- Park & Ride — P+R
- Railway & Croydon Tramlink
- Level Crossing and Tunnel
- Railway Station — KINGSTON
- Underground Station — BOND ST.
- DLR Station & Tramlink Stop — SOUTH QUAY
- Airport — LONDON CITY AIRPORT
- Airport Runway
- Built-up Area
- County Boundary
- Map Continuation — 5
- National Grid Reference — 490
- River or Canal
- Wood, Park, Cemetery, Etc.

CONGESTION CHARGING ZONE

The area contained within the Congestion Charging Zone is shown with reduced colours.

Scale: 1:63,360

1 inch (2.54cm) to 1 mile or 1.58 cm to 1 kilometre

0 — 1 — 2 Miles

0 — 1 — 2 — 3 Kilometres

Major Sporting Venues

- Cricket
- Football
- Golf Course — 9 Hole — 18 Hole
- Horse Racing
- Motor Racing
- Rugby
- Tennis
- Stadium
- Place of Interest — • Windsor Castle
- Viewpoint — 180° — 360°

Central London at 9" to 1 mile

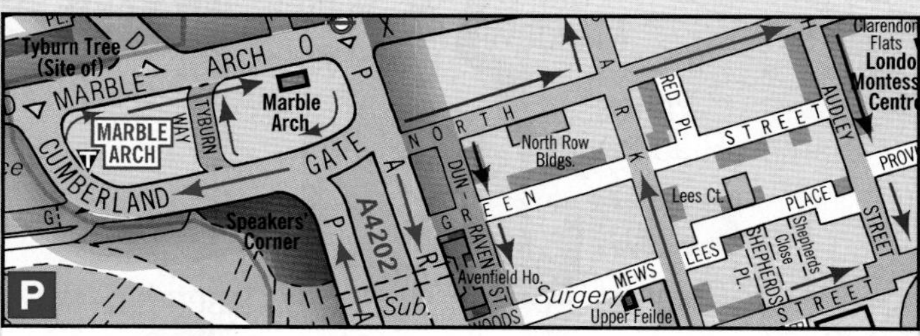

Tyburn Tree (Site of)
MARBLE ARCH
Marble Arch
CUMBERLAND GATE
Speakers' Corner
A4202
North Row Bldgs.
NORTH ROW
Lees Pl.
Avenfield Ho.
Surgery
Upper Feilde
Clarendon Flats
P

Key Page and Reference 53
Map Pages .... 54 - 93
Index to Streets & Selected Places of Interest .... 94 - 119
Index to Hospitals 120

- A Road — A10
- B Road — B326
- Dual Carriageway
- One Way Street
- Junction Name — MARBLE ARCH
- Inner Ring Road — R
- Width Restriction — 7'0"
- Restricted Access — Mon. - Sat. 7am - 7pm
- Pedestrianized Road
- House Numbers (A & B Roads only) — 34 62
- On Street Parking (Restrictions may apply)
- Car Park — P
- Railway Station
- Railway Station Entrance
  - National Rail Network
  - Underground — Symbol is the registered trade mark of Transport for London
  - Docklands Light Railway — DLR
- Borough Boundary
- Postal Boundary
- Congestion Charging Zone Boundary
- Map Continuation — 75
- Buildings
  - Educational Establishment
  - Hospital or Hospice
  - Industrial
  - Leisure or Recreational Facility
  - Office
  - Place of Interest - Public Access
  - Place of Interest - No Public Access
  - Place of Worship
  - Public Building
  - Residential
  - Shopping Centre or Market
  - Other Selected Building
- Cinema
- Fast Ferry
- Fire Station
- Information Centre
- National Grid Reference — 178
- Police Station
- Post Office
- Red Light Camera
- River Boat Trip
- Safety Camera with Speed Limit — 30
  - The position of the camera symbol does not indicate the direction of the camera
- Theatre
- Toilet
  - with facilities for the Disabled
  - without facilities for the Disabled
  - for exclusive use by the Disabled

Scale: 1:7,040

9 inches (22.86 cm) to 1 mile or 14.2 cm to 1 kilometre

0 — 100 — 200 — 300 Yards — ¼ Mile

0 — 100 — 200 — 300 — 400 Metres

Copyright of Geographers' A-Z Map Company Limited

Fairfield Road, Borough Green, Sevenoaks, Kent TN15 8PP

Telephone: 01732 781000 (Enquiries & Trade Sales) or 01732 783422 (Retail Sales)

EDITION 5 2007

www.a-zmaps.co.uk

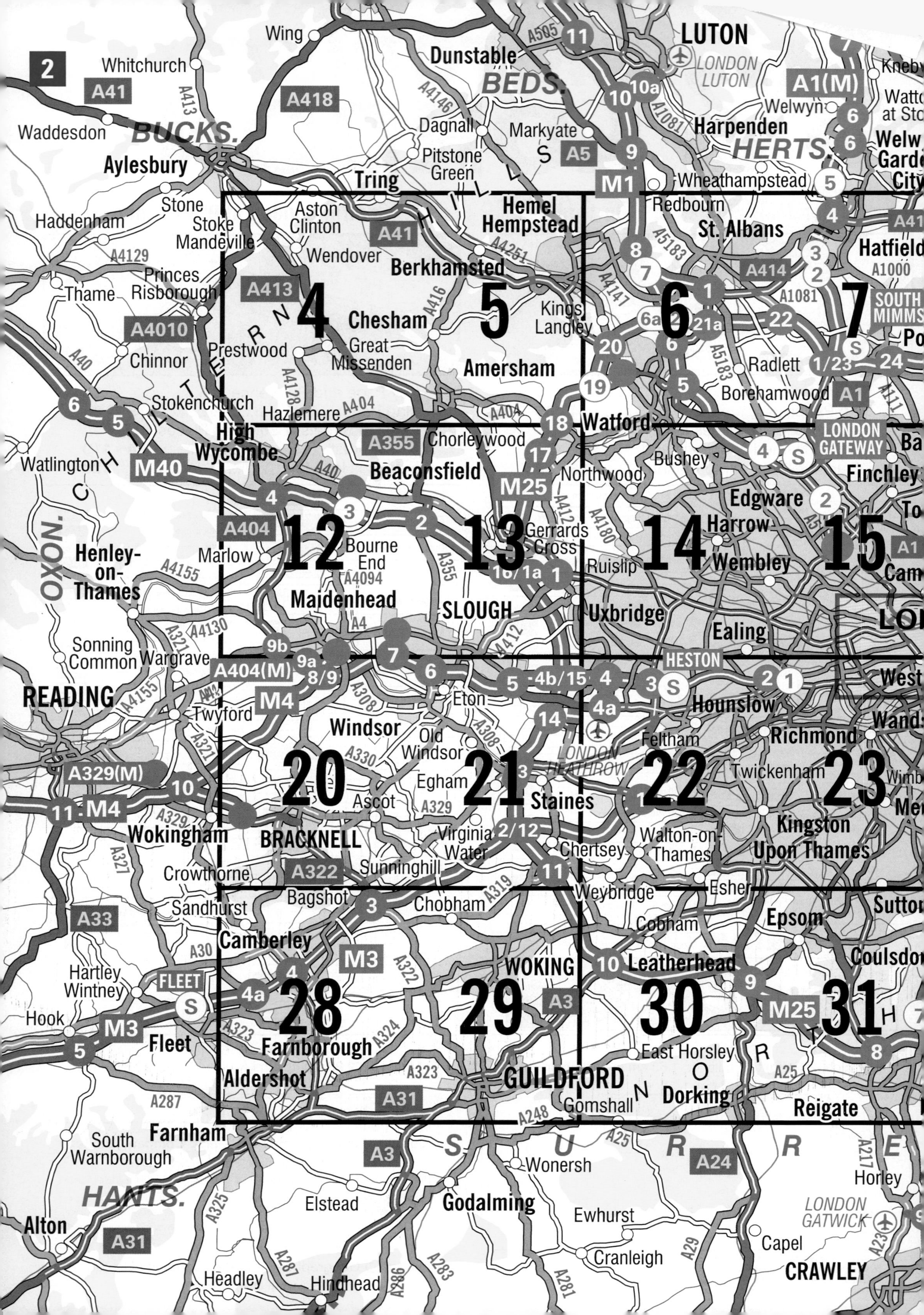

2
Wing
Whitchurch
A41
A418
A413
Waddesdon
BUCKS.
Aylesbury
Dunstable
A505
11
LUTON
LONDON LUTON
BEDS.
10
10a
A4146
Dagnall
Markyate
A5
Pitstone Green
Tring
9
M1
A1081
Harpenden
HERTS.
Wheathampstead
Welwyn
A1(M)
Knebworth
Watton at Stone
Welwyn Garden City
6
5
Haddenham
Stone
Stoke Mandeville
Aston Clinton
A41
Hemel Hempstead
Redbourn
St. Albans
4
A41
Hatfield
A4129
Wendover
Berkhamsted
A4251
8
A5183
3
2
A1000
Thame
Princes Risborough
A413
4
5
A416
A4147
7
6
A414
A1081
7
SOUTH MIMMS
A4010
Chesham
Kings Langley
6a
21a
22
A40
Chinnor
Prestwood
Great Missenden
Amersham
20
A5183
S
Radlett
1/23
24
A4128
19
Borehamwood
A1
6
5
Stokenchurch
Hazlemere
A404
A404
18
Watford
Watlington
M40
High Wycombe
A355
Chorleywood
17
LONDON GATEWAY
Bushey
4
S
A40
Beaconsfield
M25
Northwood
Finchley
4
3
2
A412
A4180
Edgware
2
OXON.
CHILTERN HILLS
A404
12
13
14
15
Henley-on-Thames
Marlow
Bourne End
Gerrards Cross
Harrow
Wembley
A1
A4155
A4094
A355
16/1a
1
Ruislip
Maidenhead
SLOUGH
Uxbridge
A4
Ealing
Sonning Common
A4130
A321
Wargrave
9b
9a
8/9
7
6
A412
A404(M)
5
4b/15
4
3
S
HESTON
2
1
Westminster
READING
A4155
A44
M4
Twyford
A308
Eton
4a
Hounslow
Windsor
Old Windsor
A308
14
Feltham
Richmond
Wandsworth
A321
A330
LONDON HEATHROW
A329(M)
20
21
22
23
Twickenham
10
Egham
3
Staines
Ascot
A329
1
11
M4
A329
Wokingham
BRACKNELL
Virginia Water
2/12
Kingston Upon Thames
A327
Walton-on-Thames
Chertsey
Crowthorne
A322
Sunninghill
11
A319
Weybridge
Esher
Bagshot
Sandhurst
3
Chobham
Sutton
A33
Epsom
Cobham
Camberley
A30
M3
A322
WOKING
10
Leatherhead
Coulsdon
Hartley Wintney
FLEET
4
9
4a
S
28
29
30
31
A3
M25
Hook
M3
A323
5
Fleet
A324
Farnborough
East Horsley
8
A25
Aldershot
A323
GUILDFORD
NORTH DOWNS
Dorking
A287
A31
Gomshall
Reigate
A248
South Warnborough
Farnham
A3
SURREY
A25
A24
A217
Wonersh
Horley
HANTS.
A325
Elstead
Godalming
Ewhurst
LONDON GATWICK
Alton
A31
Cranleigh
Capel
A29
A23
A287
Headley
Hindhead
A286
A283
A281
CRAWLEY

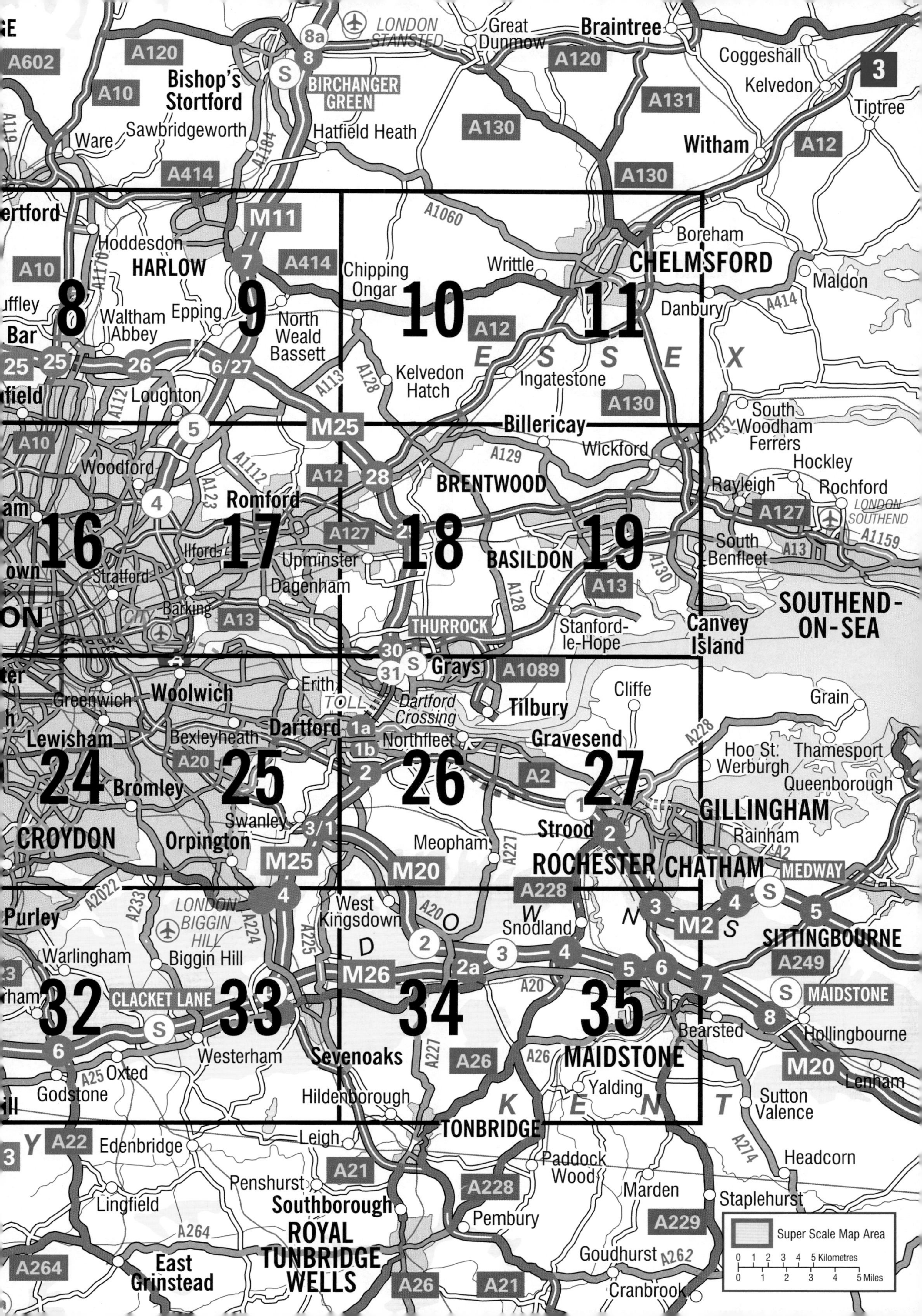
3
LONDON STANSTED
Great Dunmow
Braintree
A120
A602
A10
Bishop's Stortford
BIRCHANGER GREEN
Coggeshall
Kelvedon
Tiptree
A131
A130
Witham
A12
A119
Ware
Sawbridgeworth
A1184
Hatfield Heath
A414
Hertford
M11
A1060
Boreham
CHELMSFORD
Hoddesdon
HARLOW
A1170
Chipping Ongar
Writtle
Maldon
Cuffley
8
9
10
11
Waltham Abbey
Epping
North Weald Bassett
Danbury
Bar
A113
A128
Kelvedon Hatch
ESSEX
Ingatestone
Hatfield
A112
Loughton
M25
Billericay
South Woodham Ferrers
Wickford
A132
Hockley
A1112
A129
Woodford
BRENTWOOD
Rayleigh
Rochford
A123
Romford
LONDON SOUTHEND
A127
A1159
16
17
18
19
Ilford
Upminster
BASILDON
South Benfleet
Stratford
Dagenham
A13
Barking
CITY
THURROCK
Stanford-le-Hope
Canvey Island
SOUTHEND-ON-SEA
Grays
A1089
Erith
Woolwich
Greenwich
TOLL
Dartford Crossing
Tilbury
Cliffe
Grain
Lewisham
Bexleyheath
Dartford
Northfleet
Gravesend
A228
Hoo St. Werburgh
Thamesport
Queenborough
24
25
26
27
A20
Bromley
A2
Swanley
Strood
GILLINGHAM
CROYDON
Orpington
Meopham
A227
Rainham
M20
ROCHESTER
CHATHAM
MEDWAY
A228
Purley
A2022
A233
LONDON BIGGIN HILL
A224
A225
West Kingsdown
Snodland
M2
SITTINGBOURNE
Warlingham
Biggin Hill
M26
A249
KENT
32
33
34
35
CLACKET LANE
MAIDSTONE
Bearsted
Hollingbourne
Westerham
Sevenoaks
A26
Oxted
Godstone
A25
Hildenborough
Yalding
Lenham
Sutton Valence
A22
Edenbridge
Leigh
TONBRIDGE
A21
Paddock Wood
A274
Headcorn
Penshurst
Marden
Lingfield
Southborough
Staplehurst
Pembury
A264
ROYAL TUNBRIDGE WELLS
A229
Goudhurst
A262
East Grinstead
Cranbrook
Super Scale Map Area
0 1 2 3 4 5 Kilometres
0 1 2 3 4 5 Miles

4
AYLESBURY
A
B
C
A413
A41
ASTON CLINTON RD.
WENDOVER
Bedgrove
Buckland
Aston Clinton
Drayton Beauchamp
Wilstone Reservoir
Little Tring
Tring Wharf
New Mill
Tring
Upper Dunsley
Tring Park
Wigginton
West Leith
Weston Turville
Bye Green
Splash Covert
RAF Halton Airfield
Marl Copse
Halton
Astonhill Coppice
Aston Hill
Stoke Mandeville
STATION RD.
A4010
Marsh
North Lee
World's End
Weston Turville Reservoir
Haddington Hill
Halton Camp
Wendover Woods
Halton Wood
Bradnidge Wood
Bittam's Wood
Pavis Wood
Hastoe
Northill Wood
High Scrubs
Drayton Wood
Terrick
Nash Lee
Chalkshire
Wendover
Boddington Hill
Hengrove Wood
Chivery
Buckland Wood
Clanking
Little Kimble
Ellesborough
Butler's Cross
Bacombe Hill
Hale Wood
Baldwin's Wood
St. Leonards
Buckland Common
Coombe
Low Scrubs
Coxgrove Wood
Barn Wood
Stonehill Wood
Widow Croft
Smokey Row
Little Kimble Warren
Beacon Hill
Lodge Hill
High Scrubs
Kingsash
Lordling Wood
Great Kimble
Whorley Wood
Linton's Wood
Askett
Maple Wood
Goodmerhill Wood
Fugsdon Wood
Dunsmore
Little London
Lee Gate
Bray's Wood
Monks Risborough
Pulpit Wood
Pond Wood
Buckmoorend
Chisley Wood
Wendover Dean
Whiteleaf
Hampdenleaf Wood
The Lee
Lowndes Wood
Asheridge
Giles Wood
Hobb's Hill
The Hangings
Hengrove Wood
Little Hampden Common
Little Hampden
Cockshoots Wood
Lee Common
Lee Clump
Chartridge
Princes Risborough
Sergeant's Wood
Green Hailey
Cobblershill
Ballinger Bottom
Bellows Wood
Warren Wood
Ballinger Common
Windsor Hill
Kingsfield Wood
Hillock Wood
Furze Wood
Hampden Bottom
Redland End
Barnes's Grove
CHILTERN HILLS
3
Great Hampden
Oaken Grove
Mobwell
South Heath
Parslow's Hillock
Lodge Wood
Hotley Bottom
Rignall Wood
Keepershill Wood
A4128
B485
Loosley Row
Monkton Wood
Angling Spring Wood
Great Missenden
Wendover Woods
BUCKINGHAMSHIRE
Lacey Green
College Plantation
Prestwood
Atkins Wood
Hobbshill Wood
Hedgemoor
Mantle's Wood
Hyde Heath
Nanfan Wood
Stony Green
Bryant's Bottom
Peterley Wood
Callows Hill
Speen
Piggott's Wood
Little Boys Heath
Munt's Wood
Upper North Dean
Long Field Wood
Little Kingshill
Haleacre Wood
Little Missenden
River Misbourne
Walter's Ash
Courns Wood
Lower North Dean
Heath End
Park Wood
Little Stocking Wood
Great Kingshill
Holmer Green
Bradenham
The Coppice
Allnutt's Wood
Chalkpit Wood
Naphill Common
Cryers Hill
Beamond End
Pimlock's Wood
Widmer End
The Rough Park
Woodrow
Naphill
Great Cookshall Wood
Hughenden Valley
A404
Hearnton Wood
Common Wood
Penn Wood
Penn Street
12
Hazlemere
Downley
Hughenden Manor
Tragoe's Plantation
Little Cockshoots Wood
Charcoal Grove
West Wycombe
Great Cockshoots
Terriers
Common Wood
Penn Bottom
AMERSHAM ROAD
WYCOMBE RD.
BRADENHAM ROAD
AYLESBURY RD.
LONDON ROAD

5
D
E
F
Little Gaddesden
Hudnall
Aldbury
Aldbury Common
Ashridge Park
Thunderdell Wood
Hill Wood
Breach Wood
Gaddesden Row
Great Gaddesden
St. Margaret's
Water End
Nettleden
Rail Copse
Chestnut Wood
New Ground
Northchurch Common
Berkhamsted Common
Great Frithsden Copse
Frithsden
Heizdin's Wood
HERTFORDSHIRE
1
Grovehill
Piccotts End
Highfield
Dudswell
Berkhamsted
Northchurch
Potten End
Little Heath
Gutteridge Wood
Dell Wood
Gadebridge
Newsetts Wood
Shootersway
Fields End
Warners End
Cock Grove
Hammerfield
Counters End
HEMEL HEMPSTEAD
Pouchen End
Chaulden
Green End
Heath End
Pancake Wood
Hockeridge Wood
Geary's Wood
The Rookery
Bourne End
Boxmoor
Two Waters
2
Bennet End
Dropping's Wood
Great Wood
Felden
Apsley
Crowfoot's Wood
Bellingdon
Ashley Green
Shendish Airfield
Rucklers Lane
Whelpley Hill
Bovingdon
Great Hivings
Lye Green
Orchard Leigh
Pudds Cross
Bovingdon Green
Scatterdells Wood
Pond Park
Hilltop
Newtown
Codmore
Ley Hill
Tower Hill
Botley
Venus Hill
Chapel Croft
3
The Bury
Chesham
Hogpits Bottom
Lower Plantation
Woodman's Wood
Chipperfield
Chipperfield Common
Chessmount
Flaunden
Belsize
Pednormead End
Waterside
Commonwood
Berrybushes Wood
Lower Bois
Frith Wood
Bucks Hill
Chesham Bois
Hanginglane Wood
Sarratt
Baldwin's Wood
Chenies Bottom
Templepan Wood
Amersham on the Hill
Lane Wood
Latimer
Mount Wood
Sarratt Bottom
AMERSHAM
Mantles Green
Church End
Micklefield Green
Great Wood
Chenies
4
Amersham Old Town
Amersham Common
Little Chalfont
M25
Welling Grove
Beechengrove Wood
Loudwater
Rodgers Wood
Carpenter's Wood
Chorleywood Common
Chorleywood West
Chorleywood
Pollards Wood
Roughwood Park
Chorleywood Bottom
Rickmansworth Park
Coleshill
Brentford Wood
The Swillet
A41
A4251
A4146
A4147
A416
A404
A413
A355
A412
B4505
B4506
B485
B4442
B487

6
A
B
C
1
2
3
4
Gaddesden Row
Redbourn
Hatching Green
Harpenden
Amwell
Nomansland
Nomansland Common
Ayres End
Church End
Holtsmere End
Childwick Green
Sandridge
Grovehill
Cupid Green
Piccotts End
Highfield
New Greens
Bernard's Heath
Marshalswick
Townsend
Windmillhill Wood
Old Gorhambury House
Cypress Wood
ST. ALBANS
Fleetville
HEMEL HEMPSTEAD
Adeyfield
Leverstock Green
Westwick Row
Verulamium Roman Town
Prae Wood
The Plantation
Ladies Grove Wood
Batch Wood
The Camp
St. Stephens
St. Julians
Bennetts End
Pimlico
Potters Crouch Plantations
Potters Crouch
Chiswell Green
Sopwell
Apsley
Shendish Airfield
Nash Mills
Long Deans
Rucklers Lane
Park Street
Napsbury
London Colney
Hanging Wood
Bedmond
How Wood
Frogmore
Broad Colney
Kings Langley
Abbots Langley
Waterdale
Bloom Wood
Smug Oak
Colney Street
Bricket Wood
Chipperfield Common
Leavesden
Woodside
Bricket Wood Common
Nine Acres
Hound's Wood
Monks Wood
Berrybushes Wood
Hunton Bridge
Leavesden Green
Coldharbour Plantation
Garston Park
Peartree Wood
Radlett
Bucks Hill
Langleybury
Kingswood
LEAVESDEN GREEN
Garston
Meriden
Juniper Hill
Templepan Wood
HUNTON BRIDGE
THE DOME
North Watford
Kemprow
High Cross
Aldenham
BERRYGROVE
Battlers Green
Moses Dell
Great Wood
The Grove Park
Lees Wood
Chandler's Cross
Harrocks Wood
Whippendell Wood
Round Bush
Letchmore Heath
Welling Grove
Patchetts Green
Cassiobury Park
WATFORD
Elstree Aerodrome
Hilfield Park Reservoir
Aldenham Park
Loudwater
Croxley Green
West Watford
Aldenham Country Park
Aldenham Reservoir
Rickmansworth Park
Holywell
Watford
The Rookery
Oxhey
Bushey
M1
M10
M25
A41
A414
A405
A5183
A1081
A4147
A4146
A4251
A412
A411
A1057
A5183
B487
B4630
B556
B462

Coleman Green
Lemsford
Handside
Peartree
WELWYN GARDEN CITY
Woodhall
Hall Grove
Hatfield Hyde
Stanborough
Symondshyde Great Wood
The Commons
Mill Green
Hatfield Garden Village
Cooper's Green
Hook's Wood
Cut Field Wood
Home Covert
HATFIELD
The Ryde
Birchwood
Roe Green
Old Hatfield
Home Park
Hatfield House
Ellenbrook
Oxlease
Smallford
Nast Hyde
Sleapshyde
South Hatfield
Bullen's Green
Colney Heath
Marshmoor
Millward's Park
Roestock
Welham Green
Bush Wood
Frederick's Wood
North Mymms
North Mymms Park
Tyttenhanger Park
Water End
Bell Bar
Brick Kiln Wood
Brookmans Park
Gobions Wood
Walsingham Wood
Cobs Ash
Cangsley Grove
Hawkshead Wood
Redwell Wood
Mymmshall Wood
Swanley Bar
Little Heath
Shenleybury
South Mimms
Potters Bar
Combe Wood
Rabley
Bignells Corner
Ridge
Bigpursley Wood
Shenley
SOUTH MIMMS
BIGNELLS CORNER
Bentley Heath
Dancers Hill
Ganwick Corner
Wrotham Park
High Canons
Kitts End
Well End
Saffron Green
Monken Hadley
Hadley
Borehamwood
High Barnet
BARNET
Rowley Green
Arkley
Chipping Barnet
Ducks Island
Underhill
Barnet
Scratch Wood
Deacons Hill
Boys Hill
STIRLING CORNER
Brocket Hill
Garden Wood
Chisel Shelf
Cole Green
Birch Green
Letty Green
Staines Green
Essendon
Backhouse Wood
West End
Brickkiln Wood
Conduit Wood
Deeve Wood
Coombe Wood
Little Berkhamsted
Bedwell Park
Bayford
Bayford Wood
Home Wood
Woodside
Wildhill
Epping Green
Ashen Grove
Calves Grove
Nine Acre Wood
Tylers Causeway
Newgate Street
Northaw Great Wood (Country Park)
Grimes Bottom
Home Wood
Well Wood
Nyn Park
Leggatts Wood
Cuffley
Northaw
Hook Wood
Barvin Park
Cattlegate
Pond Wood
Little Beechhill Wood
Botany Bay
ENFIELD CHASE
Hadley Wood
Fernyhill Wood
Ride Wood
TRENT PARK (Country Park)
Williams Wood
Oak Wood
Shaws Wood
Church Wood
New Barnet
Cockfosters
East Barnet
Oakwood Park
Oakwood
Oak Hill Park
A414
A1(M)
M25
A1
A1000
A1001
A1057
A1005
A1081
A111
A411
A5135
A6129
A110
B158
B157
B156
B556
B5378
B653
B195
B197
B1455
B6426
B193

8
A414
A
B
C
HERTFORD
HERTINGFORDBURY
COLE GREEN BY-PASS
Hertingfordbury
Staines Green
WARE RD.
LONDON RD.
STANSTEAD RD.
B1502
A119
B1000
Great Amwell
Stanstead Abbots
Hunsdonbury
Bury Plantation
Lord's Wood
St. Margarets
Hertford Heath
Golding's Wood
A10
A1170
Hailey
Briggens Park
Balls Wood
A414
Roydon
B158
Broadgreen Wood
Weepings Wood
Dells Wood
Woollensbrook
Box Wood
Rye Park
RYE HOUSE
Goose Green
Bayford
Bayford Wood
Hoddesdonpark Wood
Highfield Wood
Hoddesdon
Spitalbrook
Dobb's Weir
Halls Green
Brickendon
Blackfan Wood
Cowheath Wood
HERTFORDSHIRE
Broxbourne
BROXBOURNE
Broxbourne Wood
Roydon Hamlet
B194
Epping Green
Ashen Grove
Tylers Causeway
Calves Grove
Carneles Green
Baas Hill
Nazeing
1
2
3
4
The Warren
Wormley Wood
Wormley West End
Keysers Estate
Lower Nazeing
Derry's Wood
Wormley
Thunderfield Grove
Newgate Street
Bumble's Green
Nazeing Gate
Hell Wood
Turnford
Nazeing Long Green
7
Hammond Street
Cheshunt Park
Flamstead End
Deerpark Wood
Lucas End
B156
B157
Rosedale
Holyfield
Galleyhill Wood
E
Claverhambury
Stocking Grove
Cuffley
CUFFLEY
Goff's Oak
Cheshunt
Fishers Green
Aimes Green
Churchgate
B176
B198
Cemy.
Bury Green
River Lee Navigation
Bowyer's Water
Royal Gunpowder Mills
Cattlins
Home Wood
Cattlegate
M25
25
Waltham Cross
A121
Waltham Abbey
Wood Green
26
Upshire
6
CREWS HILL
Holdbrook
Crews Hill
Whitewebbs Wood
Whitewebbs Park
Bulls Cross
Bullsmoor
A1055
A1010
Freezy Water
Botany Bay
Clay Hill
Beech Hill Park
Forty Hill
Enfield Wash
Albany Park
Enfield Lock
A112
High Beech
Hilly Fields Park
A1005
Sewardstone
Aldergrove Wood
Williams Wood
Shaws Wood
Chase Side
Brimsdown
Enfield Town
ENFIELD
Enfield Highway
Durants Park
Hill Wood
King George's Reservoir
World's End
Grange Park
Bush Hill Park
Town Park
Sewardstonebury
Bury Wood
16
Ponders End
Oakwood Park
Oakwood
Connaught Water
Warren Hill
Chingford Plain
The Hawk Wood
A104
A1069
A110
A105
THE RIDGEWAY
CAMBRIDGE ROAD
HERTFORD ROAD
MOLLISON AVENUE
SEWARDSTONE ROAD
DOWDING WAY
SOUTHBURY ROAD
WINDMILL HILL
VALLEY ROAD
Jubilee Park

D
E
F
9
1
2
3
4
M11
M25
A414
A1169
A1025
A1019
A113
A121
A1168
A1112
B181
B182
B1393
B183
B172
B175
B184
Home Wood
Gilston
Pye Corner
Eastwick
Temple Fields
Old Harlow
Harlow Mill
The Mores
Downhall Wood
Parvilles
Newman's End
Matching
Matching Tye
Matching Green
Matching Park
Churchgate Street
Mark Hall North
Mark Hall South
Little Parndon
Netteswell
Harlow Tye
Housham Tye
Carter's Green
Hobbs Cross
Loyter's Green
New Way
Church Langley
Hare Street
The High
HARLOW
Tye Green
Brays Grove
Threshers Bush
Little Laver
High Laver
Great Parndon
Passmores
Potter Street
Foster Street
Tilegate Green
Magdalen Laver
Katherines
Moreton Mill
Newhouse
Latton Bush
Kingsmoor
Stewards
Mark Bushes
Broadley Common
Sumners
Hastingwood
Moreton
Parndon Wood
Cemy.
Jack's Hatch
Rye Hill
Pedlars End
Bobbingworth
Round Spring
Tyler's Green
Bovinger
Lower Bobbingworth Green
Long Walk
Epping Green
Epping Upland
Thornwood Common
North Weald Airfield
North Weald Bassett
Dewley Wood
The Lower Forest
Orange Field Plantation
Roughtalley's Wood
Greensted Green
Ongar Wood
Chipping Ongar
Greensted
ESSEX
Cobbin's Brook
Gernon Bushes
Coopersale
High Wood
Birching Coppice
Ongar Park Wood
Toot Hill
Rookery Wood
Mount Wood
Hawkshill Wood
Colliers Hatch
Clatterford End
Epping
Gravelpit Wood
Coopersale Street
Bell Common
Gaynes Park
Tawney Common
Ivy Chimneys
Fiddlers Hamlet
Stewards Green
Knightsland Wood
Northlands Wood
Woodhatch
Stanford Rivers
Mount End
Beachet Wood
Warren Wood
Little End
Icehouse Wood
Hare Street
Barber's Wood
Long Plantation
Icehouse Plantation
Twentyacre Wood
Theydon Bois
Theydon Mount
Berwick Ham
Tenacre Wood
Aspen Wood
Navestock Park
Stapleford Tawney
Bob's Barn Wood
Theydon Garnon
Hobbs Cross
Langford Bottom
Broom Wood
Redoak Wood
Birch Wood
Shales More
Church Wood
Debden Green
Gaunt's Wood
Cemy.
River Roding
Passingford Bridge
Navestock
Long Shaw
Stapleford Tawney Airfield
Debden
Abridge
Broadfield Shaw
Curtismill Green
Sabine's Green
Great Wood
Deerbarn Wood
Horseman Side
Loughton
Lambourne
Bentleyfield Wood
Stapleford Abbotts
Navestock Common
Watton's Green
Waterhales
High Wood
Nuper's Hatch
Lambourne

Parvilles
White Roding
Manwood Green
Leaden Roding
Clatterford End
Tye Green
Margaret Roding
Margaret Roding Wood
Good Easter
Nether Street
Abbess Roding
Abbess End
Four Wantz
Farmbridge End
Mashbury
Matching Green
Chalk End
Brickles Wood
Woodend
Beech Wood
Berners Wood
Pepper's Green
Nightingale Wood
Beauchamp Roding
Blackcat
Butthatch Wood
Berners Roding
Little Laver
Birds Green
Boyton Cross
Norwood End
Nor Wood
Roxwell
Moreton Mill
Newhouse
Skreens Park
Miller's Green
Shellow Bowells
Willingale
Fyfield
Spains Wood
Clatterford End
Wall's Green
Newney Green
Pedlars End
Witney Wood
Cannon's Green
Pigstye Green
Cooksmill Green
Bobbingworth
Round Spring
Long Walk
Shelley
Radley Green
Oxney
Lady Grove
New Plantation
Norton Mandeville
Furze Woods
Norton Heath
Horsfrithpark Wood
Highwood
Edney Common
Loves Green
A414
High Ongar
Chipping Ongar
Ongar Wood
Greensted
King Street
High Woods
Writtle Deer Park
Parsons Spring
Barrow Wood
Coppice Wood
Parkponds Wood
Marden Ash
Nine Ashes
Paslow Wood Common
Blackmore
Elkins Green
Birch Spring
College Wood
Deerslade Wood
Box Wood
Stoneymore Wood
Littlebury
Bell Grove
Beggar Hill
Millgreen Common
Fryerning Wood
Mill Green
The Grove
Stanford Rivers
Menagerie Wood
Courtfield Wood
Stondon Massey
Clapgate
Portsmoorhall Wood
Little End
Park Wood
Hare Street
Bushy Wood
Tip's Cross
Hay Green
Woodbarns Spring
Green Street
Fryerning
Aspen Wood
Ireland Grove
Pole's Wood
Hook End
Wyatt's Green
A12
Ingatestone
Navestock Park
Church Wood
Doddinghurst
Swallows Cross
Beacon Hill
Kelvedon Hatch
TRUELOVES INTERCHANGE
Broom Wood
Church Wood
Brizes Wood
Peartree Green
Heybridge
Kelvedon Common
Fox Hatch
Doddinghurst Common
Long Wood
Lodge Wood
Mountnessing
Park Wood
Navestock
Navestock Side
Alders Wood
Padham's Green
Bentley
MARYLANDS INTERCHANGE
Home Wood
Sabine's Green
Crow Green
Harespring Wood
The Mores
Brick House Wood
Common
Weald
Horseman Side
Coxtie Green
Canterbury Tye Spring
Arnold's Wood
Waterhales
Bishops Hall Park
Pilgrims Hatch
Hutton
Locksmith Wood
Hall Wood
A12
Shenfield
Weald Park (Country Park)

D
E
F
1
2
3
4
Breeds
Broad's Green
Minnow End
Little Waltham
Russell Green
Blatche's Wood
Fanner's Green
Chignall Smealy
Sparrowhawk Wood
Blasford Hill
Lost Wood
Toppinghoehall Wood
Partridge Green
A130
A12
20a
HATFIELD PEVEREL INTERCHANGE (SOUTH)
Bushy Wood
Broomfield
The Grove
Mowden
Parsonage Green
Boreham
Brakey Wood
Chignall St. James
BOREHAM INTERCHANGE
19
Springfield
River Chelmer
Holybreds Wood
Scrub Wood
Little Baddow
A1060
A1016
A138
A1090
B1137
B1008
Chelmer Village
Admiral's Park
West Park
Great Oxney Green
Writtle
Long Spring Wood
Blake's Wood
Hall Wood
Lingwood Common
CHELMSFORD
Moulsham
Essex
SANDON INTERCHANGE
P+R Mon-Sat
Bellhill Wood
Danbury
Widford
A414
A1114
Great Baddow
Sandon
18
Danbury Country Park
Writtle Wood
Lower Green
Woodhill
Horne Row
South Wood
Hylands Park
Moulsham Thrift Wood
E
X
B1009
B1007
King Wood
Galleyend
HOWE GREEN INTERCHANGE
17
Thorn Wood
Butt's Green
Chapel Wood
Howe Green
Mead's Grove
Bicknacre
15
WEBBS FARM INTERCHANGE
Galleywood
Galleywood Common
A12
GALLEYWOOD / STOCK INTERCHANGE
B1418
B1002
Margaretting
Crondon
16
Temple Grove
A130
East Hanningfield
Margaretting Tye
Temple Wood
Pound Wood
Rook Wood
Forest Wood
West Hanningfield
Tye Green
Little Wood
Long Wood
Swan Wood
Blythhedges Spring Wood
RHS Garden Hyde Hall
Blythhedges Wood
Buttsbury
White's Wood
Stock
Hounden Wood
Hanningfield Reservoir
Coalhill
Rettendon
Kiln Common
South Hanningfield
Queen's Park Country Park
Forty Acre Plantation
Foxearth Wood
Thrift Wood
Brock Hill
Gorse Wood
Queen's Park
Rettendon Shaw
Lake Meadows
Downham
Morrgarden Wood
Gooseberry Green
Ramsden Heath
Rectory Wood
Norsey Wood
Meepshole Wood
BILLERICAY
Devil's Wood
A132
Battlesbridge
570
74
78
12
08
04
200
96

A
B
C
1
2
3
4
A4010
M40
A404
A404(M)
A308(M)
M4
A40
A4155
A4130
A4094
A308
A4128
A4
B482
B474
B4440
B4447
B3028
B3026
4
3
9a
9b
20
7
HIGH WYCOMBE
MARLOW
MAIDENHEAD
BEACONSFIEL
BUCKINGHA
Naphill
Naphill Common
Hughenden Valley
Cryers Hill
Widmer End
Beamond End
Woodrow
Penn Street
Downley
Hughenden Manor
Hazlemere
Terriers
West Wycombe
West Wycombe Park
Totteridge
King's Wood
Common Wood
Tylers Green
Penn
Sands
Wycombe Wanderers
Micklefield
Beacon Hill
Knotty Green
Booker
Cressex
Wycombe Marsh
Lane End
Loudwater
Forty Green
Handy Cross
Wycombe Air Park
Wooburn Moor
Holtspur
Flackwell Heath
Chisbridge Cross
Marlow Bottom
Fern
Wooburn Green
Well End
Little Marlow
Cores End
Wooburn
Wooburn Common
Lower Woodend
Bovingdon Green
Abbotsbrook
Bourne End
Dipple Wood
Littleworth Common
Bisham
Bisham Abbey
Cookham Dean
Hardings Green
Cookham
Cookham Rise
Cliveden
River Thames
Temple
Hurley
Hurley Bottom
Maidenhead Court
North Town
Furze Platt
Pinkneys Green
Taplow
Burnham
Lent
Lent Rise
Highway
Boyn Hill
Fishery
Burchett's Green
Warren Row
Holloway
Tittle Row
Knowl Hill
Littlewick Green
Woolley Green
Cox Green
Bray Wick
Bray
Lake End
Dorney Reach
Dorney
Woodlands
Hitcham Park

AMERSHAM
13
A413
A404
A355
A40
A412
A4
A4020
A4007
A408
M40
M25
M4
Little Chalfont
Chorleywood West
Chorleywood
Chorleywood Common
Chorleywood Bottom
Loudwater
Rickmansworth
Batchworth
Batchworth Heath
Moneyhill
Mill End
Heronsgate
The Swillet
HERTS
Coleshill
Pollards Wood
Philipshill Wood
Chiltern Open Air Museum
Hodgemoor Woods
Chalfont St. Giles
Chalfont Common
Seer Green
Jordans
Farm Wood
Chalfont St. Peter
Maple Cross
West Hyde
Hill End
Park Wood
Mount Pleasant
Harefield
South Harefield
Layter's Green
Austenwood
Gerrards Cross
Bulstrode Park
Oakend Wood
Denham Aerodrome
Denham Garden Village
Denham Green
Higher Denham
Tatling End
Denham
DENHAM ROUNDABOUT
SWAKELEYS ROUNDABOUT
Burtley Wood
Bower Wood
Hedgerley Green
Hedgerley
Hedgerley Hill
Hedgerley Park
Stoke Common
Fulmer
Egypt Woods
Egypt
Burnham Beeches
Farnham Common
Willowbank
New Denham
Uxbridge
Long Coppice
Round Coppice
Black Park Country Park
East Burnham
Stoke Poges
Wexham Street
Iver Heath
Farnham Royal
Britwell
Manor Park
Stoke Green
Wexham
Wexham Court
Langley Park
Shreding Green
Iver
Cowley
Cowley Peachey
Little Britain
Yiewsley
George Green
Middle Green
SLOUGH
Chalvey
Upton
Langley
Richings Park
Thorney
West Drayton
Eton Wick
Colham Green

14
A
B
C
1
2
3
4
6
13
22
WATFORD
HARROW
EALING
Uxbridge
M1
A40
A41
A312
A4180
Cassiobury Park
Croxley Green
Rickmansworth
Batchworth
Batchworth Heath
Moor Park
Eastbury
Holywell
West Watford
Watford
The Rookery
Oxhey
Watford Heath
Sherwoods Wood
Bushey
Bushey Heath
Stanmore Common
Merry Hill
Carpenders Park
Elstree Aerodrome
Hilfield Park Reservoir
Aldenham Country Park
Aldenham Reservoir
Aldenham Park
Pear Wood
Cloisters Wood
Heriot's Wood
Harrow Weald Common
Stanmore
Big Wood
Old Hangings
Oxhey Woods
South Oxhey
Northwood
Pinnerwood Park
Pinner Green
Northwood Hills
Copse Wood
Mad Bess Wood
Ruislip Common
Bayhurst Wood Country Park
Ruislip Lido
Park Wood
Duck's Hill
Woodcock Hill
Park Wood
Bishop's Wood
South Harefield
Hatch End
Pinner Park
Harrow Weald
Belmont
Wealdstone
Headstone
Greenhill
Kenton
Pinner
Eastcote Village
Eastcote
Rayners Lane
North Harrow
West Harrow
Harrow on the Hill
Roxeth
Northwick Park
North Wembley
South Harrow
Sudbury
Barham Park
Newyears Green
Ruislip
West Ruislip
Ruislip Manor
Ruislip Gardens
South Ruislip
Ickenham
Swakeleys Roundabout
Master Brewer
Willowbank
RAF Northolt Airfield
Polish War Memorial
Northolt
Gutteridge Wood
North Hillingdon
Hillingdon Court Park
Hillingdon
Target Roundabout
West End
Rectory Park
Belvue Park
Greenford
Greenford Roundabout
Perivale
Cowley
Hayes End
Hillingdon Heath
Yeading
Elthorne Heights
Cowley Peachey
Colham Green
Wood End Green
Wood End
Goulds Green
Little Britain
Country Park
Hayes
Stockley Park
Yiewsley
Dormer's Wells
Southall
Hanwell
West Ealing
West Drayton
Boston Manor
Northfields
Norwood Green
Osterley

15
Borehamwood
Elstree
High Barnet
Hadley
BARNET
Monken Hadley Common
Cockfosters
New Barnet
East Barnet
Chipping Barnet
Arkley
Rowley Green
Ducks Island
Underhill
Barnet Gate
Scratch Wood
Deacons Hill
Boys Hill Wood
LONDON GATEWAY
Edgware Bury
Edgwarebury Park
Nut Wood
Totteridge
Highwood Hill
Beech Wood
Oakleigh Park
Whetstone
Brunswick Park
Osidge
Southgate
Oakwood
Grovelands Park
Palmers Green
Friern Barnet
Woodside Park
North Finchley
Mill Hill
Stonegrove
Edgware
The Hale
Watling
Grahame Park
Burnt Oak
Little Stanmore
Queensbury
Colindale
Roe Green
Hendon
The Hyde
Kingsbury Green
Kingsbury
Fryent Country Park
Barn Hill
Preston
Church End
Holders Hill
Finchley
Colney Hatch
New Southgate
Bounds Green
Bowes Park
Muswell Hill
Hornsey
Coldfall Wood
East Finchley
Fortis Green
Cranley Gardens
Queen's Wood
Highgate Wood
Temple Fortune
Golders Green
Hampstead Garden Suburb
Big Wood
Highgate
Crouch End
Brent Cross
West Hendon
Woodfield Park
Brent Reservoir
Cricklewood
Child's Hill
Golders Hill Park
North End
HAMPSTEAD HEATH
Vale of Health
East Heath
Hampstead
Parliament Hill
Dartmouth Park
Upper Holloway
Holloway
Tufnell Park
Neasden
Dollis Hill
Gladstone Park
Wembley Park
Wembley
Tokyngton
Dudden Hill
Willesden
Church End
Fortune Green
West Hampstead
Brondesbury
Willesden Green
Brondesbury Park
Harlesden
Stonebridge
Kilburn
Kensal Rise
South Hampstead
Swiss Cottage
Chalk Farm
Primrose Hill
Gospel Oak
Kentish Town
Camden Town
Alperton
Lower Place
Park Royal
North Acton
Kensal Green
West Kilburn
St. John's Wood
Maida Vale
Regent's Park
London Zoo
Lisson Grove
Marylebone
Somers Town
St. Pancras
Bloomsbury
Old Oak Common
Wormwood Scrubs
North Kensington
Kensal Town
Westbourne Green
Paddington
Bayswater
West Acton
East Acton
White City
Acton
Notting Hill
Hyde Park
Kensington Gardens
Kensington Palace
Mayfair
Soho
West End
St. James's Park
Buckingham Palace
Westminster
Knightsbridge
Kensington
Shepherds Bush
Bedford Park
Acton Green
Gunnersbury
Gunnersbury Park
Brook Green
Brompton
Belgravia
Victoria
Olympia
HYDE PARK CORNER
MARBLE ARCH
SCOTCH HOUSE
HOLLAND PARK ROUNDABOUT
HAMMERSMITH BROADWAY
CHISWICK ROUNDABOUT
GUNNERSBURY PARK
SAVOY CIRCUS
WHITE CITY
GYPSY CORNER
HANGER LANE
PARK ROYAL JUNCTION
HARROW ROAD
NEASDEN JUNCTION
STAPLES CORNER
BRENT CROSS INTERCHANGE
HENLYS CORNER
FIVEWAYS CORNER
APEX CORNER
MILL HILL CIRCUS
STIRLING CORNER
SWISS COTTAGE
BRITANNIA JUNCTION
MARYLEBONE FLYOVER
BAKER STREET
EUSTON UNDERPASS
ARCHWAY
NAG'S HEAD
A1
M1
A41
A406
A40
A501
A400
A503
A202
A4202
A3220
A308
A4
A5
A110
A111
A1000
A5109
A411
A504
A598
A502
A407
A404
A4020
A4000
A402
A315
A1003
A109
A1201
A5200
A5205
7
16
23

16
A
B
C
1
2
3
4
15
24
8
ENFIELD
Enfield Town
Chase Side
Enfield Highway
Brimsdown
World's End
Grange Park
Bush Hill Park
Ponders End
Sewardstonebury
Epping Forest
Oakwood
Winchmore Hill
Lower Edmonton
Southgate
Palmers Green
Edmonton
Upper Edmonton
Chingford
South Chingford
Chingford Mount
Chingford Hatch
Chingford Green
Highams Park
Hale End
Buckhurst Hill
Woodford Wells
Woodford Side
Woodford Green
Woodford
Bowes Park
Bounds Green
Wood Green
Tottenham
Tottenham Hale
Muswell Hill
Noel Park
Hornsey
West Green
South Tottenham
Walthamstow
Upper Walthamstow
South Woodford
Snaresbrook
Higham Hill
Harringay
Hornsey Vale
Stroud Green
Stamford Hill
Upper Holloway
Finsbury Park
Stoke Newington
Upper Clapton
Lower Clapton
Clapton Park
Leyton
Leytonstone
Wanstead
Aldersbrook
Lea Bridge
Holloway
Tufnell Park
Highbury
Lower Holloway
Kingsland
Shacklewell
Homerton
Hackney Wick
Temple Mills
Stratford New Town
Stratford
Stratford Marsh
Forest Gate
Manor Park
Upton
West Ham
Upton Park
Plaistow
Barnsbury
Canonbury
Islington
Dalston
Hackney
De Beauvoir Town
South Hackney
Old Ford
Camden Town
Somers Town
Haggerston
Hoxton
Finsbury
Shoreditch
Bethnal Green
Globe Town
Bow
Bow Common
Bromley
Mill Meads
Canning Town
Custom House
Clerkenwell
St. Pancras
Spitalfields
Whitechapel
Mile End
Stepney
Limehouse
Poplar
City
Holborn
Soho
Shadwell
Wapping
Southwark
Rotherhithe
Bermondsey
Newington
Lambeth
Westminster
St. James's
Millwall
Cubitt Town
Silvertown
Greenwich Millennium Village
New Charlton
The O2 (Millennium Dome)
ExCeL
A10
A406
A503
A107
A12
A1
A501
A11
A13
A102
A200
A101
A100
A2
A202

17
9
25
18
88
E S S E X
M11
M25
A12
A13
A406
A1400
A1020
A117
A1112
A118
A124
A125
A123
A113
A1083
A1153
A1240
A1306
A2016
A2041
A206
B173
B174
B175
B177
B191
B1459
B1335
B213
Debden
Abridge
Stapleford Tawney Airfield
Curtismill Green
Loughton
Lambourne
Great Wood
Deerbarn Wood
Bentleyfield Wood
Stapleford Abbotts
Horseman Side
Waterhales
Navestock Common
Watton's Green
Nuper's Hatch
Pygro Wood
High Wood
Lambourne End
Bournebridge
Noak Hill
Chigwell Row
Chigwell
Hainault Forest (Country Park)
Havering-atte-Bower
Havering Park (Country Park)
Pygro Park
Foxburrow Wood
Bower Wood
Hatters Wood
Grange Hill
Hainault
Bedfords Park
Chase Cross
Harold Hill
Woodford Bridge
Hospital Hill Wood
Collier Row
Fairlop
Rise Park
Gallows Corner
Harold Wood
Clayhall
Fullwell Cross
Fairlop Waters
Marks Gate
Raphael Park
Gidea Park
Squirrel's Heath
Clayhall Park
Barkingside
Aldborough Hatch
Mawney
Mawney Park
Moby Dick
Lodge Farm Park
Ardleigh Green
Romford
Haynes Park
Gants Hill
Newbury Park
Little Heath
St. Chad's Park
Chadwell Heath
Heath Park
Hylands Park
Seven Kings Park
Crowlands
Emerson Park
Valentines Park
Seven Kings
Hornchurch
St. Andrew's Park
Cranbrook
Beacontree Heath
Rush Green
St. Leonards Hamlet
Goodmayes
Goodmayes Park
Central Park
Harrow Lodge Park
South Park
Valence Park
Becontree
Ilford
Little Ilford
Loxford
Fair Cross
Dagenham & Redbridge
Dagenham
Elm Park
Barking Park
Mayesbrook Park
Parsloes Park
Goresbrook Park
Old Dagenham Park
Hornchurch Country Park
Barking
Wallend
East Ham
South Hornchurch
Dovers Corner
Chandlers Corner
Lodge Av. Flyover Junc.
Goresbrook Interchange
Heathway
Movers Lane
Barking Riverside
Creekmouth
Channel Tunnel Rail Link
Cemetery
Rainham
Hornchurch Marshes
Beckton
River Thames
Thamesmead North
Thamesmead Central
Thames Gateway Bridge (Proposed)
London City Airport
Rainham Marshes
Wennington
Thamesmead
Thamesmead South
Erith Marshes
Thamesmead East
Wennington Marshes
North Woolwich
Woolwich Ferry
Thamesmead West
Abbey Wood
Aveley Marshes
Belvedere
Plumstead
Woolwich
Eastern Avenue
London Road
Romford Road
Whalebone Lane
Rainham Road
Longbridge Road
Ripple Road
Southend Arterial Rd.
Colchester Rd.
Hornchurch Rd.
High St.
Green Lane
Rush Green Road
Wood Lane
Cranbrook Road
Manor Way
Eastern Way
Western Way
Central Way
Alfreds Way
Thames Avenue
Woolwich Manor Way
Royal Docks Road
Barking Relief Road

18
Navestock Side
Bentley
Crow Green
10
Sabine's Green
Horseman Side
Weald
Coxtie Green
Pilgrims Hatch
Brick House Wood
Canterbury Tye Spring
MARYLANDS INTERCHANGE
MOUNTNESSING
12
Arnold's Wood
Padham's Green
Harespring Wood
Bishops Hall Park
Hall Wood
Shenfield
Hutton
Waterhales
Locksmith Wood
Weald Park (Country Park)
South Weald
St. Vincent's Hamlet
BRENTWOOD
Hutton Mount
Havering's Grove
James's Wood
Bluntswall Wood
Thrift Wood
Hall Wood
Little Bladen's Wood
Noak Hill
Dagnam Park
Front Park
Vicarage Wood
The Oaks
11
Hatters Wood
BROOK STREET INTERCHANGE
Brook Street
Ingrave Common
Harold Hill
Warley
Harts Wood
Barrack Wood
Kent's Wood
Ingrave
Thorndon Park
28
Harold Park
Herongate
Parkhill Wood
A12
A127
A128
A129
A1023
M25
Harold Wood
Tylers Common
Great Warley
Holden's Wood
Ellen's Wood
The Forest Country Park
Home Park
Foxburrow Wood
Coombe Wood
Little Warley
Thorndon Country Park
Friern Manor Wood
Squirrel's Heath
Harold Wood Park
Mill Wood
Childerditch
Ardleigh Green
Haynes Park
Codham Hall Wood
Warley Hall Wood
West Horndon
Emerson Park
17
Hornchurch
St. Andrew's Park
29
Cranham
Upminster
Upminster Park
Elm Park
Corbets Tey
Hacton
Parklands
Cemy.
Bulphan
North Ockendon
ORSETT FEN
Belhus Woods Country Park
CHANDLERS CORNER
Cemetery
Orsett
Orsett Park
Baker Street
South Ockendon
Mardyke Country Park
Belhus Park
Wennington
A1306
A13
A1013
A1089
Aveley
North Stifford
30
THURROCK
26
31
AVELEY MARSHES
Thurrock Lakeside
Chafford Hundred
Orsett Heath
Chadwell St. Mary
Grays

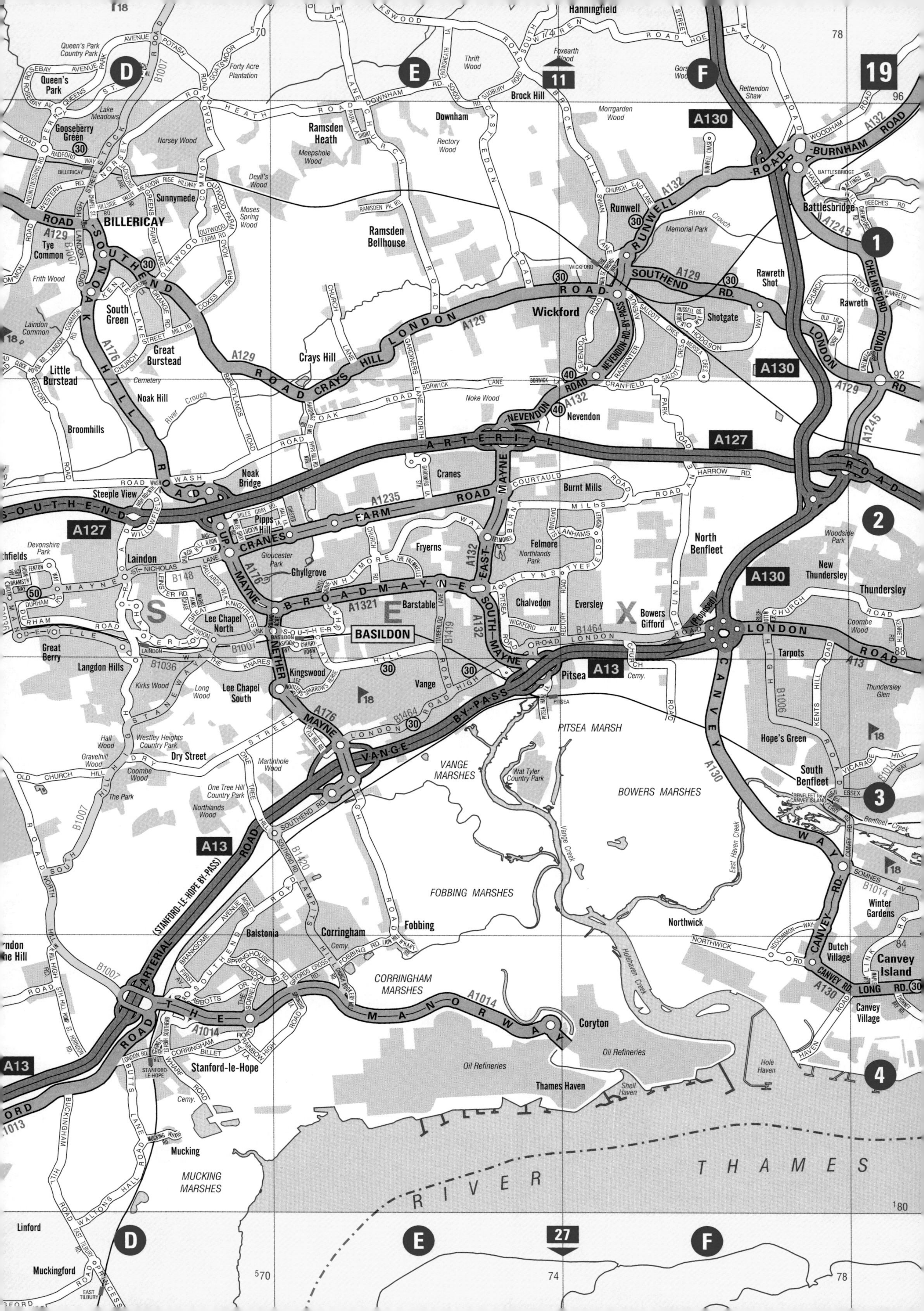

19
11
27
18
D
E
F
1
2
3
4
Billericay
Queen's Park Country Park
Queen's Park
Gooseberry Green
Lake Meadows
Norsey Wood
Sunnymede
Tye Common
Frith Wood
South Green
Laindon Common
Little Burstead
Great Burstead
Noak Hill
Broomhills
Ramsden Heath
Meepshole Wood
Downham
Thrift Wood
Brock Hill
Foxearth Wood
Hanningfield
Rectory Wood
Morrgarden Wood
Rettendon Shaw
Devil's Wood
Moses Spring Wood
Forty Acre Plantation
Ramsden Bellhouse
Crays Hill
Runwell
Memorial Park
River Crouch
Battlesbridge
Rawreth Shot
Rawreth
Wickford
Shotgate
Nevendon
Noke Wood
Cranes
Burnt Mills
Noak Bridge
Steeple View
Pipps Hill
Devonshire Park
Laindon
Gloucester Park
Ghyllgrove
Fryerns
Felmore
Northlands Park
North Benfleet
Woodside Park
New Thundersley
Thundersley
Coombe Wood
Chalvedon
Eversley
Bowers Gifford
Barstable
BASILDON
Lee Chapel North
Great Berry
Langdon Hills
Kirks Wood
Long Wood
Lee Chapel South
Kingswood
Vange
Pitsea
Tarpots
Thundersley Glen
Hope's Green
South Benfleet
PITSEA MARSH
VANGE MARSHES
Wat Tyler Country Park
BOWERS MARSHES
Hall Wood
Gravelhill Wood
Westley Heights Country Park
Dry Street
Martinhole Wood
Coombe Wood
The Park
One Tree Hill Country Park
Northlands Wood
Benfleet Creek
Winter Gardens
FOBBING MARSHES
Fobbing
Corringham
Balstonia
Northwick
Dutch Village
Canvey Island
Canvey Village
CORRINGHAM MARSHES
Coryton
Oil Refineries
Thames Haven
Shell Haven
Hole Haven
Stanford-le-Hope
Mucking
MUCKING MARSHES
Linford
Muckingford
RIVER THAMES
A127
A129
A130
A13
A132
A176
A1235
A1321
A1245
A1014
B1007
B1464
B148
B1036
B1419
B1420
B1006
B1014
(STANFORD-LE-HOPE BY-PASS)

20
A404
Warren Row
Ashley Hill Forest
Dodsley Copse
Maidenhead Thicket
Highway
Furze Hill
Knowl Hill
Littlewick Green
Woolley Green
Tittle Row
Boyn Hill
Cox Green
Woodlands Park
A404(M)
9a
9b
12
BATH ROAD
A4
MAIDENHEAD
Fishery
Bray Wick
Bray
Dorney Reach
Dorney
Lake End
M4
BUCKS.
Lindenhill Wood
Kiln Green
White Waltham Airfield
Great Thrift Wood
Shrubbery Copse
The Cut
A308(M)
8 & 9
Holyport
Water Oakley
Boveney
RIVER THAMES
White Waltham
Waltham St. Lawrence
Shottesbrook Park
Stud Green
Moneyrow Green
Fifield
Oakley Green
Milley Bridge
Gunsbrook
Burningham Wood
Paddock Wood
Paley Street
Touchen End
Great Wood
Mount Scipett Copse
B3024
West End
The Gorse
Wingwood Copse
Beenham's Heath
Pond Wood
Long Wood
Braywoodside
Holliday's Plain
Great Hazes
DRIFT ROAD
HUNGERFORD LANE
Windsor Hill
Foliejon Park
Shurlock Row
Hawthorn Hill
Home Covert
Surells Wood
Gardener's Copse
Windsor Forest
Charity Wood
Jealott's Hill
Westcott Gorse
Nuptown
Winkfield Street
Winkfield
Warren Copse
Billingbear
Tickleback Row
Moss End
Warfield
Maiden's Green
Cranbourne
Fernhill Park
Beech Wood
Pond Wood
Ashridge Wood
Tippen's Wood
Binfield
West End
Newell Green
Woodside
Round Copse
Winkfield Row
Warfield Park
Brookside
The Rough
Wood End
Paddock Wood
Long Copse
Pockets Copse
North Ascot
Ascot Heath
Birch Copse
Priestwood
Dowlesgreen
Popeswood
Big Wood
Bullbrook
Chavey Down
Fireball Hill
A329(M)
A329
A322
A330
A332
A3095
BERKSHIRE WAY
LONDON ROAD
Martin's Heron
Ascot
Sunninghill
Bowledge Hill
Wokingham
Big Wood
Tarman's Copse
Wildridings
Easthampstead
BRACKNELL
Harmanswater
Holme Green
Easthampstead Park
Great Hollands
Swinley Park
Kingsride
South Ascot
Gardeners Green
Cemy.
Hanworth
Buttersteep Hill
Old Windsor
NINE MILE RIDE
Gorrick Plantation
Hut Hill
Gravel Hill
Penny Hill
Pudding Hill
Wokingham Without
Wickham Bushes
New England Hill
Round Hill
Butter Hill
Crowthorne
Simons Wood
Bagshot Park
Windlesham
Queen's Wood
Bagshot
Fisher's Copse
Pine Hill
Poppy Hills
Edgbarrow Woods
Broadmoor Bottom
Bagshot Heath
Paschal Wood
Little
28
3

21
SLOUGH
STAINES
BUCKS.
SURREY
LONDON-HEATHROW AIRPORT
Langley Park
Shreding Green
Iver
Britain
Yiewsley
George Green
Middle Green
West Drayton
Thorney
Richings Park
Thorney Country Park
Eton Wick
Chalvey
Upton
Langley
Langley Roundabout
Sutton
Myrke
Ditton Park
Upton Court Park
Eton
Royal Windsor
Clewer Village
Windsor Castle
Windsor
The Home Park
Datchet
Datchet Common
Southlea
The Queen Mother Reservoir
Brands Hill
Colnbrook
Poyle
Longford
Harmondsworth
Sipson
Moor Junction
Old Wood
Horton
Terminal 5A (Open Spring 2008)
Terminal 5B (Open Spring 2008)
Clewer Green
Clewer New Town
New Windsor
Spital
Ham Island
Sunnymeads
Wraysbury Reservoir
Stanwell Moor
Stanwell
Old Windsor
Remenham Park
Friary Island
Wraysbury
King George VI Reservoir
Staines Reservoirs
Staines Moor
Paddockhill Copse
Bromley Hill
Newmeadow Plantation
Old Windsor Wood
Hythe End
Beehive Hill
The Village
Cookes Hill
Runnymede
Cooper's Hill Slopes
Church Lammas
Glanty
Ashford Park
Crooked Billet Roundabout
Windsor Great Park
Dell Park
Englefield Green
Runnymede Park
Egham
Pooley Green
Egham Hythe
Knowle Green
Fordbridge Roundabout
The Savill Garden
Forest Estate
Egham Wick
Ripley Springs
Thorpe Lea
Manor Hill
Cheapside
Emmet's Wood
The Valley Gardens
Great Wood
The Dell
Eastly End
Laleham
Round Copse
Virginia Water
Blacknest
Stroude
Thorpe
Thorpe Park
Belvedere Wood
Beggar's Bush
King's Copse
Duke's Copse
Thorpe Green
Laleham Burway
Laleham Park
Sunningdale Park
Sunningdale
Broom Hill
Wentworth
Trumps Green
Shrubs Hill
Broomhall
Knowle Hill
Beech Wood
Chertsey Lock
The Rough
Lyne Copse
Lyne
Hersham Copse
Chertsey
Chertsey Meads
Eastworth
Burnt Hill
Fan Grove
Little Arm
Bog Wood
King's Hill
Ship Hill
Long Arm
Dicken's Wood
Addlestone Moor
Woburn Park
Oystershell Hill
Longcross
Flutters Hill
Chertsey South
Ham Moor
Long Down
Pears Hill
Home Wood
Addlestone
Brick Hill
Birch Hill
Roundpond Clump
The Bee Garden
Heathpark Wood
Ether Hill
Ottershaw
Rowhill
Old Slade
Valley End
Burrow Hill
Langshot Bog
Butts Hill
Stonehill
Fern Hill
Stanners Hill
Timber Hill
Brox
Brox Copse
Town
New Haw
Dunstall Green
M4
M25
M3
A4
A30
A308
A3113
A332
A329
A317
A320
A319
A412
A3044

22
A
B
C
1
2
3
4
5
14
30
21
EALING
Yiewsley
West Drayton
Harmondsworth
Sipson
Harlington
Hayes
Stockley Park
Hayes Town
Southall
Southall Green
Norwood Green
Dormer's Wells
Hanwell
West Ealing
Northfields
Boston Manor
Brentford
Osterley
Heston
HESTON
Cranford
Longford
Hatton
North Feltham
Hounslow West
HOUNSLOW
Isleworth
Lampton
Spring Grove
Woodlands
Whitton
Twickenham
St. Margarets
Cole Park
RICHMOND
Stanwell
West Bedfont
East Bedfont
Feltham
Hanworth
Hanworth Park
Hounslow Heath
Ashford
Chattern Hill
Lower Feltham
Felthamhill
Ashford Common
Sunbury Common
Fulwell
Strawberry Hill
Teddington
Ham
Hampton Hill
Hampton
Hampton Wick
Hampton Court
BUSHY PARK
HAMPTON COURT PARK
Kempton Park
Marling Park
Sunbury
Charlton
Littleton
Laleham
Shepperton Green
Shepperton
Upper Halliford
Lower Halliford
East Molesey
West Molesey
Thames Ditton
Giggshill
Weston Green
Long Ditton
Hinchley Wood
Claygate
Esher
West End
Claremont Park
Sandown Park
Lower Green
Fieldcommon
Rydens
Hersham
Walton-on-Thames
Oatlands Park
Burwood Park
Weybridge
Addlestone
Ham Moor
New Haw
LONDON-HEATHROW AIRPORT
Terminal 1
Terminal 2
Terminal 3
Terminal 4
Terminal 5A (Open Spring 2008)
Terminal 5B (Open Spring 2008)
Queen Mary Reservoir
Queen Elizabeth II Reservoir
Island Barn Reservoir
SURREY
M4
M3
A4
A30
A312
A316
A308
A309
A3
A243
HENLYS ROUNDABOUT
WAGGONERS ROUNDABOUT
HATTON CROSS
CLOCKHOUSE ROUNDABOUT
CROOKED BILLET ROUNDABOUT
FORDBRIDGE ROUNDABOUT
SCHOOL RD. JUNCTION
SUNBURY CROSS
THE SHEARS
APEX CORNER
HOSPITAL BRI. ROUNDABOUT
WHITTON RD. ROUNDABOUT
LONDON RD. ROUNDABOUT
ST. MARGARETS ROUNDABOUT
GILLETTE CORNER
HARLINGTON CORNER
HAMPTON COURT
SCILLY ISLES

23
Acton
Shepherds Bush
Bayswater
Oxford
Mayfair
Soho
Hyde Park
Marble Arch
Kensington
Kensington Gardens
Kensington Palace
Knightsbridge
West End
Westminster
Victoria
Belgravia
Pimlico
Brompton
South Kensington
Chelsea
Earls Ct.
West Kensington
Hammersmith
Olympia
Brook Green
South Acton
Bedford Park
Acton Green
Gunnersbury
Chiswick
Turnham Green
Kew
Mortlake
Barnes
Castelnau
The Wetland Centre
Fulham
Parsons Green
Walham Green
West Brompton
Sands End
Battersea
Battersea Park
Nine Elms
South Lambeth
Stockwell
Clapham
Brixton
Clapham Park
Streatham Hill
Balham
Tooting Bec
Upper Tooting
Tooting
Streatham
Streatham Park
Furzedown
Streatham Common
Streatham Vale
Lonesome
Mitcham
Earlsfield
Wandsworth
Southfields
Summerstown
Putney
Putney Heath
Hurlingham
East Sheen
North Sheen
Roehampton
Richmond Park
Petersham
Kingston Vale
Putney Vale
Wimbledon
Wimbledon Park
Wimbledon Common
South Wimbledon
Merton
Merton Park
Morden
Morden Park
Raynes Park
Bushey Mead
Copse Hill
Cottenham Park
Coombe
Norbiton
Kingston upon Thames
New Malden
West Barnes
Motspur Park
Berrylands
Malden Green
Old Malden
Tolworth
Worcester Park
North Cheam
Cheam
Sutton
Stoneleigh
Nonsuch Park
West Ewell
Rosehill
Benhilton
St. Helier
The Wrythe
Hackbridge
Beddington Corner
Beddington
Carshalton
Carshalton on the Hill
Wallington
South Beddington
Roundshaw
Collier's Wood
Tooting Graveney

24
A
B
C
1
2
3
4
16
23
32
City
Holborn
Soho
West End
Westminster
Victoria
Lambeth
Vauxhall
Kennington
Walworth
Elephant & Castle
Newington
The Borough
Bermondsey
Rotherhithe
Wapping
Shadwell
Poplar
Canning Town
Silvertown
Millwall
Cubitt Town
Deptford
Greenwich
Greenwich Park
Charlton
Kidbrooke
Blackheath
New Cross
New Cross Gate
Peckham
Camberwell
Stockwell
Clapham
Brixton
Nine Elms
South Lambeth
Denmark Hill
East Dulwich
Nunhead
Brockley
Lewisham
Ladywell
Hither Green
Lee
Catford
Honor Oak
Honor Oak Park
Herne Hill
Dulwich Village
Dulwich
Forest Hill
Tulse Hill
West Dulwich
West Norwood
Streatham
Streatham Hill
Streatham Common
Norbury
Norwood New Town
Upper Norwood
Crystal Palace
National Sports Centre
Sydenham
Upper Sydenham
Lower Sydenham
Penge
Anerley
Bellingham
Southend
Downham
Grove Park
Mottingham
Sundridge
Plaistow
Bromley
Shortlands
Beckenham
New Beckenham
Elmers End
Eden Park
Park Langley
South Norwood
Thornton Heath
Selhurst
Woodside
Broad Green
Addiscombe
Shirley
Shirley Oaks
Monks Orchard
West Wickham
Hayes
Coney Hall
Upper Elmers End
Spring Park
Croydon
Waddon
Beddington
Bandonhill
Wallington
South Beddington
Roundshaw
South Croydon
Croham Hurst
Upper Shirley
Addington
New Addington
Nash
Keston
Widmore
Sutcliffe Park
A2
A3
A20
A21
A23
A100
A101
A102
A200
A202
A203
A205
A232
A2213
Lombard Roundabout
Fiveways Corner
Thornton Heath Pond
Catford Gyratory
Lewisham
Loampit Vale
The Swan
The Grove
Toll

LONDON CITY AIRPORT
THAMES GATEWAY BRIDGE (Proposed)
Thamesmead Central
Thamesmead North
Thamesmead South
Thamesmead East
Thamesmead West
Thamesmead
North Woolwich
Woolwich
Woolwich Common
Plumstead
Plumstead Common
Winn's Common
Abbey Wood
Lesnes Abbey Woods
Bostall Heath
Bostall Woods
West Heath
Lessness Heath
Belvedere
Erith
RAINHAM MARSHES
WENNINGTON MARSHES
AVELEY MARSHES
DARTFORD MARSHES
CRAYFORD MARSHES
Wennington
North End
Northumberland Heath
Slade Green
East Wickham
Welling
Shooters Hill
Eltham Common
Jack Wood
Oxleas Wood
Falconwood
Barnehurst
Barnes Cray
Crayford
Joyce Green
DARTFORD
Eltham
Eltham Park
Danson Park
Bexleyheath
Bexley
Old Bexley
Avery Hill
Avery Hill Park
Blackfen
Penhill Park
Lamorbey Park
Bexley Park Wood
New Eltham
Sidcup
Longlands
Old Farm Park
Waring Park
Coldblow
Dartford Heath
Joydens Wood
Wilmington
Hawley
Chislehurst West
Chislehurst
Ashen Grove
Beavers Wood
Foots Cray Meadows
Foots Cray
North Cray
Ruxley
Ruxley Wood
Gattons Plantation
Chalk Wood
Scadbury Park
Park Wood
St. Paul's Cray
Hockenden
Pauls Cray Hill Park
St. Mary Cray
Hextable
Swanley Village
Newbarn Park
KENT
Swanley
Bickley
Blackbrook Wood
Petts Wood
Jubilee Country Park
Poverest
Bourne Wood
Kevington
Farningham Wood
Farningham
Southborough
Derry Downs
Kynaston Wood
Crockenhill
Covet Wood
Bromley Common
Sparrow Wood
Crofton Heath
Roundabout Wood
ORPINGTON
Crofton
Ramsden
Griff's Wood
Crown Wood
Nobody's Wood
Lullingstone Roman Villa
Eynsford
Olivers Shaw
Locksbottom
Darrick Wood
Goddington
Goddington Park
Lilly's Wood
Chelsfield
Chelsfield Village
Owen Wood
Lullingstone Park
Lullingstone
Beechen Wood
Ninhams Wood
Farnborough
Green Street Green
Maypole
Well Hill
Chalkhurst Wood
Hartnips Wood
Hollows Wood
The Birches
Preston Hill Plantation
Farthing Street
FALCONWOOD
DANSON INTERCHANGE
BLACK PRINCE INTERCHANGE
FIVEWAYS
FROGNAL CORNER
CRITTALL'S CORNER
SWANLEY INTERCHANGE
THE FANTAIL
HEWITTS ROUNDABOUT
RIVER THAMES
River Cray
River Darent
A13
A2
A20
A21
A117
A205
M25
M20
THAMES GATEWAY
SHOOTERS HILL
ROCHESTER WAY RELIEF RD.
SIDCUP BY-PASS
SWANLEY BY-PASS
DARTFORD BY-PASS
BOURNE WAY
CRAY AVENUE
SEVENOAKS WAY
CROFTON ROAD
FARNBOROUGH COMMON

26
M25
A13
A
B
C
18
THURROCK
30
31
Wennington
Belhus Park
Aveley
North Stifford
Orsett Heath
Chadwell St. Mary
AVELEY MARSHES
Purfleet
Thurrock Lakeside
Chafford Hundred
West Thurrock
Grays
Little Thurrock
South Stifford
Grays Athletic
A1089
Tilbury
Tilbury Fort
DARTFORD MARSHES
DARTFORD CROSSING
QUEEN ELIZABETH II BRIDGE
Channel Tunnel Rail Link
SWANSCOMBE MARSHES
TILBURY FREE PORT
A282
LITTLEBROOK INTERCHANGE
Joyce Green
Temple Hill
DARTFORD
Greenhithe
Swanscombe
Gravesend & Northfleet
GRAVESEND
Northfleet
Rosherville
Stone
Horns Cross
Knockhall
New Town
Bluewater
1a
1b
Fleet Downs
Dartenth Country Park
Darenth Wood
PRINCES RD. INTERCHANGE
DARENTH INTERCHANGE
Perry Street
Bean
New House
Kings Farm
A2
25
Hawley
Darenth
Lane End
Ladies Wood
Lords Wood
Beacon Wood Country Park
Betsham
Southfleet
Northfleet Green
Singlewell
Estimated Completion Late 2008
Sutton at Hone
Green Street Green
Hook Green
Istead Rise
Swanley Village
South Darenth
Grubb Street
Longfield
Court Wood
Nash Street
Horton Kirby
New Barn
Walnut Wood
Cozendon Wood
Farningham Wood
Churchdown Wood
Hartley
Hartley Wood
Longfield Hill
Meopham Station
Sole Street
Hartley Green
Fawkham
Farningham
M20
Pennis Wood
Hook Green
Camer Park Country Park
Hartley Hill
Meopham
Horton Wood
Parkfield Wood
Redlibbets Wood
Eynsford
New Ash Green
Meopham Green
Olivers Shaw
Fawkham Green
West Yoke
Grubb Wood
Brands Hatch
Saxten's Wood
White Ash Wood
Elbows Wood
Priestwood
Rogers Wood
Billet Wood
Ash
Viney Wood
New Street
David Street
Maplescombe
Chalkhurst Wood
Grove Wood
Ridley Wood
South Street
Priestwood Green
West Kingsdown
34
The Roughets
Ridley
Jub's Hill Wood
Harvel
Hog Wood
Hartnips Wood
The Birches
Sidehilly Wood
Pettings Wood
Pettings
Baker's Wood
Beechen Wood
Preston Hill Plantation
High Castle Wood
Hodsoll
Culverstone Green
A206
A226
A225
A227
A1306
A1090
A126
A20
B255
B260
B262
B2175
A2260
LONDON ROAD
WATLING STREET
DARTFORD ROAD
WROTHAM ROAD
GORSE HILL

Mucking
MUCKING MARSHES
Linford
Muckingford
East Tilbury
Coalhouse Fort
EAST TILBURY MARSHES
TILBURY MARSHES
RIVER THAMES
CLIFFE MARSHES
HALSTOW MARSHES
COOLING MARSHES
HIGHAM MARSHES
SHORNE MARSHES
Cliffe
West Street
Cooling
High Halstow
Cooling Street
Spendiff
Church Street
Denton
Chalk
Lower Higham
Lower Shorne
Mockbeggar
Cliffe Woods
Great Chattenden Wood
Chattenden
Hoo St. Werburgh
Broad Street
Lower Upnor
Riverview Park
Higham
Shorne
Court Wood
Gadshill
Wainscott
Upnor Castle
Upper Upnor
St. Mary's Island
Hoo Salt Marsh
Thong
Randall Wood
Shorne Wood Country Park
Great Crabbles Wood
Brewers Wood
Shorne Ridgeway
Dickens World
Chatham Maritime
Frindsbury
Strood
Historic Dockyard
Brompton
Ashenbank Wood
West Park
Owletts
Cobham Park
Great Wood
Rochester Castle
ROCHESTER
Fort Amherst
CHATHAM
Gillingham
GILLINGHAM
Cobham
Henley Street
Cobhambury Wood
Red Wood
Lower Bush
Cuxton
Lower Luddesdown
Longbottom Wood
Clarkes Wood
Borstal
Luton
Luddesdown
Bushy Wood
North Wood
May's Wood
Wouldham Marshes
North Halling
Hale
Darland
Wayfield
Hailing Wood
Rochester Forest
Wingate Wood
Cannon Wood
Horseholders Wood
Pastead Wood
Channel Tunnel Rail Link
Saturday
Rochester Airport
Capstone Farm Country Park
Capstone
Princes Park
Hempstead
Upper Halling
Halling
Wouldham
Monk Wood
Weeds Wood
Great Buckland
Greatpark Wood
Hook Wood
Hangingbank Wood
Scarborough
Walderslade
Burham Common
Lords Wood
Holly Hill
Crookhorn Wood
A2
M2
A226
A228
A289
A229
A230
A231
A2045
B2000
B2097
B2108
B2004
19
35

Wokingham Without
A
B
C
20
A322
Crowthorne
New England Hill
Wickham Bushes
Round Hill
Butter
Windlesham
Simons Wood
Fisher's Copse
Bagshot Park
Bagshot
Queen's Wood
Wishmoor Cross
Poppy Hills
Pine Hill
Edgbarrow Woods
Bagshot Heath
M3
Little Sandhurst
Owlsmoor
Broadmoor Bottom
Paschal Wood
Penny Hill
Wildmoor Bottom
Lightwater Country Park
The Devil's Pound
Olddean Common
Black Hill
Bagshot Heath
Lightwater
High Curley
1
Sandhurst
College Town
Trilakes Sandhurst Country Park
The Yateley Lakes
Yateley
Darby Green
Frogmore
Blackwater
CAMBERLEY
York Town
Crawley Hill
Tekels Park
White Hill
Redroad Hill
Greyspot Hill
Donkey Town
Cricket Hill
Yateley Country
Common Park
WESTEND COMMON
Heatherside
Chobham Ridges
Starve Acre
Hawley Park
Frimley Ridge
Jackpond Hill
Hawley
Frith Hill
Minley
2
Minley Wood
Hawley Common
Fox Lane
Frimley
Blackdown Hill
Pirbright Common
Frimley Green
Hawley Lane
Deepcut
Old Windmill Hill
Pirbright Camp
4a
Moor Copse
M3
Cove
West Heath
North Farnborough
Ancells Copse
Farnborough Street
Mytchett
Basingstoke Canal
FARNBOROUGH
Southwood
Farnborough Park
Fleet Pond
Pyestock
Bowling H
Bridge Hill
Fleet
3
HAMPSHIRE
Pondtail
Farnborough Airport
South Farnborough
PIRBRIGHT COMMON
Peat Moor
Pyestock Wood
Eelmoor Marsh
Norris Hill West
Gelvert Bottom
Miles Copse
CLEYGATE COMMON
Ash Vale
North Camp
Ash Common
Slyfield Wood
Watts' Common
FOX HILLS
Church Crookham
Long Hill Copse
Spur Hill
Wyke Common
Centre Hill
Normandy Hill
Normandy Common
Bickley Moor
Claycart Bottom
Rushmoor Arena
South Camp
Ash
Normandy
Greendane Copse
Outridden Copse
Jubilee Plantation
North Town
A331
Wyke
Chandler's Copse
Aldershot Town
Parkhurst Hill
Burn's Hill
ALDERSHOT
Catherine Frith
Beacon Hill
Reservoirs
Skirmishing Hill
Whitegate Copse
Highfield Copse
Abury Hill
Hungry Hill
Flexford
4
Ewshot
Combe Wood
Bricksbury Hill
Heath End
Rowhill Nature Reserve
Bin Wood
Ash Green
Long Common
The Cardinals
Warren Corner
The Warren
Heath Hill
Upper Hale
Weybourne
Grubground Copse
Wanborough Wood
Wanborough
Tongham
Inwood Copse
Hale
A31
Dora's Green
Farnham Park
Badshot Lea
Seale
Williams Copse
Stony Hill
Puttenham
Claypit Wood
The Avenue
Runfold
Sandy Cross
FARNHAM
A31
Payn's Firs
Robert's Moor
Binton Wood
LONDON ROAD
PORTSMOUTH ROAD
HOG'S BACK
BLACKWATER VALLEY ROUTE
FARNBOROUGH ROAD
GUILDFORD ROAD
FARNHAM-BY-PASS

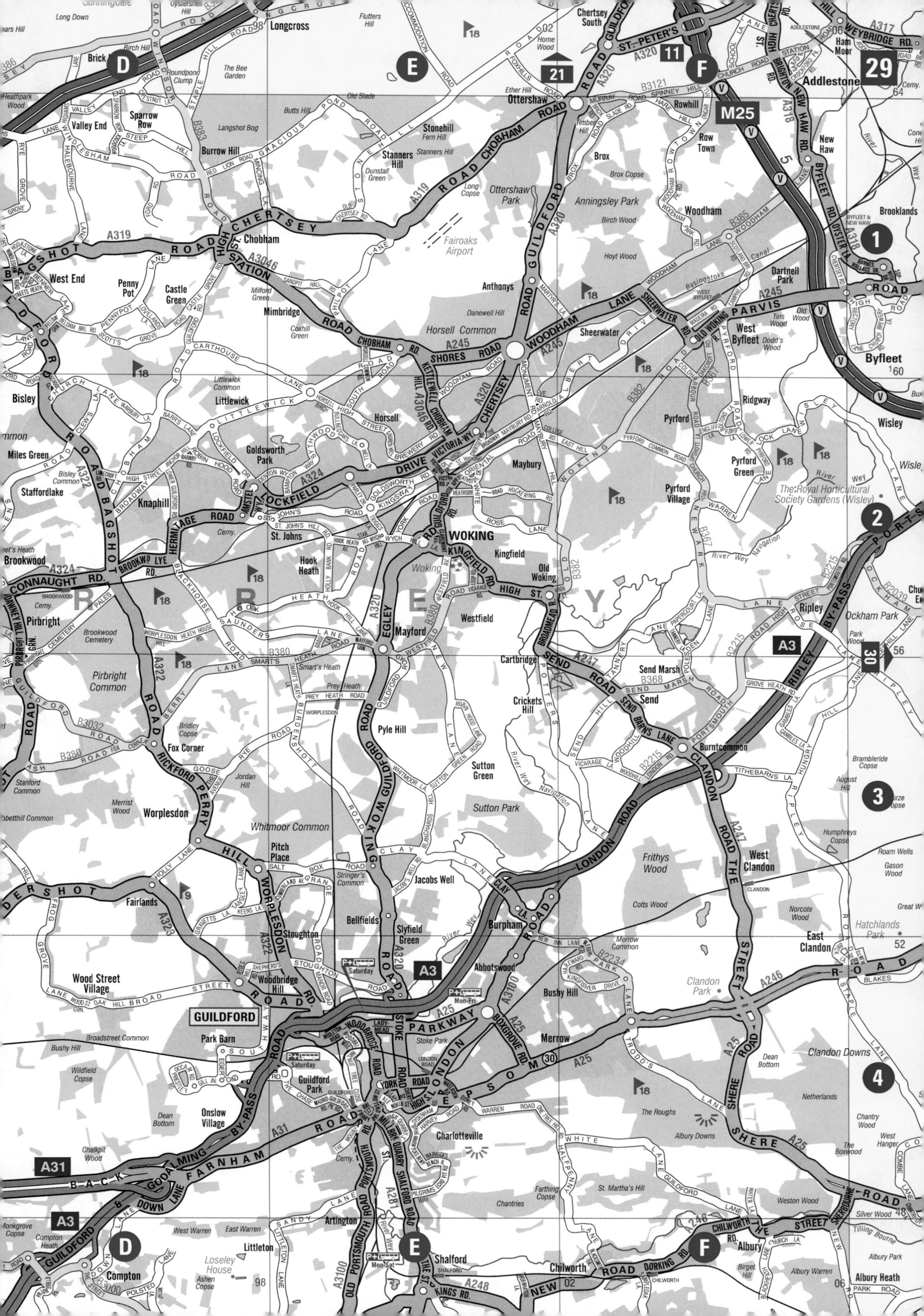

29
Longcross
Flutters Hill
Chertsey South
Home Wood
Long Down
Brick
Birch Hill
Roundpond Clump
The Bee Garden
Addlestone
Ham Moor
Weybridge Rd.
St. Peter's
11
21
D
E
F
M25
Heathpark Wood
Valley End
Sparrow Row
Burrow Hill
Butts Hill
Old Slade
Langshot Bog
Stonehill
Fern Hill
Stanners Hill
Dunstall Green
Ether Hill
Ottershaw
Rowhill
Timber Hill
Brox
Brox Copse
Row Town
New Haw
Long Copse
Ottershaw Park
Anningsley Park
Birch Wood
Woodham
Brooklands
Fairoaks Airport
Chobham
West End
Penny Pot
Castle Green
Milford Green
Mimbridge
Coxhill Green
Hoyt Wood
Anthonys
Danewell Hill
Horsell Common
Sheerwater
Dartnell Park
West Byfleet
Byfleet
Tins Wood
Old Wood
Dodd's Wood
Basingstoke Canal
Bisley
Littlewick Common
Littlewick
Horsell
Ridgway
Wisley
Pyrford
Goldsworth Park
Maybury
Pyrford Green
Miles Green
Bisley Common
Staffordlake
Knaphill
Pyrford Village
The Royal Horticultural Society Gardens (Wisley)
River Wey
Brookwood
St. Johns
WOKING
Kingfield
Old Woking
Hook Heath
River Wey Navigation
Ripley
Ockham Park
Park Wood
Pirbright
Brookwood Cemetery
Mayford
Westfield
Cartbridge
Send Marsh
Send
A3
30
Pirbright Common
Smart's Heath
Prey Heath
Crickets Hill
Burntcommon
Bridley Copse
Fox Corner
Pyle Hill
Stanford Common
Sutton Green
Brambleride Copse
August Hill
Jordan Hill
Merrist Wood
Worplesdon
Sutton Park
Humphreys Copse
Roam Wells
Gason Wood
Whitmoor Common
Pitch Place
Frithys Wood
West Clandon
Stringer's Common
Jacobs Well
Fairlands
Cotts Wood
Norcote Wood
Great Wood
Bellfields
Slyfield Green
Burpham
Stoughton
Hatchlands Park
East Clandon
Merrow Common
Abbotswood
Wood Street Village
Woodbridge Hill
Clandon Park
Bushy Hill
GUILDFORD
Broadstreet Common
Park Barn
Stoke Park
Merrow
Clandon Downs
Dean Bottom
Wildfield Copse
Guildford Park
Onslow Village
Netherlands
The Roughs
Charlotteville
Albury Downs
Chantry Wood
West Hanger
The Boxwood
Chalkpit Wood
Farthing Copse
St. Martha's Hill
Weston Wood
Chantries
Silver Wood
A31
A3
Artington
West Warren
East Warren
Littleton
Compton Heath
Monkgrove Copse
Loseley House
Ashen Copse
Compton
Shalford
Chilworth
Albury
Birget Hill
Albury Warren
Albury Park
Albury Heath
Tilling Bourne

30
Addlestone
Weybridge
Oatlands Park
Walton-on-Thames
Hersham
Esher
West End
Hinchley Wood
Claygate
Claremont Park
Esher Common
Arbrook Common
Claygate Common
Chessington World of Adventures
New Haw
Brooklands
St. George's Hill
Whiteley Village
Burnhill Park
Fairmile Common
Fairmile
Oxshott Heath
Oxshott
Prince's Coverts
Malden Rushett
Byfleet
Painshill Park
Cobham
Stoke D'Abernon
Pachesham Park
Ashtead Common
Wisley
Wisley Interchange
Wisley Common
Ockham Common
The Royal Horticultural Society Gardens (Wisley)
Pointers Green
Downside
Hatchford
Elm Corner
Martyr's Green
May's Green
Leatherhead Common
Lower Ashtead
Ripley
Bridge End
Church End
Ockham Park
Ockham
Effingham Junction
Great Bookham Common
LEATHERHEAD
Fetcham
Little Bookham
Great Bookham
Effingham
West Horsley
East Horsley
Norbury Park
Mickleham
Westhumble
Polesden Lacey
East Clandon
Hatchlands Park
Sheep Leas
Ranmore Common
Dogkennel Green
DORKING
Clandon Downs
Netherlands
Westcott
Wotton
Abinger Hammer
Gomshall
Shere
Albury Heath
North Holmwood
Tower Hill
M25
A3
A24
A25
A246
A245
A244
A307
A318
A317
A2003
B2039
B2430
B2122
B2126
Sandown Park
Scilly Isles
Kingston By-Pass
Leatherhead By-Pass
Guildford Road
Epsom Road
Portsmouth Road
Esher Road
Woodlands Lane
Randalls Road
Young Street
Oxshott Road
Kingston Road
Mickleham By-Pass
Ranmore Common Road
Dorking Road
Westcott Road
Coast Hill
Deepdene Avenue
London Road
High Street
Chapel Lane
Ockham Lane
Ripley By-Pass
Hungry Hill Lane
Hill Chapel Lane
1
2
3
4
A
B
C
6
9
10
22
29
NORTH SURREY

North Cheam
Beddington
A232
31
Stoneleigh
A240
A24
D
E
F
SUTTON
23
Carshalton
Wallington
Bandonhill
South Beddington
Roundshaw
Nonsuch Park
CHEAM VILLAGE
BEGGAR'S HILL
West Ewell
Horton Country Park
Castle Hill
ORGAN CROSSROADS
Cheam
Belmont
Carshalton Beeches
Carshalton on the Hill
Woodcote Green
Four Acre Wood
Pond Wood
Ewell
East Ewell
A217
Little Woodcote
Woodcote
1
North Looe
Banstead Downs
EPSOM
Common
DRIFT BRIDGE
Big Wood
Clock House
Coulsdon
Banstead
Woodmansterne
Nork
A240
Nork Park
Woodcote
Great Burgh
Tattenham Corner
Gt. Solom's Wood
Chipstead
Ashtead Park
Epsom Downs
Epsom
Pages Acre
Ruffett Wood
Banstead Wood
2
Farthing Fairdean
Langley Vale
Langley Bottom
Burgh Heath
A217
Walton Downs
A23
Chipstead Bottom
Poorfield Wood
Hooley
Boxer's Wood
Netherne-on-the-Hill
M25
Addlestead Wood
Tadworth
Kingswood
The Long Plantation
Porters Wood
Netherne Wood
32
Tyrell's Wood
Great Hurst Wood
Sandhill Wood
Tickners Wood
Coldroast Shaw
Alderstead Heath
Nower Wood
Costal Wood
Walton on the Hill
Banstead Heath
Beechen Copse
Mugswell
7
Alderstead Heath
M23
Cherkley Wood
Headley
Walton Park Wood
Walton Heath
Gatwick Wood
Upper Gatton Wood
Furzefield Shaw
Cockshoot Wood
Dean Wood
Lower Kingswood
A217
3
Headley Heath
Herring Grove
Little Heath
Park Shaw
Glebe Shaw
Gatton
Merstham
7
Mogador
REIGATE HILL INTERCHANGE
Margery Wood
Margery
Bullen Wood
Bramblehall Wood
Heath Plantation
White's Wood
Dawcombe Wood
Buckland Hills
M25
8
Gatton Park
Nut Wood
South Merstham
8
Colley Hill
Queen's Park
The Beeches
Mercers Park
Box Hill
Betchworth Hills Wood
Coles Meads
The Birches
Brockham Hills
Buckland
Holmethorpe
Oak Wood
REIGATE
Redhill
Nutfield
Betchworth
A25
Betchworth Park
Reigate Heath
4
Brockham
Reigate Park
Redhill Common
Earlswood
Wilderness Wood
Mead Vale
Woodhatch
South Park
Earlswood Common
Ridge Green
Strood Green
Riding's Copse
Rushetts Farm
Slipshatch Wood
Doversgreen
Fefland Copse
Roothill Wood
Highridge Wood
D
E
F
Redhill Aerodrome
Dawesgreen
Leigh
Home Grove
Benting Wood
Salfords
Sidlow

32
A
B
C
Beddington
CROYDON
A232
Spring Park
Coney Hall
Kes
FIVEWAYS CORNER
Wallington
South Beddington
Roundshaw
A23
PURLEY WAY
South Croydon
COOMBE RD.
A212
24
Lloyd Park
Coombe Wood
Addington Hills
Upper Shirley
Addington
Kennel Wood
Nash
Birch Wood
James's Wood
New Addington
Rowdown Wood
Croham Hurst
Littleheath Wood
Selsdon
Forestdale
A2022
ADDINGTON ROAD
SELSDON PARK RD.
Purley
1
FOXLEY LANE
Woodcote
Sanderstead
Selsdon Wood
Frith Wood
Puplet Wood
Frylands Wood
Crab Wood
Leaves Green
PURLEY CROSS
Riddlesdown
Foxley Wood
Mitchley Wood
Kings Wood
Fickleshole
Jewels Wood
A22
Kenley
Ansley Berry Shaw
Hamsey Green
Farleigh
Littlepark Wood
Greatpark Wood
Crewe's Wood
Holt Wood
Coulsdon
Whyteleafe
Kenley Common
Chelsham
Henley Wood
Mollards Wood
Biggin Hill
Owls Wood
Long Coppice
2
Farthing or Fairdean Downs
Old Coulsdon
Kenley Airfield
Warlingham
Lumbardine Wood
WAPSES ROUNDABOUT
Woldingham Garden Village
Ashen Shaw
Tatsfield
Boxer's Wood
Netherne-on-the-Hill
Caterham-on-the-Hill
Birch Wood
Kitchen Grove
Pitchers Wood
31
Piles Wood
Woldingham
Greenhill Shaw
Caterham
Alderstead Heath
7
Chaldon
Templehill Plantation
Great Church Wood
Whistlers Wood
Titsey Plantation
Titsey
Titsey Park
3
M23
8
Stubbs Copse
Oldpark Wood
Chalkpit Wood
Pendell Wood
Black Bushes
6
GODSTONE INTERCHANGE
Rye Wood
Limpsfield
Merstham
M25
The Abbeys
Oxted
Warwick Wold
Kitchen Copse
Tyler's Green
South Merstham
Godstone
A25
Old Oxted
Limpsfield Common
Pains Hill
Mercers Park
S U R R E Y
N O R T H
Church Town
Broadham Green
Hurst Green
Itching Com.
Nutfield
Stratton
Oldpark Park
Round Wood
Tandridge
Painscroft Wood
Bletchingley
White Post
Tilburstow Plantation
Tilburstow Common
Holland
4
NUTFIELD RD. HIGH ST. BLETCHINGLEY CASTLE ST. HIGH ST. GODSTONE
Stow Coppice
Southlands Wood
Homesland Wood
South Nutfield
Crookedfield Shaw
Piper's Wood
Merle Common
Tye Copse
Staffhurst Wood
Ridge Green
Bransland Wood
Poundhill Wood
Cinderhill Wood
South Godstone
Birchen Coppice
Crowhurst Lane End
Crowhurst
Ashen Plantations
Redhill Aerodrome
Spring Field Wood
Blindley Heath
Bradford Wood
30
34
38
48
52
56
60
64

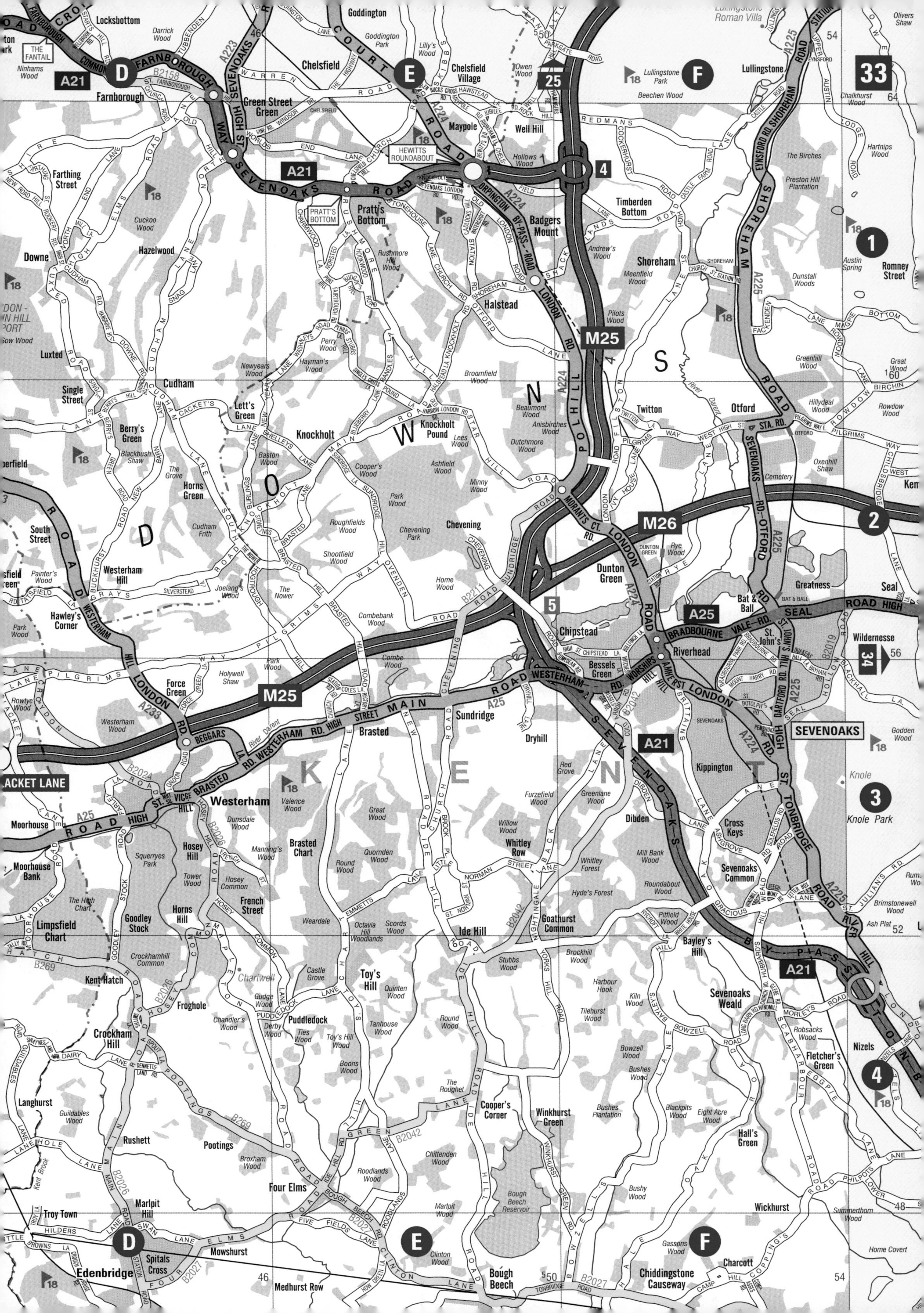
Locksbottom
Darrick Wood
Goddington
Goddington Park
Lullingstone Roman Villa
Olivers Shaw
THE FANTAIL
Ninhams Wood
A21
D
Farnborough
B2158
A223
SEVENOAKS
Chelsfield
Lilly's Wood
E
Chelsfield Village
Owen Wood
25
Lullingstone Park
F
Lullingstone
Beechen Wood
Chalkhurst Wood
Green Street Green
Maypole
Well Hill
Hartnips Wood
HEWITTS ROUNDABOUT
Hollows Wood
4
The Birches
Preston Hill Plantation
Farthing Street
A21
PRATT'S BOTTOM
Pratt's Bottom
Timberden Bottom
Cuckoo Wood
A224
Badgers Mount
1
Rushmore Hill Wood
Andrew's Wood
Austin Spring
Romney Street
Downe
Hazelwood
Shoreham
Meenfield Wood
Dunstall Woods
A225
Halstead
Pilots Wood
M25
Luxted
Perry Wood
Hayman's Wood
S
Greenhill Wood
Great Wood
Newyears Wood
Broomfield Wood
Single Street
Cudham
N
Beaumont Wood
Twitton
Otford
Hillydeal Wood
Rowdow Wood
Lett's Green
Knockholt Pound
Anisbirches Wood
Knockholt
Lees Wood
W
Dutchmore Wood
Berry's Green
Blackbush Shaw
Baston Wood
Oxenhill Shaw
Cooper's Wood
Ashfield Wood
Cemetery
The Grove
Park Wood
Minny Wood
Horns Green
O
South Street
Roughfields Wood
Chevening
M26
2
Cudham Frith
D
Chevening Park
Dunton Green
Rye Wood
Shootfield Wood
Westerham Hill
Greatness
Seal
Painter's Wood
Joeland's Wood
The Nower
Home Wood
5
Bat & Ball
A25
Hawley's Corner
Combebank Wood
Chipstead
St. John's
Wildernesse
Park Wood
Riverhead
34
Combe Wood
Bessels Green
Holywell Shaw
Force Green
M25
Rowlye Wood
Westerham Wood
Sundridge
A21
Brasted
Dryhill
SEVENOAKS
Godden Wood
River Darent
Kippington
Red Grove
K
E
N
T
Knole
ACKET LANE
A25
Valence Wood
Westerham
3
Knole Park
Furzefield Wood
Greenlane Wood
Moorhouse
Dunsdale Wood
Great Wood
Dibden
Cross Keys
Willow Wood
Brasted Chart
Whitley Row
Squerryes Park
Hosey Hill
Manning's Wood
Quornden Wood
Mill Bank Wood
Moorhouse Bank
Round Wood
Whitley Forest
Tower Wood
Hosey Common
Sevenoaks Common
Hyde's Forest
Roundabout Wood
The High Chart
French Street
Brimstonewell Wood
Limpsfield Chart
Goodley Stock
Horns Hill
Weardale
Octavia Hill Woodlands
Scords Wood
Goathurst Common
Pittfield Wood
Ash Plat
Ide Hill
Bayley's Hill
Crockhamhill Common
Stubbs Wood
Brockhill Wood
A21
Kent Hatch
Castle Grove
Toy's Hill
Quinten Wood
Harbour Hook
Sevenoaks Weald
Chartwell
Gudge Wood
Froghole
Puddledock
Kiln Wood
Chandler's Wood
Derby Wood
Tanhouse Wood
Round Wood
Tilehurst Wood
Robsacks Wood
Crockham Hill
Ties Wood
Toy's Hill Wood
Nizels
Fletcher's Green
Bowzell Wood
Boons Wood
Bushes Wood
4
Langhurst
Guildables Wood
The Roughet
Cooper's Corner
Winkhurst Green
Bushes Plantation
Blackpits Wood
Eight Acre Wood
Hall's Green
B269
Rushett
Pootings
B2042
Chittenden Wood
Broxham Wood
Roodlands Wood
Bough Beech Reservoir
Four Elms
Bushy Wood
Wickhurst
Troy Town
Marlpit Hill
Marlpit Wood
Summerthorn Wood
D
E
F
Gassons Wood
Mowshurst
Spitals Cross
Clinton Wood
Charcott
Home Covert
Edenbridge
B2027
Bough Beech
Chiddingstone Causeway
Medhurst Row
46
50
54

34
A
B
C
1
2
3
4
Olivers Shaw
Brands Hatch
West Yoke
Grubb Wood
Elbows Wood
Priestwood
Maplescombe
26
Saxten's Wood
Rogers Wood
Billet Wood
Ash
White Ash Wood
Viney Wood
New Street
David Street
South Street
Priestwood Green
Chalkhurst Wood
Grove Wood
West Kingsdown
Ridley Wood
Ridley
Harvel
The Roughets
Jub's Hill Wood
Beechen Wood
Hartnips Wood
Hog Wood
Pettings Wood
Pettings
Culverstone Green
The Birches
Sidehilly Wood
Baker's Wood
Hodsoll Street
Ridge Wood
Preston Hill Plantation
High Castle Wood
Martinhill Wood
Ashen Grove
Stacklands Wood
Stansted
Seagrove Wood
Westfield Wood
Hall Wood
East Hill
Blooming Wood
Knatts Valley
Broom Wood
Austin Spring
Romney Street
Mingram Wood
Round Wood
Fairseat
Vigo Village
Dunstall Woods
Pecken Wood
Water Wood
Knockmill
Peckham Wood
Cox's Wood
Wessells Wood
Trosley Country Park
Leize Wood
N
O
R
T
H
M20
Knockmill Wood
Thrift Wood
Grove Wood
Sandpits Wood
Woodlands
Cooper's Wood
Greenhill Wood
Great Wood
Beech Lees Wood
Whitehill Wood
Birches Wood
Trottiscliffe
A20
A227
Cotman's Ash
Summeryards Wood
Hillydeal Wood
Rowdow Wood
New Park Wood
Otford
Oxenhill Shaw
Kemsing
Heaverham
Martin Spring Wood
Wrotham
2a
Addington
M26
A25
Cockney's Wood
Noah's Ark
Borough Green
Wrotham Heath
Aldon
Valley Wood
Patchgrove Wood
Heron Shaw Wood
St. Marys Platt
Greatness
Seal
Oldbury
Offham Wood
Ightham
Styants Bottom
Long Wood
Comp
Wildernesse
33
K
E
Oldbury Wood
Great Leybourne Wood
Chance Wood
Seal Chart
Basted
Longbrook Wood
Crouch
Godden Green
Claygate Cross
Mereworth Woods
SEVENOAKS
Godden Wood
Hall Wood
Ightham Common
Stone Street
Herne Pound
Sheet Hill
Knole
Bitchet Green
Ivy Hatch
Boot Wood
Hurst Wood
Lord's Spring Wood
Yopps Green
Quarry Wood
Swanton
Knole Park
Fawke Common
Scathes Wood
Broadhoath Wood
Ightham Mote
Bitchet Common
Plaxtol
Roughway
One Tree Hill
Carter's Hill
Orchard Shaw
Home Coverts
Gover Hill
Rumshott Wood
Brakybank Wood
Dunk's Green
Sticklands Wood
South Seers Wood
West Peckham
Brimstonewell Wood
Puttenden Wood
Ash Plat
Underriver
Budds
Cold Blows
Shipbourne
Claygate
Hazel Wood
Barr Wood
Point Wood
Peacock Wood
Kiln Wood
Thomas's Wood
Twelve Acre Plantation
Claygate Wood
Clearhedges Wood
Robsacks Wood
Oakhurst
Oakhurst Wood
Lodge Wood
Sawpit Wood
Golden Stable Wood
Alder Shaw
Stallion's Green
A26
Goose Green
Nizels
Cock Wood
Cold Harbour Toll
Roughetts Wood
Coldharbour
Spring Wood
Hadlow
Starvecrow Wood
Carroty Wood
Pittswood
Fletcher's Green
Watt's Cross
A21
Trench Wood
Higham Wood
Parker's Green
Hildenborough
Cage Green
Summerhorn Wood
Stocks Green
Hilden Park
Hadlow Stair
Golden Green
Barnes Street
Home Covert
Powder Mills
TONBRIDGE
Leigh
River Medway
54
56
58
60
62
52
48

35
Hempstead
Rochester Forest
Cannon Wood
Horseholders Wood
Pastead Wood
Upper Halling
Halling
Wouldham
Rochester Airport
Saturday
Princes Park
Weeds Wood
Walderslade
Lords Wood
Lidsing
Hook Wood
Great Buckland
Greatpark Wood
Hanginghill Wood
Holly Hill
Crookhorn Wood
Monk Wood
Bridge Woods
Burham Common
Scarborough
Holborough
Paddlesworth
Snodland
Burham
Burham Court
Blue Bell Hill
Kit's Coty
Ham Hill
Horn Street
Birling
Malling Wood
Westfield Sole
Monkdown Wood
Westfield Wood
Eccles
Ryarsh
Lunsford
Lunsford Park
New Hythe
Pratling Street
Boarley
Boxley Wood
Boxley
Leybourne
Larkfield
Aylesford
Forstal
Ditton
West Malling
Manor Park Country Park
Mill Street
East Malling
Royal British Legion Village
Allington
Ringlestone
Sandling
Penenden Heath
Harbourland
Park Wood
Pope's Wood
Vinters Park
Grove Green
Well Street
East Malling Heath
Kings Hill
Oaken Wood
Barming Heath
Maidstone West
Maidstone East
MAIDSTONE
Mote Park
Mon-Sat
Fant
Tovil
Barming
Kent Street
Cattering Wood
Hoath Wood
Red Hill
Wateringbury
Teston
Shepway
Pizien Well
West Farleigh
East Farleigh
Dean Street
Loose
Farleigh Green
Nettlestead
Quarry Wood
Park Wood
Boughton Green
Cock Street
Moat Wood
Nettlestead Green
Kenward
Coxheath
Yalding
Boughton Monchelsea
Peckham Bush
Linton
Linton Park
Hunton
Brick Kiln Wood
Wierton
Hale Street
Congelow
Darnold Wood
East Peckham
Branbridges
Benover
Laddingford
Chainhurst
Stilebridge
Beltring
Hop Farm
Mockbeggar
Underling Green
Hurst Green
Rabbit's Cross
River Medway
River Teise
River Beult
M20
M2
A228
A229
A249
A20
A26
A274
B2010
B2163
B2015
B2162
B2012
B2246
B2097
A2045
D
E
F
1
2
3
4
5
6
7
27
570
74
78
64
60
56
52
48

INDEX

Including Streets, Places & Areas, Industrial Estates,
Selected Flats & Walkways, Junction Names and Selected Places of Interest.

HOW TO USE THIS INDEX

1. Each street name is followed by its Postcode District (or, if outisude the London Postcodes, by its Locality Abbreviations(s)), and then by its Locality abbreviation(s) and then by its map reference; e.g. **Abbey Rd.** DA12: Grav'nd . . . .2D **27** is in the DA12 Postcode District and the Gravesend Locality and is to be found in square 2D on page **27**. The page number being shown in bold type.

2. A strict alphabetical order is followed in which Av., Rd., St., etc. (though abbreviated) are read in full and as part of the street name; e.g. **Allsop Pl.** appears after **All Saints Rd.** but before **All Souls Av.**

3. Addresses that are in more than one part are referred to as not continuous.

4. Places and areas are shown in the index in **BLUE TYPE** and the map reference is to the actual map square in which the town centre or area is located and not to the place name shown on the map; e.g. **BARNSBURY 1A 60**

5. An example of a selected place of interest is Chiltern Open Air Mus. 1E 13

6. Junction names are shown in the index in **BOLD CAPITAL TYPE**; e.g. **ALDGATE 4A 16**

GENERAL ABBREVIATIONS

All. : Alley
App. : Approach
Av. : Avenue
Blvd. : Boulevard
Bri. : Bridge
B'way. : Broadway
C'way. : Causeway
Cen. : Centre
Chu. : Church
Circ. : Circle
Cl. : Close
Comn. : Common
Cnr. : Corner
Ct. : Court
Cres. : Crescent
Cft. : Croft
Dpt. : Depot
Dr. : Drive
E. : East
Emb. : Embankment
Flds. : Fields
Gdn. : Garden
Gdns. : Gardens
Gth. : Garth
Ga. : Gate
Gt. : Great
Grn. : Green
Gro. : Grove
Ho. : House
Info. : Information
Junc. : Junction
La. : Lane
Lit. : Little
Lwr. : Lower
Mnr. : Manor
Mkt. : Market
Mdw. : Meadow
Mdws. : Meadows
Mt. : Mount
Mus. : Museum
Nth. : North
Pal. : Palace
Pde. : Parade
Pk. : Park
Pl. : Place
Ri. : Rise
Rd. : Road
Rdbt. : Roundabout
Sth. : South
Sq. : Square
St. : Street
Ter. : Terrace
Up. : Upper
Va. : Vale
Vw. : View
Vs. : Villas
Vis. : Visitors
Wlk. : Walk
W. : West

LOCALITY ABBREVIATIONS

Abb R : **Abbess Roding**
Ab L : **Abbots Langley**
Ab C : **Abinger Common**
Ab H : **Abinger Hammer**
Abr : **Abridge**
Addtn : **Addington**
Add : **Addlestone**
Alb : **Albury**
Aldb : **Aldbury**
A'ham : **Aldenham**
Alde : **Aldershot**
Ali : **Allington**
Amer : **Amersham**
Ark : **Arkley**
Art : **Artington**
Asc : **Ascot**
Ash : **Ash**
Ashf : **Ashford**
Ash G : **Ash Green**
A Grn : **Ashley Green**
Asht : **Ashtead**
Ash V : **Ash Vale**
Ask : **Askett**
Ast C : **Aston Clinton**
Avel : **Aveley**
A'bury : **Aylesbury**
A'ford : **Aylesford**
B Lea : **Badshot Lea**
Bag : **Bagshot**
Ball : **Ballinger**
Bans : **Banstead**
Bark : **Barking**
Barm : **Barming**
Barn : **Barnet**
Bas : **Basildon**
Bat : **Battlesbridge**
B'fd : **Bayford**
B'bry : **Bayfordbury**
Beac : **Beaconsfield**
Bea E : **Beamond End**
Bean : **Bean**
Bear : **Bearsted**
Beau R : **Beauchamp Roding**
Beck : **Beckenham**
Bedd : **Beddington**
Bedf : **Bedfont**
Bedm : **Bedmond**
Bell : **Bellingdon**
Belv : **Belvedere**
Ben : **Benfleet**
Berk : **Berkhamsted**
Bern R : **Berners Roding**
Bet : **Betchworth**
Bexl : **Bexley**
Bex : **Bexleyheath**
B'acre : **Bicknacre**
Big H : **Biggin Hill**
Bill : **Billericay**
Bin : **Binfield**
Bir G : **Birch Green**
Birl : **Birling**
Bish : **Bishopstone**
Bisl : **Bisley**
Blckh : **Blackheath**
Bmore : **Blackmore**
Bla : **Blackwater**
Bled R : **Bledlow Ridge**
Blet : **Bletchingley**
B Hill : **Blue Bell Hill**
Bluew : **Bluewater**
Book : **Booker**
Bookh : **Bookham**
Bor : **Boreham**
Bore : **Borehamwood**
Bor G : **Borough Green**
B Mon : **Boughton Monchelsea**
Bou E : **Bourne End**
Bov : **Bovingdon**
B Gif : **Bowers Gifford**
Box H : **Box Hill**
Box : **Boxley**
Brac : **Bracknell**
Brad : **Bradenham**
Bras : **Brasted**
Bray : **Bray**
Bred : **Bredhurst**
Bford : **Brentford**
B'wood : **Brentwood**
Brick : **Brickendon**
Brick W : **Bricket Wood**
Brim : **Brimsdown**
Aroc : **Brockham**
Brom : **Bromley**
Brk P : **Brookmans Park**
Brkwd : **Brookwood**
Broom : **Broomfield**
Brox : **Broxbourne**
Buck H : **Buckhurst Hill**
Bkld : **Buckland**
Buck C : **Buckland Common**
Bucks : **Bucks Hill**
Bul : **Bulbourne**
Bulp : **Bulphan**
Bur G : **Burchetts Green**
Bur : **Burham**
Burn : **Burnham**
Burp : **Burpham**
Bush : **Bushey**
B Hea : **Bushy Heath**
But X : **Butlers Cross**
Byfl : **Byfleet**
Camb : **Camberley**
Can I : **Canvey Island**
Cars : **Carshalton**
Cat'm : **Caterham**
Chad H : **Chadwell Heath**
Chaf H : **Chafford Hundred**
Chal G : **Chalfont St Giles**
Chal P : **Chalfont St Peter**
Chan C : **Chandler's Cross**
Char : **Chartridge**
Cha S : **Chart Sutton**
Chat : **Chatham**
C'den : **Chattenden**
Cheam : **Cheam**
Chelm : **Chelmsford**
Chels : **Chelsfield**
Chen : **Chenies**
Chert : **Chertsey**
Ches : **Chesham**
Chesh : **Cheshunt**
Chess : **Chessington**
Chid : **Chiddingstone**
Chi J : **Chignall St James**
Chig S : **Chignall Smealy**
Chig : **Chigwell**
Chil : **Chilworth**
Chfd : **Chipperfield**
Chip : **Chipstead**
Chst : **Chislehurst**
Chis G : **Chiswell Green**
Chob : **Chobham**
Chol : **Cholesbury**
Chor : **Chorleywood**
Chu C : **Church Crookham**
Clay : **Claygate**
Cli : **Cliffe**
Cli W : **Cliffe Woods**
Cobh : **Cobham**
Cockf : **Cockfosters**
Col G : **Cole Green**
Cole : **Coleshill**
Col T : **College Town**
Col R : **Collier Row**
Coll : **Collier Street**
Coln : **Colnbrook**
Col H : **Colney Heath**
Col S : **Colney Street**
Comp : **Compton**
Cook : **Cookham**
Coo G : **Cooksmill Green**
Cool : **Cooling**
Coop : **Coopersale**
Corr : **Corringham**
Coul : **Coulsdon**
Cove : **Cove**
Cowl : **Cowley**
Cox : **Coxheath**
Cran : **Cranford**
Cray : **Crayford**
C Hill : **Crays Hill**
Crew H : **Crews Hill**
Crock : **Crockenhill**
Crock H : **Crockham Hill**
Crow : **Crowthorne**
Crox G : **Croxley Green**
C'don : **Croydon**
Cry H : **Cryers Hill**
Cud : **Cudham**
Cuff : **Cuffley**
Cux : **Cuxton**
Dag : **Dagenham**
Dan : **Danbury**
Dart : **Dartford**
Dat : **Datchet**
Deep : **Deepcut**
Den : **Denham**
Det : **Detling**
Dip : **Dippenhall**
Dit : **Ditton**
Dodd : **Doddinghurst**
Dork : **Dorking**
Dor : **Dorney**
Dor R : **Dorney Reach**
Downe : **Downe**
D'ham : **Downham**
D'ley : **Downley**
D'side : **Downside**
Dra B : **Drayton Beauchamp**
Dun G : **Dunton Green**
E Barn : **East Barnet**
E Clan : **East Clandon**
E Far : **East Farleigh**
E Han : **East Hanningfield**
E Hor : **East Horsley**
E Mal : **East Malling**
E Mos : **East Molesey**
E Pec : **East Peckham**
E Til : **East Tilbury**
Eastc : **Eastcote**
East : **Eastwick**
Ecc : **Eccles**
Eden : **Edenbridge**
Edg : **Edgware**
E Com : **Edney Common**
Eff : **Effingham**
Eff J : **Effingham Junction**
Egh : **Egham**
Ell : **Ellesborough**
E'tree : **Elstree**
Enf : **Enfield**
Enf H : **Enfield Highway**
Enf L : **Enfield Lock**
Enf W : **Enfield Wash**
Eng G : **Englefield Green**
Epp : **Epping**
Epp G : **Epping Green**
Epp U : **Epping Upland**
Eps : **Epsom**
Eps D : **Epsom Downs**
Erith : **Erith**
Esh : **Esher**
Ess : **Essendon**
Eton : **Eton**
Eton W : **Eton Wick**
Ewe : **Ewell**
Ews : **Ewshot**
Eyns : **Eynsford**
Farnb : **Farnborough**
Farnh : **Farnham**
Farn C : **Farnham Common**
Farn R : **Farnham Royal**
Farni : **Farningham**
Fawk : **Fawkham**
Felt : **Feltham**
Fet : **Fetcham**
Fidd H : **Fiddlers Hamlet**
Fifi : **Fifield**
Fin : **Finchampstead**
Five G : **Five Oak Green**
Flack H : **Flackwell Heath**
Flam : **Flamstead**
Flau : **Flaunden**
Fleet : **Fleet**
Flex : **Flexford**
Fob : **Fobbing**
F Elm : **Four Elms**
Frim : **Frimley**
F Grn : **Frimley Green**
F'mre : **Frogmore**
Fry : **Fryerning**
Ful : **Fulmer**
Fyf : **Fyfield**
Gad R : **Gaddesden Row**
Gall : **Galleywood**
G Grn : **George Green**
Ger X : **Gerrards Cross**
G'ham : **Gillingham**
G'ton : **Gilston**
G'stone : **Godstone**
G Oak : **Goff's Oak**
Gold G : **Golden Green**
Goms : **Gomshall**
G Eas : **Good Easter**
Grav'nd : **Gravesend**
Grays : **Grays**
Gt A : **Great Amwell**
Gt B : **Great Baddow**
Gt Gad : **Great Gaddesden**
Gt H : **Great Hampden**
Gt Kim : **Great Kimble**
Gt Kin : **Great Kingshill**
Gt Miss : **Great Missenden**
Gt W : **Great Waltham**
Gt War : **Great Warley**
G'frd : **Greenford**
Ghithe : **Greenhithe**
Gsted : **Greensted**
Guild : **Guildford**
Had W : **Hadley Wood**
Had : **Hadlow**
Hail : **Hailey**
Hale : **Hale**
Hall : **Halling**
Hals : **Halstead**
Hal : **Halton**
Ham : **Ham**
Hamp : **Hampton**
Ham H : **Hampton Hill**
Ham W : **Hampton Wick**
Hanw : **Hanworth**
Hare : **Harefield**
Har H : **Hare Hatch**
Harl : **Harlington**
Har : **Harlow**
Harm : **Harmondsworth**
Hrld W : **Harold Wood**
Harp : **Harpenden**
Harr : **Harrow**
Hrw W : **Harrow Weald**
Hartl : **Hartley**
Hasti : **Hastingwood**
Hasto : **Hastoe**
Hat E : **Hatch End**
Hat : **Hatfield**
Hat H : **Hatfield Heath**
Hat P : **Hatfield Peverel**
Have B : **Havering-Atte-Bower**
Hawl : **Hawley**
Hawr : **Hawridge**
Hayes : **Hayes**
Haz : **Hazlemere**
H'ly : **Headley**
H End : **Heath End**
Hedg : **Hedgerley**
Hem H : **Hemel Hempstead**
Hem : **Hempstead**
Heron : **Herongate**
Herons : **Heronsgate**
Hers : **Hersham**
Hertf : **Hertford**
Hert H : **Hertford Heath**
Herti : **Hertingfordbury**
Hest : **Heston**
Hever : **Hever**
High'm : **Higham**
H Beech : **High Beech**
H Hal : **High Halstow**
H Laver : **High Laver**
H Ongar : **High Ongar**
High : **Highwood**
H Wych : **High Wych**
H Wy : **High Wycombe**
Hild : **Hildenborough**
Hil : **Hillingdon**
Hin W : **Hinchley Wood**
Hodd : **Hoddesdon**
Holm G : **Holmer Green**
Holmw : **Holmwood**
Holy : **Holyport**
Hoo : **Hoo**
Hook E : **Hook End**
Horn : **Hornchurch**
Horn H : **Horndon-On-The-Hill**
Hort : **Horton**
Hort K : **Horton Kirby**
Houn : **Hounslow**
Howe G : **Howe Green**
Hug V : **Hughenden Valley**
Huns : **Hunsdon**
Hunt : **Hunton**
Hunt C : **Hunton Cross**
Hur : **Hurley**
Hut : **Hutton**
H Hea : **Hyde Heath**
Ick : **Ickenham**
Ide H : **Ide Hill**
Igh : **Ightham**
Ilf : **Ilford**
Inga : **Ingatestone**
Ingve : **Ingrave**
Isle : **Isleworth**
Ist R : **Istead Rise**
Iver : **Iver**
Iver H : **Iver Heath**
Ivy H : **Ivy Hatch**
Jac W : **Jacobs Well**
Jor : **Jordans**
Kel C : **Kelvedon Common**
Kel H : **Kelvedon Hatch**
Kems'g : **Kemsing**
Kenl : **Kenley**
Kent : **Kenton**
Kes : **Keston**
Kew : **Kew**
K Grn : **Kiln Green**
Kim W : **Kimble Wick**
King : **Kingsash**
Kin H : **Kings Hill**
K Lan : **Kings Langley**
King T : **Kingston Upon Thames**
Kgswd : **Kingswood**
Knap : **Knaphill**
Knat : **Knatts Valley**
Knock : **Knockholt**
K Hill : **Knowl Hill**
Lac G : **Lacey Green**
Ladd : **Laddingford**
Lain : **Laindon**
Lale : **Laleham**
L End : **Lane End**
Lan H : **Langdon Hills**
L'ly : **Langley**
Lang : **Langleybury**
Lark : **Larkfield**
Lat : **Latimer**
L Rod : **Leaden Roding**
Lea : **Leatherhead**
Lee C : **Lee Common**
Leigh : **Leigh**
Lem : **Lemsford**
Let H : **Letchmore Heath**
Let G : **Letty Green**
Leyb : **Leybourne**
Ley H : **Ley Hill**
Light : **Lightwater**
Limp : **Limpsfield**
Linf : **Linford**
Ling : **Lingfield**
Lint : **Linton**
Lit B : **Little Baddow**
L Ber : **Little Berkhamsted**
L Bur : **Little Burstead**
L Chal : **Little Chalfont**
L Gad : **Little Gaddesden**
Lit H : **Little Hampden**
Lit K : **Little Kimble**
L King : **Little Kingshill**
Lit L : **Little Laver**
Lit M : **Little Marlow**
L Mis : **Little Missenden**
Lit W : **Little Waltham**
L War : **Little Warley**
L Grn : **Littlewick Green**
Lon C : **London Colney**
H'row A : **London Heathrow Airport**
Longc : **Longcross**
Lfield : **Longfield**
Long H : **Longfield Hill**
Lford : **Longford**
Loose : **Loose**
L Row : **Loosely Row**
Lor : **Lordswood**
Loud : **Loudwater**
Lough : **Loughton**
Lwr K : **Lower Kingswood**
Lud'n : **Luddesdown**
Lye G : **Lye Green**
Lyne : **Lyne**
Mag L : **Magdalen Laver**
Maide : **Maidenhead**
Maids : **Maidstone**
Map C : **Maple Cross**
Mard : **Marden**
M Rod : **Margaret Roding**
Marg : **Margaretting**
Marl : **Marlow**
Mash : **Mashbury**
M Grn : **Matching Green**
Mat T : **Matching Tye**
Mawney : **Mawney**
Med : **Medmenham**
Med E : **Medway City Estate**
Meop : **Meopham**
Mere : **Mereworth**
Mers : **Merstham**
Mick : **Mickleham**
Mid H : **Mid Holmwood**
Mill G : **Mill Green**
Min : **Minley**
Mitc : **Mitcham**
M Ris : **Monks Risborough**
Mord : **Morden**
More : **Moreton**
Mount : **Mountnessing**
Myt : **Mytchett**
Nap : **Naphill**
Nave : **Navestock**
N'side : **Navestockside**
Naze : **Nazeing**
Nett : **Nettleden**
New Ad : **New Addington**
New A : **New Ash Green**
New Bar : **New Barnet**
New S : **Newgate Street**
New G : **New Ground**
New H : **New Haw**
N Mald : **New Malden**
Nine A : **Nine Ashes**
Noak H : **Noak Hill**
Norm : **Normandy**
N'thaw : **Northaw**
Nth B : **North Benfleet**
Nth D : **North Dean**
Nflt : **Northfleet**
Nflt G : **Northfleet Green**
N Holm : **North Holmwood**
N Mym : **North Mymms**
N Ock : **North Ockendon**
N'olt : **Northolt**
N Stif : **North Stifford**
N Weald : **North Weald**
Nwood : **Northwood**
Nor H : **Norton Heath**
Nor M : **Norton Mandeville**
Nutf : **Nutfield**
Oak G : **Oakley Green**
Ock : **Ockham**
Off : **Offham**
Old Win : **Old Windsor**
Ongar : **Ongar**
Orch : **Orchard Leigh**
Orp : **Orpington**
Ors : **Orsett**
Otf : **Otford**
Ott : **Ottershaw**
Outw : **Outwood**
Owl : **Owlsmoor**
Oxs : **Oxshott**
Oxt : **Oxted**
Pad W : **Paddock Wood**
Pal S : **Paley Street**
Pan : **Panshanger**
Park : **Park Street**
Par H : **Parslows Hillock**
Peasm : **Peasmarsh**
Pen H : **Penenden Heath**
Penn : **Penn**
Penn S : **Penn Street**
Pet W : **Petts Wood**
Pidd : **Piddington**
Pil H : **Pilgrims Hatch**
Pinn : **Pinner**
Pirb : **Pirbright**
Pit : **Pitsea**
Plax : **Plaxtol**
Pond E : **Ponders End**
Pott E : **Potten End**
Pot B : **Potters Bar**
Pot C : **Potters Crouch**
Poyle : **Poyle**
Prat B : **Pratts Bottom**
Pre : **Prestwood**
Pri R : **Princes Risborough**
Purf : **Purfleet**
Purl : **Purley**
Putt : **Puttenham**
Pyr : **Pyrford**
Rad : **Radlett**
Rad G : **Radley Green**
Rad : **Radnage**
Rain : **Rainham**
Ram : **Ramsden Bellhouse**
Ram H : **Ramsden Heath**
Ran C : **Ranmore Common**
Raw : **Rawreth**
Ray : **Rayleigh**
Redb : **Redbourn**
Redh : **Redhill**
Reig : **Reigate**
Ret : **Rettendon**
Rich P : **Richings Park**
Rich : **Richmond**
Rick : **Rickmansworth**
Ridge : **Ridge**
Rip : **Ripley**
Riv : **Riverhead**
Roch : **Rochester**
Rom : **Romford**
Rox : **Roxwell**
Roy : **Roydon**
Ruis : **Ruislip**
Runf : **Runfold**
Runw : **Runwell**
Rush G : **Rush Green**
Rya : **Ryarsh**
St A : **St Albans**
St L : **St Leonards**
St M Cry : **St Mary Cray**
St P : **St Pauls Cray**
Salf : **Salfords**
Sande : **Sanderstead**
S'urst : **Sandhurst**
S'ing : **Sandling**
Sando : **Sandon**
Sandr : **Sandridge**
Sarr : **Sarratt**
Saund : **Saunderton**
Saw : **Sawbridgeworth**
Seal : **Seal**
Seale : **Seale**
See G : **Seer Green**
Sels : **Selsdon**
Send : **Send**
S'oaks : **Sevenoaks**
Shack : **Shackleford**
Sheer : **Sheering**
Shenf : **Shenfield**
Shenl : **Shenley**
Shep : **Shepperton**
Shere : **Shere**
S'brne : **Shipbourne**
S'ham : **Shoreham**
Shorne : **Shorne**
S Row : **Shurlock Row**
Sidc : **Sidcup**
Sid : **Sidlow**
Sip : **Sipson**
Slou : **Slough**
S'ford : **Smallford**
Snod : **Snodland**
Sole S : **Sole Street**
S'hall : **Southall**
S Croy : **South Croydon**
S Dar : **South Darenth**
Sflt : **Southfleet**
S God : **South Godstone**
Sth H : **South Hanningfield**
S Hth : **South Heath**
S Mim : **South Mimms**
S Nut : **South Nutfield**
S Ock : **South Ockendon**
S Weald : **South Weald**
Sth F : **South Woodham Ferrers**
Speen : **Speen**
Spr : **Springfield**
Staines : **Staines**
Stan H : **Stanford-le-hope**
Stan : **Stanmore**
S Abb : **Stanstead Abbotts**
Stans : **Stansted**
Stanw : **Stanwell**
Stan M : **Stanwell Moor**
Stap A : **Stapleford Abbotts**
Stap T : **Stapleford Tawney**
Stap : **Staplehurst**
Stock : **Stock**
Stock P : **Stockley Park**
Stoke D : **Stoke D'Abernon**
S Man : **Stoke Mandeville**
Stoke P : **Stoke Poges**
Sto M : **Stondon Massey**
Strood : **Strood**
Sun : **Sunbury**
Sund : **Sundridge**
S'dale : **Sunningdale**
S'hill : **Sunninghill**
Surb : **Surbiton**
Sutt : **Sutton**
Sutt H : **Sutton At Hone**
Sut G : **Sutton Green**
Swan : **Swanley**
Swans : **Swanscombe**
Tad : **Tadworth**
Tand : **Tandridge**
Tap : **Taplow**
Tats : **Tatsfield**
Tatt C : **Tattenham Corner**
Tedd : **Teddington**
Ter : **Terling**
Terr : **Terrick**
Test : **Teston**
T Ditt : **Thames Ditton**
The L : **The Lee**
They B : **Theydon Bois**
They G : **Theydon Garnon**
They M : **Theydon Mount**
Thorn : **Thorney**
Thor H : **Thornton Heath**
Twood : **Thornwood**
Thorpe : **Thorpe**
Thun : **Thundersley**
Tilb : **Tilbury**
T'sey : **Titsey**
Tonb : **Tonbridge**
Tong : **Tongham**
Toot H : **Toot Hill**
Tring : **Tring**
Trin : **Tringford**
Tros : **Trottiscliffe**
Tude : **Tudeley**
Turn : **Turnford**
Twick : **Twickenham**
Twy : **Twyford**
Ty G : **Tylers Green**
Under : **Underriver**
Upm : **Upminster**
Up : **Upnor**
Up H : **Upper Hale**
Uxb : **Uxbridge**
Vange : **Vange**
Vir W : **Virginia Water**
Wadd : **Waddon**
Wain : **Wainscott**
Wald : **Walderslade**
Wall : **Wallington**
W Ash : **Walters Ash**
Walt A : **Waltham Abbey**
Walt C : **Waltham Cross**
W Law : **Waltham St Lawrence**
Walt T : **Walton-on-Thames**
Walt H : **Walton on the Hill**
Wanb : **Wanborough**
Ware : **Ware**
Warf : **Warfield**
Warl : **Warley**
Warl : **Warlingham**
W Row : **Warren Row**
W'bury : **Wateringbury**
Wat O : **Water Oakley**
Wat : **Watford**
Weald : **Weald**
W'stone : **Wealdstone**
Weav : **Weavering**
Wel G : **Welham Green**
Well : **Welling**
W City : **Welwyn Garden City**
Wemb : **Wembley**
Wend : **Wendover**
Wenn : **Wennington**
W Byf : **West Byfleet**
W Cla : **West Clandon**
W Dray : **West Drayton**
W End : **West End**
W Far : **West Farleigh**
W Han : **West Hanningfield**
W H'dn : **West Horndon**
W Hor : **West Horsley**
W Hyd : **West Hyde**
W King : **West Kingsdown**
W Mal : **West Malling**
W Mole : **West Molesey**
W Peck : **West Peckham**
W Thur : **West Thurrock**
W Til : **West Tilbury**
W W'ck : **West Wickham**
W Wyc : **West Wycombe**
Westc : **Westcott**
Westrm : **Westerham**
Westh : **Westhumble**
W Tur : **Weston Turville**
Wex : **Wexham**
Wey : **Weybourne**
Weyb : **Weybridge**
Whe : **Wheathampstead**
Whe E : **Wheeler End**
Whel : **Whelpley Hill**
White : **Whiteleaf**
W Vill : **Whiteley Village**
W Rod : **White Roding**
W Walt : **White Waltham**
Whitt : **Whitton**
Whyt : **Whyteleafe**
Wick : **Wickford**
Wid : **Widford**
Wid E : **Widmer End**
Wigg : **Wigginton**
Will : **Willingale**
Wil : **Wilstone**
Win H : **Winchmore Hill**
W'sham : **Windlesham**
Wind : **Windsor**
Wink : **Winkfield**
Wink R : **Winkfield Row**
Wis : **Wisley**
Wok : **Woking**
W'ham : **Wokingham**
Wold : **Woldingham**
Wbrn G : **Wooburn Green**
Wfd G : **Woodford Green**
Wdhm : **Woodham**
Woo V : **Wood Street Village**
Wor Pk : **Worcester Park**
Worm : **Wormley**
Worp : **Worplesdon**
Wott : **Wotton**
Woul : **Wouldham**
Wray : **Wraysbury**
Writ : **Writtle**
Wro : **Wrotham**
W Grn : **Wyatts Green**
Wyc M : **Wycombe Marsh**
Yald : **Yalding**
Yat : **Yateley**
Yead : **Yeading**
Yiew : **Yiewsley**

A

ABBESS END 1A 10
ABBESS RODING 1A 10
Abbeville Rd. SW4 2F 23
Abbey Barn La. HP11: Wyc M 2B 12
Abbey Barn Rd. HP11: Wyc M 2B 12
Abbey La. E15 4C 16
Abbey Pk. La. SL1: Burn 3D 13
Abbey Rd. DA12: Grav'nd 2D 27
DA17: Belv 1E 25
E15 4C 16
IG11: Bark 3D 17
NW6 3E 15
NW10 4D 15
Abbey St. SE1 1A 24
Abbey Vw. EN9: Walt A 3B 8
Abbey Way HP11: H Wy 1B 12
ABBEY WOOD 1E 25
ABBOTSBROOK 3B 12
Abbotsbury Rd. SM4: Mord 4E 23
ABBOTS LANGLEY 3A 6
Abbots Rd. WD5: Ab L 3A 6
ABBOTSWOOD 4E 29
Abbott Rd. E14 4C 16
(not continuous)
Abbotts Dr. SS17: Stan H 4D 19
Abbotts Rd. SM3: Cheam 4E 23
Abbs Cross La. RM12: Horn 3F 17
Aberconway Rd. SM4: Mord 3E 23
Abercorn Pl. NW8 4F 15
Abercorn Rd. HA7: Stan 2C 14
Abercrombie Way CM18: Har 1D 9
Aberdeen Rd. CR0: C'don 4A 24
NW10 3D 15
ABINGER HAMMER 4A 30
Abinger La. RH5: Ab C, Ab H 4B 30
Aboyne Rd. SW17 2F 23
ABRIDGE 4E 9
Abridge Rd.
CM16: Abr, Lough, They B 4D 9
IG7: Abr, Chig 1D 17
RM4: Abr 4E 9
Academy Rd. SE18 1D 25
Accommodation Rd.
KT16: Longc 4E 21
Acre La. SM5: Cars 4F 23
SM6: Wall 4F 23
SW2 2A 24
Acre Rd. KT2: King T 3D 23
ACTON 4D 15
ACTON GREEN 1D 23
Acton La. NW10 4D 15
ADDINGTON
CR0 4B 24
ME19 2C 34
Addington La. ME19: Tros 2C 34
Addington Rd. BR4: W W'ck 4C 24
CR2: Sande, Sels 1B 32
Addington Village Rd.
CR0: Addtn 4B 24
(not continuous)
ADDISCOMBE 4B 24
Addiscombe Gro. CR0: C'don 4A 24
Addiscombe Rd. CR0: C'don 4A 24
(not continuous)
Addison Cres. W14 1E 23
(not continuous)
Addison Rd. HP5: Ches 3D 5
W14 1E 23
ADDLESTEAD 4D 35
Addlestead Rd. TN12: E Pec 4D 35
ADDLESTONE 4F 21
ADDLESTONE MOOR 4F 21
Addlestone Rd. KT15: Add 4A 22
Adelaide Av. SE4 2B 24
Adelaide Rd. NW3 3F 15
ADEYFIELD 2A 6
Adeyfield Rd. HP2: Hem H 2A 6
Aerodrome Rd. NW9 2D 15
Aerospace Blvd. GU14: Farnb 3B 28
Agar Gro. NW1 3F 15
Agates La. KT21: Asht 2C 30
Agincourt Rd. NW3 3F 15
AIMES GREEN 3C 8
Aintree Rd. UB6: G'frd 4C 14
Airfield Way RM12: Horn 3F 17
WD25: Wat 3A 6
Akeman St. HP23: Tring 1C 4
Akerman Rd. SW9 1A 24
Alanbrooke Rd. GU11: Alde 3B 28
Albany Rd. BR7: Chst 3D 25
SE5 1A 24
SL4: Old Win 2E 21
Albany St. NW1 4F 15
Albany Ter. ME4: Chat 4F 27
Albemarle Rd. BR3: Beck 3B 24
ME5: Lor 1F 35
Albert Bri. SW11 1F 23
Albert Bri. Rd. SW11 1F 23
Albert Dr. GU21: Wok 2F 29
Albert Emb. SE1 1A 24
Albert Rd. DA17: Belv 1E 25
E16 4D 17
IG9: Buck H 1C 16
N22 2F 15
RM1: Rom 2F 17
SL4: Old Win, Wind 2D 21
Albert St. SL1: Slou 1D 21
(not continuous)
Albert Ter. NW1 4F 15
Albion Dr. E8 3B 16
Albion Pl. ME14: Maids 3F 35
Albion Rd. DA6: Bex 2E 25
N16 3A 16
ALBURY 4F 29
ALBURY HEATH 4A 30
Albyns La. RM4: Stap T 4F 9
ALDBOROUGH HATCH 2E 17
Aldborough Rd. Nth. IG2: Ilf 2D 17
Aldborough Rd. Sth. IG3: Ilf 3D 17
ALDBURY 1D 5
ALDENHAM 4B 6
Aldenham Av. WD7: Rad 4C 6
Aldenham Rd. WD6: E'tree 4C 6
WD7: Rad 4C 6
WD23: Bush 1B 14
Alderbourne La. SL0: Iver H 3E 13
SL3: Ful 3E 13
Aldermans Hill N13 1A 16
Alderney Av. TW5: Hest, Isle 1B 22
ALDERSBROOK 3C 16
Aldersbrook Rd. E11 3C 16
E12 3C 16
Aldersgate St. EC1 4A 16
ALDERSHOT 4B 28
Aldershot Rd. GU2: Guild 3D 29
GU3: Guild, Norm, Worp 3D 29
GU12: Ash 4B 28
GU24: Pirb 3C 28
GU51: Fleet 3A 28
GU52: Chu C 3A 28
Aldershot Town FC 4B 28
ALDERSTEAD HEATH 3F 31
Alderstead La. RH1: Mers 3F 31
Alderton Hill IG10: Lough 1D 17
ALDGATE 4A 16
ALDON 2C 34
Aldon La. ME19: Off 2C 34
Aldrington Rd. SW16 3F 23
Aldwych WC2 4A 16
Alexander La. CM15: Shenf 1B 18
Alexandra Av. HA2: Harr 3B 14
W4 1D 23
Alexandra Dr. KT5: Surb 4D 23
Alexandra Gro. N12 2E 15
Alexandra Pal. Way N8 2F 15
Alexandra Pk. Rd. N10 2F 15
N22 2F 15
Alexandra Rd. GU11: Alde 4A 28
(not continuous)
GU14: Farnb 3B 28
HP2: Hem H 2F 5
KT17: Eps 1D 31
SW19 3E 23
Alfreds Way IG11: Bark 4D 17
Alison's Rd. GU11: Alde 4B 28
Alkerden La.
DA9: Ghithe, Swans 2B 26
DA10: Ghithe, Swans 2B 26
Allenby Rd. UB1: S'hall 4B 14
Allende Av. CM20: Har 1D 9
(not continuous)
Allens La. TN15: Plax 3B 34
Allerds Rd. SL2: Farn R 4D 13
Alleyn Pk. SE21 2A 24
Alleyns La. SL6: Cook 3B 12
ALLINGTON 2F 35
All Saints Av. SL6: Maide 4B 12
All Saints Rd. SM1: Sutt 4E 23
Allsop Pl. NW1 4F 15
All Souls Av. NW10 4E 15
Allum La. WD6: E'tree 1D 15
Alma La. GU9: Up H 4A 28
Alma Rd. AL1: St A 2C 6
DA14: Sidc 2E 25
EN3: Pond E 1B 16
SL4: Wind 1D 21
SM5: Cars 4F 23
Almners Rd. KT16: Lyne 4E 21
(not continuous)
Alms Heath GU23: Ock 2A 30
ALPERTON 4D 15
Alperton La. HA0: Wemb 4C 14
Alphington Av. GU16: Frim 2B 28
Alston Rd. EN5: Barn 4E 7
Altwood Rd. SL6: Maide 4B 12
(not continuous)
Ambarrow La. GU47: S'urst 1A 28
Amberwood Ri. KT3: N Mald 4D 23
Ambleside Av. BR3: Beck 4B 24
SW16 3F 23
AMERSHAM 4D 5
AMERSHAM COMMON 4D 5
Amersham Hill HP13: H Wy 1B 12
AMERSHAM OLD TOWN 4D 5
AMERSHAM ON THE HILL 4D 5
Amersham Rd. HP5: Ches 4D 5
HP6: Amer 4D 5
HP6: L Chal 4E 5
HP7: Cole 1D 13
HP8: Chal G 1E 13
(not continuous)
HP9: Beac 2D 13
HP13: H Wy 1B 12
HP15: Haz, Bea E 1B 12
SL9: Chal P 1E 13
SL9: Ger X 2E 13
(not continuous)
UB9: Den 2E 13
WD3: Chen 4E 5
Amherst Hill TN13: Riv 3F 33
Amhurst Pk. N16 3A 16
Amhurst Rd. E8 3B 16
N16 3A 16
Ampere Way CR0: Wadd 4A 24
Amsbury Rd. ME15: Cox 4E 35
ME17: Cox 4E 35
Amstel Way GU21: Wok 2D 29
AMWELL 1C 6
Amwell Hill SG12: Gt A 1B 8
Amwell La. SG12: Gt A, S Abb 1B 8
Amwell St. EN11: Hodd 1B 8
(not continuous)
N1 4A 16
Amy La. HP5: Ches 3D 5
Ancells Rd. GU51: Fleet 3A 28
Anchor Hill GU21: Knap 2D 29
Anchor La. CM6: Abb R 1A 10
HP1: Hem H 2F 5
(not continuous)
Andrew Hill La. SL2: Hedg 3D 13
Andrew's La. EN7: Chesh 3A 8
(not continuous)
ANERLEY 3B 24
Anerley Hill SE19 3A 24
Anerley Rd. SE19 3B 24
SE20 3B 24
ANGEL 4A 16
ANGEL EDMONTON JUNC. 1B 16
Angel Hill SM1: Sutt 4E 23
(not continuous)
Angel La. E15 3C 16
UB3: Hayes 4A 14
Angel Rd. KT7: T Ditt 4C 22
N18 1B 16
Anson Rd. NW2 3E 15
ANTHONYS 1E 29
Anthony's Way
ME2: Med E, Strood 3F 27
(not continuous)
Anton Way HP21: A'bury 1A 4
Anyards Rd. KT11: Cobh 1B 30
APERFIELD 2D 33
APEX CORNER
Feltham 2B 22
Mill Hill 1D 15
Appleby St. EN7: Chesh 2A 8
Applecroft Rd. AL8: W City 1E 7
Approach, The KT23: Bookh 3B 30
Approach Rd. SL6: Tap 4C 12
SW20 3E 23
TN16: Tats 2C 32
Appspond La. AL2: Pot C 2B 6
APSLEY 2F 5
Arbour La. CM1: Spr 1F 11
Arbuthnot La. DA5: Bexl 2E 25
Arcadia Rd. DA13: Ist R 3C 26
ARCHWAY 3F 15
Arch Way HP13: H Wy 1B 12
Archway Rd. N6 2F 15
ARDLEIGH GREEN 2F 17
Ardleigh Grn. Rd. RM11: Horn 2F 17
Arethusa Rd. ME1: Roch 4F 27
Argall Way E10 3B 16
Argent St. RM17: Grays 1B 26
Argent Way EN7: Chesh, G Oak 2A 8
Argyle Rd. N12 1E 15
UB6: G'frd 4C 14
W13 4C 14
Arisdale Av. RM15: S Ock 4B 18
ARKLEY 1E 15
Arkwright Rd. CR2: Sande 1A 32
NW3 3F 15
Armoury Way SW18 2E 23
Arnhem Dr. CR0: New Ad 1C 32
Arnison Av. HP13: H Wy 1B 12
Arnold Rd. GU21: Wok 2E 29
Arnolds Farm La.
CM13: Mount 4C 10
Arnold's La. DA4: Sutt H 3A 26
Arnsberg Way DA7: Bex 2E 25
Arrewig La. HP5: Char 2C 4
HP23: St L 2C 4
Arrow Rd. GU14: Cove 3A 28
Arsenal FC 3A 16
Arterial Rd. RM16: N Stif 1B 26
RM19: Purf 1A 26
RM20: W Thur 1B 26
SS17: Horn H 4D 19
Arthur Rd. SL4: Wind 1D 21
SW19 3E 23
Artillery Pl. SE18 1D 25
ARTINGTON 4E 29
ASCOT 3C 20
ASCOT HEATH 3C 20
Ascot Racecourse 3C 20
Ascot Rd. RG42: Warf 2B 20
SL6: Holy, Pal S 2B 20
WD18: Wat 1A 14
Ascots La. AL9: Hat 1E 7
ASH
GU12 4B 28
TN15 4B 26
Ashburnham Rd. SW10 1F 23
Ashburton Rd. CR0: C'don 4B 24
Ash Church Rd. GU12: Ash 4B 28
Ashcombe Rd. RH4: Dork 4C 30
Ashdon Way SS16: Bas 2E 19
Ashendene Rd. SG13: B'fd 2A 8
ASHERIDGE 2C 4
Asheridge Rd. HP5: Ches 3D 5
Ashes La. TN11: Had 4B 34
Ashfield La. BR7: Chst 3D 25
(not continuous)
Ashfields WD25: Wat 4A 6
ASHFORD 3A 22
ASHFORD COMMON 3A 22
ASHFORD PARK 2F 21
Ashford Rd.
ME14: Bear, Maids, Weav 3F 35
TW13: Felt 3A 22
TW15: Ashf 3A 22
TW18: Lale, Staines 3F 21
ASH GREEN 4C 28
Ash Grn. Rd. GU12: Ash G 4C 28
Ashgrove Rd. BR1: Brom 3C 24
TN13: S'oaks 3F 33
Ash Hill Rd. GU12: Ash V 4B 28
Ash La. TN15: Ash, W King 1B 34
Ashley Av. KT18: Eps 1D 31
ASHLEY GREEN 2D 5
Ashley Grn. Rd. HP5: Ches 3D 5
ASHLEY PARK 4B 22
Ashley Pk. Rd. KT12: Walt T 4B 22
Ashley Rd. AL1: St A 2C 6
KT12: Walt T 4A 22
KT18: Eps 1D 31
TW12: Hamp 3B 22
Ashlyns SS13: Pit 2E 19
Ashlyns La. CM5: Mag L, Ongar 2F 9
Ashridge La. HP5: Ley H 3E 5
Ash Rd.
DA3: Hartl, Lfield, New A 3B 26
GU12: Alde 4B 28
GU24: Pirb 3D 29
TN15: Ash, New A 4B 26
Ash St. GU12: Ash 4B 28
ASHTEAD 2D 31
ASHTEAD PARK 2D 31
Ashton Way ME19: W Mal 2D 35
Ash Tree La. ME5: Chat 4F 27
Ashurst Rd. KT20: Tad 2E 31
ASH VALE 3B 28
Ashwells Rd. CM15: Pil H 4A 10
ASKETT 2A 4
Askew Rd. W12 1D 23
Aspen Way E14 4B 16
ASTON CLINTON 1B 4
Aston Clinton By-Pass
HP22: Ast C, Bkld 1B 4
Aston Clinton Rd. HP22: W Tur 1A 4
Atkins Rd. SW12 2F 23
Attlee Dr. DA1: Dart 2A 26
Auckland Rd. SE19 3A 24
Augustus Rd. SW19 2E 23
AUSTENWOOD 2E 13
Austenwood La. SL9: Chal P 2E 13
AVELEY 4A 18
Aveley By-Pass RM15: Avel 4A 18
Aveley Rd. RM14: Avel, Upm 3A 18
Avenue, The BR4: W W'ck 4C 24
CM13: B'wood 2B 18
DA9: Ghithe 2B 26
E4 2C 16
EN5: Barn 4E 7
GU3: Comp 3D 29
GU15: Camb 2B 28
HA6: Nwood 2A 14
HA9: Wemb 3D 15
KT4: Wor Pk 4D 23
KT20: Tad 2E 31
NW6 4E 15
RH1: S Nut 4A 32
SW4 2F 23
TW5: Cran 1B 22
TW16: Sun 3B 22
W4 1D 23
WD17: Wat 4B 6
WD23: Bush 4B 6
Avenue Rd. DA7: Bex 2E 25
GU14: Farnb 3B 28
KT18: Eps 1D 31
N14 1F 15
NW3 4F 15
NW8 3F 15
SM2: Sutt 1E 31
AVERY HILL 2D 25
Avery Hill Rd. SE9 2D 25
Avey La. EN9: Lough, Walt A 4C 8
Avignon Rd. SE4 2B 24
Avon Rd. RM14: Upm 2A 18
Avontar Rd. RM15: S Ock 4B 18
Aycliffe Dr. HP2: Hem H 1A 6
Aycliffe Rd. WD6: Bore 4D 7
AYLESBURY 1A 4
Aylesbury End HP9: Beac 2D 13
Aylesbury Rd. HP16: Gt Miss 3B 4
HP22: Ast C 1B 4
HP22: Wend 1B 4
HP23: Tring 1C 4
HP27: Ask, Pri R, M Ris 2A 4
AYLESFORD 2E 35
Ayling Hill GU11: Alde 4A 28
Aylmer Rd. N2 2F 15
AYRES END 1C 6
Ayres End La. AL3: St A 1C 6
AL5: Harp 1C 6

B

BAAS HILL 2B 8
Baas Hill EN10: Brox 2B 8
Baas La. EN10: Brox 2B 8
Babylon La. KT20: Lwr K 3E 31
Back La. CM3: E Han 3F 11
CM3: Lit W 1E 11
CM4: Fry, Mill G 3C 10
CM4: Stock 4D 11
(not continuous)
EN9: Naze 2C 8
Back La. HP8: Chal G 1E 13
ME17: B Mon, Cha S 4F 35
TN11: S'brne 4B 34
TN14: Ide H 3E 33
TN15: Igh 3B 34
WD25: Let H 4C 6
Baddow Rd. CM2: Chelm, Gt B 2E 11
(not continuous)
BADGER'S MOUNT 1E 33
Bad Godesberg Way SL6: Maide 4B 12
BADSHOT LEA 4B 28
Badshot Lea Rd. GU9: B Lea 4B 28
Bagden Hill RH5: Westh 3C 30
Bag La. CM4: Fry, Inga 4C 10
BAGSHOT 1C 28
Bagshot Rd. GU3: Worp 2D 29
GU19: Bag 3B 20
GU21: Brkwd, Knap 2D 29
GU24: Chob, W End 1D 29
GU24: Wok 2D 29
RG12: Bag, Brac 3B 20
SL5: Asc 4C 20
Bailes La. GU3: Norm 4C 28
Bailey's La. RG10: W Law 2A 20
Bakeham La. TW20: Eng G 3E 21
Bakers La. CM2: W Han 3E 11
BAKER STREET 4C 18
BAKER STREET 4F 15
Baker St. EN1: Enf 4A 8
EN6: Pot B 4E 7
KT13: Weyb 4A 22
NW1 4F 15
RM16: Ors 4C 18
W1 4F 15
Balaam St. E13 4C 16
Balaclava Rd. KT6: Surb 4C 22
Balchins La. RH4: Westc 4B 30
Baldwin's La. WD3: Crox G 4A 6
Baldwyns Pk. DA5: Bexl 2F 25
Balgores La. RM2: Rom 2F 17
BALHAM 2F 23
Balham High Rd. SW12 2F 23
SW17 2F 23
Balham Hill SW12 2F 23
Ballards La. N3 2E 15
N12 2E 15
Ballards Rd. RM10: Dag 4E 17
Ballards Wlk. SS15: Lain 2D 19
Ballards Way CR0: C'don 1B 32
CR2: Sels 1B 32
BALLINGER BOTTOM 3C 4
BALLINGER COMMON 3C 4
Ballinger Rd. HP16: S Hth 3C 4
Balls Pond Rd. N1 3A 16
Balmoral Dr. GU16: Frim 2B 28
Balmoral Rd. E7 3C 16
ME7: G'ham 3F 27
WD24: Wat 4B 6
BALSTONIA 3D 19
Bampton Way GU21: Wok 2E 29
Bancroft Rd. RH2: Reig 4E 31
BANDONHILL 4F 23
Bangors Rd. Nth. SL0: Iver H 4F 13
Bangors Rd. Sth.
SL0: Iver, Iver H 4F 13
Bank Grn. HP5: Bell 2C 4
Bank La. TN11: Hild 4A 34
TN15: Under 4A 34
Bank Mill La. HP4: Berk 2E 5
Banks La. CM16: Fidd H, They M 3E 9
Banks Rd. ME2: Strood 3F 27
BANSTEAD 2F 31
Banstead Rd. CR3: Cat'm 2A 32
CR8: Purl 1A 32
KT17: Ewe 1E 31
SM5: Cars 1F 31
SM7: Bans 1E 31
Banstead Rd. Sth. SM2: Sutt 1F 31
Barclay Rd. CR0: C'don 4A 24
Bardell Ter. ME1: Roch 3F 27
Baring Rd. SE12 2C 24
BARKING 3D 17
Barking Northern Relief Rd.
IG11: Bark 3D 17
BARKING RIVERSIDE 4E 17
Barking Rd. E6 4C 16
E13 4C 16
E16 4C 16
BARKINGSIDE 2D 17
Barlby Rd. W10 4E 15
Barleycroft Rd. AL8: W City 1E 7
Barleylands Rd. CM11: Bill, Bas 2D 19
SS15: Bas 2D 19
Barley La. IG3: Ilf 3E 17
RM6: Chad H 2E 17
Barley Mow La. AL4: St A 2D 7
Barley Mow Rd. TW20: Eng G 2E 21
BARMING 3E 35
BARMING HEATH 3E 35
Barnacres Rd. HP3: Hem H 2A 6
Barnby Rd. GU21: Knap 2D 29
BARNEHURST 2F 25
Barnehurst Rd. DA7: Bex 1F 25
Barn End La. DA2: Dart 3F 25
BARNES 1D 23
BARNES CRAY 2F 25
Barnes High St. SW13 1D 23
Barnes La. ME17: Lint 4F 35
SW20 3E 23
WD4: K Lan 3F 5
BARNES STREET 4C 34
Barnes Wallis Dr. KT13: Weyb 1A 30
BARNET 4E 7
Barnet By-Pass NW7 2D 15
Barnet By-Pass Rd. WD6: Bore 1D 15
Barnet FC 1E 15
BARNET GATE 1D 15
Barnet Ga. La. EN5: Ark 1D 15
Barnet Hill EN5: Barn 4E 7
Barnet La. EN5: Barn 1E 15
N20 1E 15
WD6: Bore, E'tree 1D 15
(not continuous)
Barnet Rd. AL2: Lon C 3D 7
EN5: Ark 1D 15
EN5: Barn 4E 7
EN6: Pot B 4E 7
Barnett Wood La. KT21: Asht 2C 30
Barnet Way NW7 1D 15
Barn Hill ME15: Hunt 4E 35
BARNSBURY 3A 16
Barnsbury Rd. N1 4A 16
Barnsole Rd. ME7: G'ham 3F 27
Barrack Rd. CM1: G Eas 1C 10
TW4: Houn 2B 22
Barracks Hill HP7: Cole 1D 13
Barra Hall Rd. UB3: Hayes 4A 14
Barrow Grn. Rd. RH8: Oxt 3B 32
Barrow La. EN7: Chesh, G Oak 3A 8
(not continuous)
Barr's La. GU21: Knap 2D 29
(not continuous)
Barry Av. SL4: Wind 1D 21
Barry Rd. SE22 2B 24
BARSTABLE 2E 19
Bartholomew Way BR8: Swan 3F 25
Barton Rd. ME15: Maids 3F 35
BASILDON 2E 19
Basildon Rd. SE2 1E 25
SS15: Lain 2D 19
Bassett's La. CM5: Will 2B 10
Bastable Av. IG11: Bark 4D 17
BASTED 3B 34
Basted La. TN15: Bor G 3B 34
Basted Mill TN15: Bor G 2B 34
Baston Rd. BR2: Hayes 4C 24
BAT & BALL 2F 33
Batchwood Dr. AL3: St A 1B 6
BATCHWORTH 1A 14
BATCHWORTH HEATH 1A 14
Batchworth Heath Hill
WD3: Rick 1A 14
Batchworth La. HA6: Nwood 1A 14
Bates Hill TN15: Igh 2B 34
Bates La. HP22: W Tur 1A 4
Bath Rd.
RG10: Har H, K Grn, K Hill 1A 20
SL3: Coln 1F 21
SL3: Coln, Poyle 1F 21
SL6: L Grn, Maide 4B 12
SL6: Tap 4C 12
TW3: Houn 1B 22
TW4: Houn 1B 22
TW5: Cran 1A 22
TW6: H'row A 1A 22
UB3: Harl 1A 22
UB7: Harm, Sip 1A 22
W4 1D 23
Bath St. DA11: Grav'nd 2C 26
EC1 4A 16
BATTERSEA 1F 23
Battersea Bri. SW11 1F 23
Battersea Bri. Rd. SW11 1F 23
Battersea Pk. Rd. SW8 1F 23
SW11 1F 23
Battersea Ri. SW11 2F 23
Battlebridge La.
RH1: Mers, Redh 3F 31
Battlefields Rd. TN15: Wro 2B 34
Battle Rd. DA8: Erith 1F 25
DA17: Belv, Erith 1F 25
BATTLERS GREEN 4C 6
BATTLESBRIDGE 1F 19
Batts Hill RH1: Redh 4F 31
RH2: Reig 4F 31
Batt's Rd. DA12: Lud'n 4D 27
BAYFORD 1A 8
Bayford La. SG13: B'fd 1A 8
Bayham Rd. TN13: S'oaks 3F 33
Bayham St. NW1 4F 15
BAYLEY'S HILL 3F 33
Bayley's Hill
TN14: S'oaks, Weald 4F 33
Bayne Hill HP9: See G 2D 13
Bay Rd. RG12: Brac 3B 20
BAYSWATER 4E 15
Bayswater Rd. W2 4E 15
W11 4E 15
BEACON HILL
CM14 4A 10
HP10 1C 12
Beacon Hill CM14: Kel H 4A 10
HP10: Penn 1C 12
Beacon Hill Rd.
CM14: Kel C, Kel H 4A 10
GU10: Ews 4A 28
GU52: Chu C 4A 28
BEACONSFIELD 2C 12
Beaconsfield Comn. La.
HP9: Beac 3D 13
Beaconsfield Rd. AL1: St A 2C 6
AL10: Hat 1E 7
SL2: Farn C, Farn R 4D 13
W4 1D 23
BEACONTREE HEATH 3E 17
Beadles La. RH8: Oxt 4C 32
Beadon Rd. W6 1E 23
BEAMOND END 4C 4
Beamond End La.
HP7: Bea E, L Mis 4C 4
BEAN 2B 26
Bean La. DA2: Bean 2B 26
Bear Rd. TW13: Hanw 3B 22
Bearsted Rd.
ME14: Maids, Weav 2F 35
Beauchamp Pl. SW3 1F 23
BEAUCHAMP RODING 1B 10
Beaufort St. SW3 1F 23
Beaumont Rd. EN7: Brox 2A 8
SW19 2E 23
BECKENHAM 3B 24
Beckenham Hill Rd. BR3: Beck 3B 24
SE6 3B 24
Beckenham La. BR2: Brom 3C 24
Beckenham Rd. BR3: Beck 3B 24
BR4: W W'ck 4C 24
BECKTON 4D 17
Beckton Rd. E16 4C 16
BECONTREE 3E 17
Becontree Av. RM8: Dag 3E 17
BEDDINGTON 4A 24
BEDDINGTON CORNER 4F 23
Beddington Farm Rd. CR0: Bedd 4A 24
Beddington La. CR0: C'don 4F 23
Beddlestead La. CR6: Warl 2C 32
Beddow Way ME20: A'ford 2E 35
Bedfont La. TW14: Felt 2A 22
Bedfont Rd. TW13: Felt 2A 22
TW14: Bedf 2A 22
TW19: Stanw 2A 22
Bedford Dr. SL2: Farn C 3D 13
Bedford Hill SW12 2F 23
SW16 2F 23
Bedford La. SL5: S'dale 4D 21
BEDFORD PARK 1D 23
Bedford Rd. SW4 2A 24
Bedford Sq. WC1 4F 15
BEDGROVE 1A 4
Bedgrove HP21: A'bury 1A 4
BEDMOND 3A 6
Bedmond La. AL2: Pot C 2B 6
AL3: St A 2B 6
WD5: Bedm 2B 6
Bedmond Rd. HP3: Hem H 2A 6
WD5: Ab L, Bedm 3A 6
Bedonwell Rd.
DA7: Belv, Bex, Erith 1E 25
DA17: Belv 1E 25
Beech Av. KT24: Eff 4B 30
Beechen Gro. WD17: Wat 4B 6
Beechenlea La. BR8: Swan 3F 25
Beeches Av. SM5: Cars 1F 31
Beeches Rd. SL2: Farn C 3D 13
SS11: Raw 1F 19
Beech Farm Rd. CR6: Warl 2C 32
Beechfield Rd. HP1: Hem H 2F 5
Beech Hill EN4: Had W 4F 7
Beech Hyde La. AL4: Whe 1D 7
Beechin Bank Rd. ME5: Wald 1F 35
Beechin Wood La. TN15: Bor G 2C 34
Beech La. GU3: Flex 4C 28
Beechmont Rd. TN13: S'oaks 3F 33
Beech Rd. AL3: St A 1C 6
CM5: Will 2B 10
ME18: Mere 3C 34
Beech St. EC2 4A 16
Beech Tree Rd. HP15: Holm G 4B 4
Beechwood Av. AL1: St A 2C 6
Beehive La. AL7: W City 1E 7
CM2: Gall, Gt B 3E 11
IG1: Ilf 2D 17
IG4: Ilf 2D 17
BEENHAM'S HEATH 2A 20
Beesfield La. DA4: Farni 4A 26
Beesonend La. AL3: St A 1B 6
AL5: Harp 1B 6
BEGGAR HILL 3C 10
Beggar Hill CM4: Fry 3C 10
BEGGAR'S BUSH 3D 21
BEGGAR'S HILL 1D 31
Beggars La. TN16: Westrm 3D 33
Bekeswell La. CM2: Chelm, Gall 3D 11
Beldam Bri. Rd.
GU24: Chob, W End 1D 29
Belgrave Pl. SW1 1F 23
Belgrave Rd. SW1 1F 23
Belgrave Sq. SW1 1F 23
BELGRAVIA 1F 23
BELL, THE 2B 16
BELL BAR 2E 7
BELL COMMON 3D 9
Bellegrove Rd. DA16: Well 1D 25
Bellevue Rd. SW17 2F 23
Bellew Rd. GU16: Deep 2B 28
Bellfield Rd. W. HP13: H Wy 1B 12
BELLFIELDS 3E 29
Bell Foundry La. RG40: W'ham 3A 20
BELL GREEN 3B 24
Bell Grn. SE26 3B 24
Bell Grn. La. SE26 3B 24
Bell Hill CM3: Dan 2F 11
BELLINGDON 2D 5
Bellingdon Rd. HP5: Ches 3D 5
BELLINGHAM 2B 24
Bellingham Rd. SE6 2C 24
Bell La. AL2: Lon C 3D 7
AL9: Brk P 2E 7
EN3: Enf H, Enf W 4B 8
EN10: Brox 2B 8
HP4: Berk 1D 5
HP6: L Chal 4E 5
KT22: Fet 3C 30
ME1: Bur 1E 35
ME14: Box 1F 35
NW4 2E 15
Bells Farm Rd. TN11: E Pec 4C 34
TN12: E Pec 4C 34
Bells Hill SL2: Stoke P 4E 13
Bells Hill Rd. SS16: Vange 3E 19
Bell's La. ME3: Hoo 2F 27
Bell St. RH2: Reig 4E 31
Bellswood La. SL0: Iver 4E 13
BELMONT
HA3 2C 14
SM2 1E 31
Belmont Hill SE13 2C 24
Belmont Pk. Av. SL6: Maide 4B 12
Belmont Ri. SM2: Sutt 1E 31
Belmont Rd. DA8: Erith 1E 25
N15 2A 16
N17 2A 16
SL6: Maide 4B 12
UB8: Uxb 3F 13
BELSIZE 3F 5
Belsize Av. NW3 3F 15
Belsize Pk. NW3 3F 15
Belsize Rd. NW6 4E 15
Belsteads Farm La. CM3: Lit W 1E 11
Belswains La. HP3: Hem H 2A 6
BELTRING 4D 35
Beltring Rd. TN12: Pad W 4D 35
BELVEDERE 1E 25
Belvedere Rd. DA7: Bex 2E 25
Benhill Av. SM1: Sutt 4F 23
(not continuous)
Benhill Rd. SM1: Sutt 4F 23
BENHILTON 4F 23
Ben Jonson Rd. E1 4B 16
Benner La. GU24: W End 1D 29
Bennett's Castle La. RM8: Dag 3E 17
BENNETTS END 2A 6
Bennetts End Rd. HP3: Hem H 2A 6
BENOVER 4E 35
Benover Rd. ME18: Yald 4D 35
Bensham La. CR0: C'don 4A 24
CR7: Thor H 4A 24
Bentham Rd. SE28 4E 17
BENTLEY 4A 10
BENTLEY HEATH 4E 7
Benton Rd. IG1: Ilf 3D 17
Beresford Av. HA0: Wemb 4D 15
Beresford Hill ME17: B Mon 4F 35
Beresford St. SE18 1D 25
Bericot Way AL7: W City 1F 7
Berkeley St. W1 4F 15
Berkhampstead Rd. HP5: Ches 3D 5
BERKHAMSTED 1E 5
Berkhamsted By-Pass
HP1: Hem H 1D 5
HP23: Wigg 1D 5
Berkhamsted La. AL9: Ess 2F 7
Berkhamsted Rd. HP1: Hem H 1F 5
(not continuous)
Berkshire Way RG12: Brac 3A 20
BERMONDSEY 1B 24
Bermondsey St. SE1 4A 16
BERNARD'S HEATH 1C 6
Bernard St. WC1 4A 16
BERNERS RODING 1B 10
BERRYGROVE 4B 6
Berry Gro. La. WD25: A'ham 4B 6
Berry Hill SL6: Tap 4C 12
BERRYLANDS 4D 23
Berry La. GU3: Worp 3D 29
(not continuous)
GU22: Wok 3D 29
WD3: Chor, Rick 1F 13
BERRY'S GREEN 2D 33
Berry's Grn. Rd. TN16: Big H 2D 33
Berry's Hill TN16: Big H 2D 33
Berwick La. CM5: Ongar, Stap T 3F 9
Berwick Pond Rd. RM14: Rain 3A 18
Berwick Pond Rd. RM13: Rain 4A 18
Berwick Rd. SL7: Marl 3A 12
Bessborough Rd. HA1: Harr 3C 14
BESSELS GREEN 3F 33
Bessels Grn. Rd. TN13: Riv 3F 33
Besson St. SE14 1B 24
Best St. ME4: Chat 4F 27
BETCHWORTH 4D 31
BETHNAL GREEN 4B 16
Bethnal Grn. Rd. E2 4A 16
Bethune Rd. N16 3A 16
BETSHAM 3B 26
Betsham Rd. DA13: Sflt 3B 26
Betts La. EN9: Naze 2C 8
Between Streets KT11: Cobh 1B 30
Beulah Hill SE19 3A 24
Beulah Rd. CR7: Thor H 3A 24
Beverley Dr. HA8: Edg 2D 15
Beverley Gdns. EN7: Chesh 3B 8
Beverley Rd. CR3: Whyt 2A 32
RM9: Dag 3E 17
Beverley Way KT3: N Mald 3D 23
SW20 3D 23
Bewley La. TN15: Plax 3B 34
BEXLEY 2E 25
BEXLEYHEATH 2E 25
Bexley High St. DA5: Bexl 2E 25
Bexley La. DA14: Sidc 3E 25
Bexley Rd. DA8: Erith 1F 25
SE9 2D 25
Beynon Rd. SM5: Cars 4F 23

BICKLEY 3D 25
Bickley Pk. Rd. BR1: Brom 3D 25
Bickley Rd. BR1: Brom 3C 24
BICKNACRE 3F 11
Bicknacre Rd. CM3: Dan 2F 11
CM3: E Han 3F 11
Big Comn. La. RH1: Blet 4A 32
Bigfrith La. SL6: Cook 3B 12
BIGGIN HILL 2C 32
Biggin La. RM16: Grays 1C 26
BIGNELL'S CORNER 3E 7
BIGNELL'S CORNER 3E 7
BILLERICAY 1D 19
Billericay Rd. CM13: Bill, Heron 2C 18
Billet Hill TN15: Ash 4B 26
Billet La. HP4: Berk 1E 5
(not continuous)
RM11: Horn 3F 17
SL0: Iver H 4E 13
SL3: L'ly 4E 13
SS17: Stan H 4D 19
Billet Rd. E17 2B 16
RM6: Chad H 2E 17
BILLINGBEAR 2A 20
Billingbear La. RG42: Bin 2A 20
Bill St. Rd. ME2: Strood 3E 27
Bilton Rd. UB6: G'frd 4C 14
Bilton Way EN3: Enf L 4B 8
Bincote Rd. EN2: Enf 4A 8
BINFIELD 3A 20
Binfield Rd. RG40: W'ham 3A 20
RG42: Bin, Brac 3A 20
Bingham Rd. CR0: C'don 4B 24
Binton La. GU10: Seale 4B 28
Birchall La. SG14: Col G, Pan 1F 7
Birchanger Rd. SE25 4B 24
BIRCH GREEN 1F 7
Birch Hill Rd. RG12: Brac 4B 20
Birchin Cross Rd. TN15: Knat 2A 34
Birch La. HP3: Flau 3E 5
BIRCHWOOD 1E 7
Birchwood Av. AL10: Hat 1E 7
Birchwood Rd. BR8: Swan 3F 25
Bird La. CM13: Gt War 2B 18
RM14: Upm 2A 18
BIRDS GREEN 1B 10
Birds Grn. CM5: Fyf, Will 2A 10
Birkbeck Rd. W3 4D 15
BIRLING 1D 35
Birling Hill DA13: Meop 1D 35
Birling Rd. ME6: Snod 1D 35
ME19: Birl, Rya 2D 35
ME19: Leyb 2D 35
Bisham Abbey National Sports Cen. 3A 12
Bishops Av., The N2 3F 15
Bishop's Bri. W2 4E 15
Bishopsford Rd. SM4: Mord 4F 23
Bishopsgate EC2 4A 16
Bishopsgate Rd. TW20: Eng G 2E 21
Bishop's La. ME15: Hunt 4E 35
RG42: Warf 2B 20
Bishops Ri. AL10: Hat 2D 7
Bishops Stortford Rd. CM1: Rox 1C 10
Bishopstone HP17: Bish 1A 4
Bishop's Way E2 4B 16
BISLEY 2D 29
BISLEY CAMP 2C 28
BITCHET GREEN 3A 34
Bittacy Hill NW7 2E 15
Blackamoor La. SL6: Maide 4B 12
Blackbird Hill NW9 3D 15
Blackborough Rd. RH2: Reig 4F 31
Black Boy La. N15 2A 16
Blackbrook La. BR1: Brom 4D 25
BR2: Brom 4D 25
Blackbrook Rd.
RH5: Holmw, N Holm 4C 30
Black Bush La. SS17: Horn H 4C 18
BLACKCAT 1A 10
Blackdown Rd. GU16: Deep 2C 28
Blacketts Wood Dr. WD3: Chor 1E 13
Black Fan Rd. AL7: W City 1E 7
(not continuous)
BLACKFEN 2E 25
Blackfen Rd. DA15: Sidc 2D 25
Blackfriars Rd. SE1 4A 16
Blackhall La. TN15: S'oaks 3A 34
BLACKHEATH 1C 24
Blackheath Hill SE10 1C 24
Blackheath La. GU5: Alb 4F 29
BLACKHEATH PARK 2C 24
Blackheath Rd. SE10 1B 24
Blackheath Village SE3 2C 24
BLACKHORSE LANE 2B 16
Blackhorse La. CR0: C'don 4B 24
E17 2B 16
EN6: S Mim 3D 7
KT20: Lwr K 3E 31
Blackhorse Rd. E17 2B 16
GU22: Wok 2D 29
Black Lion Hill WD7: Shenl 3D 7
Blackman's La. CR6: Warl 1C 32
TN11: Had 4C 34
BLACKMORE 3B 10
Blackmore Rd. CM1: Bmore 3C 10
CM4: Bmore, Fry 3B 10
CM4: Bmore, Hook E 4A 10
CM15: Bmore, Dodd, Hook E,
Kel H, Sto M 4A 10
Blackness La. BR2: Kes 1C 32
BLACKNEST 3D 21
Blacknest Rd. GU25: Vir W 3D 21
SL5: S'hill 3D 21
Black Pk. Rd. SL3: Ful, Wex 4E 13
Blackpond La.
SL2: Farn C, Farn R 3D 13
BLACK PRINCE INTERCHANGE 2E 25
Blackshaw Rd. SW17 3F 23
Blackshots La. RM16: Grays 4C 18
Blacksmith La. GU4: Guild 4F 29
Blacksmiths La. BR5: St M Cry 3E 25
UB9: Den 3F 13
Blackstock Rd. N4 3A 16
N5 3A 16
Blackstroud La. E. GU18: Light 1C 28
BLACKWALL 4C 16
Blackwall La. SE10 1C 24
Blackwall Tunnel Northern App.
E3 4C 16
E14 4C 16
Blackwall Tunnel Southern App.
SE10 1C 24
BLACKWATER 2A 28
Blackwater La. HP3: Hem H 2A 6
Blackwater Valley Relief Rd.
GU15: Camb 2A 28
Blackwater Valley Route
GU12: Alde 4B 28
GU14: Farnb 2B 28
Blackwell Dr. WD19: Wat 1B 14
Blackwell Hall La.
HP5: Ches, Lat, Ley H 3E 5
Blake Hall Rd.
CM5: Gsted, N Weald, Ongar 2F 9
E11 3C 16
Blakeney Rd. BR3: Beck 3B 24
Blakes La. GU4: E Clan 4A 30
KT24: W Hor 4A 30
Blanchards Hill
GU4: Jac W, Sut G 3E 29
Blanche La. EN6: S Mim 3D 7
Blandford Rd. Sth. SL3: L'ly 1E 21
BLASFORD HILL 1E 11
Blay's La. TW20: Eng G 3E 21
BLENDON 2E 25
Blendon Rd. DA5: Bexl 2E 25
BLETCHINGLEY 4A 32
Bletchingley Rd. RH1: Mers 3F 31
RH1: Nutf 4A 32
RH9: G'stone 4A 32
Blighton La. GU10: Runf 4B 28
Bligh Way ME2: Strood 3E 27
Blind La. CM2: W Han 3E 11
HP10: Flack H 3B 12
SL8: Bou E 3B 12
BLINDLEY HEATH 4B 32
Blindman's La. EN8: Chesh 3B 8
Bloemfontein Rd. W12 4E 15
BLOOMSBURY 4A 16
Bloomsbury St. WC1 4F 15
Blue Anchor La. RM18: W Til 1D 27
BLUE BELL HILL 1F 35
Blue Bell Hill By-Pass
ME5: Chat 1F 35
ME20: A'ford 1F 35
Blueberry La. TN14: Knock 2E 33
Bluebridge Rd. AL9: Brk P 3E 7
Bluehouse Hill AL3: St A 2B 6
Bluehouse La. RH8: Limp, Oxt 3C 32
BLUEWATER 2A 26
Bluewater Parkway
DA9: Bluew, Ghithe 2A 26
Blundel La. KT11: Stoke D 2B 30
Blunts La. AL2: Pot C 2B 6
Blyth Rd. UB3: Hayes 1A 22
Boar Head Rd. CM17: Har 1E 9
BOARLEY 2F 35
Boarley La. ME14: S'ing 2F 35
BOBBINGWORTH 2F 9
Bobbingworth Mill CM5: Ongar 2F 9
Bob Dunn Way DA1: Dart 2F 25
Bobmore La. SL7: Marl 3A 12
Bockingford La. ME15: Maids 3F 35
Bois La. HP6: Amer 4D 5
Bois Moor Rd. HP5: Ches 3D 5
Boley Hill ME1: Roch 3F 27
Boleyn Rd. N16 3A 16
Bolingbroke Gro. SW11 2F 23
Bollo La. W3 1D 23
W4 1D 23
Bolters La. SM7: Bans 2E 31
Bolton Av. SL4: Wind 2D 21
Bolton Rd. SL4: Wind 2D 21
Boltons La. GU22: Pyr 2F 29
Bolton St. W1 4F 15
Bond St. TW20: Eng G 3E 21
W5 4C 14
Boneashe La. TN15: Bor G 2C 34
Bonflower La. ME17: Lint 4F 35
Bonner Rd. E2 4B 16
Bonsor Dr. KT20: Kgswd 2E 31
BOOKER 2A 12
Bookham Rd. KT11: D'side 2B 30
Booth Rd. NW9 2D 15
Border's La. IG10: Lough 4D 9
BOREHAM 1F 11
BOREHAM INTERCHANGE 1F 11
BOREHAMWOOD 4D 7
BOROUGH, THE 1A 24
BOROUGH GREEN 2B 34
Borough Grn. Rd.
TN15: Bor G, Igh 2B 34
TN15: Wro 2B 34
Borough High St. SE1 1A 24
Borough Rd. SE1 1A 24
TW7: Isle 1C 22
BORSTAL 4E 27
Borstal Rd. ME1: Roch 4E 27
Borstal St. ME1: Roch 4E 27
Borwick La. CM11: C Hill 2E 19
(not continuous)
SS12: Wick 2E 19
Boss La. HP14: Hug V 4B 4
Bostall Hill SE2 1E 25
BOSTON MANOR 1C 22
Boston Mnr. Rd. TW8: Bford 1C 22
Boston Rd. W7 1C 22
BOTANY BAY 4F 7
BOTLEY 3E 5
Botley Rd. HP5: Ches, Ley H 3D 5
Botney Hill Rd. CM12: L Bur 2C 18
Botsom La. TN15: W King 1A 34
Bottle La. RG42: Bin, Warf 2A 20
SL6: L Grn 1A 20
Bottlescrew Hill ME17: B Mon 4F 35
Bottom Alley HP15: Holm G 4C 4
Bottom Ho. Farm La.
HP8: Chal G 1D 13
Bottom Ho. La. HP23: New G 1D 5
Bottom La. HP9: See G 2D 13
WD4: Bucks 4F 5
Bottom Rd. HP14: Rad, W Wyc 1A 12
HP23: Buck C, St L 2C 4
Bottrells La. HP7: Chal G 1D 13
HP8: Chal G 1D 13
Botwell Comn. Rd. UB3: Hayes 4A 14
Botwell La. UB3: Hayes 4A 14
BOUGH BEECH 4E 33
Bough Beech Rd. TN8: F Elm 4E 33
BOUGHTON GREEN 4F 35
Boughton La. ME15: Maids 3F 35
ME17: B Mon, Maids 3F 35
BOUGHTON MONCHELSEA 4F 35
Bounces Rd. N9 1B 16
Boundary Rd. E13 4C 16
E17 3B 16
GU14: Farnb 3B 28
HP10: Loud, Wbrn G 2C 12
NW8 4E 15
SL6: Tap 4C 12
SM6: Wall 1F 31
Boundary Way HP2: Hem H 1A 6
BOUNDS GREEN 2F 15
Bounds Grn. Rd. N11 2F 15
N22 2F 15
Bourley Rd. GU11: Alde 4A 28
GU52: Chu C 4A 28
Bourne, The N14 1F 15
BOURNEBRIDGE 1E 17
Bournebridge La. RM4: Stap A 1E 17
BOURNE END
HP1 2E 5
SL8 3C 12
Bourne End La. HP1: Hem H 2E 5
Bourne End Rd. SL6: Tap 3C 12
Bourne Hill N13 1A 16
Bourne La. TN15: Plax 3B 34
Bourne Rd. DA5: Bexl, Dart 2E 25
Bourne Way BR2: Hayes 4C 24
BOVENEY 1C 20
Boveney Rd. SL4: Dor 1C 20
Boveney Wood La. SL1: Burn 3C 12
BOVINGDON 3F 5
BOVINGDON GREEN
HP3 3E 5
SL7 3A 12
Bovingdon Grn. La. HP3: Bov 3E 5
BOVINGER 2F 9
BOW 4B 16
BOW COMMON 4B 16
Bow Comn. La. E3 4B 16
Bowerdean Rd. HP13: H Wy 1B 12
Bower Hill CM16: Epp 3E 9
Bower Hill La. RH1: S Nut 4F 31
Bower La. DA4: Eyns 4A 26
TN15: Eyns, Knat 4A 26
Bower Mt. Rd. ME16: Maids 3F 35
BOWERS GIFFORD 2F 19
BOWES PARK 2A 16
Bowes Rd. N11 1F 15
N13 1F 15
Bow Hill ME18: W'bury 3D 35
BOW INTERCHANGE 4C 16
Bowood La. HP22: Wend 2B 4
Bow Rd. E3 4B 16
ME18: W'bury 3D 35
Bow St. WC2 4A 16
Bowstridge La. HP8: Chal G 1E 13
Bowyer Pl. SE5 1A 24
Bowyer's La. RG42: Warf 2B 20
Bowzell Rd. TN14: Weald 4F 33
Bowzells La. TN8: Chid, Weald 4F 33
TN14: Chid, Weald 4F 33
Boxall's La. GU11: Alde 4B 28
Boxgrove Rd. GU1: Guild 4E 29
BOX HILL 4D 31
Boxhill Rd. KT20: Box H 4D 31
Box La. HP3: Hem H 2F 5
BOXLEY 2F 35
Boxley Rd. ME5: Wald 1F 35
(Beechin Bank Rd.)
ME5: Wald 1F 35
(Robin Hood La.)
ME14: Box, Maids, Pen H 2F 35
BOXMOOR 2F 5
Boxted Rd. HP1: Hem H 1F 5
Boxtree Rd. HA3: Hrw W 2C 14
Boyle Way TN12: E Pec 4D 35
BOYN HILL 4B 12
Boyn Hill Rd. SL6: Maide 4B 12
Boyn Valley Rd. SL6: Maide 4B 12
BOYTON CROSS 1C 10
Boyton Cross La. CM1: Rox 1C 10
BRACKNELL 3B 20
Bracknell Rd. GU19: Bag 4C 20
RG42: Warf 3B 20
RG45: Crow 4A 20
Bradbourne Pk. Rd.
TN13: S'oaks 3F 33
Bradbourne Rd. TN13: S'oaks 2F 33
Bradbourne Va. Rd.
TN13: S'oaks 2F 33
Bradcutts La. SL6: Cook 3B 12
Bradden La. HP2: Gad R 1F 5
BRADENHAM 4A 4
Bradenham La. SL7: Marl 3A 12
Bradenham Rd.
HP14: Brad, W Wyc 4A 4
Bradenham Wood La.
HP14: Brad, W Ash 4A 4
Bradmore Grn. AL9: Brk P 2E 7
Bragmans La. WD3: Sarr 3F 5
Braham St. E1 4A 16
Bramble La. RM14: Upm 4A 18
Bramley Hill CR2: S Croy 4A 24
Bramley Rd. N14 1F 15
Brampton Rd. DA7: Bex 1E 25
SE2 1E 25
Bramshot La. GU51: Fleet 3A 28
Bramston Way SS15: Lain 2D 19
BRANBRIDGES 4D 35
Branbridges Rd. TN12: E Pec 4D 35
Brancaster La. CR8: Purl 1A 32
Branch Hill NW3 3F 15
Branch Rd. AL3: St A 2B 6
Brands Hatch Motor Racing Circuit 4A 26
Brands Hatch Rd. DA3: Fawk 4B 26
BRANDS HILL 1E 21
Branksome Av. SS17: Stan H 4D 19
Branksome Hill Rd.
GU47: Col T 1A 28
Brantwood Rd. N17 2B 16
BRASTED 3E 33
BRASTED CHART 3E 33
Brasted Hill
TN14: Knock, Sund 2E 33
Brasted Hill Rd. TN16: Bras 2E 33
Brasted La. TN14: Knock 2E 33
Brasted Rd. TN16: Westrm 3D 33
Brawlings La. SL9: Chal P 1E 13
BRAY 1C 20
Bray Rd. SL6: Bray, Maide 1C 20
Brays Grn. La. HP6: H Hea 4C 4
BRAYS GROVE 1E 9
Brays La. HP6: H Hea 3C 4
BRAY WICK 1B 20
Braywick Rd. SL6: Bray, Maide 4B 12
BRAYWOODSIDE 2B 20
Braziers End HP5: Bell 2C 4
Braziers La. RG42: Wink R 3C 20
Bread and Cheese La.
EN10: Brox, Chesh 2A 8
Breakspear Rd. HA4: Ruis 2A 14
Breakspear Rd. Nth. UB9: Hare 2F 13
Breakspear Rd. Sth. UB9: Hare 3A 14
UB10: Ick 3A 14
Breakspear Way HP2: Hem H 2A 6
Brecknock Rd. N7 3F 15
N19 3F 15
BREEDS 1D 11
Breeds Rd. CM3: Gt W 1D 11
Brenchley Gdns. SE23 2B 24
Brennan Rd. RM18: Tilb 1C 26
Brent, The DA1: Dart 2A 26
BRENT CROSS 3E 15
BRENT CROSS INTERCHANGE 2E 15
Brentfield NW10 3D 15
Brentfield Rd. NW10 3D 15
BRENTFORD 1C 22
BRENTFORD END 1C 22
Brentford FC 1C 22
Brentmoor Rd. GU24: W End 1C 28
Brent St. NW4 2E 15
BRENTWOOD 1B 18
Brentwood By-Pass
CM14: B'wood, Pil H, S Weald 1A 18
Brentwood Rd. CM5: Ongar 3A 10
CM13: Heron, Ingve, W H'dn 1B 18
RM1: Rom 2F 17
RM2: Rom 2F 17
RM14: Bulp 3C 18
RM16: Grays, Ors 3C 18
Brewers Rd. DA12: Shorne 3D 27
Brewer St. RH1: Blet 4A 32
Brewery La. KT14: Byfl 1A 30
Brewery Rd. GU21: Wok 2E 29
N7 3A 16
SE18 1D 25
BRICKENDON 2A 8
Brickendon La.
SG13: Brick, Hertf 1A 8
(not continuous)
BRICKET WOOD 3B 6
BRICK HILL 4D 21
Brick Kiln La. RH8: Limp 3C 32
Brick Kiln Rd. CM2: Sando 2F 11
Brick La. E1 4A 16
E2 4A 16
BRICKLAYER'S ARMS 1A 24
Bridge, The HA3: W'stone 2C 14
BRIDGE END 2A 30
Bridge Hill CM16: Epp 3D 9
Bridge La. GU25: Vir W 4E 21
Bridgen Rd. DA5: Bexl 2E 25
Bridge Rd. BR3: Beck 3B 24
CM5: More 2F 9
DA8: Erith 1F 25
E15 4C 16
GU14: Cove 3A 28
GU19: Bag 1C 28
HA9: Wemb 3D 15
KT8: E Mos 3C 22
KT9: Chess 4D 23
KT13: Weyb 4A 22
KT16: Chert 4F 21
KT17: Eps 1D 31
N22 2A 16
RM13: Rain 4F 17
RM17: Grays 1B 26
SL6: Maide 4B 12
TW3: Houn, Isle 2C 22
WD4: Hunt C 3A 6
Bridge Rd. E. AL7: W City 1E 7
Bridge St. CM1: Writ 2D 11
GU1: Guild 4E 29
HA5: Pinn 2B 14
HP11: H Wy 2A 4
KT12: Walt T 4A 22
SL3: Coln 1F 21
Bridgewater Rd. HA0: Wemb 3C 14
HP4: Berk 1E 5
Bridle Rd. CR0: C'don 4B 24
(not continuous)
HA5: Eastc 2B 14
Bridle Rd., The CR8: Purl 1A 32
Bridle Way Nth. EN11: Hodd 1B 8
Bridle Way Sth. EN11: Hodd 1B 8
Bridport Rd. N18 1A 16
Brighton Rd. CR2: S Croy 1A 32
CR5: Coul 2F 31
(not continuous)
CR8: Purl 1A 32
KT6: Surb 4C 22
KT15: Add 4F 21
KT20: Kgswd, Lwr K, Tad 2E 31
RH1: Redh 4F 31
RH1: Salf 4F 31
SM2: Bans, Sutt 1E 31
SM7: Bans 2E 31
Brigstock Rd. CR7: Thor H 4A 24
Brimmers Hill HP15: Wid E 4B 4
Brimmers Rd. HP27: Pri R 3A 4
BRIMSDOWN 4B 8
Brimsdown Av. EN3: Enf H 4B 8
Brimstone Hill DA13: Meop 4C 26
Brimstone La. DA13: Meop 4C 26
Brishing La. ME15: Maids 3F 35
ME17: B Mon 4F 35
Brishing Rd.
ME17: Cha S, Maids 4F 35
BRITANNIA JUNC. 4F 15
Britannia Rd. ME3: H Hal 2F 27
Brittains La. TN13: S'oaks 3F 33
BRITWELL 4D 13
Britwell Rd. SL1: Burn 4C 12
BRIXTON 2A 24
Brixton Hill SW2 2A 24
Brixton Rd. SW9 2A 24
Brixton Water La. SW2 2A 24
BROAD COLNEY 3C 6
Broad Ditch Rd.
DA13: Ist R, Nflt G 3C 26
Broadfields Av. HA8: Edg 1D 15
BROAD GREEN 4A 24
Broad Grn. SG13: B'fd 1A 8
BROADGREEN WOOD 1A 8
BROADHAM GREEN 4C 32
Broadham Grn. Rd. RH8: Oxt 4C 32
Broadhurst Gdns. NW6 3E 15
Broad La. DA2: Dart 3F 25
HP9: Beac 2C 12
HP10: Wbrn G 2C 12
N15 2A 16
RG12: Brac 3B 20
TW12: Hamp 3B 22
BROADLEY COMMON 2D 9
Broadmayne SS14: Bas 2E 19
Broadmead Rd. GU23: Send 2E 29
IG8: Wfd G 2C 16
(not continuous)
UB4: Yead 4B 14
UB5: N'olt 4B 14
Broadmoor Rd. RG10: W Law 1A 20
SL6: W Walt 1A 20
Broad Sanctuary SW1 1F 23
BROAD'S GREEN 1D 11
BROAD STREET 2F 27
Broad St. GU3: Guild, Woo V 4D 29
HP5: Ches 3D 5
RM10: Dag 3E 17
TW11: Tedd 3C 22
Broad Wlk. SE3 1C 24
Broadwater Rd. AL7: W City 1E 7
ME19: W Mal 2D 35
SE28 1D 25
Broadway BR8: Crock 4F 25
DA6: Bex 2E 25
(not continuous)
E15 3C 16
GU21: Knap 2D 29
HP7: Amer 4D 5
KT6: Surb 4D 23
ME16: Maids 3F 35
RM13: Rain 4F 17
SL6: Maide 4B 12
Broadway, The GU21: Wok 2E 29
HA7: Stan 1C 14
IG10: Lough 4D 9
N8 2A 16
N9 1B 16
NW7 1D 15
NW9 2D 15
RM12: Horn 3F 17
SM3: Cheam 1E 31
SS11: Wick 1F 19
SW19 3E 23
TW18: Lale 3F 21
UB1: S'hall 4B 14
UB6: G'frd 4C 14
W13 4C 14
Broadway Mkt. E8 4B 16
Broadway Rd. GU18: Light 1C 28
GU20: W'sham 1C 28
Brockenhurst Rd. SL5: Asc 4C 20
Brocket Rd. EN11: Hodd 1B 8
BROCKHAM 4D 31
Brockhamhurst Rd. RH3: Bet 4D 31
Brockham La. RH3: Aroc 4D 31
BROCK HILL 4E 11
Brock Hill SS11: Runw 4E 11
BROCKLEY 2B 24
Brockley Gro. SE4 2B 24
Brockley Hill HA7: Stan 1C 14
Brockley Ri. SE23 2B 24
Brockley Rd. SE4 2B 24
BROMLEY
BR1 3C 24
E3 4B 16
BROMLEY COMMON 4D 25
Bromley Comn. BR2: Brom 3C 24
Bromley Hill BR1: Brom 3C 24
Bromley La. BR7: Chst 3D 25
Bromley Rd. BR1: Brom 2B 24
BR2: Brom 3C 24
BR3: Beck 3B 24
BR7: Chst 3D 25
SE6 2B 24
BROMPTON
ME7 3F 27
SW3 1F 23
Brompton Farm Rd.
ME2: Strood 3E 27
Brompton Rd. ME7: G'ham 3F 27
SW3 1F 23
BRONDESBURY 3E 15
BRONDESBURY PARK 3E 15
Brondesbury Pk. NW2 3E 15
NW6 3E 15
Brondesbury Rd. NW6 4E 15
Bronze Age Way DA8: Erith 1F 25
DA17: Belv 1F 25
Brook, The ME4: Chat 3F 27
Brook Av. HA9: Wemb 3D 15
Brookbank HP10: Wbrn G 3C 12
Brookdene Av. WD19: Wat 1B 14
Brook End HP22: W Tur 1A 4
Brook End Rd. CM2: Spr 2E 11
Brookers Row RG45: Crow 4A 20
Brookfield La. W. EN8: Chesh 3B 8
(not continuous)
BROOK GREEN 1E 23
Brook Hill CM3: Lit W 1E 11
Brookhill Rd. EN4: E Barn 1F 15
BROOKLANDS 1A 30
Brooklands Rd. KT13: Weyb 1A 30
Brook La. CM2: Gall, Gt B 3E 11
RG10: W Law 2A 20
TN15: Plax 3B 34
Brookmans Av. AL9: Brk P 2E 7
BROOKMANS PARK 3E 7
Brookmill Rd. SE8 1B 24
Brook Pl. TN14: Ide H, Sund 3E 33
Brook Rd. CM16: Epp 3E 9
IG2: Ilf 2D 17
IG9: Buck H, Wfd G 1C 16
WD6: Bore 4D 7
Brookshill HA3: Hrw W 1C 14
BROOKSIDE 3C 20
Brookside Sth. EN4: E Barn 1F 15
BROOK STREET 1A 18
Brook St. CM14: B'wood 1A 18
DA8: Erith 1E 25
DA17: Belv, Erith 1E 25
HP22: Ast C 1B 4
ME6: Snod 1E 35
BROOK STREET INTERCHANGE 1A 18
BROOKWOOD 2D 29
Brookwood Lye Rd.
GU24: Brkwd 2D 29
Broombarn La. HP16: Gt Miss 3B 4
BROOMFIELD 1E 11
Broomfield Av. N13 1A 16
Broomfield La. N13 1A 16
Broomfield Rd. CM1: Chelm 2E 11
BROOMHALL 4D 21
Broomhall La. SL5: S'dale 4D 21
Broomhill Rd. IG8: Wfd G 2C 16
(not continuous)
BROOMHILLS 2D 19
Broom Rd. TW11: Tedd 3C 22
Broomstick Hall Rd. EN9: Walt A 3C 8
Broomwood La. CM4: Stock 4E 11
CM11: Ram H 4E 11
Broomwood Rd. SW11 2F 23
Browells La. TW13: Felt 2B 22
(not continuous)
Brownhill Rd. SE6 2C 24
Browning Rd. E12 3D 17
EN2: Enf 4A 8
Brownlow Rd. HP4: Berk 1E 5
N11 2A 16
Browns La. TN8: Eden 4D 33
Browns Rd. HP15: Holm G 4C 4
HP16: H Hea 3C 4
Brownswood Rd. N4 3A 16
BROX 1F 29
BROXBOURNE 2B 8
Broxhill Rd. RM4: Have B 1F 17
Bruce Rd. KT16: Ott 1F 29
Bruce Gro. N17 2A 16
Brunel Rd. SE16 1B 24
Brunswick Av. N11 1F 15
(not continuous)
BRUNSWICK PARK 1F 15
Brunswick Pk. Rd. N11 1F 15
Brunswick Rd. W5 4C 14
Bruton St. W1 4F 15
Bryant Av. RM3: Hrld W 2F 17
BRYANT'S BOTTOM 4A 4
Bryants Bottom Rd. HP16: Gt H 3A 4
Bucketsland La. WD6: Bore 4D 7
Buckhatch La. CM3: E Han, Ret 4F 11
Buckhold Rd. SW18 2E 23
Buckhole Farm Rd. ME3: H Hal 2F 27
BUCKHURST HILL 1C 16
Buckhurst Rd. SL5: Asc, S'hill 3D 21
TN16: Westrm 2D 33
Buckhurst Way IG9: Buck H 1C 16
Buckingham Av. SL1: Slou 4D 13
Buckingham Hill Rd.
SS17: Ors, Stan H 4D 19
Buckingham Palace 1F 23
Buckingham Pal. Rd. SW1 1F 23
Buckingham Rd. HA1: Harr 2C 14
N22 2A 16
Buckingham Way GU16: Frim 2B 28
BUCKLAND
HP22 1B 4
RH3 4E 31
BUCKLAND COMMON 2C 4
Buckland Cres. NW3 3F 15
Buckland Hill ME16: Maids 2F 35
Buckland Rd. DA13: Meop 4D 27
HP22: Bkld 1B 4
KT20: Lwr K 3E 31
ME3: Cli, High'm 2E 27
RH2: Reig 4E 31
Bucks All. SG13: L Ber 2F 7
Bucks Cross Rd. BR6: Chels 4E 25
BUCKS HILL 3F 5
Bucks Hill WD4: Bucks 3F 5
BUDDS 3A 34
Budgin's Hill BR6: Prat B 1E 33
Bug Hill CR3: Wold 2B 32
CR6: Wold 2B 32
Bugsby's Way SE7 1C 24
SE10 1C 24
Bulbeggars La. RH9: G'stone 4B 32
Bulbourne Rd. HP23: Bul, Tring 1C 4
Bullbeggars La. GU21: Wok 2E 29
HP4: Berk, Pott E 2E 5
BULLBROOK 3B 20
Bullen La. TN12: E Pec 4D 35
BULLEN'S GREEN 2D 7
Bullens Grn. La. AL4: Col H 2D 7
Bullfinch La. TN13: Riv 2F 33
Bull Hill KT22: Lea 2C 30
Bull La. AL4: Whe 1C 6
ME3: High'm 2E 27
ME20: A'ford, Ecc 2E 35
N18 1A 16
Bull La. RG42: Brac 3B 20
SL9: Chal P, Ger X 2E 13
TN15: Wro 2B 34
Bullocks Farm La.
HP14: L End, Whe E, W Wyc 1A 12
Bullock's La. SG13: Hertf 1A 8
Bull Rd. ME19: Birl 1D 35
BULLS CROSS 4B 8
Bulls Cross EN2: Enf 4B 8
Bulls La. AL9: Brk P, Wel G 2E 7
BULLSMOOR 4B 8
Bullsmoor La. EN1: Enf 4B 8
EN3: Enf W 4B 8
BULPHAN 3C 18
Bulphan By-Pass RM14: Bulp 3C 18
Bulstrode La. HP3: Hem H 3F 5
WD4: Chfd, K Lan 3F 5
BUMBLE'S GREEN 2C 8
Bunce Comn. Rd. RH2: Leigh 4D 31
Buncefield La. HP2: Hem H 1A 6
(not continuous)
Bundick's Hill CM1: Chelm 2D 11
Bunhill Row EC1 4A 16
Bunkers Hill DA14: Sidc 2E 25
TN15: Ash 1B 34
Bunkers La. HP3: Hem H 2A 6
Bunns La. NW7 2D 15
(not continuous)
Bunters Hill Rd.
ME3: Cli W, Wain 2E 27
BURCHETT'S GREEN 4A 12
Burchetts Grn. La. SL6: Bur G 4A 12
Burchetts Grn. Rd.
SL6: Bur G, L Grn 4A 12
Burdenshott Rd. GU3: Worp 3E 29
Burdett Rd. E3 4B 16
E14 4B 16
Burdon La. SM2: Cheam 1E 31
Burfield Rd. SL4: Old Win 2E 21
Burford St. EN11: Hodd 1B 8
Burges Rd. E6 3D 17
BURGH HEATH 2E 31
Burgh Heath Rd.
KT17: Eps, Eps D 1D 31
Burghley Rd. SW19 3E 23
BURHAM 1E 35
BURHAM COMMON 1E 35
BURHAM COURT 1E 35
Burial Ground La. ME15: Maids 3F 35
Burkes Rd. HP9: Beac 2C 12
Burleigh Rd. EN1: Enf 4A 8
Burlings La. TN14: Knock 2D 33
Burlington La. W4 1D 23
Burlington Rd. KT3: N Mald 3D 23
Burlington Rd. W. KT3: N Mald 3E 23
Burma Rd. GU24: Chob 4D 21
BURNHAM 4C 12
BURNHAM BEECHES 3D 13
Burnham La. SL1: Slou 4C 12
Burnham Rd. DA1: Dart 2F 25
HP9: Beac 2D 13
ME1: Woul 4E 27
SS11: Bat, Sth F, Ret 1F 19
Burnt Ash Hill SE12 2C 24
Burnt Ash La. BR1: Brom 3C 24
Burnt Ash Rd. SE12 2C 24
BURNTCOMMON 3F 29
Burnthouse La.
CM4: Inga, Mount 4C 10
Burnt Mill La. CM20: Har 1D 9
BURNT MILLS 2F 19
Burnt Mills Rd. SS12: Nth B 2E 19
SS13: Bas 2E 19
BURNT OAK 2D 15
Burnt Oak B'way. HA8: Edg 2D 15
Burnt Pollard La. GU18: Light 1D 29
Burntwood La. CR3: Cat'm 2A 32
SW17 2F 23
BURPHAM 3E 29
Burrage Rd. SE18 1D 25
Burroughs, The NW4 2E 15
BURROWHILL 1D 29
Burrows La. GU5: Goms 4A 30
Burton La. EN7: G Oak 3A 8
Burton's La. HP8: Chal G 4E 5
Burton's Rd. TW12: Ham H 3B 22
Burwood Rd. KT12: Hers 1A 30
BURY, THE 2E 5
BURY GREEN 3B 8
Bury Grn. Rd.
EN7: Chesh, Walt C 3B 8
(not continuous)
Bury La. CM3: Hat P 1F 11
(not continuous)
CM16: Epp 3D 9
Bury Rd. E4 4C 8
Bury St. HA4: Ruis 2A 14
N9 1A 16
Bury St. W. N9 1A 16
Busbridge Rd. ME15: Loose 3F 35
Bushbury Rd. RH3: Bet, Aroc 4D 31
BUSHEY 1B 14
Bushey Hall Rd. WD23: Bush 4B 6
BUSHEY HEATH 1C 14
BUSHEY MEAD 3E 23
Bushey Mill La.
WD24: Bush, Wat 4B 6
(not continuous)
Bushey Rd. SW20 3E 23
Bush Hill N21 1A 16
BUSH HILL PARK 1A 16
Bush Hill Rd. N21 1A 16
Bush Rd. E11 3C 16
ME2: Cux 4D 27
SE8 1B 24
TN12: E Pec 4D 35
BUSHY HILL 4E 29
Butcher Row E1 4B 16
Butchers La. ME18: Mere 3C 34
SL6: W Walt 1A 20
TN15: Ash, Hartl 4B 26
BUTLER'S CROSS 2A 4
Butterfly La. WD6: E'tree 4C 6
Butt Grn. La. ME17: Lint 4F 35
Button St. BR8: Swan 3F 25
BUTTSBURY 4D 11
Buttsbury CM4: Inga 4C 10
BUTT'S GREEN 3F 11
Butts Grn. Rd. CM2: Sando 3F 11
RM11: Horn 2F 17
Butts La. CM3: Dan 2F 11
SS17: Stan H 4D 19
Buttway La. ME3: Cli 1E 27
Buxton La. CR3: Cat'm 2A 32
Buxton Link SS15: Lain 2D 19
BYE GREEN 1B 4
BYFLEET 1A 30
Byfleet Rd. KT15: New H 1F 29
Byron Rd. HA3: W'stone 2C 14

C

Cabbage Hill La. RG42: Bin 3A 20
Cable St. E1 4B 16
Cacket's La. TN14: Cud 2D 33
Cadbury Rd. TW16: Sun 2A 22
Cadlocks Hill TN14: Hals 1E 33
Cadmore La. EN8: Chesh, Turn 3B 8
Cadogan Ter. E9 3B 16

Cadsden Rd. HP27: White 2A 4
Caenswood Hill KT13: Weyb 1A 30
Caesars Camp Rd. GU15: Camb 1B 28
CAGE GREEN 4B 34
Cain Rd. RG12: Brac 3A 20
Cairo New Rd. CR0: C'don 4A 24
Calcutta Rd. RM18: Tilb 1C 26
Caledonian Rd. N1 4A 16
N7 3A 16
Callin's La. RG10: S Row 2A 20
Callow Hill GU25: Vir W 3E 21
Calmont Rd. BR1: Brom 3C 24
Calonne Rd. SW19 3E 23
Calthorpe St. WC1 4A 16
Calton Av. SE21 2A 24
CAMBERLEY 1B 28
CAMBERWELL 1A 24
Camberwell Chu. St. SE5 1A 24
CAMBERWELL GREEN 1A 24
Camberwell Grn. SE5 1A 24
Camberwell New Rd. SE5 1A 24
Camberwell Rd. SE5 1A 24
Camborne Av. HP21: A'bury 1A 4
Cambrian Way HP2: Hem H 1A 6
Cambridge Gdns. W10 4E 15
Cambridge Heath Rd. E1 4B 16
E2 4B 16
Cambridge Pk. E11 2C 16
Cambridge Rd. CM20: Har 1E 9
KT1: King T 3D 23
SW11 1F 23
Camden High St. NW1 4F 15
Camden Pk. Rd. NW1 3F 15
Camden Rd. N7 3A 16
NW1 3F 15
Camden St. NW1 3F 15
CAMDEN TOWN 4F 15
CAMER 4C 26
Cameron Rd. IG3: Ilf 3D 17
Camer Pk. Rd. DA13: Meop 4C 26
Camer Rd.
DA13: Meop, Sole S 4C 26
Camlet Way EN4: Barn, Had W 4E 7
CAMP, THE 2C 6
Campbell Rd. E3 4B 16
Campden Hill Rd. W8 4E 15
Camp Farm Rd. GU11: Alde 3B 28
Camp Hill TN11: Chid 4F 33
Camphill Rd. KT14: W Byf 1F 29
Camp Rd. AL1: St A 2C 6
Camrose Av. HA8: Edg 2D 15
Canada Farm Rd.
DA2: Dart, S Dar 3B 26
DA3: Fawk 3B 26
DA4: S Dar 3B 26
Canadian Av. ME7: G'ham 4F 27
SE6 2B 24
CANAL BRIDGE 1B 24
Canal Rd. DA12: Grav'nd 2C 26
ME3: High'm 2E 27
Canberra Rd. SE7 1C 24
Candlemas La. HP9: Beac 2D 13
Canes La. CM17: Hasti, Twood 2E 9
Canfield Gdns. NW6 3E 15
Canham Rd. SE25 3A 24
CANN HALL 3C 16
Cann Hall Rd. E11 3C 16
CANNING TOWN 4C 16
CANNING TOWN 4C 16
Cannizaro Rd. SW19 3E 23
Cannon Ct. Rd. SL6: Maide 4B 12
(not continuous)
Cannondown Rd. SL6: Cook 3B 12
Cannon Hill N14 1A 16
Cannon La. ME18: W'bury 3D 35
SL6: Maide 4B 12
TN9: Tonb 4B 34
CANNON'S GREEN 2A 10
Cannons La. CM5: Fyf 2A 10
Cannon St. EC2 4A 16
EC4 4A 16
Cannon St. Rd. E1 4B 16
CANONBURY 3A 16
Canonbury Pk. Nth. N1 3A 16
Canonbury Rd. N1 3A 16
CANONS PARK 2D 15
Canterbury Rd. CR0: C'don 4A 24
Canterbury St. ME7: G'ham 3F 27
CANVEY ISLAND 4F 19
Canvey Rd. SS8: Can I 4F 19
CANVEY VILLAGE 4F 19
Canvey Way
SS7: Ben, Can I, Pit 3F 19
SS8: Can I 3F 19
SS13: Ben 3F 19
SS16: Ben 3F 19
Capel Rd. E7 3C 16
E12 3C 16
Cappell La. SG12: S Abb 1C 8
CAPSTONE 4F 27
Capstone Rd. ME5: Chat, Hals 4F 27
ME7: Chat, G'ham 4F 27
Capworth St. E10 3B 16
Carbone Hill EN6: N'thaw 3F 7
CARDINALS, THE 4B 28
Carlton Av. E. HA9: Wemb 3C 14
Carlton Rd. CR2: S Croy 1A 32
DA8: Erith 1E 25
Carlton Va. NW6 4E 15
Carlyle Av. UB1: S'hall 4B 14
Carlyle Rd. SE28 4E 17
Carmichael Rd. SE25 3B 24
CARNELES GREEN 2B 8
CARPENDERS PARK 1B 14
Carpenters La. TN11: Had 4C 34
Carpenter's Rd. E15 3B 16
CARSHALTON 4F 23
CARSHALTON BEECHES 1F 31
CARSHALTON ON THE HILL 1F 31
Carshalton Pk. Rd. SM5: Cars 1F 31
Carshalton Rd. CR4: Mitc 4F 23
SM1: Sutt 4F 23
SM5: Cars 4F 23
SM7: Bans 1F 31
Carterhatch La. EN1: Enf 4A 8
Carterhatch Rd. EN3: Enf H 4B 8
CARTER'S GREEN 1F 9
CARTER'S HILL 3A 34
Carter's Hill RG42: Bin 3A 20
TN15: Under 4A 34
Carthouse La. GU21: Wok 1D 29
Cassiobury Dr. WD17: Wat 4A 6
Cassio Rd. WD18: Wat 4B 6
Cassland Rd. E9 3B 16
CASTELNAU 1E 23
Castelnau SW13 1E 23
Castlebar Hill W5 4C 14
Castlebar Rd. W5 4C 14
Castledon Rd. CM11: D'ham 1E 19
SS12: Wick 1E 19
Castle Farm Rd. TN14: S'ham 1F 33
Castlefield Rd. RH2: Reig 4E 31
CASTLE GREEN 1D 29
Castle Gro. Rd. GU24: Chob 1D 29
Castle Hill DA3: Fawk, Hartl 4B 26
GU9: Farnh 4A 28
SL6: Maide 4B 12
Castle Hill Rd. TW20: Eng G 2E 21
Castle La. DA12: Grav'nd 2D 27
Castle Rd. CR5: Chip 2F 31
DA4: Eyns 1F 33
Castle Rd. ME4: Chat 4F 27
ME16: Ali 2F 35
Castle St. GU9: Farnh 4A 28
HP4: Berk 2E 5
ME2: Up 3F 27
RH1: Blet 4A 32
Castleton Av. HA9: Wemb 3D 15
Castle Way ME19: Leyb 2D 35
TW13: Hanw 3B 22
Caterfield La. RH7: Ling 4C 32
RH8: Ling, Oxt 4C 32
CATERHAM 3A 32
Caterham By-Pass CR3: Cat'm 2B 32
CATERHAM-ON-THE-HILL 2A 32
CATFORD 2B 24
CATFORD GYRATORY 2B 24
Catford Hill SE6 2B 24
Catford Rd. SE6 2B 24
Cathall Rd. E11 3C 16
Catherine St. AL3: St A 2C 6
ME1: Roch 4F 27
Cat Hill EN4: E Barn 1F 15
Catsdell Bottom HP3: Hem H 2A 6
CATTLEGATE 3F 7
Cattlegate Rd. EN2: Crew H 3F 7
EN6: Cuff, N'thaw 3F 7
Causeway, The CM1: Writ 2C 10
EN6: Pot B 3F 7
(not continuous)
KT10: Clay 1C 30
TW4: Houn 2B 22
TW14: Felt, Houn 2B 22
TW18: Staines 3F 21
Cautherly La. SG12: Gt A 1B 8
Cave Hill ME15: Maids 3F 35
Cavendish Rd. NW6 3E 15
SW12 2F 23
Cavendish Sq. W1 4F 15
Cavendish Way AL10: Hat 1D 7
Cazenove Rd. N16 3A 16
Cecil Rd. EN2: Enf 4A 8
EN6: S Mim 3E 7
ME1: Roch 4F 27
Cedar Dr. DA4: S Dar 3A 26
Cedar Rd. EN2: Enf 4A 8
SM2: Sutt 1F 31
Cedars Av. CR4: Mitc 3F 23
Cedars Rd. SW4 2F 23
W4 1D 23
Cell Barnes La. AL1: St A 2C 6
(not continuous)
Cemetery La. TN11: Had 4C 34
Cemetery Pales GU24: Brkwd 2D 29
Central Av. CM20: Har 1D 9
DA16: Well 1D 25
KT8: W Mole 4B 22
Central Hill SE19 3A 24
Central Pde. CR0: New Ad 1C 32
Central Pk. Rd. E6 4C 16
Central Rd. KT4: Wor Pk 4E 23
SM4: Mord 4E 23
Central St. EC1 4A 16
Central Way SE28 4E 17
Centre Comn. Rd. BR7: Chst 3D 25
Centre Rd. E7 3C 16
E11 3C 16
Chadwell By-Pass RM16: Grays 1C 26
CHADWELL HEATH 2E 17
Chadwell Heath La.
RM6: Chad H 2E 17
Chadwell Rd. RM17: Grays 1C 26
CHADWELL ST MARY 1C 26
CHAFFORD HUNDRED 1B 26
CHAINHURST 4E 35
CHALDON 3A 32
Chaldon Comn. Rd. CR3: Cat'm 3A 32
Chaldon Rd. CR3: Cat'm 3A 32
Chaldon Way CR5: Coul 2A 32
CHALFONT COMMON 1E 13
Chalfont La. WD3: Chor 1E 13
WD3: W Hyd 2F 13
Chalfont Rd. HP9: See G 1D 13
WD3: Map C 1E 13
CHALFONT ST GILES 1D 13
CHALFONT ST PETER 2E 13
Chalfont St Peter By-Pass
SL9: Chal P 2E 13
CHALK 2D 27
CHALK END 1C 10
CHALKER'S CORNER 2D 23
CHALK FARM 3F 15
Chalk Farm Rd. NW1 3F 15
Chalk Hill WD19: Wat 1B 14
Chalk La. CM17: Har 1E 9
HP6: H Hea 4C 4
KT24: E Hor 4A 30
Chalkpit La. RH4: Dork 4C 30
RH8: Oxt 3C 32
SL7: Marl 3A 12
Chalk Pit Way SM1: Sutt 1F 31
Chalk Rd. DA12: Grav'nd 2D 27
ME3: High'm 2E 27
CHALKSHIRE 2A 4
Chalk St. CM3: Ret 4F 11
CHALVEDON 2E 19
CHALVEY 1D 21
Chalvey Gro. SL1: Slou 1D 21
Chalvey Rd. E. SL1: Slou 1D 21
Chalvey Rd. W. SL1: Slou 1D 21
Chamberlayne Rd. NW10 4E 15
Chambersbury La. HP3: Hem H 2A 6
(not continuous)
Chambers La. NW10 3E 15
Champion Pk. SE5 1A 24
Chancery La. WC2 4A 16
Chanctonbury Way N12 1E 15
CHANDLERS CORNER 4F 17
CHANDLER'S CROSS 4A 6
Chandlers La. GU46: Yat 1A 28
WD3: Chan C 4A 6
Chandler's Rd. DA13: Meop 4C 26
Chantilly Way KT19: Eps 1D 31
Chantry La. GU5: Shere 4A 30
CHAPEL CROFT 3F 5
Chapel Cft. WD4: Chfd 3F 5
Chapel Hill HP27: Speen 4A 4
Chapel La. CM3: Lit B 2F 11
GU14: Cove 2A 28
HA5: Pinn 2B 14
HP12: H Wy 1A 12
KT23: Bookh, Westh 3C 30
ME2: Hall 1D 35
RH5: Westh 3C 30
SG14: Bir G, Let G 1F 7
Chapel Rd. IG1: Ilf 3D 17
KT20: Tad 3E 31
RH8: Limp 3C 32
SE27 3A 24
Chapel St. CM12: Bill 1D 19
ME19: E Mal 2E 35
ME19: Rya 1D 35
NW1 4F 15
SL7: Marl 3A 12
Chapel Wood Rd. DA3: Hartl 4B 26
TN15: Ash, Hartl 4B 26
Chapman La. HP10: Flack H 2B 12
SL8: Bou E 2B 12
Chapman Rd. E9 3B 16
Chapman's Hill DA13: Meop 1C 34
Chapman Way ME19: E Mal 2D 35
Chapter Rd. NW2 3E 15
CHARCOTT 4F 33
Charing Cross Rd. WC2 4F 15
Charles St. HP4: Berk 2E 5
CHARLIE BROWN'S RDBT. 2C 16
CHARLOTTEVILLE 4E 29
CHARLTON
SE7 1C 24
TW17 3A 22
Charlton Athletic FC 1C 24
Charlton Chu. La. SE7 1C 24
Charlton La. ME15: W Far 3E 35
Charlton Pk. La. SE7 1C 24
Charlton Pk. Rd. SE7 1C 24
Charlton Rd. SE3 1C 24
SE7 1C 24
TW17: Shep 3A 22
Charlton Way EN11: Hodd 1B 8
SE3 1C 24
SE10 1C 24
Charmwood La. BR6: Prat B 1E 33
Charterhouse St. EC1 4A 16
Charteris Rd. IG8: Wfd G 2C 16
Charter Rd., The IG8: Wfd G 2C 16
Charters Rd. SL5: S'dale 4D 21
Chart Hill Rd.
ME17: B Mon, Cha S 4F 35
Chart La. RH2: Reig 4E 31
RH4: Dork 4C 30
TN16: Bras, Westrm 4E 33
Chart La. Sth.
RH5: Dork, N Holm 4C 30
CHARTRIDGE 2C 4
Chartridge La. HP5: Char, Ches 3C 4
Chartwell 4D 33
Charville La. UB4: Hayes 4A 14
Chase, The GU2: Guild 4E 29
CHASE CROSS 2F 17
Chase Cross Rd. RM5: Col R 2F 17
Chase Rd. N14 1F 15
NW10 4D 15
CHASE SIDE 4A 8
Chase Side EN2: Enf 4A 8
N14 1F 15
Chaseville Pk. Rd. N21 1A 16
Chaseway, The CM4: Stock 4E 11
Chatfield SL2: Slou 4D 13
CHATHAM 4F 27
Chatham Hill ME5: Chat 4F 27
ME7: Chat 4F 27
CHATHAM MARITIME 3F 27
Chatham Rd. ME14: S'ing 1F 35
ME20: A'ford 1F 35
Chatsworth Rd. E5 3B 16
NW2 3E 15
CHATTENDEN 2F 27
Chattenden La. ME3: C'den 2F 27
CHATTERN HILL 3A 22
CHAULDEN 2F 5
Chaulden La. HP1: Hem H 2F 5
CHAVEY DOWN 3C 20
Chavey Down Rd.
RG42: Wink R 3B 20
CHEAM 1E 31
Cheam Comn. Rd. KT4: Wor Pk 4E 23
Cheam Rd. KT17: Ewe 1E 31
SM1: Sutt 1E 31
SM2: Cheam 1E 31
CHEAM VILLAGE 1E 31
CHEAPSIDE 3D 21
Cheapside Rd. SL5: Asc 3C 20
Chelmer Rd. CM2: Chelm, Spr 2E 11
Chelmer Valley Rd.
CM1: Chelm, Spr 2E 11
CHELMER VILLAGE 2E 11
Chelmer Village Way CM2: Spr 2E 11
CHELMSFORD 2E 11
Chelmsford Crematorium
CM1: Chelm 2D 11
Chelmsford Rd.
CM1: Chelm, Writ 2D 11
CM3: E Han, Sando 3F 11
CM3: Gt W 1E 11
CM4: Bmore 3B 10
CM5: Bmore, H Ongar, Nor H 3A 10
CM5: G Eas, M Rod 1B 10
CM6: L Rod, M Rod 1B 10
CM15: Shenf 1B 18
(not continuous)
SS11: Raw 1F 19
CHELSEA 1F 23
Chelsea Bri. SW1 1F 23
SW8 1F 23
Chelsea Bri. Rd. SW1 1F 23
Chelsea Emb. SW3 1F 23
Chelsea FC 1E 23
CHELSFIELD 4E 25
Chelsfield Hill BR6: Chels 1E 33
Chelsfield La. BR5: Orp 4E 25
BR6: Chels, Orp 4E 25
BR6: Orp, Chels 1E 33
TN14: Hals, S'ham 1E 33
Chelsfield Rd. BR5: St M Cry 4E 25
CHELSFIELD VILLAGE 4E 25
CHELSHAM 2B 32
Chelsham Comn. Rd. CR6: Warl 2B 32
Chelsham Ct. Rd. CR6: Warl 2C 32
Chelsham Rd. CR6: Warl 2B 32
Cheltenham Gdns. E6 4D 17
Cheltenham Rd. SE15 2B 24
Cheney St. HA5: Eastc 2B 14
CHENIES 4E 5
CHENIES BOTTOM 4E 5
Chenies Rd. WD3: Chor 4F 5
Chenies St. WC1 4F 15
Chepstow Rd. CR0: C'don 4A 24
W2 4E 15
Chepstow Vs. W11 4E 15
Chequer La. AL3: Redb 1B 6
Chequers AL7: W City 1E 7
Chequers La. HP16: Pre 3B 4
KT20: Walt H 3E 31
RM9: Dag 4E 17
WD25: Wat 3B 6
Chequers Rd. CM1: Writ 2D 11
CM14: N'side, Rom 1A 18
RM3: Rom 1A 18
Chequer St. AL1: St A 2C 6
Cherington Rd. W7 4C 14
Cherrydown E. SS16: Bas 2E 19
Cherry Gdn. La. SL6: W Walt 1A 20
Cherry La. HP7: Amer 4C 4
UB7: W Dray 1A 22
Cherry Orchard Rd. CR0: C'don 4A 24
Cherry Tree La. HP2: Hem H 1A 6
RM13: Rain 4F 17
SL3: Ful 3E 13
Cherry Tree Rd. SL2: Farn R 3D 13
Cherrywood Rd. GU14: Farnb 2B 28
CHERTSEY 4F 21
Chertsey Bri. Rd. KT16: Chert 4F 21
Chertsey La. TW18: Staines 3F 21
CHERTSEY LOCK 4F 21
Chertsey Rd. GU20: W'sham 1C 28
GU21: Wok 2E 29
GU24: Chob 1D 29
(Alpha Rd.)
GU24: Chob 1C 28
(Windsor Rd.)
KT14: Byfl 1F 29
KT15: Add 4F 21
Chertsey Rd. TW1: Twick 2C 22
TW2: Twick 2C 22
TW13: Felt 3A 22
TW15: Ashf 3A 22
TW16: Sun 3A 22
TW17: Shep 4A 22
CHERTSEY SOUTH 4F 21
Chertsey St. GU1: Guild 4E 29
CHESHAM 3D 5
CHESHAM BOIS 4D 5
Chesham La. HP8: Chal G 1E 13
SL9: Chal P 1E 13
Chesham Pl. SW1 1F 23
(not continuous)
Chesham Rd. HP3: Bov 3E 5
HP4: Berk 2E 5
HP5: A Grn, Berk 2D 5
HP5: Bell 2D 5
HP5: Bov, Whel 3E 5
HP6: Amer 4D 5
HP16: Gt Miss, H Hea 3C 4
HP22: Wend 2B 4
HP23: Wigg 1C 4
Cheshire St. E2 4B 16
CHESHUNT 3B 8
Cheshunt Wash EN8: Chesh 3B 8
CHESSINGTON 1D 31
Chessington Rd. KT17: Ewe 1D 31
KT19: Ewe 1D 31
Chessington World of Adventures 1C 30
CHESSMOUNT 3D 5
Chester Hall La. SS14: Bas 2E 19
Chester Rd. IG10: Lough 4D 9
Chesterton Rd. W10 4E 15
Chestnut Av. HP22: Hal 1B 4
ME5: Wald 1F 35
Chestnut La. GU24: Chob 1D 29
Chetwynd Rd. NW5 3F 15
CHEVENING 2E 33
Chevening Rd. NW6 4E 15
TN13: Riv 2E 33
TN14: Sund, Riv 2E 33
Cheyne Wlk. SW3 1F 23
(not continuous)
Chichele Rd. NW2 3E 15
CHIDDINGSTONE CAUSEWAY 4F 33
Chidley Cross Rd. TN12: E Pec 4D 35
Chignall Rd.
CM1: Chelm, Chig S, Chi J 1D 11
CM1: Chig S 1D 11
CHIGNALL ST JAMES 1D 11
CHIGNALL SMEALY 1D 11
CHIGWELL 1D 17
Chigwell La. IG7: Chig, Lough 1D 17
IG10: Lough 1D 17
Chigwell Ri. IG7: Chig 1D 17
Chigwell Rd. E18 2C 16
IG8: Wfd G 2C 16
CHIGWELL ROW 1E 17
Chilbrook Rd. KT11: D'side 2B 30
CHILDERDITCH 2B 18
Childerditch La.
CM13: B'wood, L War, W H'dn 2B 18
Childsbridge La.
TN15: Kems'g, Seal 2A 34
CHILD'S HILL 3E 15
CHILDWICK GREEN 1B 6
Chilsey Grn. Rd. KT16: Chert 4F 21
Chiltern Av. HP6: Amer 4D 5
WD23: Bush 1C 14
Chiltern Dr. WD3: Rick 1F 13
Chiltern Open Air Mus. 1E 13
Chiltern Rd. SM2: Sutt 1F 31
CHILWORTH 4F 29
Chilworth Rd. GU5: Alb 4F 29
Chinbrook Rd. SE12 2C 24
CHINGFORD 1C 16
CHINGFORD GREEN 1C 16
CHINGFORD HATCH 1C 16
Chingford La. IG8: Wfd G 1C 16
CHINGFORD MOUNT 1B 16
Chingford Mt. Rd. E4 1B 16
Chingford Rd. E4 2B 16
E17 2B 16
Chinnor Rd. HP14: Bled R 1A 12
Chippendale Waye UB8: Uxb 3F 13
Chippenham Rd. W9 4E 15
CHIPPERFIELD 3F 5
CHIPPERFIELD COMMON 3F 5
Chipperfield Rd. BR5: St P 3E 25
(not continuous)
HP3: Bov 3E 5
WD4: K Lan 3F 5
CHIPPING BARNET 4E 7
CHIPPING ONGAR 3A 10
CHIPSTEAD
CR5 2F 31
TN13 2F 33
CHIPSTEAD BOTTOM 2F 31
Chipstead La. CR5: Chip, Coul 3E 31
KT20: Kgswd 3E 31
TN13: Riv 2F 33
Chipstead Valley Rd. CR5: Coul 2F 31
CHISBRIDGE CROSS 2A 12
CHISLEHURST 3D 25
Chislehurst Rd. BR1: Brom 3D 25
BR5: Orp, Pet W, St M Cry 3D 25
BR6: Orp, Pet W, St M Cry 4E 25
BR7: Chst 3D 25
DA14: Sidc 3E 25
CHISLEHURST WEST 3D 25
CHISWELL GREEN 2B 6
Chiswell Grn. La.
AL2: Chis G, Pot C 2B 6
Chiswell St. EC1 4A 16
CHISWICK 1D 23
Chiswick Bri. W4 1D 23
Chiswick High Rd. TW8: Bford 1D 23
(not continuous)
Chiswick House 1D 23
Chiswick La. Nth. W4 1D 23
CHISWICK RDBT. 1D 23
Chivers Rd. CM15: Sto M 3A 10
CHIVERY 1C 4
Choats Mnr. Way RM9: Dag 4E 17
Choats Rd. IG11: Bark 4E 17
RM9: Dag 4E 17
CHOBHAM 1D 29
Chobham La. GU24: Chob 4D 21
GU25: Vir W 4D 21
Chobham Rd. E15 3C 16
GU16: Frim 2B 28
GU21: Knap, Wok 2D 29
GU21: Wok 2E 29
(Brewery Rd., not continuous)
GU21: Wok 1E 29
(Horsell Comn. Rd.)
GU24: Chob 4D 21
KT16: Ott 1E 29
SL5: S'dale 4D 21
Choke La. SL6: Maide 4B 12
CHOLESBURY 2C 4
Cholesbury La.
HP23: Buck C, Chol 2C 4
Cholesbury Rd.
HP23: Chol, Wigg 2C 4
Chorley Rd. HP14: W Wyc 1A 12
CHORLEYWOOD 1F 13
CHORLEYWOOD BOTTOM 1F 13
Chorleywood Bottom WD3: Chor 1F 13
Chorleywood Rd. WD3: Rick 4F 5
CHORLEYWOOD WEST 4E 5
Chrisp St. E14 4B 16
(not continuous)
Christchurch Av.
HA3: Kent, W'stone 2C 14
Christ Chu. Rd. KT19: Eps 1D 31
SW14 2D 23
Christchurch Rd. GU25: Vir W 3E 21
HP23: Tring 1C 4
SW2 2A 24
SW19 3F 23
Christmas La. ME3: H Hal 2F 27
SL2: Farn C 3D 13
Church Cres. E9 3B 16
CHURCH CROOKHAM 4A 28
Church Elm La. RM10: Dag 3E 17
CHURCH END
AL3 1A 6
GU23 2A 30
N3 2E 15
NW10 3D 15
WD3 4F 5
Church End NW4 2E 15
Church End La. SS11: Runw 1F 19
Churchfield Rd. W3 4D 15
CHURCHGATE 3B 8
Churchgate EN7: Chesh 3B 8
Churchgate Rd. EN7: Chesh 3B 8
CHURCHGATE STREET 1E 9
Churchgate St. CM17: Har 1E 9
Church Gro. HP6: L Chal 4E 5
KT1: Ham W 3C 22
Church Hill CR3: Cat'm 3A 32
DA2: Dart 2F 25
E17 2B 16
GU12: Alde 4B 28
GU15: Camb 1B 28
GU21: Wok 2E 29
GU22: Pyr 2F 29
HP17: Ell 2A 4
IG10: Lough 4D 9
ME17: B Mon 4F 35
N21 1A 16
RG42: Bin 2A 20
RH1: Nutf 4A 32
SL6: W Walt 1A 20
SS15: Lain 2D 19
SS17: Stan H 4D 19
TN14: Big H 2D 33
TN15: Plax 3B 34
TN16: Tats 2C 32
UB9: Hare 2F 13
Church Hill Rd. EN4: E Barn 1F 15
SM3: Cheam 4E 23
Churchill Av. HP21: A'bury 1A 4
CHURCH LAMMAS 2F 21
Church La. CM1: Spr 2E 11
CM3: Sth H 4F 11
CM4: Inga, Marg 3D 11
CM6: W Rod 1A 10
CM11: C Hill 1E 19
CM13: Hut 1C 18
CM15: Dodd, Hook E 4B 10
CM22: Sheer 1F 9
CR3: Cat'm 3A 32
CR5: Coul 2F 31
CR6: Warl 2B 32
DA12: Grav'nd 2D 27
EN8: Chesh 3B 8
EN10: Brox, Worm 2B 8
GU5: Alb 4F 29
GU10: Ews 4A 28
GU24: Bisl 2D 29
GU24: Pirb 3C 28
HA5: Pinn 2B 14
HP3: Bov 3E 5
HP22: W Tur 1A 4
HP22: Wend 2B 4
KT9: Chess 1D 31
KT18: H'ly 3D 31
ME15: W Far 3E 35
ME16: Barm 3E 35
ME19: Tros 1C 34
N2 2F 15
N8 2A 16
NW9 2D 15
RG42: Bin 2A 20
RG42: Warf 2B 20
RH1: Blet 4A 32
RH8: Oxt 3C 32
RH9: G'stone 4B 32
RM4: Abr 4E 9
RM10: Dag 3F 17
RM14: Bulp 3C 18
SL2: Stoke P 4D 13
SL3: Wex 4E 13
SW17 3F 23
TN12: E Pec 4D 35
WD3: Rick 1F 13
WD3: Sarr 4F 5
WD4: K Lan 3A 6
WD25: A'ham 4B 6
Church La. E. GU11: Alde 4B 28
Church La. W. GU11: Alde 4A 28
CHURCH LANGLEY 1E 9
Church Langley Way CM17: Har 1E 9
Church Rd. BR2: Brom 3C 24
BR2: Kes 1C 32
BR6: Chels 1E 33
BR6: Farnb 4D 25
BR8: Crock 4F 25
BR8: Swan 3F 25
CM2: W Han 4E 11
CM3: Bor, Lit B 1F 11
CM5: More 2F 9
CM5: Ongar 3F 9
CM11: Ram H 1E 19
CM13: B'wood 2C 18
CM13: Inga, Mount 4C 10
CM14: Kel H 4A 10
CM15: Mount 4C 10
CR3: Cat'm 3A 32
CR3: Wold 2B 32
CR4: Mitc 3F 23
DA3: Hartl, New A 4B 26
DA4: Sutt H 3A 26
DA7: Bex 2E 25
DA13: Cobh, Grav'nd 3C 26
E10 3B 16
E12 3D 17
EN6: Pot B 3E 7
GU11: Alde 4B 28
GU16: Frim 2B 28
GU20: W'sham 1C 28
GU24: W End 1D 29
GU47: S'urst 1A 28
HA6: Nwood 2A 14
HA7: Stan 1C 14
HP4: Pott E 1E 5
HP10: Penn 1C 12
HP10: Ty G 1C 12
IG9: Buck H 1C 16
IG10: H Beech, Lough 4C 8
KT4: Wor Pk 4D 23
KT6: Surb 4C 22
KT10: Clay 1C 30
KT14: Byfl 1A 30
KT15: Add 4F 21
KT17: Eps 1D 31
Church Rd. KT22: Lea 2C 30
KT23: Bookh 3B 30
ME15: Maids 3F 35
ME18: W Peck 3C 34
ME19: Off 2C 34
NW4 2E 15
NW10 3D 15
RG12: Brac 3B 20
RH1: Redh 4F 31
RM4: Nave 4F 9
RM4: Noak H 1F 17
RM14: Bulp 3C 18
(not continuous)
RM18: W Til 1D 27
SE19 3A 24
SG13: L Ber, Epp G 2F 7
SL0: Iver H 4F 13
SL4: Old Win 2E 21
SL4: Wink 2C 20
SL5: S'dale 4D 21
SL6: Cook 3B 12
SL7: Lit M 2B 12
SS7: Thun 2F 19
SS11: Raw 1F 19
SS13: B Gif 2F 19
SS14: Bas 2E 19
(not continuous)
SS16: Vange 2E 19
SS17: Corr 4E 19
SW13 1D 23
SW19 3F 23
(Merton)
SW19 3E 23
(Wimbledon)
TN14: Hals 1E 33
TN14: Sund 3E 33
TN14: Weald 4F 33
TN15: Ash 4B 26
TN15: Ivy H, Seal 3A 34
TN16: Bras 3E 33
TW5: Hest 1B 22
TW10: Ham 2D 23
TW11: Tedd 3C 22
TW15: Ashf 2A 22
TW17: Shep 4A 22
TW20: Egh 3E 21
UB3: Hayes 4A 14
UB5: N'olt 4B 14
UB7: W Dray 1A 22
UB8: Cowl 4F 13
W7 4C 14
CHURCH STREET 2E 27
Church St. CM2: Gt B 2E 11
CM11: Bill 1D 19
EN2: Enf 4A 8
HP3: Bov 3E 5
HP5: Ches 3D 5
HP7: Amer 4D 5
HP11: H Wy 1B 12
KT11: Cobh 2B 30
KT12: Walt T 4B 22
KT13: Weyb 4A 22
KT17: Eps 1D 31
KT22: Lea 2C 30
(not continuous)
ME1: Bur 1E 35
ME3: Cli 2E 27
ME3: High'm 2E 27
ME3: Hoo 2F 27
ME7: G'ham 3F 27
ME15: Loose 3F 35
ME17: B Mon 4F 35
N9 1A 16
RH2: Reig 4E 31
SL1: Slou 1D 21
TN14: S'ham 1F 33
TN15: Seal 2A 34
TW12: Hamp 3C 22
TW18: Staines 3F 21
WD3: Rick 1A 14
Church St. W. GU21: Wok 2E 29
CHURCH TOWN 4B 32
Church Wlk. UB3: Hayes 4A 14
Church Way CR2: Sande 1A 32
CIPPENHAM 4D 13
Cippenham La. SL1: Slou 4D 13
Circus Rd. NW8 4F 15
CITY OF LONDON 4A 16
City Rd. N1 4A 16
City Way ME1: Roch 4F 27
Civic Sq. RM18: Tilb 1C 26
Clacket La. TN16: Westrm 3D 33
Clacton Rd. E6 4C 16
Clamp Hill HA7: Stan 1C 14
Clandon Pk. 4F 29
Clandon Rd. GU4: W Cla 3F 29
GU23: Send 3F 29
ME5: Lor 1F 35
CLANKING 2A 4
CLAPGATE 3A 10
CLAPHAM 2F 23
CLAPHAM COMMON 2F 23
Clapham Comn. Nth. Side
SW4 2F 23
Clapham Comn. Sth. Side SW4 2F 23
Clapham Comn. W. Side SW4 2F 23
(not continuous)
Clapham High St. SW4 2F 23
CLAPHAM JUNCTION 2F 23
CLAPHAM PARK 2F 23
Clapham Pk. Rd. SW4 2F 23
Clapham Rd. SW9 2A 24
Clappins La. HP14: Nap, Nth D 4A 4
Clapton Comn. E5 3A 16
(not continuous)
CLAPTON PARK 3B 16
Clare La. ME19: E Mal 2D 35
Claremont Av. GU22: Wok 2E 29
KT3: N Mald 4E 23
Claremont La. KT10: Esh 4B 22
CLAREMONT PARK 1B 30
Claremont Rd. KT6: Surb 4D 23
NW2 3E 15
Claremont Way ME4: Chat 4F 27
Clarence Av. KT3: N Mald 3D 23
Clarence La. SW15 2D 23
Clarence Rd. RM17: Grays 1B 26
SL4: Wind 1D 21
Clarence St. KT1: King T 3D 23
(not continuous)
TW18: Staines 3F 21
Clarendon Rd. HP16: Pre 3B 4
W11 4E 15
WD17: Wat 4B 6
Clare Rd. TW19: Stanw 2F 21
Clarke's Grn. Rd. TN15: Knat 1A 34
Clarks La. RH8: Warl 3C 32
TN16: Tats 3C 32
CLATTERFORD END
CM1 1B 10
CM5 2A 10
CM5 3F 9
CLAVERHAMBURY 3C 8
Claverhambury Rd. EN9: Walt A 3C 8
Claverton St. SW1 1F 23
Claycart Rd. GU11: Alde 4A 28
(not continuous)
CLAYGATE
KT10 1C 30
TN11 4B 34
CLAYGATE CROSS 3B 34

Claygate La. KT7: T Ditt 4C 22
TN11: S'brne 3B 34
Claygate Rd. ME18: Ladd 4D 35
TN12: Coll 4E 35
CLAYHALL 2D 17
Clayhall Av. IG5: Ilf 2D 17
Clayhall La. RH2: Reig 4E 31
CLAY HILL 4A 8
Clay Hill EN2: Enf 4A 8
Clay Hill Rd. SS16: Bas, Vange 2E 19
Clay La. GU4: Burp, Jac W 3E 29
KT18: H'ly 3D 31
RH1: S Nut 4F 31
SL7: Book 2A 12
Clay's La. IG10: Lough 4D 9
Clay St. HP9: Beac 1C 12
Clayton Rd. KT9: Chess 4C 22
UB3: Hayes 1A 22
Clay Tye Rd. RM14: Upm 3B 18
Cleavesland ME18: Ladd 4D 35
Clement St. BR8: Swan, Dart 3F 25
CLERKENWELL 4A 16
Clerkenwell Rd. EC1 4A 16
Cleveland Rd. W13 4C 14
Cleveland St. W1 4F 15
Cleve Rd. NW6 3E 15
CLEWER GREEN 1D 21
Clewer Hill Rd. SL4: Wind 1D 21
CLEWER NEW TOWN 1D 21
CLEWER VILLAGE 1D 21
Clew's La. GU24: Bisl 2D 29
CLIFFE 1E 27
Cliffe Rd. ME2: Strood 3E 27
CLIFFE WOODS 2E 27
Cliff Hill ME17: B Mon 4F 35
Cliff Hill Rd. ME17: B Mon 4F 35
Clifford Av. SW14 1D 23
(not continuous)
Clifford Rd. SE25 3B 24
Clifton Gdns. W9 4F 15
Clifton Marine Pde.
DA11: Nflt, Grav'nd 2C 26
(not continuous)
Clinton La. TN8: Chid 4E 33
Cliveden 3C 12
Cliveden Pl. SW1 1F 23
Cliveden Rd. SL6: Tap 4C 12
Clive Rd. CM13: Gt War 2B 18
CLOCK HOUSE 1F 31
Clockhouse La. RM5: Col R 2E 17
RM16: Chaf H 1B 26
(not continuous)
TW15: Ashf 3A 22
Clock Ho. Rd. BR3: Beck 3B 24
CM12: L Bur 1D 19
CLOCKHOUSE RDBT. 2A 22
Clubhouse Rd. GU11: Alde 3A 28
Coach Rd. TN15: Igh, Ivy H 3B 34
COALHILL 4F 11
Coalhouse Fort 1D 27
Coast Hill RH4: Westc 4B 30
Coates La. HP13: D'ley, H Wy 1A 12
Cobbett Hill GU3: Norm 3D 29
COBBLERSHILL 3B 4
Cobblershill La. HP16: Lit H 3B 4
Cobden Hill WD7: Rad 4C 6
COBHAM
DA12 3D 27
KT11 1B 30
Cobhambury Rd. DA12: Cobh 3D 27
DA13: Lud'n 3D 27
Cobham Pk. Rd. KT11: D'side 2B 30
Cobham Rd. KT11: Stoke D 2B 30
KT22: Fet 2C 30
Coborn Rd. E3 4B 16
Cockerhurst Rd. TN14: S'ham 1F 33
Cockett Rd. SL3: L'ly 1E 21
COCKFOSTERS 4F 7
Cockfosters Rd.
EN4: Cockf, Had W 4F 7
EN6: Pot B 4F 7
Cock La. CM1: High 3C 10
(not continuous)
EN11: Hodd 2B 8
HP10: Ty G 1B 12
HP13: H Wy 1B 12
Cockmannings La.
BR5: St M Cry 4E 25
Cockmannings Rd.
BR5: St M Cry 4E 25
Cockpit Rd. HP15: Gt Kin 4B 4
Cockshot Hill RH2: Reig 4E 31
Cock's La. RG42: Warf 2B 20
COCK STREET 4F 35
Cocksure La. DA14: Sidc 2E 25
CODMORE 3D 5
Codmore Wood Rd. HP5: Lat 3E 5
Cody Rd. GU14: Cove 3A 28
Coke's La. HP7: L Chal 4E 5
HP8: Chal G 4E 5
Colam La. CM3: Lit B 2F 11
Colchester Rd. CM2: Spr 1E 11
CM14: B'wood, Hrld W 2F 17
RM3: Hrld W, Rom 2F 17
Cold Arbor Rd. TN13: Riv 3F 33
COLDBLOW 2F 25
COLDHARBOUR 4B 34
Coldharbour La. RH4: Dork 4C 30
SE5 2A 24
SW9 2A 24
TN11: Hild 4A 34
TW20: Thorpe 3F 21
UB3: Hayes 4B 14
WD23: Bush 1B 14
Coldharbour Rd. DA11: Nflt 2C 26
GU22: Pyr 2F 29
KT14: W Byf 1F 29
Coldmoorholme La. SL8: Bou E 3B 12
Coleford Bri. Rd. GU16: Myt 3B 28
COLE GREEN 1F 7
Cole Grn. By-Pass
AL9: Ess 1F 7
SG14: Bir G, Herti, Pan 1F 7
Cole Grn. La. AL7: W City 1E 7
Colekitchen La. GU5: Goms 4A 30
COLEMAN GREEN 1D 7
Coleman Grn. La. AL4: Sandr 1C 6
COLE PARK 2C 22
COLESHILL 1D 13
Coleshill La. HP7: Win H 1C 12
Coles La. TN16: Bras 3E 33
COLES MEADS 4F 31
COLHAM GREEN 4A 14
Colham Grn. Rd. UB8: Hil 4A 14
COLINDALE 2D 15
Colindale Av. NW9 2D 15
Colindeep La. NW4 2D 15
NW9 2D 15
College Av. HA3: Hrw W 2C 14
College Cres. NW3 3F 15
College Hill Rd. HA3: Hrw W 2C 14
College La. AL10: Hat 2D 7
(not continuous)
COLLEGE PARK 4E 15
College Ride GU15: Camb 1B 28
College Rd. BR1: Brom 3C 24
BR8: Swan 3F 25
EN7: Chesh 3B 8
GU22: Wok 2E 29
HA1: Harr 2C 14
HP22: Ast C 1B 4
College Rd. KT17: Eps 1D 31
ME15: Maids 3F 35
SE19 3A 24
SE21 2A 24
SL6: Maide 4B 12
TW7: Isle 1C 22
WD5: Ab L 3B 6
College St. NW1 3F 15
COLLEGE TOWN 1A 28
COLLIER ROW 2E 17
Collier Row La. RM5: Col R 2E 17
Collier Row Rd. RM5: Col R 2E 17
COLLIERS HATCH 3F 9
Colliers Water La.
CR7: Thor H 3A 24
COLLIERS WOOD 3F 23
COLLIERS WOOD 3F 23
Collingwood Rd. SM1: Sutt 4E 23
Collins Cross Rd. CM17: Mat T 1F 9
Collinswood Rd. SL2: Farn C 3D 13
Collum Grn. Rd.
SL2: Farn C, Hedg, Stoke P 3D 13
Colmore Rd. EN3: Pond E 4B 8
COLNBROOK 1F 21
Colnbrook By-Pass
SL3: Coln, L'ly 1F 21
UB7: Harm 1F 21
Colne Way WD24: Wat 4B 6
WD25: Wat 4B 6
COLNEY HATCH 2F 15
Colney Hatch La. N10 2F 15
N11 2F 15
COLNEY HEATH 2D 7
Colney Heath La. AL4: St A 2D 7
COLNEY STREET 3C 6
Colonial Way WD24: Wat 4B 6
Colston Av. SM5: Cars 4F 23
Columbia Rd. E2 4A 16
Colyers La. DA8: Erith 1F 25
Colyton Rd. SE22 2B 24
Combe La. GU5: Shere 4A 30
Combe St. HP1: Hem H 2F 5
Comet Way AL10: Hat 2D 7
Commercial Rd. E1 4B 16
E14 4B 16
ME2: Strood 3E 27
Commercial St. E1 4A 16
Commercial Way SE15 1A 24
Common, The CM3: Dan 2F 11
CM3: E Han 3F 11
HA7: Stan 1C 14
HP4: Pott E 1E 5
HP10: Flack H 2B 12
HP15: Gt Kin 4B 4
HP15: Holm G 4C 4
UB2: S'hall 1B 22
W5 4D 15
(not continuous)
WD4: K Lan 3F 5
Common La. DA2: Dart 2F 25
ME3: Cli 1F 27
SL1: Burn 3C 12
WD4: K Lan 3A 6
WD7: Rad 4C 6
WD25: Let H 4C 6
Common Rd. CM4: Stock 4D 11
EN9: Naze 2D 9
HA7: Stan 1C 14
KT10: Clay 1C 30
ME3: Cli W 2E 27
ME5: Chat 1E 35
SL4: Dor, Eton W 1C 20
TN11: Had 4C 34
TN15: Igh 3B 34
WD3: Chor 4F 5
Commonside BR2: Kes 4C 24
HP13: D'ley 1A 12
Commonside E. CR4: Mitc 3F 23
(not continuous)
Commonside Rd. CM18: Har 2D 9
Commonside W. CR4: Mitc 3F 23
COMMONWOOD 3F 5
Common Wood La.
HP10: Penn, Ty G 1C 12
Commority Rd. DA13: Meop 1C 34
COMP 2C 34
Compasses Rd. TN11: Leigh 4C 34
Comp La. ME19: Off 2C 34
TN15: Bor G 2C 34
COMPTON 4D 29
Compton Rd. N21 1A 16
Conduit La. EN11: Hodd 1B 8
N18 1B 16
Conduit St. W1 4F 15
CONEY HALL 4C 24
Coney Hill Rd. BR4: W W'ck 4C 24
CONGELOW 4D 35
Coningsby La. SL6: Fifi 1C 20
Coniston Way RH2: Reig 4F 31
Connaught Bri. E16 4C 16
Connaught Gdns. N13 1A 16
Connaught Rd. GU24: Brkwd 2D 29
Connaught St. W2 4F 15
Constitution Hill ME6: Snod 1D 35
Convent Rd. TW15: Ashf 3A 22
Conways Rd. RM16: Ors 4C 18
COOKHAM 3B 12
COOKHAM DEAN 3B 12
Cookham Dean Bottom
SL6: Cook 3B 12
COOKHAM RISE 3B 12
Cookham Rd. SL6: Maide 4B 12
COOKSMILL GREEN 2C 10
COOLING 2F 27
Cooling Comn. ME3: Cli 2F 27
Cooling Rd. ME2: Strood 3E 27
ME3: Cli 2F 27
COOLING STREET 2F 27
Cooling St. ME3: Cli 2F 27
Cool Oak La. NW9 3D 15
COOMBE
HP17 2A 4
KT2 3D 23
COOMBE LANE 3D 23
Coombe La. CR0: C'don 4B 24
HP14: Hug V, Nap 4A 4
SW20 3E 23
Coombe La. Flyover SW20 3D 23
Coombe La. W. KT2: King T 3D 23
Coombe Rd. CR0: C'don 4A 24
KT2: King T 3D 23
KT3: N Mald 3D 23
Coomber Way CR0: Bedd 4F 23
COOPERSALE 3E 9
Coopersale Comn.
CM16: Coop, Epp, N Weald 3E 9
Coopersale La.
CM16: They B, They G 4E 9
COOPERSALE STREET 3E 9
Coopersale St.
CM16: Epp, Fidd H 3E 9
COOPER'S CORNER 4E 33
COOPERS GREEN 1D 7
Coopers Grn. La. AL4: St A 1D 7
AL8: W City 1D 7
AL10: Hat 1D 7
Coopers Hill CM5: Ongar 3A 10
Cooper's Hill Rd.
RH1: Nutf, S Nut 4A 32
Cooper's La. EN6: N'thaw, Pot B 3F 7
Coopers La. Rd.
EN6: N'thaw, Pot B 3F 7
Coopers Shaw Rd.
RM18: W Til 1C 26
Copenhagen St. N1 4A 16
Copes Rd. HP15: Gt Kin 4B 4
Copperfield Rd. CM1: Chelm 1D 11
Copperkins La. HP6: Amer 4D 5
Coppermill La.
WD3: Hare, W Hyd 2F 13
Coppermill Rd. TW19: Wray 2E 21
Coppetts Rd. N10 2F 15
Coppice Row CM16: They B 4D 9
Coppings Rd. TN11: Leigh 4F 33
COPSE HILL 3E 23
Copse Hill SW20 3E 23
Copsem La. KT10: Esh, Oxs 1C 30
KT22: Oxs 1C 30
Copse Rd. KT11: Cobh 1B 30
COPTHALL GREEN 3D 9
Copthall La. SL9: Chal P 2E 13
Copt Hall Rd. TN15: Igh 3B 34
Copt Hill CM3: Dan 2F 11
Copthorne Rd. KT22: Lea 2C 30
CORBETS TEY 3A 18
Corbets Tey Rd. RM14: Upm 3A 18
CORES END 3C 12
Cores End Rd. SL8: Bou E 3B 12
Corkscrew Hill BR4: W W'ck 4C 24
Cormongers La. RH1: Nutf 4F 31
Cornell Way RM5: Col R 1E 17
Cornerfield AL10: Hat 1E 7
Cornwall Cres. W11 4E 15
Cornwallis Av. ME7: G'ham 4F 27
(not continuous)
TN10: Tonb 4B 34
Cornwall Rd. HA4: Ruis 3B 14
Coronation Av. SL3: G Grn 4E 13
Coronation Dr. RM12: Horn 3F 17
Coronation Rd. HP12: H Wy 2A 12
NW10 4D 15
SL5: Asc 4C 20
SL6: L Grn 4A 12
Corporation Rd. CM1: Chelm 1E 11
Corporation St. ME1: Roch 3F 27
CORRINGHAM 3E 19
Corringham Rd.
SS17: Stan H, Corr 4D 19
(not continuous)
CORYTON 4F 19
COTMAN'S ASH 2A 34
Cotman's Ash La.
TN15: Kems'g 1A 34
Coton St. E14 4C 16
Cotswold Rd. SM2: Sutt 1E 31
COTTENHAM PARK 3E 23
Cottenham Pk. Rd. SW20 3E 23
(not continuous)
Cotton La. DA2: Dart, Ghithe 2A 26
DA9: Ghithe 2A 26
Cottonmill La. AL1: St A 2C 6
COULSDON 2F 31
Coulsdon Ct. Rd. CR5: Coul 2A 32
Coulsdon Rd.
CR3: Cat'm, Coul 2A 32
CR5: Coul 2A 32
COUNTERS END 2F 5
Country Way TW13: Hanw 3B 22
County La. RG42: Warf 3B 20
Coursers Rd. AL4: Col H 2D 7
Courtauld Rd. SS13: Bas 2E 19
Courtenay Av. HA3: Hrw W 2C 14
Courthill Rd. SE13 2C 24
Courthouse Rd. SL6: Maide 4B 12
Courtlands Dr. WD17: Wat 4A 6
WD24: Wat 4A 6
Court La. SE21 2A 24
SL1: Burn 4C 12
TN11: Had 4C 34
Court Rd. BR6: Chels, Orp 4E 25
CM1: Broom, Lit W 1E 11
ME1: Bur 1E 35
SE9 2D 25
COVE 2A 28
Cove Rd. GU14: Cove 3A 28
GU51: Fleet 3A 28
Cowbridge SG14: Hertf 1A 8
Cow La. HP23: Tring 1C 4
COWLEY 4F 13
Cowley Hill WD6: Bore 4D 7
(not continuous)
Cowley Mill Rd. UB8: Uxb 4F 13
COWLEY PEACHEY 4A 14
Cowley Rd. UB8: Uxb 4F 13
Cow Watering La. CM1: Writ 2D 11
Coxes Farm Rd. CM11: Bill 1D 19
COX GREEN 1B 20
Cox Grn. La. SL6: Maide 1B 20
Cox Grn. Rd. SL6: Maide 1B 20
COXHEATH 4F 35
Cox La. KT9: Chess 4D 23
COXTIE GREEN 1A 18
Coxtie Grn. Rd.
CM14: N'side, Pil H, S Weald 1A 18
Crabhill La. RH1: S Nut 4A 32
Craddocks Av. KT21: Asht 2D 31
Crammavill St. RM16: Grays 4B 18
Cranborne Av. EN6: Pot B 3E 7
Cranborne Rd. EN6: Pot B 3E 7
CRANBOURNE 2C 20
CRANBROOK 3D 17
Cranbrook Rd. IG1: Ilf 3D 17
IG2: Ilf 2D 17
IG6: Ilf 2D 17
CRANES 2E 19
Cranes Farm Rd. SS14: Bas 2D 19
Cranes Way WD6: Bore 1D 15
Cranfield Pk. Rd. SS12: Wick 2E 19
CRANFORD 1B 22
Cranford La. TW5: Cran, Hest 1B 22
UB3: Cran, Harl 1A 22
CRANHAM 3A 18
Cranham Rd. CM3: Lit W 1E 11
CRANLEY GARDENS 2F 15
Cranley Gdns. N10 2F 15
Cranmer Rd. CR4: Mitc 3F 23
Cranmore La. GU11: Alde 4A 28
Cranston Rd. SE23 2B 24
Craufurd Ri. SL6: Maide 4B 12
Cravells Rd. AL5: Harp 1B 6
Craven Gdns. IG6: Ilf 2D 17
Craven Hill W2 4F 15
Craven Pk. NW10 4D 15
Craven Pk. Rd. NW10 4D 15
Craven Rd. W2 4F 15
CRAWLEY HILL 2B 28
Crawley Hill GU15: Camb 1B 28
Crawley Ridge GU15: Camb 1B 28
Crawley's La. HP23: Wigg 1D 5
Cray Av. BR5: St M Cry 4E 25
CRAYFORD 2F 25
Crayford Rd. DA1: Cray 2F 25
Crayford Way DA1: Cray 2F 25
Craylands La.
DA10: Ghithe, Swans 2B 26
Cray Rd. BR8: Crock 4F 25
DA14: Sidc 3E 25
CRAYS HILL 1E 19
Crays Hill CM11: Bill, C Hill 1E 19
CREEKMOUTH 4D 17
Creek Rd. KT8: E Mos 3C 22
SE8 1B 24
SE10 1B 24
Creephedge La.
CM3: E Han, Sth F 3F 11
Creffield Rd. W3 4D 15
W5 4D 15
Creighton Av. N2 2F 15
N10 2F 15
Creighton Rd. N17 2A 16
Cremorne Rd. SW10 1F 23
Crescent, The KT22: Lea 2C 30
Crescent E. EN4: Had W 4F 7
Crescent Rd. CM14: Warl 1B 18
Crescent W. EN4: Had W 4F 7
CRESSEX 2A 12
Cressex Rd. HP12: Book, H Wy 2A 12
Crest Rd. HP11: H Wy 2A 12
Crete Hall Rd. DA11: Nflt 2C 26
CREWS HILL 4A 8
Cricketers La. RG42: Warf 3B 20
Cricketfield Rd. E5 3B 16
Cricket Grn. CR4: Mitc 3F 23
CRICKET HILL 2A 28
Cricket Hill La. GU46: Yat 2A 28
CRICKLEWOOD 3E 15
Cricklewood B'way. NW2 3E 15
Cricklewood La. NW2 3E 15
Crimp Hill SL4: Eng G, Old Win 2D 21
Cripple St. ME15: Maids 3F 35
CRITTALLS CORNER 3E 25
Critten La. RH5: Ran C 4B 30
CROCKENHILL 4F 25
Crockenhill La.
BR8: Crock, Eyns, Farni 4F 25
DA4: Eyns, Farni 4F 25
Crockenhill Rd. BR5: St M Cry 4E 25
BR8: Crock 4E 25
Crockford Pk. Rd. KT15: Add 4F 21
CROCKHAM HILL 4D 33
Crocknorth Rd. KT24: E Hor 4A 30
(not continuous)
RH5: Ran C 4A 30
CROFTON 4D 25
Crofton La. BR5: Farnb, Pet W 4D 25
BR6: Pet W 4D 25
CROFTON PARK 2B 24
Crofton Rd. BR6: Farnb, Orp 4D 25
Croham Rd. CR2: S Croy 4A 24
Croham Valley Rd. CR2: Sels 1B 32
Cromwell Av. EN7: Chesh 3B 8
Cromwell Rd. KT2: King T 3D 23
RH1: Redh 4F 31
SW5 1E 23
SW7 1E 23
TW3: Houn 2B 22
Crondall La. GU9: Farnh 4A 28
GU10: Dip 4A 28
CRONDON 3D 11
Crondon Pk. La. CM4: Stock 4D 11
Cronks Hill RH1: Redh 4F 31
RH2: Reig 4F 31
CROOKED BILLET 2B 16
CROOKED BILLET RDBT. 3F 21
Crooked Mile EN9: Walt A 3C 8
Crook Log DA6: Bex 2E 25
Crooksbury Rd. GU10: Runf 4B 28
Croom's Hill SE10 1C 24
Crossbrook St. EN8: Chesh 3B 8
Cross Deep TW1: Twick 2C 22
CROSS KEYS 3F 33
Cross Lances Rd. TW3: Houn 2B 22
Cross La. AL5: Harp 1B 6
HP9: Beac 2D 13
Cross La. E. DA12: Grav'nd 2C 26
Cross La. W. DA11: Grav'nd 2C 26
Cross Lees CM5: Fyf, More 2A 10
Crossley's Hill HP8: Chal G 1E 13
Cross Oak Rd. HP4: Berk 2E 5
Crossoaks La.
EN6: Ridge, S Mim 3D 7
Cross Rd. BR2: Brom 4D 25
KT20: Tad 2E 31
SL5: S'dale 4D 21
Cross Roads IG10: H Beech 4C 8
Cross St. N1 4A 16
Crossway SE28 4E 17
SW20 3E 23
Crossways Blvd. DA2: Dart 2A 26
DA9: Dart, Ghithe 2A 26
CROUCH 3B 34
CROUCH END 2F 15
Crouch End Hill N8 3F 15
Crouch Hill N4 2A 16
N8 2A 16
Crouch Ho. Rd. TN8: Eden 4D 33
Crouch La. EN7: Chesh, G Oak 3A 8
SL4: Wink 2C 20
TN15: Bor G 2B 34
Crowbrook Rd. HP27: M Ris 2A 4
CROW GREEN 4A 10
Crow Grn. Rd. CM15: Pil H 1B 18
CROWHURST 4C 32
Crowhurst La. RH7: Ling 4C 32
TN15: Ash, W King 1B 34
TN15: Bor G 3B 34
CROWHURST LANE END 4C 32
Crowhurst Village Rd.
RH7: Ling 4C 32
CROWLANDS 2E 17
Crow La. RM7: Rush G 3E 17
Crown Dale SE19 3A 24
Crowndale Rd. NW1 4F 15
Crownfield Rd. E15 3C 16
Crown Hill EN9: Walt A 3D 9
Crown La. BR2: Brom 4C 24
DA12: Shorne 3D 27
HP10: Penn 1C 12
SL2: Farn R 4D 13
SM4: Mord 3E 23
SW16 3A 24
Crown Rd. CM14: Kel H 4A 10
(Dudbrook Rd.)
CM14: Kel H 4A 10
(Kelvedon Hall La.)
GU25: Vir W 4E 21
SM1: Sutt 4E 23
SM4: Mord 3E 23
TW1: Twick 2C 22
Crown St. W3 4D 15
Crow Piece La. SL2: Farn R 3D 13
(not continuous)
Crowsheath La. CM11: D'ham 4E 11
CROWTHORNE 4A 20
Crowthorne Rd. GU47: S'urst 1A 28
RG12: Brac 4B 20
RG45: Crow 4A 20
CROXLEY GREEN 1A 14
Croxted Rd. SE21 2A 24
SE24 2A 24
CROYDON 4A 24
Croydon La. SM7: Bans 1F 31
Croydon Rd. BR2: Hayes, Kes 4C 24
BR3: Beck 3B 24
BR4: Hayes, W W'ck 4C 24
CR0: Bedd 4F 23
CR0: C'don 3F 23
CR3: Cat'm 3B 32
CR4: Mitc 3F 23
RH2: Reig 4F 31
SE20 3B 24
Croydon Rd. SM6: Bedd, Wall 4F 23
TN16: Westrm 3D 33
Crutches La. ME2: Strood 3E 27
ME3: High'm 3E 27
CRYERS HILL 4B 4
Cryers Hill La. HP15: Cry H 4B 4
Cryers Hill Rd. HP15: Cry H 4B 4
CRYSTAL PALACE 3A 24
Crystal Palace FC 3A 24
Crystal Palace National Sports Cen. 3B 24
Crystal Pal. Pde. SE19 3A 24
Crystal Pal. Pk. Rd. SE26 3B 24
CUBITT TOWN 1C 24
Cuckoo Hill HA5: Eastc 2B 14
Cuckoo La. TN11: Tonb 4B 34
Cucumber La. AL9: Ess 3F 7
CUDHAM 2D 33
Cudham La. Nth. BR6: Downe 1D 33
TN14: Cud 1D 33
Cudham La. Sth.
TN14: Cud, Knock 2D 33
Cudham Rd. BR6: Downe 1D 33
CUFFLEY 3A 8
Cuffley Hill EN7: Cuff, G Oak 3A 8
Culver Gro. HA7: Stan 2C 14
CULVERSTONE GREEN 1C 34
Cumberland Av. GU2: Guild 3E 29
SL2: Slou 4D 13
Cumberland Ga. W2 4F 15
Cumberland Rd. GU15: Camb 2C 28
HA7: Stan 2D 15
CUPID GREEN 1A 6
Cupid Grn. La.
HP2: Gad R, Hem H 1A 6
Curriers La. SL1: Burn 3C 12
Curtain Rd. EC2 4A 16
CURTISMILL GREEN 4F 9
Curzon St. W1 4F 15
CUSTOM HOUSE 4C 16
Cut, The SE1 1A 24
Cuton Hall La. CM2: Spr 1E 11
Cutter Ridge Rd.
DA13: Lud'n 4D 27
Cutting, The RH1: Redh 4F 31
CUXTON 4E 27
Cuxton Rd. ME2: Strood 3E 27
Cyprus Pl. E6 4D 17

D

DAGENHAM 3E 17
Dagenham & Redbridge FC 3E 17
Dagenham Av. RM9: Dag 4E 17
(not continuous)
Dagenham Rd. RM7: Rush G 3F 17
RM10: Dag 3F 17
RM13: Rain 3F 17
Dagger La. WD6: E'tree 1C 14
Dagnall Rd. HP1: Gt Gad 1E 5
Dagnam Pk. Dr. RM3: Rom 1A 18
Dagwood La. CM15: Dodd 4B 10
Daiglen Dr. RM15: S Ock 4B 18
Dairy La. TN8: Crock H 4D 33
TN12: Mard 4E 35
Dale Rd. DA13: Sflt 3B 26
Dalling Rd. W6 1E 23
DALSTON 3A 16
Dalston La. E8 3A 16
Daltons Rd. BR6: Crock, Orp 4F 25
BR8: Crock 4F 25
Dalton Way WD17: Wat 1B 14
Damases La. CM3: Bor 1F 11
Dames Rd. E7 3C 16
DANBURY 2F 11
Dancers End La. HP23: Tring 1B 4
DANCERS HILL 4E 7
Dancers Hill Rd. EN5: Barn 4E 7
Daneshill RH1: Redh 4F 31
Danns La.
ME18: W'bury, W Mal 3D 35
DANSON INTERCHANGE 2E 25
Danson La. DA16: Well 2E 25
Danson Rd. DA6: Bex 2E 25
DARBY GREEN 1A 28
Darby Grn. La. GU17: Bla 1A 28
Darby Grn. Rd. GU17: Bla 1A 28
DARENTH 3A 26
Darenth Hill DA2: Dart 3A 26
DARENTH INTERCHANGE 2A 26
Darenth Rd. DA1: Dart 2A 26
DA2: Dart 3A 26
Darenth Wood Rd. DA2: Dart 2A 26
(not continuous)
Dargets Rd. ME5: Wald 1F 35
Darkes La. EN6: Pot B 3E 7
Dark La. CM14: Gt War 2A 18
EN7: Chesh 3B 8
DARLAND 4F 27
Darland Av. ME7: G'ham 4F 27
Darman La. ME18: Ladd 4D 35
TN12: Pad W 4D 35
Darnicle Hill
EN7: New S, G Oak, Chesh 2A 8
Darnley Rd. DA11: Grav'nd 2C 26
(not continuous)
E9 3B 16
ME2: Strood 3E 27
Darr's La. HP4: Berk 1D 5
DARTFORD 2A 26
Dartford By-Pass
DA1: Bexl, Dart 2F 25
DA2: Bean, Bexl, Dart 2F 25
DA5: Bexl, Dart 2F 25
Dartford Crossing RM20: Dart 1A 26
DARTFORD HEATH 2F 25
Dartford Rd. DA1: Dart 2F 25
DA4: Farni, Hort K, Knock, S Dar 4A 26
DA5: Bexl 2F 25
TN13: S'oaks 3F 33
Dartford Tunnel RM20: Dart 1A 26
Dartmouth Hill SE10 1C 24
DARTMOUTH PARK 3F 15
Dartmouth Pk. Hill N19 3F 15
Dartmouth Pk. Rd. NW5 3F 15
Dartmouth Rd. SE23 2B 24
SE26 2B 24
DARTNELL PARK 1F 29
Darvills La. RG10: S Row 2A 20
Dashwood Av. HP12: H Wy 1A 12
Dashwood Rd. DA11: Grav'nd 2C 26
DATCHET 1E 21
DATCHET COMMON 1E 21
Datchet Rd. SL3: Hort 2E 21
SL3: Slou 1D 21
SL4: Old Win 2E 21
SL4: Wind 1D 21
Daubeney Rd. E5 3B 16
Davenants SS13: Bas 2E 19
Davidson Rd. CR0: C'don 4A 24
DAVID STREET 4C 26
David St. DA13: Meop 1C 34
DAWESGREEN 4D 31
Dawes La. WD3: Sarr 4F 5
Dawes Rd. SW6 1E 23
Dawley Rd. UB3: Harl, Hayes 4A 14
Dawney Hill GU24: Pirb 2D 29
Dawshill E4 4C 8
Daws Hill La. HP11: H Wy 2B 12
Daws La. NW7 1D 15
Days La. CM15: Dodd, Pil H 4B 10
Deacons Hill WD6: E'tree 1D 15
WD19: Wat 1B 14
Deacon's Hill Rd. WD6: E'tree 4D 7
Deadhearn La. HP8: Chal G 1E 13
Deadman's Ash La. WD3: Sarr 4F 5
Deadman's La. CM2: Gall, Gt B 3E 11
DEAN BOTTOM 3B 26
Dean La. DA13: Meop 1C 34
RH1: Mers 3F 31
SL6: Cook 3B 12
Dean Rd. DA13: Meop, Lud'n 4D 27
Deansbrook Rd. HA8: Edg 2D 15
Deans La. HA8: Edg 2D 15
KT20: Walt H 3E 31
DEAN STREET 3F 35
Dean St. ME15: E Far 4E 35
SL7: Marl 3A 12
W1 4F 15
Dean Way HP8: Chal G 1E 13
DEBDEN 4D 9
DEBDEN GREEN 4D 9
Debden La. IG10: Lough 4D 9
Debden Rd. IG10: Lough 4D 9
De Beauvoir Rd. N1 3A 16
DE BEAUVOIR TOWN 4A 16
Decoy Hill Rd. ME3: H Hal 1F 27
Dedmere Rd. SL7: Marl 3A 12
DEDWORTH 1D 21
Dedworth Rd. SL4: Wind 1C 20
DEEPCUT 2C 28
Deepcut Bri. Rd. GU16: Deep 2C 28
Deepdene Av. RH4: Dork 4C 30
Deep Mill La. HP16: L King 4C 4
Deeves Hall La. EN6: Ridge 3D 7
Delamare Rd. EN8: Chesh 3B 8
Delancey St. NW1 4F 15
Delce Rd. ME1: Roch 4F 27
Dellsome La. AL9: Wel G 2E 7
Demesne Rd. SM6: Wall 4F 23
Dene Rd. GU14: Cove 3A 28
HA6: Nwood 2A 14
KT21: Asht 2D 31
Dene St. RH4: Dork 4C 30
DENHAM 3F 13
Denham Aerodrome 2F 13
Denham Av. UB9: Den 3F 13
DENHAM GARDEN VILLAGE 2F 13
DENHAM GREEN 2F 13
Denham Grn. La. UB9: Den 2F 13
Denham La. SL9: Chal P 2E 13
Denham Rd. SL0: Iver H 3F 13
UB9: Den 3F 13
DENHAM RDBT. 3F 13
Denham Way UB9: Den 2F 13
WD3: Map C, W Hyd 2F 13
DENMARK HILL 2A 24
Denmark Hill SE5 1A 24
Dennett Rd. CR0: C'don 4A 24
Dennettsland Rd. TN8: Crock H 4D 33
Denning Av. CR0: Wadd 4A 24
Dennises La. RM14: Upm 4A 18
Dennis La. HA7: Stan 1C 14
Dennis Rd. RM15: S Ock 4B 18
Densham Rd. E15 4C 16
DENTON 2D 27
Denton Rd. DA1: Dart 2F 25
Denton Way GU21: Wok 2D 29
Denzil Rd. NW10 3D 15
DEPTFORD 1B 24
Deptford Bri. SE8 1B 24
Deptford B'way. SE8 1B 24
Deptford Chu. St. SE8 1B 24
Deptford High St. SE8 1B 24
Derby Rd. CR0: C'don 4A 24
RM17: Grays 1B 26
Deringwood Dr. ME15: Bear 3F 35
DERRY DOWNS 4E 25
Desborough Av. HP11: H Wy 2A 12
Desborough Pk. Rd.
HP12: H Wy 1A 12
Desborough Rd. HP11: H Wy 1A 12
Detillens La. RH8: Limp 3C 32
Devas St. E3 4B 16
Devenish Rd. SL5: S'dale, S'hill 4C 20
Devon Rd. DA4: S Dar, Sutt H 3A 26
Devonshire Rd. NW7 2E 15
RM16: Chaf H, Grays 1B 26
SE23 2B 24
Devons Rd. E3 4B 16
DIBDEN 3F 33
Dibden La. TN14: Ide H, S'oaks 3F 33
Dickens World 3F 27
Dickerage La. KT3: N Mald 3D 23
Dickerage Rd. KT1: King T 3D 23
Dimmocks La. WD3: Sarr 4F 5
Discovery Dr. ME19: Kin H 3D 35
Ditches La. CR3: Cat'm, Coul 2A 32
DITTON 2E 35
Ditton Hill KT6: Surb 4C 22
Ditton Hill Rd. KT6: Surb 4C 22
Ditton Pk. Rd. SL3: L'ly 1E 21
Ditton Rd. KT6: Surb 4D 23
SL3: Dat 1E 21
SL3: L'ly 1E 21
Dixons Hill Rd.
AL9: N Mym, Wel G 2E 7
DOBB'S WEIR 1C 8
Dobb's Weir Rd. CM19: Roy 1C 8
EN11: Hodd, Roy 1C 8
Dockett Eddy La. TW17: Shep 4A 22
DOCKLANDS 4D 17
Dock Rd. ME4: Chat 3F 27
RM17: Grays 1C 26
RM18: Tilb 1C 26
Dock St. E1 4B 16
Doctors La. CR3: Cat'm 3A 32
DODDINGHURST 4B 10
Doddinghurst Rd.
CM15: B'wood, Dodd, Pil H 4B 10
Dodds La. HP2: Hem H 1F 5
HP8: Chal G 1E 13
Doesgate La. RM14: Bulp 3C 18
Dogflud Way GU9: Farnh 4A 28
Doghurst La. CR5: Chip 2F 31
DOGKENNEL GREEN 4B 30
Dog Kennel Hill SE22 2A 24
Dog Kennel La. WD3: Chor 4F 5
DOLLIS HILL 3E 15
Dollis Hill La. NW2 3D 15
Dollis Rd. N3 2E 15
NW7 2E 15
DOME, THE 4B 6
Domsey La. CM3: Lit W 1E 11
Doncastle Rd. RG12: Brac 3A 20
Donkey La. DA4: Farni 4A 26
DONKEY TOWN 1E 28
Donnington Rd. NW10 3E 15
DORA'S GREEN 4A 28
Dora's Grn. La. GU10: Ews 4A 28
Dorchester Gro. W4 1D 23
DORKING 4C 30
Dorking Rd. GU4: Guild 4F 29
GU5: Goms 4A 30
KT20: Tad, Walt H 3D 31
KT22: Lea 3C 31
KT23: Bookh 3B 30
RH5: Ab H 4A 30
DORMER'S WELLS 4B 14

Dormer's Wells La. UB1: S'hall 4B 14
DORNEY 1C 20
Dorney Hill Nth. HP9: Beac 2D 13
Dorney Hill Sth. HP9: Beac 3D 13
DORNEY REACH 1C 20
Dorney Wood Rd. SL1: Burn 3C 12
Dorset Rd. SW19 3E 23
Douglas Rd. ME16: Maids 3F 35
Dover Ho. Rd. SW15 2E 23
Dover Rd. DA11: Nflt 2C 26
SL1: Slou 4D 13
Dover Rd. E. DA11: Grav'nd 2C 26
DOVERS CORNER 4F 17
DOVERSGREEN 4E 31
Dovers Grn. Rd. RH2: Reig 4E 31
Dowding Way EN9: Walt A 4C 8
DOWLESGREEN 3A 20
DOWNE 1D 33
Downe Rd. BR2: Kes 1D 33
TN14: Cud 1D 33
Downfield Rd.
SG13: Hert H, Rush G 1B 8
Down Grn. La. AL4: Whe 1C 6
Downhall Rd. CM17: M Grn 1F 9
DOWNHAM
BR1 3C 24
CM11 1E 19
Downham Rd.
CM4: D'ham, Stock 4E 11
CM11: D'ham, Ram H 4E 11
N1 3A 16
Downham Way BR1: Brom 3C 24
Downhills Pk. Rd. N17 2A 16
Down La. GU3: Comp 4D 29
DOWNLEY 1A 12
Downley Rd. HP14: Nap 4A 4
Downshills Way N17 2A 16
Downshire Way RG12: Brac 3B 20
RG42: Brac 3B 20
DOWNSIDE 2B 30
Downside Bri. Rd.
KT11: Cobh 2B 30
Downside Comn. Rd.
KT11: D'side 2B 30
Downside Rd. KT11: D'side 2B 30
SM2: Sutt 1F 31
Downs Rd. DA13: Nflt G, Ist R 3C 26
EN1: Enf 4A 8
SM2: Sutt 1E 31
Downsview Rd. SE19 3A 24
Dowsett La. CM11: Ram H 4E 11
Dowsett Rd. N17 2B 16
Doyle Gdns. NW10 4E 15
Drakefell Rd. SE4 1B 24
SE14 1B 24
Drake Rd. RM16: Chaf H 1B 26
Drakes Dr. AL1: St A 2C 6
Drakes La. CM3: Lit W 1E 11
Drapers Rd. EN2: Enf 4A 8
Draycott Av. HA3: Kent 2C 14
DRAYTON BEAUCHAMP 1C 4
Drayton Gdns. SW10 1F 23
Drayton Pk. N5 3A 16
Drayton Rd. W13 4C 14
Drewstead Rd. SW16 2F 23
DRIFT BRIDGE 1E 31
Drift Rd. SL4: Wink 2C 20
SL6: Pal S, W Walt 2A 20
Drive, The CM13: Gt War 2B 18
DA14: Sidc 2E 25
IG1: Ilf 2D 17
SM4: Mord 4F 23
WD3: Rick 1F 13
Drop La. AL2: Brick W 3B 6
Dropmore Rd. SL1: Burn 4C 12
Druid St. SE1 1A 24
Drury La. WC2 4A 16
Drury Way NW10 3D 15
Dry Arch Rd. SL5: S'dale 4D 21
Drydell La. HP5: Ches 3D 5
DRYHILL 3E 33
Dryhill La. TN14: Sund 3E 33
Dry Hill Pk. Rd. TN10: Tonb 4B 34
DRY STREET 3D 19
Dry St. SS16: Bas, Lan H, Vange 3D 19
SS16: Lan H, Bas 3D 19
Du Cane Rd. W12 4D 15
Duck La. CM16: Twood 2E 9
Duckmore La. HP23: Tring 1C 4
Duck's Hill Rd. HA6: Nwood 2A 14
DUCKS ISLAND 1E 15
Dudbrook Rd.
CM14: Kel C, Nave 4A 10
DUDDEN HILL 3E 15
Dudden Hill La. NW10 3D 15
DUDSWELL 1D 5
Dudswell La. HP4: Berk 1D 5
Duffield La. SL2: Stoke P 3D 13
Dugdale Hill La. EN6: Pot B 3E 7
Dukes Av. N10 2F 15
TW10: Ham 3C 22
Dukes La. CM5: Bern R, Will 1B 10
Duke's Ride RG45: Crow 1A 28
Duke St. CM1: Chelm 2E 11
EN11: Hodd 1B 8
DULWICH 2A 24
Dulwich Comn. SE21 2A 24
Dulwich Rd. SE24 2A 24
DULWICH VILLAGE 2A 24
Dulwich Village SE21 2A 24
Dulwich Wood Pk. SE19 3A 24
Dunbar Rd. N22 2A 16
Dunbridge St. E2 4B 16
Duncan Rd. ME7: G'ham 3F 27
Dundale Rd. HP23: Tring 1C 4
Dungells La. GU46: Yat 2A 28
Dungrove Hill La. SL6: Maide 4A 12
Dunkery Rd. SE9 3C 24
DUNK'S GREEN 3B 34
Dunk's Grn. Rd. TN11: S'brne 3B 34
Dunmow Rd.
CM5: Beau R, Bern R, Fyf 2A 10
Dunnings La.
CM13: Bulp, W H'dn 3B 18
RM14: Bulp 3B 18
Dunn St. Rd. ME7: Bred 1F 35
Dunny La. WD4: Chfd 3F 5
DUNSMORE 2B 4
Dunsmure Rd. N16 3A 16
Dunstable Rd. AL3: Redb 1B 6
DUNTON GREEN 2F 33
Dunton Rd. CM12: L Bur 2C 18
CM13: Heron, B'wood 2C 18
SE1 1A 24
SS15: Lain 2C 18
Duppas Hill Rd. CR0: Wadd 4A 24
Durants Rd. EN3: Pond E 4B 8
Durham Rd. SS15: Lain 2D 19
SW20 3E 23
Durnsford Rd. N11 2F 15
SW19 2E 23
Durrants Hill Rd. HP3: Hem H 2F 5
Durrants La. HP4: Berk 2D 5
Durrants Rd. HP4: Berk 1D 5
Dury Rd. EN5: Barn 4E 7
DUTCH VILLAGE 4F 19
Dux Ct. Rd. ME3: H Hal, Hoo 2F 27
Dux Hill TN15: Plax 3B 34
Dux La. TN15: Plax 3B 34
Dwelly La. TN8: Eden 4C 32
Dyke La. AL4: Whe 1C 6
Dytchleys La. CM14: N'side 4A 10
Dytchleys Rd. CM14: N'side 4A 10

E

Eagle Way CM13: Gt War 2B 18
Eagle Wharf Rd. N1 4A 16
EALING 4C 14
EALING COMMON 4D 15
Ealing Grn. W5 4C 14
Ealing Rd. HA0: Wemb 3D 15
TW8: Bford 1C 22
Eardley Rd. SW16 3F 23
Earl Howe Rd. HP15: Holm G 4C 4
Earl Rd. DA11: Nflt 2C 26
EARL'S COURT 1E 23
Earl's Court Exhibition Cen. 1E 23
Earls Ct. Rd. SW5 1E 23
W8 1E 23
EARLSFIELD 2F 23
Earlsfield Rd. SW18 2F 23
Earls La. EN6: Ridge, S Mim 3D 7
Earl's Path IG10: Lough 4C 8
EARLSWOOD 4F 31
EAST ACTON 4D 15
E. Acton La. W3 4D 15
East Av. E12 3D 17
EAST BARNET 1F 15
E. Barnet Rd. EN4: E Barn 4F 7
Eastbourne Rd.
RH9: G'stone, S God 4B 32
Eastbourne Ter. W2 4F 15
EAST BURNHAM 4D 13
E. Burnham La. SL2: Farn R 4D 13
EASTBURY 1A 14
Eastbury Av. HA6: Nwood 1A 14
Eastbury Rd. HA6: Nwood 2A 14
WD19: Wat 1B 14
E. Churchfield Rd. W3 4D 15
Eastchurch Rd. TW6: H'row A 1A 22
EAST CLANDON 4F 29
East Comn. SL9: Ger X 2E 13
EASTCOTE 3B 14
Eastcote La. HA2: Harr 3B 14
UB5: N'olt 3B 14
(not continuous)
Eastcote La. Nth. UB5: N'olt 3B 14
Eastcote Rd. HA4: Ruis 3A 14
HA5: Pinn 2B 14
EASTCOTE VILLAGE 2B 14
EAST DULWICH 2A 24
E. Dulwich Gro. SE22 2A 24
E. Dulwich Rd. SE15 2B 24
SE22 2A 24
(not continuous)
EASTEND 1C 8
East End Rd. N2 2E 15
N3 2E 15
Easterfields ME19: E Mal 2E 35
Eastern Av. E11 2C 16
HA5: Pinn 3B 14
IG2: Ilf 2D 17
IG4: Ilf 2D 17
RM6: Chad H 2D 17
RM20: W Thur 1A 26
Eastern Av. E. RM1: Rom 2F 17
RM2: Rom 2F 17
RM3: Rom 2F 17
Eastern Av. W. RM6: Chad H 2E 17
RM7: Chad H, Mawney, Rom
2E 17
Eastern Dene HP15: Haz 4B 4
Eastern Way RM17: Grays 1B 26
SE28 1E 25
EAST EWELL 1E 31
EAST FARLEIGH 3E 35
Eastferry Rd. E14 1B 24
Eastfield Rd. EN3: Enf W 4B 8
SL1: Burn 4C 12
Eastfields Rd. CR4: Mitc 3F 23
EAST FINCHLEY 2F 15
E. Hall Hill ME17: B Mon 4F 35
E. Hall La. RM13: Wenn 4F 17
E. Hall Rd. BR5: St M Cry 4E 25
EAST HAM 4D 17
EASTHAMPSTEAD 4B 20
Easthampstead Rd. RG12: Brac 3B 20
RG40: W'ham 3A 20
EAST HANNINGFIELD 3F 11
E. Hanningfield Rd.
CM2: Howe G, Sando 3F 11
CM3: Ret 4F 11
E. Heath Rd. NW3 3F 15
EAST HILL 1A 34
East Hill DA1: Dart 2A 26
DA4: S Dar 3A 26
GU22: Wok 2F 29
RH8: Oxt 3C 32
SW18 2F 23
E. Hill Rd. RH8: Oxt 3C 32
TN15: Knat 1A 34
EAST HORSLEY 3A 30
E. India Dock Rd. E14 4B 16
East La. HA0: Wemb 3C 14
HA9: Wemb 3C 14
RG10: W Law 1A 20
E. Lodge La. EN2: Crew H, Enf 4F 7
EASTLY END 3F 21
EAST MALLING HEATH 3D 35
East Mayne SS13: Bas 2E 19
E. Milton Rd. DA12: Grav'nd 2C 26
EAST MOLESEY 3C 22
Easton St. HP11: H Wy 1B 12
EAST PECKHAM 4D 35
East Ramp TW6: H'row A 1A 22
East Ridgeway EN6: Cuff 3A 8
East Rd. N1 4A 16
E. Rochester Way DA5: Bexl 2D 25
DA15: Bexl, Sidc 2D 25
DA16: Well 2D 25
East Row ME1: Roch 3F 27
EAST SHEEN 2D 23
East Smithfield E1 4A 16
East St. BR1: Brom 3C 24
GU9: Farnh 4A 28
KT17: Eps 1D 31
ME15: Hunt 4E 35
ME19: Addtn 2C 34
E. Thurrock Rd. RM17: Grays 1C 26
EAST TILBURY 1D 27
E. Tilbury Rd. SS17: Linf 1D 27
East Vw. CM1: Writ 2D 11
East Way E9 3B 16
EASTWICK 1D 9
Eastwick Hall La.
CM20: East, G'ton 1D 9
EAST WICKHAM 1E 25
Eastwick Rd. CM20: East, Har 1D 9
KT23: Bookh 3B 30
SG12: Huns, S Abb 1C 8
EASTWORTH 4F 21
Eastworth Rd. KT16: Chert 4F 21
Eaton Ri. W5 4C 14
Eaton Rd. EN1: Enf 4A 8
Eaton Sq. SW1 1F 23
Ebbisham La.
KT20: Eps D, Tad, Walt H 3E 31
Ebury Bri. Rd. SW1 1F 23
ECCLES 1E 35
Eccleston St. SW1 1F 23
Echo Pit Rd. GU1: Guild 4E 29
EDENBRIDGE 4D 33
EDEN PARK 4B 24
Eden Pk. Av. BR3: Beck 3B 24
(not continuous)
Edgehill Rd. CR8: Purl 1A 32
Edgemoor Rd. GU16: Frim 2C 28
Edgeworth Rd. EN4: Cockf 4F 7
Edgington Way DA14: Sidc 3E 25
EDGWARE 2D 15
EDGWARE BURY 1D 15
Edgwarebury La. HA8: Edg 1D 15
Edgware Rd. NW2 3E 15
NW9 2D 15
W2 4F 15
Edgware Way HA8: Edg 1C 14
Edinburgh Av. SL1: Slou 4D 13
Edinburgh Way CM20: Har 1D 9
Edison Gro. SE18 1D 25
Edison Rd. DA16: Well 1D 25
Edith Gro. SW10 1F 23
EDMONTON 1B 16
EDNEY COMMON 2C 10
Edward St. SE8 1B 24
SE14 1B 24
EFFINGHAM 3B 30
Effingham Comn. Rd.
KT24: Eff, Eff J 3B 30
EFFINGHAM JUNCTION 3B 30
Effingham Rd. KT6: Surb 4C 22
Effra Rd. SW2 2A 24
Egerton Dr. SE10 1B 24
Egerton Rd. GU2: Guild 4D 29
Eggar's Hill GU11: Alde 4B 28
Eggpie La. TN11: Hild 4F 33
TN14: Hild 4F 33
EGHAM 3E 21
Egham By-Pass TW20: Egh 3E 21
Egham Hill TW20: Egh, Eng G 3E 21
EGHAM HYTHE 3F 21
EGHAM WICK 3E 21
Eglantine La. DA4: Farni, Hort K 4A 26
Egley Rd. GU22: Wok 2E 29
EGYPT 3D 13
Egypt La. SL2: Farn C 3D 13
Elder Rd. SE27 3A 24
Eleanor Cross Rd. EN8: Walt C 3B 8
ELEPHANT & CASTLE 1A 24
Elgin Av. W9 4E 15
Elgin Cres. W11 4E 15
Elizabeth Rd. RM16: Chaf H 1B 26
Elizabeth Way CM19: Har 1D 9
CM20: Har 1D 9
ELKIN'S GREEN 3B 10
Elkstone Rd. W10 4E 15
ELLENBROOK 1D 7
Ellenbrook La. AL10: Hat 1D 7
Ellen Rd. HP21: A'bury 1A 4
ELLESBOROUGH 2A 4
Ellesborough Rd.
HP17: But X, Lit K, Ell 2A 4
HP22: Wend 2A 4
Ellesfield Av. RG12: Brac 3A 20
Ellesmere Rd. W4 1D 23
Elles Rd. GU14: Farnb 3A 28
Elliman Av. SL2: Slou 4D 13
Elm Av. HA4: Ruis 3B 14
Elmbridge Av. KT5: Surb 4D 23
ELM CORNER 2A 30
ELMERS END 3B 24
Elmers End Rd. BR3: Beck 3B 24
SE20 3B 24
Elm Grn. La. CM3: Dan 2F 11
Elm La. CM1: Rox 1C 10
SL8: Bou E 2B 12
Elmore Rd. CR5: Chip, Coul 2F 31
ELM PARK 3F 17
Elm Pk. Av. RM12: Horn 3F 17
Elm Pk. Rd. HA5: Pinn 2B 14
Elm Rd. CM2: Chelm 2E 11
DA14: Sidc 3E 25
HP10: Ty G 1C 12
Elmshott La. SL1: Slou 4D 13
Elms Rd. CM1: Rox 1C 10
GU11: Alde 4B 28
HA3: Hrw W 2C 14
ELMSTEAD 3D 25
Elmstead La. BR7: Chst 3D 25
Elmwood Av. TW13: Felt 2B 22
Elmwood Dr. DA5: Bexl 2E 25
Elsdale St. E9 3B 16
Elspeth Rd. SW11 2F 23
Elstead Rd. GU10: Seale 4B 28
ELSTREE 1C 14
Elstree Hill Nth. WD6: E'tree 1C 14
Elstree Hill Sth. WD6: E'tree 1C 14
Elstree Rd. WD6: E'tree 1C 14
WD23: B Hea 1C 14
Elstree Way WD6: Bore 4D 7
ELTHAM 2D 25
Eltham High St. SE9 2D 25
Eltham Hill SE9 2C 24
Eltham Palace 2D 25
Eltham Rd. SE9 2C 24
SE12 2C 24
ELTHORNE HEIGHTS 4C 14
Elton Way WD25: A'ham 4B 6
Elvetham Rd. GU51: Fleet 3A 28
Embercourt Rd. KT7: T Ditt 4C 22
Ember La. KT8: E Mos 4C 22
KT10: Esh 4C 22
EMERSON PARK 2A 18
Emmanuel Rd. SW12 2F 23
Emmet Hill La. ME18: Ladd 4D 35
Emmetts La.
TN14: Bras, Ide H 3E 33
TN16: Bras 3E 33
Empire Way HA9: Wemb 3D 15
Endell St. WC2 4A 16
Endlebury Rd. E4 1C 16
Endwell Rd. SE4 1B 24
Endymion Rd. N4 3A 16
ENFIELD 4A 8
ENFIELD HIGHWAY 4B 8
ENFIELD LOCK 4B 8
Enfield Rd. EN2: Enf 4F 7
ENFIELD TOWN 4A 8
ENFIELD WASH 4B 8
Engineers Way HA9: Wemb 3D 15
Englands La. IG10: Lough 4D 9
NW3 3F 15
ENGLEFIELD GREEN 3E 21
Englefield Rd. N1 3A 16
Engliff La. GU22: Pyr 2F 29
Enterdent Rd. RH9: G'stone 4B 32
EPPING 2E 9
EPPING GREEN
CM16 2D 9
SG13 2F 7
Epping La. RM4: Abr, Stap T 4E 9
Epping New Rd. IG9: Buck H 1C 16
IG10: Buck H, H Beech, Lough
1C 16
Epping Rd. CM5: N Weald, Ongar 2F 9
CM5: Ongar, They M, Toot H
3F 9
CM16: Epp, Epp G, Epp U, Naze
2D 9
CM16: Epp, N Weald 3E 9
CM16: Epp, They B 2F 9
CM16: Ongar, N Weald 2F 9
Epping Rd. CM19: Roy 1C 8
EN9: Naze, Roy 2D 9
EPPING UPLAND 2D 9
EPSOM 1D 31
EPSOM DOWNS 2D 31
Epsom Downs Racecourse 2D 31
Epsom La. Nth.
KT18: Tad, Tatt C 2E 31
KT20: Tad 2E 31
Epsom Rd. CR0: Wadd 4A 24
GU1: Guild 4E 29
GU4: E Clan, Guild, W Cla 4E 29
KT17: Ewe 1D 31
KT21: Asht 2D 31
KT22: Lea 2C 30
KT24: W Hor 4A 30
SM3: Sutt 4E 23
SM4: Mord 4E 23
ERITH 1F 25
Erith High St. DA8: Erith 1F 25
Erith Rd. DA7: Bex 2E 25
DA8: Erith 1F 25
DA17: Belv, Erith 1E 25
Erriff Dr. RM15: S Ock 4B 18
Erskine Rd. DA13: Meop 1C 34
ESHER 4B 22
Esher By-Pass KT9: Chess 4C 22
KT10: Esh 1B 30
KT11: Cobh 1B 30
ESHER COMMON 1C 30
Esher Rd. KT8: E Mos 4C 22
KT12: Hers 4B 22
Eskdale Av. HP5: Ches 3D 5
Esplanade ME1: Roch 4E 27
ESSENDON 1F 7
Essendon Hill AL9: Ess 1F 7
Essex Av. SL2: Slou 4D 13
Essex County Cricket Ground 2E 11
Essex Regiment Way
CM1: Spr 1E 11
CM3: Lit W 1E 11
Essex Rd. E10 2C 16
EN11: Hodd 1B 8
(not continuous)
N1 4A 16
Essex Rd. Sth. E11 3C 16
Essex Way SS7: Ben 3F 19
ETON 1D 21
Eton Rd. SL3: Dat 1D 21
Eton St. TW9: Rich 2D 23
ETON WICK 1D 21
Eton Wick Rd. SL4: Eton W 1D 21
Euston Av. WD18: Wat 1A 14
Euston Rd. NW1 4F 15
EUSTON UNDERPASS 4F 15
Evelina Rd. SE15 2B 24
Evelyn St. SE8 1B 24
Evering Rd. E5 3A 16
N16 3A 16
Eve Rd. GU21: Wok 2E 29
Eversholt St. NW1 4F 15
EVERSLEY 2F 19
Eversley Pk. Rd. N21 1A 16
EWELL 1D 31
Ewell By-Pass KT17: Ewe 1E 31
Ewell La. ME15: W Far 3E 35
Ewell Rd. KT6: Surb 4D 23
(Surbiton Hill Rd.)
KT6: Surb 4C 22
(Thornhill Rd.)
SM3: Cheam 1E 31
EWSHOT 4A 28
Ewshot La. GU52: Chu C 4A 28
ExCeL 4C 16
Exchange Rd. WD18: Wat 4B 6
Exedown Rd. TN15: Wro 1B 34
Exhibition Rd. SW7 1F 23
EYNSFORD 4A 26
Eynsford Rd. BR8: Crock 4F 25
DA4: Eyns, Farni 4A 26
TN14: Eyns, S'ham 1F 33
Eynsham Dr. SE2 1E 25

F

Fackenden La. TN14: S'ham 1F 33
Factory Rd. E16 1D 25
Faggotters La. CM17: Mat T 1F 9
Faggs Rd. TW14: Felt 2A 22
Fagnall La. HP7: Win H 1C 12
Fairchildes Rd. CR6: Warl 1C 32
FAIR CROSS 3D 17
Fairfield Av. TW18: Staines 3F 21
Fairfield La. SL2: Farn R 4D 13
Fairfield Nth. KT1: King T 3D 23
Fairfield Rd. CR0: C'don 4A 24
E3 4B 16
Fairfield Sth. KT1: King T 3D 23
Fairfield St. SW18 2E 23
FAIRLANDS 3D 29
Fair La. CR5: Coul 3F 31
Fairlie Rd. SL1: Slou 4D 13
FAIRLOP 2D 17
Fairlop Rd. E11 3C 16
Fairmeadow ME14: Maids 2F 35
Fairmead Rd.
IG10: H Beech, Lough 4C 8
FAIRMILE 1B 30
Fairmile La. KT11: Cobh 1B 30
Fairoak La. KT9: Chess 1C 30
KT22: Oxs 1C 30
Fairoaks Airport 1E 29
FAIRSEAT 1C 34
Fairseat La. TN15: Stans 1B 34
TN15: Wro 1B 34
Fairtrough Rd. BR6: Prat B 1E 33
Fairway BR5: Pet W 4D 25
RM16: Grays 4B 18
Fairway, The HA4: Ruis 3B 14
Fakenham Way GU47: Owl 1A 28
Falconer Rd. WD23: Bush 1B 14
Falcon Rd. SW11 1F 23
FALCONWOOD 2D 25
FALCONWOOD 2D 25
Falkland Rd. RH4: Dork 4C 30
Falling La. UB7: Yiew 4A 14
Falloden Way NW11 2E 15
Falmouth Av. E4 1C 16
Fane Way SL6: Maide 1B 20
FANNER'S GREEN 1D 11
Fanshawe Av. IG11: Bark 3D 17
FANT 3F 35
FANTAIL, THE 4D 25
Fant La. ME16: Maids 3E 35
Faraday Av. DA14: Sidc 2E 25
Faringdon Av. RM3: Rom 2F 17
FARLEIGH 1B 32
Farleigh Ct. Rd. CR6: Warl 1B 32
FARLEIGH GREEN 3E 35
Farleigh Hill ME15: Maids 3F 35
Farleigh La. ME16: Maids 3E 35
Farleigh Rd. CR6: Warl 2B 32
Farley La. TN16: Westrm 3D 33
Farley Rd. CR2: Sels 1B 32
FARMBRIDGE END 1C 10
Farmbridge End Rd.
CM1: G Eas, Rox 1C 10
Farm Hill Rd. EN9: Walt A 3C 8
Farm La. KT18: Eps D 2D 31
KT21: Asht 2D 31
Farm Rd. N21 1A 16
SM4: Mord 4E 23
Farm Way IG9: Buck H 1C 16
Farnaby Rd. BR1: Brom 3C 24
FARNBOROUGH
BR6 4D 25
GU14 3A 28
Farnborough Airport 3A 28
Farnborough Comn. BR6: Farnb 4D 25
FARNBOROUGH GREEN 2B 28
Farnborough Hill
BR6: Chels, Farnb 4D 25
FARNBOROUGH PARK 3B 28
Farnborough Rd. GU9: H End 4A 28
GU11: Alde 4A 28
GU14: Farnb 3B 28
FARNBOROUGH STREET 3B 28
Farnborough Way
BR6: Chels, Farnb 4D 25
FARNHAM 4A 28
Farnham By-Pass GU9: Farnh 4A 28
FARNHAM COMMON 3D 13
Farnham La. SL2: Slou 4D 13
Farnham Pk. La. SL2: Farn R 4D 13
Farnham Rd. GU2: Guild 4D 29
GU10: Ews 4A 28
SL1: Slou 4D 13
SL2: Farn R, Slou 4D 13
FARNHAM ROYAL 4D 13
FARNINGHAM 4A 26
Farningham RG12: Brac 4B 20
Farquhar Rd. SE19 3A 24
Farringdon Rd. EC1 4A 16
Fartherwell Rd. ME19: W Mal 2D 35
Farthing Grn. La. SL2: Stoke P 4E 13
FARTHING STREET 1D 33
Farthing St. BR6: Downe 1D 33
Farthing Way CR5: Coul 2F 31
Fassett Rd. KT1: King T 3D 23
Faversham Rd. SM4: Mord 4E 23
FAWKE COMMON 3A 34
Fawke Comn.
TN15: S'oaks, Under 3A 34
Fawke Wood Rd. TN15: Under 3A 34
FAWKHAM 4B 26
FAWKHAM GREEN 4B 26
Fawkham Grn. Rd.
DA3: Ash, Fawk 4B 26
Fawkham Rd. DA3: Fawk 4A 26
DA3: Fawk, Lfield 3B 26
TN15: Fawk, W King 4A 26
Featherbed La. CR0: Sels 1B 32
CR6: Warl 1B 32
HP3: Hem H 2F 5
Feenan Highway RM18: Tilb 1C 26
Felday Rd. RH5: Ab H 4A 30
FELDEN 2F 5
Felden La. HP3: Hem H 2F 5
Fellowes La. AL4: Col H 2D 7
Fellow Grn. GU24: W End 1D 29
FELMORE 2E 19
Felmores SS13: Bas 2E 19
FELTHAM 2A 22
Felthambrook Way TW13: Felt 2B 22
FELTHAMHILL 3B 22
Feltham Hill Rd. TW15: Ashf 3A 22
Feltham Rd. TW15: Ashf 3A 22
Fencepiece Rd. IG6: Chig, Ilf 1D 17
IG7: Chig 1D 17
Fen La. RM14: Bulp, N Ock 3B 18
RM16: Ors 4C 18
Fenner Rd. RM16: Chaf H 1B 26
Fenns La. GU24: W End 1D 29
Fennycroft Rd. HP1: Hem H 1F 5
Fen Pond Rd. TN15: Igh, Wro 2B 34
Fentiman Rd. SW8 1A 24
Fenton Way SS15: Lain 2D 19
Ferme Pk. Rd. N4 2A 16
N8 2A 16
FERN 2B 12
Fernbank Rd. SL5: Asc 3C 20
Fernhall La. EN9: Walt A 3C 8
Fernhead Rd. W9 4E 15
Fernhill La. GU17: Hawl 2A 28
Fernhill Rd. GU14: Cove 2A 28
GU17: Hawl 2A 28
Fernlea Rd. SW12 2F 23
Ferrers La. AL4: Whe 1C 6
AL5: Harp 1C 6
Ferry La. N17 2B 16
RM13: Rain 4F 17
SL8: Bou E 3B 12
(not continuous)
TW17: Shep 4A 22
TW18: Lale 3F 21
Ferry Rd. RM18: Tilb 2C 26
SS7: Ben 3F 19
FETCHAM 3C 30
Fetter La. EC4 4A 16
(not continuous)
FICKLESHOLE 1C 32
FIDDLERS HAMLET 3E 9
FIELDCOMMON 4B 22
Field End Rd. HA4: Ruis 3B 14
HA5: Eastc 2B 14
Field La. GU16: Frim 2B 28
(not continuous)
FIELDS END 2F 5
Fields End La. HP1: Hem H 1F 5
Field Way WD3: Rick 1F 13
Fieldway CR0: New Ad 1B 32
Fife Rd. SW14 2D 23
FIFIELD 1C 20
Fifield La. SL4: Wink 2C 20
Fifield Rd. SL6: Bray, Fifi 1C 20
Fifth Av. CM20: Har 1D 9
(not continuous)
Fifth Cross Rd. TW2: Twick 2C 22
Fifth Way HA9: Wemb 3D 15
Filston La. TN13: Otf 2F 33
TN14: Otf, S'ham 2F 33
Finborough Rd. SW10 1E 23
FINCHLEY 2E 15
Finchley La. NW4 2E 15
Finchley Rd. NW2 2E 15
NW3 2E 15
NW8 4F 15
NW11 2E 15
Fine Bush La. UB9: Hare 2A 14
Fingrith Hall La.
CM4: Bmore, Nor H 3B 10
(not continuous)
FINSBURY 4A 16
FINSBURY PARK 3A 16
Firbank Rd. AL3: St A 1C 6
RM5: Col R 1E 17
Firgrove Rd. RG27: Yat 1A 28
Firmingers Rd. BR6: Orp 4E 25
Firs La. N13 1A 16
N21 1A 16
First Av. CM20: Har 1D 9
(not continuous)
EN1: Enf 1A 16
SS17: Stan H 4D 19
First Way HA9: Wemb 3D 15
Fir Tree Av. SL2: Stoke P 4D 13
Fir Tree Hill WD3: Chan C 4A 6
Fir Tree Rd. KT17: Eps D 2E 31
SM7: Bans 2E 31
FISHERS GREEN 3B 8
FISHERY 4B 12
Fishery Rd. HP1: Hem H 2F 5
Fishponds Rd. BR2: Kes 4C 24
Fish St. AL3: Redb 1B 6
Fitzjohn's Av. NW3 3F 15
Five Elms Rd. BR2: Hayes 4C 24
Five Flds. La. TN8: F Elm 4E 33
FIVEWAYS 2D 25
FIVEWAYS CORNER
Croydon 4A 24
Hendon 2E 15
FLACKWELL HEATH 2B 12
FLAMSTEAD END 3B 8
Flamstead End Rd. EN7: Chesh 3B 8
Flanchford Rd. RH2: Leigh 4E 31
RH2: Reig 4E 31
FLAUNDEN 3E 5
Flaunden Bottom HP5: Lat 4E 5
Flaunden Hill HP3: Flau 3E 5
Flaunden La.
HP3: Bov, Flau, Hem H 3E 5
WD3: Sarr 3F 5
Fleece Rd. KT6: Surb 4C 22
FLEET 3A 28
FLEET DOWNS 2A 26
Fleet Rd. GU11: Alde 3A 28
GU14: Cove 3A 28
GU51: Cove 3A 28
GU51: Fleet 3A 28
KT11: Cobh 1A 30
NW3 3F 15
Fleet St. EC4 4A 16
FLEETVILLE 2C 6
Fleming Rd. RM16: Chaf H 1B 26
FLETCHER'S GREEN 4F 33
Fletcher Way HP2: Hem H 1F 5
FLEXFORD 4C 28
Flexford Rd. GU3: Flex 4C 28
(not continuous)
Flex Mdw. CM19: Har 1D 9
Flint Hill RH4: Dork 4C 30
Florence Rd. SE14 1B 24
Flower La. NW7 2D 15
RH9: G'stone 4B 32
Flowers Bottom La. HP27: Speen 4A 4
Floyd's La. GU22: Pyr 2F 29
FOBBING 3E 19
Fobbing Rd. SS17: Corr 4E 19
Folder's La. RG42: Brac 3B 20
Folkes La. RM14: Upm 2A 18
Folly Hill GU9: Up H 4A 28
Folly La. AL3: St A 2C 6
Fonthill Rd. N4 3A 16
FOOTS CRAY 3E 25
Foots Cray La. DA14: Sidc 2E 25
Footscray Rd. SE9 2D 25
FORCE GREEN 3D 33
Force Grn. La. TN16: Westrm 3D 33
Fordbridge Rd. TW15: Ashf 3A 22
TW16: Sun 4A 22
TW17: Shep 4A 22
FORDBRIDGE RDBT. 3A 22
Ford La. ME19: Tros 2C 34
RM13: Rain 3F 17
TN15: Wro 2C 34
Ford Rd. GU24: Bisl, W End 2D 29
GU24: Chob 1D 29
Fords Gro. N21 1A 16
Fordwater Rd. KT16: Chert 4F 21
Foreman Rd. GU12: Ash G 4B 28
Foremans Barn Rd. ME15: Hunt 4E 35
FORESTDALE 1B 32
Forest Dr. E12 3C 16
Forest Edge IG9: Buck H 1C 16
Foresters Dr. SM6: Wall 1F 31
Foresters Way RG45: Crow 4A 20
FOREST GATE 3C 16
Forest Grn. Rd. SL6: Fifi, Holy 1B 20
FOREST HILL 2B 24
Forest Hill Rd. SE22 2B 24
SE23 2B 24
Forest La. E7 3C 16
E15 3C 16
IG7: Chig 1D 17
Fore St. HA5: Eastc 2A 14
N9 2B 16
N18 2B 16
Forest Rd. E17 2B 16
IG6: Chig, Ilf 2D 17
IG10: Lough 4C 8
KT24: E Hor, Eff J 3A 30
RG42: Bin 3A 20
RG42: Warf, Wink R 3A 20
SL5: Asc 3B 20
SM3: Sutt 4E 23
TW13: Felt 2B 22
Forest Side E4 1C 16
EN9: Walt A 4C 8
Forest Way ME19: Kin H 3D 35
Forge La. DA4: Hort K 3A 26
DA12: Shorne 3D 27
GU11: Alde 3A 28
ME3: High'm 3E 27
ME15: E Far 3E 35
ME17: B Mon 4F 35
ME18: Coll 4E 35
ME18: W Peck 3C 34
Forlease Rd. SL6: Maide 4B 12
Formby Rd. ME2: Hall 4E 27
FORSTAL 2F 35
Forstal La. ME17: Cox 4F 35
Forstal Rd. ME14: S'ing 2E 35
ME20: A'ford 2E 35
Fort Amherst 3F 27
Fortess Rd. NW5 3F 15
FORTIS GREEN 2F 15
Fortis Grn. N2 2F 15
N10 2F 15
Fortis Grn. Rd. N10 2F 15
Fort Pitt Hill ME1: Chat 4F 27
Fort Rd. RM18: Tilb, W Til 2C 26
FORTUNE GREEN 3E 15
Fortune Grn. NW6 3E 15
Forty Av. HA9: Wemb 3D 15
FORTY GREEN 2C 12
Forty Grn. Rd. HP9: Beac 2C 12
FORTY HILL 4A 8
Forty Hill EN2: Enf 4A 8
Forty La. HA9: Wemb 3D 15
FOSTER STREET 1E 9
Foster St. CM17: Har 1E 9
Fostington Way ME5: Wald 1F 35
(not continuous)
Foundry La. HP27: L Row 3A 4
Fountain Dr. SE19 3A 24
Fountain La. ME16: Maids 3E 35
Fountain Rd. CM1: G Eas 1C 10
RH1: Redh 4F 31
Four Ashes Rd. HP15: Cry H 4B 4
FOUR ELMS 4E 33
Four Elms Hill ME3: C'den, Wain 3F 27
Four Elms Rd. TN8: Eden, F Elm 4D 33
Fourth Av. CM19: Har 1D 9
CM20: Har 1D 9
E12 3D 17
Fourth Way HA9: Wemb 3D 15
FOUR WANTZ 1B 10
FOX CORNER 3D 29
Fox Cnr. GU3: Worp 3D 29
FOXENDOWN 4C 26
Foxendown La. DA13: Meop 4C 26
FOX HATCH 4A 10

Foxhills Rd. KT16: Ott 4E 21
Foxhounds La. DA13: Sflt 2B 26
FOX LANE 2A 28
Fox La. BR2: Kes 4C 24
N13 1A 16
Foxley Hill Rd. CR8: Purl 1A 32
Foxley La. CR8: Purl 1F 31
Foxley Rd. SW9 1A 24
Fox Rd. CM1: Mash 1C 10
HP23: Wigg 1C 4
Foyle Dr. RM15: S Ock 4B 18
Framewood Rd.
SL2: Stoke P, Wex 3E 13
Frances Rd. SL4: Wind 1D 21
Frances St. SE18 1D 25
Francis Rd. E10 3C 16
Franks La. DA4: Hort K 4A 26
Franks Wood Av. BR5: Pet W 4D 25
Frant Rd. CR7: Thor H 4A 24
Frascati Way SL6: Maide 4B 12
Fraser Rd. DA8: Erith 1F 25
Frayes Chase CM5: Beau R 1B 10
Freelands Rd. BR1: Brom 3C 24
Freemans La. UB3: Hayes 4A 14
Freemasons Rd. E16 4C 16
Free Prae Rd. KT16: Chert 4F 21
FREEZY WATER 4B 8
Fremantle Rd. IG6: Ilf 2D 17
Fremnells, The SS14: Bas 2E 19
Frenches Rd. RH1: Redh 4F 31
French Horn La. AL10: Hat 1E 7
FRENCH STREET 3D 33
French St. TN16: Westrm 3D 33
TW16: Sun 3B 22
Frendsbury Rd. SE4 2B 24
Friars Av. CM15: Shenf 1B 18
Friars Pl. La. W3 4D 15
Friars Stile Rd. TW10: Rich 2D 23
Friary Bri. GU1: Guild 4E 29
FRIARY ISLAND 2E 21
Friary Rd. N12 1F 15
W3 4D 15
FRIDAY HILL 1C 16
Friday Hill E4 1C 16
FRIERN BARNET 1F 15
Friern Barnet La. N11 1F 15
N20 1F 15
Frieth Rd. SL7: Marl 2A 12
FRIMLEY 2B 28
Frimley By-Pass GU16: Frim 2B 28
FRIMLEY GREEN 2B 28
Frimley Grn. Rd.
GU16: Frim, F Grn 2B 28
Frimley Gro. Gdns. GU16: Frim 2B 28
Frimley High St. GU16: Frim 2B 28
FRIMLEY RIDGE 2B 28
Frimley Rd. GU12: Ash V 3B 28
GU15: Camb 1B 28
GU16: Camb, Frim 2B 28
FRINDSBURY 3F 27
Frindsbury Hill ME2: Strood 3E 27
Frindsbury Rd. ME2: Strood 3E 27
Frithe, The SL2: Slou 4E 13
Frith Hill HP16: Gt Miss, S Hth 3B 4
Frith La. NW7 2E 15
FRITHSDEN 1E 5
Frizlands La. RM10: Dag 3E 17
Frobisher Rd. AL1: St A 2C 6
Frog Gro. La. GU3: Woo V 3D 29
Froggy La. UB9: Den 3F 13
FROGHOLE 4D 33
FROGMORE
AL2 3C 6
GU17 1A 28
Frogmore AL2: F'mre 3C 6
Frogmore Rd. GU17: Bla 1A 28
Frognal NW3 3F 15
Frognal Av. DA14: Sidc 3E 25
FROGNAL CORNER 3D 25
Frognal La. NW3 3E 15
Frog St. CM15: Dodd, Kel H 4A 10
Front, The HP4: Pott E 1E 5
Front La. RM14: Upm 3A 18
Fryent Way NW9 2D 15
FRYERNING 3C 10
Fryerning La. CM4: Fry, Inga 3C 10
FRYERNS 2E 19
Fulbourne Rd. E17 2C 16
FULHAM 1E 23
FULHAM BROADWAY 1E 23
Fulham FC 1E 23
Fulham High St. SW6 1E 23
Fulham Pal. Rd. SW6 1E 23
W6 1E 23
Fulham Rd. SW3 1F 23
SW6 1E 23
SW10 1E 23
Fuller's Hill HP5: Ches 3D 5
HP6: H Hea 3D 5
Fuller St. TN15: Seal 2A 34
Fullers Way Nth. KT6: Surb 4D 23
Fullers Way Sth. KT9: Chess 4D 23
Fullers Wood La. RH1: S Nut 4F 31
Fullwell Av. IG5: Ilf 2D 17
IG6: Ilf 2D 17
FULLWELL CROSS 2D 17
Fullwell Cross IG6: Ilf 2D 17
FULMER 3E 13
Fulmer Comn. Rd. SL0: Iver H 3E 13
SL3: Ful 3E 13
Fulmer La. SL3: Ful 3E 13
SL9: Ger X 3E 13
Fulmer Rd. SL3: Ful 3E 13
SL9: Ger X 3E 13
FULWELL 3C 22
Fulwell Rd. TW11: Tedd 3C 22
Furlong Rd. SL8: Bou E 3B 12
Furness Rd. SM4: Mord 4E 23
Furzebushes La. AL2: Chis G 2B 6
FURZEDOWN 3F 23
FURZE HILL INTERCHANGE 3D 11
Furzehill Rd. WD6: Bore 4D 7
(not continuous)
Furze La. CM4: Stock 4E 11
FURZE PLATT 4B 12
Furze Platt Rd. SL6: Maide 4B 12
FYFIELD 2A 10
Fyfield Rd. CM5: Ongar 2A 10
CM5: Will 2B 10

G

Gabrielspring Rd. DA3: Fawk 4A 26
Gabrielspring Rd. E.
DA3: Fawk, Hort K 4A 26
Gadbrook Rd. RH3: Bet 4D 31
Gaddesden La.
AL3: Flam, Redb 1A 6
GADDESDEN ROW 1F 5
Gaddesden Row HP2: Gad R 1F 5
GADEBRIDGE 1F 5
Gadebridge La. HP1: Hem H 1F 5
(not continuous)
Gadebridge Rd. HP1: Hem H 1F 5
Gade Side WD25: Wat 3A 6
GADSHILL 3E 27
Gads Hill ME7: G'ham 3F 27
Gainsborough Rd. E11 3C 16
N12 1E 15
Gainsthorpe Rd. CM5: Ongar 2F 9
Gale St. RM9: Dag 3E 17
Gallants La. ME15: E Far 3E 35
Gallery Rd. SE21 2A 24
GALLEYEND 3E 11
Galley Hill HP1: Hem H 1F 5
Galley Hill Rd. DA10: Nflt 2B 26
DA11: Nflt 2B 26
Galleyhill Rd. EN9: Walt A 3C 8
(not continuous)
Galley La. EN5: Barn 4E 7
GALLEYWOOD 3E 11
Galleywood Rd. CM2: Chelm 2E 11
CM2: Gt B 2E 11
GALLEYWOOD/STOCK INTERCHANGE 3E 11
Galliard Rd. N9 1B 16
GALLOWS CORNER 2F 17
Gallows Hill WD4: Hunt C 3A 6
Gallows Hill La. WD5: Ab L 3A 6
Gallows La. HP12: H Wy 1A 12
Gallwey Rd. GU11: Alde 4B 28
Gallys Rd. SL4: Wind 1C 20
Galpins Rd. CR7: Thor H 3A 24
Galsworthy Rd. KT2: King T 3D 23
Gambles La. GU23: Rip 3F 29
Gammons La. WD24: Wat 4A 6
(not continuous)
Gander Grn. La. SM1: Sutt 4E 23
SM3: Cheam 4E 23
Gandy's La. ME17: B Mon 4F 35
Gangers Hill CR3: Wold 3B 32
RH9: G'stone 3B 32
GANTS HILL 2D 17
GANTS HILL 2D 17
Gants Hill IG2: Ilf 2D 17
GANWICK CORNER 4E 7
Ganyes Pk. Rd. RM14: Upm 3A 18
Gapemouth Rd. GU24: Pirb 2C 28
Gap Rd. SW19 3E 23
GARDENERS GREEN 4A 20
Gardens, The HA1: Harr 2C 14
Gardiners La. Nth. CM11: C Hill 1E 19
Gardiners La. Sth. SS14: Bas 2E 19
Gardner Rd. SL6: Maide 4B 12
Garfield Rd. KT15: Add 4F 21
Garlands Rd. KT22: Lea 2C 30
Garnet St. E1 4B 16
Garrad's Rd. SW16 2F 23
Garratt La. SW17 2F 23
SW18 2E 23
Garratts La. SM7: Bans 2E 31
Garrison La. KT9: Chess 1C 30
Garson's La. RG42: Warf 2B 20
GARSTON 4B 6
Garston La. WD25: Wat 3B 6
Garth Rd. SM4: Mord 4E 23
Gascoigne Rd. CR0: New Ad 1C 32
IG11: Bark 4D 17
Gascoyne Rd. E9 3B 16
Gascoyne Way SG13: Hertf 1A 8
Gaston Bri. Rd. TW17: Shep 4A 22
Gates Grn. Rd. BR2: Kes 4C 24
BR4: W W'ck 4C 24
Gateshead Rd. WD6: Bore 4D 7
Gatland La. ME16: Maids 3E 35
GATTON 3F 31
Gatton Bottom RH1: Mers 3F 31
RH2: Reig 3F 31
Gatton Pk. Rd. RH1: Redh 4F 31
RH2: Reig 4F 31
Gay Bowers La. CM3: Dan 2F 11
Gay Bowers Rd. CM3: Dan 3F 11
Gellatly Rd. SE14 1B 24
General Wolfe Rd. SE10 1C 24
Geographers' A-Z Map Company 2B 34
George V Av. HA5: Pinn 2B 14
GEORGE GREEN 4E 13
George Grn. Rd. SL3: G Grn 4E 13
George La. E18 2C 16
(not continuous)
George St. HP4: Berk 2E 5
ME15: Hunt 4E 35
TW9: Rich 2C 22
W1 4F 15
George's Wood Rd. AL9: Brk P 2E 7
Gorgewood Rd. HP3: Hem H 2A 6
Germains St. HP5: Ches 3D 5
Gerpins La. RM14: Upm 4A 18
GERRARDS CROSS 2E 13
Gerrards Cross Rd.
SL2: Stoke P 3E 13
Gervase Rd. HA8: Edg 2D 15
GHYLLGROVE 2E 19
Ghyllgrove SS14: Bas 2E 19
Gibbet La. GU15: Camb 1B 28
Gibbon Rd. SE15 1B 24
Gibbs Brook La. RH8: Oxt 4C 32
Gibbs Hill ME18: W'bury 3D 35
Gibraltar Hill ME4: Chat 4F 27
Gibson Dr. ME19: Kin H 3D 35
GIDEA PARK 2F 17
Gifford Dr. GU14: Cove 2A 28
Giffords Cross Rd. SS17: Corr 4E 19
GIGGSHILL 4C 22
Giggs Hill Rd. KT7: T Ditt 4C 22
Gighill Rd. ME20: Lark 2D 35
Gilbert Rd. DA17: Belv 1E 25
Gilbert's Hill HP23: St L 2C 4
Gildenhill Rd. BR8: Swan 3F 25
Gilden Way CM17: Har 1E 9
Gill Av. GU2: Guild 4D 29
Gillespie Rd. N5 3A 16
GILLETTE CORNER 1C 22
GILLINGHAM 3F 27
Gillingham FC 3F 27
Gillingham Rd. ME7: G'ham 3F 27
Gills Rd. DA2: Dart 3A 26
DA4: S Dar 3A 26
GILSTON 1D 9
Giltspur St. EC1 4A 16
Gipsy Hill SE19 3A 24
Gipsy Rd. SE27 3A 24
GIVONS GROVE 3C 30
Glade, The CR0: C'don 4B 24
Glade Rd. SL7: Marl 3A 12
GLANTY 3F 21
Glanty, The TW20: Egh 3F 21
Glasford St. SW17 3F 23
Glassmill La. BR2: Brom 3C 24
(not continuous)
Glaziers La. GU3: Norm 4C 28
Glebe, The CM5: Mag L 1F 9
Glebe La. ME16: Maids 3E 35
Glebe Rd. TN14: Weald 4F 33
Glebe Way BR4: W W'ck 4C 24
Glencoe Rd. UB4: Yead 4B 14
Glen Faba Rd. CM19: Roy 1C 8
Glenisters Rd. HP13: H Wy 1B 12
Glenthorne Rd. W6 1E 23
Globe Rd. E1 4B 16
E2 4B 16
GLOBE TOWN 4B 16
Gloucester Av. CM2: Chelm 2E 11
NW1 4F 15
Gloucester Pl. NW1 4F 15
W1 4F 15
Gloucester Rd. KT1: King T 3D 23
SW7 1F 23
TW12: Hamp 3B 22
Gloucester Ter. W2 4E 15
Goat Hall La. CM2: Chelm 3D 11
GOATHURST COMMON 3E 33
Goat Rd. CR4: Cars, Mitc 4F 23
Goatsmoor La. CM4: Stock 4D 11
CM11: Bill 4D 11
Goatswood La.
RM4: N'side, Noak H 1F 17
Goddard Rd. BR3: Beck 3B 24
GODDEN GREEN 3A 34
GODDINGTON 4E 25
Goddington La. BR6: Chels 4E 25
GODSTONE 3B 32
Godstone By-Pass RH9: G'stone 3B 32
Godstone Hill CR3: G'stone 3B 32
RH9: G'stone 3B 32
GODSTONE INTERCHANGE 3B 32
Godstone Rd. CR3: Cat'm 3B 32
CR8: Purl 1A 32
RH1: Blet 4A 32
RH8: Oxt 4B 32
Goffers Rd. SE3 1C 24
Goff's La. EN7: Chesh, G Oak 3A 8
GOFF'S OAK 3A 8
Goldcrest Way CR0: New Ad 1C 32
Golden Ball La. SL6: Maide 4B 12
GOLDEN GREEN 4C 34
Golden La. EC1 4A 16
GOLDERS GREEN 2E 15
Golders Grn. Rd. NW11 2E 15
Goldhawk Rd. W6 1D 23
W12 1D 23
Gold Hill E. SL9: Chal P 2E 13
Gold Hill Nth. SL9: Chal P 2E 13
Gold Hill W. SL9: Chal P 2E 13
Goldings Hill IG10: Lough 4D 9
Goldsel Rd. BR8: Crock, Swan 4F 25
Goldsmith Rd. W3 4D 15
Goldsmith's Row E2 4B 16
Gold St. DA12: Sole S, Lud'n 4D 27
GOLDSWORTH PARK 2D 29
Goldsworth Rd. GU21: Wok 2E 29
Gole Rd. GU24: Pirb 2C 28
Golf House Rd. RH8: Limp 3C 32
GOMSHALL 4A 30
Gomshall La. GU5: Shere 4A 30
GOOD EASTER 1C 10
Goodge St. W1 4F 15
GOODLEY STOCK 3D 33
Goodley Stock Rd.
TN8: Crock H 4D 33
TN16: Crock H, Westrm 4D 33
GOODMAYES 3E 17
Goodmayes La. IG3: Ilf 3E 17
Goodmayes Rd. IG3: Ilf 3E 17
Goods Way NW1 4A 16
Goodwyns Va. N10 2F 15
GOOSEBERRY GREEN 1D 19
GOOSE GREEN
EN11 1B 8
TN11 4C 34
Goose Grn. GU5: Goms 4A 30
Goose La. GU22: Wok 2E 29
Goose Rye Rd. GU3: Worp 3D 29
Gooshays Dr. RM3: Rom 1A 18
Gordon Av. HA7: Stan 2C 14
Gordon Hill EN2: Enf 4A 8
Gordon Ho. Rd. NW5 3F 15
Gordon Rd. SM5: Cars 1F 31
SS17: Corr, Stan H 4D 19
Gordon Sq. WC1 4F 15
Gordons Way RH8: Oxt 3C 32
Gore Ct. Rd. ME15: Maids 3F 35
Gore Grn. Rd. ME3: High'm 2E 27
Gore Hill HP7: Amer 4D 5
Gorelands La. HP8: Chal G 1E 13
Gore Rd. DA2: Dart 2A 26
SL1: Burn 4C 12
GORESBROOK INTERCHANGE 4E 17
Goresbrook Rd. RM9: Dag 4E 17
Gorse Hill DA4: Farni, Fawk 4A 26
Gorse Rd. BR5: St M Cry 4E 25
Goslar Way SL4: Wind 1D 21
GOSPEL OAK 3F 15
Gosport Rd. E17 2B 16
Gossamers, The WD25: Wat 4B 6
Gosset St. E2 4A 16
Gossetts, The CM6: M Rod 1B 10
Goss Hill BR8: Swan 3F 25
Gossom's End HP4: Berk 1E 5
Goswell Rd. EC1 4A 16
SL4: Wind 1D 21
GOULDS GREEN 4A 14
GOVER HILL 3C 34
Gover Hill ME18: W Peck 3C 34
TN11: S'brne 3C 34
Government Ho. Rd.
GU11: Alde 3B 28
Government Rd. GU11: Alde 4B 28
Gower St. WC1 4F 15
Graces La. CM3: Lit B 2F 11
Gracious La. TN13: S'oaks 3F 33
Gracious Pond Rd.
GU24: Chob 1E 29
Grafton Rd. KT4: Wor Pk 4D 23
Grahame Pk. Way NW7 2D 15
NW9 2D 15
Graham Rd. E8 3B 16
Grand Dpt. Rd. SE18 1D 25
Grand Dr. SW20 3E 23
Grand Pde. N4 2A 16
Grandstand Rd. KT17: Eps D 2E 31
GRANGE HILL 2D 17
Grange Hill TN15: Plax 3B 34
Grange La. DA3: Hartl 4B 26
ME14: S'ing, Box 2F 35
(not continuous)
WD25: Let H 4C 6
GRANGE PARK 1A 16
Grange Rd. CM11: Bill 1D 19
CR7: Thor H 3A 24
E13 4C 16
GU2: Guild 1E 29
GU24: Pirb 2C 28
KT22: Lea 2C 30
ME7: G'ham 3F 27
SE1 1A 24
SE25 3A 24
SL6: Cook 3B 12
TN15: Bor G 2C 34
Grants La. RH8: Limp 4C 32
TN8: Eden, Limp 4C 32
Granville Rd. HP4: Berk 1D 5
N12 2F 15
Grasmere Rd. CR8: Purl 1A 32
Gravel Hill CR0: Addtn 1B 32
DA6: Bex 2E 25
IG10: H Beech 2C 8
N3 2E 15
SL9: Chal P 2E 13
Gravel La. IG7: Chig 1D 17
Gravelly Hill CR3: Cat'm 3A 32
Gravelly La. CM1: Rox 2C 10
Gravelly Ways
ME18: Ladd, Pad W 4D 35
Gravel Path HP4: Berk 1E 5
Gravel Rd. BR2: Brom 4D 25
GRAVESEND 2C 26
Gravesend & Northfleet FC 2B 26
Gravesend Rd. DA12: Shorne 3D 27
ME2: High'm, Strood 3D 27
Gravesend Rd. ME3: High'm 3D 27
TN15: Stans, Wro 2B 34
Gravetts La. GU3: Guild 3D 29
GRAYS 1B 26
Grays Athletic FC 1B 26
Gray's Inn Rd. WC1 4A 16
Grays Pk. Rd. SL2: Stoke P 4E 13
Grays Rd. TN14: Westrm 2D 33
TN16: Westrm 2D 33
GREAT AMWELL 1B 8
GREAT BADDOW 2E 11
GREAT BERRY 2D 19
GREAT BOOKHAM 3B 30
Gt. Braitch La. AL10: Hat 1D 7
GREAT BUCKLAND 1D 35
GREAT BURGH 2E 31
GREAT BURSTEAD 1D 19
GREAT CAMBRIDGE JUNC. 1A 16
Gt. Cambridge Rd. EN1: Enf 2A 16
EN8: Chesh, Walt C 3B 8
EN10: Turn 2B 8
N9 2A 16
N17 2A 16
N18 2A 16
Gt. Central Way HA9: Wemb 3D 15
NW10 3D 15
Gt. Chertsey Rd.
TW13: Hanw, Twick 2B 22
W4 1D 23
Gt. Dover St. SE1 1A 24
Gt. Eastern Rd. E15 3C 16
Gt. Eastern St. EC2 4A 16
GREAT GADDESDEN 1F 5
GREAT HAMPDEN 3A 4
Greatham Rd. WD23: Bush 4B 6
GREAT HIVINGS 3D 5
GREAT HOLLANDS 4A 20
Gt. Hollands Rd. RG12: Brac 4A 20
GREAT KIMBLE 2A 4
GREAT KINGSHILL 4B 4
Great Knightleys SS15: Lain 2D 19
Gt. Marlborough St. W1 4F 15
GREAT MISSENDEN 3B 4
GREATNESS 2F 33
Great Norman St. TN14: Ide H 3E 33
Great Nth. Rd. AL8: W City 1E 7
(not continuous)
AL9: Brk P, Hat, Wel G 2E 7
EN5: Barn 4E 7
EN5: New Bar 1E 15
N2 2F 15
N6 2F 15
Great Nth. Way NW4 2E 15
GREAT OXNEY GREEN 2D 11
GREAT PARNDON 1D 9
Gt. Portland St. W1 4F 15
Gt. Prestons La. CM4: Stock 4E 11
Gt. Queen St. WC2 4A 16
Great Rd. HP2: Hem H 2A 6
Gt. Ropers La. CM14: Gt War 2B 18
Great Sth. W. Rd. TW4: Houn 2A 22
TW14: Bedf, Felt 2A 22
Great Tattenhams KT18: Tatt C 2E 31
GREAT WALTHAM 1D 11
GREAT WARLEY 2B 18
Gt. Warley St. CM13: Gt War 2B 18
Gt. Western Rd. W9 4E 15
W11 4E 15
Great W. Rd. TW5: Hest 1B 22
TW7: Bford, Isle 1C 22
TW8: Bford 1C 22
W4 1D 23
(Cedars Rd.)
W4 1D 23
(Dorchester Gro.)
W6 1D 23
Green, The CM1: Writ 2D 11
CM4: Bmore 3B 10
CM16: They B 4D 9
(not continuous)
CM17: Mat T 1F 9
CR6: Warl 2B 32
DA14: Sidc 3E 25
E4 1C 16
KT10: Clay 1C 30
ME15: W Far 3E 35
ME17: B Mon 4F 35
N9 1B 16
N14 1F 15
N21 1A 16
RM18: W Til 1C 26
TW2: Twick 2C 22
TW20: Eng G 3E 21
UB2: S'hall 1B 22
UB7: W Dray 1F 21
WD3: Crox G 1A 14
WD3: Sarr 4F 5
(not continuous)
Green Comn. La.
HP10: Wbrn G 3C 12
Green Ct. Rd. BR8: Crock 4F 25
Green Dene KT24: E Hor 4A 30
Green Dragon La.
HP10: Flack H 2B 12
N21 1A 16
GREEN END 2F 5
Green End St. HP22: Ast C 1B 4
Green Farm La. DA12: Shorne 2D 27
GREENFORD 4C 14
Greenford Av. W7 4C 14
Greenford Rd. HA1: Harr 4C 14
UB1: S'hall 4C 14
UB6: G'frd 4C 14
GREENFORD RDBT. 4C 14
Greengate St. E13 4C 16
GREEN HAILEY 3A 4
GREENHILL 2C 14
Green Hill HP13: H Wy 1B 12
Greenhill Pk. NW10 4D 15
Greenhill Way HA1: Harr 2C 14
GREENHITHE 2B 26
Greenhurst La. RH8: Oxt 4C 32
Greenlands La. HP16: Pre 3B 4
Green La. BR7: Chst 3D 25
CM1: Rox 2C 10
(not continuous)
CM3: Gt W 1D 11
CM14: Kel H 4A 10
CM17: Har 1E 9
CR5: Coul 3E 31
CR7: Thor H 3A 24
DA13: Meop 4C 26
GU17: Hawl 2A 28
HA1: Harr 1C 14
HA6: Nwood 4A 14
HP2: Hem H 2A 6
HP3: Bov 3E 5
HP16: Pre 3B 4
IG1: Ilf 3D 17
IG3: Ilf 3D 17
KT15: Add 4F 21
KT16: Chert 4F 21
KT20: Lwr K 3E 31
ME17: B Mon 4F 35
NW4 2E 15
RM8: Dag 3D 17
SE9 2D 25
SE20 3B 24
SL1: Burn 4C 12
SM4: Mord 4E 23
SW16 3A 24
Green La. TN8: F Elm 4E 33
TN14: F Elm 4E 33
TW4: Houn 2B 22
TW13: Hanw 3B 22
TW17: Shep 4A 22
UB8: Hil 2A 14
Green La. E. GU3: Flex 4C 28
(not continuous)
Green Lanes AL8: Lem 1D 7
AL10: Hat 1D 7
N13 2A 16
N15 2A 16
N16 3A 16
N21 2A 16
Green La. W. GU12: Ash G 4C 28
GREEN MAN RDBT. 2C 16
Green Rd. DA2: Dart 3B 26
HP13: H Wy 1B 12
TW20: Thorpe 3E 21
Greens Farm La. CM11: Bill 1D 19
GREENSTED 3F 9
GREENSTED GREEN 3F 9
Greensted Rd.
CM5: Gsted, Ongar 3F 9
GREEN STREET 3C 10
Green St. CM4: Fry, Inga 3C 10
DA1: Dart 2A 26
DA2: Dart 2A 26
E7 3C 16
E13 3C 16
EN3: Brim, Enf H 4B 8
HP11: H Wy 1A 12
TW16: Sun 3B 22
WD3: Chen, Chor 4F 5
WD6: Bore 4D 7
WD7: Shenl 4D 7
GREEN STREET GREEN
BR6 1D 33
DA2 3B 26
Green Wlk. IG8: Wfd G 2D 17
Greenway HP5: Ches 3D 5
Greenway, The UB8: Uxb 4F 13
GREENWICH 1C 24
Greenwich High Rd. SE10 1B 24
GREENWICH MILLENNIUM VILLAGE 1C 24
Greenwich Pk. 1C 24
Greenwich Sth. St. SE10 1C 24
Green Wrythe La. SM5: Cars 4F 23
Gregories Rd. HP9: Beac 2C 12
Grenfell Pl. SL6: Maide 4B 12
Grenfell Rd. SL6: Maide 4B 12
(not continuous)
Gresham Rd. TW3: Houn 1C 22
TW18: Staines 3F 21
Greville Pl. NW6 4E 15
Greyhound Hill NW4 2E 15
Greyhound La. EN6: S Mim 3E 7
SW16 3F 23
Greyhound Ter. SW16 3F 23
Griffin Rd. SE18 1D 25
Griggs App. IG1: Ilf 3D 17
Grimsdell's La. HP6: Amer 4D 5
Gringer Hill SL6: Maide 4B 12
Grosvenor Av. N5 3A 16
SM5: Cars 1F 31
Grosvenor Gdns. SW1 1F 23
Grosvenor Pl. SW1 1F 23
Grosvenor Rd. GU11: Alde 4B 28
N10 2F 15
SM6: Wall 1F 31
SW1 1F 23
WD17: Wat 4B 6
Grosvenor St. W1 4F 15
Ground La. AL10: Hat 1E 7
GROVE, THE 2B 24
Grove, The E15 3C 16
SL1: Slou 1E 21
TW7: Isle 1C 22
Grove Av. N10 2F 15
Grove Cres. KT1: King T 3D 23
Gro. Cross Rd. GU16: Frim 2B 28
Grove End GU19: Bag 1C 28
Grove End Rd. NW8 4F 15
GROVE GREEN 2F 35
Grove Grn. Rd. E10 3C 16
Grove Heath Rd. GU23: Rip 3F 29
GROVEHILL 1A 6
Grove La. HP5: Orch, Whel 3E 5
HP17: Gt Kim, Lit K 2A 4
KT1: King T 3D 23
SE5 1A 24
SL9: Chal P 2E 13
Groveley Rd. TW16: Sun 3A 22
Grovemill La. WD17: Wat 4A 6
GROVE PARK
BR1 2C 24
W4 1D 23
Grove Pk. Rd. SE9 2C 24
W4 1D 23
Grove Rd. AL5: Harp 1C 6
CR4: Mitc 3F 23
(not continuous)
E3 4B 16
E17 2B 16
HP23: Tring 1C 4
RM6: Chad H 3E 17
SL1: Burn 4C 12
SM1: Sutt 1E 31
TN15: Seal 2A 34
TW3: Houn 2B 22
Grove St. SE8 1B 24
Grove Va. SE22 2A 24
Grubbs La. AL9: Hat 2E 7
GRUBB STREET 3B 26
Grubwood La. SL6: Cook 3B 12
Gubbins La. RM3: Hrld W 2A 18
Guildables La. TN8: Eden 4D 33
GUILDFORD 4E 29
Guildford & Godalming By-Pass Rd.
GU2: Guild 4D 29
GU3: Comp 4D 29
Guildford La. GU5: Alb 4F 29
GUILDFORD PARK 4E 29
Guildford Pk. Rd. GU2: Guild 4E 29
Guildford Rd. GU3: Norm 4C 28
GU4: Sut G 3E 29
GU9: Farnh 4A 28
GU10: Farnh 4B 28
GU12: Ash 4C 28
GU16: Deep, F Grn 2B 28
GU18: Light 1C 28
GU19: Bag, Light 1C 28
(not continuous)
GU21: Wok 1E 29
GU22: Wok 1E 29
(Westfield Rd.)
GU22: Wok 2E 29
(Wych Hill La.)
GU24: Bisl, W End 1D 29
GU24: Chob 1D 29
GU24: Pirb 3D 29
KT16: Ott, Chert 1E 29
KT22: Fet 3C 30
KT24: E Hor, Eff 3A 30
RH4: Westc 4B 30
RH5: Ab H, Wott 4A 30
Guileshill La. GU23: Ock 2A 30
Guilford St. WC1 4A 16
Gun Hill GU11: Alde 4B 28
RM18: W Til 1C 26
Gun La. ME2: Strood 3E 27
GUNNERSBURY 1D 23
Gunnersbury Av. W4 1D 23
W5 4D 15
Gunnersbury Dr. W5 1D 23
Gunnersbury La. W3 1D 23
GUNNERSBURY PARK 1D 23
Gunter Gro. SW10 1F 23
GYPSY CORNER 4D 15
Gypsy La. SG12: Gt A 1B 8
SL2: Stoke P 3D 13

H

HACKBRIDGE 4F 23
Hackbridge Rd. SM6: Wall 4F 23
Hackhurst La. RH5: Ab H 4A 30
HACKNEY 4B 16
Hackney Rd. E2 4A 16
ME16: Maids 3F 35
HACKNEY WICK 3B 16
HACKNEY WICK 3B 16
HACTON 3A 18
Hacton La. RM12: Horn, Upm 3A 18
RM14: Upm 3A 18
Haddon Rd. SL6: Maide 4B 12
HADLEY 4E 7
Hadley Comn.
EN5: Barn, New Bar 4E 7
Hadley Grn. EN5: Barn 4E 7
Hadley Highstone EN5: Barn 4E 7
Hadley Rd. EN2: Enf 4A 8
EN4: Had W 4F 7
EN5: New Bar 4E 7
Hadley Way N21 1A 16
HADLEY WOOD 4F 7
HADLOW 4C 34
Hadlow Rd. TN9: Tonb 4B 34
TN10: Had, Tonb 4B 34
Hadlow Rd. E. TN11: Tonb 4B 34
HADLOW STAIR 4B 34
Hagden La. WD18: Wat 4A 6
HAGGERSTON 4A 16
Hag Hill La. SL6: Tap 4C 12
Ha Ha Rd. SE18 1D 25
HAILEY 1B 8
Hailey La.
SG13: Hail, Hert H, Hodd 1B 8
HAINAULT 2E 17
Hainault Rd. E11 3C 16
IG7: Chig 1D 17
RM6: Chad H 2E 17
HALE
GU9 4A 28
ME7 4F 27
HALE, THE 2D 15
Halebourne La.
GU24: Chob, W End 1D 29
HALE END 2C 16
Hale End Rd. E4 2C 16
E17 2C 16
IG8: Wfd G 2C 16
Hale La. HA8: Edg 1D 15
HP22: Wend 2B 4
NW7 1D 15
Hale Oak Rd. TN8: Chid, Weald 4F 33
TN14: Weald 4F 33
Hale Rd. GU9: Hale 4A 28
HP22: Wend 2B 4
N17 2B 16
SG13: Hertf 1A 8
HALE STREET 4D 35
Hale St. TN12: E Pec 4D 35
Half Acre TW8: Bford 1C 22
Halfhide La. EN8: Chesh, Turn 3B 8
Half Moon La. SE24 2A 24
Halfpence La. DA12: Cobh 3D 27
Halfpenny La. GU4: Guild 4F 29
Halfway St. DA15: Sidc 2D 25
Haling Pk. Rd. CR2: S Croy 4A 24
Hall Grn. La. CM13: Hut 1C 18
HALL GROVE 1E 7
Hall Gro. AL7: W City 1E 7
Hall Hill RH8: Oxt 4C 32
TN15: Seal 3A 34
Halliford Rd. TW16: Sun 4A 22
TW17: Shep 4A 22
Halliford St. N1 3A 16
Hallioo Valley Rd. CR3: Wold 2B 32
HALLING 4E 27
Halling By-Pass ME2: Hall 4E 27
Hall La. CM2: W Han 3E 11
CM4: Inga 4C 10
CM15: Pil H, Shenf 4B 10
E4 1B 16
GU46: Yat 1A 28
RM14: Upm 3A 18
HALL LANE JUNC. 1B 16
Hall Rd. E15 3C 16
ME1: Woul 1E 35
ME20: A'ford 2E 35
NW8 4F 15
RM15: Avel 1A 26
TW7: Isle 2C 22
HALLS GREEN
CM19 1C 8
TN14 4F 33
Halls La. RG10: W Law 1A 20
HALSTEAD 1E 33
Halstead Hill EN7: G Oak 3A 8
Halstead La. TN14: Knock, Hals 2E 33
Halstead Rd. N21 1A 16
HALTON 1B 4
HALTON CAMP 1B 4
Halton La. HP22: Hal, Wend 1B 4
HAM 2C 22
Hamberlins La. HP4: Berk 1D 5
Ham Comn. TW10: Ham 2C 22
Hamesmoor Rd. GU16: Myt 3B 28
Ham Ga. Av. TW10: Ham 2D 23
HAM HILL 1D 35
Hamilton Rd. HP13: H Wy 1B 12
WD4: Hunt C 3A 6
HAM ISLAND 2E 21
Ham La. ME7: G'ham 1F 35
SL4: Old Win 2E 21
Hamlet Hill CM19: Roy 2C 8
Hamlet Rd. SE19 3A 24
HAMMERFIELD 2F 5
Hammers La. NW7 1E 15
Hammersley La. HP10: Penn 2B 12
HP13: H Wy 2B 12
HAMMERSMITH 1E 23
Hammersmith Bri. W6 1E 23
HAMMERSMITH BROADWAY 1E 23
HAMMERSMITH FLYOVER 1E 23
Hammersmith Flyover W6 1E 23
Hammersmith Rd. W6 1E 23
W14 1E 23
Hammond's La. AL4: Sandr 1C 6
Hammonds Rd. CM2: Sando 2F 11
CM3: Lit B, Sando 2F 11
HAMMOND STREET 2A 8
Hammondstreet Rd. EN7: Chesh 2A 8
HAM MOOR 4F 21
HAMPDEN BOTTOM 3B 4
Hampden Rd. HP13: H Wy 4A 4
HP16: Pre 3A 4
Hampden Way N14 1F 15
Hampermill La. WD19: Wat 1B 14

HAMPSTEAD 3F 15
HAMPSTEAD GARDEN SUBURB 2F 15
Hampstead High St. NW3 3F 15
Hampstead La.
ME18: W'bury, Yald 4D 35
N6 3F 15
NW3 3F 15
Hampstead Rd. NW1 4F 15
Hampstead Way NW11 3E 15
HAMPTON 3B 22
Hampton Court 3C 22
HAMPTON COURT 3C 22
Hampton Ct. Bri. KT8: E Mos 3C 22
Hampton Court Palace 3C 22
Hampton Ct. Rd. KT1: Ham W 3C 22
TW12: Hamp 3C 22
Hampton Ct. Way KT7: T Ditt 4C 22
KT8: E Mos 4C 22
HAMPTON HILL 3C 22
Hampton La. TW13: Hanw 3B 22
Hampton Rd. TW2: Twick 2C 22
TW11: Tedd 3C 22
Hampton Rd. W. TW13: Hanw 2B 22
HAMPTONS 3C 34
Hamptons Rd.
TN11: Had, S'brne 3B 34
HAMPTON WICK 3C 22
Ham River Hill ME3: Cli W 2E 27
HAMSEY GREEN 2B 32
Ham St. TW10: Ham 2C 22
Handcroft Rd. CR0: C'don 4A 24
Handford La. GU46: Yat 1A 28
HANDLEY GREEN 3C 10
HANDSIDE 1E 7
HANDY CROSS 2A 12
HANGER HILL 4D 15
Hanger Hill KT13: Weyb 1A 30
HANGER LANE 4D 15
Hanger La. W5 4D 15
Hanging Hill La.
CM13: B'wood, Hut 1B 18
Hangings La. HP16: Pre 3B 4
Hangrove Hill BR6: Downe 1D 33
Hanley Rd. N4 3A 16
Hanover Pk. SE15 1B 24
HANWELL 4C 14
HANWORTH
RG12 4B 20
TW13 3B 22
Hanworth Rd. RG12: Brac 4B 20
TW3: Houn 2B 22
TW4: Houn 2B 22
TW12: Hamp 3B 22
TW13: Felt 2B 22
TW16: Sun 3B 22
(not continuous)
Harberts Rd. CM19: Har 1D 9
Harbet Rd. N18 2B 16
HARBOURLAND 2F 35
Hardings Elms Rd. CM11: C Hill 2E 19
HARDINGS GREEN 3B 12
Hardwick La. KT16: Lyne 4F 21
Hare & Billet Rd. SE3 1C 24
Harebreaks, The WD24: Wat 4B 6
HAREFIELD 2F 13
Harefield Rd. UB8: Uxb 3F 13
WD3: Rick 1F 13
Harehatch La. SL1: Burn 3D 13
SL2: Farn C 3D 13
Hare Hill KT15: Add 1F 29
Hare La. HP16: L King 4B 4
KT10: Clay 1C 30
Haresfoot Pk. HP4: Berk 2E 5
Harestone Valley Rd.
CR3: Cat'm 3A 32
HARE STREET
CM5 3A 10
CM19 1D 9
Hareward Rd. GU4: Guild 4F 29
Harfield Rd. TW16: Sun 3B 22
HARKNETT'S GATE 2D 9
Harlequins RUFC 2C 22
HARLESDEN 4D 15
Harlesden Rd. NW10 4E 15
Harleyford Rd. SE11 1A 24
HARLINGTON 1A 22
HARLINGTON CORNER 1A 22
Harlington Rd. UB8: Hil 4A 14
Harlington Rd. E. TW13: Hanw 2B 22
Harlington Rd. W. TW14: Felt 2B 22
HARLOW 1D 9
Harlow Comn. CM17: Har 1F 9
Harlow Rd. CM5: More 1F 9
CM17: Har, Mat T 1E 9
CM19: Roy 1C 8
CM21: Har, Saw 1E 9
HARLOW TYE 1F 9
HARMANS WATER 4B 20
Harman's Water Rd.
RG12: Brac 4B 20
Harmer St. DA12: Grav'nd 2C 26
HARMONDSWORTH 1A 22
Harmondsworth La.
UB7: Harm, Sip 1A 22
HAROLD HILL 1A 18
HAROLD PARK 2A 18
Harold Rd. SE19 3A 24
HAROLD WOOD 2A 18
HARPENDEN 1C 6
Harpenden La. AL3: Redb 1B 6
Harpenden Rd. AL3: St A 1C 6
Harper La. WD7: Rad, Shenl 3C 6
Harper Rd. SE1 1A 24
Harper's Rd. GU12: Ash 4C 28
Harp Farm Rd. ME14: Box 1F 35
Harple La. ME14: Det 2F 35
Harps Oak La. RH1: Mers 3F 31
HARRINGAY 2A 16
Harris La. WD7: Shenl 3D 7
HARROW 2C 14
Harrow La. SL6: Maide 4B 12
Harrow Mnr. Way SE2 1E 25
HARROW ON THE HILL 3C 14
Harrow Rd. CR6: Warl 2B 32
E11 3C 16
HA0: Wemb 3C 14
HA9: Wemb 3D 15
NW10 4E 15
SS12: Nth B 2F 19
TN14: Knock 2E 33
W9 4E 15
W10 4E 15
Harrow Vw. HA1: Harr 2C 14
HA2: Harr 2C 14
HARROW WEALD 2C 14
Hartfield Rd. SW19 3E 23
Hartforde Rd. WD6: Bore 4D 7
Harthall La. HP3: Hem H 3A 6
WD4: K Lan 3A 6
Hartington Rd. W4 1D 23
Hartlake Rd.
TN11: Tude, Five G, Gold G 4C 34
Hartland Way CR0: C'don 4B 24
HARTLEY 3B 26
Hartley Bottom Rd.
DA3: Hartl, Lfield, Long H, New A 4B 26
TN15: New A 4B 26
HARTLEY GREEN 4B 26
HARTLEY HILL 4B 26
Hartley Hill DA3: Hartl 4B 26
Hartley Rd. DA3: Lfield 3B 26
Hartmann Rd. E16 4D 17
Harts La. RH9: S God 4B 32
Hartspring La. WD23: Bush 4B 6
Hartswood Rd.
CM13: Gt War, Warl 1B 18
CM14: Warl 1B 18
HARVEL 1C 34
Harvel La. DA13: Meop 1C 34
Harvel Rd. DA13: Meop 1C 34
Harvel St. DA13: Meop 1C 34
Harvest Hill HP10: Wbrn G 3C 12
SL8: Bou E 3C 12
Harvest Hill Rd.
SL6: Bray, Maide 1B 20
Harvest Ride RG42: Warf 3B 20
Harvest Rd. TW20: Eng G 3E 21
Harvey Rd. GU1: Guild 4E 29
Harvil Rd. UB9: Hare 2F 13
UB10: Ick 3A 14
Harvist Rd. NW6 4E 15
Harwood Hall La.
RM14: Upm 3A 18
Harwood Rd. SW6 1E 23
Harwoods Rd. WD18: Wat 4B 6
Haselbury Rd. N9 1A 16
N18 1A 16
Hasted Rd.
ME2: High'm, Strood 3E 27
ME3: High'm, Wain 3E 27
Haste Hill Rd. ME17: B Mon 4F 35
Hastings Rd. BR2: Brom 4D 25
ME15: Maids 3F 35
HASTINGWOOD 2E 9
Hastingwood Rd. CM5: Mag L 2E 9
CM17: Har, Hasti, Mag L 2E 9
HASTOE 1C 4
Hastoe Hill HP23: Hasto 1C 4
Hastoe La. HP23: Tring 1C 4
HATCH END 2B 14
Hatches Farm Rd.
CM12: L Bur 1C 18
Hatches La. HP15: Gt Kin 4B 4
TN12: E Pec 4C 34
Hatchet La. SL4: Wink 3C 20
HATCHFORD 2A 30
HATCHING GREEN 1B 6
Hatchlands Pk. 3A 30
Hatch La. E4 1C 16
(not continuous)
SL4: Wind 2D 21
UB7: Harm 1F 21
Hatch Rd. CM15: Pil H 1B 18
HATFIELD 1E 7
Hatfield Av. AL10: Hat 1D 7
HATFIELD GARDEN VILLAGE 1D 7
Hatfield House 1E 7
HATFIELD HYDE 1E 7
HATFIELD PEVEREL
INTERCHANGE SOUTH 1F 11
Hatfield Rd. AL1: St A 2C 6
AL4: S'ford, St A 2C 6
AL9: Ess 3F 7
CM3: Hat P, Lit B 1F 11
EN6: Pot B 3F 7
Hatham Grn. La. TN15: Stans 1B 34
Hathaway Rd. RM17: Grays 1B 26
Hatherley Gdns. E6 4C 16
Hatterill SS15: Bas, Lain 2D 19
Hatter's La. HP13: H Wy 1B 12
HATTON CROSS 2A 22
Hatton Gdn. EC1 4A 16
Hatton Hill GU20: W'sham 4C 20
Hatton Rd. TW14: Bedf, Felt 2A 22
Havelock Rd. N17 2B 16
UB2: S'hall 1B 22
Haven Grn. W5 4C 14
Haven Hill TN15: Ash 1B 34
Haven Rd. SS8: Can I 4F 19
Haven St. ME3: Wain 2F 27
HAVERING-ATTE-BOWER 1F 17
Havering Rd.
RM1: Have B, Rom 2F 17
HAVERING'S GROVE 1C 18
Haverstock Hill NW3 3F 15
Hawk Hill SS11: Bat 1F 19
Hawkhurst Gdns. KT9: Chess 4D 23
Hawkshead La.
AL9: Brk P, N Mym 3E 7
Hawkshead Rd. EN6: Pot B 3E 7
Hawks Hill SL8: Bou E 3C 12
Hawkshill Way KT10: Esh 1B 30
Hawks Rd. KT1: King T 3D 23
Hawkstone Rd. SE16 1B 24
Hawkswood La. SL3: Ful 3E 13
SL9: Ger X 3E 13
Hawkswood Rd. CM11: D'ham 4E 11
HAWLEY
DA2 3A 26
GU17 2A 28
HAWLEY LANE 2B 28
Hawley La. GU14: Farnb 2B 28
(not continuous)
Hawley Rd. DA1: Dart 2A 26
GU17: Hawl 2A 28
NW1 3F 15
(not continuous)
HAWLEY'S CORNER 2D 33
Hawstead La. BR6: Chels 4E 25
HAWTHORN HILL 2B 20
Hawthorn Hill Rd. SL6: Pal S 2B 20
Hawthorn La. SL2: Farn C 3D 13
Hawthorn Rd. NW10 3E 15
Haydens Rd. CM20: Har 1D 9
Haydons Rd. SW19 3E 23
HAYES
BR2 4C 24
UB3 4A 14
HAYES END 4A 14
Hayes End Rd. UB4: Hayes 4A 14
Hayes Hill Rd. BR2: Hayes 4C 24
Hayes La. BR2: Brom, Hayes 4C 24
BR3: Beck 3C 24
CR8: Kenl 1A 32
Hayes Rd. BR2: Brom 3C 24
UB2: S'hall 1B 22
Hayes St. BR2: Hayes 4C 24
HAYES TOWN 1A 22
HAY GREEN 3B 10
Hay Grn. La. CM4: Bmore 4B 10
CM15: Hook E 4B 10
Hay La. NW9 2D 15
Hayle Mill Rd. ME15: Maids 3F 35
Hayle Rd. ME15: Maids 3F 35
Hayling Rd. WD19: Wat 1B 14
Haymarket SW1 4F 15
Haymill Rd. SL1: Slou 4C 12
SL2: Slou 4C 12
Hazel Av. GU14: Cove 3A 28
(not continuous)
Hazelbank Rd. SE6 2C 24
Hazellville Rd. N19 3F 15
HAZELWOOD 1D 33
Hazelwood La. CR5: Chip 2F 31
N13 1A 16
RG42: Bin, Warf 3A 20
WD5: Ab L 3A 6
Hazledene Rd. W4 2B 22
HAZLEMERE 4B 4
Hazlemere Rd. HP10: Ty G 1C 12
HEADLEY 3D 31
Headley Comn. Rd.
KT18: H'ly, Walt H 3D 31
Headley Dr. CR0: New Ad 1B 32
Headley La. RH5: Mick 3C 30
Headley Rd. KT18: Eps D 2D 31
KT18: Eps D, H'ly 3C 30
KT22: Lea 3C 30
HEADSTONE 2C 14
Headstone Dr. HA1: Harr 2C 14
Headstone Gdns. HA2: Harr 2C 14
Headstone La. HA2: Harr 2B 14
HA3: Hrw W 2B 14
Headstone Rd. HA1: Harr 2C 14
Heath, The ME19: E Mal 2D 35
Heathbourne Rd. HA7: Stan 1C 14
Heathclose Rd. DA1: Dart 2F 25
Heathcote Rd. GU15: Camb 1B 28
HEATH END
GU9 4A 28
HP4 2D 5
HP15 4B 4
Heath End HP4: Berk 2D 5
Heath End Rd.
HP10: Flack H, H Wy 2B 12
HP15: Gt Kin 4B 4
HP16: L King 4B 4
HEATHERSIDE 2C 28
Heathfield Rd. BR2: Kes 4C 24
SL6: Tap 3C 12
Heathfield Ter. W4 1D 23
Heath Ho. Rd. GU22: Wok 2D 29
Heathlands Rd. RG40: W'ham 4A 20
Heath La. GU10: Ews 4A 28
HP1: Hem H 2F 5
Heath La. Lwr. DA1: Dart 2F 25
Heath La. Up. DA1: Dart 2F 25
HEATH PARK 2F 17
Heath Pk. Rd. RM1: Rom 2F 17
RM2: Rom 2F 17
Heath Rd. CM11: Ram H 1D 19
KT13: Weyb 4A 22
KT22: Oxs 1C 30
ME15: E Far, Hunt, W Far 4E 35
ME16: Barm 3E 35
ME17: Cox, Lint 4E 35
RM16: Ors, Grays 4C 18
TW1: Twick 2C 22
TW2: Twick 2C 22
TW3: Houn, Isle 2C 22
HEATHROW AIRPORT 2A 22
Heathside Cres. GU22: Wok 2E 29
Heathside Rd. GU22: Wok 2E 29
Heath St. NW3 3F 15
Heath Vs. Bri. Rd. GU12: Ash V 3B 28
HEATHWAY 4E 17
Heathway RM9: Dag 3E 17
RM10: Dag 3E 17
Heavens Lea SL8: Bou E 3C 12
HEAVERHAM 2A 34
Heaverham Rd. TN15: Kems'g 2A 34
Hedge La. N13 1A 16
Hedgemans Rd. RM9: Dag 3E 17
Hedge Pl. Rd. DA9: Ghithe 2A 26
HEDGERLEY 3D 13
HEDGERLEY GREEN 3D 13
HEDGERLEY HILL 3D 13
Hedgerley Hill SL2: Hedg 3D 13
Hedgerley La. HP9: Beac 2D 13
SL2: Ger X, Hedg 2D 13
SL9: Ger X 2D 13
Hedsor Hill SL8: Bou E 3C 12
Hedsor La. HP10: Wbrn G 3C 12
Hedsor Rd. SL8: Bou E 3B 12
Hemel Hempstead Rd.
AL3: Redb 1A 6
AL3: St A 2B 6
HP2: Hem H 1A 6
HP3: Hem H 2A 6
Hemp La. HP23: Wigg 1D 5
HEMPSTEAD 4F 27
Hempstead La. HP4: Pott E 1E 5
Hempstead Rd. HP3: Bov 2E 5
WD4: K Lan 2A 6
Henderson Dr. DA1: Dart 2A 26
HENDON 2E 15
Hendon La. N3 2E 15
Hendon Way NW2 2E 15
NW4 2E 15
Hendon Wood La. NW7 1D 15
HENHURST 3D 27
Henhurst Rd. DA12: Cobh 3D 27
Henley Rd. SL6: Hur, Maide 4A 12
SL7: Med 3A 12
HENLEY STREET 4D 27
Henley St. DA13: Lud'n 4D 27
HENLYS CORNER 2E 15
HENLYS RDBT. 1B 22
Henniker Gdns. E6 4C 16
Henrys Av. IG8: Wfd G 1C 16
Hepworth Way KT12: Walt T 4A 22
Herbert Rd. SE18 1D 25
(not continuous)
Herberts Hole HP16: Ball 3C 4
Hercies Rd. UB10: Hil 3A 14
Heriot Rd. KT16: Chert 4F 21
Herkomer Rd. WD23: Bush 1B 14
Hermitage La. ME16: Maids 2E 35
ME17: B Mon 4F 35
ME20: A'ford, Maids 2E 35
NW2 3E 15
SW16 3A 24
Hermitage Rd. GU21: Wok 2D 29
ME3: High'm 3E 27
N4 3A 16
N15 2A 16
SE19 3A 24
Hermit Rd. E16 4C 16
HERNE HILL 2A 24
Herne Hill SE24 2A 24
Herne Hill Rd. SE24 2A 24
HERNE POUND 3C 34
Herns La. AL7: W City 1E 7
HERONGATE 2C 18
Heron Hill DA17: Belv 1E 25
HERONSGATE 1F 13
Heronsgate Rd. WD3: Chor 1E 13
Herons La. CM5: Fyf 2A 10
Heronswood Rd. AL7: W City 1E 7
Heron Way RM20: W Thur 1B 26
HERSHAM 4B 22
Hersham By-Pass KT12: Hers 4B 22
Hersham Rd.
KT12: Hers, Walt T 4B 22
HERTFORD 1A 8
HERTFORD HEATH 1B 8
Hertford Rd. AL6: Hat, Ess 1E 7
(not continuous)
EN3: Enf H, Enf W 4B 8
EN8: Walt C 4B 8
EN11: Hert H, Hodd 1B 8
N9 1B 16
HERTINGFORDBURY 1A 8
Hertingfordbury Rd.
SG14: Herti, Hertf 1A 8
Hesiers Hill CR6: Warl 2C 32
Hesiers Rd. CR6: Warl 2C 32
HESTON 1B 22
Heston Rd. TW5: Hest 1B 22
Hever Ct. Rd. DA12: Grav'nd 3C 26
Hewitts Rd. BR6: Chels 1E 33
HEWITTS RDBT. 1E 33
HEXTABLE 3F 25
HEYBRIDGE 4C 10
Hibbert Rd. SL6: Bray 1B 20
Hibernia Rd. TW3: Houn 2B 22
Hicks Farm Ri. HP13: H Wy 1B 12
Hickstars La. CM12: Bill 1D 19
HIGH, THE 1D 9
HIGHAM 3E 27
HIGHAM HILL 2B 16
Higham Hill Rd. E17 2B 16
Higham La. TN10: Tonb 4B 34
TN11: Tonb 4B 34
Higham Rd. ME3: Cli 2E 27
ME3: Wain 3F 27
Highams La. GU24: Chob 1D 29
HIGHAMS PARK 1C 16
HIGHAM WOOD 4B 34
High Banks ME15: Loose 3F 35
HIGH BARNET 4E 7
High Barn Rd. KT24: Eff, Ran C 3B 30
HIGH BEECH 4C 8
High Bri. Rd. CM2: Chelm 2E 11
Highbridge St. EN9: Walt A 3B 8
(not continuous)
HIGHBURY 3A 16
HIGHBURY CORNER 3A 16
Highbury Gro. N5 3A 16
Highbury Pk. N5 3A 16
High Canons WD6: Bore 4D 7
HIGH CROSS 4C 6
High Cross WD25: A'ham 4C 6
High Cross Rd. TN15: Ivy H 3B 34
Highcross Rd. DA13: Sflt 3B 26
HIGH CURLEY 1C 28
High Elms La. WD25: Wat 3B 6
High Elms Rd. BR6: Downe 1D 33
HIGHER DENHAM 3F 13
Higher Dr. CR8: Purl 1A 32
HIGHFIELD 1A 6
Highfield Av. NW11 3E 15
Highfield La. AL4: St A 2C 6
GU3: Putt 4C 28
SL6: Maide 1B 20
Highfield Pk. Dr. AL4: St A 2C 6
Highfield Rd. CR8: Purl 1A 32
DA1: Dart 2F 25
HIGHGATE 3F 15
Highgate High St. N6 3F 15
Highgate Hill N6 3F 15
N19 3F 15
Highgate La. GU14: Farnb 2B 28
Highgate Rd. N6 3F 15
NW5 3F 15
Highgate W. Hill N6 3F 15
HIGH HALSTOW 2F 27
High Holborn WC1 4A 16
High Ho. La. RM18: W Til 1C 26
TN11: Had 4B 34
Highlands Hill BR8: Swan 3F 25
Highlands Rd. KT22: Lea 2C 30
High La. CM22: Mat T, Sheer 1F 9
HIGH LAVER 1F 9
High Laver Rd. CM17: M Grn 1F 9
HIGH ONGAR 3A 10
High Ongar Rd.
CM5: H Ongar, Ongar 3A 10
High Rd. AL9: Ess 2F 7
CM16: Epp 3D 9
CM16: Epp, Twood 2E 9
CM16: N Weald 2E 9
CR5: Chip, Coul 3F 31
DA2: Dart 2F 25
E18 2C 16
EN10: Turn, Worm, Brox 2B 8
HA0: Wemb 3D 15
HA3: Hrw W 2C 14
HA5: Eastc 2B 14
HA9: Wemb 3D 15
IG1: Ilf 3D 17
(not continuous)
IG3: Ilf 3D 17
IG7: Chig 1D 17
IG9: Buck H 1C 16
KT14: Byfl 1A 30
N15 2A 16
N17 2A 16
N22 2A 16
NW10 3E 15
RH2: Reig 3F 31
RM16: N Stif 4B 18
RM16: Ors 4C 18
SL6: Cook 3B 12
SS7: Ben 2F 19
SS13: Pit 3E 19
SS15: Lain, Lan H 3D 19
(not continuous)
SS16: Pit, Vange 3E 19
SS17: Corr, Stan H 4D 19
SS17: Fob 3E 19
SS17: Horn H 4D 19
UB8: Cowl 4F 13
UB10: Ick 3A 14
WD23: B Hea 1C 14
WD25: Wat 3A 6
High Rd. E. Finchley N2 2F 15
High Rd. Leyton E10 2B 16
E15 2B 16
High Rd. Leytonstone E11 3C 16
High Rd. Nth. SS15: Lain 2D 19
High Rd. Nth. Finchley N12 1F 15
High Rd. Turnford EN10: Turn 2B 8
High Rd. Whetstone N20 1F 15
High Rd. Woodford Grn. E18 2C 16
IG8: Wfd G 2C 16
High St. AL2: Lon C 2C 6
AL3: St A 1B 6
AL4: Col H 2D 7
AL4: Sandr 1C 6
BR1: Brom 3C 24
BR3: Beck 3B 24
BR4: W W'ck 4B 24
BR5: St M Cry 4E 25
(not continuous)
BR6: Chels 1D 33
BR6: Downe 1D 33
BR6: Farnb 4D 25
BR6: Orp 4E 25
BR7: Chst 3D 25
BR8: Swan 3F 25
CM2: Gt B 2E 11
CM4: Inga 4C 10
CM4: Stock 4D 11
CM5: Ongar 3A 10
CM12: Bill 1D 19
CM14: B'wood 1B 18
CM16: Epp 3D 9
CM17: Har 1E 9
(not continuous)
CM19: Roy 1C 8
CR0: C'don 4A 24
(not continuous)
CR3: Cat'm 3A 32
DA1: Cray 2F 25
DA1: Dart 2A 26
DA2: Bean 2B 26
DA4: Eyns 4A 26
DA4: Farni 4A 26
DA9: Ghithe 2B 26
DA10: Swans 2B 26
DA11: Nflt 2B 26
DA14: Sidc 3E 25
High St. E11 2C 16
E13 4C 16
E15 4C 16
EN3: Pond E 1B 16
EN5: Barn 4E 7
EN6: Pot B 3F 7
EN8: Chesh 3B 8
EN8: Walt C 3B 8
(not continuous)
EN11: Brox, Hodd 2B 8
GU1: Guild 4E 29
(not continuous)
GU11: Alde 4B 28
GU19: Bag 1C 28
GU21: Knap 2D 29
GU21: Wok 2E 29
(Broadmead Rd.)
GU21: Wok 2E 29
(Horsell Birch)
GU22: Wok 2E 29
GU23: Rip 2F 29
GU24: Chob 1D 29
GU47: S'urst 1A 28
(Church Rd.)
GU47: S'urst 1A 28
(Mountbatten Ri.)
HA1: Harr 3C 14
HA3: W'stone 2C 14
(not continuous)
HA4: Ruis 3A 14
HA5: Pinn 2B 14
HA6: Nwood 2A 14
HA8: Edg 2D 15
HP1: Hem H 2F 5
HP3: Bov 3E 5
HP4: Berk 1D 5
HP5: Ches 3D 5
(not continuous)
HP7: Amer 4D 5
HP8: Chal G 1E 13
HP13: D'ley 1B 12
(Abbey Way)
HP13: D'ley 1A 12
(Plomer Grn. La.)
HP14: W Wyc 1A 12
HP16: Gt Miss 3B 4
HP16: Pre 3B 4
HP22: Wend 2B 4
HP23: Tring 1C 4
IG6: Ilf 2D 17
KT1: Ham W 3C 22
KT1: King T 3C 22
KT3: N Mald 3D 23
KT7: T Ditt 4C 22
KT8: W Mole 4B 22
KT10: Esh 4B 22
KT11: Cobh 1B 30
KT13: Weyb 4A 22
KT15: Add 4F 21
KT17: Ewe 1D 31
KT19: Eps 1D 31
KT22: Oxs 1C 30
KT23: Bookh 3B 30
ME1: Roch 3F 27
ME1: Woul 1E 35
ME2: Hall 4E 27
ME2: Strood 3E 27
ME2: Up 3F 27
ME4: Chat 4F 27
(Best St., not continuous)
ME4: Chat 3F 27
(Jeffery St.)
ME6: Snod 1E 35
(not continuous)
ME7: G'ham 3F 27
ME14: Maids 3F 35
ME18: Yald 4D 35
ME19: E Mal 2E 35
ME19: W Mal 2D 35
ME20: A'ford 2E 35
N8 2A 16
N14 1F 15
RG12: Brac 3B 20
(not continuous)
RG45: Crow 1A 28
RH1: Blet 4A 32
RH1: Mers 3F 31
RH1: Nutf 4A 32
RH1: Redh 4F 31
RH2: Reig 4F 31
RH4: Dork 4C 30
RH8: Limp 3C 32
RH8: Oxt 3C 32
RH9: G'stone 3B 32
RM11: Horn 3F 17
RM12: Horn 3F 17
RM15: Avel 4A 18
SE18 1D 25
SE20 3B 24
SE25 3A 24
SG12: S Abb 1C 8
SL0: Iver 4F 13
SL1: Burn 4C 12
SL1: Slou 1D 21
(Brammas Cl.)
SL1: Slou 1E 21
(William St., not continuous)
SL3: Coln 1F 21
SL3: Dat 1E 21
SL3: L'ly 1E 21
SL4: Eton 1D 21
SL4: Wind 1D 21
SL5: Asc 3C 20
SL5: S'dale 4D 21
SL5: S'hill 4C 20
SL6: Bray 1C 20
SL6: Cook 3B 12
SL6: Maide 4B 12
(not continuous)
SL7: Marl 3A 12
SL9: Chal P 2E 13
SM1: Sutt 4E 23
SM3: Cheam 1E 31
SM5: Cars 4F 23
SM7: Bans 2E 31
SS7: Ben 3F 19
SS12: Wick 1F 19
SS17: Stan H 4D 19
SW19 3E 23
TN9: Tonb 4B 34
TN11: Had 4C 34
TN13: Riv 2F 33
TN13: S'oaks 3F 33
TN14: Otf 2F 33
TN14: S'ham 1F 33
TN15: Bor G 2B 34
TN15: Kems'g 2A 34
TN15: Seal 2A 34
TN15: Wro 2B 34
TN16: Bras 3E 33
TN16: Westrm 3D 33
TW2: Whitt 2C 22
TW5: Cran 1B 22
TW11: Tedd 3C 22
TW12: Hamp, Ham H 3C 22
TW13: Felt 2A 22
TW17: Shep 4A 22
TW18: Staines 3F 21
TW19: Stanw 2F 21
TW19: Wray 2E 21
TW20: Egh 3E 21
High St. UB1: S'hall 4B 14
UB3: Harl 1A 22
UB7: Yiew 4F 13
UB8: Cowl 4F 13
UB8: Uxb 3F 13
UB9: Hare 2F 13
W3 4D 15
W5 4C 14
WD3: Rick 1F 13
WD4: K Lan 3A 6
WD5: Ab L 3A 6
WD5: Bedm 3A 6
WD6: E'tree 1C 14
WD23: Bush 1B 14
High St. Colliers Wood SW19 3F 23
High St. Grn. HP2: Hem H 1A 6
High St. Harlesden NW10 4D 15
High St. Nth. E6 3D 17
E12 3D 17
High St. Sth. E6 4D 17
High Vw. GU5: Goms 4A 30
HIGHWAY 4B 12
Highway, The BR6: Chels 4E 25
E1 4B 16
HIGHWOOD 2C 10
HIGHWOOD HILL 1E 15
Highwood Hill NW7 1D 15
Highwood Rd.
CM1: E Com, High 3C 10
HIGH WOODS 3C 10
High Wych Rd.
CM21: G'ton, H Wych, Saw 1D 9
HIGH WYCOMBE 1B 12
HILDENBOROUGH 4A 34
Hildenborough Rd. TN11: Leigh 4A 34
TN11: S'brne, Under 4A 34
HILDEN PARK 4A 34
Hilfield La. WD25: A'ham 4B 6
Hill, The DA11: Nflt 2C 26
HP7: Win H 1C 12
Hill Av. HP6: Amer 4D 5
Hillbury Rd. CR6: Warl 2B 32
Hillcroome Rd. SM2: Sutt 1F 31
Hillcross Av. SM4: Mord 4E 23
Hilldene Av. RM3: Rom 2F 17
HILL END 2F 13
Hill End La. AL4: St A 2C 6
Hill End Rd. UB9: Hare 2F 13
Hill Farm Av. WD25: Wat 3B 6
Hill Farm Rd. SL6: Tap 4C 12
Hillgrove Rd. NW6 3F 15
Hilliers La. CR0: Bedd 4A 24
HILLINGDON 4A 14
HILLINGDON HEATH 4A 14
Hillingdon Rd. UB8: Uxb 4F 13
UB10: Uxb 4A 14
Hillmarton Rd. N7 3A 16
Hillreach SE18 1D 25
HILLSIDE 1F 25
Hillside NW10 4D 15
Hillside Av. IG8: Wfd G 1C 16
Hillside Rd. BR2: Brom 3C 24
CM11: Bill 1D 19
HA6: Nwood 2B 14
Hills La. SL6: Cook 3B 12
TN15: Knat 1A 34
HILLTOP 3D 5
Hill Top ME15: Hunt 4E 35
Hilltop La. CR3: Cat'm 3A 32
RH1: Cat'm, Mers 3A 32
Hillway CM11: Bill 1D 19
Hillyfields IG10: Lough 4D 9
HINCHLEY WOOD 4C 22
Hindes Rd. HA1: Harr 2C 14
Hindmans Way RM9: Dag 4E 17
Hinton Rd. SE24 2A 24
Historic Dockyard, The 3F 27
Hitcham La. SL1: Burn 4C 12
Hitcham Rd. SL1: Burn 4C 12
SL6: Tap 4C 12
HITHER GREEN 2C 24
Hither Grn. La. SE13 2C 24
Hiving's Hill HP5: Ches 3D 5
HOBBS CROSS
CM16 4E 9
CM17 1E 9
Hobbs Cross Rd.
CM16: Abr, Epp, Fidd H, They G 4E 9
CM17: Har 1E 9
HOCKENDEN 3E 25
Hockenden La. BR8: Swan 3E 25
Hockering Rd. GU22: Wok 2E 29
Hockett La. SL6: Cook 3B 12
HODDESDON 1B 8
Hodford Rd. NW11 3E 15
Hodgson Way SS11: Wick 1F 19
HODSOLL STREET 1C 34
Hodsoll St. TN15: Ash 1C 34
Hoe La. CM3: Ret 4F 11
EN1: Enf 4B 8
EN3: Enf W 4B 8
EN9: Naze 2C 8
RM4: Abr 4E 9
SG12: Ware 1B 8
Hoe St. CM1: Rox 2C 10
E17 2B 16
Hogarth La. W4 1D 23
HOGARTH RDBT. 1D 23
Hogden La. KT23: Bookh 4B 30
Hogfair La. SL1: Burn 4C 12
Hogg End La. AL3: St A 1A 6
HP2: Hem H 1A 6
Hogg La. HP15: Holm G 4C 4
RM17: Grays 1B 26
Hog Hill Rd. RM5: Col R 2E 17
Hog La. HP5: A Grn 2D 5
HOGPITS BOTTOM 3E 5
Hog's Back
GU3: Guild, Putt, Wanb 4C 28
GU10: Seale 4B 28
(not continuous)
Hogscross La. CR5: Coul 2F 31
Hogtrough Hill
TN16: Bras, S'oaks 2D 33
Hogtrough La. RH1: S Nut 4F 31
Holbeck La. EN7: Chesh 2A 8
HOLBORN 4A 16
Holborn EC1 4A 16
WC1 4A 16
Holborn Viaduct EC4 4A 16
HOLBOROUGH 1E 35
Holborough Rd. ME6: Snod 1E 35
Holbrook Way BR2: Brom 4D 25
Holcombe Hill NW7 1E 15
HOLDBROOK 3B 8
HOLDERS HILL 2E 15
Holders Hill Rd. NW4 2E 15
NW7 2E 15
Holehill La. RH4: Westc 4B 30
Hole La. TN8: Eden 4D 33
Holiday Hill CM2: W Han 4E 11
HOLLAND 4C 32
Holland Av. SM2: Sutt 1E 31
Holland La. RH8: Oxt 4C 32
Holland Pk. Av. W11 4E 15
HOLLAND PARK RDBT. 1E 23
Holland Rd. ME14: Maids 2F 35
RH8: Oxt 4C 32
W14 1E 23

Hollis Rd. HP13: H Wy 1B 12
HOLLOWAY
N19 3F 15
SL6 4A 12
Holloway, The HP22: Dra B 1C 4
HP27: White 2A 4
Holloway Hill KT16: Chert 4F 21
Holloway La.
UB7: Harm, W Dray 1A 22
Holloway Rd. N7 3F 15
N19 3F 15
Holloways La. AL9: Wel G 2E 7
Hollow Hill La. SL0: Iver 4E 13
Hollow La.
CM1: Chig S, Broom, Chelm
1D 11
ME6: Snod 1D 35
RH5: Wott 4B 30
Hollow Way HP5: Ches 3C 4
Hollow Way La.
HP6: Amer, Ches 4D 5
Holly Bank Rd. GU22: Wok 2E 29
Hollybush Hill E11 2C 16
SL2: Stoke P 3E 13
Hollybush La. AL7: W City 1E 7
(not continuous)
SL0: Iver 4E 13
UB9: Den 3F 13
Hollycross Rd.
SG12: S Abb, Ware 1B 8
Hollydown Way E11 3C 16
Hollyfield Rd. KT5: Surb 4D 23
Holly Hedges La. HP3: Bov 3F 5
HOLLY HILL 1D 35
Holly Hill Rd. DA13: Meop 1D 35
Holly La. GU3: Worp 3D 29
SM7: Bans 2E 31
Hollymeoak Rd. CR5: Coul 2F 31
Holly Spring La. RG12: Brac 3B 20
Hollywood La. ME3: Wain 3F 27
HOLME GREEN 4A 20
HOLMER GREEN 4C 4
Holmer Grn. Rd. HP15: Haz 1B 12
Holmers Farm Way
HP12: Book, H Wy 2A 12
Holmesdale Hill DA4: S Dar 3A 26
Holmesdale Rd. DA4: S Dar 3A 26
Holmesdale Tunnel EN8: Walt C 3B 8
HOLMETHORPE 4F 31
Holmshill La. WD6: Bore 4D 7
Holmstall Av. HA8: Edg 2D 15
HOLTSMERE END 1A 6
HOLTSPUR 2C 12
Holtspur Av. HP10: Wbrn G 2C 12
Holtspur La. HP10: Wbrn G 2C 12
Holtspur Top La. HP9: Beac 2C 12
Holtwhite's Hill EN2: Enf 4A 8
Holybread La. CM3: Lit B 2F 11
Holy Cross Hill
EN10: Brox, Chesh, Worm 2B 8
HOLYFIELD 3C 8
Holyfield Rd. EN9: Walt A 3C 8
HOLYPORT 1B 20
Holyport Rd. SL6: Holy 1B 20
HOLYWELL 1A 14
Holywell Hill AL1: St A 2C 6
Homedean Rd. TN13: Riv 2F 33
Home Farm Rd.
CM13: B'wood, L War 2B 18
Homefield Rd. BR1: Brom 3C 24
Home Gdns. DA1: Dart 2A 26
Home Hill BR8: Swan 3F 25
Home Pk. Mill Link Rd.
WD4: K Lan 3A 6
Home Pk. Rd. SW19 3E 23
HOMERTON 3B 16
Homerton High St. E9 3B 16
Homerton Rd. E9 3B 16
Homesdale Rd. BR1: Brom 3C 24
BR2: Brom 3C 24
Homestall Rd. SE22 2B 24
Homestead La. AL7: W City 1E 7
Homestead Rd. SW6 1E 23
Honeycroft Hill UB10: Uxb 3A 14
Honey Hill RG40: W'ham 4A 20
UB10: Uxb 3A 14
Honey La. EN9: Walt A 3C 8
SL6: Bur G, Hur 4A 12
Honeypot La. CM4: Stock 4D 11
CM14: B'wood 1B 18
HA7: Stan 2C 14
NW9 2C 14
TN8: Eden 4C 32
TN15: Kems'g 2A 34
Honeysuckle Bottom
KT24: E Hor 4A 30
Honor End La. HP16: Pre 3B 4
HONOR OAK 2B 24
HONOR OAK PARK 2B 24
Honor Oak Pk. SE23 2B 24
Honor Oak Rd. SE23 2B 24
HOOK 4C 22
HOOK END 4B 10
Hook End La. CM15: Hook E 3B 10
Hook End Rd. CM15: Hook E 4B 10
HOOK GREEN
DA13, Meopham 4C 26
DA13, Southfleet 3B 26
Hook Grn. La. DA2: Dart 2F 25
Hook Grn. Rd. DA13: Sflt 3B 26
HOOK HEATH 2E 29
Hook Heath Av. GU22: Wok 2E 29
Hook Heath Rd. GU22: Wok 2D 29
Hook Hill La. GU22: Wok 2E 29
HOOK JUNC. 4C 22
Hook La. DA16: Well 2E 25
GU5: Putt 4C 28
GU5: Shere 4A 30
RM4: Abr, Stap A 1E 17
Hook Mill La. GU18: Light 1C 28
Hook Ri. Nth. KT6: Surb 4D 23
Hook Ri. Sth. KT6: Surb 4D 23
Hook Rd. KT6: Surb 4D 23
KT9: Chess 4C 22
KT19: Eps, Ewe 1D 31
Hookstone La. GU24: W End 1D 29
Hookwood Rd. BR6: Prat B 1E 33
HOOLEY 2F 31
Hooley La. RH1: Redh 4F 31
Hoop La. *NW11 2E 15*
(not continuous)
Hoo Rd. ME3: Wain 3F 27
HOO ST WERBURGH 2F 27
HOPE'S GREEN 3F 19
Hop Farm Country Pk. 4D 35
Hoppers Rd. N21 1A 16
Hopping Jacks La. CM3: Dan 2F 11
Horley Rd. RH1: Redh 4F 31
HORNCHURCH 3F 17
Hornchurch Rd. RM11: Horn 3F 17
RM12: Horn 3F 17
HORNDON ON THE HILL 4D 19
Horndon Rd. SS17: Horn H 4D 19
HORNE ROW 2F 11
Hornfair Rd. SE7 1C 24
Hornhatch La. GU4: Guild 4E 29
Hornhill Rd. WD3: Map C 1E 13
Horn La. W3 4D 15
(not continuous)
Hornsby Way SS15: Lain 2C 18
HORNS CROSS 2A 26
HORNSEY 2A 16
Hornsey N8 2A 16
Hornsey La. N19 3F 15
Hornsey Pk. Rd. N8 2A 16
Hornsey Ri. N19 3F 15
Hornsey Rd. N7 3A 16
N19 3A 16
HORNSEY VALE 2A 16
HORNS GREEN 2D 33
HORNS HILL 3D 33
Horns La. HP12: Book 2A 12
ME18: Mere 3C 34
Horns Lodge Rd. TN15: Stans 1B 34
Horns Mill Rd. SG13: Hertf 1A 8
(not continuous)
Horn's Oak Rd. DA13: Meop 4C 26
Horns Rd. IG2: Ilf 2D 17
IG6: Ilf 2D 17
HORN STREET 1D 35
Horse & Groom La.
CM2: Chelm, Gall 3E 11
Horsecroft CM5: Abb R 1A 10
Horse Fair KT1: King T 3C 22
Horseferry Rd. SW1 1F 23
Horse Hill HP5: Ley H 3E 5
HORSELL 2E 29
Horsell Birch GU21: Wok 2E 29
(not continuous)
Horsell Comn. Rd. GU21: Wok 1E 29
HORSEMAN SIDE 4A 10
Horseman Side CM14: N'side 1F 17
Horsemoor La. HP7: Win H 1C 12
Horsenden La. Nth. UB6: G'frd 3C 14
Horsenden La. Sth. UB6: G'frd 4C 14
Horseshoe Hill EN9: Walt A 3C 8
SL1: Burn 3C 12
Horseshoe La. WD25: Wat 3B 6
Horsham Rd. RH4: Dork 4C 30
RH5: Holmw, Mid H, N Holm
4C 30
Horsley Rd. KT11: D'side 2B 30
Horsted Way ME1: Roch 4F 27
HORTON
KT19 1D 31
SL3 1E 21
Horton Country Pk. 1D 31
HORTON KIRBY 3A 26
Horton La. KT19: Eps 1D 31
Horton Rd. DA4: Hort K, S Dar 3A 26
SL3: Coln, Hort 1E 21
SL3: Dat, Hort 1E 21
SL3: Poyle 2F 21
TW19: Stan M 2F 21
UB7: Yiew 4A 14
Hosey Comn. La.
TN16: Westrm 3D 33
Hosey Comn. Rd.
TN8: Crock H, Westrm 4D 33
TN16: Westrm 4D 33
HOSEY HILL 3D 33
Hosey Hill TN16: Westrm 3D 33
Hospital App. CM1: Broom 1E 11
Hospital Bri. Rd.
TW2: Twick, Whitt 2B 22
HOSPITAL BRIDGE RDBT. 2B 22
Hospital Hill GU11: Alde 4B 28
Hospital Rd. GU11: Alde 4B 28
HOTLEY BOTTOM 3B 4
Hotley Bottom La. HP16: Pre 3B 4
Houblons Hill CM16: Coop 3E 9
Hound Ho. Rd. GU5: Shere 4A 30
Houndsden Rd. N21 1A 16
HOUNSLOW 2C 22
Hounslow Rd. TW2: Whitt 2B 22
TW13: Hanw 2B 22
TW14: Felt 2B 22
HOUNSLOW WEST 2B 22
House La. AL4: Sandr 1C 6
HOUSHAM TYE 1F 9
Housham Tye Rd.
CM17: Har, Mat T 1F 9
Howard Lodge Rd. CM14: Kel C 4A 10
Howard Rd. KT24: Eff J 3B 30
Howard Way CM20: Har 1D 9
Howbury La. DA8: Erith 1F 25
HOWE GREEN 3F 11
HOWE GREEN INTERCHANGE 3F 11
Howe La. RG42: Bin 2A 20
SL6: W Walt 2B 20
How Grn. La. TN8: F Elm, Hever 4E 33
Howlands AL7: W City 1E 7
How La. CR5: Chip 2F 31
Howletts La. HA4: Ruis 2A 14
HOW WOOD 3C 6
HOXTON 4A 16
Hubbard's Hill TN13: Weald 4F 33
TN14: Weald 4F 33
Hubbard's La. ME17: B Mon 4F 35
HUDNALL 1E 5
Hudnall La. HP4: L Gad 1E 5
Hughenden Av.
HP13: D'ley, H Wy 1A 12
Hughenden Manor 1A 12
Hughenden Rd. HP13: H Wy 1B 12
HUGHENDEN VALLEY 4B 4
Huguenot Pl. SW18 2F 23
Hull's La. CM2: Sando 2F 11
Hume Av. RM18: Tilb 2C 26
Humphrey's Farm La.
CM3: Gt W 1D 11
Hungerford La. RG10: Twy 2A 20
Hungry Hill La. GU23: Rip, Send 3F 29
HUNSDONBURY 1C 8
Hunsdon Rd. SG12: Huns, S Abb 1C 8
Huntercombe La. Nth.
SL1: Slou 4C 12
Hunter's Rd. KT9: Chess 4D 23
HUNTON 4E 35
HUNTON BRIDGE 3A 6
HUNTON BRIDGE 4A 6
Hunton Bri. Hill WD4: Hunt C 3A 6
Hunton Hill ME15: Hunt 4E 35
Hunton Rd. TN12: Mard 4E 35
Hunts Hill La. HP14: Nap 4A 4
Hunts Hill Rd. GU3: Norm 3C 28
Hunts Slip Rd. SE21 2A 24
Hunt St. ME15: W Far 3D 35
ME18: Yald, W Far 3D 35
Huntswood La. SL6: Tap 3C 12
HURLEY 4A 12
HURLEY BOTTOM 4A 12
Hurley High St. SL6: Hur 4A 12
Hurley La. SL6: Hur 4A 12
HURLINGHAM 2E 23
Hurrells La. CM3: Lit B 2F 11
Hurst, The ME18: Bor G, S'brne 3C 34
TN15: Bor G 3C 34
HURST GREEN
RH8 4C 32
TN12 4F 35
Hurst Grn. Rd. RH8: Oxt 4C 32
Hurstlands RH8: Oxt 4C 32
Hurst La. KT18: H'ly 3D 31
HURST PARK 3C 22
Hurst Rd. DA5: Bexl 2E 25
DA15: Bexl, Sidc 2E 25
KT8: W Mole, E Mos 3B 22
KT12: Walt T 3B 22
KT18: H'ly 3D 31
KT20: Walt H 3D 31
HUTTON 1C 18
HUTTON MOUNT 1B 18
Hutton Rd. CM15: Shenf 1B 18
GU12: Ash V 3B 28
Hutton Village CM13: Hut 1C 18
HYDE, THE 2D 15
Hyde, The NW9 2D 15
HYDE HEATH 3C 4
Hyde Heath Rd.
HP16: H Hea 3C 4
Hyde La. HP3: Hem H 3A 6
HP16: H Hea, L King 3C 4
Hyde Pk. 4F 15
HYDE PARK CORNER 4F 15
Hyde Pk. St. W2 4F 15
Hyde Rd. N1 4A 16
Hyde Va. SE10 1C 24
HYTHE END 2E 21

I

ICKENHAM 3A 14
Ickenham Rd. HA4: Ruis 3A 14
Icknield Way HP23: Tring 1C 4
IDE HILL 3E 33
Ide Hill Rd. TN8: F Elm 4E 33
TN8: Ide H, Chid 4E 33
TN14: Ide H 3E 33
Idleigh Ct. Rd.
DA13: Hartl, Meop 4B 26
IGHTHAM 2B 34
Ightham By-Pass TN15: Igh 2B 34
IGHTHAM COMMON 3B 34
Ightham Mote 3B 34
Ightham Rd. TN11: S'brne 3B 34
TN15: S'brne 3B 34
Ilderton Rd. SE15 1B 24
SE16 1B 24
ILFORD 3D 17
Ilford Hill IG1: Ilf 3D 17
Ilford La. IG1: Ilf 3D 17
Imperial Dr. HA2: Harr 3B 14
Imperial Rd. SL4: Wind 2D 21
SW6 1E 23
INGATESTONE 4C 10
Ingatestone By-Pass
CM4: Inga, Marg 4C 10
Ingatestone Hall 4C 10
Ingatestone Rd. CM1: High 3C 10
CM4: Bmore, Fry 3B 10
CM4: Inga, Stock 4D 11
Inglis Rd. W5 4D 15
Ingram Rd. CR7: Thor H 3A 24
ME7: G'ham 3F 27
INGRAVE 2C 18
INGRAVE COMMON 1B 18
Ingrave Rd. CM13: B'wood 1B 18
CM15: B'wood 1B 18
Ingrebourne Rd. RM13: Rain 4F 17
Inholms La. RH5: N Holm 4C 30
Inner Pk. Rd. SW19 2E 23
Inner Ring E. TW6: H'row A 2A 22
Inner Ring W. TW6: H'row A 2A 22
Institute Rd. SL6: Tap 4C 12
Instone Rd. DA1: Dart 2F 25
Inverness Ter. W2 4E 15
Inwood Rd. TW3: Houn 2C 22
Iron Mill La. DA1: Cray 2F 25
Island Farm Rd. KT8: W Mole 4B 22
Isledon Rd. N7 3A 16
ISLEWORTH 2C 22
Islingham Farm Rd.
ME3: Wain 3F 27
ISLINGTON 3A 16
Islington Pk. St. N1 3A 16
Ismays Rd. TN15: Igh, Ivy H 3B 34
ISTEAD RISE 3C 26
ITCHINGWOOD COMMON 4C 32
Itchingwood Comn. Rd.
RH8: Limp 4C 32
Ively Rd. GU14: Cove 3A 28
(not continuous)
IVER 4F 13
IVER HEATH 4F 13
Iver La. SL0: Iver 4F 13
Iverson Rd. NW6 3E 15
Ivy Barn La.
CM4: Marg, Mill G, Mill G 3C 10
IVY CHIMNEYS 3D 9
Ivy Chimneys Rd. CM16: Epp 3D 9
Ivydale Rd. SE15 2B 24
IVY HATCH 3B 34
Ivy Ho. La. HP4: Berk 2E 5
TN13: Dun G, Otf 2F 33
Ivy Mill La. RH9: G'stone 4B 32

J

Jackass La. BR2: Kes 4C 24
RH8: G'stone, Tand 4B 32
JACK'S HATCH 2D 9
Jacksons La. CM11: Bill 1D 19
JACOBS WELL 3E 29
Jacob's Well Rd. GU4: Jac W 3E 29
Jail La. TN16: Big H 2D 33
Jamaica Rd. SE1 1A 24
SE16 1A 24
James La. E10 2C 16
E11 2C 16
James St. ME7: G'ham 3F 27
W1 4F 15
Jasons Hill HP5: Orch 3E 5
JEALOTT'S HILL 2B 20
Jeffery St. ME7: G'ham 3F 27
Jenkins Dale ME4: Chat 4F 27
Jenkins La. HP23: St L 2C 4
Jermyn St. SW1 4F 15
Jersey Rd. TW5: Hest 1C 22
TW7: Isle 1C 22
Jeskyns Rd.
DA13: Sole S, Cobh 3C 26
Jewels Hill TN16: Big H 1C 32
Jig's La. Nth. RG42: Warf 3B 20
Jig's La. Sth. RG42: Warf 3B 20
Jodrell Rd. E3 3B 16
Joel St. HA5: Eastc 2B 14
HA6: Nwood 2B 14
John Hall Way HP12: H Wy 2A 12
John Islip St. SW1 1F 23
John Nike Way RG12: Brac 3A 20
Johns La. HP5: A Grn 2D 5
John Wilson St. SE18 1D 25
Joiner's La. SL9: Chal P 2E 13
Jones Rd. EN7: G Oak 3A 8
JORDANS 2D 13
Jordans La. HP9: Jor 2D 13
JOYCE GREEN 2A 26
JOYDENS WOOD 3F 25
Jubilee Rd. BR6: Chels 1E 33
SL6: L Grn 4A 12
Jubilee St. E1 4B 16
Jubilee Way KT9: Chess 4D 23
SW19 3E 23
Judd St. WC1 4A 16
Judge Heath La. UB3: Hayes 4A 14
Judge's Hill EN6: N'thaw 3F 7
Junction Rd. N19 3F 15
Jupiter Dr. HP2: Hem H 1A 6
Jutsums La.
RM7: Rom, Rush G 2E 17

K

Katherine Rd. E6 3C 16
E7 3C 16
KATHERINES 1D 9
Katherine's Way CM19: Har 1D 9
Kavanaghs Rd. CM14: B'wood 1B 18
Keates La. SL4: Eton 1D 21
Keel Dr. SL1: Slou 1D 21
Keens La. GU3: Guild 3D 29
Keepers La. HP6: H Hea 4C 4
Keephatch Rd. RG40: W'ham 3A 20
KELVEDON COMMON 4A 10
Kelvedon Hall La. CM14: Kel H 4A 10
KELVEDON HATCH 4A 10
Kelvedon Rd. SW6 1E 23
KEMPROW 4C 6
Kemprow WD25: A'ham 4C 6
Kempton Pk. Racecourse 3B 22
KEMSING 2A 34
Kemsing Rd.
TN15: Kems'g, Wro 2A 34
Kendal Rd. NW10 3E 15
Kender St. SE14 1B 24
KENLEY 2A 32
Kenley Airfield 2A 32
Kenley La. CR8: Kenl 1A 32
Kenley Rd. KT1: King T 3D 23
Kennel La. CM12: Bill 1D 19
GU14: Cove 3A 28
GU20: W'sham 4D 21
Kenneth Rd. SS7: Thun 2F 19
KENNINGHALL JUNC. 1B 16
Kenninghall Rd. E5 3B 16
KENNINGTON 1A 24
Kennington La. SE11 1A 24
KENNINGTON OVAL 1A 24
Kennington Oval SE11 1A 24
Kennington Pk. Rd. SE11 1A 24
Kennington Rd. SE1 1A 24
SE11 1A 24
KENSAL GREEN 4E 15
KENSAL RISE 4E 15
Kensal Rd. W10 4E 15
KENSAL TOWN 4E 15
KENSINGTON 1E 23
Kensington Av. CR7: Thor H 3A 24
Kensington Chu. St. W8 4E 15
Kensington Gdns. 4F 15
Kensington Gore SW7 1F 23
Kensington High St. W8 1E 23
W14 1E 23
Kensington Palace 4E 15
Kensington Pk. Rd. W11 4E 15
Kensington Rd. UB5: N'olt 4B 14
W8 1F 23
Kent Gdns. W13 4C 14
Kent Ga. Way CR0: Addtn 1B 32
KENT HATCH 4D 33
Kent Hatch Rd.
RH8: Crock H, Limp 3C 32
TN8: Crock H 3C 32
Kent Ho. Rd. BR3: Beck 3B 24
SE26 3B 24
Kentish La. AL9: Brk P, Hat 2F 7
KENTISH TOWN 3F 15
Kentish Town Rd. NW1 3F 15
NW5 3F 15
Kentish Way BR1: Brom 3C 24
KENTON 2C 14
Kenton La.
HA3: Hrw W, Kent, W'stone
2C 14
Kenton Rd. E9 3B 16
HA1: Harr 3C 14
HA3: Kent 3C 14
Kent Rd. BR5: St M Cry 4E 25
ME2: Hall 4E 27
Kents Farm La. CM2: W Han 4E 11
Kents Hill Rd. SS7: Ben 3F 19
Kents La. CM16: N Weald 2F 9
KENT STREET 3D 35
Kent St. ME18: Mere 3D 35
KENWARD 4D 35
Kenward Rd. ME18: Yald 4D 35
Kenworthy Rd. E9 3B 16
KESTON 4C 24
KESTON MARK 4D 25
KESTON MARK 4C 24
Kettle La. ME15: E Far 3E 35
Kettlewell Hill GU21: Wok 1E 29
KEVINGTON 4E 25
KEW 1D 23
KEW BRIDGE 1D 23
Kew Bri. TW8: Bford 1D 23
TW9: Kew 1D 23
Kew Bri. Rd. TW8: Bford 1D 23
Kewferry Rd. HA6: Nwood 2A 14
Kew Gdns. 1D 23
Kew Gdns. Rd. TW9: Kew 1D 23
KEW GREEN 1D 23
Kew Rd. TW9: Rich 2D 23
KEYSERS ESTATE 2B 8
KIDBROOKE 1C 24
Kidbrooke Pk. Rd. SE3 1C 24
KILBURN 4E 15
Kilburn High Rd. NW6 3E 15
Kilburn La. W9 4E 15
W10 4E 15
Kilburn Pk. Rd. NW6 4E 15
Kilburn Priory NW6 4E 15
Kiln Barn Rd. ME19: E Mal 2E 35
ME20: Dit, E Mal 2E 35
KILN GREEN 1A 20
Kiln La. CM17: Har 1E 9
HP5: Ley H 3B 4
HP10: Wbrn G 3C 12
RH3: Bet, Aroc 4D 31
SL2: Hedg 3D 13
SL8: Bou E 3C 12
Kiln Rd. HP23: Hasto 1C 4
Kimberley Av. SE15 2B 24
Kimblewick Rd.
HP17: Gt Kim, Kim W 1A 4
King Charles Rd. KT5: Surb 4D 23
King Edward VII Av. SL4: Wind 1D 21
King Edward Rd. RM16: Grays 1C 26
King Edwards Rd. IG11: Bark 4D 17
KINGFIELD 2E 29
Kingfield Rd. GU22: Wok 2E 29
Kingfisher Dr. GU4: Guild 4F 29
King George Rd. ME5: Wald 1F 35
King Harolds Way
DA7: Belv, Bex 1E 25
King Harry La. AL3: St A 2B 6
King Henry's Dr. CR0: New Ad 1C 32
King Hill ME19: Kin H, W Mal 3D 35
Kings Av. IG8: Wfd G 1C 16
SW4 2F 23
SW12 2F 23
KINGSBURY 3D 15
Kingsbury Circ. NW9 2D 15
Kingsbury Rd. NW9 2D 15
Kingscroft La. RG42: Warf 2B 20
KING'S CROSS 4A 16
KING'S CROSS 4A 16
Kings Cross La. RH1: S Nut 4A 32
King's Cross Rd. WC1 4A 16
Kingsdowne Rd. KT6: Surb 4D 23
Kingsend HA4: Ruis 3A 14
KINGS FARM 2C 26
Kingsgate Rd. KT2: King T 3D 23
Kings Gro. SL6: Maide 4B 12
Kings Hall Rd. BR3: Beck 3B 24
Kings Head Hill E4 1B 16
King's Highway SE18 1D 25
KINGS HILL 3D 35
Kings Hill Av. ME19: Kin H 3D 35
Kingshill Av. UB4: Hayes 4A 14
UB5: Yead 4A 14
Kingshill Rd. HP13: H Wy 1B 12
HP15: H Wy 1B 12
Kingshill Way HP4: Berk 2E 5
KINGSLAND 3A 16
Kingsland High St. E8 3A 16
Kingsland Rd. E2 4A 16
E8 4A 16
Kings La. HP16: King 2B 4
HP16: Lit H 3B 4
HP16: S Hth 3C 4
SL6: Cook 3B 12
TW20: Eng G 3E 21
WD4: Chfd 3F 5
KINGS LANGLEY 3A 6
Kings Langley By-Pass
HP3: Hem H 2F 5
WD4: K Lan 2F 5
Kingsley Rd. TW3: Houn 1B 22
Kingsley Way N2 2F 15
Kingsmead Rd. HP11: Wyc M 2B 12
Kings Mill La. RH1: Redh, S Nut 4F 31
KINGSMOOR 2D 9
Kingsmoor Rd. CM19: Har 1D 9
King's Ride GU15: Camb 1B 28
(not continuous)
SL5: Asc 3C 20
Kings Rd. AL2: Lon C 2C 6
CM1: Chelm 2D 11
CM14: B'wood 1B 18
E4 1C 16
GU4: Chil 4E 29
GU51: Fleet 3A 28
HP4: Berk 2E 5
KT2: King T 3D 23
SL4: Wind 1D 21
SL5: S'dale, S'hill 4C 20
SW6 1E 23
SW10 1F 23
TW10: Rich 2D 23
Kings St. SS17: Stan H 4D 19
Kingston Bri. KT1: King T 3C 22
Kingston By-Pass KT6: Surb 4C 22
Kingston By-Pass Rd.
KT6: Surb 4C 22
KT10: Esh, Hin W 4C 22
Kingston Hall Rd. KT1: King T 3C 22
Kingston Hill KT2: King T 3D 23
Kingston La. TW11: Tedd 3C 22
UB8: Hil 4A 14
Kingston Rd. KT1: King T 3D 23
KT3: N Mald 3D 23
KT4: Wor Pk 4D 23
KT17: Ewe 1D 31
KT19: Ewe 4D 23
KT22: Lea 2C 30
(not continuous)
SW15 2E 23
SW19 2E 23
SW20 3E 23
TW11: Tedd 3C 22
TW15: Ashf 3A 22
TW18: Staines 3F 21
KINGSTON UPON THAMES 3D 23
KINGSTON VALE 3D 23
Kingston Va. SW15 3D 23
KING STREET 3B 10
King St. CM5: H Ongar, Ongar 3B 10
ME14: Maids 3F 35
SL6: Maide 4B 12
(not continuous)
TW1: Twick 2C 22
UB2: S'hall 1B 22
W6 1E 23
Kingsway BR4: W W'ck 4C 24
GU21: Wok 2E 29
SL2: Farn C 3D 13
SL9: Chal P 2E 13
UB3: Hayes 4A 14
WC2 4A 16
Kingsway Nth. Orbital Rd.
WD25: Wat 3B 6
KINGSWOOD
KT20 2E 31
SS16 3E 19
WD25 3B 6
Kingswood Dr. SE19 3A 24
Kingswood Rd. KT20: Tad 2E 31
KIPPINGTON 3F 33
Kirkdale SE26 2B 24
Kitchener Rd. GU11: Alde 3B 28
ME3: C'den 2F 27
KIT'S COTY 1F 35
Kitsmead La. KT16: Longc 4E 21
Kitto Rd. SE14 1B 24
KITT'S END 4E 7
Kitts End Rd. EN5: Barn 4E 7
KNAPHILL 2D 29
Knares, The SS16: Bas 3D 19
Knatts La. TN15: Knat, W King 1A 34
KNATTS VALLEY 1A 34
Knatts Valley Rd.
TN15: Farni, Knat, W King 1A 34
Knaves Beech HP10: Loud 2C 12
Knaves Beech Way HP10: Loud 2C 12
Knee Hill SE2 1E 25
Kneller Rd. TW2: Whitt 2C 22
Knight Rd. ME2: Strood 3E 27
KNIGHTSBRIDGE 1F 23
Knightsbridge SW1 1F 23
SW7 1F 23
Knights Hill SE27 3A 24
Knipp Hill KT11: Cobh 1B 30
KNOCKHALL 2B 26
Knockhall Rd. DA9: Ghithe 2B 26
KNOCKHOLT 2E 33
Knockholt Main Rd.
TN14: Knock 2D 33
KNOCKHOLT POUND 2E 33
Knockholt Rd. TN14: Hals 1E 33
KNOCKMILL 1A 34
Knock Mill La. TN15: W King 1B 34
Knole 3A 34
Knoll Rd. DA14: Sidc 3E 25
GU15: Camb 1B 28
RH4: Dork 4C 30
KNOLL RDBT. 2C 30
Knolton Way SL2: Slou 4E 13
KNOTTY GREEN 1C 12
KNOWLE GREEN 3F 21
KNOWLE HILL 4E 21
Knowle Rd. ME1: Woul 1E 35
KNOWL HILL 1A 20
Knowl Hill Comn. RG10: K Hill 1A 20

L

Labour in Vain Rd.
TN15: Stans, Wro 1B 34
LACEY GREEN 3A 4
Laceys La. ME17: Lint 4F 35
Ladbroke Gdns. W11 4E 15
Ladbroke Gro. W10 4E 15
W11 4E 15
LADDINGFORD 4D 35
Ladds La. ME6: Hall 1D 35
Ladygate La. HA4: Ruis 2A 14
Lady Margaret Rd. SL5: S'dale 4D 21
UB1: S'hall 4B 14
Ladymead GU1: Guild 4E 29
LADYWELL 2B 24
Ladywell Rd. SE4 2B 24
SE13 2B 24
Laffan's Rd. GU11: Alde 3A 28
LAINDON 2D 19
Laindon Comn. Rd.
CM12: L Bur 1D 19
Laindon Link SS15: Lain 2D 19
Laindon Rd. CM12: Bill 1D 19
Lakedale Rd. SE18 1D 25
LAKE END 1C 20
Lake End Rd. SL4: Dor 4C 12
SL6: Dor R, Tap 4C 12
Lake Ho. Rd. E11 3C 16
Lake Rd. GU16: Deep 2B 28
Lakeside Rd. GU12: Ash V 4B 28
Lakes La. HP9: Beac 2D 13
LALEHAM 3F 21
Laleham Rd. TW17: Shep 3A 22
TW18: Staines 3F 21
Lamberts Rd. KT5: Surb 4D 23
LAMBETH 1A 24
Lambeth Bri. SE1 1A 24
Lambeth Pal. Rd. SE1 1A 24
Lambeth Rd. SE1 1A 24
Lamb La. AL3: Redb 1B 6
LAMBOURNE 4E 9
LAMBOURNE END 1E 17
Lambourne Rd. IG7: Chig 1D 17
Lammas La. KT10: Esh, Hers 4B 22
Lampits Hill SS17: Corr 3E 19
LAMPTON 1C 22
Lampton Rd. TW3: Houn 2B 22
Lamson Rd. RM13: Rain 4F 17
Lanacre Av. NW9 2D 15
Lancaster Av. SE27 2A 24
Lancaster Pl. WC2 4A 16
Lancaster Rd. EN2: Enf 4A 8
HP12: H Wy 1A 12
NW10 3E 15
SE25 3A 24
Landway, The TN15: Kems'g 2A 34
LANE END
DA2 3A 26
HP14 1A 12
Lane End CM17: Har 1E 9
Lane End Rd.
HP12: Book, H Wy 1A 12
HP14: L End 1A 12
Langborough Rd. RG40: W'ham 3A 20
LANGDON HILLS 3D 19
LANGHURST 4C 32
LANGLEY 1E 21
LANGLEY BOTTOM 2D 31
LANGLEYBURY 4A 6
Langleybury La. WD4: Lang 4A 6
WD17: Wat 4A 6
Langley Dr. E11 3C 16
Langley Gro. KT3: N Mald 3D 23
Langley Hill WD4: K Lan 3A 6
Langley La. WD5: Ab L 3A 6
Langley Pk. La. SL0: Iver 4E 13
Langley Pk. Rd. SL0: Iver 4E 13
SL3: L'ly 4E 13
Langley Rd. SL3: L'ly 1E 21
WD4: Chfd 3F 5
WD17: Wat 4B 6
LANGLEY RDBT. 1E 21
Langley Va. Rd. KT18: Eps D 2D 31
Langley Way WD17: Wat 4A 6
Langthorne Rd. E11 3C 16
Lanhams SS13: Pit 2E 19
Lansbury Dr. UB4: Hayes 4A 14
Lansdell Rd. CR4: Mitc 3F 23
Lansdowne Dr. E8 3B 16
Lansdowne Rd. CR0: C'don 4A 24
N17 2B 16
Lansdown Rd. DA14: Sidc 2E 25
Larch Av. SL5: S'dale 4D 21
Larchfield Rd. SL6: Maide 4B 12
LARKFIELD 2E 35
Larkshall Rd. E4 1C 16
Lark's La. CM3: Gt W 1D 11
Lascelles Av. HA1: Harr 3C 14
Lascelles Rd. SL3: Slou 1E 21
Lascombe La. GU3: Putt 4C 28
Latchmere Rd. SW11 1F 23
LATIMER 4E 5
Latimer Rd. HP5: Ches, Lat 3D 5
WD3: Chen 4E 5
LATTON BUSH 2D 9
Lauderdale Rd. W9 4E 15
Launder's La.
RM13: Rain, Wenn 4A 18
Laundry La. EN9: Naze 2C 8
GU47: Col T 1A 28
Lauriston Rd. E9 3B 16
Lausanne Rd. SE15 1B 24
Lavender Av. CR4: Mitc 3F 23
Lavender Gdns. EN2: Enf 4A 8
Lavender Hill EN2: Enf 4A 8
SW11 2F 23
Lavender Ri. UB7: W Dray 1A 22
Lavenders Rd. ME19: W Mal 2D 35
Lawn La. CM1: Spr 1E 11
HP3: Hem H 2F 5
Lawrence La. RH3: Bkld 4E 31
Lawrence Rd. N15 2A 16
Lawrence St. NW7 1D 15
Lawrie Pk. Av. SE26 3B 24
Lawrie Pk. Rd. SE26 3B 24
Layhams Rd. BR2: Kes 4C 24
BR4: W W'ck 4C 24
LAYTER'S GREEN 2E 13
Layter's Grn. La. SL9: Chal P 2E 13
LEA BRIDGE 3B 16
Lea Bri. Rd. E5 3B 16
E10 3B 16
E17 3B 16
LEADEN RODING 1B 10
LEA INTERCHANGE 3B 16
Leamington Pk. W3 4D 15
Leamington Rd. RM3: Rom 1A 18
Leander Dr. DA12: Grav'nd 3D 27
Leapale Rd. GU1: Guild 4E 29
Leas Rd. CR6: Warl 2B 32
LEATHERHEAD 2C 30
Leatherhead By-Pass Rd.
KT22: Lea 2C 30
LEATHERHEAD COMMON 2C 30
Leatherhead Rd. KT9: Chess 1C 30
KT21: Asht 2C 30
KT22: Lea 2C 30
KT22: Oxs 1C 30
KT23: Bookh 3B 30
Leather La. HP16: Gt Miss 3B 4
Lea Valley Rd. E4 1B 16
EN3: Pond E 1B 16
Lea Valley Viaduct E4 1B 16
N18 1B 16
LEAVESDEN 4A 6
LEAVESDEN GREEN 4A 6

Leavesden Rd. WD24: Wat 4B 6
LEAVES GREEN 1C 32
Leaves Grn. Rd. BR2: Kes 1C 32
Lebanon Gdns. TN16: Big H 2C 32
Led Borough La. HP9: Beac 2C 12
Ledgemore La.
HP2: Gad R, Gt Gad 1F 5
Ledgers Rd. CR6: Warl 2B 32
SL1: Slou 1D 21
LEE 2C 24
LEE, THE 2C 4
LEE CHAPEL NORTH 2D 19
LEE CHAPEL SOUTH 3D 19
Leech La. KT18: H'ly 3D 31
LEE CLUMP 2C 4
LEE COMMON 2C 4
LEE GATE 2B 4
LEE GREEN 2C 24
Lee Grn. La. KT18: H'ly 3D 31
Lee Grn. Rd. ME3: Cli W 2E 27
Lee High Rd. SE12 . . . . .2C 24
SE13 . . . . .2C 24
Lee La. SL6: Maide 4A 12
Leeming Rd. WD6: Bore 4D 7
Lee Rd. SE3 . . . . .2C 24
Leeside Rd. N17 . . . . .2B 16
Leesons Hill BR5: St P 3D 25
BR7: Chst 3D 25
Lees Rd. ME18: Ladd, Yald 4D 35
UB8: Hil 4A 14
Lee Ter. SE3 . . . . .2C 24
Lee Woottens La. SS16: Bas 3E 19
(not continuous)
Legoland 2C 20
LEIGH
RH2 .4E 31
TN11 . . . . .4A 34
Leigham Ct. Rd. SW16 . . . . .2A 24
Leighams Rd.
CM3: B'acre, E Han 3F 11
Leigh Hill Rd. KT11: Cobh 1B 30
Leigh Pl. Rd. RH2: Leigh 4E 31
Leigh Rd. RH3: Bet 4D 31
SL1: Slou 4D 13
TN11: Hild 4A 34
TN11: Leigh 4A 34
Leighs Rd. CM3: Lit W 1E 11
Leighton Buzzard Rd.
HP1: Gt Gad, Hem H 1F 5
Leighton Rd. NW5 . . . . .3F 15
Leinster Rd. SS15: Lain 2D 19
Leinster Ter. W2 . . . . .4F 15
Leipzig Rd. GU52: Chu C 4A 28
Leman St. E1 . . . . .4B 16
LEMSFORD 1D 7
Lemsford La. AL8: W City 1E 7
Lemsford Rd. AL1: St A 2C 6
AL10: Hat 1E 7
Lemsford Village AL8: Lem 1D 7
(not continuous)
Lennard Rd. BR3: Beck 3B 24
SE20 . . . . .3B 24
Lennox Rd. DA11: Grav'nd 2C 26
LENT .4C 12
LENT RISE 4C 12
Lent Ri. Rd. SL1: Burn 4C 12
SL6: Tap 4C 12
Leonard Rd. SW16 . . . . .3F 23
Leopold Rd. SW19 . . . . .3E 23
Leret Way KT22: Lea 2C 30
Lesbourne Rd. RH2: Reig 4E 31
Leslie Pk. Rd. CR0: C'don 4A 24
LESSNESS HEATH 1E 25
LETCHMORE HEATH 4C 6
Letter Box La. TN13: S'oaks 3F 33
LETT'S GREEN 2D 33
LETTY GREEN 1F 7
LEVERSTOCK GREEN 2A 6
Leverstock Grn. Rd. HP2: Hem H . . .2A 6
HP3: Hem H 2A 6
(not continuous)
Leverstock Grn. Way
HP3: Hem H 2A 6
Lever St. EC1 . . . . .4A 16
Leverton Way EN9: Walt A 3C 8
LEWISHAM 2C 24
Lewisham High St. SE13 . . . . .2B 24
(not continuous)
Lewisham Hill SE13 . . . . .1C 24
Lewisham Rd. SE13 . . . . .1B 24
Lewisham Way SE4 . . . . .1B 24
SE14 . . . . .1B 24
Lewis Rd. DA13: Ist R 3C 26
LEYBOURNE 2D 35
Leybourne Way ME20: Lark 2D 35
Leydenhatch La.
BR8: Dart, Swan 3F 25
LEY HILL 3E 5
Ley Hill Rd. HP3: Bov 3E 5
Leys Rd. HP3: Hem H 2A 6
Ley St. IG1: Ilf 3D 17
IG2: Ilf 3D 17
LEYTON 3C 16
Leyton Cross Rd.
DA2: Bexl, Dart 2F 25
Leyton Grn. Rd. E10 . . . . .2C 16
Leyton Orient FC 3B 16
Leyton Rd. E15 . . . . .3C 16
Leywood Rd. DA13: Meop 1C 34
Liberty Av. SW19 . . . . .3F 23
Lichfield Rd. NW2 . . . . .3E 15
Liddell Gdns. NW10 . . . . .4E 15
LIDSING 1F 35
Lidsing Rd.
ME14: Box, G'ham, Bred 2F 35
Lieutenant Ellis Way
EN7: Chesh, G Oak 3B 8
(not continuous)
EN8: Chesh, Walt C 3B 8
LIGHTWATER 1C 28
Lightwater By-Pass GU18: Light . . .1C 28
Lightwater Rd. GU18: Light 1C 28
Lilford Rd. SE5 . . . . .1A 24
Lillechurch Rd. ME3: High'm 2E 27
Lilleshall Rd. SM4: Mord 4F 23
Lillie Rd. SW6 . . . . .1E 23
Lily Bottom La. HP27: Par H 3A 4
Lily Hill Dr. RG12: Brac 3B 20
Lily Hill Rd. RG12: Brac 3B 20
Lily's Wlk. HP11: H Wy 1B 12
Limbrick Rd. AL5: Harp 1B 6
Limecroft Rd. GU21: Knap 2D 29
Limeharbour E14 . . . . .1B 24
LIMEHOUSE 4B 16
LIMPSFIELD 3C 32
LIMPSFIELD CHART 3D 33
Limpsfield Rd. CR2: Sande 1B 32
CR6: Warl 2B 32
Lincoln Rd. EN1: Enf 4A 8
EN3: Pond E 4A 8
Lincolns La.
CM14: Pil H, S Weald 1A 18
Linden Av. SL6: Maide 4B 12
Linden Gro. SE15 . . . . .2B 24
Lind Rd. SM1: Sutt 4F 23
Lindsey St. CM16: Epp 3D 9
LINFORD 1D 27
Linford Rd. RM16: Grays, W Til . . .1C 26
Lingfield Av. KT1: King T 3D 23
Linkfield La. RH1: Redh 4F 31
Linkfield Rd. TW7: Isle 1C 22
Link Rd. HP16: Gt Miss 3B 4
SS8: Can I 4F 19
WD23: Bush 4B 6
WD24: Bush, Wat 4B 6
Links Av. SM4: Mord 3E 23
(not continuous)
Links Way BR3: Beck 4B 24
WD3: Crox G 4A 6
LINTON 4F 35
Linton Hill ME17: Lint 4F 35
TN12: Lint 4F 35
Linton Rd. ME15: Loose 4F 35
Lion Grn. Rd. CR5: Coul 2F 31
Lion Hill SS17: Corr 4E 19
Lippitts Hill IG10: Lough 4C 8
Lipwell Hill ME3: Cool 2F 27
LISSON GROVE 4F 15
Lisson Gro. NW1 . . . . .4F 15
NW8 . . . . .4F 15
LITTLE BADDOW 2F 11
Lit. Baddow Rd. CM3: Dan 2F 11
LITTLE BERKHAMSTED 1F 7
LITTLE BOOKHAM 3B 30
Lit. Bookham St. KT23: Bookh 3B 30
LITTLE BOYS HEATH 4C 4
LITTLE BRITAIN 4F 13
LITTLEBROOK INTERCHANGE 2A 26
Littlebrook Mnr. Way DA1: Dart . . .2A 26
LITTLE BURSTEAD 1D 19
LITTLEBURY 3A 10
Lit. Bushey La. WD23: Bush 4B 6
LITTLE CHALFONT 4E 5
Little Comn. La. RH1: Blet 4A 32
LITTLE EALING 1C 22
Lit. Ealing La. W5 . . . . .1C 22
LITTLE END 3A 10
Littlefield Grn. SL6: W Walt 1A 20
LITTLE GADDESDEN 1E 5
Lit. Gaynes La. RM14: Upm 3A 18
Lit. Gerpins La. RM14: Upm 3A 18
Little Grn. La. WD3: Crox G 4A 6
LITTLE HAMPDEN 2B 4
LITTLE HEATH
EN6 . . . . .3F 7
HP4 .1E 5
IG3 . . . . .2E 17
Little Heath SE7 . . . . .1D 25
Lit. Heath La. HP1: Berk, Pott E . . .2E 5
Littleheath La.
KT11: Cobh, Stoke D 1B 30
Lit. Heath Rd. DA7: Bex 1E 25
Lit. Hilders La. TN8: Eden 4D 33
Lit. Hundridge La. HP16: H Hea . . .3C 4
Lit. Hyde La. CM4: Fry, Inga 3C 10
LITTLE ILFORD 3D 17
Lit. Ilford La. E12 . . . . .3D 17
LITTLE KIMBLE 2A 4
Lit. Kimble Hill
HP17: Gt Kim, Lit K 2A 4
LITTLE KINGSHILL 4B 4
Little La. HP27: L Row, Saund 4A 4
LITTLE LAVER 1A 10
Lit. Laver Rd.
CM5: Lit L, More, M Grn 2A 10
CM17: M Grn 1F 9
LITTLE LONDON 2B 4
LITTLE MARLOW 3B 12
Lit. Marlow Rd. SL7: Marl 3A 12
(not continuous)
LITTLE MILL 4C 34
LITTLE MISSENDEN 4C 4
Lit. Norman St. TN14: Ide H 3E 33
Lit. Oxhey La. WD19: Wat 1B 14
LITTLE OXNEY GREEN 2D 11
LITTLE PARNDON 1D 9
LITTLE SANDHURST 1A 28
LITTLE STANMORE 2D 15
LITTLE THURROCK 1C 26
LITTLETON
GU3 . . . . .4E 29
TW17 . . . . .3A 22
Littleton La. GU3: Art 4E 29
TW17: Shep 4F 21
LITTLE TRING 1C 4
Lit. Tring Rd. HP23: Tring, Trin . . .1C 4
LITTLE WALTHAM 1E 11
Lit. Waltham Rd. CM1: Spr 1E 11
LITTLE WARLEY 2B 18
Lit. Warley Hall La.
CM13: L War 2B 18
LITTLEWICK 2D 29
LITTLEWICK GREEN 1A 20
Littlewick Rd. GU21: Knap, Wok . . .2D 29
LITTLE WOODCOTE 1F 31
Lit. Woodcote La. CR8: Purl 1F 31
SM5: Cars 1F 31
LITTLEWORTH COMMON 3C 12
Littleworth Rd. HP13: D'ley 1A 12
KT10: Esh 4C 22
SL1: Burn 3C 12
Liverpool Rd. N1 . . . . .3A 16
N7 .3A 16
SL1: Slou 4D 13
Livingstone Rd. ME7: G'ham 3F 27
Llanover Rd. HA9: Wemb 3C 14
Loampit Hill SE13 . . . . .1B 24
LOAMPIT VALE 2C 24
Loampit Va. SE13 . . . . .2B 24
Lockers Pk. La. HP1: Hem H 2F 5
Locket Rd. HA3: W'stone 2C 14
Lockfield Dr. GU21: Wok 2D 29
Lock La. GU22: Pyr 2F 29
Lock Path SL4: Dor, Eton W 1C 20
Lock Rd. TW10: Ham 3C 22
LOCKSBOTTOM 4D 25
Locks La. CR4: Mitc 3F 23
Locks Ride SL5: Asc 3B 20
Lockyers Hill DA13: Meop 4D 27
Loddington La. ME17: Lint 4F 35
Lodge Av. RM8: Dag 3E 17
RM9: Dag 3E 17
LODGE AVENUE FLYOVER JUNC.
. . . . .4E 17
Lodgebottom Rd. KT18: H'ly 3D 31
RH5: Mick 3D 31
Lodge Hill SE2: Well 1E 25
Lodge Hill La. ME3: C'den 2F 27
Lodge La. CR0: New Ad 1B 32
HP8: Chal G 4E 5
HP16: Pre 3B 4
RM5: Col R 2E 17
RM16: Grays 1B 26
Lodge Rd. CM1: Writ 2D 11
RM16: Grays 1B 26
RM5: Col R 2E 17
HP16: Pre 3B 4
HP8: Chal G 4E 5
SM5: B'acre 3F 11
Loftin Way CM2: Gt B 2E 11
Logmore La. RH4: Dork, Westc . . .4B 30
Logs Hill BR7: Chst 3D 25
Lombard Rd. SW11 . . . . .1F 23
LOMBARD RDBT. 4A 24
Lombard St. DA4: Hort K 3A 26
London Arena 1B 24
LONDON - BIGGIN HILL AIRPORT
. . . . .1D 33
London Bri. EC4 . . . . .4A 16
SE1 .4A 16
LONDON CITY AIRPORT 4D 17
LONDON COLNEY 3C 6
London End HP9: Beac 2D 13
LONDON-HEATHROW AIRPORT
. . . . .2A 22
London La. BR1: Brom 3C 24
London Rd. AL1: St A 2C 6
BR1: Brom 3C 24
BR8: Swan 3F 25
(Birchwood Rd.)
BR8: Swan 3F 25
(High St.)
CM2: Wid 2D 11
CM3: Bor, Hat P 1F 11
CM5: Ongar 4F 9
CM11: C Hill, Ram 1E 19
CM12: Bill 1C 18
CM14: B'wood 1A 18
CM17: Har 1E 9
CM17: Har, Twood 1E 9
CR0: C'don, Thor H 3A 24
CR4: Mitc 4F 23
(Carshalton Rd.)
CR4: Mitc 3F 23
(Morden Rd.)
CR7: Thor H 3A 24
DA1: Bexl, Cray 2F 25
DA2: Dart, Ghithe, Swans 2A 26
DA4: Farni 4F 25
DA9: Ghithe, Swans 2A 26
DA10: Ghithe, Swans 2A 26
DA11: Nflt 2C 26
EN2: Enf 1A 16
GU1: Guild 4E 29
(not continuous)
GU4: Burp 4E 29
GU20: W'sham 4C 20
GU23: Send 3F 29
(not continuous)
GU25: Vir W 4C 20
HA1: Harr 3C 14
HA7: Stan 1C 14
HP1: Hem H 2F 5
HP3: Hem H 2F 5
HP4: Berk 2E 5
HP8: Chal G 1E 13
HP9: Beac 2D 13
HP10: Wbrn G 2C 12
HP11: H Wy, Wyc M 1B 12
HP16: Gt Miss 3B 4
HP22: Ast C 1B 4
HP22: Wend 2B 4
HP23: Tring 1C 4
KT2: King T 3D 23
(not continuous)
KT17: Ewe 1D 31
ME2: Strood 3E 27
ME16: Ali, Maids 2E 35
ME19: Addtn, Off, Rya, W Mal
. . . . .2C 34
ME20: A'ford, Dit, E Mal,
Lark, W Mal 2C 34
RG12: Bin 3A 20
RG12: Brac 3B 20
RG27: Min, Bla 2A 28
RG40: W'ham 3A 20
RG42: Bin 3A 20
RH1: Redh 4F 31
RH2: Reig 4E 31
RH4: Dork 4C 30
RH5: Dork 4C 30
RM4: Abr 4F 9
RM4: Stap T 4E 9
RM7: Chad H, Rom 2E 17
RM15: Avel, Purf 1A 26
RM17: Grays 1B 26
RM18: Tilb 1C 26
RM19: Purf, W Thur 1A 26
(not continuous)
RM20: Purf, W Thur 1A 26
SE1 .1A 24
SE23 . . . . .2B 24
SG12: Gt A, Ware 1B 8
SG13: Hertf 1A 8
SL3: Dat 1E 21
(not continuous)
SL3: L'ly 1E 21
SL5: Asc 3B 20
SL5: Asc, S'hill 3C 20
SM3: Cheam 4E 23
SM4: Mord 4E 23
SM6: Wall 4F 23
SS6: Ray 2F 19
SS7: Ben, Thun 2F 19
SS11: Raw 1F 19
SS12: Wick 1E 19
SS13: B Gif, Pit 2F 19
SS16: Vange 3E 19
SS17: Stan H 4D 19
SW16 . . . . .3A 24
SW17 . . . . .3F 23
TN10: Tonb 4B 34
TN13: Dun G, Riv 2F 33
TN13: S'oaks 3F 33
TN14: Hals 1E 33
(not continuous)
TN15: Addtn, Off, Wro 2B 34
TN15: Bor G, W King, Wro 4A 26
TN15: S'oaks 4A 34
TN16: Westrm 3D 33
TW1: Twick 2C 22
TW3: Houn 1C 22
TW7: Bford, Isle 1C 22
TW8: Bford 1C 22
TW14: Bedf 2F 21
TW15: Ashf 2F 21
TW18: Staines 3F 21
TW20: Eng G 4C 20
WD3: Rick 1A 14
WD6: Bore 4D 7
WD7: Shenl 3D 7
WD23: Bush 1B 14
London Rd. E. HP7: Amer 4D 5
London Rd. Nth. RH1: Mers 3F 31
London Rd. Sth.
RH1: Mers, Redh 3F 31
London Rd. W. HP7: Amer 4D 5
London St. KT16: Chert 4F 21
W2 .4F 15
London Wall EC2 . . . . .4A 16
London Welsh RUFC 2C 22
London Zoo 4F 15
LONESOME 3F 23
Lonesome La. RH2: Reig, Sid 4F 31
Long Acre WC2 . . . . .4A 16
Long Barn Rd. TN14: Weald 4F 33
Longbottom La.
HP9: Beac, See G, Jor 2D 13
Longbridge Rd. IG11: Bark 3D 17
RM8: Dag 3D 17
Long Chaulden HP1: Hem H 2F 5
Longcroft La. AL8: W City 1E 7
HP3: Bov, Hem H 3F 5
LONGCROSS 4E 21
Longcross Rd. GU24: Chob 4D 21
KT16: Longc 4D 21
LONG DITTON 4C 22
Longdown Hill HP27: White 2A 4
Longdown La. Nth. KT17: Eps 1E 31
Longdown La. Sth.
KT17: Eps, Eps D 1E 31
Longdown Rd. GU47: S'urst 1A 28
Long Dr. HA4: Ruis 3B 14
Long Elmes HA3: Hrw W 2B 14
LONGFIELD 3B 26
LONGFIELD HILL 3C 26
Longfield La. EN7: Chesh 3B 8
Longfield Rd. DA3: Lfield, Meop . . .4C 26
DA13: Meop 4C 26
LONGFORD 1F 21
Long Furlong Dr. SL2: Slou 4D 13
Long Hill Rd. SL5: Asc 3B 20
Longland Dr. N20 . . . . .1E 15
LONGLANDS 2D 25
Longlands HP2: Hem H 2A 6
Longlands Rd. DA15: Sidc 2D 25
Long La. CR0: C'don 4B 24
DA7: Bex 1E 25
HP3: Bov, Flau 3E 5
ME17: B Mon 4F 35
N2 .2F 15
N3 .2E 15
(not continuous)
RM16: Grays 4B 18
(not continuous)
SE1 .1A 24
SL6: Cook 3B 12
TW19: Stanw 2A 22
UB10: Hil, Ick 4A 14
WD3: Herons 1F 13
Longleigh La. DA7: Bex 1E 25
SE2 .1E 25
Longley Rd. SW17 . . . . .3F 23
Longmead La. SL1: Burn 3C 12
Longmead Rd. KT19: Eps, Ewe 1D 31
Long Mill La. TN11: Plax, S'brne . . .3B 34
TN15: Bor G 2C 34
TN15: Plax, Bor G 3B 34
Longmore Av. EN4: E Barn 1F 15
EN5: New Bar 1F 15
Long Reach GU23: Ock 3A 30
KT24: W Hor 3A 30
Long Readings La. SL2: Slou 4D 13
Long Ridings Av. CM13: Hut 1B 18
Long Rd. SS8: Can I 4F 19
SW4 . . . . .2F 23
Longspring WD24: Wat 4B 6
Longstomps Av. CM2: Chelm 2E 11
Longstone Av. NW10 . . . . .3D 15
Long St. EN9: Walt A 3D 9
Longwood Gdns. IG5: Ilf 2D 17
Lonsdale Av. E6 . . . . .4C 16
Lonsdale Rd. SW13 . . . . .1D 23
Looe Gdns. IG6: Ilf 2D 17
Loom La. WD7: Rad 4C 6
Loop Rd. GU22: Wok 2E 29
LOOSE 3F 35
Loose Rd. ME15: Maids 3F 35
Loosley Hill HP27: L Row 3A 4
LOOSLEY ROW 3A 4
Lord's Cricket Ground 4F 15
Lordship La. N17 . . . . .2A 16
N22 .2A 16
SE22 . . . . .2A 24
Lordship Pk. N16 . . . . .3A 16
Lordship Rd. CM1: Writ 2D 11
N16 .3A 16
Lord St. EN11: Hodd 1B 8
LORDS WOOD 1F 35
Lordswood La. ME5: Lor, Wald 1F 35
Loseley House 4D 29
Lothian Rd. SW9 . . . . .1A 24
Loudoun Rd. NW8 . . . . .4F 15
LOUDWATER
HP10 . . . . .2C 12
WD3 .4F 5
Loudwater La.
WD3: Crox G, Loud 4F 5
Loughborough Rd. SW9 . . . . .1A 24
LOUGHTON 1D 17
Loughton La. CM16: They B 4D 9
Loughton Way IG9: Buck H 1C 16
Love Grn. La. SL0: Iver 4F 13
Lovelace Rd. SE21 . . . . .2A 24
Lovelands La. GU24: Chob 1D 29
Love La. RM15: Avel 1A 26
RM18: E Til 1D 27
SL0: Iver 4F 13
SM4: Mord 4E 23
WD4: K Lan 3A 6
Lovel La. SL4: Wink 3C 20
Lovel Rd. SL4: Wink 3C 20
LOVES GREEN 2C 10
Lwr. Addiscombe Rd.
CR0: C'don 4A 24
LOWER ASHTEAD 2C 30
Lwr. Bedfords Rd.
RM1: Have B, Rom 2F 17
LOWER BOBBINGWORTH GREEN . . .2F 9
LOWER BOIS 3D 5
Lwr. Boston Rd. W7 . . . . .4C 14
Lwr. Bovinger Grn. CM5: Ongar 2F 9
Lwr. Boxley Rd. ME14: Maids 2F 35
Lwr. Britwell Rd. SL2: Slou 4C 12
(not continuous)
Lwr. Bury La. CM16: Epp 3D 9
LOWER BUSH 4D 27
Lwr. Church Rd. GU47: S'urst 1A 28
Lwr. Cippenham La. SL1: Slou 4D 13
LOWER CLAPTON 3B 16
Lwr. Clapton Rd. E5 . . . . .3B 16
Lwr. Cookham Rd. SL6: Maide 4B 12
Lower Ct. Rd. KT19: Eps 1D 31
Lwr. Downs Rd. SW20 . . . . .3E 23
Lwr. Dunton Rd.
CM13: Bulp, B'wood 2C 18
RM14: Bulp 2C 18
SS17: Horn H 2C 18
LOWER EDMONTON 1A 16
Lwr. Farm Rd. ME17: B Mon 4F 35
Lwr. Farnham Rd. GU11: Alde 4B 28
GU12: Alde 4B 28
LOWER FELTHAM 3A 22
LOWER GREEN
CM2 . . . . .2F 11
KT10 . . . . .4B 22
Lower Grn. CM2: Gall 3E 11
(not continuous)
Lower Grn. Rd. KT10: Esh 4B 22
Lwr. Guildford Rd. GU21: Knap . . .2D 29
LOWER HALLIFORD 4A 22
Lwr. Hall La. E4 . . . . .1B 16
(not continuous)
Lwr. Hampton Rd. TW16: Sun 3B 22
Lwr. Hatfield Rd.
SG13: B'bry, Howe G, Hertf 1F 7
LOWER HIGHAM 2E 27
Lwr. Higham Rd.
DA12: Grav'nd, Shorne 2D 27
Lwr. High St. WD17: Wat 4B 6
LOWER HOLLOWAY 3A 16
Lwr. Icknield Way
HP17: Gt Kim 2A 4
HP22: Ast C, Bkld 1B 4
HP23: Wil 1B 4
LOWER KINGSWOOD 3E 31
Lwr. Lea Crossing E14 . . . . .4C 16
LOWER LUDDESDOWN 4D 27
Lwr. Morden La. SM4: Mord 4E 23
LOWER NAZEING 2C 8
LOWER NORTH DEAN 4A 4
Lower Pk. Rd. CR5: Chip 2F 31
LOWER PLACE 4D 15
Lwr. Pyrford Rd. GU22: Pyr 2F 29
Lwr. Richmond Rd. SW13 . . . . . . .2E 23
SW14 . . . . .2D 23
SW15 . . . . .2E 23
TW9: Rich 2D 23
Lower Rd. BR5: St M Cry 4E 25
BR8: Swan 3F 25
CM15: Mount 4C 10
DA8: Erith 1F 25
DA12: High'm, Shorne 2D 27
DA17: Belv 1E 25
HA2: Harr 3C 14
HP3: Hem H 2A 6
HP22: S Man 1A 4
HP27: L Row 3A 4
IG10: Lough 4D 9
KT22: Fet 3B 30
KT23: Bookh 3B 30
KT24: Eff 3B 30
ME15: W Far, E Far 3E 35
SE16 . . . . .1B 24
(not continuous)
SG12: Gt A 1B 8
SL6: Cook 3B 12
SL9: Chal P 2E 13
(not continuous)
SM1: Sutt 4F 23
Lwr. Rochester Rd.
ME3: High'm 2E 27
Lwr. Sandhurst Rd.
GU47: S'urst 1A 28
RG40: Fin 1A 28
LOWER SHORNE 2D 27
Lwr. Sloane St. SW1 . . . . .1F 23
Lwr. Stock Rd. CM2: W Han 4E 11
CM4: Stock, W Han 4E 11
Lower St. TN11: Hild 4A 34
Lwr. Sunbury Rd. TW12: Hamp 3B 22
LOWER SYDENHAM 3B 24
Lwr. Teddington Rd.
KT1: Ham W 3C 22
Lower Ter. NW3 . . . . .3F 15
Lwr. Thames St. EC3 . . . . .4A 16
Lower Tovil ME15: Maids 3F 35
LOWER UPNOR 3F 27
Lwr. Warren Rd. ME5: B Hill 1F 35
Lwr. Weybourne La.
GU9: B Lea, Wey 4A 28
Lwr. Wokingham Rd.
RG40: Fin 4A 20
RG45: Crow 4A 20
LOWER WOODEND 3A 12
Lower Woodside AL9: Hat 2E 7
Lowfield St. DA1: Dart 2A 26
Low Hill Rd. CM19: Roy 1C 8
Lowlands Av. HP5: Ches 3D 5
Lowlands Rd. HA1: Harr 3C 14
Low La. GU9: B Lea 4B 28
Low St. La. RM18: W Til 1D 27
Loxboro Hill HP14: Bled R 1A 12
LOXFORD 3D 17
Loxford La. IG1: Ilf 3D 17
LOYTER'S GREEN 1F 9
Lubbock Rd. BR7: Chst 3D 25
LUCAS END 3A 8
Lucas Grn. Rd. GU24: W End 2C 28
Luck's Hill ME19: W Mal 2D 35
Lucks La. ME17: B Mon 4F 35
Luckyn La. SS14: Bas 2D 19
LUDDESDOWN 4D 27
Luddesdown Rd. DA13: Lud'n 4D 27
Ludgate Hill EC4 . . . . .4A 16
Ludwick Way AL7: W City 1E 7
Lughorse La. ME15: Hunt, Yald . . .4E 35
ME18: Yald 4E 35
LULLINGSTONE 4F 25
Lullingstone La. DA4: Eyns 4F 25
Lullingstone Roman Villa 4F 25
Lullington Gth. N12 . . . . .1E 15
Lunghurst Rd. CR3: Wold 2C 33
LUNSFORD 2D 35
Lunsford La. ME20: Lark 2D 35
LUNSFORD PARK 2E 35
Lupus St. SW1 . . . . .1F 23
Lusted Hall La.
TN16: Big H, Tats 2C 32
LUTON 4F 27
Luton High St. ME5: Chat 4F 27
Luton Rd. ME4: Chat 4F 27
Luxon Rd. DA13: Meop 1D 35
LUXTED 1D 33
Luxted Rd. BR6: Downe 1D 33
Lybury La. AL3: Redb 1A 6
Lycrome Rd. HP5: Ches, Lye G 3D 5
LYE GREEN 3D 5
Lye Grn. Rd. HP5: Ches 3D 5
Lye La. AL2: Brick W 3B 6
Lymington Rd. NW6 . . . . .3E 15
Lynchford Rd. GU14: Farnb 3B 28
(not continuous)
LYNCH HILL 4D 13
Lyncroft Av. HA5: Pinn 2B 14
Lyndhurst Av. HA8: Edg 2D 15
LYNE 4E 21
Lyne Crossing Rd. KT16: Lyne 4E 21
Lyne La. GU25: Vir W 4E 21
KT16: Lyne 4E 21
Lyne Rd. GU25: Vir W 4E 21
Lynton Rd. W3 . . . . .4D 15
Lynwood Rd. KT17: Eps 1D 31
W5 .4C 14
Lyonsdown Rd. EN5: New Bar 1F 15
Lysander Way AL7: W City 1F 7
Lysons Av. GU12: Ash V 3B 28
Lyttelton Rd. N2 . . . . .2F 15

M

Mabledon Pl. WC1 . . . . .4F 15
Macdonald Rd. GU18: Light 1C 28
Mackenzie Rd. BR3: Beck 3B 24
N7 .3A 16
McLeod Rd. SE2 . . . . .1E 25
Maddox Rd. CM20: Har 1D 9
Madeira Rd. CR4: Mitc 3F 23
KT14: W Byf 1F 29
Madeley Rd. W5 . . . . .4D 15
Madles La. CM4: Stock 4D 11
Madrid Rd. GU2: Guild 4E 29
MAGDALEN LAVER 1F 9
Magdalen Rd. SW18 . . . . .2F 23
Magpie Bottom TN15: Knat 1A 34
Magpie Hall La. BR2: Brom 4D 25
Magpie Hall Rd. ME4: Chat 4F 27
WD23: B Hea 1C 14
Magpie La. CM13: L War 2B 18
HP7: Cole 1D 13
MAIDA VALE 4E 15
Maida Va. W9 . . . . .4E 15
MAIDENHEAD 4B 12
MAIDENHEAD COURT 4C 12
Maidenhead Rd. RG40: W'ham 3A 20
RG42: Warf 3B 20
SL4: Wind 1C 20
SL6: Cook, Maide 4B 12
MAIDEN'S GREEN 2B 20
Maiden's Grn. SL4: Wink 2B 20
MAIDSTONE 3F 35
Maidstone Rd. BR8: Swan 3E 25
DA14: Sidc, Swan 3E 25
ME1: Roch 4E 27
ME4: Chat, Roch 4E 27
ME5: B Hill 1F 35
(not continuous)
ME18: W Peck 4C 34
Maidstone Rd. ME18: W'bury 4D 35
TN11: Had 4C 34
TN12: Five G 4D 35
TN12: Mard 4F 35
TN12: Stap 4F 35
TN15: Bor G, Wro 2B 34
TN15: Seal 2A 34
Main Av. EN1: Enf 1B 16
Main Rd. BR2: Kes 1C 32
BR5: St P 3E 25
BR8: Crock 4F 25
BR8: Swan 3F 25
CM1: Broom 1E 11
CM3: Bor 1F 11
CM3: Broom, Chelm, Lit W 1E 11
CM3: Dan 2F 11
CM3: E Han 3F 11
CM3: Ret 4F 11
DA3: Lfield, Long H 3B 26
DA4: Sutt H 3A 26
DA14: Sidc 2D 25
DA15: Sidc 2D 25
HP27: Lac G 3A 4
ME3: C'den, Hoo 3F 27
(not continuous)
RM1: Rom 2F 17
RM2: Rom 2F 17
TN8: Crock H, Eden 4D 33
TN14: Sund 3E 33
TN16: Big H, Westrm 1C 32
Main St. HP22: W Tur 1A 4
TW13: Hanw 3B 22
Maize La. RG42: Warf 3B 20
Major Rd. E15 . . . . .3C 16
Majors Farm Rd. SL3: Dat 1E 21
Malden Cres. NW1 . . . . .3F 15
MALDEN GREEN 4E 23
MALDEN JUNC. 4D 23
Malden Rd. KT3: N Mald 4D 23
KT4: Wor Pk 4D 23
NW5 . . . . .3F 15
SM3: Cheam 4E 23
MALDEN RUSHETT 1C 30
Malden Way KT3: N Mald 4D 23
Malders La. SL6: Maide 4B 12
Maldon Rd.
CM2: Dan, Gt B, Sando 2E 11
CM2: Gt B 2E 11
CM3: Dan 2F 11
CM4: Marg 3D 11
Mall, The HA3: Kent 2D 15
W5 .4D 15
Malling Rd. ME6: Snod 1D 35
ME18: Mere 3D 35
ME18: Test 3D 35
ME19: Leyb 1D 35
Malpas Rd. SE4 . . . . .1B 24
Malt Hill RG42: Warf 3B 20
Malthouse Rd. TN15: Stans 1B 34
Maltings Hill CM5: More 2F 9
Maltings La. CM16: Epp 3E 9
Maltings Rd. SS11: Bat 1F 19
Manchester Rd. E14 . . . . .1C 24
Mandeville Rd. HP21: A'bury 1A 4
UB5: N'olt 3B 14
Mandeville St. E5 . . . . .3B 16
Mandeville Way
SS15: Bas, Lain, Lan H 2D 19
Manford Way IG7: Chig 1D 17
Mangrove La. SG13: Hertf 1A 8
Mangrove Rd. SG13: Hertf 1A 8
MANOR CIRCUS 2D 23
Manorcrofts Rd. TW20: Egh 3E 21
Manor Dr. N20 . . . . .1F 15
Mnr. Farm Rd. HA0: Wemb 4C 14
MANOR HOUSE 3A 16
Manor Ho. La. KT23: Bookh 3B 30
Manor La. DA3: Fawk 4B 26
SE12 . . . . .2C 24
TN15: Fawk 4B 26
MANOR PARK 3D 17
Manor Pk. Rd. BR4: W W'ck 4B 24
BR7: Chst 3D 25
NW10 . . . . .4D 15
Manor Rd. AL10: Hat 1D 7
BR3: Beck 3B 24
CR4: Mitc 3F 23
DA1: Cray 2F 25
DA3: Lfield, Long H 4C 26
DA8: Erith 1F 25
DA10: Swans 2B 26
E15 .4C 16
E16 .4C 16
GU2: Guild 4E 29
GU10: Tong 4B 28
GU12: Ash 4B 28
IG7: Chig 2D 17
IG8: Wfd G 2D 17
IG10: H Beech 4C 8
IG10: Lough 1C 16
N16 . . . . .3A 16
RM4: Abr, Stap A 1E 17
SE25 . . . . .3B 24
SL4: Wind 1D 21
SM6: Wall 4F 23
TW9: Rich 2D 23
TW11: Tedd 3C 22
(not continuous)
Manor Rd. Nth. KT7: T Ditt 4C 22
KT10: Hin W, T Ditt 4C 22
Manor Rd. Sth. KT10: Hin W 4C 22
Manor Vw. N3 . . . . .2E 15
Manor Way WD6: Bore 4D 7
Manorway, The
SS17: Stan H, Corr 4D 19
Mansell St. E1 . . . . .4A 16
Mansfield Hill E4 . . . . .1B 16
Mansfield Rd. NW3 . . . . .3F 15
Mansion La. SL0: Iver 4F 13
Manston Rd. CM20: Har 1D 9
Mantle Rd. SE4 . . . . .2B 24
MANTLES GREEN 4D 5
MANWOOD GREEN 1A 10
Manwood Rd. SE4 . . . . .2B 24
Mapesbury Rd. NW2 . . . . .3E 15
MAPLE CROSS 1F 13
Maple Rd. KT6: Surb 4C 22
RH1: Redh 4F 31
SE20 . . . . .3B 24
MAPLESCOMBE 4A 26
Maplescombe La. DA4: Farni 4A 26
TN15: Farni 4A 26
Mapleton Rd.
TN8: F Elm, Westrm 3D 33
TN16: Westrm 3D 33
Maple Way SS8: Can I 4F 19
MARBLE ARCH 4F 15
Marcilly Rd. SW18 . . . . .2F 23
MARDEN ASH 3A 10
Mare St. E8 . . . . .4B 16
Marford Rd. AL8: Lem 1D 7
Margaret Rd. EN4: E Barn 4F 7
MARGARET RODING 1B 10
MARGARETTING 3D 11
Margaretting Rd. CM1: Writ 3D 11
CM2: Chelm, Gall 3D 11
MARGARETTING TYE 3D 11
MARGERY 3E 31
Margery La. KT20: Lwr K 3E 31
Margery St. WC1 . . . . .4A 16
Margetts La. ME1: Bur 1E 35

Marigold La. CM4: Stock 4D 11
Markedge La. CR5: Coul 3F 31
RH1: Reig 3F 31
Marketfield Way RH1: Redh 4F 31
Market La. SL3: L'ly 1F 21
Market Pl. NW11 2E 15
RG40: W'ham 3A 20
RM4: Abr 4E 9
SL9: Chal P 2E 13
Market Rd. CM1: Chelm 2E 11
N7 3A 16
Market Sq. BR1: Brom 3C 24
(not continuous)
TN16: Westrm 3D 33
Market St. DA1: Dart 2A 26
RG12: Brac 3B 20
MARK HALL NORTH 1E 9
MARK HALL SOUTH 1E 9
Markhouse Rd. E17 2B 16
MARKS GATE 2E 17
Marks Hall La. CM6: M Rod 1B 10
Marlborough Av. HA4: Ruis 2A 14
Marlborough Rd. N19 3F 15
(not continuous)
Marley Vw. ME1: Roch 4F 27
MARLING PARK 3B 22
Marlin Hill HP23: Hasto 1C 4
MARLOW 3A 12
MARLOW BOTTOM 2A 12
Marlow Bottom SL7: Marl 2A 12
Marlow Comn. SL7: Marl 3A 12
Marlowes HP1: Hem H 2F 5
Marlow Hill HP11: H Wy 2A 12
Marlow Rd. HP11: H Wy 2A 12
HP14: L End 2A 12
SL6: Maide 4B 12
(Bad Godesberg Way)
SL6: Maide 3A 12
(Lee La.)
SL7: Lit M 3B 12
SL7: Marl 2A 12
(Clay La., not continuous)
SL7: Marl 3A 12
(Temple La.)
SL8: Bou E 3B 12
MARLPIT HILL 4D 33
Marlpit La. CR5: Coul 2A 32
Marrod's Bottom HP7: Win H 1C 12
Marroway HP22: W Tur 1A 4
Marrowbrook La. GU14: Cove 3A 28
MARSH 1A 4
Marshall Rd. GU47: Col T 1A 28
MARSHALSWICK 1C 6
Marshalswick La. AL1: St A 1C 6
Marsham St. SW1 1F 23
Marshcroft La. HP23: Tring 1C 4
Marshfoot Rd. RM16: Grays 1C 26
RM17: Grays 1C 26
Marshgate La. E15 3B 16
(not continuous)
Marsh Hill E9 3B 16
EN9: Naze, Walt A 3C 8
Marsh La. CM13: Mount 4C 10
HA7: Stan 1C 14
HP22: S Man 1A 4
NW7 1D 15
SL4: Dor 1C 20
SL6: Dor, Dor R, Tap 4C 12
MARSHMOOR 2E 7
Marsh Rd. HA5: Pinn 2B 14
Marsh Wall E14 1B 24
Marsh Way RM13: Rain 4F 17
Martime Way ME4: Chat 3F 27
Martindale Av. GU15: Camb 2C 28
Martindale Rd. TW4: Houn 2B 22
Martinsend La. HP16: Gt Miss 3B 4
MARTIN'S HERON 3B 20
Martins La. TN12: E Pec 4D 35
Martin Way SM4: Mord 3E 23
SW20 3E 23
MARTYR'S GREEN 2A 30
Martyr's La. GU21: Wok 1E 29
Marvels La. SE12 2C 24
(not continuous)
MARYLANDS INTERCHANGE 4C 10
MARYLEBONE 4F 15
MARYLEBONE FLYOVER 4F 15
Marylebone High St. W1 4F 15
Marylebone Rd. NW1 4F 15
W2 4F 15
Mascalls La.
CM14: B'wood, Gt War 1A 18
MASHBURY 1C 10
Mashbury Rd. CM1: Chi J 1D 11
CM1: Gt W, Mash 1C 10
CM3: Gt W 1C 10
Masons Av. HA3: W'stone 2C 14
Mason's Bri. Rd.
RH1: Redh, Salf 4F 31
Masons Hill BR2: Brom 3C 24
MASWELL PARK 2C 22
MATCHING 1F 9
MATCHING GREEN 1F 9
Matching La. CM6: W Rod 1A 10
Matching Rd. CM17: Har, Mat T 1E 9
CM17: M Grn, Mat T 1F 9
MATCHING TYE 1F 9
Matthews La.
ME18: Had, W Peck 4C 34
TN11: Had 4C 34
Matthias Rd. N16 3A 16
Maultway, The GU15: Camb 1B 28
Maury Rd. N16 3B 16
MAWNEY 2E 17
Mawney Rd. RM7: Mawney 2E 17
Maxted Rd. HP2: Hem H 1A 6
Maxwell Rd. HP9: Beac 2D 13
Maybank Av. HA0: Wemb 3C 14
MAYBURY 2E 29
Maybury Hill GU22: Wok 2E 29
Maybury Rd. GU21: Wok 2E 29
Mayes La. CM2: Sando 2F 11
CM3: Dan 2F 11
Mayes Rd. N22 2A 16
MAYFAIR 4F 15
Mayfield Rd. CR2: Sande 1A 32
GU14: Cove, Farnb 2A 28
KT12: Hers 4B 22
RM8: Dag 3E 17
W3 4D 15
MAYFORD 2E 29
Mayford Grn. GU22: Wok 2E 29
Maygrove Rd. NW6 3E 15
Maylands Av. HP2: Hem H 1A 6
Mayow Rd. SE23 3B 24
SE26 3B 24
Mayplace Rd. E. DA1: Cray 2F 25
DA7: Bex, Cray 2E 25
Mayplace Rd. W. DA7: Bex 2E 25
MAYPOLE 1E 33
Maypole Rd. BR6: Chels 4E 25
MAY'S GREEN 2A 30
Mays La. EN5: Ark, Barn 1E 15
Maze Hill SE3 1C 24
SE10 1C 24
Mead La. KT16: Chert 4F 21
Meadow La. SL4: Eton W 1D 21
Meadow Ri. CM11: Bill 1D 19
MEAD VALE 4F 31
Mead Way BR2: Hayes 4C 24
CR5: Coul 2A 32
Meadway EN5: Barn, New Bar 4E 7
NW11 2E 15
TW2: Twick 2C 22
Medfield St. SW15 2E 23
MEDHURST ROW 4E 33
Median Rd. E5 3B 16
Medlar St. SE5 1A 24
Medway Rd. ME7: G'ham 3F 27
(not continuous)
Medway St. ME4: Chat 3F 27
Melbourne Av. CM1: Chelm 1D 11
Melbourne Rd. WD23: Bush 1B 14
Melfort Rd. CR7: Thor H 3A 24
Melliker La. DA13: Meop 4C 26
Mellow La. E. UB4: Hayes 4A 14
Mellow La. W. UB10: Hil 4A 14
Melton St. NW1 4F 15
Melville Av. UB6: G'frd 3C 14
Melville Gdns. N13 1A 16
MEOPHAM 4C 26
MEOPHAM GREEN 4C 26
MEOPHAM STATION 4C 26
Merantun Way SW19 3F 23
Merbury Rd. SE28 4D 17
Mercian Way SL1: Slou 4C 12
Mercury Gdns. RM1: Rom 2F 17
Mere Rd. KT20: Tad 3E 31
SL1: Slou 1D 21
MEREWORTH 3C 34
Mereworth Rd.
ME18: Mere, W Peck 3C 34
MERIDEN 4B 6
Meriden Way WD25: Wat 4B 6
Meridian Way EN3: Pond E 1B 16
EN9: Walt A 3B 8
N9 1B 16
N18 1B 16
Merland Ri. KT18: Tatt C 2E 31
KT20: Tad 2E 31
MERLE COMMON 4C 32
Merlin Cres. HA8: Edg 2D 15
Merlin Way
CM16: N Weald, Twood 2E 9
Merrick Rd. UB2: S'hall 1B 22
Merrielands Cres. RM9: Dag 4E 17
Merrivale N14 1F 15
MERROW 4E 29
Merrow La. GU4: Burp, Guild 4F 29
Merrow Way CR0: New Ad 1C 32
Merryboys Rd. ME3: Cli W 2E 27
MERRY HILL 1B 14
Merry Hill Rd. WD23: Bush 1B 14
Mersea Cres. SS12: Wick 1F 19
MERSTHAM 3F 31
Merstham Rd. RH1: Blet 3A 32
MERTON 3F 23
Merton High St. SW19 3F 23
MERTON PARK 3E 23
Merton Rd. SW18 2E 23
SW19 3E 23
Merttins Rd. SE15 2B 24
Meudon Av. GU14: Farnb 3B 28
Michaels La. DA3: Fawk 4B 26
TN15: Fawk 4B 26
MICKLEFIELD 1B 12
MICKLEFIELD GREEN 4F 5
Micklefield Rd. HP13: H Wy 1B 12
MICKLEHAM 3C 30
Mickleham By-Pass RH5: Mick 3C 30
MICKLEHAM DOWNS 3C 30
Middlefield Rd. EN11: Hodd 1B 8
MIDDLE GREEN 4E 13
Middle Grn. SL3: L'ly 4E 13
Middlegreen Rd. SL3: L'ly 1E 21
Middle Hill TW20: Egh, Eng G 3E 21
Middle La. HP3: Bov 3E 5
N8 2A 16
Middlemead
CM2: Sth H, W Han 4E 11
CM3: Sth H, W Han, Ret 4E 11
Middle Pk. Av. SE9 2C 24
Middlesex CC Club 4F 15
Middle St. EN9: Naze 2C 8
GU5: Shere 4A 30
RH3: Bet, Aroc 4D 31
Middleton Hall La.
CM15: B'wood 1B 18
Middleton Rd. SM4: Mord, Cars 4E 23
Midfield Way BR5: St P 3E 25
Midland Rd. HP2: Hem H 2F 5
NW1 4F 15
Midleton Rd. GU2: Guild 4E 29
Mid St. RH1: S Nut 4A 32
Milbourne La. KT10: Esh 4C 22
Mildmay Gro. N1 3A 16
Mildmay Pk. N1 3A 16
MILE END 4B 16
MILE END GREEN 3B 26
Mile End Rd. E1 4B 16
E3 4B 16
Mile Ho. La. AL1: St A 2C 6
Miles Gray Rd. SS14: Bas 2D 19
Miles La. KT11: Cobh 1B 30
RH8: Tand 4B 32
RH9: Tand 4B 32
Milespit Hill NW7 1E 15
MILESTONE GREEN 2D 23
Milkwood Rd. SE24 2A 24
Millbank SW1 1A 24
Mill Bri. SG14: Hertf 1A 8
Millbrook GU1: Guild 4E 29
Mill Brook Rd. BR5: St M Cry 3E 25
MILL END 1F 13
Mill End Rd. HP12: H Wy 1A 12
Millennium Way SE10 1C 24
MILLER'S GREEN 2B 10
Miller's La. IG7: Chig 1E 17
Milley La. RG10: Har H 1A 20
Milley Rd. RG10: W Law 1A 20
Millfields Rd. E5 3B 16
Millfiields HP5: Ches 3D 5
(not continuous)
MILL GREEN
AL9 1E 7
CM4 3C 10
Mill Grn. AL9: Ess 1F 7
Mill Grn. La. AL7: W City 1E 7
AL9: Hat 1E 7
Mill Grn. Rd. CM4: Fry, Mill G 3C 10
CR4: Mitc 4F 23
MILL HILL 1E 15
Mill Hill CM2: Gall 3D 11
W3 1D 23
MILL HILL CIRCUS 1D 15
Mill Hill La. DA12: Shorne 3D 27
Mill Hill Rd. SW13 1E 23
Mill Ho. La. KT16: Chert 3F 21
TW20: Thorpe 3F 21
Mill La. BR6: Downe 1D 33
CM1: Broom, Chelm, Spr 1E 11
CM3: Lit B 2F 11
CM4: Mill G 3C 10
CM4: Stock 4D 11
CM5: H Ongar, Ongar 3A 10
CM5: More 1F 9
CM5: Toot H 3F 9
CM15: Hook E 4B 10
EN10: Brox 2B 8
GU24: Pirb 3C 28
GU46: Yat 1A 28
HP7: Amer 4D 5
Mill La. HP16: Gt Miss 1E 13
HP27: M Ris 2A 4
ME5: B Hill 1F 35
ME18: Yald 4E 35
NW6 3E 15
RG12: Brac 3A 20
RH8: Oxt 4C 32
RM4: Nave 4F 9
RM6: Chad H 2E 17
RM16: Ors 4C 18
(not continuous)
SL5: S'hill 3D 21
SL6: Cook 3B 12
(not continuous)
SL6: Hur 4A 12
SL6: Tap 4C 12
SL9: Ger X 2E 13
TN11: Hild 4A 34
TN15: Bor G, Igh 2B 34
TN15: Under 4A 34
TW20: Thorpe 3F 21
WD4: K Lan 3A 6
MILL MEADS 4C 16
Mill Pond Rd. DA1: Dart 2A 26
Mill Rd. CM1: G Eas 1C 10
CM4: Stock 4D 11
CM11: Bill 1D 19
KT11: Cobh 2B 30
KT17: Eps 1D 31
KT20: Tad 3E 31
ME7: G'ham 3F 27
RM15: Avel 4A 18
UB7: W Dray 1F 21
MILL STREET 2D 35
Mill St. CM17: Har 1E 9
ME15: Maids 3F 35
ME19: E Mal 2D 35
RH1: Redh 4F 31
MILLWALL 1B 24
Millwall FC 1B 24
Mill Way KT18: H'ly, Lea 3D 31
KT22: Lea 3D 31
Milman Rd. NW6 4E 15
MILTON 2C 26
Milton Rd. CR3: Cat'm 2A 32
DA10: Swans 2B 26
DA12: Grav'nd 2C 26
Milton St. DA10: Swans 2B 26
MIMBRIDGE 1E 29
Mimms Hall Rd. EN6: Pot B 3E 7
Mimms La. EN6: Ridge 3D 7
WD7: Shenl 3D 7
Mincing La. GU24: Chob 1D 29
MINLEY 2A 28
Minley La. GU17: Min 2A 28
Minley Link Rd. GU14: Cove 3A 28
Minley Rd. GU14: Cove 2A 28
GU17: Min 2A 28
GU51: Fleet 2A 28
MINNOW END 1D 11
Minories EC3 4A 16
Missenden Rd. HP5: Ches 3D 5
HP15: Gt Kin 4B 4
Miswell La. HP23: Tring 1C 4
MITCHAM 3F 23
Mitcham La. SW16 3F 23
Mitcham Rd. CR0: C'don 4A 24
SW17 3F 23
Mitchley Av. CR2: Sande 1A 32
CR8: Purl 1A 32
Mitchley Hill CR2: Sande 1A 32
Moat La. HP16: Pre 3B 4
MOBWELL 3B 4
MOBY DICK 2E 17
MOCKBEGGAR
ME3 2E 27
TN12 4E 35
MOGADOR 3E 31
Mogador Rd. KT20: Lwr K 3E 31
Mogden La. TW7: Isle 2C 22
Molesey Pk. Rd.
KT8: W Mole, E Mos 4B 22
Molesey Rd. KT8: W Mole 4B 22
KT12: Hers, Walt T, W Mole
4B 22
Molesworth St. SE13 2C 24
Mollison Av.
EN3: Brim, Enf L, Enf W,
Pond E, Walt C 4B 8
Mollison Dr. SM6: Wall 1A 32
Mollison Way HA8: Edg 2D 15
Molrams La. CM2: Gt B 2E 11
Momples Rd. CM20: Har 1E 9
Monarchs Way EN8: Walt C 3B 8
MONEYHILL 1F 13
MONEYROW GREEN 1B 20
Moneyrow Grn. SL6: Holy 1B 20
MONKEN HADLEY 4E 7
Monkham's La. IG8: Wfd G 1C 16
Monks La. TN8: Eden 4C 32
MONKS ORCHARD 4B 24
Monks Orchard Rd. BR3: Beck 4B 24
MONKS RISBOROUGH 2A 4
Monkswell La. CR5: Coul 3E 31
Monkton La. GU9: Hale 4A 28
Monmouth Rd. N9 1B 16
Monmouth St. WC2 4A 16
Montague Pl. WC1 4F 15
Montague Waye UB2: S'hall 1B 22
Montagu Rd. N9 1B 16
N18 1B 16
Montem La. SL1: Slou 1D 21
Montpelier Row SE3 1C 24
Montrose Av. HA8: Edg 2D 15
Monument Hill KT13: Weyb 4A 22
Monument La. SL9: Chal P 1E 13
Monument Rd. GU21: Wok 1E 29
Monument Way N17 2A 16
Moordale Av. RG42: Brac 3A 20
Moore's Rd. RH4: Dork 4C 30
Moorfield Rd. UB9: Den 2F 13
Moorgate EC2 4A 16
Moor Hall La.
CM3: B'acre, Dan, E Han 3F 11
Moor Hall Rd. CM17: Har 1E 9
Moorhall Rd. UB9: Hare 2F 13
MOORHOUSE 3D 33
MOORHOUSE BANK 3D 33
Moorhouse Rd.
RH8: Limp, Westrm 3D 33
TN16: Westrm 3D 33
MOOR JUNC. 1F 21
Moor La. KT9: Chess 4D 23
TW18: Staines 2F 21
TW19: Staines 2F 21
WD3: Rick 1A 14
WD3: Sarr 4F 5
MOOR PARK 1A 14
Moors Wlk. AL7: W City 1F 7
Morants Ct. Rd. TN13: Dun G 2F 33
MORDEN 3E 23
Morden Hall Rd. SM4: Mord 3F 23
MORDEN PARK 4E 23
Morden Rd. CR4: Mitc 3F 23
SW19 3E 23
Moreland St. EC1 4A 16
More La. KT10: Esh 4B 22
Mores La. CM14: Pil H 4A 10
MORETON 2F 9
Moreton Bri.
CM5: More, Ongar 2F 9
MORETON MILL 1F 9
Moreton Rd. CM5: Fyf 2A 10
CM5: More, Ongar 2F 9
CM5: Ongar 2F 9
Morgan's La. UB3: Hayes 4A 14
Morland Rd. CR0: C'don 4A 24
Morley Hill SS17: Stan H 3D 19
Morley's Rd. TN14: Weald 4F 33
Morning La. E9 3B 16
Mornington Rd. UB6: G'frd 4B 14
Morris Rd. E14 4B 16
Mortimer Rd. NW10 4E 15
Mortimer St. W1 4F 15
MORTLAKE 2D 23
Mortlake High St. SW14 2D 23
Mortlake Rd. TW9: Kew, Rich 1D 23
Morton Way N14 1F 15
Morval Rd. SW2 2A 24
MOSS END 2B 20
Moss La. HA5: Pinn 2B 14
Mote Rd. ME15: Maids 3F 35
TN11: S'brne 3A 34
TN15: S'brne, Ivy H 3A 34
Motherwell Way RM20: W Thur 1B 26
MOTSPUR PARK 4E 23
Motspur Pk. KT3: N Mald 4D 23
MOTTINGHAM 2D 25
Mottingham La. SE9 2C 24
SE12 2C 24
Mottingham Rd. SE9 2D 25
Mott St. E4 4C 8
IG10: H Beech, Lough 4C 8
MOULSHAM 2E 11
Moulsham St. CM2: Chelm 2E 11
(not continuous)
Mount, The GU2: Guild 4E 29
Mount Av. W5 4C 14
MOUNT END 3E 9
Mountgrove Rd. N5 3A 16
Mt. Harry Rd. TN13: S'oaks 3F 33
Mount La. UB9: Den 3F 13
MOUNTNESSING 4C 10
Mountnessing By-Pass
CM15: Mount, Shenf 4C 10
Mountnessing La. CM15: Dodd 4B 10
Mountnessing Rd.
CM4: Bmore, Mount, W Grn
3B 10
CM12: Bill 4C 10
CM15: Mount, W Grn 3B 10
Mount Nugent HP5: Ches 2D 5
MOUNT PLEASANT 2F 13
Mt. Pleasant EN4: Cockf 4F 7
HA0: Wemb 4D 15
Mt. Pleasant La. AL2: Brick W 3B 6
Mt. Pleasant Rd. N17 2A 16
Mount Rd.
CM16: Fidd H, Stap T, They M
3E 9
RM4: Stap T 3E 9
Mounts Hill SL4: Wink 2C 20
Mounts Rd. DA9: Ghithe 2B 26
MOVERS LANE 4D 17
Movers La. IG11: Bark 4D 17
MOWDEN 1F 11
Mowden Hall La. CM3: Hat P 1F 11
MOWSHURST 4D 33
MUCKING 4D 19
MUCKINGFORD 1D 27
Muckingford Rd. RM18: W Til 1C 26
SS17: Linf, W Til 1C 26
Mucking Wharf Rd.
SS17: Stan H 4D 19
MUGSWELL 3F 31
Mulberry Grn. CM17: Har 1E 9
Mulberry Way E18 2C 16
Mulgrave Rd. SM2: Sutt 1E 31
Mumfords La. SL9: Chal P 2E 13
Mundaydean La. SL7: Marl 2A 12
Mungo Pk. Rd. RM13: Rain 3F 17
Munster Rd. SW6 1E 23
Murchison Av. DA5: Bexl 2E 25
Murdoch Rd. RG40: W'ham 3A 20
Murray Rd. KT16: Ott 1F 29
Murrell Hill La. RG42: Bin 3A 20
Murthering La.
RM4: Nave, Stap A 1F 17
Mussenden La.
DA3: Fawk, Hort K 4A 26
DA4: Fawk, Hort K 4A 26
MUSWELL HILL 2F 15
Muswell Hill N10 2F 15
Muswell Hill B'way. N10 2F 15
Muswell Hill Rd. N6 2F 15
N10 2F 15
Mutton La. EN6: Pot B, S Mim 3E 7
Myddelton Av. EN1: Enf 4A 8
Myddelton Pk. N20 1F 15
Myddleton Rd. N22 2A 16
MYRKE 1D 21
MYTCHETT 3B 28
Mytchett Pl. Rd. GU12: Ash V 3B 28
GU16: Myt 3B 28
Mytchett Rd. GU16: Myt 3B 28

N

NAG'S HEAD 3A 16
Nags Head La.
CM14: B'wood, Upm 2A 18
HP16: Gt Miss 4B 4
(not continuous)
RM14: Upm 2A 18
Nags Head Rd. EN3: Pond E 4B 8
Nairdwood La. HP16: Pre 3B 4
Nallhead Rd. TW13: Hanw 3B 22
Nap, The WD4: K Lan 3A 6
NAPHILL 4A 4
Napier Rd. ME7: G'ham 4F 27
NAPSBURY 2C 6
Napsbury La. AL1: St A 2C 6
Narcot La. HP8: Chal G 1E 13
SL9: Chal P 1E 13
Narrow La. CR6: Warl 2B 32
Narrow St. E14 4B 16
Nascot Wood Rd. WD17: Wat 4A 6
NASH 4C 24
Nash Bank DA13: Meop, Ist R 3C 26
Nashdom La. SL1: Burn 3C 12
Nash La. BR2: Kes 1C 32
NASH LEE 1A 4
Nash Lee Rd. HP17: Terr 1A 4
Nashleigh Hill HP5: Ches 3D 5
NASH MILLS 2A 6
Nash Mills La. HP3: Hem H 2A 6
NASH STREET 3C 26
NAST HYDE 2D 7
Nathan's La. CM1: E Com, Writ 2C 10
Nathan Way SE28 1D 25
NAVESTOCK 4F 9
NAVESTOCK SIDE 4A 10
Navestockside
CM14: Kel C, N'side 4A 10
NAZEING 2C 8
Nazeing Comn. EN9: Naze 2C 8
NAZEING GATE 2C 8
NAZEING LONG GREEN 2C 8
Nazeing New Rd. EN10: Brox 2B 8
Nazeing Rd. EN9: Brox, Naze 2C 8
NEASDEN 3D 15
NEASDEN JUNC. 3D 15
Neasden La. NW10 3D 15
Neasden La. Nth. NW10 3D 15
Nelson Rd. E4 2B 16
ME7: G'ham 4F 27
TW2: Whitt 2B 22
TW3: Houn 2B 22
TW6: H'row A 1A 22
Nene Rd. TW6: H'row A 1A 22
Nepicar La. TN15: Wro 2C 34
Netherhall Rd. CM19: Roy 1C 8
Nether Mayne
SS16: Bas, Vange 2E 19
Netherne Dr. CR5: Coul 2F 31
Netherne La. CR5: Coul 3F 31
RH1: Coul 3F 31
NETHERNE-ON-THE-HILL 2F 31
NETHER STREET 1B 10
Nether St. CM5: Abb R, Beau R 1A 10
N3 2E 15
N12 2E 15
NETTESWELL 1D 9
NETTLEDEN 1E 5
Nettleden Rd. HP1: Hem H, Nett 1E 5
HP4: Pott E 1E 5
NETTLESTEAD 3D 35
NETTLESTEAD GREEN 4D 35
Nettlestead La. ME18: W'bury 3D 35
NEVENDON 2F 19
Nevendon Rd. SS13: Bas 2E 19
(not continuous)
NEW ADDINGTON 1C 32
Newark La. GU22: Pyr 2F 29
GU23: Rip 2F 29
Newarks Rd. CM1: G Eas 1C 10
NEW ASH GREEN 4B 26
NEW BARN 3C 26
NEW BARNET 4F 7
New Barn La. TN14: Cud 2D 33
TN16: Cud, Westrm 2D 33
Newbarn La. HP9: See G 1D 13
New Barn Rd. BR8: Swan 3F 25
DA3: Ist R, Lfield 3B 26
DA13: Ist R, Lfield, Nflt G, Sflt
3B 26
New Barn St. E13 4C 16
NEW BECKENHAM 3B 24
New Bond St. W1 4F 15
New Bowers Way CM1: Spr 1E 11
New Bri. St. EC4 4A 16
Newbury Av. EN3: Enf L 4B 8
NEWBURY PARK 2D 17
Newbury Rd. TW6: H'row A 1A 22
New Cavendish St. W1 4F 15
NEW CHARLTON 1C 24
New City Rd. E13 4C 16
NEW CROSS 1B 24
NEW CROSS 1B 24
NEW CROSS GATE 1B 24
NEW CROSS GATE 1B 24
New Cross Rd. SE14 1B 24
New Cut ME15: E Far 3F 35
New Cut Rd. ME14: Weav 3F 35
NEW DENHAM 3F 13
NEWELL GREEN 3B 20
NEW ELTHAM 2D 25
New Farm Dr. RM4: Abr 4E 9
New Forest Ride RG12: Brac 4B 20
Newgate St Village
SG13: New S 2A 8
NEWGATE STREET 2F 7
Newgate St. SG13: New S 2F 7
Newgatestreet Rd. EN7: G Oak 2A 8
NEW GREENS 1C 6
NEW GROUND 1D 5
Newground Rd.
HP23: Aldb, New G 1D 5
Newham Way E6 4C 16
E16 4C 16
NEW HAW 1F 29
New Haw Rd. KT15: Add 4F 21
New Heston Rd. TW5: Hest 1B 22
NEW HOUSE 2C 26
NEWHOUSE 1A 10
New Ho. La. DA11: Nflt, Grav'nd 2C 26
NEW HYTHE 2E 35
New Hythe La. ME20: Lark 2E 35
NEWINGTON 1A 24
Newington Butts SE11 1A 24
Newington C'way. SE1 1A 24
Newington Grn. N1 3A 16
Newington Grn. Rd. N1 3A 16
New Inn La. GU4: Burp 4E 29
New Kent Rd. SE1 1A 24
New Kings Rd. SW6 1E 23
Newlands La. DA13: Meop 1C 34
Newlands Pk. SE26 3B 24
New La. GU4: Sut G 3E 29
New Lodge Chase CM3: Lit B 2F 11
New London Rd. CM2: Chelm 2E 11
(not continuous)
NEW MALDEN 3D 23
NEWMAN'S END 1F 9
New Mile Rd. SL5: Asc 3C 20
NEW MILL 1C 4
New Nabbotts Way CM1: Spr 1E 11
NEWNEY GREEN 2C 10
New Nth. Rd. IG6: Ilf 2D 17
N1 3A 16
New Oxford St. WC1 4F 15
New Pk. Rd. SW2 2A 24
New Plaistow Rd. E15 4C 16
New Pond Rd. HP15: Holm G 4C 4
Newport Rd. TW6: H'row A 1A 22
New Pound La. ME18: Mere 3C 34
New Rd. E1 4B 16
E4 1B 16
GU4: Chil, Guild 4E 29
GU4: E Clan 4A 30
GU5: Alb 4F 29
GU19: Bag 1C 28
HP4: Berk 1E 5
(Brownlow Rd.)
HP4: Berk 1D 5
(High St.)
HP7: Cole 4D 5
HP10: Ty G 1C 12
HP12: Book, H Wy 1A 12
HP14: W Ash 4A 4
HP22: W Tur 1A 4
HP27: Lac G, W Ash 4A 4
HP27: Pri R 3A 4
(not continuous)
KT8: W Mole 3B 22
KT20: Tad 3E 31
ME1: Roch 4F 27
ME4: Chat 4F 27
ME19: E Mal 2E 35
ME20: Dit 2E 35
RH8: Limp 3C 32
RH8: Tand 4B 32
RM4: Abr 1E 17
RM9: Dag 4E 17
RM10: Dag 4E 17
RM13: Rain 4E 17
SE2 1E 25
SL5: Asc 3C 20
TN14: Sund 3E 33
TW14: Bedf 2A 22
TW17: Shep 3A 22
TW18: Staines 4F 21
New Rd. UB8: Hil 4A 14
WD3: Crox G 1A 14
WD3: Sarr 4F 5
WD7: Rad 4C 6
New Rd. Av. ME4: Chat 4F 27
New Rd. Hill BR2: Kes 1D 33
BR6: Downe 1D 33
NEW SOUTHGATE 2F 15
NEW STREET 4C 26
New St. CM1: Chelm 2E 11
New St. Rd.
DA13: Meop, New A 4C 26
TN15: Ash, New A 4C 26
New Tank Hill Rd. RM15: Avel 1A 26
RM19: Avel, Purf 1A 26
NEW THUNDERSLEY 2F 19
NEW TOWN 2A 26
NEWTOWN 3D 5
Newtown Rd. SL7: Marl 3A 12
New Wanstead E11 2C 16
NEW WAY 1F 9
New Way La. CM17: Har, Mat T 1F 9
New Wickham La. TW20: Egh 3E 21
NEW WINDSOR 2D 21
New Windsor St. UB8: Uxb 4F 13
New Wokingham Rd.
RG45: Crow 4A 20
NEWYEARS GREEN 3A 14
Newyears Grn. La. UB9: Hare 2A 14
New Years La. BR6: Knock 1E 33
TN14: Knock 2D 33
New Zealand Av. KT12: Walt T 4A 22
Nightingale La. AL1: St A 2C 6
BR1: Brom 3C 24
SW4 2F 23
SW12 2F 23
TN14: Ide H 3E 33
Nightingale Pl. SE18 1D 25
Nightingale Rd. N9 1B 16
SM5: Cars 4F 23
WD3: Rick 1F 13
Nightingales La. HP8: Chal G 4E 5
NINE ASHES 3B 10
Nine Ashes Rd.
CM4: Bmore, Nine A 3B 10
CM15: Sto M 3B 10
NINE ELMS 1F 23
Nine Elms La. SW8 1F 23
Ninehams Rd. CR3: Cat'm 2A 32
Nine Mile Ride RG12: Brac 4B 20
RG45: Brac 4A 20
NIZELS 4A 34
Nizels La. TN11: Hild 4A 34
NOAH'S ARK 2A 34
Noah's Ark TN15: Kems'g 2A 34
NOAK BRIDGE 2D 19
NOAK HILL
CM12 2D 19
RM4 1F 17
Noak Hill Rd. CM12: Bill 1D 19
RM3: Rom 1F 17
SS15: Bas, Lain 1D 19
Noble Tree Rd. TN11: Hild 4A 34
NOEL PARK 2A 16
Noel Rd. W3 4D 15
Noke La. AL2: Chis G 2B 6
NOMANSLAND 1C 6
NORBITON 3D 23
NORBURY 3A 24
Norbury Av. SW16 3A 24
Norbury Cres. SW16 3A 24
Norden Rd. SL6: Maide 4B 12
Norfolk Rd. DA12: Grav'nd 2C 26
(not continuous)
SL6: Maide 4B 12
Norheads La. TN16: Big H 2C 32
NORK 2E 31
Norlands La. TW20: Thorpe 3F 21
NORMANDY 4C 28
Normandy Rd. AL3: St A 1C 6
Norman Rd. ME19: W Mal 2D 35
SE10 1B 24
Norreys Dr. SL6: Maide 1B 20
Norris Hill Rd. GU51: Fleet 3A 28
Norsey Rd. CM11: Bill 1D 19
Norsted La. BR6: Prat B 1E 33
NORTH ACTON 4D 15
Nth. Acton Rd. NW10 4D 15
Northall Rd. DA7: Bex 1F 25
North App. WD25: Wat 3B 6
NORTH ASCOT 3C 20
Nth. Ash Rd. DA3: New A 4B 26
Nth. Audley St. W1 4F 15
North Av. CM1: Chelm 1D 11
NORTHAW 3F 7
Northaw Rd. E. EN6: Cuff 3F 7
Northaw Rd. W. EN6: N'thaw 3F 7
NORTH BENFLEET 2F 19
Nth. Birkbeck Rd. E11 3C 16
Northborough Rd. SL2: Slou 4D 13
SW16 3F 23
Northbrook Rd. IG1: Ilf 3D 17
NORTH CAMP 3B 28
NORTH CHEAM 4E 23
NORTHCHURCH 1D 5
Nth. Circular Rd. N3 3E 15
N12 2F 15
N13 1A 16
NW2 3E 15
NW4 3E 15
NW10 4D 15
NW11 3E 15
Northcote Rd. CR0: C'don 4A 24
ME2: Strood 3E 27
SW11 2F 23
NORTH CRAY 3E 25
Nth. Cray Rd. DA5: Bexl 3E 25
DA14: Sidc 3E 25
Northcroft Rd. TW20: Eng G 3E 21
Nth. Dane Way ME5: Chat, Lor 4F 27
Northdown Rd. CR3: Wold 3B 32
NORTH END
DA8 1F 25
NW3 3F 15
North End W14 1E 23
Northend HP3: Hem H 2A 6
North End La. BR6: Downe 1D 33
North End Rd. NW11 3E 15
Northend Rd. DA8: Erith 1F 25
North End Way NW3 3F 15
Northern Perimeter Rd.
TW6: H'row A 1A 22
Northern Perimeter Rd. (West)
TW6: H'row A 1A 22
Northern Rd. SL2: Slou 4D 13
Northern Woods
HP10: Flack H 2C 12
Northey Av. SM2: Cheam 1E 31
NORTH FELTHAM 2B 22
Northfield Av. W5 1C 22
W13 4C 14
NORTHFIELDS 1C 22
NORTH FINCHLEY 1F 15
NORTHFLEET 2B 26
NORTHFLEET GREEN 3C 26
Northfleet Grn. Rd. DA13: Sflt 3C 26
Nth. Folly Rd. ME15: E Far 4E 35
North Ga. ME1: Roch 3F 27
NORTH HALLING 4E 27
NORTH HARROW 2B 14
Nth. Hatton Rd. TW6: H'row A 1A 22

North Hill CM3: Lit B 1F 11
N6 2F 15
SS17: Horn H 3D 19
WD3: Chor 4F 5
North Hill Dr. RM3: Rom 1F 17
NORTH HILLINGDON 4A 14
NORTH HOLMWOOD 4C 30
Nth. Hyde La. TW5: Hest 1B 22
UB2: S'hall 1B 22
Nth. Hyde Rd. UB3: Harl 1A 22
Northiam N12 1E 15
(not continuous)
NORTH KENSINGTON 4E 15
North La. GU12: Alde 4B 28
NORTH LEE 1A 4
North Lee La. HP22: Terr 1A 4
NORTH LOOE 1E 31
North Mdw. ME19: Off 2C 34
NORTH MYMMS 2D 7
NORTH OCKENDON 3B 18
NORTHOLT 3B 14
Northolt Rd. HA2: Harr 3B 14
Nth. Orbital Rd. AL1: St A 2C 6
AL2: Brick W, Chis G 3B 6
WD3: W Hyd 2F 13
WD25: Wat 3B 6
Northover BR1: Brom 2C 24
Nth. Pole La. BR2: Kes 1C 32
Nth. Pole Rd. ME16: Test, Barm 3D 35
ME18: E Mal 3D 35
W10 4E 15
Northridge Way HP1: Hem H 2F 5
North Rd. HP6: Amer 4D 5
HP15: Wid E 1B 12
N6 3F 15
N7 3A 16
RM4: Have B 1F 17
RM15: S Ock, Upm 4B 18
SG14: Hertf 1A 8
UB1: S'hall 4B 14
NORTH SHEEN 2D 23
NORTH STIFFORD 4B 18
North St. EN9: Naze 2C 8
GU1: Guild 4E 29
ME2: Strood 3E 27
ME16: Barm 3E 35
RM1: Rom 2F 17
(not continuous)
RM11: Horn 3F 17
SL4: Wink 2C 20
SM5: Cars 4F 23
SW4 2F 23
NORTH TOWN
GU12 4B 28
SL6 4B 12
Northumberland Av. DA16: Well 2D 25
WC2 4A 16
NORTHUMBERLAND HEATH 1F 25
Northumberland Pk. N17 2B 16
Northumberland Rd.
ME15: Maids 3F 35
North Vw. HA5: Eastc 3B 14
NORTH WATFORD 4B 6
NORTH WEALD BASSETT 2F 9
NORTH WEMBLEY 3C 14
Nth. Western Av. WD25: A'ham 4C 6
WD25: A'ham, Wat 4A 6
NORTHWICK 3F 19
Northwick Rd. SS8: Can I 4F 19
Northwold Rd. E5 3A 16
N16 3A 16
NORTHWOOD 2B 14
NORTHWOOD HILLS 2A 14
Northwood Rd. CR7: Thor H 3A 24
UB9: Hare 2F 13
Northwood Way HA6: Nwood 2B 14
NORTH WOOLWICH 4D 17
Nth. Woolwich Rd. E16 4C 16
NORTON HEATH 2B 10
Norton Heath Rd. CM5: Will 2B 10
Norton La. CM4: Nor H 2B 10
CM5: Nor M 2B 10
NORTON MANDEVILLE 2B 10
Norwich Rd. HA6: Nwood 2A 14
NORWOOD 3A 24
NORWOOD END 1A 10
Norwood End CM5: Fyf 1A 10
NORWOOD GREEN 1B 22
Norwood High St. SE27 2A 24
Norwood La. DA13: Meop 4C 26
SL0: Iver 4F 13
NORWOOD NEW TOWN 3A 24
Norwood Rd. SE24 2A 24
SE27 2A 24
UB2: S'hall 1B 22
NOTTING HILL 4E 15
Notting Hill Ga. W11 4E 15
Nower, The TN14: Knock 2D 33
Nower Hill HA5: Pinn 2B 14
NUNHEAD 2B 24
Nunhead La. SE15 2B 24
NUPER'S HATCH 1F 17
Nupton Dr. EN5: Barn 1E 15
NUPTOWN 2B 20
Nuptown La. RG42: Warf 2B 20
Nursery La. CM3: Dan 2F 11
Nursery Rd. IG10: H Beech 4C 8
TW16: Sun 3A 22
NURSTEAD 3C 26
Nurstead Chu. La.
DA13: Meop, Sole S 3C 26
Nurstead La.
DA3: Lfield, Long H, Meop 3C 26
NUTFIELD 4A 32
Nutfield Marsh Rd. RH1: Nutf 4F 31
Nutfield Rd. RH1: Mers 3F 31
RH1: Redh, Nutf 4F 31
Nuxley Rd. DA17: Belv 1E 25

O

O2, The
(Millennium Dome) 4C 16
Oak Av. TW12: Hamp 3B 22
Oakcroft Rd. KT14: W Byf 1F 29
Oakdene Rd. KT11: Cobh 1B 30
Oakenden Rd.
DA13: Meop, Lud'n 4C 26
Oak End Way SL9: Ger X 2E 13
Oaken La. KT10: Clay 4C 22
Oak Farm La. TN15: Stans 1C 34
Oakfield La. DA1: Dart 2F 25
DA2: Bexl 2F 25
Oakfield Rd. CR0: C'don 4A 24
SE20 3B 24
Oak Hill GU3: Woo V 4D 29
IG8: Wfd G 2C 16
Oak Hill Rd. RM4: Stap A 1F 17
OAKHURST 4A 34
Oakington Av. HA9: Wemb 3D 15
Oaklands La. AL4: S'ford 1D 7
TN16: Big H 1C 32
Oak La. HP5: Bell 2C 4
HP23: St L 2C 4
TN13: S'oaks 3F 33
Oaklawn Rd. KT22: Lea 2C 30
OAKLEIGH PARK 1F 15
Oakleigh Pk. Nth. N20 1F 15
Oakleigh Pk. Sth. N20 1F 15
Oakleigh Rd. Nth. N20 1F 15
Oakleigh Rd. Sth. N11 1F 15
OAKLEY GREEN 1C 20
Oakley Grn. Rd.
SL4: Oak G, Wat O 1C 20
(not continuous)
Oakley Rd. BR2: Brom 4D 25
Oakley Sq. NW1 4F 15
Oakley St. SW3 1F 23
Oakridge La. WD25: A'ham, Rad 4C 6
Oak Rd. CM11: C Hill 2E 19
Oaks Rd. CR0: C'don 4B 24
TW19: Stanw 2F 21
Oakthorpe Rd. N13 1A 16
OAKWOOD 1F 15
Oakwood Av. BR3: Beck 3C 24
Oakwood Hill IG10: Lough 1D 17
Oakwood Rd. AL2: Brick W 3B 6
ME16: Maids 3F 35
Oatlands Av. KT13: Weyb 4A 22
Oatlands Chase KT13: Weyb 4A 22
Oatlands Dr. KT13: Weyb 4A 22
SL1: Slou 4D 13
OATLANDS PARK 4A 22
Occam Rd. GU2: Guild 4D 29
Ockendon Rd.
RM14: N Ock, Upm 3A 18
OCKHAM 2A 30
Ockham La. GU23: Ock 2A 30
KT11: Cobh 2A 30
Ockham Rd. Nth. GU23: Ock 2A 30
KT24: E Hor, W Hor 3A 30
Ockham Rd. Sth. KT24: E Hor 3A 30
Ockwells Rd. SL6: Maide 1B 20
Odessa Rd. E7 3C 16
Odiham Rd. GU10: Up H 4A 28
OFFHAM 2C 34
Offham Rd. ME19: W Mal 2D 35
Offord Rd. N1 3A 16
Okehampton Cres. DA16: Well 1E 25
Old Bethnal Grn. Rd. E2 4B 16
OLD BEXLEY 2E 25
Old Bexley La. DA5: Bexl, Dart 2F 25
Old Bisley Rd. GU16: Frim 2B 28
OLD BRENTFORD 1C 22
Old Brompton Rd. SW5 1E 23
SW7 1F 23
OLDBURY 2B 34
Oldbury La. TN15: Igh 2B 34
Old Chapel Rd. BR8: Crock 4F 25
Old Chatham Rd.
ME14: Maids, S'ing 2F 35
Old Chertsey Rd. GU24: Chob 1E 29
Old Church Hill SS16: Lan H 3D 19
Old Church La. CM13: Mount 4C 10
HA7: Stan 1C 14
NW9 3D 15
TN12: E Pec 3D 35
Old Church Rd. CM3: E Han 3F 11
CM13: Bill, Mount 4C 10
E4 1B 16
ME1: Bur 1E 35
Oldchurch Rd. RM7: Rush G 3F 17
Old Coach Rd., The
SG14: Bir G, Herti 1F 7
OLD COULSDON 2A 32
Old Dover Rd. SE3 1C 24
Old Farleigh Rd. CR2: Sels 1B 32
CR6: Warl 1B 32
Oldfield La. Nth. UB6: G'frd 4C 14
Oldfield La. Sth. UB6: G'frd 4C 14
Oldfield Rd. SL6: Maide 4B 12
Oldfields Rd. SM1: Sutt 4E 23
OLD FORD 4B 16
OLD FORD 4B 16
Old Ford Rd. E2 4B 16
E3 4B 16
Old Gorhambury House 2B 6
Old Hall Ri. CM17: Har 1E 9
OLD HARLOW 1E 9
OLD HATFIELD 1E 7
Old Highway EN11: Hodd 1B 8
Old Hill BR6: Downe 1D 33
BR7: Chst 3D 25
Old Ho. La. CM19: Har, Roy 1C 8
Oldhouse La. WD4: Bucks, Lang 4A 6
OLD ISLEWORTH 1C 22
Old Kent Rd. SE1 1A 24
SE15 1A 24
Old La. KT11: Cobh 2A 30
TN16: Tats 2C 32
Old Lodge La. CR8: Kenl, Purl 1A 32
Old London Rd. AL1: St A 2C 6
CM17: Har 1E 9
(not continuous)
RH5: Mick 3C 30
SS11: Raw 1F 19
TN14: Hals 1E 33
TN14: Knock 2E 33
TN15: Wro 2B 34
Old Loose Hill ME15: Loose 4F 35
Old Maidstone Rd. DA14: Sidc 3E 25
OLD MALDEN 4D 23
Old Malden La. KT4: Wor Pk 4D 23
Old Marylebone Rd. W1 4F 15
Old Mill La. UB8: Cowl 4F 13
Old Mill Rd. UB9: Den 3F 13
WD4: Hunt C 3A 6
Old Nazeing Rd. EN10: Brox 2B 8
OLD OAK COMMON 4D 15
Old Oak Comn. La. NW10 4D 15
W3 4D 15
Old Oak La. NW10 4D 15
Old Oak Rd. W3 4D 15
Old Oxford Rd. HP14: Pidd 1A 12
OLD OXTED 4C 32
Old Park Av. EN2: Enf 4A 8
Old Pk. Ridings N21 1A 16
Old Portsmouth Rd.
GU7: Art, Peasm 4E 29
Old Rectory La. UB9: Den 3F 13
Old Rectory Rd. CM5: Ongar 3F 9
Old Redding HA3: Hrw W 1B 14
Old Reigate Rd. RH3: Bet 4D 31
Old Rd. CM14: Nave, N'side 4F 9
CM17: Har 1E 9
DA1: Cray 2F 25
ME18: W'bury 3D 35
RH3: Bkld 4D 31
RM4: Nave 4F 9
TN12: E Pec 4D 35
Old Rd. E. DA12: Grav'nd 2C 26
Old Rd. W. DA11: Grav'nd 2C 26
Old Roxwell Rd. CM1: Writ 2D 11
Old School La. RH3: Aroc 4D 31
Old Soar Rd. TN15: Plax 3B 34
Old Southend Rd. CM2: Howe G 3F 11
Old Station Rd. IG10: Lough 1D 17
OLD STREET 4A 16
Old St. EC1 4A 16
Old Terry's Lodge Rd.
TN15: W King 2A 34
Old Tilburstow Rd. RH9: S God 4B 32
Old Tovil Rd. ME15: Maids 3F 35
Old Town CR0: C'don 4A 24
SW4 2F 23
Old Tree La. ME17: B Mon 4F 35
Old Uxbridge Rd.
WD3: Map C, W Hyd 1F 13
Old Watling St. ME2: Strood 3E 27
OLD WINDSOR 2E 21
OLD WOKING 2E 29
Old Wokingham Rd.
RG40: W'ham 4A 20
RG45: Crow 4A 20
Old Woking Rd. GU22: Wok, Pyr 2F 29
KT14: W Byf 1F 29
Oliver Rd. E10 3B 16
RM20: W Thur 1B 26
(not continuous)
Oliver Way CM1: Chelm 1D 11
Olleberrie La. WD3: Sarr 3F 5
Olympia 1E 23
One Pin La. SL2: Farn C 3D 13
One Tree Hill
SS17: Bas, Fob, Vange 3D 19
One Tree Hill Rd. GU4: Guild 4E 29
Ongar Hill KT15: Add 1F 29
Ongar Rd. CM1: Coo G, Writ 2C 10
CM4: Coo G, Rad G, Writ 2C 10
(not continuous)
CM5: Fyf, Ongar 2A 10
CM5: M Rod 1B 10
CM5: Ongar, Sto M 3A 10
CM6: M Rod 1B 10
CM15: B'wood, Kel H, Pil H 3A 10
CM15: Sto M 3A 10
RM4: Abr, Stap T 4E 9
Onslow Sq. SW7 1F 23
Onslow St. GU1: Guild 4E 29
ONSLOW VILLAGE 4D 29
Opladen Way RG12: Brac 4B 20
Orange Hill Rd. HA8: Edg 2D 15
Orange Tree Hill RM4: Have B 1F 17
Orchard Av. CM12: Bill 4D 11
CR0: C'don 4B 24
Orchard Gdns. KT9: Chess 4D 23
Orchard Rd. BR1: Brom 3C 24
HP9: See G 1D 13
KT1: King T 3D 23
Orchard Way BR3: Beck 4B 24
CR0: C'don 4B 24
Ordnance Cres. SE10 1C 24
Ordnance Rd. EN3: Enf L, Enf W 4B 8
GU11: Alde 4B 28
ORGAN CROSSROADS 1E 31
Oriental Rd. GU22: Wok 2E 29
Orient Way E10 3B 16
Orphanage Rd. WD24: Wat 4B 6
ORPINGTON 4E 25
Orpington By-Pass Rd.
BR6: Hals 1E 33
TN14: Hals 1E 33
Orpington Rd. BR7: Chst 3D 25
ORSETT 4C 18
ORSETT HEATH 4C 18
Orsett Rd. RM16: Horn H, Ors 4C 18
RM17: Grays 1B 26
SS17: Horn H 4C 18
Orwell Dr. HP21: A'bury 1A 4
Osborne La. RG42: Warf 3B 20
Osborne Rd. SL4: Wind 2D 21
OSIDGE 1F 15
Osidge La. N14 1F 15
Ossulton Way N2 2F 15
OSTERLEY 1C 22
Osterley Rd. TW7: Isle 1C 22
OTFORD 2F 33
Otford La. TN14: Hals 1E 33
Otford Rd. TN14: S'oaks 2F 33
OTTERSHAW 1E 29
Otterspool Way WD25: A'ham 4B 6
(not continuous)
Ottways La. KT21: Asht 2C 30
Ouseley Rd. SL4: Old Win 2E 21
(not continuous)
Outing's La.
CM15: Dodd, Hook E 4B 10
Outram Rd. CR0: C'don 4A 24
Outwood Comn. Rd. CM11: Bill 1D 19
Outwood Farm Rd. CM11: Bill 1D 19
Outwood La. CR5: Chip, Kgswd 2E 31
KT20: Kgswd 2E 31
RH1: Blet, S Nut 4A 32
Oval Cricket Ground, The 1A 24
Oval Rd. Nth. RM10: Dag 4E 17
Ovenden Rd. TN14: Sund 2E 33
Overcliffe DA11: Grav'nd 2C 26
Overton Dr. E11 3C 16
Overy St. DA1: Dart 2A 26
Owletts 3D 27
OWLSMOOR 1A 28
Owlsmoor Rd. GU47: Col T, Owl 1A 28
(not continuous)
Oxenden Rd. GU10: Tong 4B 28
Oxenhoath Rd.
TN11: Had, S'brne 4C 34
Oxestall's Rd. SE8 1B 24
Oxford Rd. HP9: Beac 2D 13
HP11: H Wy 1A 12
HP14: Pidd, W Wyc 1A 12
SL7: Marl 3A 12
SL9: Ger X 2D 13
UB9: Den 3F 13
Oxford St. HP16: Lee C 2C 4
W1 4F 15
Oxgate La. NW2 3E 15
OXHEY 1B 14
Oxhey Dr. HA6: Nwood 1B 14
WD19: Wat 1B 14
Oxhey La. WD19: Wat 1B 14
Oxhey Rd. WD19: Wat 1B 14
OXLEASE 2E 7
Oxlease Dr. AL10: Hat 2E 7
Oxlow La. RM9: Dag 3E 17
RM10: Dag 3E 17
OXSHOTT 1C 30
Oxshott Rd. KT22: Lea 2C 30
OXTED 3C 32
Oxted Rd. RH9: G'stone 3B 32
Oyster La. KT14: Byfl 1F 29
(not continuous)

P

PACHESHAM PARK 2C 30
Packet Boat La. UB8: Cowl 4F 13
Packhorse La. EN6: Ridge 3D 7
Packhorse Rd. SL9: Ger X 2E 13
Paddenswick Rd. W6 1E 23
PADDINGTON 4F 15
Paddington St. W1 4F 15
PADDLESWORTH 1D 35
Paddlesworth Rd. ME6: Snod 1D 35
Paddocks, The HA9: Wemb 3D 15
PADHAM'S GREEN 4C 10
Padham's Grn. Rd. CM4: Inga 4C 10
Page Heath La. BR1: Brom 3C 24
Pages La. N10 2F 15
Page St. NW7 2E 15
Pagnell St. SE14 1B 24
Paines La. HA5: Pinn 2B 14
PAINS HILL 4C 32
PAINSHILL 1A 30
Pains Hill RH8: Limp 4C 32
Painters Rd. IG2: Ilf 2E 17
Palace Av. ME15: Maids 3F 35
Palace Gdns. Ter. W8 4E 15
Palace Ga. W8 1F 23
Palace Gates Rd. N22 2F 15
Palermo Rd. NW10 4E 15
PALEY STREET 1B 20
Paley St. SL6: Pal S 1B 20
Pall Mall SW1 4F 15
Palmers Av. RM17: Grays 1C 26
PALMERS GREEN 1A 16
Palmers Hill CM16: Epp 3E 9
Palmerston Rd. E17 2B 16
IG9: Buck H 1C 16
ME4: Chat 4F 27
N22 2A 16
Pampisford Rd. CR2: S Croy 1A 32
CR8: Purl 1A 32
Pancake La. HP2: Hem H 2A 6
Pancras Rd. NW1 4F 15
Pan La. CM3: E Han, Ret 3F 11
Panshanger Dr. AL7: W City 1E 7
Papercourt La. GU23: Rip 2F 29
Parade, The SL8: Bou E 3B 12
Paradise Rd. TW9: Rich 2D 23
Parchmore Rd. CR7: Thor H 3A 24
Paringdon Rd. CM18: Har 2D 9
CM19: Har 2D 9
Parish La. SE20 3B 24
SL2: Farn C 3D 13
Park Av. CM1: Chelm 2D 11
EN1: Enf 1A 16
N22 2A 16
UB1: S'hall 1B 22
WD23: Bush 4B 6
PARK BARN 4D 29
Park Cnr. Rd. DA13: Sflt 3B 26
Park Cres. W1 4F 15
Parker's Farm Rd.
RM16: Bulp, Ors 3C 18
PARKER'S GREEN 4B 34
Parker's Hill KT21: Asht 2D 31
Park Farm Rd. ME19: Rya 1D 35
RM14: Upm 3A 18
Park Flds. ME2: Strood 3E 27
Parkfields AL8: W City 1E 7
Parkgate Rd. BR6: Orp 4E 25
SM6: Wall 4F 23
SW11 1F 23
Park Hall Rd. SE21 2A 24
Park Hill DA13: Meop 3C 26
SM5: Cars 1F 31
Park Hill Rd. CR0: C'don 4A 24
NW3 3F 15
Parkhill Rd. DA5: Bexl 2E 25
Parkhurst Rd. N7 3A 16
Park La. CM11: Ram H 1E 19
CR0: C'don 4A 24
EN7: Chesh 2A 8
EN10: Brox, Hodd 2B 8
GU4: Guild 4F 29
HA9: Wemb 3D 15
HP9: Beac 2D 13
HP14: L End 1A 12
KT21: Asht 2D 31
ME17: B Mon 4F 35
RH2: Reig 4E 31
RM11: Horn 2F 17
SL1: Burn 3D 13
SM5: Cars 4F 23
TN15: Seal, S'oaks 2A 34
TW5: Cran 1B 22
UB4: Hayes 4A 14
UB9: Hare 2F 13
W1 4F 15
Park La. E. RH2: Reig 4E 31
Park La. Paradise
EN7: Brox, Chesh 2B 8
PARK LANGLEY 3C 24
Parkpale La. RH3: Bet, Aroc 4D 31
Park Pde. NW10 4D 15
Park Rd. BR7: Chst 3D 25
CR6: Warl 1C 32
CR8: Kenl 2A 32
DA1: Dart 2A 26
GU5: Alb 4A 30
GU14: Farnb 3B 28
GU15: Camb 2B 28
HP5: Ches 3D 5
HP23: Tring 1C 4
KT1: Ham W 3C 22
KT2: King T 3D 23
ME18: E Pec, W'bury 3D 35
ME19: Addtn 2C 34
ME19: Leyb 2D 35
N8 2F 15
N18 1B 16
NW1 4F 15
NW4 3E 15
NW8 4F 15
RG12: Brac 3B 20
RH7: Ling 4C 32
SE25 3A 24
SL2: Farn R, Stoke P 4D 13
SM7: Bans 2F 31
TN11: Had 3C 34
TW11: Tedd 3C 22
TW12: Ham H 3B 22
TW16: Sun 3B 22
TW19: Stanw, Stan M 2F 21
UB8: Uxb 3A 14
WD3: Rick 1A 14
WD7: Rad 4C 6
PARK ROYAL 4D 15
PARK ROYAL JUNC. 4D 15
Park Royal Rd. NW10 4D 15
Parkside SW19 2E 23
Parkside Av. DA7: Bex 1F 25
Parkside Gdns. EN4: E Barn 1F 15
Parkside Way HA2: Harr 2B 14
PARK STREET 2C 6
Park St. AL2: Park 3C 6
GU15: Camb 1B 28
SL3: Coln 1F 21
W1 4F 15
Park St. La. AL2: Park 3B 6
Park Vw. EN11: Hodd 1B 8
Park Vw. Rd. DA16: Well 2E 25
N17 2B 16
UB8: Hil 4A 14
Park Way HA4: Ruis 3B 14
Parkway AL8: W City 1E 7
(not continuous)
CM1: Chelm 2E 11
CM2: Chelm 2E 11
CM19: Har 1D 9
CR0: New Ad 1C 32
GU1: Guild 4E 29
NW1 4F 15
Parkway, The TW4: Cran 1B 22
TW5: Cran 1B 22
UB2: S'hall 1B 22
UB4: Yead 1B 22
UB5: N'olt 1B 22
PARK WOOD 3F 35
Parlaunt Rd. SL3: L'ly 1E 21
(not continuous)
Parley Dr. GU21: Wok 2E 29
Parliament La. SL1: Burn 3C 12
Parnall Rd. CM18: Har 1D 9
Parndon Wood Crematorium
CM19: Har 2D 9
Parndon Wood Rd. CM19: Har 2D 9
Parnell Rd. E3 4B 16
(not continuous)
Parrock Rd. DA12: Grav'nd 2C 26
Parrock St. DA12: Grav'nd 2C 26
Parrott's La. HP23: Buck C, Chol 2C 4
Parry St. SW8 1A 24
Parsloe Rd. CM16: Epp G 2D 9
CM19: Har 2D 9
Parsloes Av. RM9: Dag 3E 17
PARSLOW'S HILLOCK 3A 4
PARSONAGE GREEN 1D 11
Parsonage La. CM4: Marg 3D 11
DA14: Sidc 3E 25
EN1: Enf 4A 8
EN2: Enf 4A 8
ME2: Strood 3F 27
SL2: Farn C, Farn R 3D 13
SL4: Wind 1D 21
Parsonage Manorway
DA17: Belv 1E 25
Parsonage Rd. TW20: Eng G 3E 21
PARSONS GREEN 1E 23
Parson's Grn. La. SW6 1E 23
Parsons La. DA2: Dart 2F 25
Parson's Mead CR0: C'don 4A 24
Parson St. NW4 2E 15
Partridge Av. CM1: Chelm 1D 11
Partridge Rd. CM18: Har 1D 9
Parvis Rd. KT14: W Byf, Byfl 1F 29
PASLOW WOOD COMMON 3B 10
PASSINGFORD BRIDGE 4F 9
PASSMORES 1D 9
Pastures, The HP13: D'ley 1A 12
PATCHETTS GREEN 4C 6
Patching Hall La.
CM1: Broom, Chelm 1D 11
Paternoster Hill EN9: Walt A 3C 8
Patmos Rd. SW9 1A 24
Pattens La. ME1: Roch 4F 27
Pauls Hill HP10: Penn 1C 12
Paul St. EC2 4A 16
Pawsons Rd. CR0: C'don 4A 24
Paycock Rd. CM19: Har 1D 9
Peabody Rd. GU14: Farnb 3B 28
Peach St. RG40: W'ham 3A 20
Peacock La. RG12: Brac 4A 20
RG40: W'ham 4A 20
Peakes La. EN7: Chesh 3A 8
Peakes Way EN7: Chesh 3A 8
Pea La. RM14: Upm 3B 18
PEARTREE 1E 7
PEARTREE GREEN 4B 10
Pear Tree La.
DA12: High'm, Shorne 3D 27
ME7: G'ham, Hem 4F 27
Peartree La. AL7: W City 1E 7
(not continuous)
Peascod St. SL4: Wind 1D 21
Peascroft Rd. HP3: Hem H 2A 6
Pease Hill TN15: Ash 1B 34
Pebble Hill Rd. RH3: Bet 4D 31
PECKHAM 1B 24
PECKHAM BUSH 4D 35
Peckham High St. SE15 1B 24
Peckham Hill St. SE15 1B 24
Peckham Hurst Rd.
TN11: S'brne 3C 34
Peckham Pk. Rd. SE15 1B 24
Peckham Rd. SE5 1A 24
SE15 1A 24
Peckham Rye SE15 2B 24
SE22 2B 24
Peck's Hill EN9: Naze 2C 8
PEDLARS END 2F 9
Pedlars End CM5: More 2F 9
Pednor Bottom HP5: Ches 3C 4
PEDNORMEAD END 3D 5
Pednor Rd. HP5: Ches 3C 4
Peeble Hill KT24: W Hor 4A 30
Peens La. ME17: B Mon 4F 35
Pegmire La. WD25: A'ham 4C 6
Pegs La. SG13: Hertf 1A 8
Pelham Rd. DA11: Grav'nd 2C 26
Pelham Rd. Sth.
DA11: Grav'nd, Nflt 2C 26
Pelham St. SW7 1F 23
Pells La. TN15: W King 1B 34
Pembridge La.
EN10: Brick, Brox 2A 8
Pembridge Rd. W11 4E 15
Pembridge Vs. W2 4E 15
W11 4E 15
Pembroke B'way. GU15: Camb 1B 28
Pembroke Rd. DA8: Erith 1F 25
HA4: Ruis 3A 14
HA9: Wemb 3C 14
TN13: S'oaks 3F 33
W8 1E 23
Pembury Rd. E5 3B 16
Pendell Rd. RH1: Blet 4A 32
Pendleton Rd. RH1: Redh 4F 31
PENENDEN HEATH 2F 35
Penenden Heath Rd.
ME14: Pen H 2F 35
Penfold La. HP7: L Mis 4C 4
HP15: Holm G 4C 4
PENGE 3B 24
Penge Rd. SE20 3B 24
SE25 3B 24
Penhill Rd. DA5: Bexl 2E 25
Penman's Grn. WD4: Bucks 3F 5
PENN 1C 12
PENN BOTTOM 1C 12
Penn Rd. HP9: Beac 1C 12
HP15: Haz 1B 12
PENN STREET 4C 4
Penn St. N1 4A 16
PENNY POT 1D 29
Pennypot La. GU24: Chob 1D 29
Penny Royal Rd. CM3: Dan 2F 11
Penrhyn Rd. KT1: King T 3D 23
Penton St. N1 4A 16
Pentonville Rd. N1 4A 16
Penwith Rd. SW18 2E 23
Pepper Hill SG12: Gt A 1B 8
PEPPER'S GREEN 1C 10
Pepys Rd. SE14 1B 24
Percival St. EC1 4A 16
Percy Rd. N21 1A 16
TW2: Whitt 2B 22
TW12: Hamp 3B 22
PERIVALE 4C 14
Perks La. HP16: Pre 4B 4
Perry Hall Rd. BR6: St M Cry 4D 25
Perry Hill GU3: Worp 3D 29
(not continuous)
ME3: Cli 2F 27
SE6 2B 24
Perry Ri. SE23 2B 24
Perrys La. BR6: Prat B 1E 33
PERRY STREET 2C 26
Perry St. BR7: Chst 3D 25
CM12: Bill 1D 19
DA1: Cray 2F 25
DA11: Nflt 2C 26
Perry Va. SE23 2B 24
Perth Rd. IG2: Ilf 2D 17
N22 2A 16
Pested Bars Rd. ME17: B Mon 3F 35
Peterborough Rd. HA1: Harr 3C 14
Peterley La. HP16: Pre 4B 4
Petersfield Av. RM3: Rom 2A 18
PETERSHAM 2D 23
Petersham Rd.
TW10: Rich, Ham 2C 22
Peters La.
HP27: M Ris, White, Par H 3A 4
Petherton Rd. N5 3A 16
PETTINGS 1B 34
Pettits La. CM15: W Grn 4B 10
RM1: Rom 2F 17
Pettits La. Nth. RM1: Rom 2F 17
Pettman Cres. SE28 1D 25
Pett's Hill UB5: N'olt 3B 14
PETTS WOOD 4D 25
Petts Wood Rd. BR5: Pet W 4D 25
Pheasant Hill HP8: Chal G 1E 13
Pheasant La. ME15: Maids 3F 35
Philanthropic Rd. RH1: Redh 4F 31
Philip La. N15 2A 16
Philpot La. GU24: Chob 1E 29
Philpots La. TN11: Leigh, Hild 4A 34
Phipps Hatch La. EN2: Enf 4A 8
Picardy Manorway DA17: Belv 1E 25
Picardy Rd. DA17: Belv 1E 25
Picardy St. DA17: Belv 1E 25
Piccadilly W1 4F 15
PICCOTTS END 1F 5
Piccotts End HP1: Hem H 1F 5
Piccotts End Rd. HP1: Hem H 1F 5
Picketts Lock La. N9 1B 16
Pickford La. DA7: Bex 1E 25
Pickhurst La. BR4: W W'ck 4C 24
Pield Heath Rd. UB8: Cowl, Hil 4A 14
Pierce Mill Rd. TN11: Had 4C 34
Pier Rd. E16 1D 25
ME4: Chat 3F 27
ME7: Chat, G'ham 3F 27
Pigeonhouse La. SL4: Wink 2C 20
Piggott's Hill HP14: Nth D 4A 4
PIGSTYE GREEN 2B 10
Pigstye Grn. Rd. CM5: Will 2B 10
Pikefish La. ME18: Ladd 4D 35
Pike La. RM14: Upm 3A 18
Pikey La. ME19: E Mal 2D 35
PILGRIMS HATCH 1B 18
Pilgrims La. RH8: T'sey 3C 32
RM16: N Stif 4B 18
TN16: Tats 3C 32
Pilgrims Rd. ME2: Hall 4D 27
Pilgrims Way GU4: Guild 4E 29
(not continuous)
ME2: Hall 1D 35
ME14: Box, Det 2F 35
ME19: Tros 1C 34
ME20: A'ford 1E 35
TN14: Otf 2A 34
TN14: Sund 2E 33
TN15: Kems'g 2A 34
TN15: Wro 2B 34
TN16: Westrm, Bras 3D 33
Pilgrims Way E. TN14: Otf 2F 33
Pilgrims Way W. TN14: Otf 2F 33
Pillar Box Rd. TN15: Seal 2A 34
Pimlico Rd. SW1 1F 23
PINDEN 3B 26
Pinesfield La. ME19: Tros 1C 34
Pines Rd. BR1: Brom 3D 25
Pine Tree La. TN15: Ivy H 3B 34
Pinewood Rd. SL0: Iver H 3E 13
Pinkham Way N11 2F 15
Pink Hill HP27: Par H 3A 4
Pink La. SL1: Burn 4C 12
Pinkneys Dr. SL6: Maide 4A 12
PINKNEYS GREEN 4A 12
Pinkneys Rd. SL6: Maide 4B 12
Pink Rd. HP27: Lac G, Par H 3A 4
PINNACLES 1D 9
PINNER 2B 14
PINNER GREEN 2B 14
Pinner Grn. HA5: Pinn 2B 14
Pinner Hill Rd. HA5: Pinn 2B 14
Pinner Rd. HA1: Harr 2B 14
HA2: Harr 2B 14
HA5: Pinn 2B 14
HA6: Nwood 2A 14
WD19: Wat 1B 14
Pinner Vw. HA1: Harr 2C 14
PINNERWOOD PARK 2B 14
Piper's Hill HP1: Gt Gad, Nett 1F 5
Pipers La. AL5: Harp 1C 6
HP15: Gt Kin 4B 4
Piper's Tye CM2: Gall 3E 11
PIPPS HILL 2D 19
Pipps Hill Rd. Nth. CM11: C Hill 2E 19
PIRBRIGHT 2D 29
PIRBRIGHT CAMP 2C 28
Pirbright Grn. GU24: Pirb 3D 29
Pirbright Rd. GU3: Norm 4C 28
PITCH PLACE 3E 29
Pitfield St. N1 4A 16
PITSEA 3F 19
Pitsea Hall La. SS13: Pit 3E 19
Pitsea Rd. SS13: Pit 2E 19
Pitshanger La. W5 4C 14
Pitt Rd. KT17: Eps 1D 31
PITTSWOOD 4B 34
Pix Farm La. HP1: Hem H 2E 5
PIXHAM 4C 30
Pixham La. RH4: Dork 4C 30
PIZIEN WELL 3D 35
Pizien Well Rd. ME18: W'bury 3D 35
Place Farm La.
CM15: Dodd, Kel H 4B 10
Place Farm Rd. RH1: Blet 3A 32
Placehouse La. CR5: Coul 2A 32
Plain, The CM16: Epp 3E 9
PLAISTOW
BR1 3C 24
E13 4C 16
Plaistow La. BR1: Brom 3C 24
(not continuous)
Plaistow Rd. E13 4C 16
E15 4C 16
Plantagenet Rd. EN5: New Bar 4F 7
Plantation Rd. CM3: Bor 1F 11
HP6: Amer 4D 5
PLASHET 3D 17
Plashet Gro. E6 3C 16
Plashet Rd. E13 4C 16
Platt Ho. La. TN15: Stans, Wro 1C 34
Platt's La. NW3 3E 15
Plaxdale Grn. Rd. TN15: Stans 1B 34
PLAXTOL 3B 34
Plaxtol La. TN15: Plax 3B 34
Pleasure Pit Rd. KT21: Asht 2D 31
Plevna Rd. N9 1B 16
Plomer Grn. La. HP13: D'ley 1A 12
Plomer Hill HP13: D'ley 1A 12
Plough Hill EN6: Cuff 3A 8
TN15: Bor G 3B 34
Plough La. CR8: Purl 1A 32
KT11: Cobh 2B 30
RG40: W'ham 3A 20
SL2: Stoke P 4E 13
SM6: Bedd 4A 24
SW17 3F 23
SW19 3F 23
WD3: Sarr 3F 5
Plough Rd. SW11 2F 23
Plough Way SE16 1B 24
Ployters Rd. CM18: Har 2D 9
Plug La. DA13: Meop 4C 26
PLUMSTEAD 1D 25
PLUMSTEAD COMMON 1D 25
Plumstead Comn. Rd. SE18 1D 25

Plumstead High St. SE18 1D 25
Plumstead Rd. SE18 1D 25
Pococks La. SL4: Eton 1D 21
POINTERS GREEN 2A 30
Polehanger La. HP1: Hem H 1F 5
Pole Hill Rd. UB10: Hil 4A 14
Polesden Lacey 3B 30
Polesden La. GU23: Rip 3F 29
Polesden Rd. KT23: Bookh 3B 30
Poles Hill WD3: Sarr 3F 5
Polesteeple Hill TN16: Big H 2C 32
Polhill TN14: Hals 2F 33
POLISH WAR MEMORIAL 3B 14
Pollard Rd. N20 1F 15
Pollards Wood Hill RH8: Oxt 3C 32
Pollards Wood Rd. RH8: Oxt 4C 32
Polsted La. GU3: Comp 4D 29
Pomeroy St. SE15 1B 24
Pond Approach HP15: Holm G 4C 4
PONDERS END 1B 16
Pondfield La. CM13: B'wood 1B 18
Pond La. TN15: Ivy H 3A 34
POND PARK 3D 5
Pond Pk. Rd. HP5: Ches 3D 5
Ponds Rd. CM2: Gall 3E 11
Pond St. NW3 3F 15
PONDTAIL 3A 28
Pont St. SW1 1F 23
POOLEY GREEN 3F 21
Pooley Grn. Rd. TW20: Egh 3E 21
Pool Rd. KT8: W Mole 4B 22
POOTINGS 4D 33
Pootings Rd.
TN8: F Elm, Crock H 4D 33
Popes La. RH8: Oxt 4C 32
SL6: Cook 3B 12
W5 1C 22
POPESWOOD 3A 20
Popeswood Rd. RG42: Bin 3A 20
POPLAR 4B 16
Poplar High St. E14 4B 16
Poplar Row CM16: They B 4D 9
Poplar Way TW13: Felt 2B 22
Porchester Rd. W2 4E 15
Porlock Av. HA2: Harr 3C 14
Porters Av. RM8: Dag 3E 17
RM9: Dag 3E 17
Porters Way UB7: W Dray 1A 22
Port Hill BR6: Prat B 1E 33
SG14: Hertf 1A 8
(not continuous)
Portland Pl. W1 4F 15
Portland Rd. SE25 3B 24
Portman Sq. W1 4F 15
Portnalls Rd. CR5: Coul 2F 31
Portsmouth Rd. GU2: Guild 4E 29
GU15: Camb 1B 28
GU16: Frim 2B 28
GU23: Rip 2F 29
GU23: Send, Rip 3F 29
KT1: King T 3C 22
KT7: T Ditt 4C 22
KT10: Esh 1B 30
(Old Chestnut Av.)
KT10: Esh 4C 22
(Sandown Rd.)
KT11: Cobh 1B 30
Portway E15 4C 16
Potash La. TN15: Bor G 2C 34
Potash Rd. CM11: Bill 4D 11
CM17: Abb R, M Grn 1F 9
Potkiln La. HP9: Jor 2D 13
Potley Hill Rd. GU46: Yat 1A 28
POTTEN END 1F 5
Potten End Hill HP1: Hem H 1F 5
Potter Row
HP16: Gt Miss, S Hth 3B 4
POTTERS BAR 3E 7
POTTERS CROUCH 2B 6
Potterscrouch La. AL2: Pot C 2B 6
AL3: St A 2B 6
Potters La. GU23: Send 3E 29
WD6: Bore 4D 7
Potter's Rd. EN5: New Bar 4E 7
POTTER STREET 1E 9
Potter St. CM17: Har 1E 9
HA5: Pinn 2B 14
HA6: Nwood 2B 14
POUCHEN END 2F 5
Pouchen End La. HP1: Hem H 2F 5
Pound, The SL6: Cook 3B 12
Pound Farm La.
GU12: Ash, Ash G 4C 28
Pound La. GU20: W'sham 1C 28
KT19: Eps 1D 31
NW10 3E 15
SL7: Marl 3A 12
SS12: Nth B 2F 19
SS13: B Gif 2F 19
TN14: Knock 2E 33
Pound Rd. TN12: E Pec 4D 35
Pound St. HP22: Wend 2B 4
SM5: Cars 4F 23
POVEREST 4E 25
Poverest Rd. BR5: St M Cry 4D 25
Powder Mill La. TW2: Whitt 2B 22
POWDER MILLS 4A 34
Powerscroft Rd. E5 3B 16
Powys La. N13 1A 16
N14 1A 16
POYLE 1F 21
Poyle La. SL1: Burn 4C 12
Poyle Rd. GU10: Tong 4B 28
SL3: Poyle 2F 21
Poynders Rd. SW4 2F 23
Praed St. W2 4F 15
PRATLING STREET 2F 35
Pratling St. ME20: A'ford 2E 35
PRATT'S BOTTOM 1E 33
PRATT'S BOTTOM 1E 33
Pratts Farm La. CM3: Lit W 1E 11
(not continuous)
Pratt St. NW1 4F 15
Prebendal Av. HP21: A'bury 1A 4
Prebend St. N1 4A 16
PRESTON 3D 15
Preston Hill HA3: Kent 3D 15
Preston La. KT20: Tad 2E 31
Preston Rd. HA3: Kent 3D 15
HA9: Kent, Wemb 3D 15
Prestons Rd. BR2: Hayes 4C 24
E14 4C 16
Prestwick Rd. WD19: Wat 1B 14
PRESTWOOD 3B 4
Pretoria Rd. N17 2A 16
Pretoria Rd. Nth. N18 2A 16
Prey Heath Rd. GU22: Wok 3E 29
Prices La. RH2: Reig 4E 31
Priestfield ME1: Roch 4E 27
Priest Hill SL4: Old Win 2E 21
TW20: Eng G, Old Win 2E 21
Priest La. GU24: W End 2C 28
Priestley Rd. GU2: Guild 4D 29
Priests Bri. SW13 2D 23
SW14 2D 23
Priests La.
CM15: B'wood, Shenf 1B 18
PRIESTWOOD
DA13 4C 26
RG42 3A 20
PRIESTWOOD GREEN 4C 26
Priestwood Rd. DA13: Meop 1C 34
PRIMROSE HILL 4F 15
Primrose Hill HP15: Wid E 4B 4
WD4: K Lan 3A 6
Primrose Hill Rd. NW3 3F 15
Prince Albert Rd. NW1 4F 15
NW8 4F 15
Prince Arthur Rd. ME7: G'ham 3F 27
Prince Charles Av. ME5: Wald 1F 35
RM16: Ors 4C 18
Prince Charles Rd. SE3 1C 24
Prince George Av. N14 1F 15
Prince Imperial Rd. BR7: Chst 3D 25
Prince of Wales Dr. SW11 1F 23
Prince of Wales Rd. NW5 3F 15
RH1: Outw 4A 32
SE3 1C 24
Prince Regent La. E13 4C 16
E16 4C 16
Princes Av. GU11: Alde 3B 28
ME5: Wald 1F 35
PRINCES PARK 4F 27
PRINCES RISBOROUGH 3A 4
Princes Rd. CM2: Chelm 2E 11
CM14: Kel C, N'side 4A 10
DA1: Dart 2F 25
DA2: Dart 2A 26
PRINCES ROAD INTERCHANGE 2A 26
Princess Margaret Rd.
RM18: E Til 1D 27
SS17: Linf, E Til 1D 27
Princess Way RH1: Redh 4F 31
Printinghouse La. UB3: Hayes 1A 22
Prior Rd. GU15: Camb 1B 28
Priorsfield Rd. GU3: Comp 4D 29
Priory Av. CM17: Har 1E 9
HP13: H Wy 1B 12
Priory La. RG42: Brac 3B 20
SW15 2D 23
Priory Rd. CM3: B'acre 3F 11
HP13: H Wy 1B 12
ME2: Strood 3E 27
N8 2F 15
NW6 4E 15
SL1: Slou 4C 12
SL5: Asc 3B 20
SM3: Cheam 4E 23
Priory Rd. Sth. DA1: Dart 2F 25
Pritchard's Rd. E2 4B 16
Prospect Av. GU14: Farnb 2B 28
Prospect Hill E17 2B 16
Prospect Rd. AL1: St A 2C 6
GU12: Ash V 3B 28
GU14: Cove, Farnb 3B 28
Prune Hill TW20: Egh, Eng G 3E 21
Pudding La. IG7: Chig 1D 17
PUDDLEDOCK 4E 33
Puddledock La.
DA2: Dart, Swan 3F 25
TN16: Westrm 4D 33
PUDDS CROSS 3E 5
Pumpkin Hill SL1: Burn 3D 13
Pump La. CM1: Spr 1E 11
UB3: Hayes 1B 22
Pump La. Nth. SL7: Marl 2A 12
Pump St. SS17: Horn H 4D 19
Punch Bowl La. AL3: St A 1A 6
HP2: Hem H 1A 6
Punchbowl La. RH5: Dork 4C 30
PURFLEET 1A 26
Purfleet By-Pass RM19: Purf 1A 26
Purfleet Rd. RM15: Avel 1A 26
PURLEY 1A 32
PURLEY CROSS 1A 32
Purley Downs Rd. CR2: Sande 1A 32
CR8: Purl 1A 32
Purley Way CR0: C'don, Wadd 4A 24
CR8: Purl 4A 24
Pursley Rd. NW7 2E 15
Purton La. SL2: Farn C, Farn R 3D 13
PUTNEY 2E 23
Putney Bri. SW6 2E 23
SW15 2E 23
Putney Bri. Rd. SW15 2E 23
SW18 2E 23
PUTNEY HEATH 2E 23
Putney Heath SW15 2E 23
Putney High St. SW15 2E 23
Putney Hill SW15 2E 23
(not continuous)
PUTNEY VALE 2E 23
Puttenden Rd. TN11: S'brne 4B 34
PUTTENHAM 4C 28
Puttenham Heath Rd.
GU3: Comp, Putt 4C 28
Puttenham Hill GU3: Putt 4C 28
Puttenham Rd. GU10: Seale 4B 28
PYE CORNER 1D 9
Pyenest Rd. CM19: Har 1D 9
PYESTOCK 3A 28
PYLE HILL 3E 29
Pynest Grn. La.
EN9: Lough, Walt A 4C 8
Pyrcroft Rd. KT16: Chert 4F 21
PYRFORD 2F 29
Pyrford Comn. Rd. GU22: Pyr 2F 29
PYRFORD GREEN 2F 29
Pyrford Rd. GU22: Pyr 1F 29
KT14: W Byf 1F 29
PYRFORD VILLAGE 2F 29
Pyrles La. IG10: Lough 4D 9

Q

Quadrant, The TW9: Rich 2C 22
Quaker La. EN9: Walt A 3C 8
Quakers Hall La. TN13: S'oaks 2F 33
Quarries, The ME17: B Mon 4F 35
Quarry Hill Rd. TN15: Bor G 2B 34
Quarry St. GU1: Guild 4E 29
Quarry Wood Rd. SL6: Cook 3A 12
SL7: Cook, Marl 3A 12
Queen Alexandra Rd.
HP11: H Wy 1B 12
Queen Anne Av. BR2: Brom 3C 24
Queen Elizabeth II Bri.
RM20: Dart, W Thur 1A 26
Queen Elizabeth Rd.
KT2: King T 3D 23
Queens Av. GU11: Alde 4B 28
N10 2F 15
WD18: Wat 1A 14
Queensbridge Rd. E2 4A 16
E8 3A 16
QUEENSBURY 2D 15
Queen's Club (Tennis) 1E 23
Queens Dr. W3 4D 15
W5 4D 15
Queen's Farm Rd.
DA12: Shorne, Grav'nd 2D 27
Queen's Ga. SW7 1F 23
Queen's Mead Rd.
BR2: Brom 3C 24
QUEEN'S PARK 4D 11
Queens Pk. Av. CM12: Bill 4D 11
Queen's Pk. Rangers FC 4E 15
Queens Ride SW13 2E 23
SW15 2E 23
Queens Rd. CM14: B'wood 1B 18
CR0: C'don 4A 24
Queens Rd. DA8: Erith 1F 25
E17 2B 16
GU11: Alde 4A 28
GU14: Farnb 3B 28
GU24: Bisl, Brkwd 2D 29
IG9: Buck H 1C 16
KT2: King T 3D 23
KT12: Hers 4A 22
KT13: Weyb 4A 22
ME16: Maids 3E 35
NW4 2E 15
SE14 1B 24
SE15 1B 24
SL3: Dat 1E 21
SW19 3E 23
TW10: Rich 2D 23
TW11: Tedd 3C 22
WD17: Wat 4B 6
Queenstown Rd. SW8 1F 23
Queen St. CM5: Fyf 2A 10
GU5: Goms 4A 30
SL6: Maide 4B 12
(not continuous)
Queensway AL10: Hat 1E 7
BR5: Pet W 4D 25
HP1: Hem H 2F 5
HP2: Hem H 2F 5
W2 4E 15
QUEEN VICTORIA 4E 23
Queen Victoria St. EC4 4A 16
Quex Rd. NW6 4E 15
Quickley La. WD3: Chor 1F 13
Quickmoor La. WD4: Bucks 3F 5
Quinta Dr. EN5: Barn 1E 15

R

Raans Rd. HP6: Amer 4D 5
RABBIT'S CROSS 4F 35
Rabbits Rd. DA4: S Dar 3A 26
Rabies Heath Rd. RH1: Blet 4A 32
RABLEY 3D 7
Rackstraw Rd. GU47: Col T, Owl 1A 28
Radford Way CM12: Bill 1D 19
RADLETT 4C 6
Radlett La. WD7: Rad, Shenl 3C 6
Radlett Rd. WD24: Wat 4B 6
WD25: A'ham 4B 6
RADLEY GREEN 2C 10
Radley Grn. Rd. CM4: Rad G 2C 10
CM5: Rad G, Will 2B 10
Radwinter Av. SS12: Wick 1F 19
Raeburn Av. KT5: Surb 4D 23
RAF Halton Airfield 1B 4
RAF Mus. Hendon 2D 15
RAF NORTHOLT AERODROME 3A 14
Ragged Hall La.
AL2: Chis G, Pot C 2B 6
Rag Hill Rd. TN16: Tats 2D 33
Raglan Rd. RH2: Reig 4E 31
Ragmans La. SL7: H Wy, Marl 2A 12
Rags La. EN7: Chesh, G Oak 3A 8
Ragstone Rd. SL1: Slou 1D 21
Raikes La. RH5: Ab H 4B 30
Railton Rd. SE24 2A 24
Railway App. HA3: Harr 2C 14
Railway St. ME4: Chat 4F 27
ME7: G'ham 3F 27
Railway Ter. WD4: K Lan 3A 6
Rainbow La. SS17: Stan H 4D 19
Rainbow Rd. CM17: Mat T 1F 9
RM16: Chaf H 1B 26
RAINHAM 4F 17
Rainham Rd. ME5: Chat 4F 27
ME7: G'ham 4F 27
RM12: Horn, Rain 3F 17
RM13: Rain 3F 17
Rainham Rd. Nth. RM10: Dag 3E 17
Rainham Rd. Sth. RM10: Dag 3F 17
Rainsford La. CM1: Chelm 2D 11
Rainsford Rd. CM1: Chelm 2D 11
Ralph's Ride RG12: Brac 3B 20
(not continuous)
RAMSDEN 4E 25
RAMSDEN BELLHOUSE 1E 19
RAMSDEN HEATH 1E 19
Ramsden Pk. Rd. CM11: Ram 1E 19
Ram St. SW18 2E 23
Rances La. RG40: W'ham 3A 20
Rancliffe Rd. E6 4D 17
Randalls Rd. KT22: Lea 2C 30
Randles La. TN14: Knock 1E 33
Ranger's Rd. E4 1C 16
IG10: Lough 1C 16
RANMORE COMMON 4C 30
Ranmore Comn. Rd.
RH5: Ran C, Westh 4B 30
Ranmore Rd. RH4: Dork 4C 30
Ravensbourne Pk. SE6 2B 24
Ravenscourt Gro. RM12: Horn 3A 18
Ravens La. HP4: Berk 2E 5
Ravensworth Rd. BR4: W W'ck 4C 24
Rawlings La. HP9: See G 1D 13
RAWRETH 1F 19
Rawreth La. SS11: Raw, Ray 1F 19
RAWRETH SHOT 1F 19
Rayleigh Rd. CM13: Hut 1B 18
Rayley La.
CM16: N Weald, Twood 2E 9
Ray Mead Rd. SL6: Maide 4C 12
Ray Mill Rd. E. SL6: Maide 4B 12
Ray Mill Rd. W. SL6: Maide 4B 12
Raymouth Rd. SE16 1B 24
RAYNERS LANE 3B 14
Rayners La. HA2: Harr 2B 14
RAYNES PARK 3E 23
Ray Pk. Av. SL6: Maide 4B 12
Ray Pk. Rd. SL6: Maide 4B 12
Rays Hill DA4: Hort K 3A 26
HP5: Bell 2C 4
Ray St. SL6: Maide 4B 12
Reading Rd. GU14: Farnb 3B 28
GU17: Bla 1A 28
GU46: Yat 1A 28
Reading Rd. Sth. GU51: Fleet 3A 28
Rectory Hill HP6: Amer 4D 5
HP7: Amer 4D 5
Rectory La. CM1: Chelm 2E 11
DA14: Sidc 3E 25
IG10: Lough 4D 9
KT6: Surb 4C 22
KT14: Byfl 1A 30
KT21: Asht 2D 31
KT23: Bookh 3B 30
ME16: Maids 3E 35
RG12: Brac 3B 20
RH3: Bkld 4D 31
SM7: Bans 2F 31
SW17 3F 23
TN15: Igh 2B 34
TN16: Bras 3E 33
TN16: Tats 3D 33
WD4: K Lan 3A 6
WD7: Shenl 3D 7
Rectory Pk. CR2: Sande 1A 32
Rectory Rd. BR3: Beck 3B 24
CM12: L Bur 2D 19
CR5: Coul 3F 31
GU14: Farnb 3B 28
ME3: Cli 2E 27
Rectory Rd. N16 3A 16
RG40: W'ham 3A 20
RM16: Ors 4C 18
RM17: Grays 1C 26
RM18: W Til 1C 26
SL6: Tap 4C 12
SS13: Pit 2F 19
(not continuous)
TN15: Ash 4B 26
WD3: Rick 1F 13
Redan Rd. GU12: Alde 4B 28
REDBOURN 1B 6
Redbournbury La. AL3: St A 1B 6
Redbourn La. AL3: Redb 1B 6
AL5: Harp 1B 6
Redbourn Rd. AL3: St A 1B 6
HP2: Hem H 1A 6
REDBRIDGE 2C 16
Redbridge La. E. IG4: Ilf 2C 16
Redbridge La. W. E11 2C 16
REDBRIDGE RDBT. 2C 16
Redcliffe Gdns. SW5 1E 23
SW10 1E 23
Rede Ct. Rd. ME2: Strood 3E 27
Redhall La. WD3: Chan C 4A 6
RED HILL 3D 35
REDHILL 4F 31
Red Hill BR7: Chst 3D 25
ME18: W'bury 3D 35
Redhill Aerodrome and Heliport 4F 31
Redhill Rd. DA3: New A 4B 26
REDLAND END 3A 4
Red La. KT10: Clay 1C 30
RH8: Oxt 4C 32
Red Lion La. SE18 1D 25
WD3: Sarr 4F 5
Red Lion Rd. GU24: Chob 1D 29
KT6: Surb 4D 23
Red Lion St. HP5: Ches 3D 5
TW9: Rich 2C 22
WC1 4A 16
Red Lodge Rd. BR4: W W'ck 4C 24
Redmans La. TN14: S'ham 1F 33
Red Post Hill SE24 2A 24
Redricks La. CM21: Saw 1D 9
Redriff Rd. SE16 1B 24
Red Rd. GU18: Light 1C 28
Redrose La. CM4: Bmore 3B 10
RED ROVER 2D 23
Redstone Hill RH1: Redh 4F 31
Redstone Hollow RH1: Redh 4F 31
Red St. DA13: Sflt 3B 26
Redvers Buller Rd. GU11: Alde 3B 28
Redwall La. ME15: Hunt 4E 35
ME17: Hunt, Lint 4E 35
Redwell La. TN15: Igh 3B 34
Reede Rd. RM10: Dag 3E 17
Reed's Hill RG12: Brac 4B 20
Reeds La. TN11: S'brne 3B 34
Reed St. ME3: Cli 1E 27
Reeves La. CM19: Roy 2C 8
REGENT'S PARK 4F 15
Regent's Pk. 4F 15
Regents Pk. Rd. N3 2E 15
NW1 4F 15
(not continuous)
Regent St. SW1 4F 15
W1 4F 15
Regent Way GU16: Frim 2B 28
Regina Rd. UB2: S'hall 1B 22
REIGATE 4E 31
Reigate Av. SM1: Sutt 4E 23
Reigate Hill RH2: Reig 4E 31
REIGATE HILL INTERCHANGE 3E 31
Reigate Rd. KT17: Eps D, Tad 1E 31
KT17: Eps, Ewe 1D 31
KT20: Tad 1E 31
KT22: Lea 3C 30
RH1: Redh 4F 31
RH2: Reig 4F 31
RH3: Bet, Bkld 4C 30
RH4: Dork 4C 30
Renfree Way TW17: Shep 4A 22
Renwick Rd. IG11: Bark 4E 17
Replingham Rd. SW18 2E 23
Repository Rd. SE18 1D 25
Reservoir Rd. IG10: H Beech 4C 8
RETTENDON 4F 11
Rettendon Rd. CM3: E Han 3F 11
Rhodeswell Rd. E14 4B 16
(not continuous)
RHS Garden (Hyde Hall) 4F 11
RICHINGS PARK 1F 21
Richings Way SL0: Rich P 1F 21
RICHMOND 2D 23
Richmond Bri. TW1: Twick 2C 22
RICHMOND CIRCUS 2D 23
Richmond Hill TW10: Rich 2D 23
Richmond Pk. 2D 23
Richmond Rd. E8 3A 16
KT2: King T 3C 22
ME7: G'ham 3F 27
TW1: Twick 2C 22
TW7: Isle 2C 22
Ricketts Hill Rd. TN16: Tats 2C 32
Rickford GU3: Worp 3D 29
RICKMANSWORTH 1A 14
Rickmansworth La. SL9: Chal P 2E 13
Rickmansworth Rd. HA5: Pinn 2B 14
HA6: Nwood 1A 14
HP6: Amer 4D 5
UB9: Hare 2F 13
WD3: Chor 4F 5
WD18: Wat 4A 6
RIDDLESDOWN 1A 32
Riddlesdown Rd. CR8: Purl 1A 32
RIDGE 3D 7
Ridge, The CM3: Lit B 2F 11
CR3: Wold 3B 32
CR6: Warl 3C 32
Ridge Av. N21 1A 16
RIDGE GREEN 4A 32
Ridge La. WD17: Wat 4A 6
Ridgemead Rd. TW20: Eng G 2E 21
Ridgemount Rd. SL5: S'dale 4D 21
Ridge Rd. N21 1A 16
SM3: Sutt 4E 23
Ridge Way HP13: H Wy 1B 12
Ridgeway AL7: W City 1E 7
Ridgeway, The AL4: St A 1C 6
DA12: Shorne 3D 27
E4 1B 16
EN2: Enf 3F 7
EN6: N'thaw, Cuff 3F 7
EN6: Pot B 3F 7
HA2: Harr 2B 14
(not continuous)
KT22: Fet 3C 30
ME4: Chat 4F 27
NW7 1E 15
TN10: Tonb 4B 34
Ridgeway Rd. TW7: Isle 1C 22
RIDGWAY 2F 29
Ridgway SW19 3E 23
Riding Ct. Rd. SL3: Dat, L'ly 1E 21
Riding La. TN11: Hild 4A 34
Ridlands La. RH8: Limp 3C 32
RIDLEY 4B 26
Riefield Rd. SE9 2D 25
Riffhams Chase CM3: Lit B 2F 11
Riffhams La. CM3: Dan, Lit B 2F 11
Rignall Rd. HP16: Gt Miss 3B 4
Rignals La. CM2: Gall 3E 11
Ring, The RG12: Brac 3B 20
RINGLESTONE 2F 35
Ringmead RG12: Brac 4A 20
(not continuous)
Rings Hill TN11: Hild 4A 34
RIPLEY 2F 29
Ripley By-Pass GU23: Rip 3F 29
Ripley La. GU23: Rip 3A 30
KT24: W Hor 3A 30
Ripley Rd. GU4: E Clan 3F 29
GU23: Send 3F 29
RIPLEY SPRINGS 3E 21
Ripon Way WD6: Bore 1D 15
Ripple Rd. IG11: Bark, Dag 4D 17
RM9: Dag 4E 17
Risborough Rd.
HP22: S Man, Terr 1A 4
RISE PARK 2F 17
Rise Rd. SL5: S'dale 4D 21
River Bank KT8: E Mos 3C 22
RIVERHEAD 2F 33
River Hill TN15: S'oaks 3A 34
River Rd. IG11: Bark 4D 17
Riverside DA4: Eyns 4F 25
Riverside Dr. TW10: Ham 2C 22
WD3: Rick 1F 13
Riverside Rd. TW19: Stanw 2F 21
(not continuous)
Riverside Wlk. TW7: Isle 2C 22
Riverside Way GU15: Camb 2B 28
River Vw. RM16: Grays 1C 26
RIVERVIEW PARK 3D 27
Roberts La. SL9: Chal P 1E 13
Robert St. NW1 4F 15
Robert Way SS11: Wick 1F 19
ROBIN HOOD 2D 23
Robin Hood La. GU4: Sut G 3E 29
ME5: Wald 1F 35
Robin Hood Rd.
GU21: Knap, Wok 2D 29
(not continuous)
Robin Hood Way SW15 3D 23
SW20 3D 23
Robins Nest Hill
SG13: Howe G, L Ber 1F 7
Robinsway KT12: Hers 4B 22
Robson Av. NW10 3E 15
Robson Rd. SE27 2A 24
Rocfort Rd. ME6: Snod 1E 35
ROCHESTER 3F 27
ROCHESTER AIRPORT 4F 27
Rochester Av. BR1: Brom 3C 24
Rochester Castle 3E 27
Rochester Rd. DA12: Grav'nd 2D 27
ME1: Bur, Woul 4E 27
ME1: Roch, Chat 4F 27
ME2: Cux 4E 27
ME5: Chat, Roch 4F 27
ME20: A'ford 2E 35
Rochester Row SW1 1F 23
Rochester Way DA1: Dart 2F 25
SE3 2C 24
SE9 2D 25
Rochester Way Relief Rd. SE3 1C 24
SE9 1C 24
Rock Av. ME7: G'ham 4F 27
Rockfield Rd. RH8: Oxt 3C 32
Rock Hill BR6: Chels 1E 33
Rockingham Rd. UB8: Uxb 4F 13
Rock Rd. TN15: Bor G 2B 34
Rockshaw Rd. RH1: Mers 3F 31
Rocks La. SW13 2E 23
Rocks Rd., The ME19: E Mal 2E 35
Rocky La. RH2: Reig 3F 31
Rodborough Rd. NW11 3E 15
Roding La. IG7: Chig 1D 17
IG9: Buck H 1D 17
(not continuous)
Roding La. Nth. IG8: Wfd G 2C 16
Roding La. Sth.
IG4: Ilf, Wfd G 2C 16
(not continuous)
IG8: Wfd G 2C 16
Roding Rd. IG10: Lough 1D 17
Rodney Rd. SE17 1A 24
(not continuous)
ROE GREEN
AL10 1E 7
NW9 2D 15
Roe Grn. NW9 2D 15
ROEHAMPTON 2E 23
Roehampton High St. SW15 2E 23
ROEHAMPTON LANE 2E 23
Roehampton La. SW15 2E 23
Roehampton Va. SW15 2D 23
Roehyde Way AL10: Hat 2D 7
ROESTOCK 2D 7
Roestock La. AL4: Col H 2D 7
Roffe's La. CR3: Cat'm 3A 32
Rogers La. SL2: Stoke P 3D 13
Rogers Wood La. DA3: Fawk 4B 26
Rokesly Av. N8 2A 16
Rolls Rd. SE1 1A 24
Roman Rd. CM4: Inga 4C 10
CM4: Marg 3D 11
CM15: Mount, Shenf 4C 10
E2 4B 16
E3 4B 16
Roman Villa Rd.
DA2: Dart, S Dar, Sutt H 3A 26
DA4: S Dar, Sutt H 3A 26
Roman Way CR0: C'don 4A 24
ME2: Strood 4E 27
ROMFORD 2F 17
Romford Rd. CM5: Ongar 3A 10
E7 3C 16
E15 3C 16
IG7: Chad H, Chig 1E 17
RM5: Col R 2E 17
RM15: Avel 4A 18
Romney Rd. SE10 1C 24
ROMNEY STREET 1A 34
Romney St. TN15: Knat 1A 34
Rom Valley Way RM7: Rush G 3F 17
Ron Leighton Way E6 4D 17
Roodlands La. TN8: F Elm 4E 33
ROOKERY, THE 1B 14
Rookery Hill SS17: Corr 4E 19
Rookery Rd. BR6: Downe 1D 33
CM4: Bmore 3B 10
Rook La. CR3: Cat'm 3A 32
Roothill La. RH3: Bet 4D 31
Roper's La. ME3: Hoo 2F 27
Roscommon Way SS8: Can I 4F 19
Rosebay Av. CM12: Bill 4D 11
Rosebery Av. EC1 4A 16
ROSEDALE 3B 8
Rosedale Way EN7: Chesh 3B 8
ROSEHILL 4F 23
Rose Hill SL1: Burn 3C 12
SM1: Sutt 4E 23
ROSE HILL RDBT. 4F 23
Rose La. GU23: Rip 2F 29
RM6: Chad H 2E 17
Rosemary La. GU17: Bla 1A 28
TN15: Ash 1C 34
Rosendale Rd. SE21 2A 24
SE24 2A 24
Rose St. RG40: W'ham 3A 20
Rose Va. EN11: Hodd 1B 8
ROSHERVILLE 2C 26
Rosherville Way DA11: Nflt 2C 26
Rosslyn Hill NW3 3F 15
Rossmore Rd. NW1 4F 15
Rossway HP4: Berk 2D 5
Rossway La. HP23: Wigg 1D 5
Rothbury Rd. E9 3B 16
ROTHERHITHE 1B 24
Rotherhithe New Rd. SE16 1B 24
Roughetts Rd. ME19: Rya 2D 35
ROUGHWAY 3B 34
Roughway La. TN11: S'brne 3B 34
Roughwood La. HP8: Chal G 1E 13
Roundacre SS15: Lain 2D 19
ROUND BUSH 4C 6
Round Cl. GU46: Yat 1A 28
ROUNDSHAW 1A 32
ROUND STREET 3C 26
Round St. DA13: Sole S 3C 26
Roundway, The N17 2A 16
Roundwood Rd. NW10 3D 15
Rousebarn La.
WD3: Chan C, Crox G 4A 6
Rowan Rd. SW16 3F 23
Rowdow TN14: Otf 2A 34
Row Dow La. TN14: Knat 1F 33
TN15: Knat 1F 33
ROWHILL 1F 29
ROWLEY GREEN 1D 15
Rowley Grn. Rd. EN5: Ark 1E 15
Rowley La. EN5: Ark 4D 7
SL3: Wex 4E 13
WD6: Bore 4D 7
Rowley Rd. RM16: Ors 4C 18
ROW TOWN 1F 29
Row Town KT15: Add 1F 29
ROXETH 3C 14
Roxeth Grn. Av. HA2: Harr 3B 14
Roxeth Hill HA2: Harr 3C 14
ROXWELL 1C 10
Roxwell Rd.
CM1: Chelm, Rox, Writ 1D 11
Royal Albert Way E16 4C 16
ROYAL BRITISH LEGION VILLAGE 2E 35
Royal Docks Rd. E6 4D 17
IG11: Bark 4D 17
Royal Engineers Rd.
ME14: S'ing, Maids 2F 35
Royal Gunpowder Mills 3B 8
Royal Hill SE10 1C 24
Royal Horticultural Society Gardens, The (Wisley) 2A 30
Royal Hospital Rd. SW3 1F 23
Royal La. UB7: Yiew 4A 14
UB8: Hil 4A 14
Royal Mint St. E1 4A 16
Royal Pde. BR7: Chst 3D 25
SE3 1C 24
Royal Windsor Racecourse 1D 21
ROYDON 1C 8
Roydon Hall Rd. TN12: E Pec 4D 35
ROYDON HAMLET 2C 8
Roydon Rd. CM19: Har 1D 9
SG12: S Abb 1C 8
Royds La. CM14: Kel H 4A 10
Roystons, The KT5: Surb 4D 23
Ruckholt Rd. E10 3B 16
RUCKLERS LANE 2F 5
Rucklers La. WD4: K Lan 3F 5
Ruddlesway SL4: Wind 1C 20
(not continuous)
Rugby Rd. TW1: Twick 2C 22
RUISLIP 3A 14
RUISLIP COMMON 2A 14
RUISLIP GARDENS 3A 14
RUISLIP MANOR 3B 14
Ruislip Rd. UB5: N'olt 4B 14
UB6: G'frd 4B 14
Ruislip Rd. E. W7 4C 14
RUNFOLD 4B 28
Running Waters CM13: B'wood 1B 18
(not continuous)
RUNNYMEDE 2E 21
Runnymede 2E 21
Runsell La. CM3: Dan 2F 11
RUNWELL 1F 19
Runwell Chase SS11: Runw 1F 19
Runwell Rd. SS11: Wick 1F 19
Rushbottom La. SS7: Thun 2F 19
RUSHETT 4D 33
Rushett La. KT9: Chess 1C 30
RUSHETTS FARM 4F 31
Rushey Grn. SE6 2B 24
RUSH GREEN 3F 17
Rush Grn. Rd. RM7: Rush G 3F 17
Rushgrove Av. NW9 2D 15
Rushley SS13: Bas, Pit 2F 19
Rushmere La. HP5: Orch 3E 5
Rushmoor Arena 4A 28
Rushmoor Rd. GU11: Alde 4A 28
Rushmore Hill BR6: Prat B 1E 33
TN14: Knock, Prat B 1E 33
Rushworth Rd. RH2: Reig 4E 31
Ruskin Rd. SM5: Cars 4F 23
Russell Gdns. SS11: Wick 1F 19
RUSSELL GREEN 1F 11
Russell La. N20 1F 15
Russell Rd. EN1: Enf 4A 8
TW17: Shep 4A 22
Russell St. WC1 4A 16
Rutts, The WD23: B Hea 1C 14
Ruxbury Rd. KT16: Chert 4F 21
RUXLEY 3E 25
Ruxley La. KT19: Ewe 1D 31
RYARSH 2D 35
Ryarsh Rd. ME19: Birl 1D 35
Rycroft La. TN14: S'oaks 3F 33
RYDE, THE 1E 7
RYDENS 4B 22
Rydens Rd. KT12: Walt T 4B 22
Ryde's Hill Rd. GU2: Guild 4D 29
Rye Gro. GU18: Light 1D 29
RYE HILL 2D 9
Rye Hill Rd. CM18: Har 2D 9
Ryehurst La. RG42: Bin 3A 20
Rye La. SE15 1B 24
TN14: Dun G, Otf 2F 33
RYE PARK 1B 8
Rye Rd. EN11: Hodd 1B 8
SG12: S Abb, Hodd 1B 8

S

SABINE'S GREEN 4A 10
Sabine's Rd.
CM14: Nave, N'side 4A 10
RM4: Nave, N'side 4F 9
SAFFRON GREEN 4E 7
St Agnells La. HP2: Hem H 1A 6
ST ALBANS 2C 6
St Albans Hill HP3: Hem H 2A 6
St Albans La. WD5: Bedm 2B 6
St Albans Rd. AL3: Redb 1B 6
AL4: St A 1C 6
AL5: Harp 1B 6
EN5: Barn 4E 7
EN6: S Mim 3D 7

St Albans Rd. HP2: Hem H 2F 5
WD17: Wat 4B 6
WD24: Wat 4B 6
St Albans Rd. E. AL10: Hat 1E 7
St Albans Rd. W. AL10: Hat 1D 7
St Andrews Dr. HA7: Stan 2C 14
St Andrew's Rd. RM18: Tilb 1C 26
St Andrew St. SG14: Hertf 1A 8
St Andrew's Way SL1: Slou 4C 12
St Anne's Rd. AL2: Lon C 3C 6
CM15: Mount, Shenf 4C 10
St Ann's Hill SW18 2E 23
St Ann's Hill Rd. KT16: Chert 4F 21
St Ann's Rd. KT16: Chert 4F 21
N15 2A 16
St Asaph Rd. SE4 2B 24
St Augustine's Rd. DA17: Belv 1E 25
St Barnabas Rd. IG8: Wfd G 2C 16
SM1: Sutt 4F 23
St Blaise Av. BR1: Brom 3C 24
St Botolph's Rd. TN13: S'oaks 3F 33
St Bride's Av. HA8: Edg 2D 15
St Catherines Rd. GU16: Frim 2B 28
(not continuous)
St Chads Rd. RM16: Grays 1C 26
RM18: Grays, Tilb 1C 26
St Clements Way
DA9: Bluew, Ghithe 2B 26
St Clere Hill Rd. TN15: W King 1A 34
St Cloud Way SL6: Maide 4B 12
St Davids Rd. BR8: Swan 3F 25
ST DUNSTAN'S 1E 31
St Dunstans Av. W3 4D 15
St Dunstan's Hill SM1: Sutt 1E 31
St Dunstan's Rd. TW13: Felt 2A 22
St Edith's Rd. TN15: Kems'g 2A 34
St Edwards Way RM1: Rom 2F 17
St George's Av. KT13: Weyb 1A 30
St George's Dr. SW1 1F 23
ST GEORGE'S HILL 1A 30
St George's Rd. E7 3C 16
GU9: B Lea 4B 28
(not continuous)
SE1 1A 24
St Helens La. ME15: E Far 3E 35
ST HELIER 4F 23
St Helier Av. SM4: Mord 4F 23
St Hubert's La. SL9: Ger X 3E 13
St James La. DA9: Dart, Ghithe 2A 26
St James Rd. EN7: G Oak 3A 8
ST JAMES'S 4F 15
St James's Dr. SW17 2F 23
St James's Rd. CR0: C'don 4A 24
SE1 1B 24
SE16 1B 24
St James's St. E17 2B 16
SW1 4F 15
ST JOHNS
GU21 2E 29
SE8 1B 24
TN13 2F 33
St John's Gro. N19 3F 15
St John's Hill SW11 2F 23
TN13: S'oaks 2F 33
St John's Hill Rd. GU21: Wok 2E 29
St Johns Rd. GU14: Cove 2A 28
GU21: Wok 2E 29
HA9: Wemb 3D 15
HP1: Hem H 2F 5
HP10: Ty G 1B 12
TW7: Isle 1C 22
UB8: Uxb 4F 13
St John St. EC1 4A 16
St John's Way N19 3F 15
ST JOHN'S WOOD 4F 15
St John's Wood Rd. NW8 4F 15
St Judes Rd. TW20: Eng G 3E 21
ST JULIANS 2C 6
St Julians Rd.
TN15: S'oaks, Under 3A 34
St Katherine's La. ME6: Snod 1D 35
ST LEONARD'S 2C 4
St Leonards Av. ME4: Chat 4F 27
St Leonards Rd.
EN9: Naze, Walt A 2C 8
(not continuous)
KT7: T Ditt 4C 22
KT10: Clay 1C 30
SL4: Wind 2D 21
St Leonard's St. ME19: W Mal 2D 35
ST LUKE'S 4A 16
St Luke's Rd. SL4: Old Win 2E 21
ST MARGARETS
HP1 1E 5
SG12 1C 8
TW1 2C 22
St Margarets Rd.
DA2: Dart, S Dar 3A 26
DA4: S Dar 3A 26
TW1: Twick 2C 22
ST MARGARETS RDBT. 2C 22
St Margaret's St. ME1: Roch 4E 27
St Margaret St. SW1 1A 24
St Mark's Cres. SL6: Maide 4B 12
St Mark's Hill KT6: Surb 4D 23
St Marks Rd. CR4: Mitc 3F 23
EN1: Enf 1A 16
RG42: Bin 3A 20
SL6: Maide 4B 12
W10 4E 15
St Martin's La. WC2 4A 16
ST MARY CRAY 3E 25
St Marys Cl. ME18: Ladd 4D 35
St Mary's Hill SL5: S'hill 4C 20
ST MARY'S ISLAND 3F 27
St Mary's La. CM13: W H'dn 3B 18
RM14: Upm 3A 18
SG14: Herti, Hertf 1A 8
ST MARYS PLATT 2C 34
St Marys Rd. KT6: Surb 4C 22
KT13: Weyb 4A 22
SL3: L'ly 4E 13
SW19 3E 23
W5 1C 22
St Mary's Way HP5: Ches 3D 5
St Matthew's Rd. SW2 2A 24
St Michael's St. AL3: St A 2B 6
St Mildreds Rd. SE12 2C 24
St Nazaire Rd. CM1: Chelm 1D 11
St Nicholas La. SS15: Lain 2D 19
St Nicholas Way SM1: Sutt 4E 23
St Norbert Rd. SE4 2B 24
ST PANCRAS 4A 16
St Pancras Way NW1 3F 15
St Paul's Av. NW2 3E 15
ST PAUL'S CRAY 3E 25
St Paul's Cray Rd. BR7: Chst 3D 25
St Paul's Rd. IG11: Bark 4D 17
N1 3A 16
St Paul's Way E3 4B 16
St Paul's Wood Hill BR5: St P 3D 25
St Peter's Rd. CR0: C'don 4A 24
St Peter's St. AL1: St A 2C 6
ME16: Maids 2F 35
St Peter's Way KT15: Add 4F 21
KT16: Chert 4F 21
St Philip's Av. ME15: Maids 3F 35
St Quintin Av. W10 4E 15
ST STEPHENS 2B 6
St Stephen's Hill AL1: St A 2C 6
St Thomas' Dr. HA5: Pinn 2B 14
St Thomas St. SE1 4A 16
St Vincents Av. DA1: Dart 2A 26
ST VINCENT'S HAMLET 1A 18
St Vincents La. ME19: Addtn 2C 34
St Vincents Rd. DA1: Dart 2A 26
St William's Way ME1: Roch 4F 27
Salcott Cres. SS12: Wick 1F 19
Sale Pl. W2 4F 15
SALFORDS 4F 31
Salisbury Rd. KT4: Wor Pk 4D 23
Salmon La. E14 4B 16
Salmons La. CR3: Whyt 2A 32
CR3: Whyt, Cat'm 2A 32
Salmons La. W. CR3: Cat'm 2A 32
Salmon St. NW9 3D 15
Saltbox Hill TN16: Big H 1C 32
Salt Box Rd. GU3: Guild 3E 29
GU4: Guild 3E 29
Salter Rd. SE16 4B 16
Salter's Hill SE19 3A 24
Salt La. ME3: Cli 2E 27
Salts La. ME15: Loose 4F 35
Salusbury Rd. NW6 4E 15
Sampleoak La.
GU4: Blckh, Guild 4F 29
Sandbanks Hill DA2: Bean, Dart 3B 26
Sandcross La. RH2: Reig 4E 31
Sanders La. NW7 2E 15
SANDERSTEAD 1B 32
Sanderstead Hill CR2: Sande 1A 32
Sanderstead Rd.
CR2: Sande, S Croy 1A 32
Sandford Mill Rd.
CM2: Gt B, Spr 2E 11
(not continuous)
Sandford Rd. CM2: Chelm 2E 11
Sandhill La. ME3: High'm 2E 27
Sandhills La. GU25: Vir W 4E 21
SANDHURST 1A 28
Sandhurst La. GU17: Bla 1A 28
Sandhurst Rd. GU46: Yat 1A 28
RG40: Fin 4A 20
RG45: Crow 1A 28
SE6 2C 24
SANDLING 2F 35
Sandling La.
ME14: Maids, Pen H, S'ing 2F 35
SANDON 2F 11
SANDON INTERCHANGE 2F 11
Sandown Pk. Racecourse 4C 22
Sandpit Hall Rd. GU24: Chob 1E 29
Sandpit La. AL1: St A 2C 6
AL4: St A 2C 6
CM14: Pil H, S Weald 1A 18
Sandpit Rd. RH1: Redh 4F 31
SANDRIDGE 1C 6
Sandridgebury La. AL3: St A 1C 6
Sandridge Rd. AL1: St A 1C 6
Sandringham Cres. AL4: St A 1C 6
Sandringham Rd. E8 3A 16
SANDS 1A 12
SANDS END 1F 23
Sands Rd. GU10: Runf 4B 28
Sandycombe Rd.
TW9: Kew, Rich 2D 23
SANDY CROSS 4B 28
Sandy La. BR5: St P 3E 25
DA2: Bean, Sflt 2B 26
(not continuous)
DA14: Sidc 3E 25
GU3: Art 4E 29
GU5: Shere 4A 30
GU14: Cove 2A 28
GU47: S'urst 1A 28
GU52: Chu C 4A 28
HA6: Nwood 1A 14
KT1: Ham W 3C 22
KT11: Cobh 1B 30
KT22: Oxs 1B 30
ME19: Addtn, Wro 2C 34
ME19: Rya 2D 35
RH1: Blet 4A 32
RH1: S Nut 4A 32
RH3: Bet 4D 31
RH8: Oxt 3C 32
RM15: Avel, Wenn 4A 18
SM2: Cheam 1E 31
SM6: Wall 1F 31
TN15: Ivy H, Igh 3B 34
TW11: Tedd 3C 22
WD23: Bush 4C 6
WD25: A'ham 4C 6
Sandy La. Nth. SM6: Wall 4F 23
Sandy La. Sth. SM6: Wall 1F 31
Sandy Lodge HA6: Nwood 1A 14
Sanford St. SE14 1B 24
Sangley Rd. SE6 2B 24
Santers La. EN6: Pot B 3E 7
SARRATT 4F 5
SARRATT BOTTOM 4F 5
Sarratt La. WD3: Chor, Loud, Sarr 4F 5
Sarratt Rd.
WD3: Sarr, Chan C, Crox G 4F 5
Saunders La. GU22: Wok 2D 29
Savernake Way RG12: Brac 4B 20
Savill Garden, The 3D 21
SAVOY CIRCUS 4D 15
Sawpit Hill HP15: Haz 4B 4
Sawyers La. EN6: Pot B 3E 7
Saxbys Rd. TN15: Seal 2A 34
Scabharbour Rd. TN11: Hild 4F 33
TN14: Weald, Hild 4F 33
SCARBOROUGH 1E 35
Scarborough La. ME1: Bur 1E 35
Scarletts La. RG10: K Grn 1A 20
School Cl. GU24: Bisl 2D 29
School Hill RH1: Mers 3F 31
School La. BR8: Swan 3F 25
CM1: Broom 1E 11
CM4: Stock 4D 11
CM5: Abb R, Beau R, Will 1A 10
(not continuous)
DA2: Bean 3B 26
DA3: Fawk, S Dar 3A 26
DA4: Hort K, S Dar, Fawk 3A 26
GU3: Norm 4C 28
GU24: Pirb 2D 29
HP7: Amer 4D 5
HP7: Penn S 4C 4
HP9: See G 2D 13
HP22: W Tur 1A 4
KT15: Add 4F 21
KT22: Fet 2C 30
ME1: Woul 4E 27
ME3: High'm 2E 27
ME19: Tros 1C 34
RM16: Ors 4C 18
SL6: Cook 3B 12
SL7: Lit M 2B 12
TN11: Plax, S'brne 3B 34
TN15: Seal 2A 34
TN15: W King 1A 34
WD23: Bush 1B 14
School Rd. CM1: G Eas 1C 10
CM5: Ongar, Toot H 3F 9
CM11: D'ham 4E 11
CM15: Dodd, Kel H 4A 10
GU20: W'sham 4C 20
HP10: Ty G 1C 12
RG10: W Law 2A 20
TW15: Ashf 3A 22
SCHOOL ROAD JUNC. 3A 22
SCILLY ISLES 4C 22
Scotch Comn. W13 4C 14
SCOTCH HOUSE 1F 23
Scotland Bri. Rd. KT15: New H 1F 29
Scotland Grn. Rd. EN3: Pond E 1B 16
Scotshall La. CR6: Warl 2C 32
Scots Hill WD3: Crox G 1A 14
Scott's Gro. Rd. GU24: Chob 1D 29
Scott's La. BR2: Brom 3C 24
Scratchers La. DA3: Fawk 4A 26
Scrubbs La. NW10 4E 15
W10 4E 15
Scudders Hill DA3: Fawk 4B 26
SEAL 2A 34
SEAL CHART 3A 34
SEALE 4C 28
Seale La. GU3: Putt 4C 28
GU10: Seale 4B 28
Seal Hollow Rd. TN13: S'oaks 3F 33
Seal Rd. TN14: S'oaks 2F 33
TN15: S'oaks 2A 34
Second Av. CM18: Har 1D 9
Sedge Grn. CM19: Roy 2C 8
EN9: Naze, Roy 2C 8
SEER GREEN 2D 13
SELHURST 4A 24
Selhurst Rd. SE25 4A 24
SELSDON 1B 32
Selsdon Pk. Rd. CR0: Sels 1B 32
CR2: Sels 1B 32
Selsdon Rd. CR2: S Croy 4A 24
Selvage La. NW7 1D 15
Selwyn Av. E4 2C 16
SEND 3F 29
Send Barns La. GU23: Send 3F 29
Send Hill GU23: Send 3F 29
SEND MARSH 3F 29
Send Marsh Rd.
GU23: Rip, Send 3F 29
Send Rd. GU23: Send 3F 29
Sergehill La. WD5: Bedm 3B 6
Seven Arches Rd.
CM14: B'wood 1B 18
Seven Hills Rd. KT11: Cobh 1A 30
KT12: Hers, W Vill 1A 30
SL0: Iver H 3E 13
SEVEN KINGS 3D 17
Seven Kings Rd. IG3: Ilf 3D 17
Seven Mile La. ME18: Mere 2C 34
TN12: E Pec 3C 34
(not continuous)
TN15: Bor G, Wro 2C 34
(not continuous)
SEVENOAKS 3F 33
Sevenoaks By-Pass
TN14: Ide H, S'oaks, Sund, Weald 3F 33
SEVENOAKS COMMON 3F 33
Sevenoaks Rd. BR6: Chels, Orp 4D 25
BR6: Prat B 1D 33
TN14: Hals 1E 33
TN14: Otf, S'oaks 2F 33
TN15: Bor G 2B 34
TN15: Igh, Seal 3A 34
Sevenoaks Way BR5: St P 3E 25
SEVENOAKS WEALD 4F 33
SEVEN SISTERS 2A 16
Seven Sisters Rd. N4 3A 16
N7 3A 16
N15 2A 16
SEWARDSTONE 4C 8
SEWARDSTONEBURY 4C 8
Sewardstone Rd. E2 4B 16
E4 1B 16
EN9: Enf, Walt A 3C 8
Seymour Ct. Rd. SL7: Marl 2A 12
Seymour Pl. W1 4F 15
Seymour St. W1 4F 15
Shacklands Rd.
TN14: Hals, S'ham 1F 33
Shacklegate La. TW11: Tedd 3C 22
Shackleton Way AL7: W City 1F 7
SHACKLEWELL 3A 16
Shacklewell La. E8 3A 16
SHADWELL 4B 16
Shaftesbury Av. HA2: Harr 3B 14
W1 4F 15
WC2 4F 15
Shaggy Calf La. SL2: Slou 4E 13
SHALFORD 4E 29
Shalford Rd. GU1: Guild 4E 29
SHANNON CORNER 3E 23
Shantock Hall La. HP3: Bov 3E 5
Shantock La. HP3: Bov 3E 5
Shardeloes Rd. SE4 1B 24
SE14 1B 24
Sharpes La. HP1: Hem H 2E 5
Shawfield Rd. GU12: Ash 4B 28
Shawstead Rd. ME7: G'ham 4F 27
Sheal's Cres. ME15: Maids 3F 35
SHEARS, THE 3A 22
Sheen Comn. Dr. TW10: Rich 2D 23
Sheen La. SW14 2D 23
Sheen Rd. TW9: Rich 2D 23
TW10: Rich 2D 23
Sheepbarn La. CR6: Big H 1C 32
Sheepcote Dell Rd.
HP7: Bea E 4C 4
HP15: Holm G 4C 4
Sheepcote La. BR5: St M Cry 4E 25
SL6: Pal S 2B 20
Sheepcote Rd. HA1: Harr 2C 14
Sheepcot La. WD25: Wat 3B 6
(not continuous)
Sheephouse La.
RH5: Ab C, Wott 4B 30
(not continuous)
Sheephouse Rd. SL6: Maide 4B 12
Sheepridge La. HP10: Flack H 2B 12
SL7: Lit M 2B 12
Sheep Wlk. TW17: Shep 4A 22
Sheering Lwr. Rd. CM17: Har 1E 9
Sheering Rd. CM17: Har 1E 9
(not continuous)
SHEERWATER 1F 29
Sheerwater Rd. KT14: W Byf 1F 29
KT15: Wdhm 1F 29
SHEET HILL 3B 34
Sheet Hill TN15: Plax 3B 34
Sheet St. SL4: Wind 1D 21
Sheet St. Rd. SL4: Wind 3C 20
Sheffield Rd. SL1: Slou 4D 13
Shelbourne Rd. N17 2B 16
Shellbank La. DA2: Bean, Dart 3B 26
SHELLEY 2A 10
Shelleys La. TN14: Knock 2E 33
SHELLOW BOWELLS 2B 10
Shelvers Way KT20: Tad 2E 31
Shendish Airfield 2F 5
SHENFIELD 1B 18
Shenfield Rd.
CM15: B'wood, Shenf 1B 18
SHENLEY 3D 7
SHENLEYBURY 3D 7
Shenleybury WD7: Shenl 3D 7
Shenley Hill WD7: Rad 4C 6
Shenley La. AL2: Lon C 2C 6
Shenley Rd. HP2: Hem H 1A 6
WD6: Bore 4D 7
WD7: Rad 3C 6
Shepherd & Flock Rdbt.
GU9: Farnh 4A 28
Shepherdess Wlk. N1 4A 16
SHEPHERD'S BUSH 1E 23
Shepherd's Bush Grn. W12 1E 23
Shepherd's Bush Rd. W6 1E 23
Shepherds Hill N6 2F 15
RH1: Mers 3F 31
RM3: Hrld W 2A 18
Shepherds La. DA1: Dart 2F 25
GU2: Guild 4D 29
RG42: Brac 3B 20
SL6: Hur 4A 12
WD3: Chor, Rick 1F 13
Shepherds Way AL9: Brk P 3F 7
Shepiston La. UB3: Harl 1A 22
SHEPPERTON 4A 22
SHEPPERTON GREEN 3A 22
Shepperton Rd. N1 4A 16
TW18: Lale, Shep 3F 21
SHEPWAY 3F 35
Sherard Rd. SE9 2D 25
Sherbourne GU5: Alb 4F 29
SHERE 4A 30
Shere La. GU5: Shere 4A 30
Shere Rd. GU4: Guild, W Cla 4F 29
GU5: Alb, Goms, Shere 4F 29
KT24: W Hor 3A 30
(not continuous)
Sherfield Rd. RM17: Grays 1B 26
Shernhall St. E17 2C 16
Sherwood Pk. Rd. CR4: Mitc 3F 23
Shillitoe Av. EN6: Pot B 3E 7
Shingle Barn La. ME15: W Far 4E 35
Shingle Hall Rd. CM16: Epp U 2D 9
SHIPBOURNE 3B 34
Shipbourne Rd. TN10: Tonb 4B 34
TN11: Tonb 4B 34
Ship Hill SL1: Burn 3D 13
TN16: Tats 2C 32
Ship La. DA4: Sutt H, Swan 3A 26
GU14: Farnb 2B 28
RM15: Avel, Purf 1A 26
RM19: Purf 1A 26
Shipley Hills Rd. DA13: Meop 4D 27
Ship Rd. CM2: W Han 3E 11
Shirehall Rd. DA2: Dart 3F 25
Shire La. BR2: Kes 1D 33
BR6: Chels, Downe 1D 33
(not continuous)
SL9: Chal P 1E 13
(not continuous)
WD3: Chor 1E 13
Shirland Rd. W9 4E 15
SHIRLEY 4B 24
Shirley Chu. Rd. CR0: C'don 4B 24
Shirley Hills Rd. CR0: C'don 4B 24
SHIRLEY OAKS 4B 24
Shirley Rd. CR0: C'don 4B 24
Shirley Way CR0: C'don 4B 24
Shoe La. GU11: Alde 3B 28
Shonks Mill Rd.
RM4: Nave, Ongar 4F 9
SHOOTERS HILL 1D 25
Shooters Hill DA16: Well 1D 25
SE18 1D 25
Shooters Hill Rd. SE10 1C 24
SE18 1C 24
SHOOTERSWAY 2D 5
Shootersway HP4: Berk 1D 5
Shoot Up Hill NW2 3E 15
Shoppenhangers Rd.
SL6: Maide 1B 20
Shore, The DA11: Nflt 2C 26
SHOREDITCH 4A 16
Shoreditch High St. E1 4A 16
SHOREHAM 1F 33
Shoreham La. BR6: Chels 1E 33
TN14: Hals 1E 33
Shoreham Rd. DA4: Eyns 1F 33
TN14: Otf, S'ham 1F 33
Shores Rd. GU21: Wok 1E 29
SHORNE 3D 27
Shorne Ifield Rd. DA12: Shorne 3D 27
SHORNE RIDGEWAY 3D 27
Shorne Wood Country Pk. 3D 27
SHORTLANDS 3C 24
Shortlands Rd. BR2: Brom 3C 24
Short La. CM11: Ram H 1E 19
RH8: Limp 4C 32
TW19: Stanw 2A 22
Shorts Way ME1: Roch 4E 27
SHOTGATE 1F 19
SHREDING GREEN 4E 13
Shrubbery Rd. DA4: S Dar 3A 26
Shrublands Rd. HP4: Berk 1E 5
SHRUBS HILL 4D 21
SHURLOCK ROW 2A 20
SIDCUP 3E 25
Sidcup By-Pass DA14: Sidc 3D 25
Sidcup Hill DA14: Sidc 3E 25
Sidcup Rd. SE9 2C 24
SE12 2C 24
Sidmouth Rd. NW2 3E 15
Sidmouth St. WC1 4A 16
Sidney St. E1 4B 16
(not continuous)
Silver Hill HP8: Chal G 1E 13
Silverstead La. TN16: Westrm 2D 33
Silver St. EN1: Enf 4A 8
EN7: Walt C, G Oak 3A 8
ME3: Wain 2E 27
N18 1A 16
Silverthorne Rd. SW8 1F 23
SILVERTOWN 4C 16
Silvertown Way E16 4C 16
(not continuous)
Silwood Rd. SL5: S'dale, S'hill 3D 21
Simmons La. E4 1C 16
Singles Cross La. TN14: Knock 1E 33
SINGLE STREET 2D 33
Single St. TN16: Big H 2D 33
SINGLEWELL 3C 26
Singlewell Rd. DA11: Grav'nd 2C 26
SIPSON 1A 22
Sipson La. UB3: Harl 1A 22
UB7: Sip 1A 22
Sipson Rd. UB7: Sip, W Dray 1A 22
(not continuous)
Sittingbourne Rd. ME14: Det 2F 35
ME14: Maids 2F 35
(not continuous)
Siviter Way RM10: Dag 3E 17
Sixth Cross Rd. TW2: Twick 2C 22
Skeet Hill La. BR5: Orp 4E 25
BR6: Orp 4E 25
Skibbs La. BR5: Orp, St M Cry 4E 25
BR6: Chels, Orp 4E 25
Skid Hill La. CR6: Warl 1C 32
Skimped Hill La. RG12: Brac 3B 20
Skinner St. EC1 4A 16
Skinney La. DA4: Hort K, S Dar 3A 26
Slade, The SE18 1D 25
SLADE GREEN 1F 25
Slade Grn. Rd. DA8: Erith 1F 25
Slade Oak La. SL9: Den, Ger X 2F 13
UB9: Den 2F 13
Slade Rd. KT16: Ott 1F 29
Slades Hill EN2: Enf 4A 8
Slade's La. CM2: Gall 3F 11
Slad La. HP27: Lac G, Speen 4A 4
SLEAPSHYDE 2D 7
Sleapshyde La. AL4: S'ford 2D 7
Slewins La. RM11: Horn 2F 17
Slines Oak Rd. CR3: Wold 3B 32
CR6: Warl, Wold 2B 32
Slipshatch Rd. RH2: Reig 4E 31
Sloane St. SW1 1F 23
Slough La. HP14: Bled R, Saund 4A 4
KT18: H'ly 3D 31
Slough Rd. SL0: Iver H 4F 13
SL3: Dat 1E 21
SL4: Eton 1D 21
SLYFIELD GREEN 4E 29
Smalldean La.
HP14: Lac G, Saund 4A 4
HP27: Lac G 4A 4
SMALLFORD 2D 7
Smallford La. AL4: S'ford 2D 7
Smallgains La. CM4: Stock 4D 11
Small Profits ME18: Yald 4D 35
Smallshoes Hill CM1: G Eas 1C 10
Smart's Heath La. GU22: Wok 3E 29
Smart's Heath Rd. GU22: Wok 3D 29
Smeaton Rd. EN3: Enf L 4B 8
Smewins Rd. SL6: W Walt 1A 20
Smitham Bottom La. CR8: Purl 1F 31
Smitham Downs Rd. CR8: Purl 1F 31
Smith's Hill ME15: W Far 4E 35
Smiths La. EN7: Chesh 2A 8
SL4: Wind 1D 21
TN8: Crock H 4D 33
SMUG OAK 3B 6
Smug Oak La.
AL2: Brick W, Col S 3B 6
Snag La. TN14: Cud 1D 33
Snakes Hill CM14: N'side, Pil H 4A 10
Snakes La. E.
IG8: Buck H, Wfd G 2C 16
Snakes La. W. IG8: Wfd G 1C 16
SNARESBROOK 2C 16
Snaresbrook Rd. E11 2C 16
Snatts Hill RH8: Oxt 3C 32
SNODLAND 1E 35
Snodland By-Pass
ME6: Hall, Snod 1E 35
Snodland Rd. ME6: Snod 1D 35
ME19: Birl 1D 35
Snoll Hatch Rd. TN12: E Pec 4D 35
Snowerhill Rd. RH3: Bet 4D 31
Snow's Ride GU20: W'sham 4C 20
SOHO 4F 15
Solefields Rd. TN13: S'oaks 3F 33
Solesbridge La.
WD3: Chor, Sarr 4F 5
SOLE STREET 4C 26
Sole St. DA12: Cobh, Sole S 4C 26
Solway HP2: Hem H 1A 6
Somerset Rd. RH1: Redh 4F 31
UB1: S'hall 4B 14
SOMERS TOWN 4F 15
Somnes Av. SS8: Can I 3F 19
SOPWELL 2C 6
Sopwith Dr. KT13: Weyb 1A 30
Sorrells, The SS17: Stan H 4D 19
SOUTH ACTON 1D 23
SOUTHALL 4B 14
SOUTHALL GREEN 1B 22
Southall La. TW5: Cran 1B 22
UB2: S'hall 1B 22
Southampton Rd. NW5 3F 15
Southampton Row WC1 4A 16
Southampton Way SE5 1A 24
SOUTH ASCOT 4C 20
Sth. Ash Rd. TN15: Ash 1B 34
Sth. Audley St. W1 4F 15
SOUTH BEDDINGTON 1F 31
SOUTH BENFLEET 3F 19
SOUTHBOROUGH
BR2 4D 25
KT6 4C 22
Southborough La. BR2: Brom 4D 25
Southborough Rd. BR1: Brom 4D 25
Southbridge Rd. CR0: C'don 4A 24
SOUTH BROMLEY 4C 16
Southbrook Rd. SE12 2C 24
Southbury Av. EN1: Enf 4A 8
SOUTH CAMP 4B 28
SOUTH CHINGFORD 1B 16
SOUTHCOURT 1A 4
Southcroft Rd. SW16 3F 23
SW17 3F 23
Sth. Croxted Rd. SE21 2A 24
SOUTH CROYDON 4A 24
SOUTH DARENTH 3A 26
Sth. Ealing Rd. W5 1C 22
Sth. Eden Pk. Rd. BR3: Beck 4B 24
SOUTHEND 3C 24
South End CR0: C'don 4A 24
Southend Arterial Rd.
CM13: Gt War, L War, W H'dn 2F 17
RM2: Hrld W 2F 17
RM3: Hrld W 2F 17
RM11: Horn, Upm 2F 17
RM14: Gt War, Upm 2F 17
SS6: Ray 2D 19
SS12: Wick 2D 19
SS14: Bas 2D 19
SS15: Bas, Lain 2D 19
Southend Cres. SE9 2D 25
Southend La. SE6 3B 24
SE26 3B 24
South End Rd. NW3 3F 15
RM12: Horn 3F 17
RM13: Horn, Rain 4F 17
Southend Rd. BR3: Beck 3B 24
CM2: E Han, Howe G, Ret 3F 11
CM3: Ret 3F 11
CM11: Bill 1D 19
CM12: Bill 1D 19
E4 2B 16
E17 2B 16
E18 2C 16
IG8: Wfd G 2C 16
RM17: Grays 1C 26
SS11: Wick 1F 19
(not continuous)
SS17: Corr, Fob, Horn H, Stan H 4D 19
Souther Cross CM1: G Eas 1C 10
Southernhay SS14: Bas 2E 19
(not continuous)
Southern Perimeter Rd.
TW6: H'row A 2F 21
Southerns La. CR5: Coul 3F 31
Southern Way CM17: Har 1E 9
CM18: Har 1D 9
CM19: Har 1D 9
Sth. Essex Crematorium
RM14: Upm 3A 18
SOUTH FARNBOROUGH 3B 28
Southfield Rd. W4 1D 23
SOUTHFIELDS
SS15 2D 19
SW18 2E 23
SOUTHFLEET 3B 26
Southfleet Rd. DA2: Bean 3B 26
DA10: Swans 2B 26
SOUTHGATE 1F 15
Southgate Rd. EN6: Pot B 3F 7
N1 4A 16
SOUTH GODSTONE 4B 32
SOUTH GREEN 1D 19
South Gro. E17 2B 16
N6 3F 15
SOUTH HACKNEY 3B 16
SOUTH HAMPSTEAD 3F 15
SOUTH HANNINGFIELD 4F 11
Sth. Hanningfield Rd.
CM3: Ret, Sth H 4E 11
SS11: Runw, Sth H, Ret 4E 11
SOUTH HAREFIELD 2F 13
SOUTH HARROW 3C 14
SOUTH HATFIELD 2E 7
SOUTH HEATH 3C 4
South Hill GU1: Guild 4E 29
SS16: Horn H, Lan H 3D 19
SS17: Horn H 3D 19
(High Rd.)
SS17: Horn H 4D 19
(Saffron Cl.)
Sth. Hill Rd. RG12: Brac 4B 20
SOUTH HORNCHURCH 4F 17
Southill La. HA5: Eastc 2B 14
SOUTH KENSINGTON 1F 23
SOUTH LAMBETH 1A 24
Sth. Lambeth Rd. SW8 1A 24
Southlands La. RH8: Oxt, Tand 4B 32
Southlands Rd. BR1: Brom 3C 24
BR2: Brom 3C 24
UB9: Den 3F 13
South La. KT3: N Mald 3D 23
South La. W. KT3: N Mald 3D 23
SOUTHLEA 1E 21
Southlea Rd. SL3: Dat 1E 21
SL4: Wind 2E 21
Sth. Lodge Av. CR4: Mitc 3A 24
South Mayne SS13: Bas, Pit 2E 19
South Mdw. La. SL4: Eton 1D 21
SOUTH MERSTHAM 3F 31
SOUTH MIMMS 3E 7
SOUTH NORWOOD 3B 24
Sth. Norwood Hill SE25 3A 24
SOUTH NUTFIELD 4A 32
SOUTH OCKENDON 4B 18
Sth. Ordnance Rd. EN3: Enf L 4B 8
Southover N12 1E 15
SOUTH OXHEY 1B 14
South Pde. W4 1D 23
SOUTH PARK 4E 31
South Pk. Dr. IG3: Ilf 3D 17
IG11: Bark 3D 17
Sth. Pk. Hill Rd. CR2: S Croy 4A 24
Sth. Pk. La. RH1: Blet 4B 32
South Rd. GU21: Wok 2E 29
RM15: S Ock 4B 18
(not continuous)
TW2: Twick 2C 22
UB1: S'hall 1B 22
SOUTH RUISLIP 3B 14
Southside Comn. SW19 3E 23
SOUTH STIFFORD 1B 26
SOUTH STREET
DA13 1C 34
TN16 2D 33
South St. CM3: Gt W 1D 11
DA13: Meop 1C 34
EN3: Pond E 1B 16
GU9: Farnh 4A 28
HP22: Wend 2B 4
ME16: Barm 3E 35
RH4: Dork 4C 30
RM1: Rom 2F 17
TW7: Isle 2C 22
TW18: Staines 3F 21
SOUTH TOTTENHAM 2A 16
SOUTHWARK 4A 16
Southwark Bri. SE1 4A 16
Southwark Bri. Rd. SE1 1A 24
Southwark Pk. Rd. SE16 1B 24
Southwark St. SE1 4A 16
South Way AL9: Hat 2E 7
AL10: Hat 2E 7
HA9: Wemb 3D 15
WD5: Ab L 3A 6
Southway GU2: Guild 4D 29
SOUTH WEALD 1A 18
Southwell Pk. Rd. GU15: Camb 1B 28
SOUTH WIMBLEDON 3E 23
SOUTHWOOD 3A 28
SOUTH WOODFORD 2C 16
Sth. Woodford to Barking Relief Rd.
E6 2C 16
E11 2C 16
E12 2C 16
IG1: Ilf 2C 16
IG4: Ilf 2C 16
IG11: Bark 2C 16
Southwood La. N6 3F 15
Southwood Rd. GU14: Cove 3A 28
SE9 2D 25
Sovereign Blvd. ME7: G'ham 4F 27
Spa Hill SE19 3A 24
Spains Hall Rd. CM5: Will 2B 10
Spaniards Rd. NW3 3F 15
Sparepenny La.
DA4: Eyns, Farni 4F 25
SPARROW ROW 1D 29
Sparrow Row GU24: Chob 1D 29
Sparrows Herne SS16: Bas 3E 19
WD23: Bush 1B 14
Sparrows La.
CM22: Abb R, M Grn, Hat H 1A 10
Speedgate Hill DA3: Fawk 4B 26
SPEEN 4A 4
Speen Rd. HP14: Hug V, Nth D 4A 4
Speer Rd. KT7: T Ditt 4C 22
Spelthorne La. TW15: Ashf 3A 22
Spencer Pk. SW18 2F 23
Spencer Rd. KT8: E Mos 4C 22
Spencers Rd. SL6: Maide 4B 12
Spencer St. EC1 4A 16
SPENDIFF 2F 27
Spinfield La. SL7: Marl 3A 12
Spinney Hill KT15: Add 4F 21
SPITAL 2D 21
SPITALBROOK 1B 8
SPITALS CROSS 4D 33
SPITALFIELDS 4B 16
Spittal St. SL7: Marl 3A 12
Spook Hill RH5: N Holm 4C 30
Sporehams La. CM2: Sando 3F 11
CM3: Dan 3F 11
Spout Hill CR0: Addtn 4B 24
Spout La. TN8: Crock H 4D 33
Spriggs La. CM4: Bmore 3B 10
Springbottom La. RH1: Blet 3A 32
Springbridge Rd. W5 4C 14
Spring Coppice La.
HP27: Speen 4A 4
Spring Elms La. CM3: Lit B 2F 11
SPRINGFIELD 1E 11
Springfield Grn. CM1: Spr 1E 11
Springfield Rd.
CM2: Chelm, Spr 2E 11
(not continuous)
SPRING GROVE 1C 22
Spring Gro. Rd.
TW3: Houn, Isle 1B 22
TW7: Isle 1B 22
Springhead Rd. DA11: Nflt 2C 26

Springhouse La. SS17: Corr 4E 19
Springhouse Rd. SS17: Corr 4D 19
Spring La.
HP10: Flack H, Wyc M 2B 12
RH8: Oxt 4C 32
SE25 . . . . .4B 24
SL2: Farn R 3D 13
SL6: Cook 3B 12
TN15: Igh 2B 34
SPRING PARK 4B 24
Spring St. KT17: Ewe 1D 31
W2 .4F 15
Spring Wlk. EN10: Brox 2B 8
Springwell La. UB9: Hare 1F 13
WD3: Rick 1F 13
Spurlands End Rd. HP15: Gt Kin 4B 4
Spur Rd. BR6: Orp 4E 25
HA8: Edg 1D 15
TW7: Isle 1C 22
Square, The CM4: Stock 4D 11
Square Hill Rd. ME15: Maids 3F 35
Squire's Bri. Rd. TW17: Shep 3A 22
Squires La. N3 . . . . .2E 15
SQUIRREL'S HEATH 2F 17
Squirrels Heath La.
RM2: Horn, Rom 2F 17
RM11: Horn, Rom 2F 17
Squirrels Heath Rd.
RM3: Hrld W 2A 18
Stablebridge Rd. HP22: Ast C 1B 4
Stack La. DA4: Hort K 3A 26
Staffhurst Wood Rd.
TN8: Limp 4C 32
STAFFORDLAKE 2D 29
Stafford Rd. CR0: Wadd 1F 31
CR3: Cat'm 3A 32
SM6: Wall 1F 31
Stagg Hill EN4: Had W 4F 7
STAG LANE 2D 23
Stag La. HA8: Edg 2D 15
HP15: Gt Kin 4B 4
NW9 . . . . .2D 15
WD3: Chor 1F 13
STAINES 3F 21
Staines By-Pass TW15: Ashf 2F 21
TW18: Staines 2F 21
TW19: Staines 2F 21
STAINES GREEN 1A 8
Staines Rd. KT16: Chert 4F 21
TW2: Twick 2B 22
TW3: Houn 2A 22
TW4: Houn 2A 22
TW14: Bedf, Felt 2A 22
(not continuous)
TW18: Lale, Staines 3F 21
TW19: Wray 2E 21
Staines Rd. E. TW16: Sun 3B 22
Staines Rd. W. TW15: Ashf 3A 22
TW16: Sun 3A 22
STALLIONS GREEN 4C 34
Stamford Brook Rd. W6 . . . . .1D 23
Stamford Hill N16 . . . . .3A 16
Stamford Rd. N1 . . . . .3A 16
Stamford St. SE1 . . . . .4A 16
STANBOROUGH 1D 7
Stanborough Rd. AL8: W City 1E 7
Staneway SS16: Bas 3D 19
Stanford La. TN11: Had 4C 34
STANFORD-LE-HOPE 4D 19
Stanford-le-Hope By-Pass
SS17: Horn H, Lan H, Stan H
. . . . .3D 19
STANFORD RIVERS 3F 9
Stanford Rivers Rd.
CM5: Ongar 3A 10
Stanford Rd. RM16: Grays, Ors 1C 26
SS17: Stan H 4C 18
Stangate Rd. ME19: Birl 1D 35
Stanhope Gdns. SW7 . . . . .1F 23
Stanhope Rd. AL1: St A 2C 6
DA10: Swans 2B 26
Stan La. ME18: W Peck 3C 34
Stanley Hill GU24: Pirb 2C 28
HP7: Amer 4D 5
Stanley Pk. Rd. SM5: Cars 1F 31
SM6: Wall 1F 31
Stanley Rd. RM17: Grays 1B 26
TW11: Tedd 3C 22
STANMORE 2C 14
Stanmore Hill HA7: Stan 1C 14
STANNERS HILL 1E 29
Stansfeld Rd. E6 . . . . .4C 16
STANSTEAD ABBOTTS 1C 8
Stanstead Rd. CR3: Cat'm 3A 32
EN11: Hodd 1B 8
SE6 .2B 24
SE23 . . . . .2B 24
SG12: Gt A, Rush G, Ware 1B 8
SG13: Hertf, Hert H, Rush G . . .1B 8
STANSTED 1B 34
Stansted Hill TN15: Stans 1B 34
Stansted La. TN15: Ash 1B 34
STANWELL 2A 22
STANWELL MOOR 2F 21
Stanwell Moor Rd.
TW18: Staines 2F 21
TW19: Lford, Stan M 2F 21
TW19: Staines, Stan M 2F 21
UB7: Lford 1F 21
Stanwell Rd. SL3: Hort 2E 21
TW14: Bedf 2A 22
TW15: Ashf 2A 22
STAPLEFORD ABBOTTS 1F 17
Stapleford Rd.
RM4: Stap A, Stap T 4E 9
STAPLEFORD TAWNEY 4E 9
Stapleford Tawney Airfield 4E 9
Staple Hill Rd. GU24: Chob 1D 29
Staplehurst Rd. SM5: Cars 1F 31
TN12: Mard 4F 35
Staple La. GU4: E Clan 4F 29
STAPLES CORNER 3E 15
Stapleton Hall Rd. N4 . . . . .3A 16
Stapleton Rd. WD6: Bore 4D 7
Star & Garter Hill TW10: Rich 2D 23
Star Hill ME1: Roch 3F 27
Star Hill Rd. TN14: Dun G 2E 33
Star La. BR5: St M Cry 3E 25
CR5: Coul 2F 31
E16 .4C 16
Startins La. SL6: Cook 3B 12
Starts Hill Rd. BR6: Farnb 4D 25
Station App. BR2: Hayes 4C 24
CM16: They B 4D 9
GU22: Wok 2E 29
HA4: Ruis 3B 14
HP16: Gt Miss 3B 4
RH8: Oxt 3C 32
WD3: Chor 4F 5
Station Av. CR3: Cat'm 3B 32
KT12: Walt T 4B 22
Station Hill BR2: Hayes 4C 24
ME15: E Far 3E 35
SL5: Asc 3C 20
SL6: Cook 3B 12
Station La. CM4: Inga 4C 10
RM12: Horn 3A 18
Station Rd. AL2: Brick W 3B 6
AL4: S'ford 2D 7
AL9: Brk P, N Mym, Wel G 2E 7
BR2: Brom 3C 24
Station Rd. BR4: W W'ck 4C 24
BR5: St P 3E 25
BR6: Orp 4D 25
CM13: W H'dn 2C 18
CM16: Epp 3E 9
CM17: Har 1E 9
CR3: Wold 2B 32
DA1: Cray 2F 25
DA3: Lfield 3B 26
DA4: Eyns 4F 25
DA9: Ghithe 2B 26
(not continuous)
DA13: Sflt 3B 26
DA15: Sidc 2E 25
E4 .1C 16
E12 . . . . .3D 17
EN5: New Bar 1E 15
EN6: Cuff 3A 8
EN9: Walt C, Walt A 3B 8
EN10: Brox 2B 8
GU5: Goms 4A 30
GU11: Alde 4B 28
GU24: Chob 1D 29
HA1: Harr 2C 14
HA2: Harr 2B 14
HA8: Edg 2D 15
HP1: Hem H 2F 5
HP6: Amer 4D 5
HP7: Amer 4D 5
HP9: Beac 2C 12
HP10: Loud 2C 12
HP22: S Man 1A 4
HP23: Tring, Aldb 1C 4
IG10: Lough 1D 17
KT7: T Ditt 4C 22
KT10: Esh 4C 22
KT11: Stoke D 2B 30
KT15: Add 4F 21
KT22: Lea 2C 30
ME2: Cux 4E 27
ME2: Strood 3E 27
ME3: Cli 2E 27
ME18: W'bury 4D 35
ME20: Dit, A'ford 2E 35
N11 . . . . .1F 15
N21 . . . . .1A 16
N22 . . . . .2A 16
NW4 . . . . .2E 15
NW10 . . . . .4D 15
RH1: Redh 4F 31
(not continuous)
RH3: Bet 4D 31
(not continuous)
RH4: Dork 4C 30
RM2: Rom 2F 17
RM6: Chad H, Dag 3E 17
RM14: Upm 3A 18
RM18: E Til, W Til 1D 27
SG12: S Abb 1C 8
SG14: Let G 1F 7
SL1: Slou 4D 13
SL3: L'ly 1E 21
SL5: S'dale 4D 21
SL6: Tap 4C 12
SL7: Marl 3A 12
SL8: Bou E 3B 12
SM2: Sutt 1E 31
SW13 . . . . .1D 23
TN8: Eden 4D 33
TN13: Dun G 2F 33
TN14: Hals 1E 33
TN14: Otf 2F 33
TN14: S'ham 1F 33
TN15: Bor G 2B 34
TN16: Bras 3E 33
TW19: Wray 2E 21
UB3: Harl, Hayes 1A 22
UB7: W Dray 1A 22
UB8: Cowl 4F 13
WD4: K Lan 3A 6
WD17: Wat 4B 6
Station Rd. E. RH8: Oxt 3C 32
Station Rd. W. RH8: Oxt 3C 32
Station Way IG9: Buck H 1C 16
SM3: Cheam 1E 31
Staveley Rd. W4 . . . . .1D 23
Staverton Rd. NW2 . . . . .3E 15
Steel's La. KT22: Oxs 1B 30
Steep Hill GU24: Chob 1D 29
STEEPLE VIEW 2D 19
Stephenson St. E16 . . . . .4C 16
Stephenson Way WD23: Bush 4B 6
STEPNEY 4B 16
Stepney Grn. E1 . . . . .4B 16
Stepney Way E1 . . . . .4B 16
Sterling Way N18 . . . . .1A 16
Sternhold Av. SW2 . . . . .2A 24
Stevens Hill GU46: Yat 1A 28
Stevens La. KT10: Clay 1C 30
STEWARDS 2D 9
STEWARD'S GREEN 3E 9
Stewards Grn. Rd.
CM16: Epp, Fidd H 3E 9
Stewart's Dr. SL2: Farn C 3D 13
Steyne Rd. W3 . . . . .4D 15
Stickens La. ME19: E Mal 2D 35
Stifford Clays Rd. RM16: Grays 4B 18
RM16: Ors 4C 18
Stifford Hill
RM15: N Stif, S Ock 4B 18
RM16: N Stif 4B 18
Stifford Rd. RM15: Avel, S Ock 4A 18
STILEBRIDGE 4F 35
Stilebridge La. ME17: B Mon 4F 35
TN12: B Mon 4F 35
TN12: Mard 4F 35
(not continuous)
STIRLING CORNER 1D 15
Stites Hill Rd. CR5: Coul 2A 32
Stoats Nest Rd. CR5: Coul 1A 32
STOCK 4D 11
Stockett La. ME15: E Far, Maids . . .3F 35
ME17: Cox 4F 35
Stock Hill TN16: Big H 2C 32
Stocking La. HP14: Hug V, Nap 4A 4
Stock La. CM4: Inga 4C 10
STOCKLEY PARK 4A 14
Stockley Rd. UB7: W Dray 4A 14
UB11: Stock P 4A 14
Stock Rd.
CM2: Gall, Stock, W Han 3E 11
(not continuous)
CM4: Stock 1D 19
(not continuous)
CM12: Bill 1D 19
STOCKS GREEN 4A 34
Stocks Grn. Rd. TN11: Hild 4A 34
Stocks La. CM15: Kel H 4A 10
Stocks Rd. HP23: Aldb 1D 5
STOCKWELL 1A 24
Stockwell Rd. SW9 . . . . .1A 24
STOKE COMMON 3E 13
Stoke Comn. Rd. SL3: Ful 3E 13
STOKE D'ABERNON 2B 30
STOKE GREEN 4E 13
Stoke Grn. SL2: Stoke P 4E 13
STOKE MANDEVILLE 1A 4
STOKE NEWINGTON 3A 16
Stoke Newington Chu. St. N16 . . . .3A 16
Stoke Newington High St. N16 . . . .3A 16
Stoke Newington Rd. N16 . . . . . . .3A 16
STOKE POGES 4D 13
Stoke Poges La. SL1: Slou 4D 13
SL2: Slou, Stoke P 4D 13
Stoke Rd. GU1: Guild 4E 29
HP21: A'bury 1A 4
KT11: Cobh, Stoke D 2B 30
ME3: Hoo 2F 27
SL2: Slou, Stoke P 4D 13
Stompond La. KT12: Walt T 4B 22
Stomp Rd. SL1: Burn 4C 12
Stonard Rd. N13 . . . . .1A 16
Stonards Hill CM16: Coop, Epp 3E 9
STONDON MASSEY 3B 10
Stondon Pk. SE23 . . . . .2B 24
Stondon Rd. CM5: Ongar 3A 10
STONE 2A 26
STONEBRIDGE 4D 15
Stonebridge Rd. DA11: Nflt 2B 26
Stonecot Hill SM3: Sutt 4E 23
Stonecross AL1: St A 2C 6
Stonegrove HA8: Edg 1D 15
STONEHILL 1E 29
Stonehill Rd. CM1: Rox 2C 10
GU24: Chob 1E 29
KT16: Ott 1E 29
Stonehorse La. ME2: Strood 3E 27
ME3: Strood 3E 27
Stonehouse La. RM19: Purf 1A 26
TN14: Hals 1E 33
Stoneings La. TN14: Knock 2D 33
STONELEIGH 4E 23
Stoneness Rd. RM20: W Thur 1B 26
Stone Pk. Av. BR3: Beck 3B 24
Stone Pl. Rd. DA9: Ghithe 2A 26
Stones Cross Rd. BR8: Crock 4F 25
STONE STREET 3A 34
Stone St. Rd. TN15: Ivy H, Seal 3A 34
Stoney La. HP1: Hem H 2E 5
Stoney Rd. RG42: Brac 3B 20
Stony Cnr. DA13: Lfield, Meop 3C 26
STONY GREEN 4B 4
Stony Hill KT10: Esh 1B 30
Stony La. CM5: Ongar 2F 9
HP6: L Chal 4E 5
Stopford Rd. E13 . . . . .4C 16
Stortford Rd.
CM6: L Rod, W Rod 1A 10
STOUGHTON 3E 29
Stoughton Rd. GU1: Guild 4E 29
GU2: Guild 4E 29
Straight Bit HP10: Flack H 2B 12
Straight Mile, The
RG10: S Row, Twy 2A 20
RG40: W'ham 2A 20
Straight Rd. RM3: Rom 1F 17
SL4: Old Win 2E 21
Strand WC2 . . . . .4A 16
STRATFORD 3C 16
STRATFORD MARSH 3B 16
STRATFORD NEW TOWN 3C 16
Stratford Rd. GU12: Ash V 3B 28
WD17: Wat 4B 6
Strathearn Rd. SW19 . . . . .3E 23
Stratheden Rd. SE3 . . . . .1C 24
Strath Ter. SW11 . . . . .2F 23
Strathyre Av. SW16 . . . . .3A 24
STRATTON 4B 32
STRAWBERRY HILL 3C 22
Strawberry Hill RG42: Warf 3B 20
Strawberry Va. TW1: Twick 2C 22
(not continuous)
Straw Mill Hill ME15: Maids 3F 35
Streatfield Rd. HA3: Kent 2C 14
STREATHAM 3A 24
STREATHAM COMMON 3A 24
Streatham Comn. Nth. SW16 . . . . .3A 24
Streatham High Rd. SW16 . . . . . . .3A 24
STREATHAM HILL 2A 24
Streatham Hill SW2 . . . . .2A 24
STREATHAM PARK 3F 23
Streatham Pl. SW2 . . . . .2A 24
Streatham Rd. CR4: Mitc 3F 23
SW16 . . . . .3F 23
STREATHAM VALE 3F 23
Streatham Va. SW16 . . . . .3F 23
Street, The CM1: Rox 1C 10
CM3: Hat P 1F 11
CM3: Lit W 1E 11
CM5: H Ongar 3A 10
DA4: Hort K 3A 26
DA12: Cobh 3D 27
DA12: Shorne 3D 27
DA13: Meop 4C 26
GU3: Comp 4D 29
GU3: Putt 4C 28
GU4: Chil 4E 29
GU4: E Clan 4A 30
GU4: W Cla 4F 29
GU5: Alb 4F 29
GU10: Tong 4B 28
KT21: Asht 2D 31
KT22: Fet 2C 30
KT24: Eff 3B 30
KT24: W Hor 3A 30
ME2: Hall 4D 27
ME3: H Hal 2E 27
ME14: Box 2F 35
ME18: Mere 3C 34
ME18: Test 3E 35
ME19: Rya 2D 35
RG10: S Row 2A 20
RG10: W Law 1A 20
RH3: Bet 4D 31
TN15: Ash 4B 26
TN15: Igh 2B 34
TN15: Plax 3B 34
WD4: Chfd 3F 5
Street End Rd. ME5: Chat 4F 27
Streets Heath GU24: W End 1D 29
(not continuous)
STROOD 3E 27
STROOD GREEN 4D 31
STROUDE 3E 21
Stroude Rd. GU25: Vir W 3E 21
TW20: Egh 3E 21
STROUD GREEN 3A 16
Stuart Rd. DA11: Grav'nd 2C 26
Stubbers La. RM14: Upm 3A 18
Stubbles La. SL6: Cook 3B 12
Stubbs Hill BR6: Prat B 1E 33
RG42: Bin 2A 20
Stubbs La. KT20: Lwr K 3E 31
STUD GREEN 1B 20
Studio Way WD6: Bore 4D 7
Studland St. W6 . . . . .1E 23
Studridge La. HP27: Speen 4A 4
Stumble Hill TN11: S'brne 3B 34
Stump La. CM1: Spr 2E 11
Sturdee Av. ME7: G'ham 4F 27
Sturt Grn. SL6: Holy 2B 20
Sturt Rd. GU16: F Grn 2B 28
STYANTS BOTTOM 2A 34
Styants Bottom Rd. TN15: Seal 2A 34
Styles Cl. TN8: F Elm 4E 33
Succombs Hill CR6: Warl 2B 32
SUDBURY 3C 14
Sudbury Ct. Dr. HA1: Harr 3C 14
Sudbury Hill HA1: Harr 3C 14
Sudbury Rd. CM11: D'ham 4E 11
Suffield La. GU8: Putt, Shack 4C 28
Suffield Rd. HP11: H Wy 1A 12
Suffolk Rd. HA2: Harr 2B 14
Sugden Rd. KT7: T Ditt 4C 22
Summer Hill BR7: Chst 3D 25
Summerhouse Dr. DA2: Dart 2F 25
DA5: Bexl, Dart 2F 25
Summerhouse La. WD25: A'ham . . .4C 6
Summerleaze Rd. SL6: Maide 4B 12
Summer Rd. KT7: T Ditt 4C 22
Summers La. N12 . . . . .2F 15
SUMMERSTOWN 2F 23
Summerstown SW17 . . . . .2F 23
Summerswood La. WD6: Bore 3D 7
Summit Av. GU14: Cove 3A 28
Sumner Rd. CR0: C'don 4A 24
SUMNERS 2D 9
SUNBURY 3B 22
SUNBURY COMMON 3A 22
SUNBURY CROSS 3B 22
Sunbury Rd. TW13: Felt 3A 22
Sunbury Way TW13: Hanw 3B 22
Sunderland Rd. SE23 . . . . .2B 24
SUNDRIDGE
BR1 . . . . .3C 24
TN14 . . . . .3E 33
Sundridge Av. BR1: Brom 3C 24
BR7: Chst 3D 25
Sundridge Hill
ME2: Cux, Strood 4E 27
TN14: Knock, Sund 2E 33
Sundridge La. TN14: Knock 2E 33
Sundridge Rd. TN14: Dun G 2E 33
Sun Hill DA3: Fawk 4B 26
SUN-IN-THE-SANDS 1C 24
SUNNINGDALE 4D 21
Sunningdale Golf Course 4D 21
SUNNINGHILL 3C 20
Sunninghill Rd. GU20: W'sham 4C 20
SL4: Wink 3C 20
SL5: Asc 3C 20
SL5: S'hill 3C 20
Sunnings La. RM14: Upm 3A 18
Sunningvale Av. TN16: Big H 2C 32
Sunny Bank CR6: Warl 2B 32
SUNNYMEADS 2E 21
SUNNYMEDE 1D 19
Sunnyside Rd. HP5: Ches 3D 5
Sunray Av. SE24 . . . . .2A 24
Sun St. EC2 . . . . .4A 16
SURBITON 4C 22
Surbiton Cres. KT1: King T 3C 22
Surbiton Hill Pk. KT5: Surb 4D 23
Surbiton Hill Rd. KT6: Surb 4D 23
Surbiton Rd. KT1: King T 3D 23
Surrey Canal Rd. SE14 . . . . .1B 24
SE15 . . . . .1B 24
Surrey County Cricket Club (The Oval)
. . . . .1A 24
Surrey Quays Rd. SE16 . . . . .1B 24
Sussex Gdns. W2 . . . . .4F 15
Sussex Pl. SL1: Slou 1E 21
(not continuous)
W2 .4F 15
Sussex Ring N12 . . . . .1E 15
Sutherland Av. W9 . . . . .4E 15
SUTTON
SL3 . . . . .1F 21
SM1 . . . . .4E 23
SUTTON AT HONE 3A 26
Sutton Comn. Rd. SM1: Sutt 4E 23
SM3: Sutt 4E 23
Sutton Ct. Rd. W4 . . . . .1D 23
SUTTON GREEN 3E 29
Sutton Grn. Rd. GU4: Sut G 3E 29
Sutton La. SL3: L'ly 1E 21
SM2: Sutt 1E 31
SM7: Bans 1E 31
TW3: Houn 1B 22
Sutton Pk. Rd. SM1: Sutt 4E 23
Sutton Rd. ME15: Maids 3F 35
SL6: Cook 3B 12
TW5: Hest 1B 22
Suttons Av. RM12: Horn 3F 17
Suttons La. RM12: Horn 3F 17
Swains La. HP10: Flack H 2B 12
Swakeleys Rd. UB10: Ick 3A 14
SWAKELEYS RDBT. 3A 14
Swallowdale La. HP2: Hem H 1A 6
SWALLOWS CROSS 4B 10
Swallows Cross Rd.
CM15: Mount 4B 10
Swallow St. SL0: Iver, Iver H 4F 13
SWAN, THE 4C 24
Swan Bottom HP16: The L 2C 4
Swandon Way SW18 . . . . .2F 23
Swanland Rd. AL9: N Mym 2E 7
EN6: S Mim 3E 7
Swan La. CM4: Marg, Stock 3D 11
DA1: Dart 2F 25
GU47: S'urst 1A 28
HP16: The L 2C 4
HP23: St L 2C 4
SS11: Runw 1F 19
TN8: Eden 4D 33
SWANLEY 3F 25
SWANLEY BAR 3E 7
Swanley Bar La. EN6: Pot B 3E 7
Swanley By-Pass BR8: Swan 3E 25
DA14: Swan 3E 25
SWANLEY INTERCHANGE 4F 25
Swanley La. BR8: Swan 3F 25
SWANLEY VILLAGE 3F 25
Swanley Village Rd. BR8: Swan . . .3F 25
Swan Rd. TW13: Hanw 3B 22
UB7: W Dray 1F 21
SWANSCOMBE 2B 26
Swanscombe St. DA10: Swans 2B 26
Swansea Rd. TW14: Felt 2A 22
Swan St. ME19: W Mal 2D 35
SWANTON 3C 34
Swanton Rd.
ME18: Mere, W Peck 3C 34
Swanton Valley La.
ME18: S'brne 3C 34
Swaynesland Rd. TN8: Crock H 4D 33
Sweeps La. BR5: St M Cry 4E 25
Sweetcroft La. UB10: Hil 3A 14
Sweets La. ME19: E Mal 3E 35
Swift Cres. ME5: Lor 4F 27
SWILLET, THE 1E 13
Swingate La. SE18 . . . . .1D 25
Swing Ga. La. HP4: Berk 2E 5
Swinley Rd. GU19: Bag 4C 20
SL5: Asc 4C 20
SWISS COTTAGE 3F 15
Switchback Rd. Nth.
SL6: Maide 4B 12
Switchback Rd. Sth. SL6: Maide . . .4B 12
(not continuous)
Swyncombe Av. W5 . . . . .1C 22
Sycamore Rd. GU14: Farnb 3B 28
(not continuous)
HP6: Amer 4D 5
SYDENHAM 3B 24
Sydenham Hill SE23 . . . . .3B 24
SE26 . . . . .3B 24
Sydenham Rd. CR0: C'don 4A 24
GU1: Guild 4E 29
SE26 . . . . .3B 24
Sydney Rd. EN2: Enf 4A 8
(not continuous)
GU1: Guild 4E 29
Sydney St. SW3 . . . . .1F 23
Sylvan Av. RM11: Horn 2A 18
Sylvan Hill SE19 . . . . .3A 24
Sylvan Way AL7: W City 1F 7
Symonds La. ME18: Ladd 4D 35
Syon House 1C 22
Syon La. TW7: Isle 1C 22
Syon Pk. 1C 22
Sythwood GU21: Wok 2E 29

T

Tabor's Hill CM2: Gt B 2E 11
Taddington ME5: Wald 1F 35
Tadpole La. GU10: Ews 4A 28
TADWORTH 2E 31
Tadworth St. KT20: Tad 3E 31
Talgarth Rd. W. W14 . . . . .1E 23
Tally Rd. RH8: Limp 4D 33
Tamworth La. CR4: Mitc 3F 23
TANDRIDGE 4B 32
Tandridge Hill La. RH9: G'stone . . .3B 32
Tandridge La. RH7: Ling 4B 32
RH8: Tand 4B 32
Tanfield Av. NW2 . . . . .3D 15
Tangley La. GU3: Guild 3D 29
Tan Ho. La. CM14: N'side 4A 10
Tanhouse Rd. RH8: Oxt 4C 32
Tank Hill Rd. RM19: Avel, Purf 1A 26
Tank Rd. GU47: Col T 1A 28
Tanner's Hill RH3: Aroc 4D 31
Tanners La. IG6: Ilf 2D 17
Tanner St. SE1 . . . . .1A 24
(not continuous)
Tannery La. GU23: Send 3F 29
Tanyard Hill DA12: Shorne 3D 27
TAPLOW 4C 12
Taplow Comn. Rd. SL1: Burn 3C 12
Taplow Rd. SL6: Tap 4C 12
Tapner's Rd. RH2: Leigh 4D 31
TARGET RDBT. 4B 14
TARPOTS 2F 19
Tate Rd. SM1: Sutt 4E 23
TATLING END 3E 13
TATSFIELD 2C 32
TATSFIELD GREEN 2D 33
Tatsfield La. TN16: Tats 2D 33
TATTENHAM CORNER 2E 31
Tattenham Cres. KT18: Tatt C 2E 31
Tattenham Way KT20: Tad 2E 31
Taunton Way HA7: Stan 2D 15
Taverners Way EN11: Hodd 1B 8
Tavistock Pl. WC1 . . . . .4A 16
Tavistock Sq. WC1 . . . . .4F 15
Tawney Comn. CM16: They M 3E 9
Tawney La. CM5: Stap T, They M . . .3F 9
RM4: Stap T 3F 9
Tawneys Rd. CM18: Har 1D 9
Taylor's La. ME3: High'm 3E 27
ME19: Tros 1C 34
Teasaucer Hill ME15: Maids 3F 35
TEDDINGTON 3C 22
Tees Dr. RM3: Rom 1F 17
Teignmouth Gdns. UB6: G'frd 4C 14
Telegraph Hill ME3: High'm 3E 27
Telford Dr. SL1: Slou 1D 21
Telford Rd. N11 . . . . .1F 15
TEMPLE 3A 12
TEMPLE FIELDS 1E 9
TEMPLE FORTUNE 2E 15
Temple Fortune La. NW11 . . . . . .2E 15
TEMPLE HILL 2A 26
Temple Hill DA1: Dart 2A 26
Temple Hill Sq. DA1: Dart 2A 26
Temple La. SL7: Marl 3A 12
Temple Mill La. E15 . . . . .3C 16
E15 . . . . .3C 16
(not continuous)
TEMPLE MILLS 3B 16
Temple Rd. KT19: Eps 1D 31
Temple St. HP11: H Wy 1B 12
Temple Way RG42: Bin 3A 20
Templewood La.
SL2: Farn C, Stoke P 3D 13
Ten Acre La. TW20: Thorpe 3F 21
Tendring Rd. CM18: Har 1D 9
(not continuous)
Tennison Rd. SE25 . . . . .3A 24
Tentelow La. UB2: S'hall 1B 22
Terling Hall Rd. CM3: Hat P, Ter . . .1F 11
Terling Rd. CM3: Hat P 1F 11
Terrace, The DA12: Grav'nd 2C 26
(not continuous)
IG8: Wfd G 2C 16
SW13 . . . . .1D 23
Terrace Rd. KT12: Walt T 4B 22
Terrace Rd. Nth. RG42: Bin 3A 20
Terrace Rd. Sth. RG42: Bin 3A 20
TERRICK 1A 4
TERRIERS 1B 12
Terry's La. SL6: Cook 3B 12
Terry's Lodge Rd. TN15: Wro 1B 34
TESTON 3E 35
Teston La. ME15: W Far 3E 35
ME18: Test 3E 35
Teston Rd. ME18: E Mal 3D 35
ME19: Kin H, Off, W Mal 2C 34
Tetherdown N10 . . . . .2F 15
THAMES DITTON 4C 22
Thames Gateway RM9: Dag 4E 17
Thames Gateway Bri. E6 . . . . .4D 17
SE28 . . . . .4D 17
THAMES HAVEN 4E 19
Thameside KT16: Chert 3F 21
TW18: Lale 3F 21
THAMESMEAD 4E 17
THAMESMEAD CENTRAL 4E 17
THAMESMEAD EAST 1E 25
THAMESMEAD NORTH 4E 17
THAMESMEAD SOUTH 1E 25
THAMESMEAD WEST 1D 25
Thames Rd. DA1: Cray 1F 25
IG11: Bark 4D 17
Thames St. KT13: Weyb 4A 22
SL4: Wind 1D 21
TW12: Hamp 3B 22
TW16: Sun 3B 22
TW18: Staines 3F 21
Thames Way
DA11: Nflt, Grav'nd 2B 26
The . . .
Names prefixed with 'The' for example 'The Approach' are indexed under the main name such as 'Approach, The'
Theberton St. N1 . . . . .4A 16
Theobalds La.
EN8: Chesh, Walt C 3B 8
Theobalds Pk. Rd.
EN2: Crew H, Enf 4A 8
Theobald's Rd. WC1 . . . . .4A 16
Theobald St. WD6: Bore 4D 7
WD7: Rad 4C 6
Thesiger Rd. SE20 . . . . .3B 24
THEYDON BOIS 4D 9
THEYDON GARNON 4E 9
THEYDON MOUNT 4E 9
Theydon Pk. Rd. CM16: They B 4D 9
Theydon Rd. CM16: Epp 4D 9
Thicket Rd. SE20 . . . . .3B 24
Thieves La. SG14: Pan 1A 8
Third Av. CM18: Har 1D 9
CM19: Har 1D 9
Thoby La. CM15: Mount 4C 10
Thomas More St. E1 . . . . .4B 16
Thompkins La. SL2: Farn R 3D 13
THONG 3D 27
Thong La.
DA12: Grav'nd, Shorne 3D 27
TN15: Bor G 2B 34
Thorkhill Rd. KT7: T Ditt 4C 22
Thornbury Rd. TW7: Isle 1C 22
Thorncliffe Rd. UB2: S'hall 1B 22
Thorndon Av. CM13: W H'dn 2C 18
Thorndown La. GU20: W'sham 1C 28
THORNEY 1F 21
Thorney Bay Rd. SS8: Can I 4F 19
Thorney La. Nth. SL0: Iver 4F 13
Thorney La. Sth. SL0: Rich P 1F 21
Thorney Mill Rd. SL0: Thorn 1F 21
(not continuous)
Thornhill Av. SE18 . . . . .1D 25
Thornhill Rd. GU11: Alde 1D 28
KT6: Surb 4D 23
N1 .3A 16
Thornton Av. SW2 . . . . .2F 23
THORNTON HEATH 3A 24
THORNTON HEATH POND 4A 24
Thornton Rd. CR0: C'don 4A 24
CR7: Thor H 4A 24
SW12 . . . . .2F 23
THORNWOOD COMMON 2E 9
Thornwood Rd.
CM16: Epp, Twood 3E 9
THORPE 3F 21
Thorpe By-Pass TW20: Thorpe 3E 21
THORPE GREEN 3E 21
THORPE LEA 3F 21
Thorpe Lea Rd.
TW20: Egh, Thorpe 3E 21
Thorpe Pk. 3F 21
Thorpe Rd. KT16: Chert 4F 21
TW18: Staines 3F 21
Thrale Rd. SW16 . . . . .3F 23
Three Arch Rd. RH1: Redh 4F 31
Three Cherry Trees La.
HP2: Hem H 1A 6
Three Colts La. E2 . . . . .4B 16
Three Elm La.
TN11: Tonb, Gold G 4B 34
Three Gates Rd. DA3: Fawk 4A 26
Three Households HP8: Chal G 1D 13
Three Mile Hill CM2: Wid 3D 11
CM4: Chelm, Marg, Writ 3D 11
THRESHERS BUSH 1F 9
Throwley Way SM1: Sutt 4E 23
THUNDERSLEY 2F 19
Thurloe Gdns. RM1: Rom 2F 17
Thurlow Pk. Rd. SE21 . . . . .2A 24
Thurlow St. SE17 . . . . .1A 24
(not continuous)
THURROCK LAKESIDE 1B 26
Thurston Rd. SE8 . . . . .1B 24
TIBBET'S CORNER 2E 23
Tibbet's Ride SW15 . . . . .2E 23
Tibbs Hill Rd. WD5: Ab L 3A 6
TICKLEBACK ROW 2B 20
Tideway, The ME1: Roch 4F 27
Tiepigs La. BR4: W W'ck 4C 24
Tilburstow Hill Rd.
RH9: G'stone 4B 32
RH9: S God 4B 32
TILBURY 1C 26
Tilbury Fort 2C 26
Tilbury Rd. CM13: W H'dn 2C 18
Tilden La. TN12: Mard 4F 35
TILEGATE GREEN 2F 9
Tilegate Rd.
CM5: H Laver, Mag L 2F 9
Tilehouse La. UB9: Den 2F 13
WD3: W Hyd 2F 13
Tilehurst La. RG42: Bin 3A 20
RH5: Dork 4D 31
Tile Kiln La. DA5: Bexl 2F 25
Tilley La. KT18: Eps D, H'ly 2D 31
Tilling Rd. NW2 . . . . .3E 15
Tillwicks Rd. CM18: Har 1D 9
Timbercroft La. SE18 . . . . .1D 25
TIMBERDEN BOTTOM 1F 33
Timberlog La. SS14: Bas 2E 19
Tinker Pot La. TN15: W King 1A 34
Tinkers La. SL4: Wind 2C 20
Tippendell La. AL2: Chis G, Park . . .2B 6
Tipps Cross La. CM15: Hook E 3B 10
TIP'S CROSS 3B 10
Tite Hill TW20: Egh, Eng G 3E 21
Tithebarns La. GU23: Send 3F 29
Tithepit Shaw La. CR6: Warl 2B 32
TITSEY 3C 32
Titsey Hill RH8: T'sey 3C 32
Titsey Rd. RH8: Limp, T'sey 3C 32
TITTLE ROW 4B 12
Tiverton Rd. NW10 . . . . .4E 15
Tofts Chase CM3: Lit B 1F 11
TOKYNGTON 3D 15
Tollgate Rd. AL4: Col H 2D 7
AL9: N Mym 2E 7
E6 .4C 16
E16 . . . . .4C 16
Tollhouse Way N19 . . . . .3F 15
Tollington Pk. N4 . . . . .3A 16
Tollington Rd. N7 . . . . .3A 16
Tollington Way N7 . . . . .3A 16
Tolpits La. WD18: Wat 1A 14
TOLWORTH 4D 23
TOLWORTH JUNC. (TOBY JUG) 4D 23
Tolworth Ri. Nth. KT5: Surb 4D 23
Tolworth Ri. Sth. KT5: Surb 4D 23
Tomkyns La. RM14: Upm 2A 18
Toms Hill Rd. HP23: Aldb 1D 5
Toms La. WD4: K Lan 3A 6
WD5: Bedm 3A 6
Tomswood Hill IG6: Ilf 2D 17
Tomswood Rd. IG7: Chig 2D 17
Tonbridge By-Pass
TN11: S'oaks, Tonb 4A 34
Tonbridge Rd.
ME16: Barm, Maids, Test 3D 35
ME18: Mere, W'bury 3D 35
TN8: Chid 4E 33
TN11: Had 4B 34
TN11: Hild 4A 34
TN11: S'brne, Tonb 4B 34
TN12: E Pec 4C 34
TN13: S'oaks 3F 33
TN15: Igh, Plax 3B 34
TONGHAM 4B 28
Tooley St. SE1 . . . . .4A 16
TOOT HILL 3F 9
Toot Hill Rd.
CM5: Gsted, Ongar, Toot H 3F 9
TOOTING 3F 23
TOOTING BEC 2F 23
Tooting Bec Gdns. SW16 . . . . . . .3F 23
(not continuous)
Tooting Bec Rd. SW16 . . . . .3F 23
SW17 . . . . .2F 23
TOOTING GRAVENEY 3F 23
Tooting High St. SW17 . . . . .3F 23
Top Dartford Rd. BR8: Swan 3F 25
DA2: Dart 3F 25

Torbay TN12: Pad W 4D 35
Torriano Av. NW5 .....3F 15
Torridon Rd. SE6 .....2C 24
SE13 .....2C 24
Torrington Pk. N12 .....1F 15
Torrington Pl. WC1 .....4F 15
Torrington Rd. HA4: Ruis 3B 14
TOTTENHAM 2A 16
Tottenham Ct. Rd. W1 .....4F 15
TOTTENHAM HALE 2B 16
TOTTENHAM HALE GYRATORY 2A 16
Tottenham Hotspur FC 2B 16
Tottenham La. N8 .....2A 16
TOTTERIDGE
HP13 .....1B 12
N20 .....1E 15
Totteridge Comn. N20 .....1E 15
Totteridge La. HP13: H Wy 1B 12
N20 .....1E 15
Totteridge Rd. HP13: H Wy 1B 12
Totteridge Village N20 .....1E 15
TOUCHEN END 1B 20
Touchen End Rd. SL6: Holy 1B 20
TOVIL 3F 35
Tovil Hill ME15: Maids 3F 35
Tovil Rd. ME15: Maids 3F 35
Tower Bri. SE1 .....4A 16
Tower Bri. Rd. SE1 .....1A 24
TOWER HILL 3F 5
TOWER HILL 4A 16
Tower Hill ME19: Off 2C 34
WD4: Chfd 3F 5
Tower Hill La. AL4: Sandr 1D 7
Tower Rd. BR6: Orp 4D 25
HP7: Cole 1D 13
TW1: Twick 2C 22
Tower Vw. ME19: Kin H 2D 35
Town, The EN2: Enf 4A 8
Towncourt La. BR5: Pet W 4D 25
Town End CR3: Cat'm 2A 32
Town Hill ME19: W Mal 2D 35
Town La. HP10: Wbrn G 3C 12
TW19: Stanw 2F 21
(not continuous)
Townley Rd. DA6: Bex 2E 25
Townmead Rd. SW6 .....2E 23
Town Rd. ME3: Cli W 2E 27
N9 .....1B 16
TOWNSEND 1C 6
Towpath TW17: Shep 4A 22
TOY'S HILL 4E 33
Toy's Hill TN8: F Elm, Westrm 4E 33
TN16: Westrm 4E 33
Trafalgar Av. SE15 .....1A 24
Trafalgar Rd. SE10 .....1C 24
Tranquil Va. SE3 .....1C 24
Trap's Hill IG10: Lough 4D 9
Traps La. KT3: N Mald 3D 23
Travellers La. AL10: Hat 2E 7
Treadaway Rd. HP10: Flack H 2B 12
Tredegar Rd. E3 .....4B 16
Tree La. TN15: Plax 3B 34
Trelawney Av. SL3: L'ly 1E 21
Trenches La. SL3: L'ly 4E 13
TRENCH WOOD 3B 34
Treve Av. HA1: Harr 3C 14
Trevor Rd. UB3: Hayes 1A 22
Trevithick Dr. DA1: Dart 2A 26
Trigg's La. GU22: Wok 2E 29
TRING 1C 4
Tring Ford Rd. HP23: Tring, Trin 1C 4
Tring Hill HP22: Bkld 1B 4
HP23: Tring 1B 4
Tring Rd. HP4: Berk 1D 5
HP22: Hal, Wend 1B 4
TRING WHARF 1C 4
Trinity Rd. SW17 .....2F 23
SW18 .....2F 23
Tripton Rd. CM18: Har 1D 9
Trodd's La. GU1: Guild 4F 29
GU4: Guild 4F 29
Trooper Rd. HP23: Aldb 1D 5
Trotters Bottom EN5: Barn 4E 7
Trotters Rd. CM18: Har 1E 9
TROTTISCLIFFE 1C 34
Trottiscliffe Rd.
ME19: Addtn, Rya, Tros 2C 34
Trott Rd. N10 .....2F 15
Troy La. TN8: Eden 4D 33
TROY TOWN 4D 33
TRUELOVES INTERCHANGE 4C 10
Trueloves La. CM4: Inga 4C 10
Trumpets Hill Rd. RH2: Reig 4E 31
TRUMPS GREEN 4E 21
Trumpsgreen Rd. GU25: Vir W 4E 21
Trundleys Rd. SE8 .....1B 24
Trunk Rd. GU14: Cove 3A 28
Truro Rd. N22 .....2A 16
Tubbenden La. BR6: Orp 4D 25
Tubbs Rd. NW10 .....4D 15
Tudor Dr. KT2: King T 3D 23
SM4: Mord 4E 23
Tudor Gdns. NW9 .....3D 15
Tudor Way BR5: Pet W 4D 25
TUFNELL PARK 3F 15
TULSE HILL 2A 24
Tulse Hill SW2 .....2A 24
Tumber St. KT18: H'ly 3D 31
Tumblefield Rd.
TN15: Stans, Wro 1B 34
Tunnel App. SE16 .....1B 24
Tunnel Av. SE10 .....1C 24
(not continuous)
Tuns La. SL1: Slou 1D 21
Tupwood La. CR3: Cat'm 3B 32
Tupwood Scrubbs Rd.
CR3: Cat'm 3B 32
TURKEY STREET 4B 8
Turkey St. EN1: Enf 4B 8
EN3: Enf W 4B 8
Turner Rd. HA8: Edg 2D 15
Turner's Hill EN8: Chesh 3B 8
Turney Rd. SE21 .....2A 24
TURNFORD 2B 8
Turnfurlong La. HP21: A'bury 1A 4
TURNHAM GREEN 1D 23
Turnham Grn. Ter. W4 .....1D 23
Turnpike La. N8 .....2A 16
RM18: W Til 1C 26
Turpington La. BR2: Brom 4D 25
Tweedy Rd. BR1: Brom 3C 24
Tweseldown Rd. GU52: Chu C 4A 28
TWICKENHAM 2C 22
Twickenham Bri. TW1: Twick 2C 22
TW9: Rich 2C 22
Twickenham Rd. TW7: Isle 2C 22
TW11: Tedd 3C 22
(not continuous)
TW13: Hanw 2B 22
Twickenham Rugby Union
Football Ground 2C 22
Twist, The HP23: Wigg 1C 4
Twitchell La. HP22: Ast C 1B 4
Twitchell's La. HP9: Jor 1D 13
TWITTON 2F 33
Twitton La. TN14: Otf 2F 33
Two Dells La. HP5: A Grn, Orch 2D 5
Twogates Hill
ME3: High'm, Cli W 2E 27
TWO WATERS 2F 5
Two Waters Rd. HP3: Hem H 2F 5
Two Waters Way HP3: Hem H 2F 5
Twyford Abbey Rd. NW10 .....4D 15
Twyford Av. W3 .....4D 15
Tye, The CM3: E Han 3F 11
CM4: Marg 3D 11
TYE COMMON 1D 19
Tye Comn. Rd.
CM12: Bill, L Bur 1C 18
Tyefields SS13: Pit 2F 19
TYE GREEN
CM1 .....1C 10
CM4 .....4D 11
CM18 .....1D 9
Tyland La. ME14: S'ing 2F 35
TYLERS CAUSEWAY 2F 7
Tylers C'way. SG13: New S 2F 7
TYLERS GREEN
CM16 .....2F 9
HP10 .....1C 12
RH9 .....3B 32
Tylers Grn. Rd. BR8: Crock 4F 25
Tylers Rd. CM19: Roy 2C 8
Tylers Way WD25: A'ham 4B 6
Tylney Rd. E7 .....3C 16
Tylney Rd. BR1: Brom 3C 24
TYRRELL'S WOOD 3D 31
Tysea Hill RM4: Noak H, Stap A 1F 17
Tysea Rd. CM18: Har 1D 9
TYTTENHANGER 2C 6
Tyttenhanger Grn. AL4: St A 2D 7

U

UNDERHILL 1E 15
UNDERLING GREEN 4F 35
UNDERRIVER 3A 34
Underriver Ho. Rd.
TN15: Under 3A 34
Union St. GU14: Farnb 3B 28
SE1 .....4A 16
Upchat Rd. ME2: Up, C'den 3F 27
ME3: C'den, Up 3F 27
Updown Hill GU20: W'sham 1C 28
Upland Rd.
CM16: Epp, Epp U, Twood 2D 9
Uplands Pk. Rd. EN2: Enf 4A 8
UPMINSTER 3A 18
Upminster Rd. RM11: Horn 3A 18
RM12: Horn 3A 18
RM14: Upm 3A 18
Upminster Rd. Nth. RM13: Rain 4F 17
Upminster Rd. Sth. RM13: Rain 4F 17
Upney La. IG11: Bark 3D 17
Upnor Castle 3F 27
Upnor Rd. ME2: Strood, Up 3F 27
Up. Austin Lodge Rd.
DA4: Eyns 4F 25
Up. Barn Hill ME15: Hunt 4E 35
Up. Beulah Hill SE19 .....3A 24
Up. Bray Rd. SL6: Bray 1C 20
Up. Brentwood Rd. RM2: Rom 2F 17
Up. Brighton Rd. KT6: Surb 4C 22
Up. Chobham Rd. GU15: Camb 2B 28
UPPER CLAPTON 3B 16
Up. Clapton Rd. E5 .....3B 16
Up. College Ride GU15: Camb 1B 28
UPPER DUNSLEY 1C 4
UPPER EDMONTON 1B 16
UPPER ELMERS END 4B 24
Up. Elmers End Rd. BR3: Beck 3B 24
Up. Fant Rd. ME16: Maids 3F 35
Upper Grn. Rd. TN11: S'brne 3B 34
Upper Grn. W. CR4: Mitc 3F 23
(not continuous)
Up. Grosvenor St. W1 .....4F 15
UPPER HALE 4A 28
Up. Hale Rd. GU9: Up H 4A 28
UPPER HALLIFORD 3A 22
Up. Halliford By-Pass
TW17: Shep 4A 22
Up. Halliford Rd. TW17: Shep 3A 22
UPPER HALLING 4D 27
Up. Ham Rd. TW10: Ham 3C 22
Up. High St. KT17: Eps 1D 31
Upper Highway WD4: Hunt C 3A 6
WD5: Ab L 3A 6
UPPER HOLLOWAY 3F 15
Up. Hunton Hill ME15: E Far 4E 35
Up. Icknield Way
HP22: Ast C, Hal 1B 4
HP27: Pri R, White 2A 4
(not continuous)
Upper Mayne SS15: Lain 2D 19
Up. Mulgrave Rd. SM2: Cheam 1E 31
UPPER NORTH DEAN 4A 4
Upper Nth. St. E14 .....4B 16
UPPER NORWOOD 3A 24
Upper Pk. Rd. DA17: Belv 1E 25
GU15: Camb 1B 28
Up. Rainham Rd. RM12: Horn 3F 17
Up. Richmond Rd. SW15 .....2D 23
Up. Richmond Rd. W. SW14 .....2D 23
TW10: Rich 2D 23
Upper Rd. E13 .....4C 16
Up. Selsdon Rd.
CR2: Sande, Sels 1A 32
UPPER SHIRLEY 4B 24
Up. Shirley Rd. CR0: C'don 4B 24
Up. Stone St. ME15: Maids 3F 35
Upper St. GU5: Shere 4A 30
(not continuous)
N1 .....4A 16
Up. Sunbury Rd. TW12: Hamp 3B 22
Up. Sutton La. TW5: Hest 1B 22
UPPER SYDENHAM 3B 24
Up. Teddington Rd.
KT1: Ham W 3C 22
Up. Thames St. EC4 .....4A 16
Up. Tollington Pk. N4 .....3A 16
(not continuous)
UPPER TOOTING 2F 23
Up. Tooting Rd. SW17 .....3F 23
UPPER UPNOR 3F 27
UPPER WALTHAMSTOW 2C 16
Up. Weybourne La.
GU9: H End 4A 28
Up. Wickham La. DA16: Well 1E 25
UPSHIRE 3C 8
Upshire Rd. EN9: Walt A 3C 8
Upshot La. GU22: Pyr 2F 29
UPTON
E7 .....3C 16
SL1 .....1E 21
Upton Ct. Rd. SL3: L'ly, Slou 1E 21
Upton La. E7 .....3C 16
UPTON PARK 4C 16
Upton Rd. DA6: Bex 2E 25
Urswick Rd. E9 .....3B 16
UXBRIDGE 3F 13
Uxbridge Rd. HA3: Hrw W 2B 14
HA5: Hat E, Pinn 2B 14
HA7: Stan 2B 14
KT1: King T 4C 22
SL1: Slou 1E 21
SL2: Slou 4E 13
TW12: Hamp, Ham H 3B 22
TW13: Felt 2B 22
UB1: S'hall 4B 14
UB4: Hayes, Yead 4A 14
UB10: Hil 4A 14
Uxbridge Rd. W3 .....4D 15
W5 .....4B 14
W7 .....4B 14
W12 .....4E 15
W13 .....4B 14
WD3: Rick 1F 13

V

Vache La. HP8: Chal G 1E 13
Vale, The HP5: Ches, Hawr 2D 5
NW11 .....3E 15
W3 .....4D 15
Valence Av. RM8: Dag 3E 17
VALE OF HEALTH 3F 15
Vale Rd. DA11: Nflt 2C 26
GU12: Ash V 3B 28
HP5: Ches 3D 5
SL4: Wind 1D 21
WD23: Bush 1B 14
Vallance Rd. E1 .....4B 16
E2 .....4B 16
Vallentin Rd. E17 .....2C 16
Valley Bri. CM1: Chelm 1E 11
Valley Dr. DA12: Grav'nd 3C 26
VALLEY END 1D 29
Valley End Rd. GU24: Chob 1D 29
Valley Hill IG10: Lough 1D 17
Valley Rd. AL3: St A 1C 6
AL8: W City 1E 7
BR2: Brom 3C 24
CM11: Bill 1D 19
CR8: Kenl 2A 32
DA3: Fawk 4B 26
HP14: Hug V 4B 4
SW16 .....3A 24
WD3: Rick 1F 13
Vanbrugh Hill SE3 .....1C 24
SE10 .....1C 24
Vanbrugh Pk. SE3 .....1C 24
Van Dieman's Rd. CM2: Chelm 2E 11
VANGE 3E 19
Vange By-Pass
SS16: Fob, Pit, Vange 3E 19
Vanguard Way ME2: Med E, Up 3F 27
Vanity La. ME17: Lint 4F 35
Vansittart Rd. SL4: Wind 1D 21
Vapery La. GU24: Pirb 2C 28
Vaughan Rd. HA1: Harr 3C 14
VAUXHALL 1A 24
Vauxhall Bri. SE1 .....1A 24
SW1 .....1A 24
Vauxhall Bri. Rd. SW1 .....1F 23
VAUXHALL CROSS 1A 24
VENUS HILL 3E 5
Venus Hill HP3: Bov 3E 5
Verdant La. SE6 .....2C 24
Vernon Pl. WC1 .....4A 16
Verulamium Roman Town 2B 6
Verulam Rd. AL3: St A 2C 6
Vesta Rd. SE4 .....1B 24
Vicarage C'way. SG13: Hert H 1B 8
Vicarage Cres. SW11 .....1F 23
Vicarage Farm Rd. TW3: Houn 1B 22
TW4: Houn 1B 22
Vicarage Hill SS7: Ben 3F 19
TN16: Westrm 3D 33
Vicarage La. CM2: Gt B 3E 11
CM16: N Weald 2E 9
(not continuous)
DA12: Grav'nd 2D 27
E15 .....3C 16
GU23: Send 3F 29
GU46: Yat 1A 28
HP3: Bov 3E 5
IG7: Chig 1D 17
ME3: Hoo 3F 27
ME15: E Far 3E 35
WD4: K Lan 3A 6
Vicarage Rd. CM1: Rox 1C 10
DA5: Bexl 2E 25
GU17: Hawl 2A 28
GU22: Wok 2E 29
GU46: Yat 1A 28
HP4: Pott E 1E 5
HP23: Wigg 1C 4
ME2: Hall 4D 27
ME18: Yald 4E 35
TW16: Sun 3A 22
TW20: Egh 3E 21
WD18: Wat 1B 14
Victoria Dock Rd. E16 .....4C 16
Victoria Dr. SW19 .....2E 23
Victoria Emb. EC4 .....4A 16
SW1 .....1A 24
WC2 .....4A 16
Victoria Pk. Rd. E9 .....4B 16
Victoria Rd. CM1: Chelm 2E 11
(not continuous)
CM1: Writ 2D 11
DA1: Dart 2A 26
GU11: Alde 4B 28
GU14: Farnb 3B 28
GU22: Wok 2E 29
HA4: Ruis 3B 14
IG9: Buck H 1C 16
KT6: Surb 4C 22
N9 .....1A 16
N18 .....1A 16
NW10 .....4D 15
RM1: Rom 2F 17
TN11: Gold G, Had 4C 34
W3 .....4D 15
Victoria Rd. Sth. CM1: Chelm 2E 11
Victoria St. AL1: St A 2C 6
ME1: Roch 3F 27
SL4: Wind 1D 21
SW1 .....1F 23
TW20: Eng G 3E 21
Victoria Way GU21: Wok 2E 29
View Rd. ME3: Cli W 2E 27
Vigilant Way DA12: Grav'nd 3D 27
Vigo Hill ME19: Tros 1C 34
Vigo La. GU46: Yat 1A 28
Vigo Rd. TN15: Stans 1B 34
VIGO VILLAGE 1C 34
VILLAGE, THE 2D 21
Village, The CM5: Will 2B 10
SE7 .....1C 24
Village La. SL2: Hedg 3D 13
Village Rd. EN1: Enf 1A 16
HP7: Cole 1D 13
SL4: Dor 1C 20
TW20: Thorpe 3E 21
UB9: Den 3F 13
Village Way BR3: Beck 3B 24
HA5: Pinn 3B 14
SE21 .....2A 24
Villa Rd. ME3: High'm 3E 27
Villiers Av. KT5: Surb 4D 23
Villiers Rd. KT1: King T 3D 23
SL2: Slou 4D 13
WD19: Wat 1B 14
Vincent La. RH4: Dork 4C 30
Vine La. UB10: Hil 4A 14
Vine Rd. BR6: Chels 1D 33
Vines La. ME1: Roch 3F 27
TN11: Hild 4A 34
Vineyards Rd. EN6: N'thaw 3F 7
VINTERS PARK 2F 35
Violet Rd. E3 .....4B 16
Virginia Rd. CR7: Thor H 3A 24
VIRGINIA WATER 3E 21
Vivian Av. NW4 .....2E 15

W

WADDON 4A 24
Waddon New Rd. CR0: C'don 4A 24
Waddon Rd. CR0: C'don, Wadd 4A 24
Waddon Way CR0: Wadd 1A 32
Wadham Rd. E4 .....2B 16
Waggon Rd. EN5: Barn 4E 7
WAINSCOTT 3F 27
Wainscott Rd. ME2: Wain 3F 27
Wake Rd. IG10: H Beech 4C 8
Waldegrave Rd. TW1: Twick 3C 22
TW11: Tedd 3C 22
Waldens Rd. BR5: St M Cry 4E 25
WALDERSLADE 1F 35
Walderslade Rd. ME4: Chat 4F 27
ME5: Chat, Wald 4F 27
Walderslade Woods ME5: Chat 1F 35
Waldram Pk. Rd. SE23 .....2B 24
Wales Farm Rd. W3 .....4D 15
WALHAM GREEN 1E 23
Walk, The EN6: Pot B 3E 7
Wallace La. CM3: Bor 1F 11
WALLEND 3D 17
WALLINGTON 1F 31
WALLINGTON GREEN 4F 23
Wallis Av. ME15: Maids 3F 35
WALL'S GREEN 2B 10
Walm La. NW2 .....3E 15
Walnut Hill Rd.
DA13: Meop, Ist R 3C 26
Walnut Tree Cl. GU1: Guild 4E 29
Walnut Tree Rd. RM8: Dag 3E 17
Walpole Rd. N17 .....2A 16
(not continuous)
Walterton Rd. W9 .....4E 15
WALTHAM ABBEY 3C 8
WALTHAM CROSS 3B 8
Waltham Rd. CM3: Bor 1F 11
EN9: Naze 2C 8
SL6: W Walt 1A 20
WALTHAM ST LAWRENCE 1A 20
WALTHAMSTOW 2B 16
Waltham Way E4 .....1B 16
Walton Bri. TW17: Shep 4A 22
WALTON COURT 1A 4
Walton Heath Golf Course 3E 31
Walton La. KT13: Weyb 4A 22
SL2: Farn R 4D 13
TW17: Shep 4A 22
WALTON-ON-THAMES 4B 22
WALTON ON THE HILL 3E 31
Walton Rd. KT8: W Mole, E Mos 3B 22
KT12: Walt T 4B 22
KT18: Eps D, H'ly 2D 31
Walton's Hall Rd. SS17: Stan H 1D 27
Walton St. KT20: Walt H 3E 31
WALWORTH 1A 24
Walworth Rd. SE17 .....1A 24
WANBOROUGH 4C 28
Wanborough Hill GU3: Wanb 4C 28
Wandle Rd. SM4: Mord 3F 23
WANDSWORTH 2E 23
Wandsworth Bri. SW6 .....2E 23
Wandsworth Bri. Rd. SW6 .....1E 23
WANDSWORTH COMMON 2F 23
WANDSWORTH GYRATORY 2E 23
Wandsworth High St. SW18 .....2E 23
Wandsworth Rd. SW8 .....2F 23
WANSTEAD 2C 16
Wantz Rd. CM4: Marg 3D 11
WAPPING 4B 16
Wapping High St. E1 .....4B 16
Wapping La. E1 .....4B 16
Wapping Wall E1 .....4B 16
WAPSES LODGE RDBT. 2B 32
Wapseys La. SL2: Hedg 3D 13
Warbury La. GU21: Knap 2D 29
War Coppice Rd. CR3: Cat'm 3A 32
Wardour St. W1 .....4F 15
Wardrobes La. HP27: L Row 3A 4
Warepoint Dr. SE28 .....1D 25
Ware Rd. EN11: Hodd 1B 8
SG13: Gt A, Hail 1B 8
SG13: Hertf 1A 8
Wares Rd. CM1: G Eas 1C 10
WARFIELD 2B 20
Warfield Rd. RG12: Brac 3B 20
RG42: Brac 3B 20
Warfield St. RG42: Warf 3B 20
Warham Rd. CR2: S Croy 4A 24
Warkworth Gdns. TW7: Isle 2A 22
WARLEY 1B 18
Warley Gap
CM13: Gt War, L War 2B 18
Warley Hall La. RM14: Upm 3B 18
Warley Hill CM13: Gt War, Warl 2B 18
CM14: Warl 1B 18
Warley Rd. CM13: Gt War 2B 18
RM14: Gt War, Upm 2A 18
Warley St. CM13: Gt War, Upm 2B 18
RM14: Upm 2B 18
WARLINGHAM 2B 32
Warner Pl. E2 .....4B 16
WARNERS END 2F 5
Warners End Rd. HP1: Hem H 2F 5
Warners Hill SL6: Cook 3B 12
Warren Av. BR1: Brom 3C 24
WARREN CORNER 4A 28
Warrendene Rd. HP14: Hug V 4B 4
Warrengate Rd. AL9: N Mym 2E 7
Warren Ho. Rd. RG40: W'ham 3A 20
Warren La. CM15: Dodd, Kel H 4A 10
GU22: Pyr 2F 29
KT22: Oxs 1C 30
RH8: Oxt 4C 32
RM16: Chaf H 1B 26
Warren Rd. BR2: Hayes 4C 24
BR6: Chels 4D 25
CM3: Runw, Sth H, Ret 4E 11
CR8: Purl 1A 32
DA13: Lud'n 4D 27
DA13: Sflt 3B 26
E10 .....3C 16
GU1: Guild 4E 29
ME5: B Hill 1F 35
TW2: Whitt 2C 22
WARREN ROW 4A 12
Warren Row Rd. RG10: W Row 4A 12
Warren St. W1 .....4F 15
Warwick Av. W9 .....4E 15
Warwick Gdns. W14 .....1E 23
Warwick La. RM13: Rain 4A 18
RM14: Avel, Upm 4A 18
Warwick Rd. SW5 .....1E 23
W5 .....1C 22
W14 .....1E 23
Warwicks Bench GU1: Guild 4E 29
Warwick's Bench Rd.
GU1: Guild 4E 29
Warwick Ter. SE18 .....1D 25
Warwick Way SW1 .....1F 23
WARWICK WOLD 3A 32
Warwick Wold Rd. RH1: Mers 3A 32
Wash Hill HP10: Wbrn G 3C 12
Washneys Rd. BR6: Prat B 1E 33
Washpond La. CR6: Warl 2C 32
Wash Rd. CM13: Hut, Mount 1C 18
SS15: Bas, Lain 2D 19
(not continuous)
Watchet La. HP15: Holm G 4B 4
HP16: L King 4B 4
Watchouse Rd. CM2: Gall 3E 11
Watercroft Rd. TN14: Hals 1E 33
WATERDALE 3B 6
Waterden Rd. E15 .....3B 16
GU1: Guild 4E 29
WATER END
AL9 .....2E 7
HP1 .....1F 5
Water End Rd. HP4: Pott E 1F 5
Waterfall Rd. N11 .....1F 15
N14 .....1F 15
Waterfields Way WD17: Wat 4B 6
WATERHALES 1F 17
Waterhouse La. CM1: Chelm 2D 11
KT20: Kgswd 2E 31
RH1: Blet 4B 32
WATERINGBURY 3D 35
Wateringbury Rd.
ME19: E Mal 3D 35
Water La. CM19: Har, Roy 2D 9
E15 .....3C 16
GU5: Alb 4F 29
GU9: Farnh 4A 28
HP3: Bov 3E 5
IG3: Ilf 3D 17
KT11: Cobh 1B 30
ME19: W Mal 2D 35
WD4: K Lan 3A 6
WD17: Wat 4B 6
Waterloo Bri. SE1 .....4A 16
SE1 .....4A 16
Waterloo Rd. KT19: Eps 1D 31
RG40: W'ham 3A 20
RG45: Crow 1A 28
RM7: Rom, Rush G 2F 17
SE1 .....1A 24
UB8: Uxb 4F 13
Waterlow Rd. DA13: Meop 1C 34
Watermead Way N17 .....2B 16
WATER OAKLEY 1C 20
WATERSIDE 3D 5
Waterside HP5: Ches 3D 5
WD4: K Lan 3A 6
Waterside Dr. KT12: Walt T 4B 22
Watersplash La. SL5: Asc 3D 21
Waterway Rd. KT22: Lea 2C 30
Watery La. CM5: H Laver, Lit L 1F 9
DA14: Sidc 3E 25
HP10: Wbrn G 2C 12
TN15: Kems'g, Seal 2A 34
WATFORD 4B 6
Watford By-Pass HA8: Edg 1D 15
WD6: E'tree 1C 14
Watford FC 1B 14
WATFORD HEATH 1B 14
Watford Heath WD19: Wat 1B 14
Watford Rd. AL1: St A 2B 6
AL2: Chis G 2B 6
HA0: Wemb 3C 14
HA1: Harr 3C 14
HA6: Nwood 2A 14
WD3: Crox G 3A 6
WD4: Hunt C, K Lan 3A 6
WD6: E'tree 1C 14
WD7: Rad 4C 6
Watford Way NW4 .....2E 15
NW7 .....1D 15
Watling Av. HA8: Edg 2D 15
Watling St. AL1: St A 2C 6
AL2: Park 2C 6
DA1: Dart 2A 26
DA2: Bean, Bluew, Dart, Ghithe, Sflt 2B 26
DA6: Bex 2E 25
DA9: Ghithe, Bluew 2A 26
DA11: Nflt, Sflt 2B 26
DA12: Cobh, Grav'nd 2B 26
ME2: Strood 3D 27
ME5: Chat, G'ham 4F 27
WD6: E'tree 3C 6
WD7: Rad 3C 6
Watney's Rd. CR4: Mitc 4F 23
Watson's Wlk. AL1: St A 2C 6
WATTON'S GREEN 1F 17
Watts Av. ME1: Roch 4F 27
WATT'S CROSS 4A 34
Watt's Cross Rd. TN11: Hild 4A 34
Watts La. BR7: Chst 3D 25
Watts Rd. KT7: T Ditt 4C 22
Wat Tyler Rd. SE3 .....1C 24
Wat Tyler Way ME15: Maids 3F 35
Waverley Cres. SE18 .....1D 25
Waverley Rd. AL3: St A 1C 6
Waxwell La. HA5: Pinn 2B 14
WAYFIELD 4F 27
Wayfield Rd. ME5: Chat 4F 27
Wayside NW11 .....3E 15
Weald Bri. Rd. CM16: N Weald 2F 9
Weald Hall La. CM16: Twood 2E 9
Weald Pk. Way
CM14: S Weald 1A 18
Weald Rd. CM14: S Weald 1A 18
TN13: S'oaks 3F 33
WEALDSTONE 2C 14
Weald Way CR3: Cat'm 3A 32
WEBBS FARM INTERCHANGE 3D 11
Weedon Hill HP6: H Hea 3C 4
WEEDS WOOD 1F 35
Weigall Rd. SE12 .....2C 24
Weir Rd. KT16: Chert 4F 21
Welders La. HP9: Jor 2D 13
SL9: Chal P 2D 13
WELHAM GREEN 2E 7
Wellbrook Rd. BR6: Farnb 4D 25
WELL END
SL8 .....2B 12
WD6 .....4D 7
Well End Rd. WD6: Bore 4D 7
Weller Av. ME1: Roch 4F 27
Weller's La. RG42: Warf 2B 20
Wellesley Rd. CR0: C'don 4A 24
GU11: Alde 4A 28
(not continuous)
TW2: Twick 2C 22
W4 .....1D 23
Welley Rd. SL3: Hort 2E 21
TW19: Wray 2E 21
Wellfield Rd. AL10: Hat 1E 7
Well Hall Rd. SE9 .....2D 25
WELL HALL RDBT. 2D 25
WELL HILL 4E 25
Well Hill BR6: Orp 4E 25
WELLING 2E 25
Welling High St. DA16: Well 2E 25
Wellington Av. GU11: Alde 4A 28
GU25: Vir W 4E 21
Wellington Hill
IG10: H Beech, Lough 4C 8
Wellingtonia Av. RG45: Crow 1A 28
Wellington Rd. NW8 .....4F 15
TW12: Ham H 3C 22
Wellington Rd. Nth.
TW4: Houn 2B 22
Wellington Rd. Sth. TW4: Houn 2B 22
Wellington St. DA12: Grav'nd 2C 26
SE18 .....1D 25
SL1: Slou 4D 13
WC2 .....4A 16
Welling Way DA16: Well 2D 25
SE9 .....2D 25
Well La. CM3: Dan 2F 11
CM4: Stock 4D 11
GU21: Wok 2E 29
Well Rd. EN6: N'thaw 3F 7
ME14: Maids 2F 35
Well Row SG13: B'fd 1A 8
Wells Pk. Rd. SE26 .....2B 24
WELL STREET 2D 35
Well St. E9 .....3B 16
ME15: Loose 4F 35
ME19: E Mal 2D 35
Wells Way SE5 .....1A 24
WELWYN GARDEN CITY 1E 7
Welwyn Rd. SG14: Hertf 1A 8
WEMBLEY 3D 15
Wembley Hill Rd. HA9: Wemb 3D 15
WEMBLEY PARK 3D 15
Wembley Pk. Dr. HA9: Wemb 3D 15
Wembley Stadium 3D 15
Wemborough Rd. HA7: Stan 2C 14
WENDOVER 2B 4
Wendover By-Pass HP22: Wend 1A 4
WENDOVER DEAN 2B 4
Wendover Rd. HP21: A'bury 1A 4
HP22: S Man, W Tur 1A 4
Wendover Way DA16: Well 2E 25
HP21: A'bury 1A 4
Wenlock's La. CM4: Bmore 3B 10
WENNINGTON 4A 18
Wennington Rd.
RM13: Rain, Wenn 4F 17
Wensleydale Rd. TW12: Hamp 3B 22
WENTWORTH 4D 21
Wentworth Golf Course (East Course) 4D 21
Wentworth Golf Course (West Course) 4D 21
Wessex Way SL6: Maide 1B 20
Westacott Way SL6: L Grn 4A 12
WEST ACTON 4D 15
WEST BARNES 3E 23
W. Barnes La. SW20: N Mald 3E 23
WEST BEDFONT 2A 22
Westbere Rd. NW2 .....3E 15
WESTBOURNE GREEN 4E 15
Westbourne Gro. W2 .....4E 15
W11 .....4E 15
Westbourne Pk. Rd. W11 .....4E 15
Westbourne Rd. N7 .....3A 16
Westbourne Ter. W2 .....4F 15
Westbridge Rd. SW11 .....1F 23
WEST BROMPTON 1E 23
Westbrook Rd. TW5: Hest 1B 22
Westbury Av. N22 .....2A 16
WEST BYFLEET 1F 29
Westcar La. KT12: Hers 4B 22
WEST CLANDON 3F 29
Westcombe Hill SE3 .....1C 24
West Comn. SL9: Ger X 2E 13
(not continuous)
West Comn. Rd. BR2: Hayes 4C 24
Westcote Rd. SW16 .....3F 23
WESTCOTT 4B 30
Westcott Rd. RH4: Dork 4C 30
Westcott St. RH4: Westc 4C 30
WESTCOURT 2D 27
WEST DRAYTON 1A 22
W. Drayton Rd. UB8: Hil 4A 14
West Dr. SW16 .....3F 23
WEST DULWICH 2A 24
WEST EALING 4C 14
Wested La. BR8: Crock, Swan 4F 25
(not continuous)
WEST END
AL9 .....1F 7
GU24 .....1D 29
KT10 .....1B 30
RG10 .....2A 20
RG42 .....3B 20
SW1 .....1F 23
UB5 .....4B 14
West End TN15: Kems'g 2A 34
West End La. AL9: Ess, Hat 2F 7
HA5: Pinn 2B 14
KT10: Esh 1B 30
NW6 .....3E 15
(not continuous)
SL2: Stoke P 4D 13
West End Rd. EN10: Brox 2A 8
HA4: Ruis 3A 14
UB5: N'olt 3B 14
WESTERHAM 3D 33
WESTERHAM HILL 2D 33
Westerham Hill TN16: Westrm 2D 33
Westerham Rd. BR2: Kes 4D 25
RH8: Limp, Oxt, Westrm 3C 32
TN13: Riv 3E 33
TN14: Sund 3E 33
TN16: Westrm 3C 32
TN16: Westrm, Bras 3E 33
Westerhill Rd. ME17: Lint, Cox 4F 35
Western Av. CM14: B'wood 1B 18
HA4: Ruis 3F 13
ME4: Chat 3F 27
UB5: N'olt 3B 14
UB6: G'frd 4C 14
UB9: Den, Uxb 3F 13
UB10: Hil 3F 13
W5 .....4C 14
Western Dene HP15: Haz 4B 4
Western Perimeter Rd.
TW6: H'row A 1F 21
Western Rd. CM12: Bill 1D 19
CM14: B'wood 1B 18
CR4: Mitc 3F 23
HP23: Tring 1C 4
RG12: Brac 3A 20
RM1: Rom 2F 17
SW19 .....3F 23
TN15: Bor G 2B 34
UB2: S'hall 1B 22
Western Way SE28 .....1D 25
WEST EWELL 1D 31
WEST FARLEIGH 3E 35
Westferry Rd. E14 .....4B 16
WESTFIELD 2E 29
Westfield Av. GU22: Wok 2E 29
Westfield Rd. GU22: Wok 2E 29
HP4: Berk 1D 5
WESTFIELD SOLE 1F 35
Westfield Sole Rd. ME14: Lor 1F 35
Westgate Rd. DA1: Dart 2F 25
WEST GREEN 2A 16
West Grn. Rd. N15 .....2A 16
West Gro. KT12: Hers 4B 22
Westhall Rd. CR6: Warl 2B 32
WEST HAM 4C 16
W. Ham La. E15 .....3C 16
(not continuous)
WEST HAMPSTEAD 3E 15
West Ham United FC 4C 16
WEST HANNINGFIELD 4E 11
W. Hanningfield Rd.
CM2: Gt B, W Han 3E 11
WEST HARROW 3C 14

Westhatch La. RG42: Warf 2B 20
WEST HEATH
GU14 2A 28
SE2 1E 25
W. Heath Rd. GU14: Cove 3A 28
NW3 3E 15
SE2 1E 25
WEST HENDON 3D 15
WEST HILL 2E 23
West Hill DA1: Dart 2F 25
KT19: Eps 1D 31
RH8: Oxt 3C 32
SW15 2E 23
SW18 2E 23
WEST HORNDON 2C 18
Westhorne Av. SE9 2C 24
SE12 2C 24
WEST HORSLEY 3A 30
WESTHUMBLE 4C 30
Westhumble St. RH5: Westh 4C 30
WEST HYDE 2F 13
W. Hyde La. SL9: Chal P 2F 13
W. India Dock Rd. E14 4B 16
(not continuous)
WEST KENSINGTON 1E 23
WEST KILBURN 4E 15
WEST KINGSDOWN 1A 34
West La. RH5: Wott 4B 30
WEST LEITH 1C 4
WEST MALLING 2D 35
West Mayne SS15: Lain 2C 18
Westmead Rd. SM1: Sutt 4F 23
WESTMINSTER 1A 24
Westminster Bri. SE1 1A 24
SW1 1A 24
Westminster Bri. Rd. SE1 1A 24
WEST MOLESEY 3B 22
Westmoreland Rd. BR2: Brom 4C 24
Westmorland Dr. RG42: Warf 3B 20
Westmount Rd. SE9 1D 25
WEST NORWOOD 3A 24
Weston Av. RM20: W Thur 1A 26
Weston Dr. HA7: Stan 2C 14
WESTON GREEN 4C 22
Weston Grn. Rd. KT10: Esh 4C 22
Weston Rd. HP22: Ast C 1B 4
WESTON TURVILLE 1A 4
Westow Hill SE19 3A 24
Westow St. SE19 3A 24
West Pk. SE9 2D 25
WEST PECKHAM 3C 34
Westpole Av. EN4: Cockf 4F 7
West Ramp TW6: H'row A 1A 22
West Riding AL2: Brick W 3B 6
West Rd. RH2: Reig 4E 31
RM15: S Ock 4B 18
WEST RUISLIP 3A 14
W. Side Comn. SW19 3E 23
West Smithfield EC1 4A 16
WEST STREET 1E 27
West St. BR1: Brom 3C 24
DA8: Erith 1F 25
DA11: Grav'nd 2C 26
HA1: Harr 3C 14
ME15: Hunt 4E 35
ME19: W Mal 2D 35
RH2: Reig 4E 31
RH4: Dork 4C 30
SM1: Sutt 4E 23
SM5: Cars 4F 23
WEST THURROCK 1B 26
W. Thurrock Way
RM20: Chaf H, Grays, W Thur 1B 26
WEST TILBURY 1D 27
WEST WATFORD 4B 6
Westway CM1: Wid 2D 11
CR3: Cat'm 3A 32
SW20 3E 23
W12 4E 15
WEST WICKHAM 4C 24
Westwick Row HP2: Hem H 2A 6
Westwood Hill SE26 3B 24
Westwood La. DA16: Well 2D 25
GU3: Norm 4C 28
Westwood Rd. DA13: Sflt 3B 26
GU20: W'sham 4C 20
WEST WYCOMBE 1A 12
West Wycombe Pk. 1A 12
W. Wycombe Rd. HP11: H Wy 1A 12
HP12: H Wy 1A 12
WEST YOKE 4B 26
West Yoke TN15: Ash 4B 26
W. Yoke Rd. DA3: New A 4B 26
Wetland Cen., The 1E 23
WEXHAM 4E 13
WEXHAM COURT 4E 13
Wexham Pk. La. SL3: Wex 4E 13
Wexham Rd. SL1: Slou 1E 21
SL2: Slou, Wex 1E 21
WEXHAM STREET 4E 13
Wexham St. SL2: Stoke P, Wex 4E 13
SL3: Stoke P, Wex 4E 13
WEYBOURNE 4A 28
Weybourne Rd. GU9: Farnh 4A 28
WEYBRIDGE 4A 22
Weybridge Rd. KT15: Add 4A 22
Wey La. HP5: Ches 3D 5
Weymouth St. W1 4F 15
Whalebone La. Nth.
RM6: Chad H, Col R 2E 17
Whalebone La. Sth.
RM6: Chad H, Dag 3E 17
RM8: Dag 3E 17
Wharfdale Rd. N1 4A 16
Wharf La. HP23: Berk 1D 5
Wharf Rd. EN10: Worm 2B 8
GU12: Ash V 4B 28
GU16: F Grn 2B 28
ME7: G'ham 3F 27
(not continuous)
SS17: Fob 4E 19
Wharncliffe Rd. SE25 3A 24
Wheatfield Way KT1: King T 3D 23
Wheeler's Hill CM3: Lit W 1E 11
Wheelers La.
CM14: N'side, Pil H 4A 10
ME17: Lint 4F 35
RH3: Aroc 4D 31
WHELPLEY HILL 2E 5
Whelpley Hill HP4: Berk 2E 5
HP5: Whel 2E 5
Whetsted Rd. TN12: Five G 4D 35
WHETSTONE 1E 15
Whielden La. HP7: Amer, Win H 1D 13
HP7: Win H, Amer 1C 12
Whielden St. HP7: Amer 4D 5
Whinchat Rd. SE28 1D 25
Whippendell Rd. WD18: Wat 1A 14
Whipps Cross Rd. E11 2C 16
(not continuous)
Whiston Rd. E2 4A 16
Whitchurch La. HA8: Edg 2C 14
Whitchurch Rd. RM3: Rom 1F 17
WHITECHAPEL 4B 16
Whitechapel Rd. E1 4B 16
WHITE CITY 4E 15
WHITE CITY 4E 15
Whitefoot La. BR1: Brom 3C 24
(not continuous)
Whitehall SW1 1A 24
Whitehall La. DA8: Erith 1F 25
RH2: Reig 4E 31
TW20: Egh 3E 21
Whitehall Rd. E4 1C 16
IG8: Wfd G 1C 16
White Hart La. CM1: Spr 1E 11
N17 2A 16
N22 2A 16
RM7: Col R, Mawney 2E 17
SW13 2D 23
White Hart Rd. HP2: Hem H 2A 6
White Hill CR5: Chip 3F 31
HP4: Berk 1E 5
HP5: Ches 3D 5
HP10: Wbrn G 1B 12
HP14: Hug V 2C 12
WD3: Rick 2A 14
White Hill La. RH1: Blet 3A 32
Whitehill La. DA12: Grav'nd 2C 26
Whitehill Rd. DA3: Dart, Lfield 3B 26
DA12: Grav'nd 2C 26
DA13: Meop 4C 26
White Horse Hill BR7: Chst 3D 25
White Horse La. AL2: Lon C 2C 6
E1 4B 16
Whitehorse La. SE25 3A 24
Whitehorse Rd. DA13: Meop 1C 34
Whitehorse Rd. CR0: C'don 4A 24
CR7: Thor H 4A 24
Whitehouse La. HP10: Wbrn G 2C 12
WD5: Bedm 2B 6
White Ho. Rd. TN14: S'oaks 3F 33
Whitelands Way RM3: Hrld W 2A 18
White La. GU4: Guild 4F 29
GU5: Alb 4F 29
GU10: Tong 4C 28
GU12: Ash G 4C 28
RH8: T'sey 3C 32
TN16: Tats, T'sey 3C 32
WHITELEAF 2A 4
WHITELEY VILLAGE 1A 30
White Lion Rd.
HP7: Amer, L Chal 4D 5
Whitepit La.
HP10: Flack H, Wbrn G 2C 12
WHITE POST 4A 32
Whitepost Hill RH1: Redh 4F 31
(not continuous)
White Post La. DA13: Sole S 3C 26
Whitepost La. DA13: Meop 1C 34
WHITE RODING 1A 10
White Rose La. GU22: Wok 2E 29
White's Hill CM4: Stock 4D 11
White Stubbs La. EN10: Brox 2A 8
SG13: B'fd, Brick, Brox, Epp G 2A 8
WHITE WALTHAM 1A 20
White Waltham Airfield 1A 20
Whitewebbs Rd.
EN2: Crew H, Enf 4A 8
Whitmoor La. GU4: Sut G 3E 29
Whitmore La. SL5: S'dale, S'hill 4D 21
Whitmore Rd. HA1: Harr 3C 14
Whitmore Way SS14: Bas 2E 19
Whittington Rd. N22 2A 16
Whittington Way HA5: Pinn 2B 14
WHITTON 2B 22
Whitton Av. E. UB6: G'frd 3C 14
Whitton Av. W. UB5: N'olt 3C 14
UB6: G'frd 3C 14
Whitton Dene TW3: Houn 2C 22
TW7: Isle 2C 22
Whitton Rd. TW1: Twick 2C 22
TW2: Twick 2C 22
TW3: Houn 2B 22
WHITTON ROAD RDBT. 2C 22
Whitworth Rd. SE25 3A 24
Whyteladyes La. SL6: Cook 3B 12
WHYTELEAFE 2B 32
Whyteleafe Hill CR3: Whyt 2A 32
(not continuous)
Whyteleafe Rd. CR3: Cat'm 3A 32
WICKFORD 1F 19
Wickford Av. SS13: Pit 2E 19
Wickham Ct. Rd. BR4: W W'ck 4C 24
Wickham La. SE2 1E 25
Wickham Rd. BR3: Beck 3B 24
CR0: C'don 4B 24
SE4 2B 24
Wickham St. DA16: Well 1E 25
Wickham Way BR3: Beck 3C 24
WICKHURST GREEN 4F 33
Wick La. E3 4B 16
TW20: Eng G 3D 21
Wick Rd. E9 3B 16
Wick's Grn. RG42: Bin 3A 20
Wide Way CR4: Mitc 3F 23
WIDFORD 2D 11
Widmere La. SL7: Marl 2A 12
WIDMER END 4B 4
WIDMORE 3C 24
Widmore Rd. BR1: Brom 3C 24
WIERTON 4F 35
Wierton Hill ME17: B Mon 4F 35
Wierton Rd. ME17: B Mon 4F 35
Wiggenhall Rd. WD18: Wat 1B 14
WIGGINTON 1C 4
WIGGINTON BOTTOM 1D 5
Wightman Rd. N4 2A 16
N8 2A 16
Wigley Bush La.
CM14: B'wood, S Weald 1A 18
Wigmore St. W1 4F 15
Wilbury Way N18 1A 16
WILDERNESSE 2A 34
WILDHILL 2F 7
WILDRIDINGS 3B 20
Wildridings Rd. RG12: Brac 3B 20
Wildwood Rd. NW11 2F 15
Wilkin's Grn. La. AL4: S'ford 2D 7
WILLESDEN 3E 15
WILLESDEN GREEN 3E 15
Willesden La. NW2 3E 15
NW6 3E 15
WILLEY GREEN 4D 29
William Barefoot Dr. SE9 3D 25
William St. SL1: Slou 4D 13
WILLINGALE 2B 10
Willingale Rd. CM4: Nor H 2B 10
CM5: Fyf, Will 2A 10
CM5: Nor H, Will 2B 10
IG10: Lough 4D 9
Willington St. ME15: Maids 3F 35
Willoughby La. N17 2B 16
WILLOWBANK 3F 13
Willow Brook Rd. SE15 1A 24
Willowfield SS15: Lain 2D 19
Willow Rd. EN1: Enf 4A 8
Willow Tree La. UB4: Yead 4B 14
Willow Wents ME18: Mere 3C 34
Wilmerhatch La. KT18: Eps 2D 31
Wilmer Way N14 1F 15
WILMINGTON 3F 25
Wilson La. DA4: S Dar 3A 26
Wilsons La. ME15: E Far 3E 35
Wilson St. EC2 4A 16
Wiltshire Rd. RG40: W'ham 3A 20
SL7: Marl 3A 12
WIMBLEDON 3E 23
Wimbledon
All England Lawn Tennis &
Croquet Club 2E 23
Wimbledon Hill Rd. SW19 3E 23
WIMBLEDON PARK 2E 23
Wimbledon Pk. Rd. SW18 2E 23
SW18 2E 23
Wimbledon Pk. Side SW19 2E 23
Wimbledon Rd. SW17 3F 23
Winchbottom La.
HP10: H Wy 2A 12
SL7: Lit M 2B 12
Winchelsea Rd. NW10 4D 15
Winchester Rd. E4 2C 16
N9 1B 16
Winchester St. W3 1D 23
WINCHMORE HILL
HP7 1C 12
N21 1A 16
Winchmore Hill CM1: G Eas 1C 10
Winchmore Hill Rd. N14 1F 15
N21 1F 15
Windermere Av.
HA9: Kent, Wemb 3C 14
Wind Hill CM5: Mag L 2F 9
WINDLESHAM 4C 20
Windlesham Rd. GU24: Chob 1D 29
GU24: W End 1D 29
Windmill Hill EN2: Enf 4A 8
HA4: Ruis 3A 14
HP7: Cole 1D 13
TN15: Bor G, Wro 2C 34
WD4: Chfd 3F 5
Windmill La. E15 3C 16
EN8: Chesh 3B 8
HP15: Wid E 4B 4
KT17: Eps 1D 31
TW7: Isle 1C 22
UB2: S'hall 1C 22
Windmill Rd. CR0: C'don 4A 24
CR4: Mitc 3F 23
SL3: Ful 3E 13
SW18 2F 23
TN13: S'oaks 3F 33
TN14: Weald 4F 33
TW8: Bford 1C 22
TW16: Sun 3A 22
W5 1C 22
Windmill St. DA12: Grav'nd 2C 26
(not continuous)
WINDSOR 1D 21
Windsor & Eton Relief Rd.
SL4: Eton, Wind 1D 21
Windsor Av. SW19 3F 23
Windsor Castle 1D 21
Windsor Dr. BR6: Chels 1E 33
SG14: Hertf 1A 8
Windsor End HP9: Beac 2D 13
Windsor Great Pk. 2D 21
Windsor Hill HP10: Wbrn G 2C 12
Windsor La. HP16: L King 4B 4
SL1: Burn 4C 12
Windsor Rd. GU24: Chob 4D 21
SL1: Slou 1D 21
SL2: Ger X, Stoke P 3E 13
SL3: Dat 1E 21
SL4: Old Win 2E 21
SL4: Wat O, Wind 1C 20
SL4: Wink 3C 20
Windsor Rd. SL5: Asc 3C 20
SL6: Bray 1B 20
SL9: Ger X 3E 13
TW19: Wray 2E 21
TW20: Egh 2E 21
Windsor St. KT16: Chert 4F 21
Windsor Way GU11: Alde 4B 28
Winfield La. TN15: Bor G 3B 34
Wingletye La. RM11: Horn 2A 18
Wingrave Rd. HP23: Tring 1C 4
WINKFIELD 2C 20
Winkfield La. SL4: Wink 2C 20
Winkfield Rd. SL4: Wink 3C 20
SL5: Asc 3C 20
WINKFIELD ROW 3B 20
Winkfield Row RG42: Wink R 3B 20
WINKFIELD STREET 2C 20
Winkfield St. SL4: Wink 2C 20
WINKHURST GREEN 4E 33
Winkhurst Grn. Rd.
TN8: Ide H, Chid 4E 33
Winkworth Rd. SM7: Bans 1E 31
Winn Rd. SE12 2C 24
Winston Churchill Way
EN8: Walt C 3B 8
Winston Way IG1: Ilf 3D 17
Winterfield La. ME19: W Mal 2D 35
WINTER GARDENS 3F 19
Winter Hill SL6: Cook 3B 12
Winter Hill Rd.
SL6: Cook, Maide 3B 12
Wise La. NW7 2E 15
WISLEY 2A 30
WISLEY INTERCHANGE 2A 30
Wisley La. GU23: Wis 2F 29
Witches La. TN13: Riv 3F 33
Witheridge La. HP9: Beac 1C 12
HP10: Penn 1C 12
Withies La. GU3: Comp 4D 29
Woburn Hill KT15: Add 4F 21
Woburn Pl. WC1 4A 16
WOKING 2E 29
WOKINGHAM 3A 20
Wokingham Rd. GU47: S'urst 1A 28
RG42: Brac 3A 20
RG45: Crow 1A 28
WOKINGHAM WITHOUT 4A 20
Woking Rd. GU1: Guild 3E 29
GU4: Jac W 3E 29
WOLDINGHAM 3B 32
WOLDINGHAM GARDEN VILLAGE 2B 32
Woldingham Rd. CR3: Wold 2B 32
Wolf La. SL4: Wind 2C 20
Wolf's Hill RH8: Oxt 4C 32
Wolfs Hill RH8: Limp 3C 32
Wolf's Row RH8: Limp 3C 32
Wolseley Rd. N8 2F 15
Wolves La. N22 2A 16
Wonham La. RH3: Bet 4D 31
WOOBURN 3C 12
WOOBURN COMMON 3C 12
Wooburn Comn. Rd.
HP10: Wbrn G 3C 12
SL1: Burn 3C 12
WOOBURN GREEN 2C 12
Wooburn Grn. La. HP9: Beac 2C 12
WOOBURN MOOR 2C 12
Woodberry Gro. N4 3A 16
WOODBRIDGE HILL 4E 29
Woodbridge Mdws. GU1: Guild 4E 29
Woodbridge Rd. GU1: Guild 4E 29
(not continuous)
Woodcock Hill HA3: Kent 2C 14
WD6: E'tree 1D 15
Woodcockhill AL4: Sandr 1C 6
Woodcock La. GU24: Chob 1D 29
WOODCOTE
CR8 1F 31
KT18 2D 31
WOODCOTE GREEN 1F 31
Woodcote Grn. SM6: Wall 1F 31
Woodcote Gro. Rd. CR5: Coul 2F 31
Woodcote Rd. CR8: Purl 1F 31
SM6: Wall 1F 31
Woodcote Valley Rd. CR8: Purl 1F 31
Woodcroft Av. HA8: Edg 2D 15
WOOD END
SL4 3C 20
UB4 4A 14
WOODEND 1A 10
Wood End SL7: Med 3A 12
UB3: Hayes 4A 14
WOOD END GREEN 4A 14
Wood End Grn. Rd. UB3: Hayes 4A 14
Wood End La. UB5: N'olt 3B 14
(not continuous)
Woodfield Av. SW16 2F 23
Woodfield La. AL9: Hat 2F 7
KT21: Asht 2D 31
Woodfield Rd. W5 4C 14
WOODFORD 2C 16
Woodford Av. IG2: Ilf 2D 17
IG4: Ilf, Wfd G 2D 17
WOODFORD BRIDGE 2D 17
WOODFORD GREEN 1C 16
Woodford New Rd. E17 2C 16
E18 2C 16
Woodford Rd. E7 3C 16
WD17: Wat 4B 6
WOODFORD SIDE 1C 16
WOODFORD WELLS 1C 16
Woodgate Rd. ME19: Rya 2C 34
Woodgrange Rd. E7 3C 16
WOOD GREEN
EN9 3C 8
N22 2A 16
Woodgreen Rd. EN9: Walt A 3C 8
WOODHALL 1E 7
Woodhall Hill
CM1: Chig S, Chi J 1D 11
Woodhall La. AL7: W City 1E 7
WOODHAM 1F 29
Woodham La. GU21: Wok 1E 29
KT15: Wdhm, New H 1F 29
KT15: Wok 1E 29
Woodham Pk. Rd. KT15: Wdhm 1F 29
Woodham Rd. GU21: Wok 2E 29
SS11: Bat, Ret 1F 19
WOODHATCH
CM16 3F 9
RH2 4F 31
Woodhatch Rd. RH1: Redh 4F 31
RH2: Reig 4F 31
Woodhayes Rd. SW19 3E 23
WOODHILL 2F 11
Wood Hill DA13: Meop 4C 26
Woodhill GU23: Send 3F 29
Woodhill Rd. CM2: Sando 2F 11
Woodhouse La.
CM1: Broom, Lit W 1D 11
CM3: Lit W 1E 11
Woodhouse Rd. N12 2F 15
Woodhurst La. RH8: Oxt 4C 32
Woodland Av. CM13: Hut 1C 18
Woodland Rd. WD3: Map C 1F 13
WOODLANDS
TN15 1A 34
TW7 2C 22
Woodlands Av. RM11: Horn 2F 17
Woodlands Hill HP9: Beac 2D 13
Woodlands La. DA12: Shorne 3D 27
GU20: W'sham 1D 29
KT11: Lea, Stoke D 2B 30
WOODLANDS PARK 1B 20
Woodlands Pk. Rd. SL6: Maide 1B 20
Woodlands Rd. KT22: Lea 2C 30
ME7: G'ham 4F 27
TW7: Isle 1C 22
Wood La. CM5: Will 2B 10
HA4: Ruis 3A 14
HA7: Stan 1C 14
ME5: Wald 1F 35
NW9 3D 15
RM8: Dag 3E 17
RM9: Dag 3E 17
RM10: Dag 3E 17
RM12: Horn 3F 17
SL0: Iver, Iver H 4F 13
TW7: Isle 1C 22
W12 4E 15
Wood La. End HP2: Hem H 2A 6
Woodman Rd. CM14: Warl 1B 18
WOODMANSTERNE 2F 31
Woodmansterne La. SM5: Cars 1F 31
SM6: Wall 1F 31
SM7: Bans 2F 31
Woodmansterne Rd. SM5: Cars 1F 31
Woodmansterne St. SM7: Bans 2F 31
Woodmere Av. WD24: Wat 4B 6
Woodplace La. CR5: Coul 2F 31
Woodridden Hill
EN9: Epp, They B, Walt A 4C 8
WOODROW 3C 12
Woods, The HA6: Nwood 1B 14
Woods Av. AL10: Hat 1E 7
WOODSIDE
AL9 2E 7
SE25 4B 24
SL4 3C 20
WD25 3B 6
Woodside CM16: N Weald, Twood 2E 9
SW19 3E 23
Woodside Av. N6 2F 15
N10 2F 15
Woodside Grn. SE25 4B 24
(not continuous)
Woodside Hill AL9: Hat 2E 7
WOODSIDE PARK 1E 15
Woodside Pk. Rd. N12 1E 15
Woodside Rd. HP6: Amer 4D 5
WD5: Ab L 3B 6
WD25: Wat 3B 6
Woodstock La. Nth. KT6: Surb 4C 22
Woodstock La. Sth. KT9: Chess 4C 22
KT10: Clay 4C 22
WOOD STREET 2C 16
Wood St. BR8: Swan 3F 25
CM2: Wid 2E 11
E17 2C 16
EN5: Barn 4E 7
KT1: King T 3D 23
(not continuous)
ME7: G'ham 3F 27
Wood St. Grn. GU3: Woo V 4D 29
WOOD STREET VILLAGE 4D 29
Woodthorpe Rd. TW15: Ashf 3F 21
Wood Va. SE23 2B 24
Wood Vw. RM16: Grays 1C 26
Woodward Rd. RM9: Dag 3E 17
Woodway HP27: L Row, Pri R 3A 4
WOOLLENSBROOK 1B 8
WOOLLEY GREEN 1A 20
Woolmead Rd. GU9: Farnh 4A 28
Woolmers La. SG14: Let G 1F 7
Woolmonger's La. CM4: Nine A 3B 10
Woolstone Rd. SE23 2B 24
WOOLWICH 1D 25
Woolwich Chu. St. SE18 1D 25
Woolwich Comn. SE18 1D 25
Woolwich Mnr. Way E6 4D 17
E16 4D 17
Woolwich New Rd. SE18 1D 25
Woolwich Rd. DA7: Bex 2E 25
DA17: Belv 1E 25
SE2 1E 25
SE7 1C 24
SE10 1C 24
Wootton Way SL6: Maide 4B 12
WORCESTER PARK 4E 23
Worcester Pk. Rd.
KT4: Wor Pk 4D 23
Workers Rd. CM5: H Laver 1F 9
CM17: Har, H Laver 1F 9
Workhouse La. ME15: E Far 3F 35
Workhouse Rd. ME19: Rya 2D 35
WORLD'S END
EN2 4A 8
HP22 1A 4
Worlds End La. BR6: Chels 1D 33
EN2: Enf 4A 8
HP22: W Tur 1A 4
N21 1A 16
WORMLEY 2B 8
WORMLEY WEST END 2A 8
Worple Rd. SW19 3E 23
SW20 3E 23
TW18: Staines 3F 21
(not continuous)
WORPLESDON 3D 29
Worplesdon Hill GU22: Wok 2D 29
Worplesdon Rd. GU2: Guild 3D 29
Worships Hill TN13: Riv 3F 33
Worship St. EC2 4A 16
Worton Rd. TW7: Isle 2C 22
WOTTON 4B 30
WOULDHAM 4E 27
Wouldham Rd. ME1: Woul 4E 27
Wrangling La. DA13: Meop 1D 35
Wray La. RH2: Reig 3F 31
WRAYSBURY 2E 21
Wraysbury Rd. TW18: Staines 2F 21
TW19: Staines 2E 21
Wrentham Av. NW10 4E 15
Wren Way GU14: Farnb 2A 28
Wrightsbridge Rd.
CM14: S Weald 1A 18
WRITTLE 2D 11
Writtle Rd. CM1: Chelm 2D 11
CM4: Marg 3D 11
WROTHAM 2B 34
Wrotham By-Pass TN15: Wro 2B 34
WROTHAM HEATH 2C 34
Wrotham Hill Rd. TN15: Wro 1B 34
Wrotham Rd.
DA11: Grav'nd, Nflt 2C 26
DA13: Meop 1C 34
DA13: Meop, Ist R 4C 26
TN15: Bor G, Wro 2B 34
Wrotham Water La. ME19: Tros 2C 34
Wrotham Water Rd. TN15: Tros 1C 34
Wrottesley Rd. NW10 4E 15
WRYTHE, THE 4F 23
Wrythe Grn. Rd. SM5: Cars 4F 23
Wrythe La. SM5: Cars 4F 23
Wulfere Way ME2: Wain 3F 27
WYATT'S GREEN 4B 10
Wyatt's Grn. Rd.
CM15: Dodd, W Grn 4B 10
Wych Hill GU22: Wok 2E 29
Wych Hill La. GU22: Wok 2E 29
Wycombe Air Pk. 2A 12
Wycombe End HP9: Beac 2D 13
Wycombe La. HP10: Wbrn G 2C 12
WYCOMBE MARSH 1B 12
Wycombe Rd. HP14: Brad, Saund 4A 4
HP15: Holm G 4B 4
HP16: Pre 3B 4
SL7: Marl 3A 12
Wycombe Wanderers FC 1A 12
WYKE 4C 28
Wyke La. GU12: Ash 4C 28
Wymer's Wood Rd. SL1: Burn 4C 12
Wyndham Rd. SE5 1A 24
Wyse's Rd. CM1: Coo G, High 2C 10

Y

YALDING 4D 35
Yalding Hill ME18: Yald 4D 35
Yardley Pk. Rd. TN9: Tonb 4B 34
Yarnton Way DA18: Belv, Erith 1E 25
SE2 1E 25
YATELEY 1A 28
Yateley Rd. GU47: S'urst 1A 28
YEADING 4B 14
Yeading La. UB4: Yead 4B 14
UB5: Yead 4B 14
Yelsted La. ME14: Box 1F 35
Yeovil Rd. GU47: Owl 1A 28
Yester Rd. BR7: Chst 3D 25
Yew Tree Bottom Rd.
KT17: Eps D 2E 31
Yew Tree Rd. SL1: Slou 1E 21
YIEWSLEY 4F 13
YOPPS GREEN 3B 34
Yopps Grn. TN15: Plax 3B 34
York Cres. WD6: Bore 4D 7
York Rd. E10 3C 16
EN5: New Bar 1F 15
GU1: Guild 4E 29
GU11: Alde 4A 28
GU22: Wok 2E 29
SE1 1A 24
SL6: Maide 4B 12
SM1: Sutt 1E 31
SM2: Sutt 1E 31
SW11 2F 23
UB8: Uxb 3F 13
Yorks Hill Rd. TN14: Ide H 4E 33
YORKSHIRE GREY 2C 24
York St. TW1: Twick 2C 22
W1 4F 15
YORK TOWN 2B 28
Yorktown Rd. GU47: S'urst 1A 28
York Way N1 4A 16
N7 3F 15
Young St. KT22: Fet, Lea 3C 30

Z

Zigzag, The KT20: Box H 3C 30
RH5: Mick 3C 30

CENTRAL LONDON

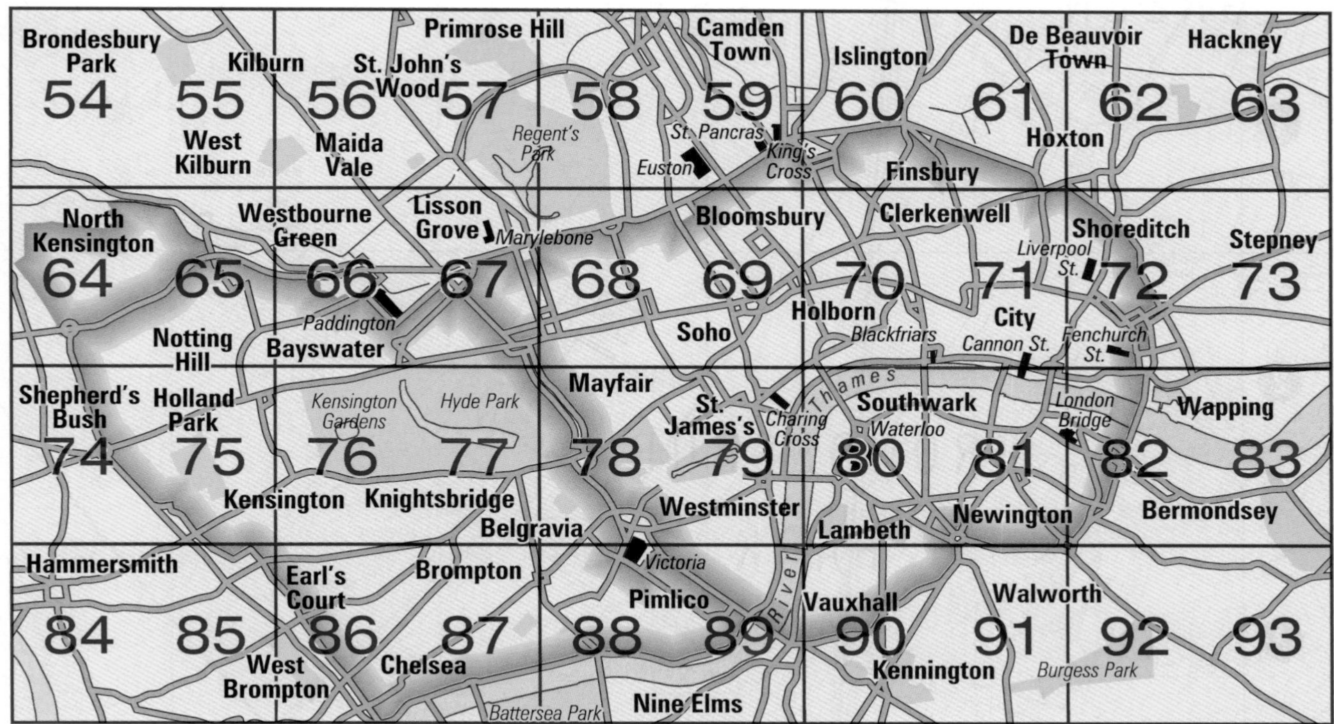

Brondesbury Park
54
Kilburn
55
West Kilburn
St. John's Wood
56
Maida Vale
Primrose Hill
57
Regent's Park
58
Camden Town
59
St. Pancras
Euston
King's Cross
Islington
60
Finsbury
De Beauvoir Town
61
62
Hoxton
Hackney
63
North Kensington
64
65
Westbourne Green
66
Paddington
Lisson Grove
Marylebone
67
68
Bloomsbury
69
Soho
Clerkenwell
70
Holborn
Blackfriars
Liverpool St.
71
City
Cannon St.
Shoreditch
72
Fenchurch St.
Stepney
73
Notting Hill
Bayswater
Shepherd's Bush
74
Holland Park
75
Kensington Gardens
76
Hyde Park
77
Kensington
Knightsbridge
Mayfair
78
St. James's
79
Charing Cross
Thames
Southwark
Waterloo
80
81
London Bridge
82
Wapping
83
Belgravia
Westminster
Lambeth
Newington
Bermondsey
Hammersmith
84
85
Earl's Court
86
West Brompton
Brompton
87
Chelsea
Victoria
88
Pimlico
89
River
Vauxhall
90
Kennington
Walworth
91
92
Burgess Park
93
Battersea Park
Nine Elms

REFERENCE

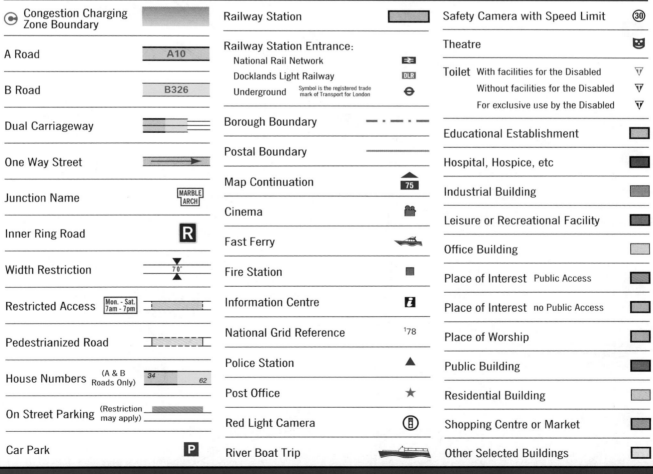

Congestion Charging Zone Boundary	Railway Station	Safety Camera with Speed Limit (30)
A Road (A10)	Railway Station Entrance: National Rail Network; Docklands Light Railway (DLR); Underground (Symbol is the registered trade mark of Transport for London)	Theatre
B Road (B326)	Borough Boundary	Toilet: With facilities for the Disabled; Without facilities for the Disabled; For exclusive use by the Disabled
Dual Carriageway	Postal Boundary	Educational Establishment
One Way Street	Map Continuation (75)	Hospital, Hospice, etc
Junction Name (MARBLE ARCH)	Cinema	Industrial Building
Inner Ring Road (R)	Fast Ferry	Leisure or Recreational Facility
Width Restriction (7'0")	Fire Station	Office Building
Restricted Access (Mon. - Sat. 7am - 7pm)	Information Centre	Place of Interest Public Access
Pedestrianized Road	National Grid Reference (178)	Place of Interest no Public Access
House Numbers (A & B Roads Only) (34, 62)	Police Station	Place of Worship
On Street Parking (Restriction may apply)	Post Office	Public Building
Car Park (P)	Red Light Camera	Residential Building
	River Boat Trip	Shopping Centre or Market
		Other Selected Buildings

SCALE

0 50 100 200 300 Yards ¼ ½ Mile

0 50 100 200 300 400 500 750 Metres

1:7,040 9 inches (22.7cm) to 1 mile
14.2cm to 1km

WILLESDEN GREEN
54
NW2
BRONDESBURY PARK
BRENT
NW10
KENSAL RISE
KENSAL GREEN
QUEENS
W10
KENSINGTON and CHELSEA
KENSAL GREEN CEMETERY
Willesden Sports Stadium
Stand
King Edward VII Recreation Ground
Cannons Health Club
Cricket Ground
Tennis Cts.
Pavs.
Pav.
Elstow Grange
Queens Park Community School
Sports Centre
Playing Field
Netball Ct.
Netball Cts.
Malorees Junior & Infant Schools
Brondesbury College for Boys
Christ Ch.
BRONDESBURY PARK
Comm. Cen.
Manor School
Youth Cen.
Doyle Nursery Sch.
Library
Princess Frederica C of E Prim. Sch.
KENSAL RISE
Kensal Rise Primary School
Warehouse
Bridge Ho.
Keslake Mans.
Bandstand
Tennis Courts
Playground
St. Martin's Ch.
KENSAL GREEN
Factory
Depot
Moberly Spts. & Educ. Cen.
Queens Park Court
Bales Coll.
St. John's Ch.
West London Crematorium
Catacombs
Basin
Kensal Wharf
Quayside Ho.
Lib.
B413
B450
B451
A404
Avenue
Willesden Lane
Chamberlayne Road
Harrow Road
Kilburn Lane
Ladbroke Grove
College Road
Harvist Road
Mortimer Road
Brondesbury Park
Christchurch Avenue
Okehampton Road
Wrentham Avenue
Chevening Road
Keslake Road
Kempe Road
Whitmore Gardens
Leigh Gardens
Clifford Gardens
Purves Road
Ashburnham Road
Burrows Road
Hazel Road
Wakeman Road
Rainham Road
Pember Road
Buller Rd.
Milman Road
Peploe Road
Creighton Road

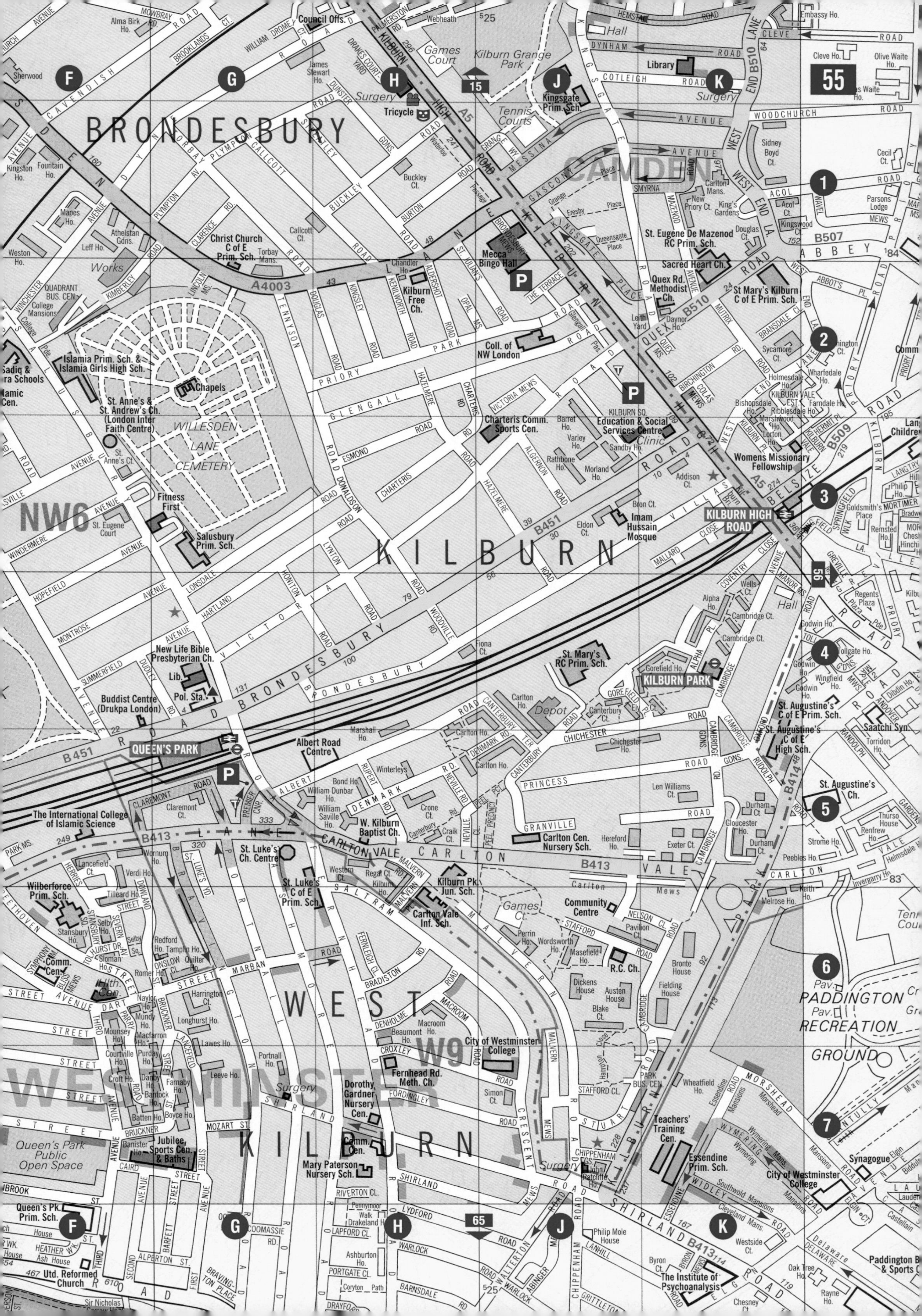
55
BRONDESBURY
CAMDEN
KILBURN
NW6
W9
WEST KILBURN
WESTMINSTER
F
G
H
J
K
1
2
3
4
5
6
7
15
56
65
A5
A4003
B451
B413
B414
B507
B509
B510
End B510
Council Offs.
Alma Birk Ho.
Mowbray Rd.
Brooklands Ct.
William Dromey Ct.
Palmerston Rd.
Webheath
Games Court
Kilburn Grange Park
Hemstal Rd.
Hall
Dynham Road
Library
Cotleigh Road
Surgery
Embassy Ho.
Cleve Road
Cleve Ho.
Olive Waite Ho.
Woodchurch Road
Sherwood
Cavendish
James Stewart Ho.
Drakes Courtyard
Dunster Gdns.
Tricycle
Kingsgate Prim. Sch.
Tennis Courts
Kingsgate Avenue
Messina Avenue
Sidney Boyd Ct.
Cecil Ct.
Kilburn High Road
Plympton Av.
Plympton Rd.
Callcott Rd.
Buckley Rd.
Buckley Ct.
Burton Rd.
Waterloo Passage
Grange Wy.
Gascony Place
Smyrna Rd.
Mazenod Avenue
Carlton Mans.
New Priory Ct.
King's Gardens
Acol Road
Acol Ct.
Kingswood
Wavel Mews
Parsons Lodge
Kingston Ho.
Fountain Ho.
Mapes Ho.
Athelstan Gdns.
Leff Ho.
Weston Ho.
Works
Christ Church C of E Prim. Sch.
Torbay Mans.
Callcott Ct.
Chandler Ho.
Aldershot Rd.
Kilburn Free Ch.
St Julian's Rd.
Brondesbury Mews
Mecca Bingo Hall
Grange
Eresby Place
Queensgate Place
Kingsgate Place
St. Eugene De Mazenod RC Prim. Sch.
Douglas Ct.
Sacred Heart Ch.
Abbey Road
Abbot's Pl.
Quadrant Bus. Cen.
College Mansions
Winchester Avenue
Kimberley Rd.
Lincoln Ms.
Tennyson Rd.
Douglas Rd.
Kingsley Rd.
Kenilworth Rd.
Opal Ms.
The Terrace
Quex Rd. Methodist Ch.
Daynor Ho.
Quex Road
Quex Ms.
Mutrix Rd.
St Mary's Kilburn C of E Prim. Sch.
Bransdale Cl.
Sycamore Ct.
Leith Yard
Glengall Pas.
Coll. of NW London
Priory Park Road
Islamia Prim. Sch. & Islamia Girls High Sch.
Sadiq & ...ra Schools
Chapels
St. Anne's & St. Andrew's Ch. (London Inter Faith Centre)
Willesden Lane Cemetery
St. Anne's Ct.
Glengall Road
Victoria Mews
Charteris Rd.
Hazelmere Rd.
Kilburn Sq.
Charteris Comm. Sports Cen.
Education & Social Services Centre
Clinic
Barret Ho.
Varley Ho.
Rathbone Ho.
Sandby Ho.
Morland Ho.
Addison Ct.
Birchington Rd.
Colas Mews
Holmesdale Ho.
Wharfedale Ho.
Kilburn Vale Est.
Bishopsdale Ho.
Ribblesdale Ho.
Farndale Ho.
Marshwood Ho.
Lorton Ho.
Hermit Pl.
Womens Missionary Fellowship
Belsize Road
Kilburn Priory
Esmond Road
Donaldson Road
Algernon Road
Fitness First
Salusbury Prim. Sch.
Salusbury Road
St. Eugene Court
Windermere Avenue
Bron Ct.
Imam Hussain Mosque
Eldon Ct.
Kilburn Villas
Kilburn High Road
Mallard Close
Goldsmith's Place
Mortimer
Remsted Ho.
Philip Ho.
Springfield Wlk.
Greville Road
Hopefield Avenue
Lonsdale Road
Hartland
Honiton Road
Lynton Road
Victoria Road
Montrose Avenue
Coventry Close
Wells Ct.
Manor Ms.
Alpha Ho.
Cambridge Ct.
Alpha Pl.
Regents Plaza
Godwin Ho.
Tollgate Ho.
Tollgate Gdns.
Wingfield Ho.
Wingfield Mews
Dibdin Ho.
Andover Road
Summerfield Avenue
New Life Bible Presbyterian Ch.
Dudley Rd.
Lib.
Pol. Sta.
Buddist Centre (Drukpa London)
Brondesbury Road
Brondesbury Villas
Woodville Rd.
Fiona Ct.
St. Mary's RC Prim. Sch.
Gorefield Ho.
Gorefield Pl.
Kilburn Park
Carlton Ho.
Depot
Canterbury Ho.
Ely Ct.
Cambridge Road
St. Augustine's C of E Prim. Sch.
St. Augustine's C of E High Sch.
Saatchi Syn.
Torridon Ho.
Randolph Gdns.
Queen's Park
Albert Road Centre
Marshall Ho.
Canterbury Road
Canterbury Ter.
Denmark Rd.
Chichester Road
Chichester Ho.
Cambridge Gdns.
Oxford Road
Rudolph Road
Claremont Road
Claremont Ct.
Premier Cnr.
The International College of Islamic Science
Park Ms.
Winterleys
Bond Ho.
William Dunbar Ho.
William Saville Ho.
Denmark Rd.
Rupert Rd.
Crone Ct.
Neville Rd.
Peel Precinct
Princess Road
Len Williams Ct.
Durham Ct.
St. Augustine's Ch.
Thurso House
Renfrew Ho.
Strome Ho.
Peebles Ho.
Helmsdale Ho.
Invergarry Ho.
W. Kilburn Baptist Ch.
Craik Ct.
Granville Road
Carlton Cen. Nursery Sch.
Hereford Ho.
Exeter Ct.
Gloucester Ho.
Keith Ho.
Melrose Ho.
Lancefield Ct.
Verdi Ho.
Wornum Ho.
St. Luke's Yd.
St. Luke's Ch. Centre
Carlton Vale
Western Ct.
Regal Ct.
Malvern Rd.
Kilburn Pk Jun. Sch.
Carlton Mews
Wilberforce Prim. Sch.
Tilleard Ho.
Herries Street
Beethoven Street
Stansbury Ho.
Selby Ho.
Severn Avenue
Dowland Street
St. Luke's C of E Prim. Sch.
Saltram Cres.
Carlton Vale Inf. Sch.
Games Ct.
Community Centre
Nelson Cl.
Pavilion Ct.
Stafford Road
Perrin Ho.
Wordsworth Ho.
Masefield Ho.
R.C. Ch.
Bronte House
Fielding House
Dickens House
Austen House
Blake Ct.
Symphony Mews
Comm. Cen.
Bliss Mews
Hlth. Cen.
Redford Ho.
Tamplin Ho.
Onslow Cl.
Quilter Ct.
Romer Ho.
Marban Road
Fernleigh Cl.
Bradiston Rd.
Harrington Ct.
Longhurst Ho.
Lawes Ho.
Macroom Road
Denholme Rd.
Macroom Ho.
Beaumont Ho.
City of Westminster College
Croxley Rd.
Fernhead Rd. Meth. Ch.
Portnall Ho.
Leeve Ho.
Naylor Ho.
Mundy Ho.
Mounsey Ho.
Macfarron Ho.
Courtville Ho.
Purday Ho.
Croft Ho.
Danby Ho.
Farnaby Ho.
Bantock Ho.
Boyce Ho.
Batten Ho.
Lancefield Street
Fordingley Road
Simon Ct.
Dorothy Gardner Nursery Cen.
Shirland Road
Surgery
Stafford Cl.
Hamilton Close
Park Bus. Cen.
Wheatfield Ho.
Morshead Road
Wymering Mans.
Mozart St.
Bruckner Street
Banister Ho.
Jubilee Sports Cen. & Baths
Comm. Cen.
Mary Paterson Nursery Sch.
Chippenham Road
John Ratcliffe Ho.
Teachers' Training Cen.
Essendine Prim. Sch.
Southwold Mansions
Widley Road
Synagogue
City of Westminster College
Queen's Park Public Open Space
Caird Street
Third Avenue
Fifth Avenue
Fourth Avenue
Fernhead Road
Ashmore Road
Walterton Road
Elgin Avenue
Lauderdale
Castellain
Paddington Recreation Ground
Pav.
Bristol Gdns.
Queen's Pk. Prim. Sch.
Heather Wk.
Ash House
Utd. Reformed Church
Second Avenue
Barfett Street
Alperton St.
Bravington Place
Coomassie Rd.
Riverton Cl.
Pennymoor Walk
Drakeland Ho.
Lapford Cl.
Ashburton Ho.
Portgate Cl.
Coryton Path
Barnsdale Rd.
Warlock Road
Abinger
Lydford Road
Lanhill
Philip Mole House
Grittleton
Cleveland Mans.
Westside Ct.
Byron Ct.
The Institute of Psychoanalysis
Oak Tree Ho.
Rayne Ho.
Delaware Road
Paddington Bowls & Sports Cl.
Chesney
Drayford
Sir Nicholas Garrow Ho.

56
SOUTH HAMPSTEAD
NW6
W9
MAIDA VALE
PADDINGTON RECREATION GROUND
Cricket Ground
Tennis Courts
Sports Ground
15
55
66
A
B
C
D
E
1
2
3
4
5
6
7
526
CLEVE ROAD
CANFIELD GARDENS
GREENCROFT GARDENS
FAIRHAZEL GDNS.
WOODCHURCH ROAD
ABERDARE GARDENS
GOLDHURST TERRACE
ACOL ROAD
PRIORY ROAD
ABBEY ROAD
BELSIZE ROAD
HILGROVE ROAD
BOUNDARY ROAD
LOUDOUN ROAD
MARLBOROUGH HILL
FINCHLEY ROAD
SPRINGFIELD ROAD
CARLTON HILL
CLIFTON HILL
BLENHEIM ROAD
GREVILLE ROAD
KILBURN HIGH ROAD
KILBURN PARK ROAD
MAIDA VALE
RANDOLPH AVENUE
ELGIN AVENUE
LAUDERDALE ROAD
SUTHERLAND AVENUE
HAMILTON TERRACE
GROVE END ROAD
CARLTON VALE
ABERCORN PLACE
WEST END LANE
SOUTH HAMPSTEAD
KILBURN HIGH ROAD
MAIDA VALE
SWISS COTTAGE
ST. JOHN'S WOOD
St. Mary's Church
St Mary's Kilburn C of E Prim. Sch.
Health Cen.
Comm. Cen.
Langtry Children's Cen.
Womens Missionary Fellowship
Jack Taylor School
Grace Chapel
George Eliot Jun. & Inf. Schools
Quintin Kynaston Sch.
The American School in London
Arnold House Sch.
St. John's Wood Syn.
Hospital of St. John & St. Elizabeth
St. John's Hospice
Convent of Mercy
Abbey Rd. Baptist Ch.
Recording Studio
New London Synagogue
Clinic
Islamic Centre England
St. Augustine's C of E Prim. Sch.
St. Augustine's C of E High Sch.
St. Augustine's Ch.
Saatchi Syn.
St. George's Catholic Sch.
North Paddington Boys' Club
St. Mark's Ch.
Violet Hill Gdns.
Lauderdale Rd. Syn.
St. Joseph's R.C. Prim. Sch.
Synagogue
City of Westminster College
Essendine Prim. Sch.
Paddington Bowling & Sports Club
Institute of Psychoanalysis
M.C.C. Cricket Museum & Tours
Odeon Swiss Cott.
Surgery
A5
A41
B507
B509
B510
B413
B414

57
F
G
H
J
K
1
2
3
4
5
6
7
83
NW3
NW8
NW1
CAMDEN
PRIMROSE HILL
REGENT'S PARK
ADELAIDE ROAD
B509
15
67
Surgery
Blashford
Burnham
Dorney
Bray
Hornby
Fellows Road
Winchester Road
Kings College Rd.
Quickswood
Elliott Sq.
Lower Merton Rise
Elsworthy Rise
Conybeare
Hawtrey Road
King Henry's Road
Sports Cen.
Visage
Frank Barnes Sch.
Swiss Cottage School
St. John's Lodge
St. Mary's Ch.
St. Paul's C of E Prim. Sch.
Elsworthy Ct.
Elsworthy Road
Wadham Gardens
Harley Road
Avenue Lodge
The Polygon
Park Lodge
Sheringham
Walsingham
Primrose Hill Court
Whitton
Oppidans Road
Meadowbank
Ainger Road
Erskine Rd.
Chalcot Square
Chalcot Cr.
Sharpleshall St.
Primrose Mews
St. George's Ter.
Rothwell St.
Regent's Park Road
Gloucester Avenue
Fitzroy Yd.
Primrose Hill Studios
Manley
Oldstown Street
Albert Ter.
Church
Lib.
Factory
Depot
Works
Hill View
Carole Ho.
Jacqueline Ho.
Marion Ho.
Reservoir
Barrow Hill
St. Stephen's Close
Rudgwick Ter.
Kingsland
Broxwood Way
Avenue Cl.
Guinness Ct.
St. Edmund's Ter.
Danes Ct.
Ormonde Ct.
Kings Ct.
Parkwood
Consort Lodge
Prince Albert Ct.
St. James's Ter.
St. Christina's Sch.
Prince Regent Ct.
Stockleigh Hall
Prince Albert Road
Snowdon Aviary
Primrose Hill Bri.
Regent's Canal
Main Entrance
London Zoo
Running Track
Macclesfield Bri
Tennis Courts
Regents Park Golf & Tennis School
Cricket Ground
The Hub
Outer Circle
CLOSED Midnight - 7am
Avenue Road
Norfolk Road
Townshend Road
B525
Henstridge Place
Robinsfield Inf. Sch.
Acacia Pl.
Tatham Pl.
Ordnance Hill
St. Ann's Terrace
Kingsmill
Surgery
Clinic
Charlbert St.
Allitsen Road
Swallow Ho.
Starling Ho.
Barrow Hill Est.
Mallard Ho.
Robin Ho.
Barrow Hill Jun. Sch.
Newcourt
Pol. Sta.
Culworth St.
Oslo Ct.
Bentinck Ct.
Viceroy Ct.
Tower Ct.
Eamont Ct.
Townshend Est.
Turner Ho.
Cruikshank Ho.
Opie Ho.
Cameron Ho.
Ramsay Ho.
Calderon Ho.
Cotman Ho.
London Ho.
Imperial Ct.
Elgood Ho.
Lib.
Fettes Ho.
Reynolds Ho.
Cicely Ho.
George Eyre Ho.
Densham Ho.
Lebus Ho.
Cochrane Mews
Wellington Circus
The Wellington Hosp.
The Wellington Hospital
Cavendish Ho.
Hanover Ho.
North Gate
St. John's Wood Church Gardens
St. John the Baptist's Ch.
Prince Albert Road
A5205
Wellington Road
A41
Cavendish Cl.
Media Cen.
Middlesex County Cricket Club & Marylebone C.C.
Lord's Cricket Ground
Lords View
Pavilion
The Liberal Jewish Synagogue
Church of Our Lady
Blazer Ct.
Lisson Green
Strathmore Ct.
Regent Court
Durham Ho.
Crown Ct.
London Central Mosque
Hanover Gate
Abbey Lodge
Hanover Terrace
Macmillan Ho.
Park Lorne
Monroe Ho.
Regent's Park Ho.
Winfield House
Playground
Children's Boating Pond
Boating Lake
The Holme
Regent's Park Open Air
Queen Mary's Gardens
Bandstand
Jubilee Gate
Regent's College
London Business Sch.
College
Lisson Green Estate
Tickford Ho.
Simpson Ho.
Olney Ho.
Padbury Ho.
Missenden Ho.
Linslade Ho.
Lavendon Ho.
Chetwode Ho.
Dinton Ho.
Horwood Ho.
Cottesloe Ho.
Verney Ho.
Chequers Ho.
Turville Ho.
Kenneth Campbell Ho.
Bazelgette Ho.
Castleford Ct.
Ashby Ct.
Gateway Prim. Sch.
Marylebone Road
Rossmore Ct.
Elizabeth Ct.
Annes Ct.
Alberts Ct.
Park Road
Lisson Grove
Grove End Road
P
Marys

58
CHALK FARM
The Roundhouse
The Stables Market
Superstore
Camden Lock Market
Canal Market
REGENT'S CANAL
CAMDEN ROAD
CAMDEN TOWN
BRITANNIA JUNCTION
The Cavendish School
Jewish Museum
Cecil Sharp House
Primrose Hill Prim. Sch.
St. Mark's Ch.
St. Mark's Bri.
Cumberland Basin
Car & Coach Park
CLOSED Midnight - 7am
CLOSED 10am - 7pm
Snowdon Aviary
Main Entrance
Refreshment Rooms
London Zoo
CAMDEN
NW1
St. Martin's Gardens
Harrington Sq. Gardens
Carriage Shed
Regent's Park Barracks
Cricket Ground
The Hub
REGENT'S
WESTMINSTER
PARK
Refreshments
Cumberland Gate
REGENT'S PARK
St. John's Lodge
Frazer Lodge
Parks Department
Regent's Park Open Air
Chester Road Gates
QUEEN MARY'S GARDENS
Chester Wlk Gate
Avenue Gdns.
English Gdns.
Lake
Bandstand
The Holme
Jubilee Gates
Regent's College
Tennis Courts
Playground
Royal College of Physicians
St. Mary Magdalene's Ch.
St. Anne's Ch.
Univ. of Westminster
Westminster Kingsway Coll.
Netley Prim. Sch.
Comm. Cen.
Library
68
57

CAMDEN TOWN
ISLINGTON
N1
KING'S CROSS
SOMERS TOWN
ST. PANCRAS
ST. PANCRAS INTERNATIONAL
KING'S CROSS
KING'S CROSS ST. PANCRAS
EUSTON
EUSTON SQUARE
British Library
The Raceway (Go-Kart Track)
Goods Shed
St. Pancras Basin
Oblique Bridge
Sorting Office
St. Pancras Hospital
Royal Veterinary College
Beaumont Animals Hosp.
Jubilee Waterside Youth Cen.
Canal Side Studios
Cedar Way Ind. Est.
Depots
Warehouse
Warehouses
Works
Factory
Community Centre
Agar Grove Estate
North Western Comm. Cen.
Acorn Production Centre
Bemerton Estate
Bingfield Park
Paget Christian Cen.
Cally Swimming Pool
Caithness Ho.
Dunoon Ho.
Lib.
Copenhagen Street B154
Blessed Sacrament RC Prim. Sch.
Battlebridge Youth Cen.
Copenhagen Prim. Sch.
Regents Canal
London Canal Mus.
London Wildlife Trust
Camley St. Natural Pk.
Gasholder
St. Pancras Gardens
Coroners' Ct.
St. Pancras Old Church
South Camden Comm. Sch.
Edith Neville Prim. Sch.
Somers Town Community Sports Cen.
Adventure Playground
Richard Cobden Prim. Sch.
Working Men's Coll.
Theatre Technis
Training Cen.
Health Cen.
Oakley Sq. Gardens
St. Aloysius Jun. Sch.
St. Aloysius RC Inf. Sch.
St. Aloysius Ch.
Convent Maria Fidelis Convent Sch.
Parcels Depot
St. James Gardens
Maria Fidelis Convent Sch.
Euston Sq. Gardens
Fire Sta.
London Contemporary Dance Sch.
St. Pancras Ch.
The Place
Bentham Hall
Hughes Hall
Canterbury Hall
Commonwealth Hall
St. Mary's German Ch.
Holy Cross Ch.
Town Hall Lib.
Argyle Prim. Sch.
Argyle Sq. Gdns.
King's Cross Mission Ch.
City & Guilds of London Inst.
Royal National Throat, Nose & Ear Hosp.
Nuffield Cen.
Winton Prim. Sch.
Westminster Kingsway College (Gray's Inn Centre)
Regent Sq. Presbyterian Ch.
Utd. Ref. Ch.
Goodenough College
Thomas Coram Early Childhood Cen.
The Foundling Mus.
Mecklenburgh Sq. Gdns.
The Wolfson Assessment Cen.
St. George's Gdns.
Sch. of Pharmacy
British Medical Association
U.C.L. (Campbell Ho.)
U.C.L. (Chemistry Bldg.)
Wellcome Collection
Government Offs.
Friends Ho.
Mary Ward Hall
Gov. Offs.
Tavistock Sq.
Bloomsbury
CLOSED FRIDAY 11am - 2.30pm
BUSES ONLY
A5202
A5200
A4200
A400
A501
B512
B504
EUSTON ROAD
PENTONVILLE ROAD
GRAY'S INN ROAD
CALEDONIAN ROAD
YORK WAY
PANCRAS ROAD
MIDLAND ROAD
GOODS WAY
WHARF ROAD
CAMLEY STREET
ST. PANCRAS WAY
AGAR GROVE
EVERSHOLT STREET
ACTON STREET
SWINTON STREET
WHARFDALE ROAD
CROMER STREET
JUDD STREET
HUNTER STREET
TAVISTOCK PLACE
15
16
60
69

CALEDONIAN RD. & BARNSBURY
N7
BARNSBURY
A
B
C
D
E
16
Works
Surgery
Warehouse
Offord Rd.
Huntingdon St.
Carnoustie Dr.
Lyon St.
Kember St.
Bemerton Estate
Airdrie Cl.
Port Cl.
Perth Ho.
Tilloch St.
Freeling St.
Ranraer Wy.
Earlsferry Way
Story St.
Pembroke St.
Gifford St.
St. Andrew's Ch.
Thornhill Crescent
Bridgeman Road
Liby. Buddhist Cen.
Rec. Grnd.
Thornhill Square
Lofting Road
Ripplevale Grove
Barnsbury Sq.
Barnsbury Mount
Mountfort Cr.
Fort Ter.
Barnes Ct.
Brayfield Ter.
Thornhill Prim. Sch.
Bewdley Street
Brooksby Street
Brooksby Ho.
Lofting Ho.
Cara Ho.
Pugin Ct.
Morland Mews
Gissing Walk
Liverpool Road
B515
College Cross
Islington Ms.
New College Mews
Haven Mews
Milner Square
Lonsdale Square
Lonsdale Pl.
Waterloo Gdns.
Waterloo Ter.
Almeida St.
Almeida
Post Office Depot
King's Head
Upper Street
Town Hall Mus.
Richmond Cres.
Tyndale Ter.
Evelyn Denington Ct.
Cadmore Ho.
Adstock Ho.
Datchworth Ho.
Flitton Ho.
Garston Ho.
Premier Ho.
Terretts Place
Florence Ct.
Fire Stn.
Paget Christian Cen.
Bingfield Park
Bingfield Street
Havelock St.
Cally Swimming Pool
Stanmore St.
Twyford St.
Caithness Ho.
Orkney Ho.
Dunoon Ho.
Clayton Cr.
Copenhagen Street
B154
Lib.
Bramwell Ms.
Richmond Avenue
Malvern Ter.
Thornhill Gdns.
St. Andrew's C of E Prim. School
Barnard Park
Play-ground
Matilda Street
Hemingford Road
Everilda St.
Pulteney Ter.
Prices Yd.
Bryan St.
Dowrey St.
Samuel Rhodes School
Cloudesley Square
Cloudesley Road
The Celestial Church of Christ
Stonefield Street
Gibson Square
Theberton Street
Moon St.
Studd St.
Screen on the Green
Islington
Water Pl.
Old Royal Free Sq.
Southwood Smith St.
St. Albans Pl.
Islington Grn. Gdns.
Islington Grn.
Copenhagen Ho.
Blackmore Ho.
Mavor Ho.
Jocelin Ho.
Messiter Ho.
Molton Ho.
Barnsbury Est.
Kenwick Ho.
Thorpe Ho.
Venn Ho.
Adrian Ho.
Redmond Ho.
Roding Ho.
Samford Ho.
Fisher Ho.
Payne Ho.
Vittoria Ho.
Corbet Ho.
Berners Ho.
Vittoria Prim. Sch.
Young Actors Theatre Sch.
Elsinore Ho.
Denmark Gro.
Olive Ct.
Barford Street
Business Design Centre
Batchelor St.
Wollaton Ho.
Newstead Ho.
Ritchie St.
Surgery
Bromfield St.
Parkfield St.
N1 Shop. Centre
Vue Cin.
Camden Pas.
Charlton Pl.
St. Johns Ch.
St. John Prim. Sch.
Clerkenwell County Ct.
Duncan Street
Duncan Ter.
Convent
Camden Walk
Copenhagen
Blessed Sacrament RC Prim. Sch.
Ch. of the Blessed Sacrament
Battlebridge Youth Cen.
Copenhagen Prim. Sch.
Surg.
Ewen Ho.
Ritson Ho.
Thornhill Bridge Wharf
Carnegie St.
Thornhill Bridge
Regents Canal
Islington Tunnel
Ice Wharf Marina
Regents Wharf
All Saints St.
Killick St.
London Canal Mus.
Health Cen.
Gattis Wharf
Battle Bridge Rd.
Wharfdale Road
Wynford Road
Maygood St.
Dewey Rd.
Tolpuddle St.
Police Sta.
Calshot Ho.
Wynford Ho.
Grimaldi Ho.
Foliot Ho.
Tornay Ho.
Paveley Ho.
Grendon Ho.
Priory Green Estate
Redington Ho.
Kendal Ho.
Hugh Cubitt Ho.
Chalbury Walk
Hayward Ho.
St. Silas's Ch.
Elizabeth Garrett Anderson Language Coll.
Rising Hill St.
Chapel Market
White Conduit St.
Baron St.
Penton St.
White Lion Street
White Lion Youth Cen.
Utd. Reformed Ch.
Crafts Council
Angel Mews
Angel
Islington High St.
Southern St.
Winton Prim. Sch.
Bonnington Ho.
Donegal Street
Mos.
Collier St.
Joseph Grimaldi Park
Rodney Ho.
Prospect Ho.
Penton Ho.
Henley Prior
Manneby Prior
Hales Prior
Stuart Mill Ho.
Pollard Ho.
Radius Apartments
Cynthia St.
Hermes St.
Pentonville
Pentonville Road
A501
Buses Only
Reservoir
Claremont Sq.
The Angel Centre
Old Red Lion
Fitness First
Elia St.
Wildford Ho.
City Road
Dame Alice Owen Building
College
RNIB
Alice Owen Tech. Cen.
Copperworks
Albion Yd.
Albion Buildings
Railway St.
Balfe St.
Wharfdale Yard
Caledonia St.
Joiners Yard
Varnishers Yard
Courtyard
Omega Pl.
Keystone Cres.
Kings Cross
Myddelton House
Holford Yard
Foxcroft
Hurst Ho.
Sharwood
Frearson Ho.
Stelfox Ho.
Cobden Bldgs.
Holford Gdns.
Kingsway Coll. (Vernon Sq. Cen.)
Bevin Ct.
Sanders Ho.
Cruikshank St.
Myddelton St.
St. Mark's Ch.
Gdns.
Chadwell St.
Baptist Chap.
Arlington Ho.
Sadler's Wells
Inglebert St.
Worthington Ho.
Benyon Ho.
Myddelton Pas.
River St.
The Nautilus Bldg.
New River Head
Sadler Ho.
Spa Grn. Estate
Wells Ho.
Tunbridge Ho.
Rawstorne St.
Southwood Ct.
Lloyd's Row
King's Cross Mission Ch.
City & Guilds Inst.
Field St.
Leeke St.
Derby Lodge
Pioneer Ho.
Britannia St.
Wicklow St.
Inst. Royal National Throat, Nose & Ear Hosp.
Nuffield Cen.
Riverside
Riverfleet
Argyle Sq. Gdns.
Depot
Fleetway
Fleetfield
Swinton St.
Baptist Ch.
Holford Ho.
Percy Circus
Great Percy St.
Cable Ho.
Lloyd Sq.
Prideaux Ho.
Clerkenwell Magistrates Court
Great Percy St.
WC1
Whatton Cotts.
Clerkenwell Parochial C of E Prim. Sch.
Surgery
The Remus Bldg.
The Hydra Bldg.
Merlin Ct.
Charles Rowan Ho.
St. Pauls View App.
RC Ch.
Finsbury TH
Family Records Centre
Hugh Myddelton Prim. Sch.
Connaught Bldg.
Gloucester Bldg.
City University
Joseph Trotter Cl.
Michael Cliffe Ho.
Finsbury Estate
Patrick Coman Ho.
Lib.
Kings Bldg.
Spencer St.
Brunswick Cl. Est.
Emberton Ct.
Argyle Square
Acton St.
Gatesden
Bedefield
Sandfield
Cromer St.
Peperfield
Mulletsfield
Hollisfield
Chadswell
Northiam
Harrison St.
Rodmell
Regent Sq.
Linfield
Warnham
St. Peter's Ho.
Sidmouth St.
Seaford St.
Camden
Frederick St.
Ampton St.
Wells Square
Comm. Cen.
Sage Wy.
Gray's Inn Road
A5200
Westminster Kingsway College (Gray's Inn Centre)
Regent Sq. Presbyterian Ch.
Ref. Ch.
St. George's Gdns.
Heathcote St.
Goodenough College
Mecklenburgh Pl.
Byron Ct.
The Eastman Dental Hosp. & Institute
St. Andrews Gdns.
Trinity Ct.
Granville Square
Wharton St.
Gwynne Pl.
Riceyman Ho.
Bagnigge Ho.
Greenaway Ho.
Gwynne Ho.
Earlsm Ho.
Spring Ho.
St. Helena Ho.
St. Ann's Ho.
Charles Simmons Ho.
Sherston Ct.
Margery St.
Attneave St.
Yardley St.
Wilmington Sq.
Tysoe St.
Rosoman St.
Farringdon Road
B502
Skinner St.
Mount Pleasant Sorting Office
Ch. of Our Most Holy Redeemer
Exmouth Ho.
Hlth. Cen.
Spa Flds. Open Space
London Metropolitan Archives
Northampton Rd.
Corporation Row
Kingsway Place
The Bridge Sch.
Art Studies
Walmsley Bldg.
Paramount Bldg.
Stirling Ct.
Percival St.
Thomas Coram Early Childhood Cen.
Mecklenburgh Sq. Gdns.
Handel Mans.
Pharmacy
The Foundling Mus.
The Wolfson Assessment Cen.
Jubilee Ho.
Calthorpe St.
Phoenix Pl.
Langton Cl.
Pakenham St.
Model Buildings
Wren St.
70
59

61
32
33
CANONBURY ROAD
ESSEX ROAD
NEW NORTH ROAD
NORTHCHURCH ROAD
DOWNHAM ROAD
SOUTHGATE GROVE
BALMES ROAD
PENN STREET
HYDE ROAD
MINTERN STREET
EAGLE WHARF ROAD
REGENT'S CANAL
SHEPHERDESS WALK
WENLOCK STREET
CITY ROAD
OLD STREET
GREAT EASTERN STREET
PITFIELD STREET
PROVOST ST.
EAST ROAD
BATH STREET
GOSWELL ROAD
ASTEY'S ROW
ESSEX RD.
St. Stephen's Ch.
Community Centre
Mecca Bingo
St. Mary's Prim. Sch.
Church
Liby.
PEABODY ESTATE
Charles Lamb Prim. Sch.
Council Offs.
Ecclesbourne Prim. School
Rotherfield Primary School
CANONBURY BUS. CEN.
City & Islington Coll. Shepperton Arts Centre
Rosemary
Playground
Tennis Cts.
Rosemary Gdns.
Rosemary Branch Bri.
DE BEAUV
The Bridge Sch.
St. James's Ch.
Islington Green Sec. Sch.
Surgery
Polish Catholic Ch.
N1
Whitmore Prim. Sch.
Britannia Leisure Centre
Shoreditch Park
Tennis Courts
Play Park
Surgeries
Packington St. Bri.
Hanover Prim. Sch.
City Road Lock
City Road Basin
Wenlock Basin
Comm. Cen.
Thomas Fairchild Prim. Sch.
HACKNEY
HOXTON
Holy Trinity Ch.
Mail Sorting Office
Crusoe House School
Police Sta.
City Coll.
True Jesus Ch.
Youth Cen.
St. John the Baptist C of E Prim. Sch.
St. John the Baptist Ch.
St. Monica's RC Church
Moreland Prim. Sch.
St. Clement with St. Barnabas & St. Matthew Ch.
EC1
CITY FORUM
King's Square Gardens
Moorfields Eye Hosp.
Inst. of Ophthalmology
ST. LUKE'S
Ironmonger Row Baths
St. Lukes Prim. Sch.
Finsbury Leisure Cen.
Finsbury & Heyworth Halls
LSO St. Lukes
OLD STREET
Fire Sta.
Central Foundation Boys Sch.
Shoreditch County Ct.
Gallery
Saddlers Sport Cen.
St. Peter's & St. Paul's RC Sch.
Dallington Sch.
Fitness First
A1200
A104
B144
A501
B502
A5201

62
DALSTON
DE BEAUVOIR TOWN
N1
HACKNEY
E8
HOXTON
HAGGERSTON
EC2
BET
Queensbridge Sports & Comm. Centre
Surgery
St. Peter De Beauvoir Town Church
Metropolitan Bus. Cen.
Fire Sta.
Oscar Faber Place
Queensbridge Infants Sch.
All Saints Church
Northern Extension (Und. Const.)
Kingsland Basin
Quebec Wharf
Kings Wharf
Regent's Canal
Rosemary Branch Bri.
The Comet Nursery Sch.
New Era Estate
Whitmore Prim. Sch.
Britannia Leisure Centre
Mosque
Shoreditch Park
Tennis Courts
Play Park
St. Annes Ch.
St. Columba Church
Trust HQ & Hlth. Cen.
Burbage Schools
Randal Cremer Prim. Sch.
St. Mary's Community Garden
Haggerston Park
Football Pitch
Haggerston Sch.
Church
Sebright Prim. Sch.
Geffrye Mus.
Geffrye's Gdns.
Hoxton Hall
True Jesus Ch.
Youth Cen.
Mecca Bingo
St. John the Baptist C of E Prim. Sch.
St. John the Baptist Ch.
The Comm. Coll. Hackney (Shoreditch Campus)
Lib.
Cremer Bus. Cen.
Ravenscroft Park
Columbia Prim. Sch.
Jesus Green
Ion Square Gdns.
St. Monica's RC Prim. Sch.
St. Monica's RC Church
Playground
Columbia Mkt. Nursy. Sch.
Magistrates Court
Shoreditch Town Hall
St. Leonard's Ch.
Baptist Ch.
Mildmay Mission Hosp. (Hospice)
Sports Cen.
Bethnal Green Technology College
Tower Hamlets Coll. (Bethnal Green Centre)
Boundary Gds.
Arnold Circus
London Coll. of Fashion
Central Foundation Boys Sch.
Gallery
St. Matthias CE Prim. Sch.
St. Matthew's Church
Kingsland Road
Queensbridge Road
Hackney Road
Columbia Road
Old Street
Great Eastern Street
Shoreditch High Street
Bethnal Green Road
A10
A1208
A5201
A1202
A1209
B101
B108
B118
B122

63
HACKNEY
London Fields Lido
Gayhurst Prim. Sch.
LONDON FIELDS
London Fields Prim. Sch.
Closed SATURDAY 07.30 - 17.30
Mare Street
The London Coll. of Fashion
Superstore
Warehouses
Cassland Road
Well Street
Well St. Comn.
Orchard Prim. Sch.
Church
Lauriston Sch.
The Comm. College Hackney
The Triangle
Revenues & Benefits Service
St. Josephs Hospice
R.C. Ch.
E9
Victoria Park Road
A106
St. Agnes Gate
Gore Gate
VICTORIA PARK
Bonner Hall Bri.
Sewardstone Road
Bus Garage
Gas Holders
Factories
Works
Warehouse
Mowlem Prim. Sch.
Bethnal Green Methodist Ch.
London Chest Hospital
Gatehouse Sch.
St. James the Less Ch.
Raines Foundation School
Cambridge Heath
A107
A1208
Hackney Road
TOWER HAMLETS
E2
Town Hall
York Hall Leisure Cen.
St. John's C of E Prim. Sch.
Museum of Childhood
Bethnal Green Gdns.
Police Sta.
Fire Sta.
Globe Prim. Sch.
London Buddhist Cen.
Bonner Prim. Sch.
Globe Town Market
Morpeth School
Oakslands Secondary Sch.
Elizabeth Selby Inf. Sch.
Lawdale Jun. Sch.
Raine's Foundation School
Beatrice Tate Sch.
St. Peter with St. Thomas Ch.
B118
B135
A1209
Roman Road
Bethnal Green
Bethnal Green Gardens
Bangabandhu Prim. Sch.
Weavers Fields
Hague Prim. Sch.
St. Peter's Ch.
Harpley Sch.
E1
NAL GREEN

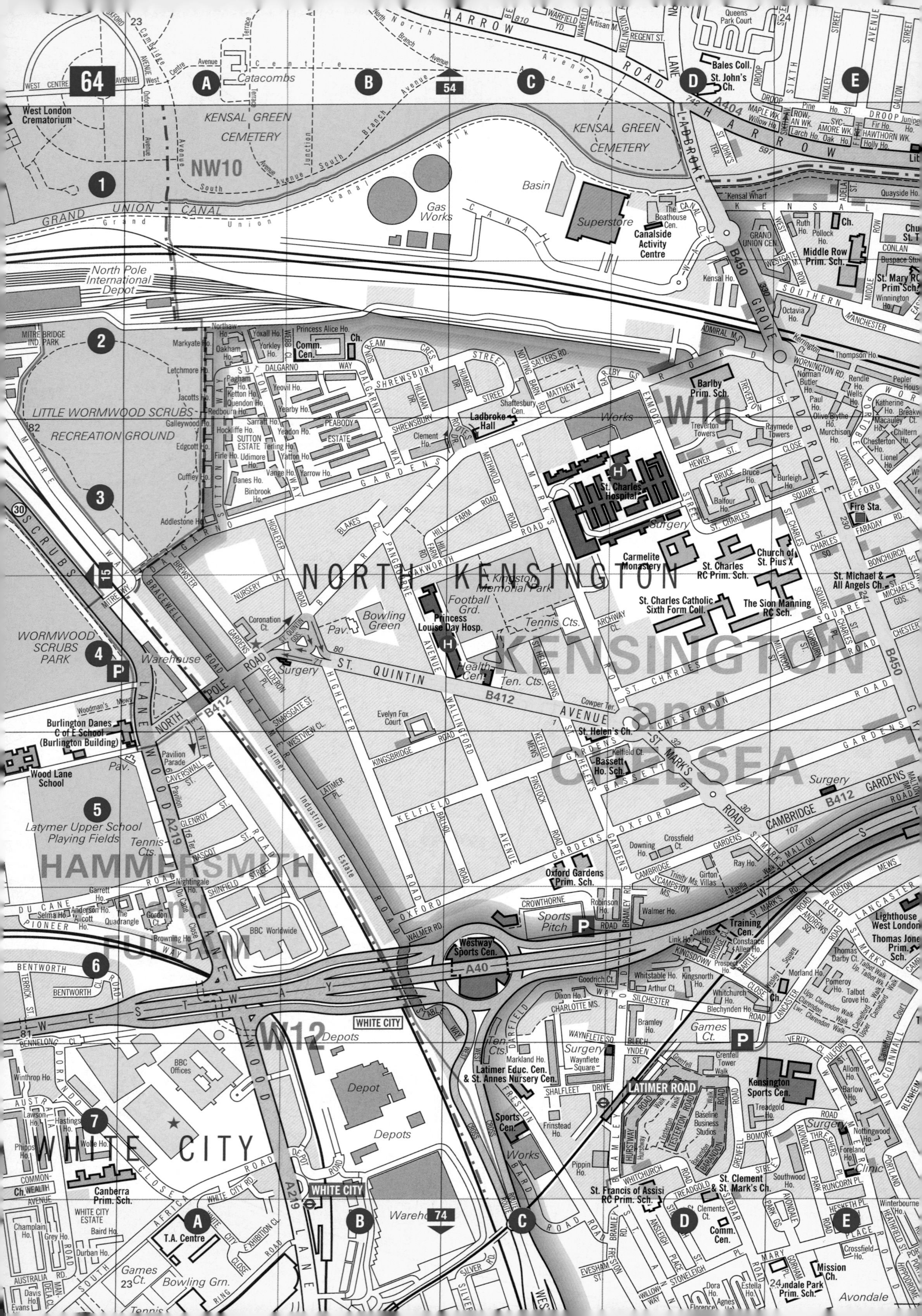
64
54
74
NORTH KENSINGTON
KENSINGTON and CHELSEA
HAMMERSMITH and FULHAM
WHITE CITY
NW10
W10
W12
KENSAL GREEN CEMETERY
GRAND UNION CANAL
West London Crematorium
Catacombs
Gas Works
Superstore
Canalside Activity Centre
North Pole International Depot
LITTLE WORMWOOD SCRUBS RECREATION GROUND
WORMWOOD SCRUBS PARK
St. Charles Hospital
Carmelite Monastery
St. Charles RC Prim. Sch.
Church of St. Pius X
St. Charles Catholic Sixth Form Coll.
The Sion Manning RC Sch.
Princess Louise Day Hosp.
Kingston Memorial Park
Bowling Green
Ladbroke Hall
Barlby Prim. Sch.
Burlington Danes C of E School (Burlington Building)
Wood Lane School
Latymer Upper School Playing Fields
BBC Worldwide
Westway Sports Cen.
Oxford Gardens Prim. Sch.
LATIMER ROAD
WHITE CITY
Kensington Sports Cen.
Latimer Educ. Cen. & St. Annes Nursery Cen.
St. Francis of Assisi RC Prim. Sch.
St. Clement & St. Mark's Ch.
Canberra Prim. Sch.
T.A. Centre
BBC Offices
Depot
Depots
HARROW ROAD
LADBROKE GROVE
ST. QUINTIN AVENUE
WOOD LANE
WESTWAY
A40
A219
B412
B450
A404
Lighthouse West London
Thomas Jones Prim. Sch.
Avondale Park Prim. Sch.
Mission Ch.

65
KILBURN
MAIDA HILL
WESTMINSTER
W9
W2
W11
NOTTING HILL
55
75
66
F
G
H
J
K
B
1
2
3
4
5
6
7
Queen's Park Public Open Space
Jubilee Sports Cen. & Baths
Queen's Pk. Prim. Sch.
Utd. Reformed Church
Mary Paterson Nursery Sch.
Teachers' Training Cen.
Essendine Prim. Sch.
City of Westminster College
Synagogue
Paddington Bowl & Sports Club
The Institute of Psychoanalysis
B.B.C. Studios
Paddington Academy
Ch. of Our Lady of the Holy Souls
Comm. Cen.
Queen Elizabeth II Jubilee Sch.
Emmanuel Ch.
St. Peter's Ch.
St. Peter's C of E Prim. School
St. Thomas C of E Prim. Sch.
The Kensington and Chelsea College
R.C. Ch.
Pol. Sta.
Council Offs.
Westminster Adult Educ. Cen.
St. Mary Magdalene C of E Prim. Sch.
Mosque
Golborne Rd. Ch.
The Muslim Cultural Heritage Cen.
Bevington Prim. Sch.
Westbourne Park
Ainsworth Nursery Sch.
Spanish Bilingual School
Ch. of Our Lady of Sorrows
Our Lady of Dolours RC Prim. Sch.
Next Generation Carlton Club
Westbourne Youth Activity Cen.
West London Buddhist Cen.
St. Stephen's Ch.
St. Mary of the Angels RC Prim. Sch.
Isaac Newton Centre
Ladbroke Grove
Serbian Orthodox Ch.
Talbot Tabernacle
All Saints Ch.
Salv. Army Hall
Health Cen.
Mus. of Brands
Colville Prim. Sch.
Peniel Chap.
Baptist Ch.
The New Church Cen.
College Park School
Greek Orthodox Cathedral
St. Matthew's Ch.
St. Peter's Ch.
St. John's Ch.
Ladbroke Square Gardens
Training Cen.
Portobello Green
Grand Union Canal
Westway
A40
A404
A4207
A4206
B412
B413
B414
B415
B450
Harrow Road
Great Western Road
Westbourne Park Road
Westbourne Grove
Ledbury Road
Chepstow Road
Pembridge Villas
Kensington Park Road
Ladbroke Grove
Elgin Crescent
Lancaster Road
Portobello Road
Shirland Road
Elgin Avenue
Sutherland Avenue
Chippenham Road
Kilburn Park Rd.
Golborne Road
Cambridge Gardens
Notting Hill

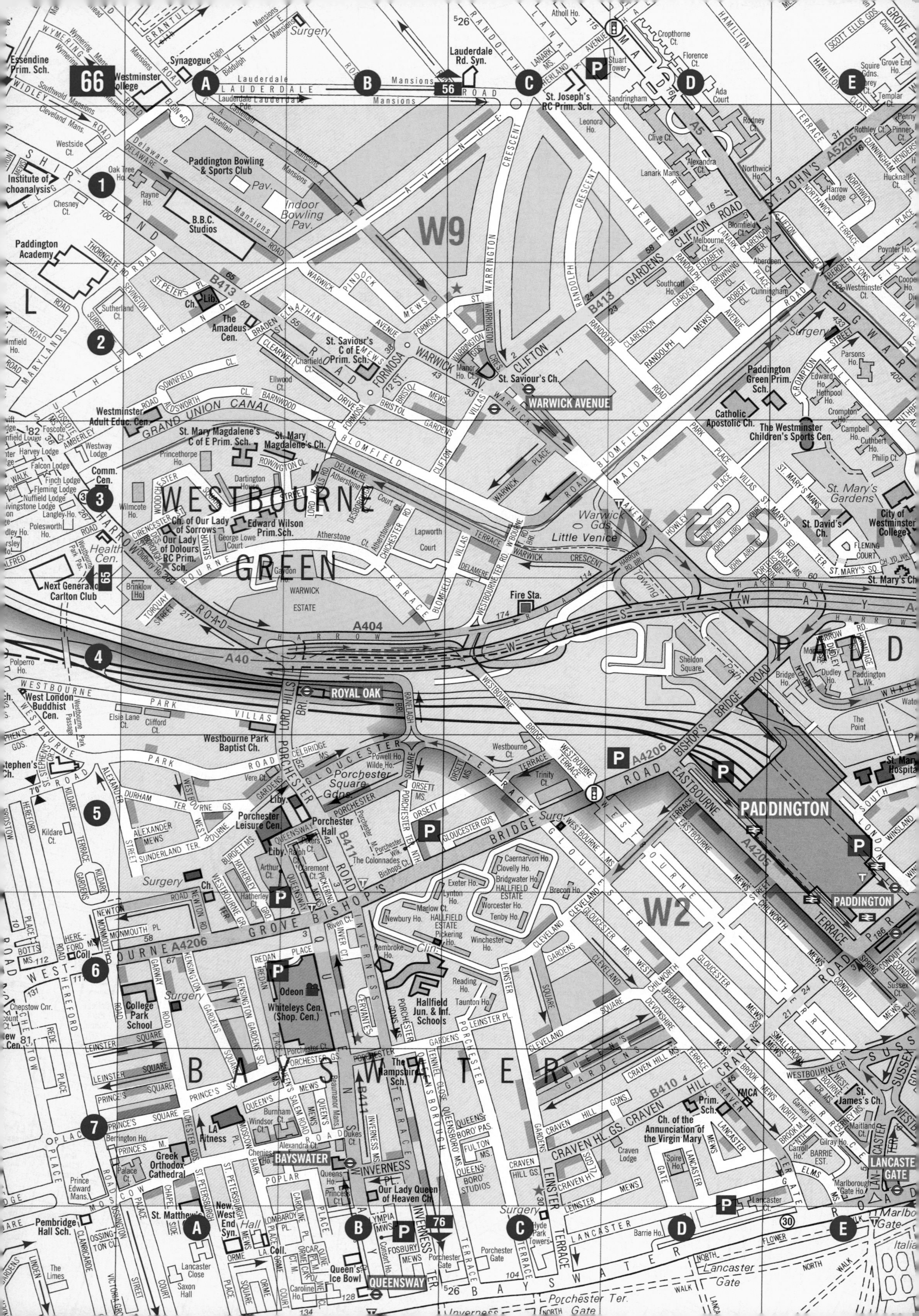

66
56
65
76
A
B
C
D
E
1
2
3
4
5
6
7
W9
W2
WESTBOURNE
GREEN
BAYSWATER
PADD
Essendine Prim. Sch.
Westminster College
Synagogue
Surgery
Lauderdale Rd. Syn.
Lauderdale Mansions
LAUDERDALE ROAD
St. Joseph's RC Prim. Sch.
Atholl Ho.
Cropthorne Ct.
Florence Ct.
Stuart Tower
Ada Court
Sandringham Ct.
Leonora Ho.
Clive Ct.
Alexandra Ct.
Rodney Ct.
Lanark Mans.
Northwick Ho.
Harrow Lodge
Hucknall Ct.
Rothley Ct.
Pinner Ct.
Penny
Grove End Ho.
Templar Ct.
Squire Gdns.
Institute of Psychoanalysis
Oak Tree Ho.
Rayne Ho.
Chesney Ct.
Paddington Bowling & Sports Club
Pav.
Indoor Bowling Pav.
B.B.C. Studios
Paddington Academy
CASTELLAIN ROAD
RANDOLPH AVENUE
MAIDA VALE
HAMILTON TERRACE
ST. JOHN'S WOOD ROAD
CLIFTON GARDENS
CLIFTON ROAD
WARRINGTON CRESCENT
ELGIN AVENUE
SHIRLAND ROAD
Sutherland Ct.
St. Peter's Pl.
Lib.
Ch.
The Amadeus Cen.
St. Saviour's C of E Prim. Sch.
St. Saviour's Ch.
WARWICK AVENUE
Manor Ho. Ct.
Southcott Ho.
Melbourne Ct.
Blomfield Ho.
Aberdeen Ct.
Cunningham Ct.
Westminster Ct.
Poynter Ho.
Parsons Ho.
Paddington Green Prim. Sch.
Catholic Apostolic Ch.
The Westminster Children's Sports Cen.
Edward Ho.
Hethpool Ho.
Crompton Ho.
Campbell Ho.
Cuthbert Ho.
Philip Ct.
St. Mary's Gardens
City of Westminster College
St. David's Ch.
Fleming Court
St. Mary's Ch.
Westminster Adult Educ. Cen.
GRAND UNION CANAL
BLOMFIELD ROAD
St. Mary Magdalene's C of E Prim. Sch.
St. Mary Magdalene's Ch.
Princethorpe Ho.
Dartington House
Comm. Cen.
Ch. of Our Lady of Sorrows
Our Lady of Dolours RC Prim. Sch.
Edward Wilson Prim.Sch.
George Lowe Court
Lapworth Court
Atherstone Ct.
Warwick Gds.
Little Venice
WARWICK CRESCENT
Health Cen.
Next Generation Carlton Club
Brinklow Ho.
Gaydon Ho.
WARWICK ESTATE
Fire Sta.
HARROW ROAD
A404
A40
WESTWAY
ROYAL OAK
Sheldon Square
Bridge Ho.
Dudley Ho.
Paddington Wk.
The Point
St. Mary's Hospital
Polperro Ho.
West London Buddhist Cen.
Elsie Lane Ct.
Clifford Ct.
Westbourne Park Baptist Ch.
WESTBOURNE PARK VILLAS
St. Stephen's Ch.
Powell Ho.
Wilde Ho.
Porchester Square Gdns.
Westbourne Ct.
Trinity Ct.
A4206
BISHOP'S BRIDGE ROAD
PADDINGTON
A4205
EASTBOURNE TERRACE
Kildare Ct.
Porchester Leisure Cen.
Porchester Hall
Liby.
The Colonnades
Caernarvon Ho.
Clovelly Ho.
Bridgwater Ho.
HALLFIELD ESTATE
Worcester Ho.
Tenby Ho.
Brecon Ho.
Exeter Ho.
Lynton Ho.
Marlow Ct.
Newbury Ho.
Pickering Ho.
Winchester Ho.
Surgery
Arthur Ct.
Hatherley Ct.
Claremont Ct.
Bishops Ct.
Riven Ct.
Coll.
College Park School
Odeon
Whiteleys Cen. (Shop. Cen.)
Pembroke Ho.
Clin.
Hallfield Jun. & Inf. Schools
Reading Ho.
Taunton Ho.
Chepstow Cnr.
LEINSTER SQUARE
PRINCE'S SQUARE
The Hampshire Sch.
B411
B410
CRAVEN HILL GDS.
YMCA
Ch. of the Annunciation of the Virgin Mary
Prim. Sch.
Craven Lodge
Spire Ho.
Gilray Ho.
Carroll Ho.
Maitland Ct.
BARRIE EST.
St. James's Ch.
LANCASTER GATE
Marlborough Gate Ho.
LA Fitness
Greek Orthodox Cathedral
Berrington Ho.
Palace Ct.
Prince Edward Mans.
Burnham Ct.
Windsor Ct.
Dukes Ct.
Alexandra Ct.
Chenies Ho.
BAYSWATER
Queens Ho.
INVERNESS PL.
Our Lady Queen of Heaven Ch.
St. Matthew's Ch.
New West End Syn.
Hall
Coll.
Pembridge Hall Sch.
The Limes
Lancaster Close
Saxon Hall
Queen's Ice Bowl
QUEENSWAY
Porchester Gate
Hyde Park Towers
Barrie Ho.
Lancaster Ct.
BAYSWATER ROAD
Lancaster Gate
Porchester Ter. North Gate

67
57
77
68
F
G
H
J
K
M
1
2
3
4
5
6
7
LISSON GROVE
MARYLEBONE
NW8
NW1
W1
Boating Lake
The Holme
Bandstand
Regent's College
Jubilee Gates
Clarence Gate
The Liberal Jewish Synagogue
Grand Union Canal
Lisson Green
LISSON GREEN ESTATE
Royal Coll. of Obstetricians & Gynaecologists
London Business Sch.
Francis Holland Sch.
St. Cyprian's Ch.
The Sherlock Holmes Mus.
BAKER STREET
Madame Tussaud's
Lost Property Off.
University of Westminster
BAKER ST.
MARYLEBONE
Gateway Prim. Sch.
Cockpit
City of Westminster Coll.
Ch. Sylvia Young Theatre Sch.
St. Edward's RC Prim. Sch. & Convent
Nightingale Capio Day Hospital
Nightingale Capio Hosp.
Vocational Education Cen.
LA Fitness
Town Hall
Lib.
Screen on Baker St.
Western Eye Hosp.
St. Mary's Prim. Sch.
Magistrates Court
St. Dunstans
Swedish Ch.
St. Mary's Ch.
EDGWARE ROAD
EDGWARE RD.
MARYLEBONE FLYOVER
Police Sta.
MARYLEBONE ROAD
A501
A404
A41
A5
A4209
A5204
A402
A4202
B507
Ch. of the Holy Rosary
Seymour Leisure Cen.
St. Mark's Ch.
Baptist Ch.
Eleventh Ch. of Christ Scientist
Hampden Gurney C of E Prim. Sch.
Imperial Coll. (Wilson Ho.)
Medical Sch.
St. Mary's Hospital
Alexander Fleming Lab. Mus.
PADDINGTON BASIN
West End Quay
Westcliffe Apartments
The Water Gardens
The Quadrangle
St. John's Ch.
West London Synagogue
Ch. Army HQ Ch.
Ch. of the Annunciation
Police Sta.
MARBLE ARCH
Odeon
Tyburn Tree (Site of)
Marble Arch
Speakers' Corner
Animals in War Memorial
PORTMAN SQUARE
OXFORD STREET
BAYSWATER ROAD
Stanhope Place Gate
Albion Gate
Clarendon Gate
Victoria Gate
Westbourne Gate
NORTH CARRIAGE DRIVE
CLOSED Midnight - 5am
ENTRANCE TO UNDERGROUND CAR PARK
Refreshment Kiosk
Underground Car Park
HYDE PARK
Fountains
PARK LANE
HYDE PARK SQUARE
CONNAUGHT SQUARE
DORSET SQ.
BRYANSTON SQUARE
MONTAGU SQUARE
SUSSEX SQUARE
NORFOLK CRESCENT
GLOUCESTER PLACE
BAKER STREET

68
58
78
A
B
C
D
E
1
2
3
4
5
6
7
QUEEN MARY'S GARDENS
Chester Road Gates
Chester Wlk Gate
Avenue Gdns.
English Gdns.
Bandstand
Jubilee Gates
New Lodge
Tennis Courts
Playground
REGENT'S PARK
CLOSED Midnight - 7am
Clarence Gate
Park Square Gardens
NW1
Regent's College
Royal College of Physicians
Pol. Sta.
St. Mary Magdalene's Ch.
St. Anne's Ch.
Univ. of Westminster
Euston Cen.
EUSTON UNDERPASS
Holy Trinity Ch.
The White Ho.
Regency Ho.
Marlborough Ho.
Jellicoe Ho.
International Comm. Sch.
Harley House
Ryl. Academy of Music Mus.
REGENT'S PARK
GT. PORTLAND ST.
Ryl. Nat. Orthopaedic Hosp.
St. Luke's Hosp. for the Clergy
Sherlock Holmes Mus.
BAKER STREET
Lost Property Off.
Madame Tussaud's
Crescent Gardens
Central London Civil Justice Centre
The London Clinic
St. Marylebone Ch.
The Portland Hosp.
Inst. for the Blind
University of Westminster
The Princess Grace Hospl.
St. Marylebone Sch.
Christie's Education
BAKER ST.
MARYLEBONE
Meth. Ch.
RIBA
The London Telecom Tower
Latimer Day Hosp.
Hosp. (Outpatients)
King Edward VII's Hosp.
Portland Pl. Sch.
Central Synagogue
Univ. of Westminster
The Harley St. Clinic
St. Charles Ch.
Paddington Street Gdns.
B.B.C. Offs.
The Heart Hospital
Hlth. Cen.
BBC Broadcasting House
West London Coll.
St. Vincent's RC Sch.
Fire Sta.
Queen's Coll.
All Souls' Ch.
St. James's Ch. in Spanish Pl.
London Welbeck Hospital
Wallace Collection
College
Chapel Convent
St. Paul's Ch.
Meth. Ch.
Wigmore Hall
CAVENDISH SQUARE
Univ. of Westminster
W1
Portman Towers
ENTRANCE TO UNDERGROUND CAR PARK
London Coll. of Fashion
OXFORD CIRCUS
St. Peter's Ch.
Buses & Taxis only Mon. - Sat. 7am - 7pm
Selfridges
College
West London Coll.
Regent Hall
Fitness First
London Palladium
Police
MARBLE ARCH
BOND ST.
West One Shop. Cen.
Kings Weigh Ho. Ch.
College
TA Cen.
Hanover Sq Gdns
London Montessori Centre
Marble Arch
St. George's Ch.
St. Thomas Ch.
Roosevelt Mem.
American Embassy
Animals in War Memorial
Pol. Sta.
MAYFAIR
OXFORD STREET
WIGMORE STREET
MARYLEBONE ROAD
EUSTON ROAD
PORTLAND PLACE
REGENT STREET
BAKER STREET
GLOUCESTER PLACE
PARK LANE
NEW BOND STREET
GROSVENOR SQUARE
PORTMAN SQUARE
MANCHESTER SQUARE

69
F
G
H
J
K
1
2
3
4
5
6
7
EUSTON
EUSTON SQUARE
GOODGE STREET
RUSSELL SQUARE
TOTTENHAM COURT ROAD
HOLBORN
COVENT GARDEN
LEICESTER SQ.
PICCADILLY CIRCUS
BLOOMSBURY
WC1
WC2
SOHO
COVENT GARDEN
EUSTON ROAD
GOWER STREET
TOTTENHAM COURT ROAD
WOBURN PL.
TAVISTOCK SQ.
GORDON SQUARE
BEDFORD SQUARE
RUSSELL SQUARE
BLOOMSBURY SQUARE
NEW OXFORD ST.
OXFORD ST.
SHAFTESBURY AV.
CHARING CROSS RD.
ST. MARTIN'S LA.
LONG ACRE
GREAT QUEEN ST.
SOUTHAMPTON ROW
KINGSWAY
GUILFORD ST.
THEOBALD'S ROAD
HIGH HOLBORN
BRUNSWICK SQ.
MECKLENBURGH SQ.
GREAT RUSSELL ST.
MONTAGUE PL.
MALET ST.
STORE ST.
CHENIES ST.
GOODGE ST.
CHARLOTTE ST.
PERCY ST.
RATHBONE PL.
BERNERS ST.
WARDOUR ST.
DEAN ST.
GREEK ST.
FRITH ST.
OLD COMPTON ST.
GERRARD ST.
LISLE ST.
COVENTRY ST.
BREWER ST.
BROADWICK ST.
NEAL ST.
ENDELL ST.
DRURY LANE
BOW ST.
WELLINGTON ST.
KING ST.
HENRIETTA ST.
MAIDEN LA.
STRAND
British Museum
Great Court
University College
University College Hospital
Univ. Coll. Sch. of Medicine
The Elizabeth Garrett Anderson & Obstetric Hospital
Wellcome Collection
Friends Ho.
Government Offs.
The Centre for the Magic Arts
Wolfson Ho.
St. Pancras Ch.
The Place
London Contemporary Dance Sch.
British Medical Association
Mary Ward Hall
Gov. Offs.
Tavistock Sq. Gardens
Gordon Sq. Garden
Percival David Foundation
Inst. of Latin Studies
Connaught Hall
U.C.L. (Chemistry Bldg.)
U.C.L. (Campbell Ho.)
Strang Print Room
Petrie Mus.
Christ the King Gordon Sq. Ch.
Inst. of Education
Inst. of Advanced Legal Studies
Warburg Inst.
Univ. of London Union
Sch. of Oriental & African Studies
Birkbeck Coll.
College Hall
RADA
School of Hygiene & Tropical Medicine
Brunei Gallery
University of London (Senate House)
Russell Sq. Gardens
American Church
Drill Hall Arts
Ch. of Scientology
Cavendish Coll.
British Transport Police
Coll. of Law
Health Cen.
Toy Mus.
Mosque
Sch. of Architecture
Odeon
YMCA Central
Dominion
Sorting Office
Int. Studies Cen.
The Plaza Shop. Cen.
French Protestant Ch.
Centrepoint
The Astoria
Bloomsbury Cen. Baptist Ch.
St. Giles Ct.
St. Giles-in-the-Fields Ch.
Phoenix
Central St. Martins Coll. of Art and Design
Prince Edward
Palace
New Ambassadors
Cambridge
Donmar
Thomas Neal's Cen.
Shaftesbury
Oasis Sports Centre
Swiss Ch.
St. Patrick's Ch.
NHS Cen.
Soho
Curzon
City of Westminster Coll.
St. Anne's Ch.
Queen's
Gielgud
Apollo
Lyric
Piccadilly
Trocadero Cen.
Prince of Wales
Criterion
Eros
Empire
Prince Charles
Vue
Odeon
Wyndham's
Noel Coward
Garrick
Duke of York's
Central Lending Lib.
Coliseum
Fitness First
Charing Cross Pol. Sta.
Adelphi
Vaudeville
Savoy
Queen's Chapel of the Savoy
Corpus Christie Ch.
St. Paul's Ch.
The Market
London Transport Mus.
Royal Opera House
Fortune
Drury Lane
Aldwych
Lyceum
Duchess
Novello
St. Clement Danes Prim. Sch.
Freemasons' Hall
Connaught Rooms
City Lit. Cen.
New London
St. Joseph's R.C. Prim. Sch.
City Lit. Inst.
Town Hall
Holy Trinity with St. John Ch.
Cen. St. Martins Coll. of Art & Design
Conway Hall
Cochrane
Cartoon Mus.
St. George's Ch.
Bloomsbury Sq. Gdns.
St. George the Martyr Ch.
Mary Ward Cen.
Jeff Wooller Coll.
St. Giles Coll. London Cen.
The National Hospital for Neurology and Neurosurgery
Gt. Ormond Street Hospital for Children
The Royal London Homoeopathic Hosp.
The Foundling Mus.
The Wolfson Assessment Cen.
Coram's Fields
Mecklenburgh Sq. Gdns
Thomas Coram Early Childhood Cen.
Goodenough College
Regent Sq. Presbyterian Ch.
St. George's Gdns.
Utd. Ref. Ch.
Hunter St. Health Cen.
Sch. of Pharmacy
Brunswick Centre
Renoir
Fitness First
TA Cen.
Comm. Cen.
Depot
Holy Cross Ch.
St. Mary's German Ch.
Canterbury Hall
Hughes Hall
Bentham Hall
Fire Sta.
Surgery
Kingsway Inn Centre
Sadler's Wells

70
60
80
A
B
C
D
E
1
2
3
4
5
6
7
Westminster Kingsway College (Gray's Inn Centre)
Regent Sq. Presbyterian Ch.
St. George's Gdns.
Thomas Coram Early Childhood Cen.
Goodenough College
Mecklenburgh Sq. Gdns.
The Wolfson Assessment Cen.
The Foundling Mus.
Coram's Fields
The Eastman Dental Hosp. & Institute
St. Andrews Gdns.
Mount Pleasant Sorting Office
Family Records Centre
City University
Connaught Bldg.
Gloucester Bldg.
Ch. of Our Most Holy Redeemer
Spa Flds. Open Space
London Metropolitan Archives
The Bridge Sch.
Art Studies
Walmsley Bldg.
Woodbridge Chapel
St. James's Church
Church of St. John
CLERKENWELL
WC1
Dickens' House
Independent Television News
Gt. Ormond Street Hospital for Children
The National Hospital for Neurology and Neurosurgery
The Royal London Homoeopathic Hosp.
St. George the Martyr C of E Prim. Sch.
Buddhist Cen. London
Library
Pol. Sta.
London Weather Cen.
St. Alban's C of E Prim. Sch.
Gray's Inn Gdns
Gray's Inn
Chapel
Islamic Cen.
St. Etheldreda's Ch.
FARRINGDON
Conway Hall
Cen. St. Martins Coll. of Art & Design
CHANCERY LANE
HOLBORN
Holy Trinity with St. John Ch.
Min. Offs.
Inns of Court & City Yeomanry Mus.
TA Centre
Sir John Soane's Museum
Lincoln's Inn
Lincoln's Inn Hall
Lincoln's Inn Fields
Land Registry Office
Royal Coll. of Surgeons
Old Curiosity Shop
The Hunterian Mus.
Royal Courts of Justice
WC2
WESTMINSTER
London School of Economics
King's College Library
St. Dunstan-in-the-West Ch.
Dr. Johnson's H.
City Temple
St. Andrew's Ch.
CITY THAMESLINK
Connaught Rooms
Freemasons' Hall
City Lit. Cen.
St. Joseph's R.C. Prim. Sch.
Royal Opera House
Drury Lane
Fortune
Aldwych
Novello
Duchess
London Transport Mus.
Lyceum
Savoy
Vaudeville
Adelphi
Peacock
St. Clement Danes Prim. Sch.
St. Clement Danes Ch.
Australia Ho.
India Ho.
Bush Ho.
Inland Revenue
St. Mary-le-Strand Ch.
Courtauld Galleries
Somerset House
King's Coll. (Strand Campus)
Hermitage Rooms
Gilbert Collection
Queen's Chapel of the Savoy
TEMPLE
Victoria Embankment Gardens
Temple Bar
Temple Ch.
Inner Temple Hall
Mid. Temple Hall
Middle Temple
Inner Temple Garden
Fleetbank Ho.
The Patent Off.
St. Bride's Ch.
BLACKFRIARS
Blackfriars Millennium Pier
H.M.S. President
HQS. Wellington
St. Katharine
Lifeboat Station
Queen Mary
RIVER
HOLBORN
FLEET STREET
STRAND
KINGSWAY
THEOBALD'S ROAD
GRAY'S INN ROAD
FARRINGDON ROAD
VICTORIA EMBANKMENT

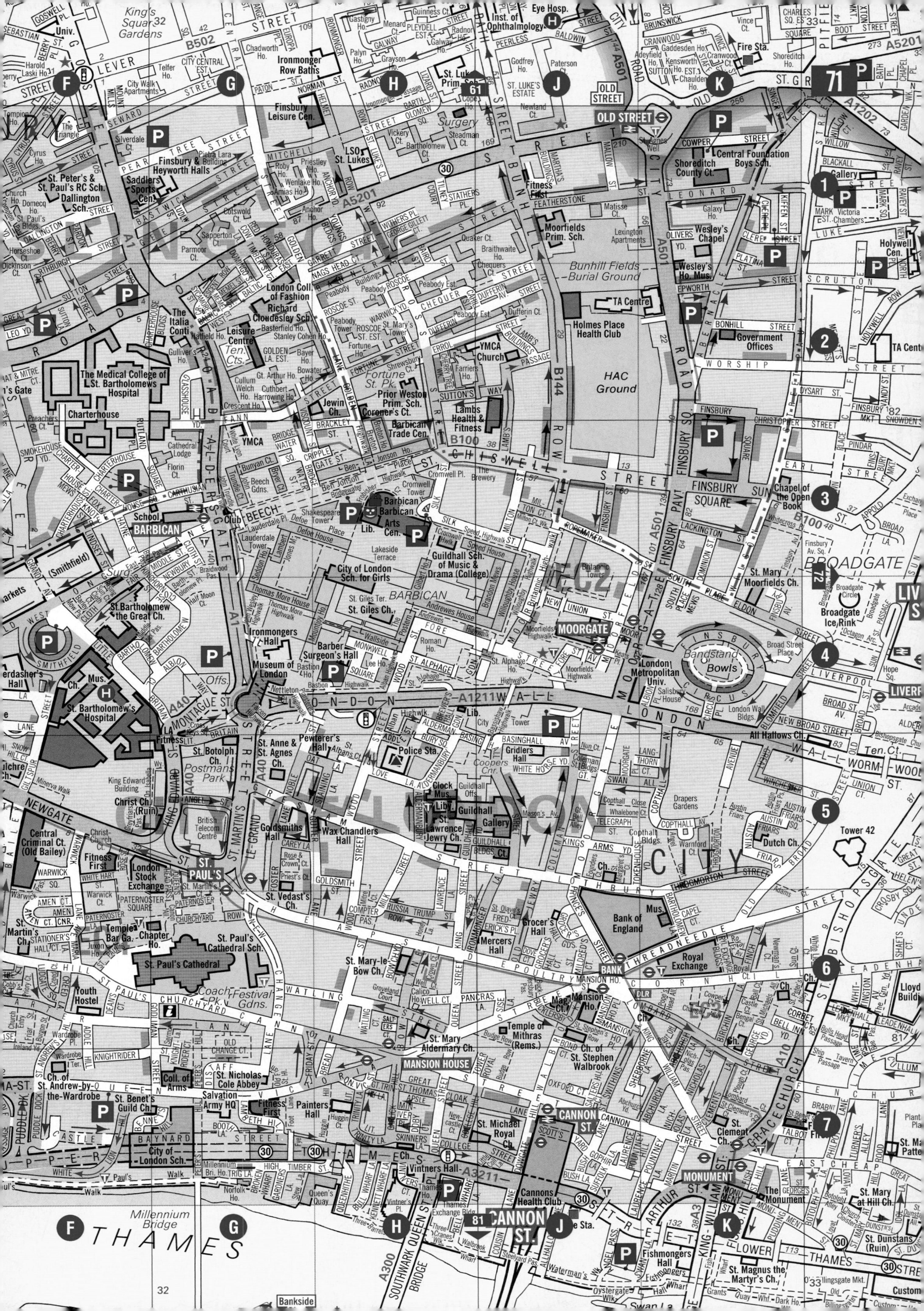

King's Square Gardens
Eye Hosp.
Inst. of Ophthalmology
Ironmonger Row Baths
St. Luke's Prim. Sch.
ST. LUKE'S ESTATE
OLD STREET
Fire Sta.
Finsbury Leisure Cen.
LSO St. Lukes
Surgery
Shoreditch County Ct.
Central Foundation Boys Sch.
Gallery
Finsbury & Heyworth Halls
Saddlers Sports Cen.
St. Peter's & St. Paul's RC Sch.
Dallington Sch.
Fitness First
Moorfields Prim. Sch.
Wesley's Chapel
Wesley's Ho. Mus.
Holywell Cen.
Bunhill Fields Burial Ground
TA Centre
Holmes Place Health Club
HAC Ground
Government Offices
London Coll. of Fashion
Richard Cloudesley Sch.
The Italia Conti
Leisure Centre
YMCA Church
The Medical College of St. Bartholomews Hospital
Charterhouse
Jewin Ch.
Prior Weston Prim. Sch.
Coroner's Ct.
Barbican Trade Cen.
Lambs Health & Fitness
FINSBURY SQUARE
Chapel of the Open Book
BARBICAN
Barbican Arts Cen.
Lib.
Guildhall Sch. of Music & Drama (College)
City of London Sch. for Girls
BARBICAN
St. Giles Ch.
E.C.2
BROADGATE
Broadgate Ice Rink
St. Mary Moorfields Ch.
MOORGATE
London Metropolitan Univ.
Bandstand Bowls
FINSBURY CIRCUS
(Smithfield)
St. Bartholomew the Great Ch.
Mus.
St. Bartholomew's Hospital
Ironmongers Hall
Barber Surgeons' Hall
Museum of London
LONDON WALL
All Hallows Ch.
Police Sta.
Gridlers Hall
St. Botolph Ch.
Postmans Park
Christ Ch. (Ruin)
British Telecom Centre
Goldsmiths Hall
Wax Chandlers Hall
Clock Mus.
Guildhall
Gallery
St. Lawrence Jewry Ch.
Drapers Gardens
Dutch Ch.
Tower 42
CITY OF LONDON
CITY
Central Criminal Ct. (Old Bailey)
Fitness First
London Stock Exchange
ST. PAUL'S
St. Vedast's Ch.
Bank of England
Royal Exchange
BANK
St. Paul's Cathedral
St. Paul's Cathedral Sch.
Temple Bar Ga.
Chapter Ho.
Youth Hostel
St. Mary-le-Bow Ch.
Mercers Hall
Grocer's Hall
Mansion Ho.
Temple of Mithras (Rems.)
Ch. of St. Stephen Walbrook
St. Mary Aldermary Ch.
MANSION HOUSE
Coll. of Arms
St. Nicholas Cole Abbey
Salvation Army HQ
Fitness First
Painters Hall
St. Benet's Guild Ch.
St. Andrew-by-the-Wardrobe
City of London Sch.
St. Michael Royal Ch.
CANNON ST.
St. Clement Ch.
Vintners Hall
Cannons Health Club
MONUMENT
The Monument
St. Mary at Hill Ch.
St. Dunstans (Ruin)
Fishmongers Hall
St. Magnus the Martyr's Ch.
Millennium Bridge
THAMES
SOUTHWARK BRIDGE
32
Bankside

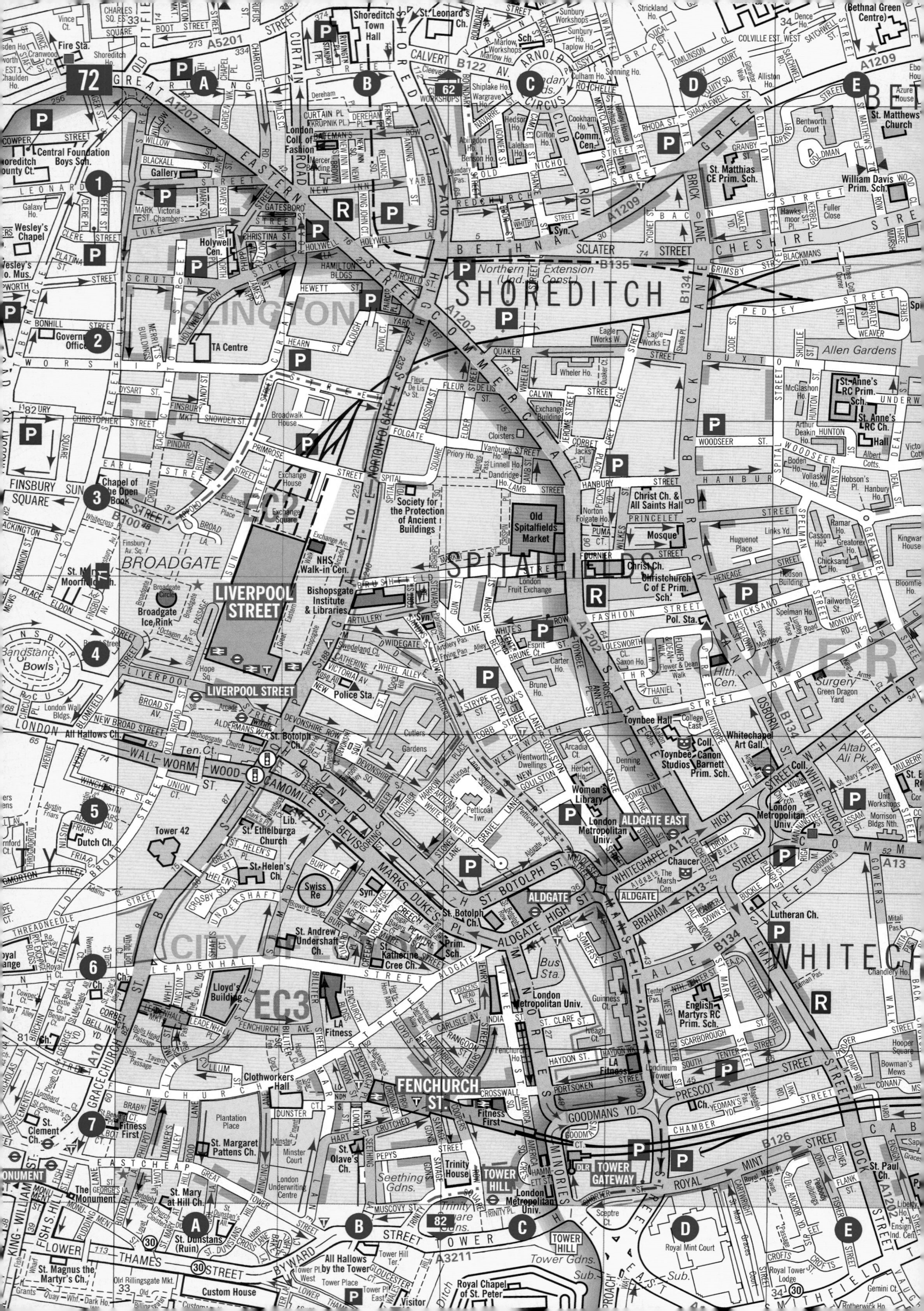

SHOREDITCH
SPITALFIELDS
TOWER
WHITECH
ISLINGTON
CITY
EC2
EC3
BROADGATE
LIVERPOOL STREET
FENCHURCH ST.
ALDGATE EAST
ALDGATE
TOWER HILL
TOWER GATEWAY
MONUMENT
Shoreditch Town Hall
St. Leonard's Ch.
Fire Sta.
Central Foundation Boys Sch.
Wesley's Chapel
Wesley's Ho. Mus.
Gallery
Holywell Cen.
London Coll. of Fashion
TA Centre
Chapel of the Open Book
Broadgate Ice Rink
Broadwalk House
Exchange House
Exchange Square
NHS Walk-in Cen.
Bishopsgate Institute & Libraries
Society for the Protection of Ancient Buildings
Old Spitalfields Market
London Fruit Exchange
Christ Ch. & All Saints Hall
Mosque
Christ Ch.
Christchurch C of E Prim. Sch.
Pol. Sta.
Police Sta.
Toynbee Hall
Toynbee Studios
Canon Barnett Prim. Sch.
Whitechapel Art Gall.
London Metropolitan Univ.
Women's Library
Chaucer
Tower 42
St. Ethelburga Church
St. Helen's Ch.
Swiss Re
St. Andrew Undershaft Ch.
St. Katherine Cree Ch.
Lloyd's Building
LA Fitness
St. Botolph Ch.
Dutch Ch.
All Hallows Ch.
Clothworkers Hall
Plantation Place
St. Margaret Pattens Ch.
Minster Court
London Underwriting Centre
St. Olave's Ch.
Trinity House
Seething Gdns.
St. Mary at Hill Ch.
St. Dunstans (Ruin)
The Monument
St. Magnus the Martyr's Ch.
Custom House
All Hallows by the Tower
Royal Chapel of St. Peter
Tower Gdns.
Royal Mint Court
Fitness First
Lutheran Ch.
English Martyrs RC Prim. Sch.
Allen Gardens
St. Anne's RC Prim. Sch.
St. Anne's RC Ch.
St. Matthias CE Prim. Sch.
William Davis Prim. Sch.
St. Matthews' Church
Bethnal Green Centre
Huguenot Place
Green Dragon Yard
Altab Ali Pk.
St. Paul Ch.
Petticoat Twr.
Cutlers Gardens
Bus Sta.
Finsbury Square
Bandstand
Bowls
GREAT EASTERN STREET
COMMERCIAL STREET
BISHOPSGATE
NORTON FOLGATE
BETHNAL GREEN ROAD
SCLATER STREET
CHESHIRE STREET
BRICK LANE
HANBURY STREET
FASHION STREET
WHITECHAPEL HIGH ST.
ALDGATE HIGH ST.
LEADENHALL STREET
FENCHURCH STREET
GRACECHURCH ST.
EASTCHEAP
LOWER THAMES STREET
TOWER HILL
MINORIES
ROYAL MINT STREET
CAMOMILE ST.
HOUNDSDITCH
WORSHIP STREET
LEONARD STREET
CURTAIN ROAD
OLD STREET
A1202
A10
A1209
A11
A13
A1211
A3211
B134
B135
Northern Extension (Und. Const.)

73
BETHNAL GREEN
STEPNEY
Weavers Fields
Bethnal Green Gardens
Burial Ground
Swanlea Secondary School
Whitechapel Sports Centre
The Royal London Hospital
NHS Walk-in-Cen.
East London Mosque
Superstore
Tower Hamlets Mission
John Scurr Prim. Sch.
Anchor Retail Park
Stepney Green
Stepney Green Park
Alice Model Nsy. Sch.
London Independent BMI Hosp.
Redlands Prim. Sch.
Smithy Street Prim. Sch.
St. Bartholomew School of Nursing & Midwifery
Madani Girls Sch.
London Metropolitan University
Mulberry Sch. for Girls
Bigland Green Prim. Sch.
Darul Ummah Masjid
Jubilee Gdns.
St. Mary & St. Michael RC Prim. Sch.
The Bishop Challoner Sch.
Tower Hamlets Coll.
Blue Gate Fields Jun & Inf. Schs.
St. George's Gdns.
St. George in the East Ch.
St. George's Pools
St. Paul's C of E Prim. Sch.
St. Paul's Church
Shadwell Basin
King Edward Memorial Park
Bowling Green
Tennis Courts
Free Trade Wharf
Whitechapel
Bethnal Green
Shadwell
Whitechapel Road
Mile End Road
Commercial Road
Cable Street
The Highway
Cambridge Heath Road
New Road
Cannon Street Road
Jamaica Street
Three Colts Street
Vallance Road
A11
A13
A107
A1203
B108
B126
B135
B140
63
83
16

WHITE CITY
SHEPHERD'S BUSH
HAMMERSMITH and FULHAM
BROOK GREEN
W12
W6
W14
White City
Wood Lane (Due Open Late 2008)
Shepherd's Bush (Market)
Shepherd's Bush
Goldhawk Road
Holland Park
BBC Television Centre
Hammersmith Park
Queen's Park Rangers FC (Loftus Road)
Westfield London (Under Construction - Due Open Late 2008)
Multiplex Cinema (Due Open Late 2008)
Bus Station (Due Open Late 2008)
Library (Due Open Late 2008)
Shepherd's Bush Common
Shepherds Bush Empire
Vue Cinema
Warehouse
Warehouses
Depots
Depot
Works
T.A. Centre
Games Ct.
Bowling Grn.
Tennis Cts.
Canberra Prim. Sch.
St. Stephen's C of E Prim. Sch.
Miles Coverdale Prim. Sch.
Mosque
Hindu Tem.
Police Sta.
Baptist Ch.
St. Simon's Ch.
Methodist Ch.
Addison Prim. Sch.
Lena Gdns. Prim. Sch.
St. Marys Cath. Prim. Sch.
St. Matthew's Church
St. John the Baptist's Church
Central Gurdwara (London)
Spanish & Portuguese Syn.
St. James's Church
Islamic Centre
St. Clement & St. James C of E Prim. Sch.
Avondale Park Prim. Sch.
Avondale Park
Mission Ch.
St. Francis of Assisi RC Prim. Sch.
St. Clement & St. Mark's Ch.
Chinese Church
St. Paul's Girls School
Bute Ho. Prep. Sch.
Fire Station
Osram Court
Playing Field
Cambridge Sch.
The Godolphin & Latymer Sch.
Uxbridge Road
Goldhawk Road
Wood Lane
Shepherd's Bush Road
Holland Road
West Cross Route
A4020
A219
A402
A3220
A B C D E
1 2 3 4 5 6 7
64
84
15
23

75
65
85
F
G
H
J
K
1
2
3
4
5
6
7
NOTTING
HILL
HOLLAND
PARK
KENSINGTON
and
CHELSEA
KENSINGTON
W11
W2
W8
HOLLAND
PARK
Ladbroke Square Gardens
St. John's Ch.
St. Peter's Ch.
Ladbroke Grove Ho.
Lansdowne Ct.
Hillcrest
Bartok Ho.
Chartwell Ho.
Weller Ct.
Lansdowne Ho.
Bonham Ho.
Kent Ho.
Police Sta.
The Square Montessori Sch.
NOTTING HILL GATE
Coronet
Gate
Coll.
Chap.
Surg.
Lib.
Kensington Temple
Training Cen.
Pembridge Hall Sch.
The Limes
Prince Edward Mans.
Unitarian Ch.
St. Matthew's Ch.
Greek Orthodox Cathedral
Lancaster Close
Saxon Hall
LA Fitness
Surgery
Rodney Ho.
Latimer Ho.
Princes Ho.
Buckingham Ct.
Matlock Ct.
Kelvin Ct.
Sch.
HOLLAND PARK
St. Nicholas' Convent
Tennis Crt.
Holland Park Tennis Grd.
Abbotsbury Ho.
Redlynch Ct.
Fox Prim. Sch.
Coll. & Fox Cen.
Palmerston Ho.
Melbourne Ho.
Campden Houses
Kensington Heights
The Mount
St. George's Ch.
Bedford Gardens Ho.
Campden House Ter.
Campden Ho.
Tor Ct.
Laurie Ho.
Tennis Courts
Holland Park School
The Kensington and Chelsea College
St. Mary Abbot Church Hall
Vicarage Ct.
Winchester Ct.
Bullingham Mans.
Newton Ct.
Carmel Ct.
Holland Pl. Cham.
Lancer Square
Campden Hill Ct.
Academy Gardens
Duchess of Bedford Ho.
Campden Hill Gate
Holland House King George VI Mem. Youth Hostel
Holland Park
The Orangery Gallery
Cricket Field
Town Hall
Library
St. Mary Abbots Ch. Prim. Sch.
Ingelow Ho.
Hornton Ct.
Phillimore Ct.
Linley Sambourne Ho.
Commonwealth Institute
HIGH STREET KENSINGTON
Kensington Arcade
First Ch. of Christ Scientist
Sovereign Ct.
William Cobbett Ho.
St. Sarkis Armenian Ch.
Our Lady of Victories Ch.
Odeon
Monarch Ct.
Warwick Chambers
Abingdon Mans.
Kensington Chapel
TA Cen.
Allen Ho.
Allen Mans.
Manderley
Serlby Ct.
Oakwood Mans.
St. Barnabas' Ch.
Farley Ct.
Stavordale Lodge
Leighton House Art Gall. & Museum
Kingfisher Ho.
Monckton Ct.
Kenbrook Ho.
Park Lodge
Prim. Sch.
Pol. Sta.
Coptic Orthodox Church
Sandalwood Mans.
Cedar Ho.
Zetland Ho.
Rutland Ho.
Falkland Ho.
Sutherland Ho.
KENSINGTON OLYMPIA
Olympia
Ashmore Ho.
Ibberton Ho.
Manston Ho.
Oakeford Ho.
Rushmore Ho.
Chillingstone Ho.
Kenton Ct.
Tollard Ho.
Charles House
Abbot's Ho.
St. Mary Abbot's Ct.
Pembroke Ct.
Pembroke Cotts.
WARWICK GARDENS Restricted Access between 9pm & 6am
Lizmans Ter.
St. Philip's Ch.
Alexa Ct.
Sherbourne Ct.
Moscow Mans.
Chatsworth Ct.
Marlborough Ct.
Durrels Ho.
Palace Mans.
Argyll Mans.
Richmond Cotts.
St. James Sch.
Avonmore Prim. Sch.
Welbeck Court
Broadwood Ter.
A402
A4206
A4204
A315
A3220
B450
B415
B405
B316
ADDISON CRES.
HOLLAND ROAD
KENSINGTON HIGH STREET
NOTTING HILL GATE
HOLLAND PARK AVENUE
LADBROKE GROVE
CAMPDEN HILL ROAD
KENSINGTON CHURCH STREET
PEMBROKE ROAD
CROMWELL ROAD
EARLS COURT ROAD
HOLLAND WALK
PHILLIMORE GARDENS
ABINGDON ROAD
WARWICK GARDENS
EDWARDES SQUARE
ADDISON ROAD
HAMMERSMITH ROAD
PEMBRIDGE ROAD
PORTOBELLO ROAD
LANSDOWNE CRESCENT
KENSINGTON PARK ROAD

76
BAYSWATER
QUEENSWAY
KENSINGTON GARDENS
ROUND POND
Kensington Palace
The Royal Ceremonial Dress Collection
The Orangery
Diana, Princess of Wales Memorial Playground
Diana, Princess of Wales Memorial Walk
Refreshment Kiosk
Bandstand
Speke's Monument
Peter Pan Statue
Queen's Temple
Albert Memorial
Royal Albert Hall
Royal Coll. of Art
Royal Geographical Soc
Royal College of Music
Imperial College
Natural History Museum
HIGH STREET KENSINGTON
GLOUCESTER ROAD
KENSINGTON
W8
NOTTING HILL GATE
BAYSWATER ROAD
KENSINGTON HIGH STREET
KENSINGTON ROAD
KENSINGTON CHURCH STREET
CROMWELL ROAD
QUEEN'S GATE
GLOUCESTER ROAD
Kensington Palace Green
Town Hall
Library
Heythrop College
Thomas's Preparatory School
The Cromwell Hosp.
David Lloyd Leisure
Lycee Francais Charles de Gaulle
Queen's Ice Bowl
Greek Orthodox Cathedral
St. Mary Abbots Ch.
Christian Science Ch.
Holy Trinity Ch.
A402
A315
A4204
A4
B411
B405
B325

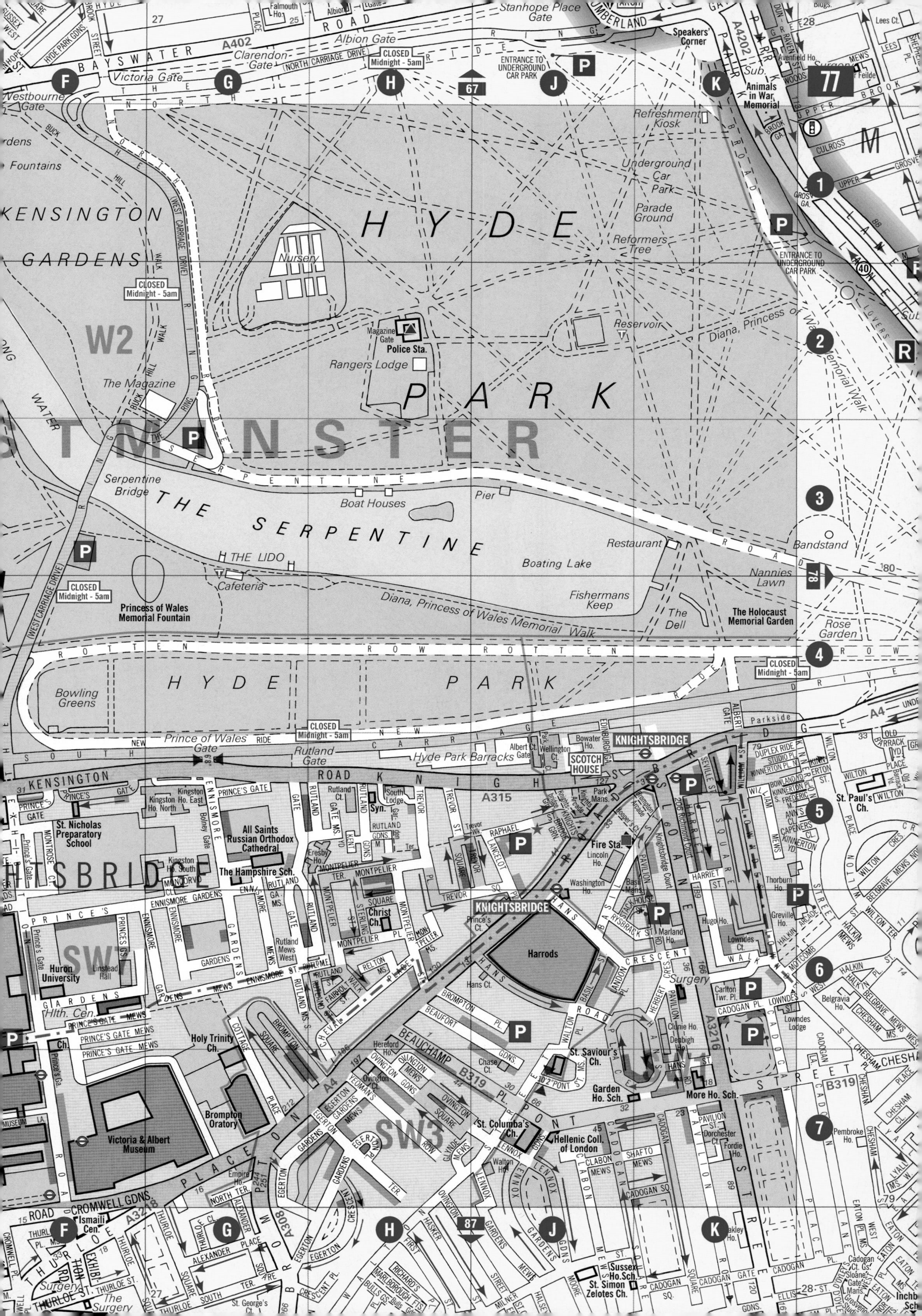
HYDE PARK
KENSINGTON GARDENS
THE SERPENTINE
WESTMINSTER
KNIGHTSBRIDGE
W2
SW7
SW3
Speakers' Corner
Animals in War Memorial
Refreshment Kiosk
Underground Car Park
Parade Ground
Reformers Tree
Nursery
Magazine Gate
Police Sta.
Rangers Lodge
Reservoir
Diana, Princess of Wales Memorial Walk
The Magazine
Serpentine Bridge
Boat Houses
Pier
Restaurant
Bandstand
Nannies Lawn
Boating Lake
Fishermans Keep
The Dell
The Holocaust Memorial Garden
Rose Garden
THE LIDO
Cafeteria
Princess of Wales Memorial Fountain
Bowling Greens
Rotten Row
Prince of Wales' Gate
Rutland Gate
Hyde Park Barracks
Albert Gate
Bayswater Road
Victoria Gate
Clarendon Gate
Albion Gate
Stanhope Place Gate
Westbourne Gate
Fountains
CLOSED Midnight - 5am
ENTRANCE TO UNDERGROUND CAR PARK
Knightsbridge
Scotch House
Harrods
All Saints Russian Orthodox Cathedral
St. Nicholas Preparatory School
The Hampshire Sch.
Christ Ch.
Fire Sta.
St. Paul's Ch.
Huron University
Holy Trinity Ch.
Brompton Oratory
Victoria & Albert Museum
St. Saviour's Ch.
Garden Ho. Sch.
More Ho. Sch.
St. Columba's Ch.
Hellenic Coll. of London
Ismaili Cen.
St. Simon Zelotes Ch.
Sussex Ho. Sch.
Surgery
67
78
87
76

MAYFAIR
W1
HYDE PARK
W2
GREEN PARK
WESTMI
PALACE GARDENS
BELGRAVIA
Speakers' Corner
Animals in War Memorial
Roosevelt Mem.
American Embassy
Grosvenor Chapel
Library
St. George's Gdns.
St. George's Hanover Sq. Prim. Sch.
Ch. of the Immaculate Conception
Faraday Mus.
Royal Arcade
Third Ch. of Christ Scientist
Curzon
Mos.
Christ Ch.
Park Towers
Achilles Statue
Queen Elizabeth Gate
Bandstand
Diana, Princess of Wales Memorial Walk
The Holocaust Memorial Garden
Rose Garden
Wellington Museum
Apsley Ho.
HYDE PARK CORNER
Wellington Mon.
Wellington Arch
Australian War Meml.
CLOSED Midnight - 5am
ENTRANCE TO UNDERGROUND CAR PARK
Canada Memorial
CLOSED SUNDAY
Commonwealth Memorial Gates
Queen Victoria Memorial
The Forecourt
The Quadrangle
Buckingham Palace
Ambassadors' Court
Queen's Gallery
The Royal Mews
Royal Mews
Dept. for Transport
LA Fitness
Spencer Ho.
Arlington Ho.
St. Paul's Ch.
European Academy & Accademia Italiana
Montrose Ho.
St. Peter's Ch.
St. Peter's Prim. Sch.
Instituto Cervantes
Belgravia Ho.
Lowndes Lodge
Pembroke Ho.
More Ho. Sch.
Inchbald Sch.
St. Michael's Ch.
Victoria Place Shop. Cen.
VICTORIA
Victoria Palace
Apollo Victoria
Bus Sta.
Convent
GREEN PARK
HYDE PARK CORNER
A4202
A4
A302
A3217
A3214
A202
A3123
B310
B312
B319
KNIGHTSBRIDGE
CONSTITUTION HILL
DUKE OF WELLINGTON PL.
GROSVENOR PLACE
BUCKINGHAM PALACE ROAD
BUCKINGHAM GATE
VAUXHALL BRIDGE RD.
PICCADILLY
PARK LANE
BELGRAVE SQUARE
EATON SQUARE
CHESHAM PLACE
LOWNDES SQUARE
SLOANE STREET
68
88

79
F
G
H
J
K
1
2
3
4
5
6
7
80
89
PICCADILLY CIRCUS
LEICESTER SQ.
CHARING CROSS
EMBANKMENT
WESTMINSTER
ST. JAMES'S PARK
WC2
SW1
ST. JAMES'S
WESTMINSTER
GARDEN
RIVER THAMES
ST. JAMES'S PARK
Piccadilly
Trocadero Cen.
Cineworld
London Pav.
Prince of Wales
Eros
Criterion
Haymarket
Comedy
Odeon
Empire
Queen's
Gielgud
Apollo
Lyric
China Town
Prince Charles
Wyndham's
Noel Coward
Duke of York's
Garrick
Coliseum
Vaudeville
Adelphi
Savoy
Lyceum
The Market
Transport Mus.
St. Paul's Ch.
Corpus Christie Ch.
Queen's Chapel of the Savoy
Central Lending Lib.
Friends' Meet. Ho.
National Portrait Gallery
National Gallery
Sainsbury Wing
St. Martin-in-the-Fields Ch.
Charing Cross Underground Shop. Cen.
Charing Cross Pol. Sta.
South Africa Ho.
Canada Ho.
Nelson's Column
Her Majesty's
Britain & London Visitor Centre
Jermyn St.
St. James's Ch.
Apollo W. End
London Library
HQ of the Inst. of Directors
Admiralty Arch
Mall Galleries
ICA
Duke of York Column
Waterloo Gdns.
RAC
Marlborough House (Commonwealth Conference Centre)
King George VI Memorial
Queen's Chapel
St. James's Palace
Clarence Ho.
Stable Yard Gate
Cleopatra's Needle
Savoy Pier
Embankment Pier
Hungerford Bridge
Festival
Bandstand
New Players
Playhouse
Northumberland Ho.
Police Sta.
Government Offices
Trafalgar Studios
Old Admiralty Offices
Horse Guards
Horse Guards Parade
Guards Mem.
Old War Office
Banqueting House
Wales Office
Scotland Office
Min. of Defence
Victoria Embankment Gardens
Hispaniola
PS Tattershall Castle
The Golden Jubilee Bridges
RAF Memorial
Whitehall Stairs
Waterloo Millennium Pier
London Eye
Dali Universe
London Aquarium
Refreshments
Duck Island
Lake
Bandstand
CLOSED SUNDAY
Foreign and Commonwealth Office
Cenotaph
Former New Scotland Yard
Clive Steps
HM Treasury
Churchill Mus. with the Cabinet War Rooms
Northern Ireland Office
Westminster Millennium Pier
Portcullis Ho.
Diana, Princess of Wales Mem. Walk
Play Ground
Queen Anne's Gate
Queen Elizabeth II Conference Cen.
Middlesex Guildhall
Big Ben
New Palace Yard
Westminster Hall
Houses of Parliament
Guards' Chapel
Guards' Mus.
Wellington Barracks
Caxton Ho. (Dept. of Education & Skills)
Methodist Central Hall
St. Margaret's Ch.
Westminster Abbey
The Cloisters
Poets' Corner
Westminster Abbey Choir Sch.
Westminster Abbey Mus.
Jewel Tower
Abbey Garden
Westminster Sch.
Black Rod Garden
Victoria Tower Gardens
Caxton Hall
New Scotland Yard
Dept. of Trade & Industry
Dept. for Educ. & Skills
Westminster Chapel
Westminster Kingsway College
Westminster City Sch.
Westminster City Hall
Lib.
Ashdown Ho. (Dept. for Transport)
St. Matthew's Prim. Sch.
St. Matthew's Ch.
Fire Sta.
Home Office
Emmanuel Cen. Ch.
Chapel
St. John's Concert Hall
Dept. for Enviroment
The Grey Coat Hosp. Sch.
Channel 4 TV
TA Cen.
RHS Lawrence Hall & Conf. Cen.
RHS Lindley Hall
Westminster Coll.
Prim. Sch.
St. Stephen's Ch.
Magistrates Court
Ryl. Coll. of Vet. Surgeons
Coroner's Ct.
Dept. for Transport
St. John's Gdns.
Northern Ireland Office (Thames House)
Health Cen.
St. Thomas' Hospital
King's College London
King's College London (St. Thomas' Campus)
Lambeth Palace
Mus. of Garden History
Lambeth Pier
Parliament View
A302
A3203
A3212
A3211
A400
A4
B308
B323
B324
B326
WESTMINSTER BRIDGE
LAMBETH BRIDGE
WHITEHALL
PARLIAMENT ST.
MILLBANK
VICTORIA EMBANKMENT
NORTHUMBERLAND AV.
THE MALL
PALL MALL
HORSE GUARDS ROAD
BIRDCAGE WALK
VICTORIA STREET
BROAD SANCTUARY
GREAT GEORGE ST.
GREAT SMITH ST.
MARSHAM STREET
HORSEFERRY RD.
STRAND
LAMBETH PALACE ROAD
COCKSPUR ST.
REGENT STREET
HAYMARKET
CHARING CROSS RD.
ST. MARTIN'S PL.

80
A
B
C
D
E
1
2
3
4
5
6
7
70
90
TEMPLE
BLACKFRIARS
EMBANKMENT
WATERLOO
WATERLOO EAST
SOUTHWARK
LAMBETH NORTH
R I V E R
Courtauld Galleries
Somerset House
King's Coll. (Strand Campus)
Hermitage Rooms
Gilbert Collection
Victoria Embankment Gardens
Inner Temple Garden
Middle Temple Gdn.
HMS President
Blackfriars Millennium Pier
HQS Wellington
St. Katharine
Temple Pier
Lifeboat Station
Queen Mary
Savoy Pier
Cleopatra's Needle
Stamford Wharf
OXO TOWER WHARF
Gabriels Wharf
Bernie Spain Gardens
The London Television Centre
MULBERRY HOUSING CO-OPERATIVE
The London Nautical Sch.
Christ Church
The National Film Theatre
National Theatre
Purcell Room
Queen Elizabeth Hall
Royal Festival Hall
Hayward Gallery
King's College London (Waterloo Campus)
Schiller Univ.
King's College London
The Warehouse
PEABODY ESTATE
Sports & Comm. Cen.
Festival Pier
Embankment Pier
Hungerford Bridge
Hispaniola
PS Tattershall Castle
The Golden Jubilee Bridges
IMAX
RAF Memorial
Waterloo Millennium Pier
London Eye
Jubilee Gardens
Dali Universe
London Aquarium
County Hall (Former)
Westminster Millennium Pier
The Young Vic
Southwark Coll. (Waterloo Cen.)
St. Andrews Ch.
The Old Vic
Rec. Grnd.
Baylis Rd. Open Space
Johanna Prim. Sch.
Teacher Training Cen.
WESTMINSTER BRIDGE RD.
Florence Nightingale Mus.
St. Thomas' Hospital
Evelina Children's Hosp.
King's College London
Houses of Parliament
Kagyu Samye Dzong London
Christ Ch. & Upton Chapel
Morley College
Morley Coll. The Abbey Churchill London
St. George's RC Cathedral
Notre Dame School
St. Judes C of E Prim. Sch.
ARCHBISHOP'S PARK
L A M B E T H
King's College London (St. Thomas' Campus)
Marine Institute
Imperial War Museum
Charlotte Sharman Foundation Prim. Sch.
Geraldine Mary Harmsworth Park
Paddling Pool
West Sq. Gdn.
Lambeth Palace
Mus. of Garden History
St. Thomas' Youth Cen.
Lambeth Pier
LAMBETH BRIDGE
Police Support Headquarters
Walnut Tree Walk Prim. Sch.
Police Sta.

81
THAMES
Millennium Bridge
Bankside Pier
Bankside Art Gallery
Shakespeare's Globe & Exhibition
Tate Modern
CANNON ST.
EC4
Fishmongers Hall
St. Magnus the Martyr's Ch.
Swan La. Pier
Regalia
Upper Pool
London Bridge City Pier
The Monument
St. Mary at Hill Ch.
St. Dunstans (Ruin)
Custom
Golden Hinde
Glaziers Hall
Clink Exhibition
Vinopolis
Southwark Cath.
Borough Market
LONDON BRIDGE
London Dungeon
Operating Theatre Mus.
Chapel
Guy's Hospital
Guy's Hosp. Extension
Guy's Nuffield Ho.
Bramah Tea & Coffee Mus.
Menier Chocolate Factory
Precious Blood Ch.
Southwark Playhouse
Jerwood Space Art Gallery
Knightsbridge Crown Court
London Fire Brigade Museum
Cathedral Sch. of St. Saviours & St. Mary Overie
St. Joseph's RC Prim. Sch.
Lit. Dorrit Park
St. George The Martyr Ch.
BOROUGH
Charles Dickens Prim. Sch.
St. George's Gdns
Nelson Rec. Grd.
Snowsfields Prim. Sch.
Leathermarket Gdns.
Community Park
City Banking Ch.
Greenwood
The Glass Art Gall.
St. Hugh's Ch.
Beormund Sch.
Tabard Gardens
TABARD GARDEN ESTATE
Police Sta.
Southwark County Ct.
The Henry Wood Hall
Inner London Sessions House
Newington Gardens
Mosque
Dickens Sq. Park
Deeper Life Bible Ch.
London South Bank University
London South Bank Univ. Technopark
Perry Lib.
Pilgrim Fathers Memorial Ch.
Geoffrey Chaucer Technology College
Joseph Lancaster Prim. Sch.
St. Saviour's & St. Olave's School
Brotherhood of the Cross & Star Church
St. Matthews Ch.
Comm. Cen.
ELEPHANT & CASTLE
London College of Communication
Metropolitan Tabernacle
Shopping Centre
Palace Bingo Superbowl
Fusion Health & Leis. Cen.
Crossway Ch.
Victory Comm. Park
BRICKLAYER'S ARMS
THE BOROUGH
NEWINGTON
SOUTHWARK
A3200
B300
A3201
A3202
A300
A3
A2
A2198
A200
A201
B240

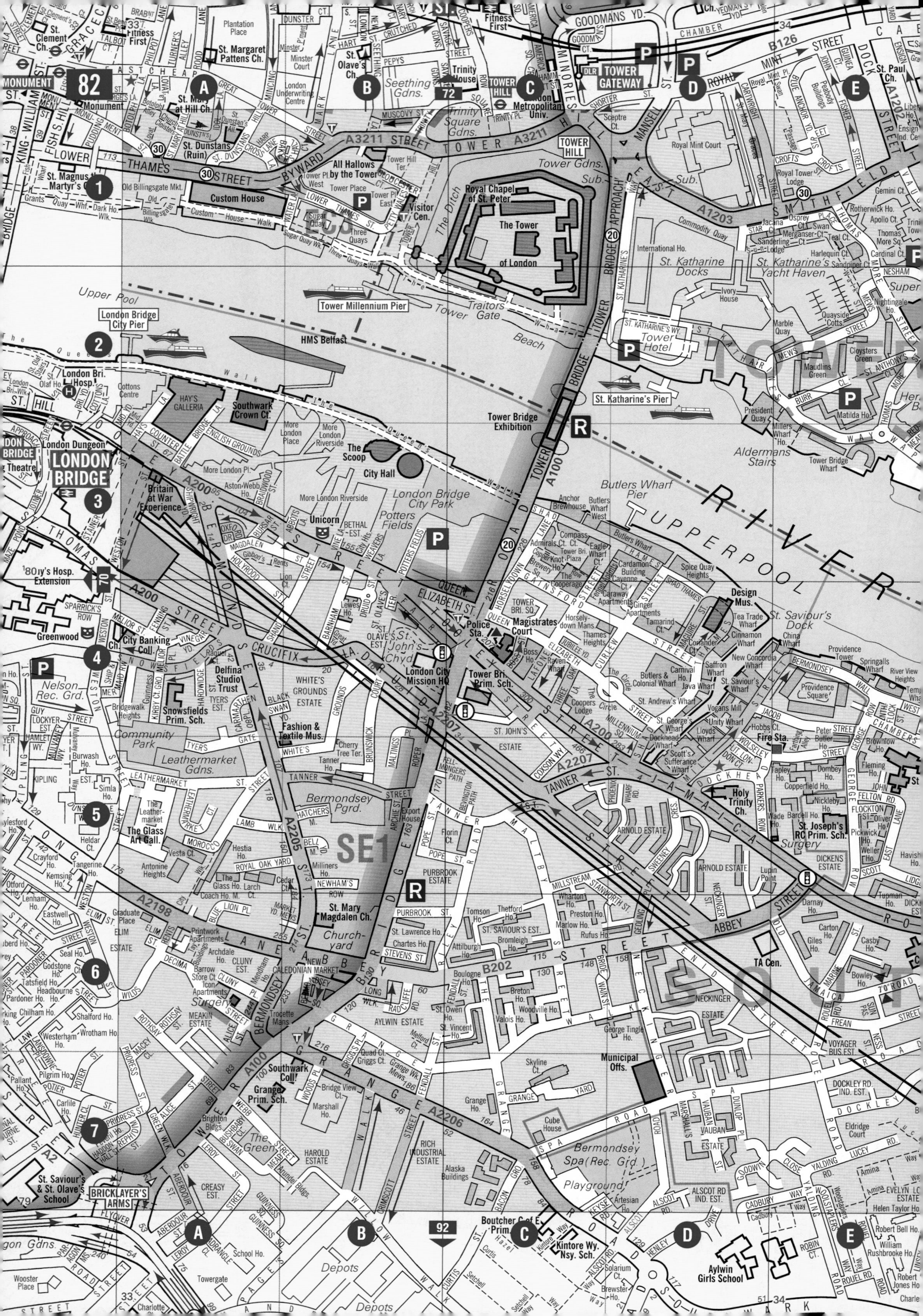

82
MONUMENT
Monument
St. Clement Ch.
Fitness First
St. Margaret Pattens Ch.
EASTCHEAP
St. Mary at Hill Ch.
St. Dunstans (Ruin)
St. Olave's Ch.
Seething Gdns.
Trinity House
72
TOWER HILL
London Metropolitan Univ.
MINORIES
GOODMANS YD.
TOWER GATEWAY
ROYAL MINT STREET
St. Paul Ch.
Royal Mint Court
LOWER THAMES STREET
St. Magnus the Martyr's Ch.
Old Billingsgate Mkt.
Custom House
All Hallows by the Tower
Tower Place
Visitor Cen.
The Ditch
Royal Chapel of St. Peter
The Tower of London
Tower Gdns.
TOWER HILL
BYWARD
A3211
TOWER BRIDGE APPROACH
EAST SMITHFIELD
A1203
Commodity Quay
International Ho.
St. Katharine Docks
St. Katharine's Yacht Haven
Ivory House
Tower Hotel
Upper Pool
Tower Millennium Pier
Traitors Gate
Tower Beach
London Bridge City Pier
HMS Belfast
St. Katharine's Pier
Tower Bridge Exhibition
Aldermans Stairs
Tower Bridge Wharf
London Bri. Hosp.
Hay's Galleria
Southwark Crown Ct.
More London Place
More London Riverside
The Scoop
City Hall
London Bridge City Park
Potters Fields
Butlers Wharf Pier
RIVER
UPPER POOL
TOWER BRIDGE ROAD
A100
London Dungeon
LONDON BRIDGE
Theatre
Britain at War Experience
TOOLEY STREET
A200
Unicorn
Guy's Hosp. Extension
Greenwood
City Banking Coll.
CRUCIFIX LANE
Delfina Studio Trust
Snowsfields Prim. Sch.
White's Grounds Estate
St. John's Chyd.
London City Mission HQ
Police Sta.
Magistrates Court
Tower Bri. Prim. Sch.
Design Mus.
St. Saviour's Dock
SHAD THAMES
Butlers Wharf
Cinnamon Wharf
China Wharf
Providence Square
Fire Sta.
JAMAICA ROAD
A2207
Holy Trinity Ch.
St. Joseph's RC Prim. Sch.
Dickens Estate
Nelson Rec. Grd.
Community Park
Leathermarket Gdns.
Fashion & Textile Mus.
Bermondsey Pgrd.
SE1
The Leathermarket
The Glass Art Gall.
Tanner Ho.
St. Mary Magdalen Ch.
Churchyard
Purbrook Estate
Arnold Estate
BERMONDSEY STREET
A2205
ABBEY STREET
B202
Neckinger Estate
TA Cen.
SOUTH
Voyager Bus. Est.
Municipal Offs.
Long Lane
A2198
Caledonian Market
Southwark Coll.
Grange Prim. Sch.
Harold Estate
The Green
Rich Industrial Estate
Alaska Buildings
GRANGE ROAD
A2206
Bermondsey Spa (Rec. Grd.)
Playground
SPA ROAD
Alscot Rd Ind. Est.
Dockley Rd. Ind. Est.
St. Saviour's & St. Olave's School
BRICKLAYER'S ARMS
FLYOVER
Creasy Est.
Kintore Wy. Nsy. Sch.
Aylwin Girls School
Depots
92
A B C D E
1 2 3 4 5 6 7

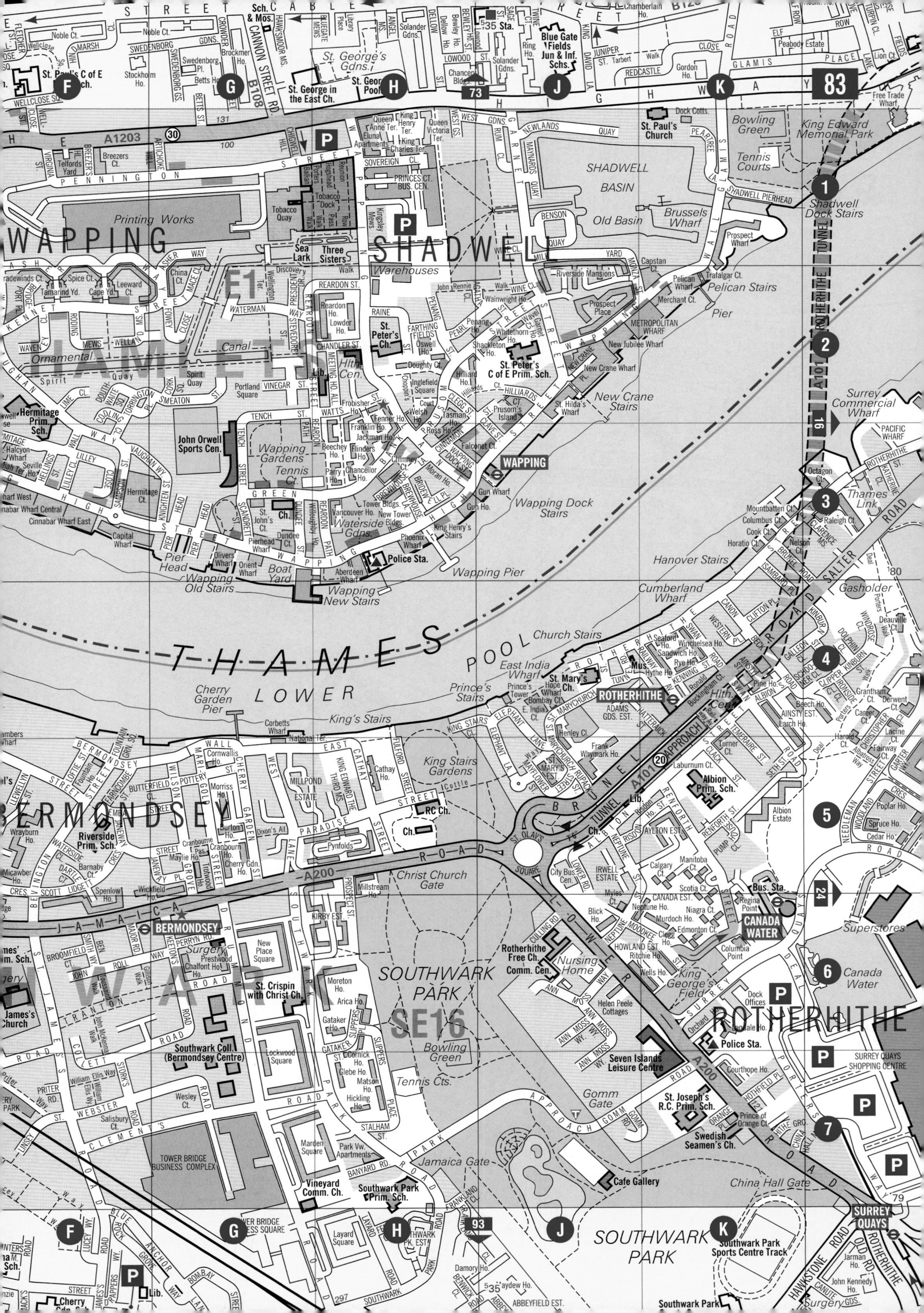

83
WAPPING
SHADWELL
E1
HAMLETS
THAMES
LOWER
POOL
BERMONDSEY
SOUTHWARK
SOUTHWARK PARK
SE16
ROTHERHITHE
A1203
A101
A200
B108
CANNON STREET RD.
CABLE STREET
HIGHWAY
PENNINGTON STREET
WAPPING LANE
WAPPING HIGH STREET
WAPPING WALL
GLAMIS RD.
SHADWELL BASIN
Old Basin
Brussels Wharf
Shadwell Pierhead
Shadwell Dock Stairs
King Edward Memorial Park
Bowling Green
Tennis Courts
St. Paul's Church
Printing Works
Tobacco Dock
Tobacco Quay
Sea Lark
Three Sisters
Warehouses
Ornamental Canal
Spirit Quay
Portland Square
John Orwell Sports Cen.
Wapping Gardens
Tennis Ct.
St. Peter's Ch.
St. Peter's C of E Prim. Sch.
Hermitage Prim. Sch.
Police Sta.
WAPPING
Wapping Dock Stairs
Wapping Pier
Wapping Old Stairs
Wapping New Stairs
Pier Head
Boat Yard
Waterside Gdns.
New Crane Stairs
Pelican Stairs
Surrey Commercial Wharf
Pacific Wharf
Thames Link
Hanover Stairs
Cumberland Wharf
Church Stairs
East India Wharf
Prince's Stairs
King's Stairs
Cherry Garden Pier
King Stairs Gardens
St. Mary's Ch.
ROTHERHITHE
Albion Prim. Sch.
Albion Estate
SALTER ROAD
BRUNEL ROAD
ROTHERHITHE TUNNEL
Gasholder
St. Olav's Square
Christ Church Gate
Riverside Prim. Sch.
BERMONDSEY
JAMAICA ROAD
LOWER ROAD
Canada Water
CANADA WATER
Bus. Sta.
Superstores
Rotherhithe Free Ch. Comm. Cen.
Nursing Home
King George's Field
St. Crispin with Christ Ch.
Southwark Coll (Bermondsey Centre)
Bowling Green
Tennis Cts.
Seven Islands Leisure Centre
St. Joseph's R.C. Prim. Sch.
Swedish Seamen's Ch.
Gomm Gate
Jamaica Gate
China Hall Gate
Cafe Gallery
SURREY QUAYS SHOPPING CENTRE
SURREY QUAYS
TOWER BRIDGE BUSINESS COMPLEX
Vineyard Comm. Ch.
Southwark Park Prim. Sch.
Southwark Park Sports Centre Track
F
G
H
J
K
1
2
3
4
5
6
7
16
24
73
93

84
BROOK GREEN
HAMMERSMITH
W6
SW13
CASTELNAU
RICHMOND UPON THAMES
HAMMERSMITH and FULHAM
RIVER THAMES
LONDON WETLAND CENTRE
FULHAM CEMETERY
Hammersmith Cemetery
Recreation Ground
Park
Playing Field
Games Ct.
Tennis Cts.
Pumping Station
HAMMERSMITH IND. EST.
The Godolphin & Latymer Sch.
Cambridge Sch.
St. John's Ch.
Fire Station
Police Sta.
Fitness First Health Club
Lib.
Bute Ho. Prep. Sch.
Surgery
St. Paul's Girls School
Holy Trinity RC Ch.
Chinese Church
Larmenier & Sacred Cath. Prim. Sch.
St. Joseph's House
St. Joseph's Almshouses
Kensington Centre
St. Mary's Church
James Lee Nursery Sch.
Sacred Heart High Sch.
Cadet Cen.
Convent
Health Club
Squash Cen.
Hotel
HAMMERSMITH BROADWAY
HAMMERSMITH
THE BROADWAY CEN.
Bus Station
St. Paul's Church
HAMMERSMITH FLYOVER
KINGS MALL
Lyric
Ealing, Hammersmith & West London College (Barons Ct. Site)
Energize Fitness Club
BARONS COURT
LAMDA
The Ark
West London Magistrates Ct.
London Apollo
St. Augustine's R.C. Church
St. Paul's C of E Prim. Sch.
The Hungarian Reformed Ch.
William Morris Academy
Clinic
Mortuary Chapel
Riverside Studios
Charing Cross Hospital
Chapel
Charing Cross Sports Club
Melcombe Prim. Sch.
William Morris House
St. Alban's Church
Comm. Cen.
Tasso Baptist Ch.
Bayonne Nursery Sch.
Play-ground
Fitness Centre
Twynholm Baptist Ch.
Fulham Cross Secondary School
St. Clement's Ch.
Queen's Manor Sch. & Special Needs Unit
GLENTHORNE ROAD A315
KING STREET A315
HAMMERSMITH ROAD
TALGARTH ROAD A4
GREAT WEST ROAD A4
SHEPHERD'S BUSH ROAD A219
FULHAM PALACE ROAD A219
LILLIE ROAD A3218
HAMMERSMITH BRIDGE
CASTELNAU A306
MARGRAVINE GARDENS
GREYHOUND ROAD
MUNSTER ROAD
23
24
74

85
KENSINGTON OLYMPIA
Olympia
WEST KENSINGTON
EARLS COURT
W8
W14
SW5
SW6
Charles House
Superstore
WARWICK GARDENS Restricted Access between 9pm & 6am
LAMDA
West London County Court
Avonmore Prim. Sch.
St. James Sch.
Shaftesbury Place Superstore
EARL'S COURT
London Electronics College
Earls Court Exhibition Building
Earls Court 2
Empress State Building
Piazza Buildings
WEST BROMPTON
Gibbs Green School
Inst. of Indian Culture
St. Cuthbert's Ch.
Normand Croft Sch.
Fulham Pools
NORMAND PARK
St. Augustine's RC Prim. Sch.
Sir John Lillie Prim. Sch.
St. Thomas's RC Ch.
St. Thomas RC Prim. Sch.
Baptist Church
Fulham Prim. Sch.
FARM LANE TRADING ESTATE
Methodist Ch.
Mecca Bingo
St. John's Ch.
Vue Cinema
FULHAM BROADWAY
FULHAM BROADWAY (SHOP. CEN.)
Town Hall
London Oratory School
Brompton Park
The Sir Oswald Stoll Foundation
Sir Oswald Stoll Mansions
Coptic Orthodox Church
St. Philip's Ch.
A4 WEST CROMWELL ROAD
CROMWELL ROAD
WARWICK ROAD
NORTH END ROAD
LILLIE ROAD
FULHAM ROAD
OLD BROMPTON ROAD
A3220
A3218
A3219
A304
B317
B318
75
23

86
SOUTH KENSINGTON
KENSINGTON
WEST BROMPTON
BROMPTON CEMETERY
SW5
SW6
SW7
SW10
W6
CROMWELL ROAD
GLOUCESTER ROAD
EARL'S COURT
WEST BROMPTON
FULHAM BROADWAY
OLD BROMPTON ROAD
FULHAM ROAD
KING'S ROAD
REDCLIFFE GARDENS
EDITH GROVE
THE BOLTONS
Natural History Museum
Science Mu
Lycee Francais Charles de Gaulle
Institute of Cancer Research
Chelsea & Westminster Hospital
Chelsea FC (Stamford Bridge)
The Cromwell Hosp.
Brompton Park
Chapel
St. Mary the Boltons Ch.
St. Luke's Ch.
London Oratory School
Cremorne Gardens
Cremorne Wharf
Westfield Park
Coptic Orthodox Church
David Lloyd Leisure
Point West
Gloucester Arcade
A4
A308
A3218
A3220
A304
A3217
B325
B318
76
77
23
A
B
C
D
E
1
2
3
4
5
6
7

Victoria & Albert Museum
Brompton Oratory
St. Columba's Ch.
Hellenic Coll. of London
Walton Ho.
Pembroke Ho.
F
G
H
J
K
77
CROMWELL GDNS.
CROMWELL ROAD
Ismaili Cen.
THURLOE PLACE
THURLOE SQUARE
ALEXANDER PLACE
THURLOE ST.
BROMPTON ROAD
EGERTON CRESCENT
EGERTON GARDENS
SOUTH KENSINGTON
PELHAM STREET
ONSLOW SQUARE
PELHAM CRESCENT
SYDNEY STREET
SLOANE AVENUE
DRAYCOTT AVENUE
CADOGAN SQUARE
CADOGAN GARDENS
CADOGAN GATE
SLOANE STREET
SLOANE SQ.
LOWER SLOANE STREET
SLOANE GARDENS
HOLBEIN MEWS
Cadogan Hall
Holy Trinity Ch.
Royal Ct.
Sloane Sch.
Saatchi Gallery
Sussex Ho.Sch.
St. Simon Zelotes Ch.
St. Mary's Ch.
St. Thomas More & St. Joseph Schs.
Marlborough Prim. Sch.
The Kensington & Chelsea Coll. (Marlborough Cen.)
Chelsea Cloisters
Police Sta.
CRANMER COURT
THE SUTTON ESTATE
Oratory RC Prim. Sch.
St. Luke's Ch.
The Royal Marsden Hosp. (Fulham)
Imperial College London
Royal Brompton Hospital
FULHAM ROAD
KINGS ROAD
BRITTEN STREET
ELYSTAN STREET
MARKHAM SQUARE
SMITH STREET
WELLINGTON SQUARE
ROYAL AVENUE
ST. LEONARD'S TERRACE
KINGS WALK SHOP. CEN.
Burton's Court
ROYAL HOSPITAL ROAD
Royal Hospital Chelsea
Great Hall
Chap.
FIGURE CT.
COLLEGE CT.
INFIRMARY CT.
National Army Mus.
Convent
Royal Hospital Chelsea
Chelsea Physic Garden
CHELSEA
SW1
SW3
SW11
Chelsea Coll. of Art & Design
Fire Sta.
Dovehouse Grn.
Old Town Hall
Lib.
Registry Off.
Chelsea Sports Cen.
Meth. Ch.
Welsh United Reformed Chapel
Chelsea Affiliated Synagogue
Hosp.
Clinic
CHEYNE WALK
CHELSEA EMBANKMENT
Christ Ch. C of E Prim. Sch.
Christ Ch.
Carlyle's Ho.
R.C. Ch.
Chelsea Old Church
Chelsea Open Air Nursery Sch.
Cineworld
Cameron Ho. Sch.
Cadogan Pier
RIVER THAMES
Chelsea Reach
ALBERT BRIDGE
BATTERSEA BRIDGE
A3220
A3212
A3031
B302
B304
A308
A3216
A3217
Nipponzan Myohoji Peace Pagoda
Battersea Park Children's Zoo
Tennis Courts
WANDSWORTH
BATTERSEA PARK
CARRIAGE DRIVE
CENTRAL AVENUE
Albion Riverside Building
Waterside Point
Riverside
Thames Walk
Ransome's Dock
RANSOME'S DOCK BUS. CEN.
St. Mary-le-Park Ch.
Police Sta.
Royal Coll. of Art
Gov. Offs.
Bowling Green
Pav.
23
88
1
2
3
4
5
6
7

88
BELGRAVIA
VICTORIA
SW1
SW3
SW11
WESTMINSTER
WANDSWORTH
RIVER
BATTERSEA PARK
Instituto Cervantes
St. Peter's Prim. Sch.
Bus Sta.
Apollo Victoria
Victoria Place Shop. Cen.
St. Michael's Ch.
Inchbald Sch.
Cadogan Hall
Holy Trinity Ch.
Sloane Ter. Mans.
Prim. Sch.
Royal Ct.
SLOANE SQ.
Victoria Coach Sta. (Arrivals)
Victoria Coach Sta. (Departures)
Chester Ho.
Liby.
Fountain Square
Coach Station
Passport Office
The Queen Mother Sports Cen.
Civil Service Coll.
National Audit Office
The Buddhist Society UK
Inchbald Sch. of Design
St. Mary's Ch.
Francis Holland C of E Sch.
Carmel Hall
Police Sta.
Saatchi Gallery
St. Barnabas C of E Prim. Sch.
Church of St. Barnabas
St. Gabriel's Ch.
Church of the Holy Apostles
Royal Hospital Chelsea
Mus.
LIGHT HORSE COURT
Great Hall
Chap.
FIGURE CT.
COLLEGE CT.
INFIRMARY CT.
National Army Mus.
RANELAGH GARDENS
Chilianwallan Memorial
Grosvenor Canal
Inner Basin
Lock
Carriage Shed
The Lister Hospital
St. Gabriel's C of E Prim. Sch.
CHELSEA EMBANKMENT
GROSVENOR ROAD
CHELSEA BRIDGE
Grosvenor Bridge
Chelsea Bridge Wharf
Pier
Refuse Transfer Station
Battersea Power Station (Disused)
Nipponzan Myohoji Peace Pagoda
Battersea Park Children's Zoo
British Genius Site
Tennis Courts
Millennium Arena
Rec. Grd.
Duck Pond
Boating Lake
The Pump Ho. Gall.
Ladies Pond
Bowling Green
Police Sta.
Gas Holder Station
Battersea Dogs' Home
Marco Polo House
QUEENSTOWN ROAD
CARRIAGE DRIVE
CENTRAL AVENUE
BATTERSEA PARK ROAD
A3216
A3212
A3214
A3217
A3123
A202
A3205
B302
B313
78
87
23

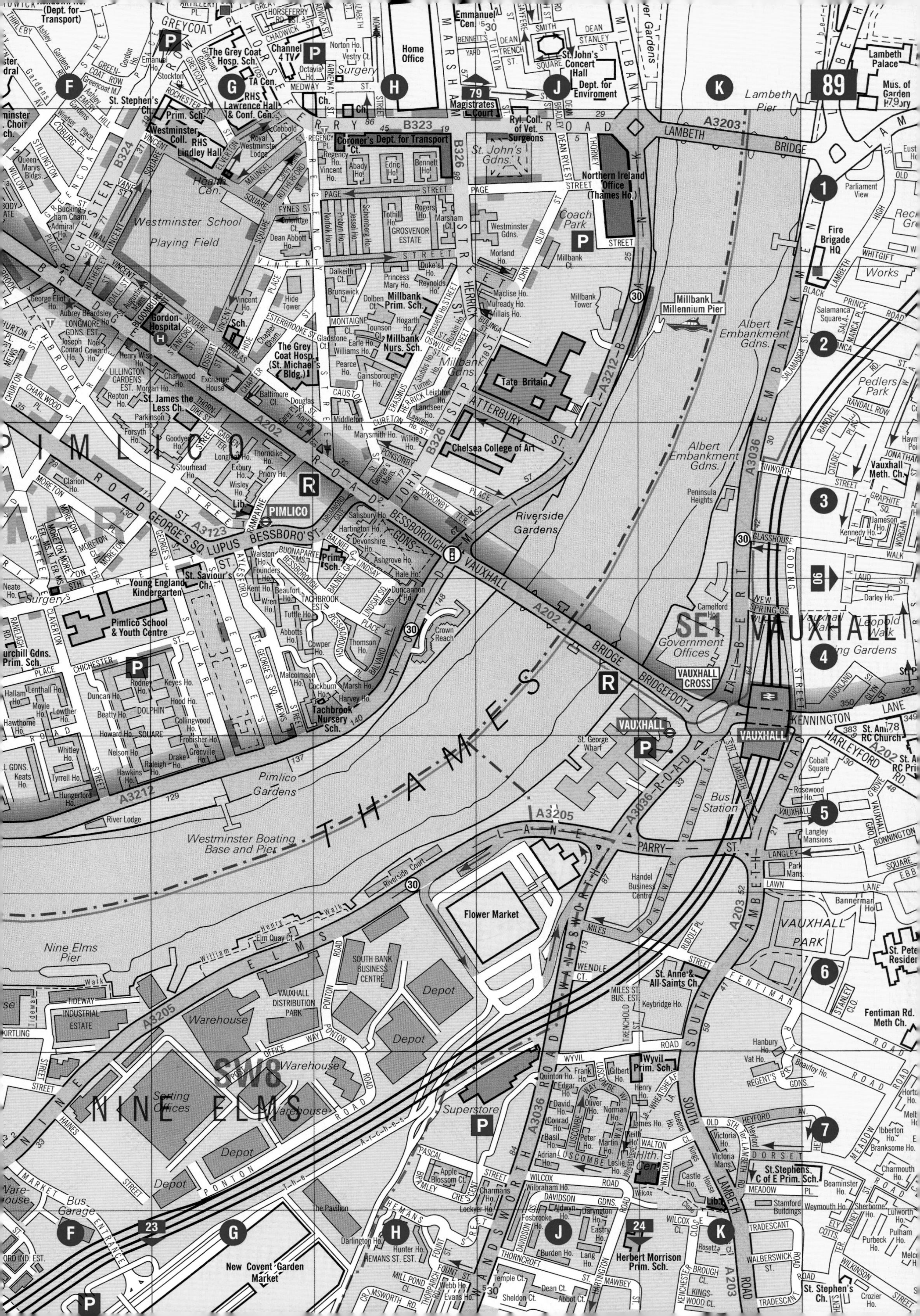

89
Home Office
Channel 4 TV
The Grey Coat Hosp. Sch.
TA Cen.
RHS Lawrence Hall & Conf. Cen.
RHS Lindley Hall
Westminster Coll.
St. John's Concert Hall
Dept. for Enviroment
Magistrates Court
Ryl. Coll. of Vet. Surgeons
Coroner's Ct.
Dept. for Transport
Lambeth Palace
Mus. of Garden History
Lambeth Pier
LAMBETH BRIDGE
A3203
B323
B324
B326
Northern Ireland Office (Thames Ho.)
Westminster School Playing Field
Heath Cen.
GROSVENOR ESTATE
Coach Park
Fire Brigade HQ
Works
Parliament View
Millbank Millennium Pier
Millbank Tower
Albert Embankment Gdns.
Tate Britain
Chelsea College of Art
Millbank Prim. Sch.
Millbank Nurs. Sch.
The Grey Coat Hosp. (St. Michael's Bldg.)
Gordon Hospital
St. James the Less Ch.
LILLINGTON GARDENS EST.
LONGMORE GDNS. EST.
Pedlers Park
Vauxhall Meth. Ch.
PIMLICO
A202
A3123
A3212
A3036
A3205
A203
Riverside Gardens
Peninsula Heights
Crown Reach
Young England Kindergarten
Pimlico School & Youth Centre
Tachbrook Nursery Sch.
SE1 VAUXHALL
Government Offices
VAUXHALL CROSS
VAUXHALL
St. George Wharf
Bus Station
THAMES
Pimlico Gardens
River Lodge
Westminster Boating Base and Pier
Nine Elms Pier
Flower Market
Handel Business Centre
SOUTH BANK BUSINESS CENTRE
VAUXHALL DISTRIBUTION PARK
TIDEWAY INDUSTRIAL ESTATE
Warehouse
Depot
Sorting Offices
SW8
NINE ELMS
Superstore
St. Anne's & All Saints Ch.
Wyvil Prim. Sch.
Hlth. Cen.
Herbert Morrison Prim. Sch.
New Covent Garden Market
Bus Garage
VAUXHALL PARK
St. Stephens C of E Prim. Sch.
Fentiman Rd. Meth Ch.
St. Peter's Residences
KENNINGTON LANE
HARLEYFORD RD.
SOUTH LAMBETH ROAD
WANDSWORTH ROAD
NINE ELMS LANE
PARRY ST.
VAUXHALL BRIDGE
BESSBOROUGH GDNS.
GROSVENOR ROAD
ALBERT EMBANKMENT
MILLBANK
23
24
79
90

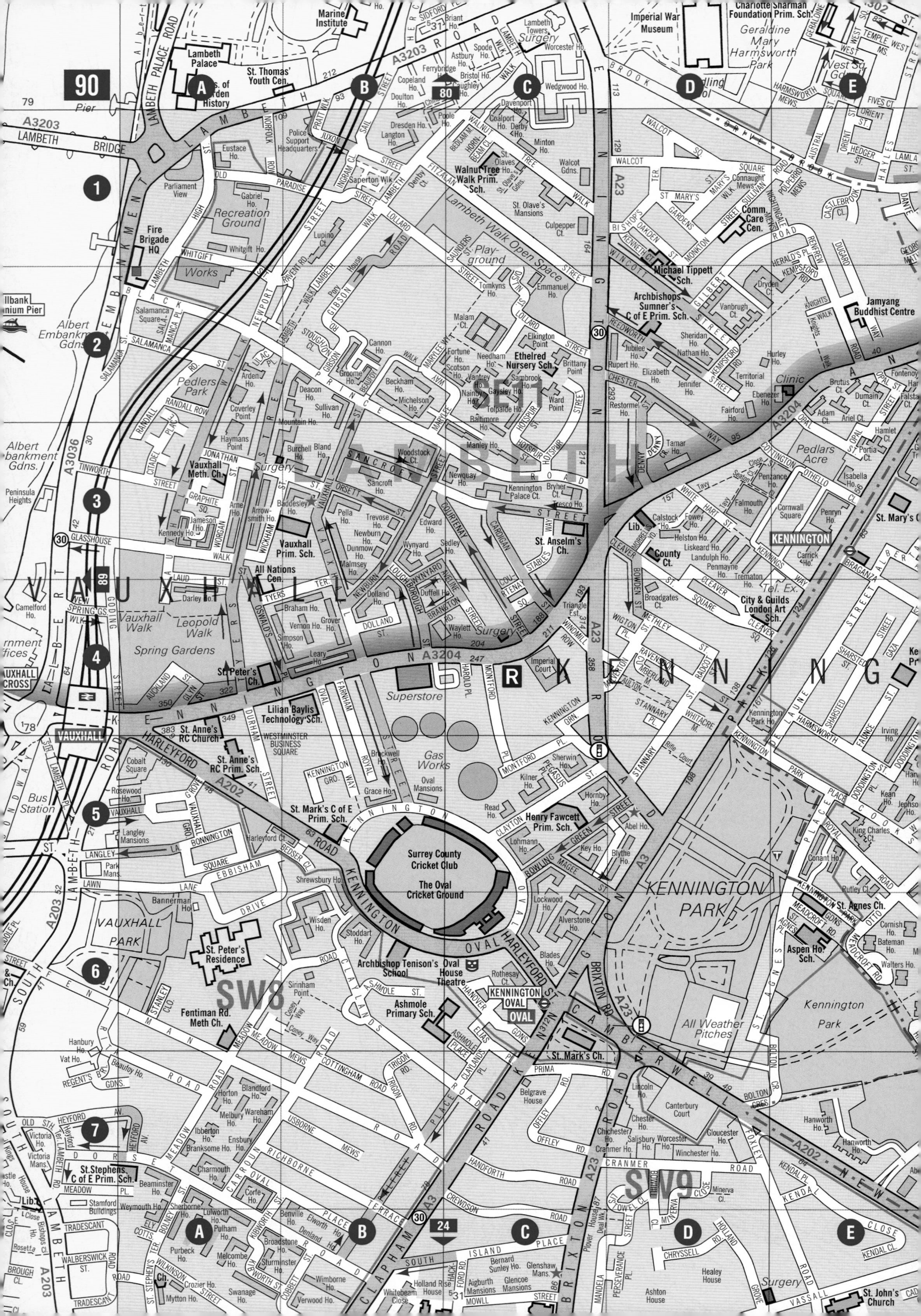

90
A
B
C
D
E
1
2
3
4
5
6
7
Lambeth Palace
Mus. of Garden History
St. Thomas' Youth Cen.
Marine Institute
Imperial War Museum
Charlotte Sharman Foundation Prim. Sch.
Geraldine Mary Harmsworth Park
80
A3203
LAMBETH BRIDGE
LAMBETH PALACE ROAD
LAMBETH ROAD
Pier
Police Support Headquarters
Parliament View
Recreation Ground
Fire Brigade HQ
Works
Lambeth Walk Open Space
Playground
Walnut Tree Walk Prim. Sch.
Lambeth Towers
Surgery
Wedgwood Ho.
Walcot Gdns.
Culpepper Ct.
St. Olave's Mansions
St. Mary's Gardens
Comm. Care Cen.
Michael Tippett Sch.
Archbishops Sumner's C of E Prim. Sch.
Jamyang Buddhist Centre
Albert Embankment Gdns.
Salamanca Square
Pedlers Park
Vauxhall Meth. Ch.
Vauxhall Prim. Sch.
All Nations Cen.
SE11
LAMBETH
Ethelred Nursery Sch.
St. Anselm's Ch.
Clinic
Pedlars Acre
KENNINGTON
County Ct.
Lib.
City & Guilds London Art Sch.
Tel. Ex.
St. Mary's Ch.
A3204
A23
A3036
Peninsula Heights
VAUXHALL
Vauxhall Walk
Leopold Walk
Spring Gardens
St. Peter's Ch.
KENNINGTON LANE
Imperial Court
Superstore
Lilian Baylis Technology Sch.
St. Anne's RC Church
St. Anne's RC Prim. Sch.
Westminster Business Square
Gas Works
Oval Mansions
VAUXHALL CROSS
Bus Station
Cobalt Square
A202
HARLEYFORD ROAD
St. Mark's C of E Prim. Sch.
Surrey County Cricket Club
The Oval Cricket Ground
Henry Fawcett Prim. Sch.
KENNINGTON PARK
Kennington Park
St. Agnes Ch.
Aspen Ho. Sch.
VAUXHALL PARK
St. Peter's Residence
SW8
Archbishop Tenison's School
Oval House Theatre
Ashmole Primary Sch.
KENNINGTON OVAL
OVAL
Fentiman Rd. Meth Ch.
St. Mark's Ch.
All Weather Pitches
Canterbury Court
SW9
St. Stephens C of E Prim. Sch.
Stamford Buildings
Lib.
24
Surgery
St. John's Church
CAMBERWELL NEW ROAD
CLAPHAM ROAD
BRIXTON ROAD
A3
A203
SOUTH LAMBETH ROAD

91
NEWINGTON
WALWORTH
SOUTHWARK
SE1
SE17
SE5
ELEPHANT & CASTLE
Elephant & Castle Shopping Centre
Palace Bingo Superbowl
London College of Communication
Metropolitan Tabernacle
Fusion Health & Leis. Cen.
St. Mary's Churchyard
NEW KENT ROAD
A201
Bricklayer's Arms
Flyover
Technology College
Joseph Lancaster Prim. Sch.
Brotherhood of the Cross & Star Church
St. Matthews Ch.
London Sth. Bank Univ. (Halls of Residence)
Comm. Cen.
Crossway Ch.
Victory Comm. Park
Victory Prim. Sch.
Lady Margaret's Ch.
Townsend Prim. Sch.
Paragon Gdns.
Heygate
Municipal Offices
Lib.
St. John's Ch.
Cuming Museum
Clinic
St. John's Prim. Sch.
Nursery Row Park
English Martyrs Ch.
English Martyrs RC Prim. Sch.
St. Christopher's Ch.
Crampton Prim. Sch.
Newington Ind. Est.
Police Station
Surgery
Robert Browning Prim. Sch.
Walworth Sch.
Faraday Gdns.
St. Peter's C of E Prim. Sch.
St. Peter's Ch.
TA Cen.
Walworth Gdn. Farm
St. Paul's C of E Prim. Sch.
Surrey Sq. Inf. & Jun.
Michael Faraday Prim. Sch.
Pelier Park
St. Paul's Ch.
St. Wilfred's Ch.
John Ruskin Prim. Sch.
Clubland Meth. Hostel
Aylesbury Day Cen.
Burgess Park Kart Track
BURGESS PARK
ALBANY ROAD
B214
CAMBERWELL ROAD
A215
Chiltern Ho.
St. George's Prim. Sch.
Burgess Business Park
Blue Elephant
Camberwell Evangelical Ch.
St. Joseph's RC Inf. & Jun. Schs.
Archbishop Michael Ramsey Technology College
St. Michael & All Angels Ch.
Comber Hall
Comber Gro. Prim. Sch.
Brunswick Park Prim. Sch.
Ichthus Prim. Sch. & Ch.
Southwark Coll. (Camberwell Cen.)
Wyndham Estate
Elmington Estate
Bowyer Place
New Church Road
B217
Southampton Way

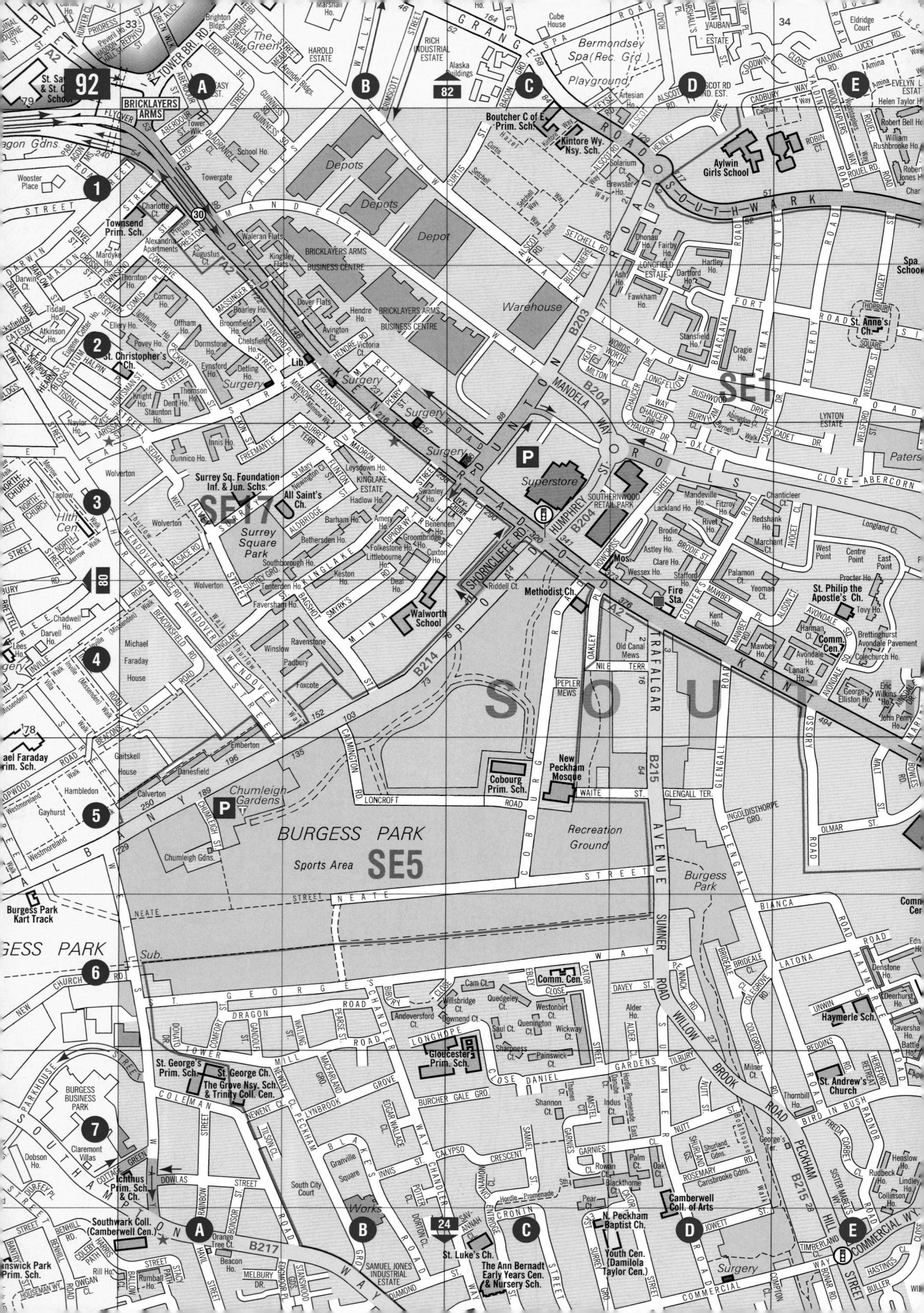

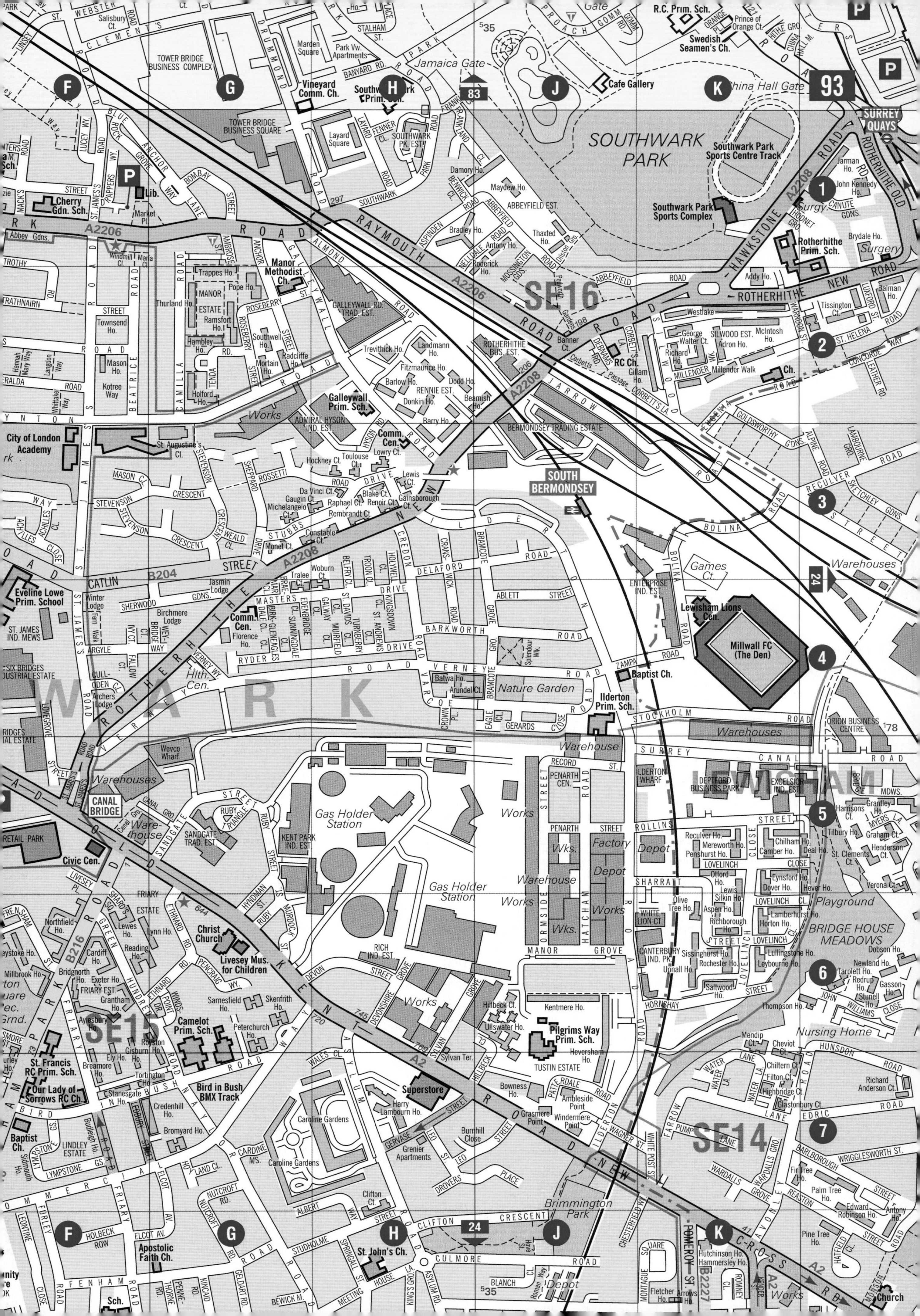
SOUTHWARK PARK
SE16
SE15
SE14
LEWISHAM
Millwall FC (The Den)
SOUTH BERMONDSEY
SURREY QUAYS
83
24
Gas Holder Station
BRIDGE HOUSE MEADOWS
Brimmington Park

INDEX

Including Streets, Places & Areas, Industrial Estates,
Selected Flats & Walkways, Junction Names and Selected Places of Interest.

HOW TO USE THIS INDEX

1. Each street name is followed by its Postcode District and then by its map reference; e.g. **Abbey Gdns.** NW8 . . . .5C **56** is in the NW8 Postcode District and is to be found in square 5C on page **56**. The page number being shown in bold type.
2. A strict alphabetical order is followed in which Av., Rd., St., etc. (though abbreviated) are read in full and as part of the street name; e.g. **Allsop Pl.** appears after **All Saints St.** but before **All Souls Av.**
3. Streets and a selection of flats and walkways too small to be shown on the maps, appear in the index with the thoroughfare to which it is connected shown in brackets; e.g. **Alluvium Ct.** *SE1 . . . .6A **82** (off Long La.)*
4. Addresses that are in more than one part are referred to as not continuous.
5. Places and areas are shown in the index in **BLUE TYPE** and the map reference is to the actual map square in which the town centre or area is located and not to the place name shown on the map; e.g. **BARNSBURY 1A 60**
6. An example of a selected place of interest is Alexander Fleming Laboratory Mus. 5F 67
7. Junction names are shown in the index in **BOLD CAPITAL TYPE**; e.g. **ALDGATE 6D 72**

GENERAL ABBREVIATIONS

All. : Alley
App. : Approach
Arc. : Arcade
Av. : Avenue
Bk. : Back
Bri. : Bridge
B'way. : Broadway
Bldg. : Building
Bldgs. : Buildings
Bus. : Business
C'way. : Causeway
Cen. : Centre
Chu. : Church
Chyd. : Churchyard
Circ. : Circle
Cir. : Circus
Cl. : Close
Coll. : College
Cnr. : Corner
Cotts. : Cottages
Ct. : Court
Cres. : Crescent
Cft. : Croft
Dr. : Drive
E. : East
Emb. : Embankment
Est. : Estate
Flds. : Fields
Gdn. : Garden
Gdns. : Gardens
Ga. : Gate
Gt. : Great
Grn. : Green
Gro. : Grove
Hgts. : Heights
Ho. : House
Ho's. : Houses
Ind. : Industrial
Info. : Information
Junc. : Junction
La. : Lane
Lit. : Little
Lwr. : Lower
Mnr. : Manor
Mans. : Mansions
Mkt. : Market
Mdws. : Meadows
M. : Mews
Mt. : Mount
Mus. : Museum
Nth. : North
Pal. : Palace
Pde. : Parade
Pk. : Park
Pas. : Passage
Pav. : Pavilion
Pl. : Place
Pct. : Precinct
Prom. : Promenade
Ri. : Rise
Rd. : Road
Rdbt. : Roundabout
Shop. : Shopping
Sth. : South
Sq. : Square
Sta. : Station
St. : Street
Ter. : Terrace
Twr. : Tower
Trad. : Trading
Up. : Upper
Va. : Vale
Vw. : View
Vs. : Villas
Vis. : Visitors
Wlk. : Walk
W. : West
Yd. : Yard

A

Abady Ho. SW1 . . . .1H **89**
Abbey Ct. NW8 . . . .4C **56**
SE17 . . . .4H **91**
Abbey Est. NW8 . . . .3B **56**
Abbeyfield Est. SE16 . . . .1J **93**
Abbeyfield Rd. SE16 . . . .1J **93**
(not continuous)
Abbey Gdns. NW8 . . . .5C **56**
SE16 . . . .1F **93**
W6 . . . .5E **84**
Abbey Ho. NW8 . . . .6D **56**
Abbey Lodge NW8 . . . .7H **57**
Abbey Orchard St.
SW1 . . . .6G **79**
Abbey Orchard St. Est.
SW1 . . . .6H **79**
(not continuous)
Abbey Rd. NW6 . . . .1A **56**
NW8 . . . .2B **56**
Abbey St. SE1 . . . .6B **82**
Abbot Ct. SW8 . . . .7J **89**
Abbotsbury NW1 . . . .1G **59**
Abbotsbury Cl. W14 . . . .5F **75**
Abbotsbury Ho. W14 . . . .4F **75**
Abbotsbury Rd. W14 . . . .4F **75**
Abbots Ct. W8 . . . .5B **76**
Abbot's Ho. W14 . . . .7G **75**
Abbots La. SE1 . . . .3B **82**
Abbots Mnr. SW1 . . . .3C **88**
Abbot's Pl. NW6 . . . .2A **56**
Abbots Wlk. W8 . . . .7A **76**
Abbotts Ho. SW1 . . . .4G **89**
Abchurch La. EC4 . . . .7K **71**
(not continuous)
Abchurch Yd. EC4 . . . .7J **71**
Abdale Rd. W12 . . . .2A **74**
Abel Ho. SE11 . . . .5D **90**
Abercorn Cl. NW8 . . . .5C **56**
Abercorn Cotts. NW8 . . . .6C **56**
Abercorn Mans. NW8 . . . .5D **56**
Abercorn Pl. NW8 . . . .6C **56**
Abercorn Wlk. NW8 . . . .6C **56**
Abercorn Way SE1 . . . .3E **92**
Aberdare Gdns. NW6 . . . .1B **56**
Aberdeen Ct. W9 . . . .1D **66**
Aberdeen Mans. WC1 . . . .1J **69**
Aberdeen Pl. NW8 . . . .2E **66**
Aberdeen Wharf E1 . . . .3H **83**
Aberdour St. SE1 . . . .7A **82**
Aberfeldy Ho. SE5 . . . .7E **90**
(not continuous)
Ability Towers EC1 . . . .6G **61**
Abingdon W14 . . . .2H **85**
Abingdon Cl. SE1 . . . .2D **92**
Abingdon Ct. W8 . . . .7K **75**
Abingdon Gdns. W8 . . . .7K **75**
Abingdon Ho. E2 . . . .1C **72**
Abingdon Lodge W8 . . . .7A **76**
Abingdon Mans. W8 . . . .6J **75**
Abingdon Rd. W8 . . . .6J **75**
Abingdon St. SW1 . . . .6J **79**
Abingdon Vs. W8 . . . .7J **75**
Abinger Ho. SE1 . . . .5J **81**
Abinger M. W9 . . . .1J **65**
Ablett St. SE16 . . . .4J **93**
Acacia Gdns. NW8 . . . .4F **57**
Acacia Pl. NW8 . . . .4F **57**
Acacia Rd. NW8 . . . .4F **57**
Academy Bldgs. N1 . . . .6A **62**
Academy Ct. E2 . . . .6K **63**
Academy Gdns. W8 . . . .4J **75**
Acanthus Dr. SE1 . . . .3F **93**
Achilles Cl. SE1 . . . .3F **93**
Achilles Ho. E2 . . . .5H **63**
Achilles Statue 3B **78**
Achilles Way W1 . . . .3B **78**
Acklam Rd. W10 . . . .4F **65**
(not continuous)
Acol Ct. NW6 . . . .1K **55**
Acol Rd. NW6 . . . .1K **55**
Acorn Production Cen.
N7 . . . .1J **59**
Acton Ho. E8 . . . .2C **62**
Acton M. E8 . . . .2C **62**
Acton St. WC1 . . . .7A **60**
Ada Ct. N1 . . . .3G **61**
W9 . . . .7D **56**
Ada Ho. E2 . . . .3F **63**
Adair Ho. SW3 . . . .6H **87**
Adair Rd. W10 . . . .2F **65**
Adair Twr. W10 . . . .2F **65**
Adam & Eve Ct. W1 . . . .5F **69**
Adam & Eve M. W8 . . . .6K **75**
Adam Ct. SE11 . . . .2E **90**
SW7 . . . .1D **86**
Adams Ct. EC2 . . . .5K **71**
Adams Gdns. Est.
SE16 . . . .4J **83**
Adam's Row W1 . . . .1B **78**
Adam St. WC2 . . . .1K **79**
Adam Wlk. SW6 . . . .7B **84**
Ada Pl. E2 . . . .3F **63**
Adastral Ho. WC1 . . . .3A **70**
Ada St. E8 . . . .3G **63**
Ada Workshops E8 . . . .3G **63**
Addington Sq. SE5 . . . .6J **91**
(not continuous)
Addington St. SE1 . . . .5B **80**
Addis Ho. E1 . . . .3J **73**
Addisland Ct. W14 . . . .4E **74**
Addison Av. W11 . . . .2E **74**
Addison Bri. Pl. W14 . . . .1G **85**
Addison Ct. NW6 . . . .3K **55**
Addison Cres. W14 . . . .6F **75**
(not continuous)
Addison Gdns. W14 . . . .6C **74**
Addison Ho. NW8 . . . .6E **56**
Addison Pk. Mans.
W14 . . . .6D **74**
Addison Pl. W11 . . . .3E **74**
Addison Rd. W14 . . . .4E **74**
Addle Hill EC4 . . . .6F **71**
Addlestone Ho. W10 . . . .3A **64**
Addle St. EC2 . . . .5H **71**
Addy Ho. SE16 . . . .2K **93**
Adela Ho. W6 . . . .3A **84**
Adelaide Ct. NW8 . . . .5D **56**
Adelaide Ho. W11 . . . .6G **65**
Adelaide Rd. NW3 . . . .1E **56**
Adelaide St. WC2 . . . .1J **79**
Adela St. W10 . . . .1E **64**
Adelina Gro. E1 . . . .3J **73**
Adelina Yd. E1 . . . .3J **73**
Adeline Pl. WC1 . . . .4H **69**
Adelphi Ct. E8 . . . .1D **62**
Adelphi Ter. WC2 . . . .1K **79**
Adelphi Theatre 1K **79**
Adeney Cl. W6 . . . .6D **84**
Adeyfield Ho. EC1 . . . .7K **61**
Adie Rd. W6 . . . .7A **74**
Adler St. E1 . . . .5E **72**
Admiral Ct. W1 . . . .4A **68**
Admiral Ho. SW1 . . . .1F **89**
Admiral Hyson Ind. Est.
SE16 . . . .2G **93**
Admiral M. W10 . . . .2D **64**
Admirals Ct. SE1 . . . .3C **82**
Admiralty Arch 2H **79**
Admiral Wlk. W9 . . . .3K **65**
Adpar St. W2 . . . .3E **66**
Adrian Boult Ho. E2 . . . .6G **63**
Adrian Ho. N1 . . . .3B **60**
SW8 . . . .7J **89**
Adrian M. SW10 . . . .5B **86**
Adron Ho. SE16 . . . .2K **93**
Adstock Ho. N1 . . . .1E **60**
Affleck St. N1 . . . .5B **60**
Afsil Ho. EC1 . . . .4D **70**
Aftab Ter. E1 . . . .1G **73**
Agar Gro. NW1 . . . .1F **59**
Agar Gro. Est. NW1 . . . .1G **59**
Agar Pl. NW1 . . . .1F **59**
Agar St. WC2 . . . .1J **79**
Agate Rd. W6 . . . .6A **74**
Agatha Cl. E1 . . . .2J **83**
Agdon St. EC1 . . . .1E **70**
Agnes Ho. W11 . . . .1D **74**
Aigburth Mans. SW9 . . . .7C **90**
Ainger M. NW3 . . . .1K **57**
Ainger Rd. NW3 . . . .1J **57**
Ainsdale NW1 . . . .5E **58**
Ainsdale Dr. SE1 . . . .4E **92**
Ainsley St. E2 . . . .7H **63**
Ainsty Est. SE16 . . . .4K **83**
Ainsty St. SE16 . . . .4K **83**
Ainsworth Ho. NW8 . . . .3B **56**
W10 . . . .6E **54**
Ainsworth Rd. E9 . . . .1K **63**
Ainsworth Way NW8 . . . .2C **56**
Aintree Est. SW6 . . . .7F **85**
Aintree St. SW6 . . . .7F **85**
Aird Ho. SE1 . . . .7G **81**
Airdrie Cl. N1 . . . .1A **60**
Airlie Gdns. W8 . . . .3J **75**
Air St. W1 . . . .1F **79**
Aisgill Av. W14 . . . .4H **85**
(not continuous)
Aitken Cl. E8 . . . .2E **62**
Ajax Ho. E2 . . . .5H **63**
Alan Preece Ct.
NW6 . . . .1D **54**
Alaska Bldgs. SE1 . . . .7C **82**
Alaska St. SE1 . . . .3C **80**
Alban Highwalk EC2 . . . .4H **71**
(not continuous)
Albany W1 . . . .1E **78**
Albany Ct. NW8 . . . .5E **56**
Albany Courtyard W1 . . . .1F **79**
Albany Mans. SW11 . . . .7H **87**
Albany M. SE5 . . . .6H **91**
Albany Rd. SE5 . . . .6H **91**
Albany St. NW1 . . . .4C **58**
Albany Ter. NW1 . . . .2D **68**
Alba Pl. W11 . . . .5G **65**
Albatross Way SE16 . . . .5K **83**
Albemarle St. W1 . . . .1D **78**
Albemarle Way EC1 . . . .2E **70**
Alberta Est. SE17 . . . .3F **91**
Alberta St. SE17 . . . .3E **90**
Albert Barnes Ho.
SE1 . . . .7G **81**
Albert Bri. SW11 . . . .6H **87**
Albert Bri. Rd. SW11 . . . .7H **87**
Albert Cl. E9 . . . .3H **63**
Albert Cotts. E1 . . . .3E **72**
Albert Ct. SW7 . . . .5E **76**
Albert Ct. Ga. SW1 . . . .5J **77**
Albert Emb. SE1 . . . .7A **80**
(Lambeth Pal. Rd.)
SE1 . . . .4K **89**
(Vauxhall Bri.)
Albert Gdns. E1 . . . .6K **73**
Albert Ga. SW1 . . . .4K **77**
Albert Gray Ho.
SW10 . . . .7E **86**
Albert Hall Mans.
SW7 . . . .5E **76**
(not continuous)
Albert Memorial 5E **76**
Albert M. W8 . . . .6C **76**
Albert Pl. W8 . . . .5B **76**
Albert Rd. NW6 . . . .5G **55**
Alberts Ct. NW1 . . . .1H **67**
Albert St. NW1 . . . .3D **58**
Albert Ter. NW1 . . . .2A **58**
Albert Ter. M. NW1 . . . .2A **58**
Albert Way SE15 . . . .7G **93**
Albert Westcott Ho.
SE17 . . . .3F **91**
Albery Ct. E8 . . . .1C **62**
Albion Bldgs. N1 . . . .5K **59**
Albion Cl. W2 . . . .7H **67**
Albion Dr. E8 . . . .1C **62**
Albion Est. SE16 . . . .5K **83**
Albion Ga. W2 . . . .7H **67**
(not continuous)
Albion M. N1 . . . .1C **60**
W2 . . . .7H **67**
Albion Pl. EC1 . . . .3E **70**
EC2 . . . .4K **71**
Albion Riverside Bldg.
SW11 . . . .7G **87**
Albion Sq. E8 . . . .1C **62**
(not continuous)
Albion St. SE16 . . . .5J **83**
W2 . . . .6H **67**
Albion Ter. E8 . . . .1C **62**
Albion Wlk. N1 . . . .5K **59**
Albion Way EC1 . . . .4G **71**
Albion Yd. E1 . . . .3H **73**
N1 . . . .5K **59**
Albury Ho. SE1 . . . .5F **81**
Aldbridge St. SE17 . . . .3B **92**
Aldburgh M. W1 . . . .5B **68**
(not continuous)
Aldbury Ho. SW3 . . . .2G **87**
Aldenham Ho. NW1 . . . .5F **59**
Aldenham St. NW1 . . . .5F **59**
Alden Ho. E8 . . . .2G **63**
Aldensley Rd. W6 . . . .7A **74**
Alder Cl. SE15 . . . .6D **92**
Alder Ho. SE15 . . . .6D **92**
Aldermanbury EC2 . . . .5H **71**
Aldermanbury Sq.
EC2 . . . .4H **71**
Aldermans Wlk. EC2 . . . .4A **72**
Alderney Rd. E1 . . . .1K **73**
Alderney St. SW1 . . . .2D **88**
Aldersgate St. EC1 . . . .3G **71**
Aldershot Rd. NW6 . . . .2H **55**
Alderson St. W10 . . . .1F **65**
Aldford Ho. W1 . . . .2A **78**
Aldford St. W1 . . . .2A **78**
ALDGATE 6D 72
Aldgate EC3 . . . .6C **72**
Aldgate Av. E1 . . . .5C **72**
Aldgate Barrs E1 . . . .5D **72**
Aldgate High St. EC3 . . . .6C **72**
Aldgate Triangle E1 . . . .5E **72**
Aldine Ct. W12 . . . .3B **74**
Aldine Pl. W12 . . . .4B **74**
Aldine St. W12 . . . .4B **74**
Aldington Ct. E8 . . . .1F **63**
Aldrick Ho. N1 . . . .3B **60**
Aldridge Ct. W11 . . . .4H **65**
Aldridge Rd. Vs.
W11 . . . .4H **65**
Aldsworth Cl. W9 . . . .2A **66**
Aldwych WC2 . . . .7A **70**
Aldwych Ct. E8 . . . .1D **62**
Aldwych Theatre 6A **70**
Aldwyn Ho. SW8 . . . .7J **89**
Alexa Ct. W8 . . . .1K **85**
Alexander Av. NW10 . . . .1A **54**
Alexander Fleming
Laboratory Mus. 5F **67**
Alexander M. W2 . . . .5A **66**
Alexander Pl. SW7 . . . .1G **87**
Alexander Sq. SW3 . . . .7G **77**
Alexander St. W2 . . . .5K **65**
Alexandra Ct. SW7 . . . .6D **76**
W2 . . . .7B **66**
W9 . . . .1D **66**
Alexandra Ho. W6 . . . .4A **84**
Alexandra Mans.
SW3 . . . .6E **86**
Alexandra Pl. NW8 . . . .2D **56**
Alexandra Rd. NW8 . . . .2D **56**
Alexandra Yd. E9 . . . .2K **63**
Alexandria Apartments
SE17 . . . .1A **92**
Alexis St. SE16 . . . .1F **93**
Alford Ct. N1 . . . .5H **61**
(not continuous)
Alford Pl. N1 . . . .5H **61**
Alfred M. W1 . . . .3G **69**
Alfred Pl. WC1 . . . .3G **69**
Alfred Rd. W2 . . . .3K **65**
Algar Ho. SE1 . . . .5E **80**
Algernon Rd. NW6 . . . .3J **55**
Alice Gilliatt Ct. W14 . . . .5G **85**
Alice Owen Technology Cen.
EC1 . . . .6E **60**
Alice St. SE1 . . . .7A **82**
(not continuous)
Alie St. E1 . . . .6D **72**
Alison Ct. SE1 . . . .4E **92**
Allcott Ho. W12 . . . .6A **64**
Allen Ho. W8 . . . .6K **75**
Allen Mans. W8 . . . .6K **75**
Allensbury Pl. NW1 . . . .1H **59**
Allen St. W8 . . . .6K **75**
Allerton Ho. N1 . . . .6J **61**
Allerton St. N1 . . . .6J **61**
Allestree Rd. SW6 . . . .7E **84**
Alleyn Ho. SE1 . . . .7K **81**
Allgood St. E2 . . . .5D **62**
Allhallows La. EC4 . . . .1J **81**
Allingham M. N1 . . . .4G **61**
Allingham St. N1 . . . .4G **61**
Allington Ct. SW1 . . . .7D **78**
Allington Rd. W10 . . . .5E **54**
Allington St. SW1 . . . .7D **78**
Alliston Ho. E2 . . . .7D **62**
Allitsen Rd. NW8 . . . .5G **57**
(not continuous)
All Nations Ho. E8 . . . .1G **63**
Allom Ho. W11 . . . .7E **64**
Allport M. E1 . . . .2K **73**
All Saints Ct. E1 . . . .7K **73**
All Saints Ho. W11 . . . .4G **65**
All Saints Rd. W11 . . . .4G **65**
All Saints St. N1 . . . .4A **60**
Allsop Pl. NW1 . . . .2K **67**
All Souls Av. NW10 . . . .4A **54**
All Souls' Pl. W1 . . . .4D **68**
Alluvium Ct. *SE1 . . . .6A **82***
(off Long La.)
Alma Birk Ho. NW6 . . . .1F **55**
Alma Gro. SE1 . . . .2D **92**
Alma Pl. NW10 . . . .7A **54**
Alma Sq. NW8 . . . .5D **56**
Alma Ter. W8 . . . .7K **75**
Almeida St. N1 . . . .2E **60**
Almeida Theatre 2E **60**
Almond Rd. SE16 . . . .1H **93**
Almorah Rd. N1 . . . .1J **61**
Alperton St. W10 . . . .1F **65**
Alpha Cl. NW1 . . . .7H **57**
Alpha Ho. NW6 . . . .4K **55**
NW8 . . . .2G **67**
Alpha Pl. NW6 . . . .4K **55**
SW3 . . . .5H **87**
Alpine Gro. E9 . . . .1K **63**
Alpine Rd. SE16 . . . .3K **93**
Alsace Rd. SE17 . . . .3A **92**
Alscot Rd. SE1 . . . .1C **92**
(not continuous)
Alscot Rd. Ind. Est.
SE1 . . . .7D **82**
Alscot Way SE1 . . . .1C **92**
Alverstone Ho. SE11 . . . .6C **90**
Alverstone Rd. NW2 . . . .1B **54**
Alvey St. SE17 . . . .3A **92**
Alwyne Rd. N1 . . . .1G **61**
Alwyne Vs. N1 . . . .1F **61**
Alzette Ho. E2 . . . .5K **63**
Amazon St. E1 . . . .6G **73**
Ambassadors Ct. E8 . . . .1D **62**
SW1 . . . .3F **79**
Ambergate St. SE17 . . . .3F **91**
Amberley Rd. W9 . . . .3K **65**
Amber Wharf E2 . . . .3C **62**
Ambleside NW1 . . . .5D **58**
Ambleside Point
SE15 . . . .7J **93**
Ambrosden Av. SW1 . . . .7F **79**
Ambrose St. SE16 . . . .1G **93**
Amelia Ho. W6 . . . .3A **84**
Amelia St. SE17 . . . .3F **91**
Amen Cnr. EC4 . . . .6F **71**

Amen Ct. EC4 6F 71
America Sq. EC3 7C 72
America St. SE1 3G 81
Amery Gdns. NW10 3A 54
Amery Ho. SE17 3B 92
Ames Ho. E2 5K 63
Amias Ho. EC1 1G 71
Amiel St. E1 1K 73
Amigo Ho. SE1 6D 80
Amina Way SE16 7E 82
Amor Rd. W6 7A 74
Amory Ho. N1 3B 60
Ampthill Est. NW1 5F 59
Ampthill Sq. NW1 5F 59
Ampton Pl. WC1 7A 60
Ampton St. WC1 7A 60
Amstel Ct. SE15 7C 92
Amwell St. N1 6C 60
Anchor Brewhouse SE1 3C 82
Anchor Ct. SW1 2G 89
Anchor Ho. EC1 1G 71
SW10 6F 87
Anchor Retail Pk. E1 2K 73
Anchor St. SE16 1G 93
Anchor Ter. E1 2K 73
Anchor Yd. EC1 1H 71
Ancill Cl. W6 6D 84
Anderson Ho. W12 6A 64
Anderson Sq. N1 3E 60
Anderson St. SW3 3J 87
Andover Pl. NW6 4A 56
Andoversford Ct. SE15 6B 92
Andrew Borde St. WC2 5H 69
Andrewes Highwalk EC2 4H 71
Andrewes Ho. EC2 4H 71
Andrews Crosse WC2 6C 70
Andrew's Rd. E8 3G 63
Andrews Wlk. SE17 6F 91
ANGEL 5D 60
Angel All. E1 5D 72
Angel Cen., The N1 5D 60
Angel Ct. EC2 5K 71
SW1 3F 79
Angel Ga. EC1 6F 61
(not continuous)
Angelis Apartments N1 5F 61
Angel M. E1 7H 73
N1 5D 60
Angel Pas. EC4 1J 81
Angel Pl. SE1 4J 81
Angel Sq. EC1 5E 60
Angel St. EC1 5G 71
Angel Wlk. W6 2A 84
Anglebury W2 5J 65
Angrave Ct. E8 2D 62
Angrave Pas. E8 2D 62
Anhalt Rd. SW11 7H 87
Anley Rd. W14 5C 74
Anna Cl. E8 2D 62
Anne Goodman Ho. E1 5J 73
Annes Ct. NW1 1H 67
Annette Cres. N1 1H 61
Anning St. EC2 1B 72
Ann La. SW10 7E 86
Ann Moss Way SE16 6J 83
Ann's Cl. SW1 5K 77
Ann's Pl. E1 4C 72
Ansdell St. W8 6B 76
Ansdell Ter. W8 6B 76
Ansell Ho. E1 3J 73
Anselm Rd. SW6 6J 85
Ansleigh Pl. W11 1D 74
Anson Ho. SW1 5E 88
Anstey Ho. E9 2J 63
Antenor Ho. E2 5G 63
Anthony Cope Ct. N1 6K 61
Anthony Ho. NW8 2G 67
Anthony St. E1 5H 73
Antill Ter. E1 5K 73
Antonine Hgts. SE1 5A 82
Antony Ho. SE14 7K 93
SE16 1J 93
Apollo Ct. E1 1E 82
Apollo Ho. E2 5H 63
SW10 6E 86
Apollo Pl. SW10 7E 86
Apollo Theatre
Soho 7G 69
Victoria 7E 78
Apollo West End Cinema 1G 79
Apothecary St. EC4 6E 70
Apple Blossom Ct. SW8 7H 89
Appleby Rd. E8 1F 63
Appleby St. E2 4C 62
Appleford Ho. W10 2F 65
Appleford Rd. W10 2F 65
Applegarth Ho. SE1 4F 81
SE15 7E 92
Applegarth Rd. W14 7C 74
Apple Tree Yd. SW1 2F 79
Appold St. EC2 3A 72
Approach Rd. E2 5J 63
April Ct. E2 4F 63
Apsley House 4B 78
Apsley Ho. E1 4K 73
NW8 4E 56
Apsley Way W1 4B 78
(not continuous)
Aquila St. NW8 4F 57
Aquinas St. SE1 3D 80
Arbon Ct. N1 3H 61
Arbour Ho. E1 5K 73
Arbour Sq. E1 5K 73
Arbutus St. E8 2C 62
Arcade, The EC2 4A 72
Arcadia Ct. E1 5C 72
Archdale Ho. SE1 6A 82
Archel Rd. W14 5G 85
Archer Apartments N1 4A 62
Archer Ho. N1 3B 62
W11 7H 65
Archers Lodge SE16 4F 93
Archer St. W1 7G 69
Archery Cl. W2 6H 67
Archery Steps W2 7H 67
Arches, The NW1 1C 58
SW8 7G 89
WC2 2K 79
Archibald M. W1 1C 78
Archie St. SE1 5B 82
Arch St. SE1 7G 81
Archway Cl. W10 4C 64
Arden Est. N1 5A 62
Arden Ho. N1 5A 62
SE11 2A 90
Argon M. SW6 7K 85
Argos Ho. E2 5G 63
Argyle Pl. W6 2A 84
Argyle Rd. E1 1K 73
Argyle Sq. WC1 6K 59
Argyle St. WC1 6J 59
Argyle Wlk. WC1 7J 59
Argyle Way SE16 4F 93
Argyll Mans. SW3 5F 87
W14 1F 85
Argyll Rd. W8 5J 75
Argyll St. W1 6E 68
Arica Ho. SE16 6H 83
Ariel Ct. SE11 2E 90
Ariel Way W12 2B 74
Ark, The W6 3C 84
Arklow Ho. SE17 6J 91
Arlidge Ho. EC1 3D 70
Arlington Av. N1 4H 61
(not continuous)
Arlington Ho. EC1 6D 60
SW1 2E 78
W12 3A 74
Arlington Rd. NW1 2C 58
Arlington Sq. N1 3H 61
Arlington St. SW1 2E 78
Arlington Way EC1 6D 60
Armadale Rd. SW6 7J 85
Armitage Ho. NW1 3H 67
Armsby Ho. E1 4J 73
Armstrong Rd. SW7 7E 76
Arncliffe NW6 4B 56
Arne Ho. SE11 3A 90
Arne St. WC2 6K 69
Arneway St. SW1 7H 79
Arnold Cir. E2 7C 62
Arnold Est. SE1 5D 82
(not continuous)
Arnold Ho. SE17 4F 91
Arnold Mans. W14 5F 85
Arnside Ho. SE17 5J 91
Arnside St. SE17 5H 91
Arrol Ho. SE1 7H 81
Arrow Ct. SW5 2J 85
Arrow Ho. *N1 3B 62*
(off Wilmer Gdns.)
Arrows Ho. SE15 7K 93
Arrowsmith Ho. SE11 3A 90
Arta Ho. E1 6K 73
Artesian Ho. SE1 7D 82
Artesian Rd. W2 6J 65
Arthur Ct. W2 5A 66
W10 6D 64
Arthur Deakin Ho. E1 3E 72
Arthur Ho. *N1 3A 62*
(off New Era Est.)
Arthur St. EC4 1K 81
Artichoke Hill E1 1G 83
Artillery La. E1 4B 72
Artillery Pas. E1 4B 72
Artillery Pl. SW1 7G 79
Artillery Row SW1 7G 79
Artisan M. NW10 7C 54
Artisan Quarter NW10 7C 54
Artizan St. E1 5B 72
Arts Theatre 7J 69
Arundel Bldgs. SE1 7B 82
Arundel Ct. SE16 4H 93
SW3 3H 87
SW13 5A 84
Arundel Gdns. W11 7G 65
Arundel Gt. Ct. WC2 7B 70
Arundel St. WC2 7B 70
Arundel Ter. SW13 5A 84
Ascalon Ho. SW8 7E 88
Ascot Ct. NW8 7E 56
Ascot Ho. NW1 6D 58
W9 2J 65
Ascot Lodge NW6 3B 56
Ashbee Ho. E2 7K 63
Ashbridge St. NW8 2G 67
Ashburn Gdns. SW7 1C 86
Ashburnham Mans. SW10 7D 86
Ashburnham Rd. NW10 6A 54
SW10 7D 86
Ashburnham Twr. SW10 7E 86
Ashburn Pl. SW7 1C 86
Ashburton Ho. W9 1H 65
Ashby Ct. NW8 1F 67
Ashby Ho. N1 1H 61
Ashby St. EC1 7F 61
Ashcroft Sq. W6 2A 84
Ashdown Ho. SW1 7F 79
Ashenden SE17 1G 91
Ashentree Ct. EC4 6D 70
Asher Way E1 1F 83
Ashfield Ho. W14 3H 85
Ashfield St. E1 4G 73
Ashfield Yd. E1 4J 73
Ashford St. N1 6A 62
Ash Gro. E8 3H 63
Ashgrove Ct. W9 3J 65
Ashgrove Ho. SW1 3H 89
Ash Ho. SE1 2D 92
W10 1F 65
Ashington Ho. E1 1H 73
Ashland Pl. W1 3A 68
Ashley Ct. SW1 7E 78
Ashley Gdns. SW1 7F 79
(not continuous)
Ashley Pl. SW1 7E 78
(not continuous)
Ashmill St. NW1 3G 67
Ashmole Pl. SW8 6C 90
(not continuous)
Ashmole St. SW8 6B 90
Ashmore NW1 1G 59
Ashmore Ho. W14 7F 75
Ashmore Rd. W9 6G 55
Ashton Ho. SW9 7D 90
Ash Tree Ho. SE5 7G 91
Ashworth Mans. W9 7B 56
Ashworth Rd. W9 6B 56
Aske Ho. N1 6A 62
(not continuous)
Aske St. N1 6A 62
Asolando Dr. SE17 2H 91
Aspen Gdns. W6 3A 84
Aspen Ho. SE15 6K 93
Aspenlea Rd. W6 5C 84
Aspen Lodge W8 7A 76
Aspinden Rd. SE16 1H 93
Assam St. E1 5E 72
Assembly Pas. E1 3K 73
Association Gallery, The 1A 72
Astbury Ho. SE11 7C 80
Astell Ho. SW3 3H 87
Astell St. SW3 3H 87
Astey's Row N1 2F 61
Astley Ho. SE1 3D 92
SW13 6A 84
W2 3J 65
Aston Ho. W11 7H 65
Aston Webb Ho. SE1 3A 82
Astor Ct. SW6 7C 86
Astoria, The 5H 69
Astoria Ct. E8 1D 62
Astrop M. W6 6A 74
Astrop Ter. W6 6A 74
Astwood M. SW7 1B 86
Asylum Rd. SE15 6H 93
Athelstan Gdns. NW6 1F 55
Athene Pl. *EC4 5D 70*
(off St Andrew St.)
Athens Gdns. W9 2J 65
Atherstone Ct. W2 3B 66
Atherstone M. SW7 1D 86
Athlone Ho. E1 5J 73
Atholl Ho. W9 7C 56
Atkin Bldg. WC1 3B 70
Atkinson Ho. E2 4F 63
SE17 2K 91
Atrium Apartments N1 3K 61
Atterbury St. SW1 2J 89
Attilburgh Ho. SE1 6C 82
Attneave St. WC1 1C 70
Atunbi Ct. NW1 1E 58
Atwood Ho. W14 2H 85
Aubrey Beardsley Ho. SW1 2F 89
Aubrey Mans. NW1 3G 67
Aubrey Pl. NW8 5C 56
Aubrey Rd. W8 2H 75
Aubrey Wlk. W8 3H 75
Auckland St. SE11 4A 90
Auden Pl. NW1 2A 58
Audley Sq. W1 2B 78
Augustas St. E2 4E 62
Augustine Rd. W14 7C 74
Augustus Cl. W12 5A 74
Augustus Ct. SE1 1A 92
Augustus Ho. NW1 5E 58
Augustus St. NW1 5D 58
Aulton Pl. SE11 4D 90
Auriol Ho. W12 2A 74
Auriol Mans. *W14 2E 84*
(off Edith Rd.)
Auriol Rd. W14 2E 84
Austen Ho. NW6 6J 55
Austin Friars EC2 5K 71
(not continuous)
Austin Friars Pas. EC2 5K 71
Austin Friars Sq. EC2 5K 71
Austin St. E2 7C 62
Austin Ter. SE1 6D 80
Australian War Memorial 4B 78
Australia Rd. W12 7A 64
Austral St. SE11 1E 90
Avebury Ct. N1 3J 61
Avebury St. N1 3J 61
Aveline St. SE11 4C 90
Ave Maria La. EC4 6F 71
Avenfield Ho. W1 7K 67
Avenue, The NW6 3D 54
Avenue Cl. NW8 3H 57
Avenue Ct. SW3 2J 87
Avenue Ho. NW8 5G 57
Avenue Lodge NW8 1F 57
Avenue Rd. NW3 1E 56
NW8 2G 57
Averill St. W6 6C 84
Avery Farm Row SW1 2C 88
Avery Row W1 7C 68
Avington Ct. SE1 2B 92
Avocet Cl. SE1 3E 92
Avon Ct. W9 3J 65
Avondale Ho. SE1 4E 92
Avondale Pk. Gdns. W11 1E 74
Avondale Pk. Rd. W11 7E 64
Avondale Pavement SE1 4E 92
Avondale Sq. SE1 4E 92
Avon Ho. W8 6K 75
W14 2H 85
Avonley Rd. SE14 7K 93
Avonmore Gdns. W14 2H 85
Avonmore Pl. W14 1F 85
Avonmore Rd. W14 1F 85
Avonmouth St. SE1 6G 81
Avon Pl. SE1 5H 81
Axis Ct. *SE16 4E 82*
(off East La.)
Aybrook St. W1 4A 68
Aycliffe Ho. SE17 5K 91
Aylesbury Ho. SE15 6F 93
Aylesbury Rd. SE17 4K 91
Aylesbury St. EC1 2E 70
Aylesford Ho. SE1 5K 81
Aylesford St. SW1 3G 89
Aylestone Av. NW6 1C 54
Aylton Est. SE16 5K 83
Aylward St. E1 5K 73
(Jamaica St.)
E1 5J 73
(Jubilee St.)
Aylwin Est. SE1 6B 82
Aynhoe Mans. W14 1D 84
Aynhoe Rd. W14 1D 84
Ayres St. SE1 4H 81
Ayrton Rd. SW7 6E 76
Ayshford Ho. E2 7G 63
Ayton Ho. SE5 7K 91
Azure Ho. E2 7E 62

B

Babington Ct. WC1 3A 70
Babington Ho. SE1 4H 81
Babmaes St. SW1 1G 79
Bacchus Wlk. N1 5A 62
Bache's St. N1 7K 61
Back All. EC3 6B 72
Bk. Church La. E1 6E 72
Back Hill EC1 2D 70
Backhouse Pl. SE17 2B 92
Back Passage EC1 3F 71
Bacon Gro. SE1 7C 82
Bacon St. E1 1D 72
E2 1D 72
Bacton St. E2 6K 63
Baddesley Ho. SE11 3B 90
Baddow Wlk. N1 2H 61
Baden Pl. SE1 4J 81
Baden Powell Ho. SW7 7D 76
Bagnigge Ho. WC1 7C 60
Bagshot Ho. NW1 6D 58
Bagshot St. SE17 4B 92
Baildon E2 5K 63
Bailey Ho. SW10 7B 86
Bainbridge St. WC1 5H 69
Baird Ho. W12 1A 74
Baird St. EC1 1H 71
Baker Ho. WC1 2K 69
Bakers Hall Ct. EC3 1A 82
Baker's M. W1 5A 68
Baker's Rents E2 7C 62
Baker's Row EC1 2C 70
BAKER STREET 3K 67
Baker St. NW1 2K 67
W1 3K 67
Baker's Yd. EC1 2C 70
Balaclava Rd. SE1 2D 92
Balcombe Ho. NW1 1H 67
Balcombe St. NW1 1J 67
Balcorne St. E9 1K 63
Balderton Flats W1 6B 68
Balderton St. W1 6B 68
Baldwins Gdns. EC1 3C 70
Baldwin St. EC1 7J 61
Baldwin Ter. N1 4G 61
Balfe St. N1 4K 59
Balfour Ho. W10 3D 64
Balfour M. W1 2B 78
Balfour Pl. W1 1B 78
Balfour St. SE17 1J 91
Balin Ho. SE1 4J 81
Balkan Wlk. E1 1G 83
Ball Ct. EC3 6K 71
Balliol Rd. W10 5B 64
Ballow Cl. SE5 7A 92
Balman Ho. SE16 2K 93
Balmes Rd. N1 2K 61
Balmoral Apartments *W2 4G 67*
(off Praed St.)
Balmoral Ct. SE17 4J 91
Balmoral Ho. W14 1E 84
Balniel Ga. SW1 3H 89
Baltic Pl. N1 3B 62
Baltic St. E. EC1 2G 71
Baltic St. W. EC1 2G 71
Baltimore Ct. SW1 2G 89
Baltimore Ho. SE11 2C 90
Balvaird Pl. SW1 4H 89
Bamborough Gdns. W12 5B 74
Banbury Ct. WC2 7J 69
Bancroft Ho. E1 1J 73
Bancroft Rd. E1 7K 63
Banister Ho. W10 7F 55
Banister Rd. W10 6D 54
Bank End SE1 2H 81
Bank of England 6J 71
Bank of England Mus. 6K 71
Banks Ho. SE1 7G 81
Bankside SE1 1G 81
(not continuous)
Bankside Art Gallery 1F 81
Banner Ct. SE16 2J 93
Bannerman Ho. SW8 6A 90
Banner St. EC1 2H 71
Banqueting House 3J 79
Bantock Ho. W10 7F 55
Bantry St. SE5 7K 91
Banyard Rd. SE16 7H 83
Barandon Rd. W11 7D 64
Barandon Wlk. W11 7D 64
Barbanel Ho. E1 1K 73
Barbara Brosnan Ct. NW8 5E 56
Barbara Castle Cl. SW6 6H 85
Barbican Arts Cen. 3H 71
Barbican Cinema
Silk Street 3H 71
Barbican Theatre 3H 71
Barbican Trade Cen. EC1 3H 71
Barb M. W6 7B 74
Barbon All. EC2 5B 72
Barbon Cl. WC1 3K 69
Barclay Ho. E9 1J 63
Barclay Rd. SW6 7J 85
Bardell Ho. SE1 5E 82
Bard Rd. W10 7C 64
Bardsey Pl. E1 2J 73
Barfett St. W10 1G 65
Barford St. N1 3D 60
Barge Ho. St. SE1 2D 80
Barham Ho. SE17 3B 92
Baring Ct. N1 3J 61
Baring St. N1 3J 61
Barker Dr. NW1 1F 59
Barkers Arc. W8 5A 76
Barker St. SW10 5C 86
Barkham Ter. SE1 6D 80
Bark Pl. W2 7A 66
Barkston Gdns. SW5 2A 86
Barkworth Rd. SE16 4H 93
Barlborough St. SE14 7K 93
Barlby Gdns. W10 2C 64
Barlby Rd. W10 4B 64
Barley Mow Pas. EC1 4F 71
Barley Shotts Bus. Pk. W10 3G 65
Barlow Ho. N1 6J 61
SE16 2H 93
W11 7E 64
Barlow Pl. W1 1D 78
Barlow St. SE17 2K 91
Barnaby Ct. SE16 5F 83
Barnaby Pl. SW7 2E 86
Barnard Ho. E2 6G 63
Barnard Lodge *W9 3K 65*
(off Admiral Wlk.)
Barnardo Gdns. E1 7K 73
Barnardo St. E1 6K 73
Barnard's Inn EC1 5D 70
Barnbrough NW1 3E 58
Barnby St. NW1 5F 59
Barnes Ct. N1 1C 60
Barnes Ho. E2 4J 63
Barnet Gro. E2 6E 62
Barnett St. E1 5G 73
Barnham St. SE1 4B 82
BARNSBURY 1A 60
Barnsbury Est. N1 3B 60
(not continuous)
Barnsbury Pk. N1 1C 60
Barnsbury Rd. N1 4C 60
Barnsbury Sq. N1 1C 60
Barnsbury St. N1 1D 60
Barnsbury Ter. N1 1B 60
Barnsdale Rd. W9 1H 65
Barnsley St. E1 1H 73
Barnston Wlk. N1 2G 61
Barnwood Cl. W9 2A 66
Baroness Rd. E2 6D 62
BARONS COURT 4E 84
Baron's Ct. Rd. W14 3E 84
Barons Court Theatre *3F 85*
(off Comeragh Rd.)
Barons Keep W14 3E 84
Baron's Pl. SE1 5D 80
Baron St. N1 4C 60
Barratt Ho. N1 1F 61
Barret Ho. NW6 3J 55
Barrett Ho. SE17 3H 91
Barrett St. W1 6B 68
Barrie Est. W2 7E 66
Barrie Ho. W2 1D 76
Barrow Hill Est. NW8 5G 57
Barrow Hill Rd. NW8 5G 57
Barrow Store Ct. SE1 6A 82
Barry Ho. SE16 2H 93
Barter St. WC1 4K 69
Bartholomew Cl. EC1 4F 71
(not continuous)
Bartholomew Ct. EC1 1H 71
Bartholomew La. EC2 6K 71
Bartholomew Pl. EC1 4G 71
Bartholomew Sq. E1 1H 73
EC1 7H 61
Bartholomew St. SE1 7K 81
Bartle Rd. W11 6D 64
Bartlett Ct. EC4 5D 70
Bartletts Pas. EC4 5D 70
Bartok Ho. W11 2G 75
Barton Ct. W14 4E 84
Barton Ho. N1 1F 61
Barton Rd. W14 4E 84
Barton St. SW1 6J 79
Bartonway NW8 4E 56
Barwell Ho. E2 1F 73
Baseline Bus. Studios W11 7D 64
Basildon Ct. W1 3B 68
Basil Ho. SW8 7J 89
Basil Mans. SW3 5J 77
Basil St. SW3 6J 77
Basinghall Av. EC2 5J 71
Basinghall St. EC2 5H 71
Basing Ho. Yd. E2 6B 62
Basing Pl. E2 6B 62
Basing St. W11 5G 65
Basire St. N1 2G 61
Bassett Rd. W10 5D 64
Bassingbourn Ho. N1 1D 60
Bassishaw Highwalk EC2 4J 71
Basterfield Ho. EC1 2G 71
Bastion Highwalk EC2 4H 71
Bastion Ho. EC2 4G 71
Bastwick St. EC1 1G 71
Batchelor St. N1 4D 60
Bateman Ho. SE17 6E 90
Bateman's Bldgs. W1 6G 69
Bateman's Row EC2 1B 72
Bateman St. W1 6G 69
Bath Ct. EC1 2C 70
Bath Gro. E2 5E 62
Bath Ho. E2 1F 73
SE1 6G 81
Bath Pl. EC2 7A 62
W6 3B 84
Baths App. SW6 7H 85
Bath St. EC1 7H 61
Bath Ter. SE1 7G 81
Bathurst Gdns. NW10 5A 54
Bathurst M. W2 7F 67
Bathurst St. W2 7F 67
Batman Cl. W12 1A 74
Batoum Gdns. W6 6B 74
Batson Ho. E1 6F 73
Batten Ho. W10 7F 55
Battersea Bri. SW11 7F 87
Battersea Bri. Rd. SW11 7G 87
Battersea Church Rd. SW11 7G 87
Battersea Pk. 7K 87

Battersea Pk. Children's Zoo 7A 88
Battersea Pk. Rd. SW8 7D 88
Battishill St. N1 1E 60
Battlebridge Ct. N1 4K 59
Battle Bri. La. SE1 3A 82
Battle Bri. Rd. NW1 5J 59
Battle Ho. SE15 6E 92
Batty St. E1 5F 73
Batwa Ho. SE16 4H 93
Baxendale St. E2 6E 62
Bay Ct. E1 2K 73
Bayer Ho. EC1 2G 71
Bayford M. E8 1H 63
Bayford Rd. NW10 7C 54
Bayford St. E8 1H 63
Bayford St. Bus. Cen. E8 1H 63
Bayham Pl. NW1 3E 58
Bayham St. NW1 2D 58
Bayley St. WC1 4G 69
Baylis Rd. SE1 5C 80
Baynes St. NW1 1F 59
Bayonne Rd. W6 6E 84
BAYSWATER 7C 66
Bayswater Rd. W2 1A 76
Bayton Ct. E8 1F 63
Baytree M. SE17 1J 91
Bazalgette Ho. NW8 1F 67
Bazeley Ho. SE1 5E 80
BBC Broadcasting House 4D 68
BBC Maida Vale Studios 1A 66
BBC Television Cen. 1A 74
BBC Worldwide 6A 64
Beach Ho. SW5 3J 85
Beacon Ho. SE5 7A 92
Beaconsfield Rd. SE17 5K 91
Beaconsfield Ter. Rd. W14 7E 74
Beadon Rd. W6 2A 84
Beak St. W1 7F 69
Beaminster Ho. SW8 7A 90
Beamish Ho. SE16 2H 93
Bear All. EC4 5E 70
Bear Gdns. SE1 2G 81
Bear La. SE1 2F 81
Bear St. WC2 7H 69
Beatrice Ho. W6 3A 84
Beatrice Pl. W8 7A 76
Beatrice Rd. SE1 2F 93
Beatrix Ho. SW5 3B 86
Beatty Ho. NW1 1E 68
SW1 4F 89
Beatty St. NW1 4E 58
Beauchamp Pl. SW3 6H 77
Beauchamp St. EC1 4C 70
Beauclerc Rd. W6 6A 74
Beaufort Ct. SW6 5J 85
Beaufort Gdns. SW3 6H 77
Beaufort Ho. SW1 4G 89
SW3 6F 87
Beaufort Mans. SW3 6F 87
Beaufort M. SW6 5H 85
Beaufort St. SW3 4E 86
Beaufoy Ho. SW8 7A 90
Beaufoy Wlk. SE11 2B 90
Beaumanor Mans. W2 7B 66
Beaumont W14 2H 85
Beaumont Av. W14 3G 85
Beaumont Bldgs. WC2 6K 69
Beaumont Ct. NW1 2F 59
W1 3B 68
Beaumont Cres. W14 3G 85
Beaumont Gro. E1 2K 73
Beaumont Ho. W9 6H 55
Beaumont M. W1 3B 68
Beaumont Pl. W1 1F 69
Beaumont Sq. E1 3K 73
Beaumont St. W1 3B 68
Beaumont Wlk. NW3 1K 57
Bechtel Ho. W6 2C 84
Becket Ho. SE1 5J 81
Becket St. SE1 6J 81
Beckett Ho. E1 4J 73
Beckfoot NW1 5F 59
Beckford Cl. W14 1H 85
Beckford Pl. SE17 4H 91
Beckham Ho. SE11 2B 90
Beck Rd. E8 2G 63
Beckway St. SE17 2K 91 (not continuous)
Beckwith Ho. E2 4H 63
Bedale St. SE1 3J 81
Bedefield WC1 7K 59
Bedford Av. WC1 4H 69
Bedfordbury WC2 1J 79
Bedford Ct. WC2 1J 79 (not continuous)
Bedford Ct. Mans. WC1 4H 69
Bedford Gdns. W8 3J 75
Bedford Gdns. Ho. W8 3K 75
Bedford Pas. SW6 7F 85
W1 3F 69
Bedford Pl. WC1 3J 69
Bedford Row WC1 3B 70
Bedford Sq. WC1 4H 69
Bedford St. WC2 7J 69
Bedford Way WC1 2H 69
Bedlam M. SE11 1C 90
Bedmond Ho. SW3 3G 87
Bedser Cl. SE11 5B 90
Beech Ct. W9 3J 65
Beechey Ho. E1 3H 83
Beech Gdns. EC2 3G 71
Beech Ho. SE16 4K 83
Beech St. EC2 3G 71
Beech Tree Cl. N1 1C 60
Beechwood Ho. E2 4F 63
Beechworth NW6 1E 54
Beehive Cl. E8 1C 62
Bee Pas. EC3 6A 72
Beeston Ho. SE1 7J 81
Beeston Pl. SW1 7D 78
Beethoven St. W10 6F 55
Belford Ho. E8 2D 62
Belfry Cl. SE16 3H 93
Belgrave Ct. E2 5G 63
Belgrave Gdns. NW8 3B 56
Belgrave Ho. SW9 7C 90
Belgrave Mans. NW8 3B 56
Belgrave M. Nth. SW1 6A 78
Belgrave M. Sth. SW1 6B 78
Belgrave M. W. SW1 6A 78
Belgrave Pl. SW1 6B 78
Belgrave Rd. SW1 2D 88
Belgrave Sq. SW1 6A 78
Belgrave Yd. SW1 7C 78
BELGRAVIA 7B 78
Belgravia Ct. SW1 7C 78
Belgravia Ho. SW1 6A 78
Belgrove St. WC1 6K 59
Belitha Vs. N1 1B 60
Bella Best Ho. *SW1 3D 88* *(off Westmoreland Ter.)*
W1 6H 69 *(off Westmoreland Ter.)*
Bellamy Cl. W14 4H 85
Bellevue Pl. E1 2J 73
Bell Inn Yd. EC3 6K 71
Bell La. E1 4C 72
Bell St. NW1 3G 67
Bell Wharf La. EC4 1H 81
Bell Yd. WC2 6C 70
Bell Yd. M. SE1 5B 82
Belmont St. NW1 1B 58
Belsize Rd. NW6 3K 55
Belvedere Bldgs. SE1 5F 81
Belvedere Ct. N1 2A 62
Belvedere Pl. SE1 5F 81
Belvedere Rd. SE1 4B 80
Bembridge Cl. NW6 1E 54
Bemerton Est. N1 1A 60
Bemerton St. N1 2A 60
Benbow Ct. W6 6A 74
Benbow Rd. W6 6A 74
Bendall Ho. NW1 3H 67
Bendall M. NW1 3H 67
Benenden Ho. SE17 3B 92
Ben Ezra Ct. SE17 2H 91
Benfleet Ct. E8 2D 62
Bengal Ct. EC3 6K 71
Benham Ho. SW10 7B 86
Benhill Rd. SE5 7K 91
Benjamin Cl. E8 2F 63
Benjamin Franklin House *2J 79* *(off Craven St.)*
Benjamin St. EC1 3E 70
Ben Jonson Ct. N1 4B 62
Ben Jonson Ho. EC2 3H 71
Ben Jonson Pl. EC2 3H 71
Bennelong Cl. W12 6A 64
Bennet's Hill EC4 7F 71
Bennet St. SW1 2E 78
Bennett Ho. SW1 1H 89
Bennett's Yd. SW1 7H 79
Ben Smith Way SE16 6F 83
Benson Ho. E2 1C 72
SE1 3D 80
Benson Quay E1 1J 83
Bentham Ct. N1 1G 61
Bentham Ho. SE1 6J 81
Bentinck Cl. NW8 5H 57
Bentinck Mans. W1 5B 68
Bentinck M. W1 5B 68
Bentinck St. W1 5B 68
Bentworth Ct. E2 1E 72
Bentworth Rd. W12 6A 64
Benville Ho. SW8 7B 90
Benwick Cl. SE16 1H 93
Benyon Ct. N1 2A 62
Benyon Ho. EC1 6D 60
Benyon Rd. N1 2K 61
Benyon Wharf N1 2B 62
Berenger Twr. SW10 7E 86
Berenger Wlk. SW10 7E 86
Berens Rd. NW10 7C 54
Berghem M. W14 7D 74
Bergholt M. NW1 1F 59
Berkeley Ct. NW1 2K 67
Berkeley Gdns. W8 3K 75
Berkeley M. W1 6K 67
Berkeley Sq. W1 1D 78
Berkeley St. W1 1D 78
Berkley Gro. NW1 1K 57
Berkley Rd. NW1 1K 57
BERMONDSEY 5E 82
Bermondsey Sq. SE1 6B 82
Bermondsey St. SE1 3A 82
Bermondsey Trad. Est. SE16 3J 93
Bermondsey Wall E. SE16 5F 83
Bermondsey Wall W. SE16 4E 82
Bernard Hegarty Lodge E8 1F 63
Bernard Mans. WC1 2J 69
Bernard Shaw Ct. NW1 1E 58
Bernard St. WC1 2J 69
Bernard Sunley Ho. SW9 7C 90
Berners Ho. N1 4C 60
Berners M. W1 4F 69
Berners Pl. W1 5F 69
Berners Rd. N1 3E 60
Berners St. W1 4F 69
Berner Ter. E1 6F 73
Bernhardt Cres. NW8 1G 67
Berrington Ho. W2 7K 65
Berryfield Rd. SE17 3F 91
Berry Ho. E1 2H 73
Berry Pl. EC1 7F 61
Berry St. EC1 1F 71
Berwick Ct. SE1 5H 81
Berwick St. W1 5F 69
Beryl Rd. W6 4C 84
Besant Ho. NW8 2C 56
Besford Ho. E2 4F 63
Bessborough Gdns. SW1 3H 89
Bessborough Pl. SW1 3G 89
Bessborough St. SW1 3G 89
Bessemer Ct. NW1 1F 59
Bessy St. E2 6K 63
Bethal Est. SE1 5K 81
Bethersden Ho. SE17 3B 92
BETHNAL GREEN 7G 63
Bethnal Green Cen. for Sports & Performing Arts 7D 62
Bethnal Green Mus. of Childhood 6J 63
Bethnal Grn. Rd. E1 1C 72
E2 7F 63
Bethwin Rd. SE5 7F 91
Betsham Ho. SE1 4J 81
Betterton Ho. WC2 6K 69
Betterton St. WC2 6K 69
Betts Ho. E1 7G 73
Betts St. E1 7G 73
Bevan Ho. *N1 3A 62* *(off New Era Est.)*
WC1 3K 69
Bevan St. N1 3H 61
Bevenden St. N1 6K 61
Beverston M. W1 4J 67
Bevin Ct. WC1 6B 60
Bevington Path *SE1 5C 82* *(off Tanner St.)*
Bevington Rd. W10 3F 65
Bevington St. SE16 5F 83
Bevin Ho. E2 6K 63
Bevin Way WC1 6C 60
Bevis Marks EC3 5B 72
Bewdley St. N1 1C 60
Bewick M. SE15 7G 93
Bewley Ho. E1 7H 73
Bewley St. E1 7H 73
Bianca Ho. N1 5A 62
Bianca Rd. SE15 6D 92
Bibury Cl. SE15 6B 92 (not continuous)
Bickenhall Mans. W1 3K 67 (not continuous)
Bickenhall St. W1 3K 67
Bicknell Ho. E1 6F 73
Bidborough St. WC1 7J 59
Biddesden Ho. SW3 2J 87
Biddulph Mans. W9 7A 56
Biddulph Rd. W9 7A 56
Big Ben 5K 79
Bigland St. E1 6G 73
Billingley NW1 3E 58
Billing Pl. SW10 7B 86
Billing Rd. SW10 7B 86
Billing St. SW10 7B 86
Billiter Sq. EC3 6B 72
Billiter St. EC3 6B 72
Bilton Towers W1 6K 67
Bina Gdns. SW5 2C 86
Binbrook Ho. W10 3A 64
Bingfield St. N1 2K 59 (not continuous)
Bingham Ct. N1 1F 61
Bingham Pl. W1 3A 68
Binney St. W1 6B 68
Binnie Ho. SE1 7G 81
Birch Ho. W10 1F 65
Birchington Ct. NW6 2A 56
Birchington Rd. NW6 2K 55
Birchin La. EC3 6K 71
Birchmere Lodge SE16 4G 93
Birch Va. Ct. NW8 1F 67
Birdbrook Ho. N1 1G 61
Birdcage Wlk. SW1 5E 78
Bird in Bush BMX Track 7G 93
Bird in Bush Rd. SE15 7E 92
Bird St. W1 6B 68
Birkbeck College 2H 69
Birkbeck St. E2 7H 63
Birkdale Cl. SE16 4G 93
Birkenhead St. WC1 6K 59
Birley Lodge NW8 4F 57
Biscay Rd. W6 4C 84
Bishopgate Chu. Yd. EC2 5A 72
Bishop King's Rd. W14 1F 85
Bishop's Bri. Rd. W2 6B 66
Bishops Ct. EC4 5E 70
W2 5B 66
WC2 5C 70
Bishopsdale Ho. NW6 2K 55
Bishopsgate EC2 5A 72
Bishopsgate Arc. EC2 4B 72
Bishopsgate Institute & Libraries 4B 72
Bishops Ho. SW8 7K 89
Bishops Mead SE5 7H 91
Bishops Rd. SW6 7H 85
SW11 7H 87
Bishops Sq. E1 3B 72
Bishop's Ter. SE11 1D 90
Bishop St. N1 2G 61
Bishop's Way E2 4H 63
Bittern Ho. SE1 5G 81
Bittern St. SE1 5G 81
Blackall St. EC2 1A 72
Blackbird Yd. E2 6D 62
Black Bull Yd. EC1 3C 70
Blackburne's M. W1 7A 68
Blackfriars Bri. SE1 1E 80
Blackfriars Ct. EC4 7E 70
Black Friars La. EC4 7E 70 (not continuous)
Blackfriars Pas. EC4 7E 70
Blackfriars Rd. SE1 5E 80
Blackfriars Underpass EC4 7E 70
Black Horse Ct. SE1 6K 81
Blacklands Ter. SW3 2J 87
Blackmans Yd. E2 1E 72
Blackmore Ho. N1 3B 60
Black Prince Rd. SE1 2A 90
SE11 2A 90
Blacks Rd. W6 2A 84
Blackstone Est. E8 1F 63
Blackstone Ho. SW1 4E 88
Black Swan Yd. SE1 4A 82
Blackthorne Ct. SE15 7D 92
Blackwater Ho. NW8 3F 67
Blackwood Ho. E1 2H 73
Blackwood St. SE17 3J 91
Bladen Ho. E1 5K 73
Blades Ct. W6 3A 84
Blades Ho. SE11 6C 90
Blagrove Rd. W10 4F 65
Blair Ct. NW8 2E 56
Blake Ct. NW6 6J 55
SE16 3H 93
Blake Ho. SE1 6C 80
Blakeney Cl. NW1 1G 59
Blakes Cl. W10 3B 64
Blake's Rd. SE15 7B 92
Blanch Cl. SE15 7J 93
Blandford Ct. N1 1B 62
NW6 1E 54
Blandford Ho. SW8 7A 90
Blandford Sq. NW1 2H 67
Blandford St. W1 5K 67
Bland Ho. SE11 3B 90
Blantyre St. SW10 7E 86
Blantyre Twr. SW10 7E 86
Blantyre Wlk. SW10 7E 86
Blashford NW3 1J 57
Blazer Ct. NW8 7F 57
Blechynden Ho. W10 6D 64
Blechynden St. W10 7D 64
Bledlow Cl. NW8 2F 67
Bleeding Heart Yd. EC1 4D 70
Blemundsbury WC1 3A 70
Blendon Row SE17 2J 91
Blenheim Cres. W11 7E 64
Blenheim Ho. SW3 4H 87
Blenheim Pas. NW8 4C 56 (not continuous)
Blenheim Rd. NW8 4D 56
Blenheim St. W1 6C 68
Blenheim Ter. NW8 4C 56
Bletchley Ct. N1 5J 61 (not continuous)
Bletchley St. N1 5H 61
Bletsoe Wlk. N1 4H 61
Blick Ho. SE16 6J 83
Bliss M. W10 6F 55
Blisworth Ho. E2 3F 63
Blithfield St. W8 7A 76
Blomfield Ct. W9 1D 66
Blomfield Mans. W12 3A 74
Blomfield Rd. W9 3B 66
Blomfield St. EC2 4K 71
Blomfield Vs. W2 4B 66
Bloomburg St. SW1 2F 89
Bloomfield Ho. E1 4E 72
Bloomfield Pl. W1 7D 68
Bloomfield Ter. SW1 3B 88
BLOOMSBURY 3K 69
Bloomsbury Ct. WC1 4K 69
Bloomsbury Pl. WC1 4K 69
Bloomsbury Sq. WC1 4K 69
Bloomsbury St. WC1 4H 69
Bloomsbury Theatre 1G 69
Bloomsbury Way WC1 4J 69
Blore Ct. W1 7G 69
Blore Ho. SW10 7C 86
Blossom St. E1 2B 72
Blue Anchor La. SE16 1F 93
Blue Anchor Yd. E1 7E 72
Blue Ball Yd. SW1 3E 78
Bluebell Cl. E9 2J 63
Blue Elephant Theatre 7G 91
Bluegate M. E1 7H 73
Blue Lion Pl. SE1 6A 82
Blythe Ho. SE11 5D 90
Blythe M. W14 6C 74
Blythendale Ho. E2 5F 63
Blythe Rd. W14 6C 74 (not continuous)
Blythe St. E2 6G 63
Boadicea St. N1 3A 60
Boarley Ho. SE17 2A 92
Boathouse Cen., The W10 1D 64
Boathouse Wlk. SE15 7D 92 (not continuous)
Bocking St. E8 2G 63
Boddington Ho. SW13 6A 84
Boden Ho. E1 3E 72
Bodington Ct. W12 4C 74
Boisseau Ho. E1 4K 73
Boldero Pl. NW8 2G 67
Bolina Rd. SE16 3K 93
Bolingbroke Rd. W14 6C 74
Bolney Ga. SW7 5G 77
Bolney St. SW8 7A 90
Bolsover St. W1 2D 68
Bolt Ct. *EC4 6D 70* *(off Fleet St.)*
Bolton Cres. SE5 7E 90
Bolton Gdns. NW10 5C 54
SW5 3A 86
Bolton Gdns. M. SW10 3B 86
Bolton Pl. NW8 3B 56
Bolton Rd. NW8 3B 56
Boltons, The SW10 3C 86
Boltons Ct. SW5 3B 86
Boltons Pl. SW5 3C 86
Bolton St. W1 2D 78
Bolton Studios SW10 4D 86
Bombay Ct. SE16 4J 83
Bombay St. SE16 1G 93
Bomore Rd. W11 7D 64
Bonar Rd. SE15 7E 92
Bonchurch Rd. W10 3E 64
Bond Ct. EC4 6J 71
Bond Ho. NW6 5H 55
Bondway SW8 6K 89
Bonham Ho. W11 2G 75
Bonhill St. EC2 2K 71
Bonner Rd. E2 4J 63
Bonner St. E2 5K 63
Bonnington Ho. N1 5A 60
Bonnington Sq. SW8 5A 90
Bonny St. NW1 1E 58
Bonsor St. SE5 7A 92
Booth Cl. E9 3H 63
Booth La. EC4 7G 71
Booth's Pl. W1 4F 69
Boot St. N1 7A 62
Boreas Wlk. N1 5F 61
BOROUGH, THE 5H 81
Borough High St. SE1 5H 81
Borough Mkt. SE1 3J 81
Borough Rd. SE1 6E 80
Borough Sq. SE1 5G 81
Borrett Cl. SE17 4G 91
Borrowdale NW1 7E 58
Boscobel Pl. SW1 1B 88
Boscobel St. NW8 2F 67
Boss Ho. SE1 4C 82
Boss St. SE1 4C 82
Boston Ho. SW5 2B 86
Boston Pl. NW1 2J 67
Boswell Ct. W14 7D 74
WC1 3K 69
Boswell Ho. WC1 3K 69
Boswell St. WC1 3K 69
Bosworth Ho. W10 2F 65
Bosworth Rd. W10 2F 65
Bothwell St. W6 6D 84
Botolph All. EC3 7A 72
Botolph La. EC3 1A 82
Botts M. W2 6K 65
Boughton Ho. SE1 4J 81
Boulogne Ho. SE1 6C 82
Boundary Ho. SE5 7G 91
W11 2D 74
Boundary La. SE17 6H 91
Boundary Pas. E2 1C 72
Boundary Rd. NW8 3B 56
Boundary Row SE1 4E 80
Boundary St. E2 7C 62
Bourchier St. W1 7G 69 (not continuous)
Bourdon Pl. W1 7D 68
Bourdon St. W1 7D 68
Bourlet Cl. W1 4E 68
Bourne Est. EC1 3C 70
Bourne M. W1 5B 68
Bourne St. SW1 2A 88
Bourne Ter. W2 3A 66
Bouverie Pl. W2 5F 67
Bouverie St. EC4 6D 70
Bowater Ho. EC1 2G 71
SW1 5J 77
Bow Chyd. EC4 6H 71
Bowden St. SE11 3D 90
Bowfell Rd. W6 6B 84
Bowhill Cl. SW9 7D 90
Bowland Yd. SW1 5K 77
Bow La. EC4 6H 71
Bowl Ct. EC2 2B 72
Bowles Rd. SE1 5E 92
Bowley Ho. SE16 6E 82
Bowling Grn. Ho. SW10 7E 86
Bowling Grn. La. EC1 1D 70
Bowling Grn. Pl. SE1 4J 81
Bowling Grn. St. SE11 5C 90
Bowling Grn. Wlk. N1 6A 62
Bowman's Bldgs. NW1 3G 67
Bowman's M. E1 7E 72
Bowmore Wlk. NW1 1H 59
Bowness Ho. SE15 7J 93
Bow St. WC2 6K 69
Bowyer Ho. N1 3B 62
Bowyer Pl. SE5 7H 91
Bowyer St. SE5 7H 91
Boxmoor Ho. E2 3F 63
W11 3D 74
Boxworth Gro. N1 2B 60
Boyce Ho. W10 7G 55
Boydell Ct. NW8 1E 56 (not continuous)
Boyd St. E1 6F 73
Boyfield St. SE1 5F 81
Boyle St. W1 7E 68
Boyne Ter. M. W11 2G 75
Boyson Rd. SE17 5H 91 (not continuous)
Boyson Wlk. SE17 5H 91
Boyton Cl. E1 1K 73
Boyton Ho. NW8 4F 57
Brabant Ct. EC3 7A 72
Brabner Ho. E2 6E 62
Bracer Ho. N1 3B 62
Bracewell Rd. W10 4A 64
Brackenbury Gdns. W6 6A 74
Brackenbury Rd. W6 7A 74
Brackley Ct. NW8 1E 66
Brackley St. EC1 3H 71
Bracklyn Ct. N1 4J 61 (not continuous)
Bracklyn St. N1 4J 61
Bradbeer Ho. E2 7J 63
Bradby Ho. NW8 5B 56
Bradenham SE17 5J 91
Bradenham Cl. SE17 5J 91
Braden St. W9 2A 66
Bradfield Ct. NW1 1D 58
Bradford Ho. W14 7D 74
Bradiston Rd. W9 6H 55
Bradley Ho. SE16 1H 93
Bradley's Cl. N1 4D 60
Brad St. SE1 3D 80
Bradwell Ho. NW6 3A 56
Brady St. E1 1G 73
Braemar Cl. SE16 4G 93
Braemar Ho. W9 7C 56
Braemar Mans. SW7 7B 76
Braes St. N1 1F 61
Braganza St. SE17 3E 90
Braham Ho. SE11 4B 90
Braham St. E1 6D 72
Braidwood Pas. EC1 3G 71
Braidwood St. SE1 3A 82
Braintree Ho. E1 1J 73
Braintree St. E2 1J 73
Braithwaite Ho. EC1 1J 71
Braithwaite Twr. W2 3E 66
Bramah Tea & Coffee Mus. 3H 81
Bramber WC1 7J 59
Bramber Ct. W14 5H 85
Bramber Rd. W14 5G 85

Bramcote Gro. SE16 ....3J 93
Bramerton St. SW3 ....5G 87
Bramham Gdns. SW5 ....3A 86
Bramley Cres. SW8 ....7H 89
Bramley Ho. W10 ....6D 64
Bramley Rd. W10 ....1D 74
(not continuous)
Brampton WC1 ....4A 70
Bramshurst NW8 ....3B 56
Bramwell Ho. SE1 ....7H 81
SW1 ....4E 88
Bramwell M. N1 ....2B 60
Branch Pl. N1 ....3K 61
Brandon Est. SE17 ....6E 90
Brandon Mans. W14 ....5F 85
Brandon M. EC2 ....4J 71
Brandon Rd. N7 ....1J 59
Brandon St. SE17 ....2H 91
(not continuous)
Brangton Rd. SE11 ....4B 90
Brangwyn Ct. W14 ....7E 74
Branksome Ho. SW8 ....7A 90
Branscombe NW1 ....3F 59
Bransdale Cl. NW6 ....2K 55
Brantwood Ho. SE5 ....7G 91
Brasenose Dr. SW13 ....6A 84
Brathay NW1 ....5F 59
Bratley St. E1 ....2E 72
Bravington Pl. W9 ....1G 65
Bravington Rd. W9 ....5G 55
Bravingtons Wlk. *N1 ....5K 59*
(off York Way)
Brawne Ho. SE17 ....6F 91
Bray NW3 ....1G 57
Brayfield Ter. N1 ....1C 60
Brayford Sq. E1 ....5K 73
Bray Pl. SW3 ....3J 87
Bread St. EC4 ....7H 71
(not continuous)
Breakwell Ct. W10 ....2E 64
Breamore Ho. SE15 ....7F 93
Bream's Bldgs. EC4 ....5C 70
Brechin Pl. SW7 ....3D 86
Brecon Ho. W2 ....5C 66
Brecon Rd. W6 ....6F 85
Bredin Ho. SW10 ....7B 86
Breezers Ct. E1 ....1F 83
Breezer's Hill E1 ....1F 83
Bremner Rd. SW7 ....6D 76
Brendon St. W1 ....5H 67
Brenley Ho. SE1 ....4J 81
Bressenden Pl. SW1 ....6D 78
Breton Highwalk EC1 ....3H 71
Breton Ho. EC2 ....3H 71
SE1 ....6C 82
Brettell St. SE17 ....4K 91
Brettinghurst SE1 ....4E 92
Brewer's Grn. SW1 ....6G 79
Brewer's Hall Gdn.
EC2 ....4H 71
Brewer St. W1 ....1F 79
Brewery, The EC2 ....3J 71
Brewery Ind. Est., The
N1 ....5H 61
Brewery Sq. EC1 ....1F 71
SE1 ....3C 82
Brewhouse La. E1 ....3H 83
Brewhouse Yd. EC1 ....1E 70
Brewster Gdns. W10 ....3A 64
Brewster Ho. SE1 ....1D 92
Briant Ho. SE1 ....7C 80
Briar Wlk. W10 ....1F 65
Briary Cl. NW3 ....1G 57
Brickbarn Cl. SW10 ....7D 86
Brick Ct. EC4 ....6C 70
Brick La. E1 ....1D 72
E2 ....7D 62
BRICKLAYER'S ARMS
....7K 81
Bricklayers Arms Bus. Cen.
SE1 ....1B 92
Brick St. W1 ....3C 78
Brideale Cl. SE15 ....6D 92
Bride Ct. EC4 ....6E 70
Bride La. EC4 ....6E 70
Bridel M. N1 ....3E 60
Brides Pl. N1 ....1A 62
Bridewain St. SE1 ....6C 82
(not continuous)
Bridewell Pl. E1 ....3H 83
EC4 ....6E 70
Bridford M. W1 ....3D 68
Bridge, The SW8 ....7C 88
Bridge App. NW1 ....1A 58
Bridge Av. W6 ....2A 84
Bridge Av. Mans. W6 ....3A 84
Bridge Cl. W10 ....6D 64
Bridgefoot SE1 ....4K 89
Bridge Ho. NW3 ....1A 58
NW10 ....4C 54
SW1 ....3C 88
W2 ....4E 66
Bridgehouse Ct. SE1 ....4E 80
Bridgeman Ho. E9 ....1J 63
Bridgeman Rd. N1 ....1A 60
Bridgeman St. NW8 ....5G 57
Bridge Mdws. SE14 ....5K 93
Bridgen Ho. E1 ....5H 73
Bridge Pl. SW1 ....1D 88
Bridgeport Pl. E1 ....2F 83
Bridges Ho. SE5 ....7J 91
Bridgeside Ho. N1 ....5G 61
Bridge St. SW1 ....5J 79
Bridge Vw. W6 ....3A 84
Bridge Vw. Ct. SE1 ....7B 82
Bridgewalk Hgts.
SE1 ....4K 81
Bridgewater Highwalk
EC2 ....3H 71
Bridgewater Sq. EC2 ....3G 71
Bridgewater St. EC2 ....3G 71
Bridgeway St. NW1 ....5F 59
Bridge Yd. SE1 ....2K 81
Bridgnorth Ho. SE15 ....6F 93
Bridgwater Ho. W2 ....5C 66
Bridle La. W1 ....7F 69
Bridport SE17 ....4J 91
Bridport Ho. N1 ....3K 61
Bridport Pl. N1 ....3K 61
(not continuous)
Bridstow Pl. W2 ....5K 65
Brierfield NW1 ....3E 58
Brierly Gdns. E2 ....5K 63
Briggs Ho. E2 ....6D 62
Brighton Bldgs. SE1 ....7A 82
Brill Pl. NW1 ....5H 59
Brindley Ho. W2 ....3K 65
Brinklow Ho. W2 ....4A 66
Brinsley Ho. E1 ....6J 73
Brinsley St. E1 ....6H 73
Brinton Wlk. SE1 ....3E 80
Brisbane St. SE5 ....7J 91
Briset St. EC1 ....3E 70
Bristol Gdns. W9 ....2B 66
Bristol Ho. SE11 ....7C 80
SW1 ....3A 88
WC1 ....3K 69
Bristol M. W9 ....2B 66
Britain & London Vis. Cen.
....2G 79
Britain at War Experience
....3A 82
Britannia Bldg. N1 ....6J 61
BRITANNIA JUNC. 2D 58
Britannia Leisure Cen.
....3K 61
Britannia Rd. SW6 ....7A 86
(not continuous)
Britannia Row N1 ....2F 61
Britannia St. WC1 ....6A 60
Britannia Wlk. N1 ....5J 61
(not continuous)
Britannic Highwalk
EC2 ....4J 71
Britannic Twr. EC2 ....3J 71
British Genius Site 7A 88
British Library 6H 59
British Mus. 4H 69
British Telecom Cen.
EC1 ....5G 71
Brittany Point SE11 ....2C 90
Britten Ho. SW3 ....3G 87
Britten St. SW3 ....4G 87
Britton St. EC1 ....2E 70
Brixton Rd. SE11 ....6C 90
SW9 ....7C 90
Broadbent St. W1 ....7C 68
Broad Ct. WC2 ....6K 69
Broadfield La. NW1 ....1J 59
Broadgate EC2 ....4A 72
Broadgate Circ. EC2 ....4A 72
Broadgate Ice Rink 4A 72
Broadgates Ct. SE11 ....4D 90
Broad La. EC2 ....3A 72
Broadley St. NW8 ....3F 67
Broadley Ter. NW1 ....2H 67
Broadmayne SE17 ....3J 91
Broadmead W14 ....2E 84
Broadoak Ho. NW6 ....3A 56
Broad Sanctuary
SW1 ....5H 79
Broadstone NW1 ....1G 59
Broadstone Ho. SW8 ....7A 90
Broadstone Pl. W1 ....4A 68
Broad St. Av. EC2 ....4A 72
Broad St. Pl. EC2 ....4K 71
Broad Wlk. NW1 ....4B 58
W1 ....1K 77
Broad Wlk., The W8 ....1B 76
Broadwalk Ct. W8 ....2K 75
Broadwalk Ho. EC2 ....2A 72
SW7 ....5C 76
Broadwall SE1 ....2D 80
Broadway SW1 ....5G 79
SW1 ....6G 79
Broadway Arc. W6 ....2B 84
Broadway Cen., The
W6 ....2B 84
Broadway Chambers
W6 ....2B 84
Broadway Ho. E8 ....3G 63
Broadway Mans.
SW6 ....7K 85
Broadway Mkt. E8 ....3G 63
Broadway Mkt. M. E8 ....3F 63
Broadway Shop. Mall
SW1 ....6G 79
Broadwick St. W1 ....7F 69
Broadwood Ter. W8 ....1H 85
Broad Yd. EC1 ....2E 70
Brocas Cl. NW3 ....1H 57
Brockham Ho. NW1 ....3F 59
Brockham St. SE1 ....6H 81
Brockmer Ho. E1 ....7G 73
Brockweir E2 ....5K 63
Brockwell Ho. SE11 ....5B 90
Brodie Ho. SE1 ....3D 92
Brodie St. SE1 ....3D 92
Brodlove La. E1 ....7K 73
Broken Wharf EC4 ....7G 71
Broke Wlk. E8 ....2D 62
Bromfield St. N1 ....4D 60
Bromhead Rd. E1 ....5J 73
Bromhead St. E1 ....5J 73
Bromleigh Ho. SE1 ....6C 82
Bromley Pl. W1 ....3E 68
BROMPTON 7H 77
Brompton Arc. SW3 ....5K 77
Brompton Cotts.
SW10 ....5C 86
Brompton Oratory 7G 77
Brompton Pk. Cres.
SW6 ....6K 85
Brompton Pl. SW3 ....6H 77
Brompton Rd. SW1 ....1G 87
SW3 ....1G 87
Brompton Sq. SW3 ....6G 77
Brompton Vs. SW6 ....5J 85
Bromyard Ho. SE15 ....7G 93
Bron Ct. NW6 ....3K 55
BRONDESBURY 1H 55
Brondesbury M. NW6 ....1J 55
BRONDESBURY PARK
....3A 54
Brondesbury Pk.
NW6 ....1C 54
Brondesbury Rd.
NW6 ....4G 55
Brondesbury Vs.
NW6 ....4H 55
Bronsart Rd. SW6 ....7E 84
Bronte Ct. W14 ....7D 74
Bronte Ho. NW6 ....6K 55
Bronti Cl. SE17 ....4H 91
Bronwen Ct. NW8 ....7E 56
Brook Dr. SE11 ....7D 80
Brooke's Ct. EC1 ....4C 70
Brooke's Mkt. EC1 ....3C 70
Brooke St. EC1 ....3C 70
Brook Ga. W1 ....1K 77
BROOK GREEN 1D 84
Brook Grn. W6 ....7C 74
Brook Grn. Flats W14 ....7C 74
Brook Ho. W6 ....2B 84
Brook Ho's. NW1 ....5F 59
Brooklands Ct. NW6 ....1G 55
Brooklyn Pas. W12 ....5A 74
Brook M. WC2 ....6H 69
Brook M. Nth. W2 ....7D 66
Brooksby Ho. N1 ....1D 60
Brooksby M. N1 ....1D 60
Brooksby St. N1 ....1C 60
Brooks Ct. SW8 ....7F 89
Brooks Lodge N1 ....4B 62
Brooks M. W1 ....7C 68
Brook St. W1 ....7B 68
W2 ....7F 67
Brooksville Av. NW6 ....3F 55
Brookville Rd. SW6 ....7G 85
Brookwood Ho. SE1 ....5F 81
Broome Way SE5 ....7J 91
Broomfield Ct. SE16 ....6F 83
Broomfield Ho. SE17 ....2A 92
Brougham Rd. E8 ....2F 63
Brough Cl. SW8 ....7K 89
Brown Hart Gdns.
W1 ....7B 68
Browning Cl. W9 ....2D 66
Browning Ct. W14 ....5G 85
Browning Ho. W12 ....6A 64
Browning M. W1 ....4B 68
Browning St. SE17 ....3H 91
Brownlow Ho. SE16 ....5E 82
Brownlow M. WC1 ....2B 70
Brownlow Rd. E8 ....2D 62
Brownlow St. WC1 ....4B 70
Browns Arc. W1 ....1F 79
Brown's Bldgs. EC3 ....6B 72
Brown St. W1 ....5J 67
Broxwood Way NW8 ....3H 57
Bruce Cl. W10 ....3D 64
Bruce Ho. W10 ....3D 64
Bruckner St. W10 ....6G 55
Bruges Pl. NW1 ....1F 59
Brune Ho. E1 ....4C 72
Brunei Gallery 3H 69
Brunel Engine House Mus.
....4J 83
Brunel Est. W2 ....4J 65
Brunel M. W10 ....6D 54
Brunel Rd. SE16 ....3K 83
Brunel Wlk. SW10 ....7F 87
Brune St. E1 ....4C 72
Brunlees Ho. SE1 ....7G 81
Brunswick Cen. WC1 ....1J 69
Brunswick Cl. Est.
EC1 ....7E 60
Brunswick Ct. EC1 ....7E 60
SE1 ....5B 82
SW1 ....2H 89
Brunswick Flats W11 ....6J 65
Brunswick Gdns. W8 ....3K 75
Brunswick Ho. E2 ....4D 62
Brunswick Mans.
WC1 ....1K 69
Brunswick M. W1 ....5K 67
Brunswick Pl. N1 ....7K 61
NW1 ....2B 68
(not continuous)
Brunswick Sq. WC1 ....1K 69
Brushfield St. E1 ....4B 72
Bruton La. W1 ....1D 78
Bruton Pl. W1 ....1D 78
Bruton St. W1 ....1D 78
Brutus Ct. SE11 ....2E 90
Bryan Av. NW10 ....1A 54
Bryan Ho. NW10 ....1A 54
Bryanston Ct. W1 ....5J 67
(not continuous)
Bryanston Mans. W1 ....3J 67
Bryanston M. E. W1 ....4J 67
Bryanston M. W. W1 ....4J 67
Bryanston Pl. W1 ....4J 67
Bryanston Sq. W1 ....4J 67
Bryanston St. W1 ....6J 67
Bryant Ct. E2 ....4C 62
(not continuous)
Brydale Ho. SE16 ....1K 93
Brydges Pl. WC2 ....1J 79
Brydon Wlk. N1 ....2K 59
Bryer Ct. EC2 ....3G 71
Bryher Ct. SE11 ....3C 90
Buchanan Gdns.
NW10 ....5A 54
Buckfast St. E2 ....7F 63
Buck Hill Wlk. W2 ....1F 77
Buckhurst St. E1 ....2H 73
Buckingham Arc.
WC2 ....1K 79
Buckingham Chambers
SW1 ....1F 89
Buckingham Ct. W11 ....1J 75
Buckingham Ga.
SW1 ....6E 78
Buckingham M. SW1 ....6E 78
Buckingham Palace 5D 78
Buckingham Pal. Rd.
SW1 ....2C 88
Buckingham Pl. SW1 ....6E 78
Buckingham St. WC2 ....1K 79
Buckland Ct. N1 ....4A 62
Buckland Ho. SW1 ....3C 88
Buckland St. N1 ....5K 61
Bucklebury NW1 ....7E 58
Bucklers All. SW6 ....7H 85
(not continuous)
Bucklersbury EC4 ....6J 71
Bucklersbury Pas.
EC4 ....6J 71
Buckle St. E1 ....6D 72
Buckley Ct. NW6 ....1H 55
Buckley Ho. *W11 ....4E 74*
(off Holland Pk. Av.)
Buckley Rd. NW6 ....1H 55
Bucknall St. WC2 ....5H 69
Bucknill Ho. SW1 ....3C 88
Buckridge Ho. EC1 ....3C 70
Buckshead Ho. W2 ....4J 65
Buck St. NW1 ....1D 58
Budge Row EC4 ....6J 71
Budge's Wlk. W2 ....3C 76
Budleigh Ho. SE15 ....7F 93
Bulbarrow NW8 ....3B 56
Bulinga St. SW1 ....2J 89
Bullard's Pl. E2 ....6K 63
Bulleid Way SW1 ....2D 88
Bullen Ho. E1 ....2H 73
Buller Cl. SE15 ....7E 92
Buller Rd. NW10 ....7D 54
Bullingham Mans.
W8 ....4K 75
Bull Inn Ct. WC2 ....1K 79
Bulls Gdns. SW3 ....1H 87
Bulls Head Pas. EC3 ....6A 72
Bull Wharf La. EC4 ....7H 71
Bull Wharf Wlk. *EC4 ....1H 81*
(off Bull Wharf La.)
Bulmer M. W11 ....2J 75
Bulmer Pl. W11 ....2H 75
Bulrington Cnr. NW1 ....1E 58
Bulstrode Pl. W1 ....4B 68
Bulstrode St. W1 ....5B 68
Bulwer St. W12 ....3B 74
Bunhill Row EC1 ....1J 71
Bunhouse Pl. SW1 ....3A 88
Bunning Way N7 ....1K 59
Bunyan Ct. EC2 ....3G 71
Buonaparte M. SW1 ....3G 89
Burbage Cl. SE1 ....7J 81
Burbage Ho. N1 ....3K 61
Burchell Ho. SE11 ....3B 90
Burcher Gale Gro.
SE15 ....7B 92
Burden Ho. SW8 ....7J 89
Burdett M. W2 ....5A 66
Burgess Bus. Pk.
SE5 ....7K 91
Burgess Ho. SE5 ....7G 91
Burgess Pk. Kart Track
....6K 91
Burge St. SE1 ....7K 81
Burgh St. N1 ....4F 61
Burgon St. EC4 ....6F 71
Burleigh Ho. SW3 ....6F 87
W10 ....3E 64
Burleigh St. WC2 ....7A 70
Burlington Arc. W1 ....1E 78
Burlington Cl. W9 ....1J 65
Burlington Gdns. W1 ....1E 78
Burnaby St. SW10 ....7D 86
Burnand Ho. W14 ....6D 74
Burne Jones Ho. W14 ....2F 85
Burnell Wlk. SE1 ....3D 92
Burne St. NW1 ....3G 67
Burnham NW3 ....1G 57
Burnham Ct. W2 ....7A 66
Burnham Est. E2 ....6J 63
Burnham St. E2 ....6J 63
Burnhill Cl. SE15 ....7H 93
Burnsall St. SW3 ....3H 87
Burns Ho. E2 ....7J 63
SE17 ....4F 91
Burnthwaite Rd.
SW6 ....7H 85
Buross St. E1 ....5H 73
Burrard Ho. E2 ....4J 63
Burr Cl. E1 ....2E 82
Burrell St. SE1 ....2F 81
Burrows M. SE1 ....4E 80
Burrows Rd. NW10 ....6A 54
Bursar St. SE1 ....3A 82
Burslem St. E1 ....6G 73
Burton Bank N1 ....1J 61
Burton Ct. SW3 ....3K 87
(not continuous)
Burton Gro. SE17 ....4J 91
Burton Ho. SE16 ....5G 83
Burton M. SW1 ....2B 88
Burton Pl. WC1 ....7H 59
Burton Rd. NW6 ....1H 55
Burton St. WC1 ....7H 59
Burtt Ho. N1 ....6A 62
Burwash Ho. SE1 ....5K 81
Burwell Cl. E1 ....6H 73
Burwood Pl. W2 ....5H 67
Bury Ct. EC3 ....5B 72
Bury Pl. WC1 ....4J 69
Bury St. EC3 ....6B 72
SW1 ....2E 78
Bury Wlk. SW3 ....2G 87
Bushbaby Cl. SE1 ....7A 82
Bush Ct. W12 ....4D 74
Bushell St. E1 ....3F 83
Bush La. EC4 ....7J 71
Bush Rd. E8 ....3G 63
Bush Theatre 4B 74
Bushwood Dr. SE1 ....2D 92
Business Design Cen.
N1 ....3D 60
Buspace Studios
W10 ....1E 64
Bute Gdns. W6 ....2C 84
Bute St. SW7 ....1E 86
Butler Ho. E2 ....6K 63
Butler Pl. SW1 ....6G 79
Butlers & Colonial Wharf
SE1 ....4D 82
Butler St. E2 ....6K 63
Butlers Wharf SE1 ....3D 82
Butlers Wharf W.
SE1 ....3C 82
Butterfield Cl. SE16 ....5F 83
Buttermere NW1 ....6D 58
Buttermere Cl. SE1 ....2C 92
Buttermere Ct. NW8 ....2E 56
Butterwick W6 ....2C 84
Butterworth Ter.
SE17 ....4H 91
Buttesland St. N1 ....6K 61
Buxted Rd. E8 ....1C 62
Buxton Ct. N1 ....6H 61
(not continuous)
Buxton St. E1 ....2D 72
Byng Pl. WC1 ....2H 69
Byron Cl. E8 ....2E 62
Byron Ct. NW6 ....1D 56
SW3 ....2H 87
W9 ....1K 65
WC1 ....1A 70
Byron M. W9 ....1K 65
Byward St. EC3 ....1B 82
Bywater St. SW3 ....3J 87
Bywell Pl. W1 ....4E 68

C

Cabbell St. NW1 ....4G 67
Cable Ho. WC1 ....6C 60
Cable St. E1 ....7E 72
Caci Ho. W14 ....2G 85
Cadbury Way SE16 ....7D 82
Cadell Cl. E2 ....5D 62
Cadet Dr. SE1 ....3D 92
Cadiz St. SE17 ....4H 91
Cadman Cl. SW9 ....7E 90
Cadmore Ho. N1 ....1E 60
Cadogan Ct. SW3 ....2J 87
Cadogan Ct. Gdns.
SW1 ....1A 88
Cadogan Gdns. SW3 ....1K 87
Cadogan Ga. SW1 ....1K 87
Cadogan Ho. SW3 ....6F 87
Cadogan La. SW1 ....6A 78
Cadogan Mans. SW3 ....2K 87
Cadogan Pl. SW1 ....6K 77
Cadogan Sq. SW1 ....7J 77
Cadogan St. SW3 ....2J 87
Caernarvon Ho. W2 ....5C 66
Cafe Gallery 7J 83
Cahill St. EC1 ....2H 71
Caird St. W10 ....7F 55
Caithness Ho. N1 ....2A 60
Caithness Rd. W14 ....1C 84
Calcott Ct. W14 ....7E 74
Calcraft Ho. E2 ....4J 63
Calderon Ho. NW8 ....4G 57
Calderon Pl. W10 ....4A 64
Caldew St. SE5 ....7J 91
Caldwell Ho. SW13 ....7A 84
Caleb St. SE1 ....4H 81
Caledonian Rd. N1 ....5K 59
N7 ....1A 60
Caledonia St. N1 ....5K 59
Cale St. SW3 ....3G 87
Calgarth NW1 ....5F 59
Calgary Ct. SE16 ....5K 83
Caliban Twr. N1 ....5A 62
Calico Ho. EC4 ....6H 71
Callahan Cotts. E1 ....3J 73
Callcott Ct. NW6 ....1G 55
Callcott Rd. NW6 ....1G 55
Callcott St. W8 ....2J 75
Callendar Rd. SW7 ....6E 76
Callow St. SW3 ....5D 86
Cally Swimming Pool
....2A 60
Calmington Rd. SE5 ....5B 92
Calshot Ho. N1 ....4A 60
Calshot St. N1 ....4A 60
Calstock NW1 ....3G 59
Calstock Ho. SE11 ....3D 90
Calthorpe St. WC1 ....1B 70
Calvert Av. E2 ....7B 62
Calverton SE5 ....5A 92
Calvert's Bldgs. SE1 ....3J 81
Calvert St. NW1 ....2A 58
Calvin St. E1 ....2C 72
Calypso Cres. SE15 ....7C 92
Camber Ho. SE15 ....5K 93
Camberley Ho. NW1 ....5D 58
Camberwell New Rd.
SE5 ....6C 90
Camberwell Rd. SE5 ....5H 91
Cambourne M. W11 ....6E 64
Cambridge Av. NW6 ....4K 55
NW10 ....7A 54
Cambridge Cir. WC2 ....6H 69
Cambridge Ct. E2 ....5H 63
NW6 ....4K 55
W2 ....4G 67
W6 ....1B 84
Cambridge Cres. E2 ....5G 63
Cambridge Gdns.
NW6 ....4K 55
W10 ....5D 64
Cambridge Ga. NW1 ....1C 68
Cambridge Ga. M.
NW1 ....1D 68
Cambridge Gro. W6 ....1A 84
Cambridge Heath Rd.
E1 ....3H 73
E2 ....5H 63
Cambridge Ho. W6 ....1A 84
Cambridge Pl. W8 ....5B 76
Cambridge Rd. NW6 ....6K 55
Cambridge Sq. W2 ....5G 67
Cambridge St. SW1 ....2D 88
Cambridge Ter. NW1 ....7C 58
Cambridge Ter. M.
NW1 ....7D 58
Cambridge Theatre 6J 69
Cam Ct. SE15 ....6C 92
Camden Ct. NW1 ....1F 59
Camden Gdns. NW1 ....1D 58
Camden High St.
NW1 ....1D 58
Camden Lock Market
....1C 58
Camden Lock Pl.
NW1 ....1C 58
Camden Market 2D 58
Camden Markets 1C 58
Camden Pas. N1 ....4E 60
Camden Peoples Theatre
....1E 68
Camden Rd. NW1 ....1E 58
Camden St. NW1 ....1E 58
Camden Studios NW1 ....3F 59
CAMDEN TOWN 2D 58
Camden Wlk. N1 ....3E 60
Camelford NW1 ....3F 59
Camelford Ct. W11 ....7E 64
Camelford Ho. SE1 ....4K 89
Camelford Wlk. W11 ....6E 64
Camera Pl. SW10 ....6E 86
Cameret Ct. W11 ....4D 74
Cameron Ho. NW8 ....4G 57
SE5 ....7G 91
Cameron Pl. E1 ....5H 73
Camgate Mans. SE5 ....5H 91
Camilla Rd. SE16 ....2G 93
Camlet St. E2 ....1C 72

Camley St. NW1 ... 1G 59
Camomile St. EC3 ... 5A 72
Campbell Ct. SW7 ... 7C 76
Campbell Ho. SW1 ... 4E 88
W2 ... 3E 66
Campbell Wlk. N1 ... 2K 59
Campden Gro. W8 ... 4K 75
Campden Hill W8 ... 4H 75
Campden Hill Ct. W8 ... 4K 75
Campden Hill Gdns. W8 ... 2J 75
Campden Hill Ga. W8 ... 4J 75
Campden Hill Mans. W8 ... 2K 75
Campden Hill Pl. W11 ... 2H 75
Campden Hill Rd. W8 ... 2J 75
Campden Hill Sq. W8 ... 2H 75
Campden Hill Towers W11 ... 2J 75
Campden Ho. NW6 ... 1E 56
W8 ... 3K 75
Campden Ho. Cl. W8 ... 4K 75
Campden Ho's. W8 ... 3J 75
Campden Ho. Ter. W8 ... 3K 75
Campden Mans. W8 ... 2K 75
Campden St. W8 ... 3J 75
Camperdown St. E1 ... 6D 72
Canada Est. SE16 ... 6K 83
Canada Memorial ... 4D 78
CANAL BRIDGE ... 5F 93
Canal Bldg. N1 ... 4G 61
Canal Cl. W10 ... 1D 64
Canal Gro. SE15 ... 5F 93
Canal Market ... 1C 58
Canal Path E2 ... 3C 62
Canalside Activity Cen. ... 1D 64
Canal Side Studios NW1 ... 2G 59
Canal St. SE5 ... 6J 91
Canal Wlk. N1 ... 2K 61
Canal Way W10 ... 1C 64
Candover St. W1 ... 4E 68
Canfield Gdns. NW6 ... 1A 56
Cann Ho. W14 ... 7F 75
Canning Pas. W8 ... 6C 76 (not continuous)
Canning Pl. W8 ... 6C 76
Canning Pl. M. W8 ... 5C 76
Cannon Ct. EC1 ... 1F 71
Cannon Ho. SE11 ... 2B 90
Cannons Health Club
Cannon Street ... 7J 71
Willesden Green ... 1B 54
Cannon St. EC4 ... 6G 71
Cannon St. Rd. E1 ... 5G 73
Canon All. *EC4 ... 6G 71 (off Queen's Head Pas.)*
Canon Beck Rd. SE16 ... 4K 83
Canonbury Bus. Cen. N1 ... 2H 61
Canonbury Ct. N1 ... 1F 61
Canonbury Cres. N1 ... 1H 61
Canonbury Gro. N1 ... 1G 61
Canonbury Rd. N1 ... 1F 61
Canonbury St. N1 ... 1G 61
Canonbury Vs. N1 ... 1F 61
Canon Row SW1 ... 5J 79 (not continuous)
Canon St. N1 ... 3G 61
Canrobert St. E2 ... 5G 63
Canterbury Ct. NW6 ... 4J 55
SW9 ... 7D 90
Canterbury Ho. SE1 ... 6B 80
Canterbury Ind. Pk. SE15 ... 6K 93
Canterbury Pl. SE17 ... 2F 91
Canterbury Rd. NW6 ... 5H 55 (not continuous)
Canterbury Ter. NW6 ... 4J 55
Cantium Retail Pk. SE1 ... 5E 92
Canute Gdns. SE16 ... 1K 93
Canvey St. SE1 ... 2G 81
Capel Ct. EC2 ... 6K 71
Capel Ho. E9 ... 1J 63
Capener's Cl. SW1 ... 5K 77
Cape Yd. E1 ... 2F 83
Capital Wharf E1 ... 3F 83
Capland Ho. NW8 ... 1F 67
Capland St. NW8 ... 1F 67
Caple Ho. SW10 ... 7D 86
Capper St. WC1 ... 2F 69
Capstan Ct. E1 ... 1K 83
Caradoc Cl. W2 ... 5J 65
Cara Ho. N1 ... 1D 60
Caranday Vs. W11 ... 3D 74
Caraway Apartments SE1 ... 4D 82
Carbrooke Ho. E9 ... 2J 63
Carburton St. W1 ... 3D 68
Cardamon Bldg. SE1 ... 3D 82
Cardiff Ho. SE15 ... 6F 93
Cardigan St. SE11 ... 3C 90
Cardinal Bourne St. SE1 ... 7K 81
Cardinal Cap All. SE1 ... 2G 81
Cardinal Ct. E1 ... 1E 82
Cardinal Mans. SW1 ... 1E 88
Cardinal Pl. SW1 ... 6E 78 (not continuous)
Cardinal Wlk. SW1 ... 7E 78
Cardine M. SE15 ... 7G 93
Cardington St. NW1 ... 6F 59
Career Ct. SE16 ... 4K 83
Carey Ct. SE5 ... 7G 91
Carey La. EC2 ... 5G 71
Carey Mans. SW1 ... 1G 89
Carey Pl. SW1 ... 2G 89
Carey St. WC2 ... 6B 70
Carfree Cl. N1 ... 1D 60
Carisbrooke Ct. W1 ... 4B 68
Carisbrooke Gdns. SE15 ... 7D 92
Carlile Ho. SE1 ... 7K 81
Carlisle Av. EC3 ... 6C 72
Carlisle La. SE1 ... 7B 80
Carlisle Mans. SW1 ... 1E 88
Carlisle Pl. SW1 ... 7E 78
Carlisle Rd. NW6 ... 2E 54
Carlisle St. W1 ... 6G 69
Carlos Pl. W1 ... 1B 78
Carlow St. NW1 ... 4E 58
Carlton Ct. W9 ... 4B 56
Carlton Gdns. SW1 ... 2G 79
Carlton Hill NW8 ... 5B 56
Carlton Ho. NW6 ... 4J 55 (not continuous)
Carlton Ho. Ter. SW1 ... 3G 79
Carlton Mans. NW6 ... 1K 55
W9 ... 6A 56
W14 ... 4F 75
Carlton M. NW6 ... 5J 55
Carlton Sq. E1 ... 1K 73 (not continuous)
Carlton St. SW1 ... 1G 79
Carlton Twr. Pl. SW1 ... 6K 77
Carlton Va. NW6 ... 5H 55
Carlyle Ho. SE5 ... 7G 91
SW3 ... 5F 87
Carlyle Mans. SW3 ... 6G 87
W8 ... 2K 75 (off Kensington Mall.)
Carlyle's House ... 6G 87
Carlyle Sq. SW3 ... 4F 87
Carmarthen Pl. SE1 ... 4A 82
Carmel Ct. W8 ... 4A 76
Carmelite St. EC4 ... 7D 70
Carmel Lodge SW6 ... 5J 85
Carnaby St. W1 ... 6E 68
Carnegie St. N1 ... 3A 60
Carnival Ho. SE1 ... 4D 82
Carnoustie Dr. N1 ... 1A 60 (not continuous)
Carole Ho. NW1 ... 2K 57
Caroline Cl. W2 ... 1B 76
Caroline Gdns. E2 ... 6B 62
SE15 ... 7G 93
Caroline Ho. W2 ... 1B 76
W6 ... 4A 84
Caroline Pl. W2 ... 7B 66
Caroline Pl. M. W2 ... 1B 76
Caroline Ter. SW1 ... 2A 88
Caroline Wlk. W6 ... 6E 84
Carol St. NW1 ... 2E 58
Carpenters Ct. NW1 ... 2E 58
Carpenter St. W1 ... 1C 78
Carriage Dr. E. SW11 ... 7B 88
Carriage Dr. Nth. SW11 ... 6A 88 (Carriage Dr. E.)
SW11 ... 7J 87 (The Parade)
Carriage Dr. W. SW11 ... 7J 87
Carrick Ho. SE11 ... 3E 90
Carrington Ho. W1 ... 3C 78
Carrington St. W1 ... 3C 78
Carroll Ho. W2 ... 7E 66
Carroun Rd. SW8 ... 7A 90
Carter Ct. EC4 ... 6F 71
Carteret St. SW1 ... 5G 79
Carter Ho. E1 ... 4C 72
Carter La. EC4 ... 6F 71
Carter Pl. SE17 ... 4H 91
Carter St. SE17 ... 5G 91
Carthew Vs. W6 ... 6A 74
Carthusian St. EC1 ... 3G 71
Carting La. WC2 ... 1K 79
Cartmel NW1 ... 6E 58
Carton Ho. SE16 ... 6E 82
W11 ... 1D 74
Cartoon Mus. ... 4J 69
Cartwright Gdns. WC1 ... 7J 59
Cartwright Ho. SE1 ... 7H 81
Cartwright St. E1 ... 7D 72
Cartwright Way SW13 ... 7A 84
Casby Ho. SE16 ... 6E 82
Casey Cl. NW8 ... 7G 57
Caspian St. SE5 ... 7J 91
Cassidy Rd. SW6 ... 7J 85 (not continuous)
Cassland Rd. E9 ... 1K 63
Casson Ho. E1 ... 3E 72
Casson St. E1 ... 4E 72
Castellain Mans. W9 ... 1A 66 (not continuous)
Castellain Rd. W9 ... 1A 66
Castelnau SW13 ... 5A 84
Castelnau Gdns. SW13 ... 5A 84
Castelnau Mans. SW13 ... 5A 84 (not continuous)
Casterbridge NW6 ... 2B 56
W11 ... 5H 65
Castleacre W2 ... 6G 67
Castle Baynard St. EC4 ... 7F 71
Castlebrook Ct. SE11 ... 1E 90
Castle Ct. EC3 ... 6K 71
Castleden Ho. NW3 ... 1E 56
Castleford Ct. NW8 ... 1F 67
Castlehaven Rd. NW1 ... 1C 58
Castle Ho. SE1 ... 1G 91
SW8 ... 7K 89
Castle Ind. Est. SE17 ... 1G 91
Castle La. SW1 ... 6E 78
Castlemain St. E1 ... 3G 73
Castle Mead SE5 ... 7H 91
Castlereagh St. W1 ... 5J 67
Castletown Rd. W14 ... 4F 85
Castle Yd. SE1 ... 2F 81
Catesby Ho. E9 ... 1K 63
Catesby St. SE17 ... 2K 91
Cathay Ho. SE16 ... 5H 83
Cathay St. SE16 ... 5H 83
Cathcart Rd. SW10 ... 5B 86
Cathedral Lodge EC1 ... 3G 71
Cathedral Mans. SW1 ... 1E 88
Cathedral Piazza SW1 ... 7E 78
Cathedral St. SE1 ... 2J 81
Cathedral Wlk. SW1 ... 6E 78
Catherine Ct. SW10 ... 5D 86
Catherine Griffiths Ct. EC1 ... 1D 70
Catherine Ho. N1 ... 3B 62
Catherine Pl. SW1 ... 6E 78
Catherine St. WC2 ... 7A 70
Catherine Wheel All. E1 ... 4B 72
Catherine Wheel Yd. SW1 ... 3E 78
Catherwood Ct. N1 ... 5J 61 (not continuous)
Catlin St. SE16 ... 4F 93
Cator St. SE15 ... 7D 92 (Commercial Way)
SE15 ... 6C 92 (Ebley Cl.)
Cato St. W1 ... 4H 67
Catton St. WC1 ... 4A 70
Caughley Ho. SE11 ... 7C 80
Causton Ho. SE5 ... 7H 91
Causton St. SW1 ... 2H 89
Cavaye Ho. SW10 ... 5D 86
Cavaye Pl. SW10 ... 4D 86
Cavell Ho. N1 ... 3A 62
Cavell St. E1 ... 3H 73
Cavendish Av. NW8 ... 5F 57
Cavendish Cl. NW8 ... 6F 57
Cavendish Ct. EC3 ... 5B 72
Cavendish Ho. NW8 ... 5F 57
Cavendish Mans. EC1 ... 2C 70
Cavendish M. Nth. W1 ... 3D 68
Cavendish M. Sth. W1 ... 4D 68
Cavendish Pl. W1 ... 5D 68
Cavendish Rd. NW6 ... 1F 55
Cavendish Sq. W1 ... 5D 68
Cavendish St. N1 ... 5J 61
Caversham Ho. SE15 ... 6E 92
Caversham St. SW3 ... 5J 87
Caverswall St. W12 ... 5A 64
Cavour Ho. SE17 ... 3F 91
Caxton Rd. W12 ... 3C 74
Caxton St. SW1 ... 6F 79
Caxton Wlk. WC2 ... 6H 69
Cayenne Ct. SE1 ... 3D 82
Cayton Pl. EC1 ... 7J 61
Cayton St. EC1 ... 7J 61
Cecil Ct. NW6 ... 1A 56
SW10 ... 5C 86
WC2 ... 7J 69
Cecil Rhodes Ho. NW1 ... 4G 59
Cecil Sharp House ... 2B 58
Cedar Ct. N1 ... 1H 61
SE1 ... 5B 82
Cedar Ho. E2 ... 4J 63
SE16 ... 5K 83
W8 ... 6A 76
Cedarne Rd. SW6 ... 7A 86
Cedar Way NW1 ... 1G 59
Cedar Way Ind. Est. NW1 ... 1G 59
Celandine Dr. E8 ... 1D 62
Celbridge M. W2 ... 5B 66
Celia Ho. N1 ... 5A 62
Cenotaph ... 4J 79
Centaur St. SE1 ... 6B 80
Central Av. SW11 ... 7J 87
Central Markets (Smithfield) ... 4E 70
Central St Martins College of Art & Design ... 4K 69
Central St. EC1 ... 6G 61
Centre Av. NW10 ... 7A 54
Cen. for the Magic Arts, The ... 1F 69
Centre Hgts. NW3 ... 1E 56
Centre Point SE1 ... 3E 92
Centrepoint WC2 ... 5H 69
Centre Point Ho. WC2 ... 5H 69
Centre St. E2 ... 5G 63
Centric Cl. NW1 ... 2C 58
Centurion Bldg. SW8 ... 6C 88
Cephas Av. E1 ... 1K 73
Cephas Ho. E1 ... 2J 73
Cephas St. E1 ... 2J 73
Cerney M. W2 ... 7E 66
Cervantes Ct. W2 ... 6B 66
Cester St. E2 ... 3E 62
Ceylon Rd. W14 ... 7D 74
Chadston Ho. N1 ... 1F 61
Chadswell WC1 ... 7K 59
Chadwell Ho. SE17 ... 4K 91
Chadwell St. EC1 ... 6D 60
Chadwick St. SW1 ... 7H 79
Chadworth Ho. EC1 ... 7G 61
Chagford St. NW1 ... 2J 67
Chalbury Wlk. N1 ... 4B 60
Chalcot Cres. NW1 ... 1K 57
Chalcot Rd. NW1 ... 1A 58
Chalcot Sq. NW1 ... 1K 57 (not continuous)
Chaldon Rd. SW6 ... 7E 84
Chalfont Ct. NW1 ... 2K 67
Chalfont Ho. SE16 ... 6G 83
CHALK FARM ... 1B 58
Chalk Farm Rd. NW1 ... 1A 58
Chalk Hill Rd. W6 ... 2C 84
Challoner Ct. W14 ... 4G 85
Challoner Cres. W14 ... 4G 85
Challoner Mans. W14 ... 4G 85
Challoner St. W14 ... 3G 85
Chalmers Wlk. SE17 ... 6F 91
Chalton Ho. NW1 ... 6G 59
Chalton St. NW1 ... 4F 59 (not continuous)
Chamberlain Ho. E1 ... 7J 73
NW1 ... 5G 59
SE1 ... 5C 80
Chamberlain St. NW1 ... 1K 57
Chamberlayne Mans. NW10 ... 6D 54
Chamberlayne Rd. NW10 ... 1A 54
Chambers La. NW10 ... 1A 54
Chambers St. SE16 ... 4E 82
Chamber St. E1 ... 7D 72
Chambers Wharf SE16 ... 4F 83
Chambord St. E2 ... 6D 62
Champlain Ho. W12 ... 1A 74
Chancellor Ho. E1 ... 3H 83
SW7 ... 6D 76
Chancellors Ct. WC1 ... 3A 70
Chancellor's Rd. W6 ... 4A 84
Chancellor's St. W6 ... 4A 84
Chancellors Wharf W6 ... 4A 84
Chancel St. SE1 ... 3E 80
Chancery Bldgs. E1 ... 7H 73
Chancery La. WC2 ... 4B 70
Chance St. E1 ... 1C 72
E2 ... 1C 72
Chandler Ho. NW6 ... 2H 55
WC1 ... 2K 69
Chandler St. E1 ... 2H 83
Chandler Way SE15 ... 6B 92
Chandlery, The SE1 ... 6D 80
Chandlery Ho. E1 ... 6E 72
Chandos Pl. WC2 ... 1J 79
Chandos St. W1 ... 4D 68
Change All. EC3 ... 6K 71
Channel 4 TV ... 7G 79
Chanticleer Ct. SE1 ... 3E 92
Chantry Cl. W9 ... 2H 65
Chantry Sq. W8 ... 7A 76
Chantry St. N1 ... 3F 61
Chapel Ct. SE1 ... 4J 81
Chapel Mkt. N1 ... 4C 60
Chapel of St John the Evangelist ... *1C 82 (in The Tower of London)*
Chapel Pl. EC2 ... 7A 62
N1 ... 4D 60
W1 ... 6C 68
Chapel Side W2 ... 7A 66
Chapel St. NW1 ... 4G 67
SW1 ... 6B 78
Chaplin Cl. SE1 ... 4D 80
Chapman Ho. E1 ... 6H 73
Chapman St. E1 ... 7G 73
Chapone Pl. W1 ... 6G 69
Chapter Chambers SW1 ... 2G 89
Chapter House ... 6F 71
Chapter Rd. SE17 ... 4F 91
Chapter St. SW1 ... 2G 89
Charcroft Ct. W14 ... 5C 74
Charecroft Way W12 ... 5C 74
Charfield Ct. W9 ... 2B 66
Charing Cross SW1 ... 2J 79
Charing Cross Rd. WC2 ... 5H 69
Charing Cross Sports Club ... 5C 84
Charing Cross Underground Shop. Cen. WC2 ... 1J 79
Charing Ho. SE1 ... 4D 80
Charlbert Ct. NW8 ... 4G 57
Charlbert St. NW8 ... 4G 57
Charles II Pl. SW3 ... 4H 87
Charles II St. SW1 ... 2G 79
Charles Auffray Ho. E1 ... 4K 73
Charles Darwin Ho. *E2 ... 6G 63 (off Canrobert St.)*
Charles Dickens Ho. E2 ... 6F 63
Charles Gardner Ct. N1 ... 6K 61
Charles Harrod Ct. SW13 ... 6A 84
Charles House ... *1G 85 (off Kensington High St.)*
Charles La. NW8 ... 5F 57
Charles Mackenzie Ho. SE16 ... 1E 92
Charles Pl. NW1 ... 7F 59
Charles Rowan Ho. WC1 ... 7C 60
Charles Simmons Ho. WC1 ... 7B 60
Charles Sq. N1 ... 7K 61
Charles Sq. Est. N1 ... 7K 61
Charles St. W1 ... 2C 78
Charleston St. SE17 ... 2H 91
Charles Townsend Ho. EC1 ... 7E 60
Charleville Ct. W14 ... 4G 85
Charleville Mans. W14 ... 4F 85
Charleville Rd. W14 ... 4F 85
Charlie Chaplin Wlk. SE1 ... 3B 80
Charlotte Ct. SE1 ... 1A 92
Charlotte Ho. W6 ... 4A 84
Charlotte M. W1 ... 3F 69
W10 ... 6C 64
W14 ... 1E 84
Charlotte Pl. SW1 ... 2E 88
W1 ... 4F 69
Charlotte Rd. EC2 ... 7A 62
Charlotte St. W1 ... 3F 69
Charlotte Ter. N1 ... 3B 60
Charlton Ct. E2 ... 3D 62
Charlton Pl. N1 ... 4E 60
Charlwood Ho. SW1 ... 2G 89
Charlwood Ho's. *WC1 ... 7K 59 (off Midhope St.)*
Charlwood Pl. SW1 ... 2F 89
Charlwood St. SW1 ... 4E 88 (not continuous)
Charmans Ho. SW8 ... 7J 89
Charmian Ho. N1 ... 5A 62
Charmouth Ho. SW8 ... 7A 90
Charrington St. NW1 ... 4G 59
Charterhouse ... 2F 71
Charter Ho. WC2 ... 6K 69
Charterhouse Bldgs. EC1 ... 2G 71
Charterhouse M. EC1 ... 3F 71
Charterhouse Sq. EC1 ... 3F 71
Charterhouse St. EC1 ... 4D 70
Charteris Community Sports Cen. ... 3J 55
Charteris Rd. NW6 ... 2H 55
Chartes Ho. SE1 ... 6B 82
Chartham Ho. SE1 ... 6K 81
Chartridge SE17 ... 5J 91
Chart St. N1 ... 6K 61
Chartwell Ho. W11 ... 2H 75
Chase Ct. SW3 ... 7J 77
Chasemore Ho. SW6 ... 7F 85
Chater Ho. E2 ... 6K 63
Chatham St. SE17 ... 1J 91
Chatsworth Ct. W8 ... 1J 85
Chaucer Dr. SE1 ... 2D 92
Chaucer Ho. SW1 ... 4E 88
Chaucer Mans. W14 ... 5F 85
Chaucer Theatre ... 5D 72
Chaulden Ho. EC1 ... 7K 61
Cheadle Ct. NW8 ... 1F 67
Cheapside EC2 ... 6G 71
Chearsley SE17 ... 1H 91
Cheddington Ho. E2 ... 3E 62
Cheesemans Ter. W14 ... 4G 85 (not continuous)
Chelmsford Cl. W6 ... 5D 84
Chelmsford Sq. NW10 ... 3A 54
CHELSEA ... 4G 87
Chelsea Bri. SW1 ... 5C 88
Chelsea Bri. Rd. SW1 ... 3A 88
Chelsea Bri. Wharf SW8 ... 6D 88
Chelsea Cinema ... 4H 87
Chelsea Cloisters SW3 ... 2H 87
Chelsea College of Art & Design ... 4G 87
Chelsea Ct. SW3 ... 5A 88
Chelsea Emb. SW3 ... 6G 87
Chelsea Farm Ho. Studios SW10 ... 6E 86
Chelsea FC ... 7A 86
Chelsea Gdns. SW1 ... 4B 88
Chelsea Ga. SW1 ... 4B 88
Chelsea Lodge SW3 ... 5K 87
Chelsea Mnr. Ct. SW3 ... 5H 87
Chelsea Mnr. Gdns. SW3 ... 5G 87
Chelsea Mnr. St. SW3 ... 4G 87
Chelsea Mnr. Studios SW3 ... 4H 87
Chelsea Pk. Gdns. SW3 ... 5E 86
Chelsea Physic Garden ... 5J 87
Chelsea Reach Twr. SW10 ... 7E 86
Chelsea Sports Cen. ... 4H 87
Chelsea Sq. SW3 ... 3F 87
Chelsea Studios SW6 ... 7B 86
Chelsea Towers SW3 ... 4H 87
Chelsea Village SW6 ... 7B 86
Chelsea Wharf SW10 ... 7E 86
Chelsfield Ho. SE17 ... 2A 92
Cheltenham Ter. SW3 ... 3K 87
Chelwood Ho. W2 ... 6F 67
Chenies, The NW1 ... 4H 59
Chenies Ho. W2 ... 7A 66
Chenies M. WC1 ... 2G 69
Chenies Pl. NW1 ... 4H 59
Chenies St. WC1 ... 3G 69
Cheniston Gdns. W8 ... 6A 76
Chepstow Cnr. W2 ... 6K 65
Chepstow Ct. W11 ... 7J 65
Chepstow Cres. W11 ... 7J 65
Chepstow Pl. W2 ... 6K 65
Chepstow Rd. W2 ... 4J 65
Chepstow Vs. W11 ... 7H 65
Chequers Ct. EC1 ... 2J 71
Chequers Ho. NW8 ... 1G 67
Chequer St. EC1 ... 2H 71 (not continuous)
Cherbury Ct. N1 ... 5K 61
Cherbury St. N1 ... 5K 61
Cherry Gdn. Ho. SE16 ... 5G 83
Cherry Gdn. St. SE16 ... 5G 83
Cherry Tree Cl. E9 ... 2K 63
Cherry Tree Ter. SE1 ... 5B 82
Cherry Tree Wlk. EC1 ... 2H 71
Cherwell Ho. NW8 ... 2F 67
Chesham Cl. SW1 ... 7A 78
Chesham Flats W1 ... 7B 68
Chesham M. SW1 ... 6A 78
Chesham Pl. SW1 ... 7A 78 (not continuous)
Chesham St. SW1 ... 7A 78
Cheshire Ct. EC4 ... 6D 70
Cheshire St. E2 ... 1D 72
Cheshunt Ho. NW6 ... 3A 56
Chesil Ct. E2 ... 4J 63
SW3 ... 5H 87
Chesney Ct. W9 ... 1K 65
Chesson Rd. W14 ... 5G 85
Chester Cl. SW1 ... 5C 78
Chester Cl. Nth. NW1 ... 6D 58
Chester Cl. Sth. NW1 ... 7D 58
Chester Cotts. SW1 ... 2A 88
Chester Ct. NW1 ... 6D 58 (not continuous)
SE5 ... 7J 91
W6 ... 2C 84
Chesterfield Gdns. W1 ... 2C 78
Chesterfield Hill W1 ... 2C 78
Chesterfield Ho. W1 ... 2B 78
Chesterfield St. W1 ... 2C 78
Chesterfield Way SE15 ... 7J 93
Chester Ga. NW1 ... 7C 58
Chester Ho. SE8 ... 1C 88
SW9 ... 7D 90
Chester M. SW1 ... 6C 78
Chester Pl. NW1 ... 6C 58
Chester Rd. NW1 ... 7B 58
Chester Row SW1 ... 2A 88
Chester Sq. SW1 ... 1B 88
Chester Sq. M. SW1 ... 7C 78
Chester St. E2 ... 1F 73
SW1 ... 6B 78
Chester Ter. NW1 ... 6C 58 (not continuous)
Chesterton Ho. W10 ... 3E 64

Chesterton Rd. W10 ... 4D 64
Chesterton Sq. W8 ... 1H 85
Chester Way SE11 ... 2D 90
Chestnut All. SW6 ... 5H 85
Chestnut Ct. SW6 ... 6H 85
W8 ... 7A 76
Chettle Cl. SE1 ... 6J 81
Chetwode Ho. NW8 ... 1G 67
Cheval Pl. SW7 ... 6H 77
Chevening Rd. NW6 ... 5C 54
Cheverell Ho. E2 ... 4F 63
Cheviot Ct. SE14 ... 6K 93
Cheviot Ho. E1 ... 5H 73
Cheylesmore Ho.
SW1 ... 4C 88
Cheyne Ct. SW3 ... 5J 87
Cheyne Gdns. SW3 ... 5H 87
Cheyne M. SW3 ... 6H 87
Cheyne Pl. SW3 ... 5J 87
Cheyne Row SW3 ... 6G 87
Cheyne Wlk. SW3 ... 6G 87
(not continuous)
SW10 ... 7E 86
Chicheley St. SE1 ... 4B 80
Chichester Ho. NW6 ... 5J 55
SW9 ... 7C 90
Chichester Rents
WC2 ... 5C 70
Chichester Rd. NW6 ... 5J 55
W2 ... 3B 66
Chichester St. SW1 ... 4F 89
Chicksand Ho. E1 ... 3E 72
Chicksand St. E1 ... 4D 72
(not continuous)
Chigwell Hill E1 ... 1G 83
Child's M. SW5 ... 2K 85
Child's Pl. SW5 ... 2K 85
Child's St. SW5 ... 2K 85
Child's Wlk. SW5 ... 2K 85
Chilham Ho. SE1 ... 6K 81
SE15 ... 5K 93
Chilianwallan Memorial
... 5A 88
Chiltern Ct. NW1 ... 2K 67
SE14 ... 7K 93
Chiltern Ho. W10 ... 3E 64
Chiltern St. W1 ... 3A 68
Chilton St. E2 ... 1D 72
Chilworth M. W2 ... 6E 66
Chilworth St. W2 ... 6D 66
Chimney Ct. E1 ... 3H 83
China Ct. E1 ... 2G 83
China Hall M. SE16 ... 7K 83
China Wlk. SE11 ... 7B 80
China Wharf SE1 ... 4E 82
Ching Ct. WC2 ... 6J 69
Chippendale Ho.
SW1 ... 4D 88
Chippenham Gdns.
NW6 ... 7J 55
Chippenham M. W9 ... 2J 65
Chippenham Rd. W9 ... 1J 65
Chipperfield Ho.
SW3 ... 3G 87
Chiswell St. EC1 ... 3H 71
SE5 ... 7K 91
Chitty St. W1 ... 3F 69
Chocolate Studios N1 ... 6J 61
Choppin's Ct. E1 ... 2H 83
Christchurch Av.
NW6 ... 2D 54
Christchurch Ct. EC4 ... 5F 71
Christchurch Sq. E9 ... 3J 63
Christchurch St. SW3 ... 5J 87
Christchurch Ter.
SW3 ... 5J 87
Christian Pl. E1 ... 6F 73
Christian St. E1 ... 5F 73
Christina St. EC2 ... 1A 72
Christopher Cl. SE16 ... 5K 83
Christopher Pl. NW1 ... 6H 59
Christophers M. W11 ... 2E 74
Christopher St. EC2 ... 2K 71
Chryssell Rd. SW9 ... 7D 90
Chudleigh Rd. NW6 ... 1C 54
Chumleigh Gdns.
SE5 ... 5A 92
Chumleigh St. SE5 ... 5A 92
Church Cloisters EC3 ... 1A 82
Church Cl. W8 ... 4A 76
Church Cres. E9 ... 1K 63
Church Entry EC4 ... 6F 71
Church Ho. *EC1 ... 1F 71*
(off Compton St.)
SW1 ... 6H 79
Churchill Gdns. SW1 ... 4E 88
(not continuous)
Churchill Gdns. Rd.
SW1 ... 4D 88
Churchill Mus.
(Cabinet War Rooms)
... 4H 79
Church Mead SE5 ... 7H 91
Church Pas. *EC2 ... 5H 71*
(off Guildhall Yd.)
Church Pl. SW1 ... 1F 79
Church Row SW6 ... 7A 86
Church St. NW8 ... 2F 67
W2 ... 3F 67
Church St. Est. NW8 ... 2F 67
(not continuous)
Churchward Ho. SE17 ... 5F 91
W14 ... 4H 85
Churchway NW1 ... 6H 59
(not continuous)
Churchyard Row
SE11 ... 1F 91
Church Yd. Wlk. W2 ... 3E 66
Churston Mans. WC1 ... 2B 70
Churton Pl. SW1 ... 2F 89
Churton St. SW1 ... 2F 89
Chuter Ede Ho. SW6 ... 6H 85
Cicely Ho. NW8 ... 5F 57
Cine Lumiere ... 1E 86
Cineworld
Chelsea ... 5F 87
Fulham Rd. ... 4D 86
Haymarket ... 1G 79
Shaftesbury Av. ... 1G 79
Cinnabar Wharf Central
E1 ... 3F 83
Cinnabar Wharf E. E1 ... 3F 83
Cinnabar Wharf W.
E1 ... 3E 82
Cinnamon Cl. SE15 ... 7C 92
Cinnamon St. E1 ... 3H 83
Cinnamon Wharf SE1 ... 4D 82
Circa Apartments
NW1 ... 1A 58
Circle, The SE1 ... 4D 82
Circus Lodge NW8 ... 6E 56
Circus M. W1 ... 3J 67
Circus Pl. EC2 ... 4K 71
Circus Rd. NW8 ... 6E 56
Cirencester St. W2 ... 3A 66
Citadel Pl. SE11 ... 3A 90
City Apartments *E1 ... 5E 72*
(off White Chu. La.)
City Bus. Cen. SE16 ... 5J 83
City Central Est. EC1 ... 7G 61
City Forum EC1 ... 6G 61
City Gdn. Row N1 ... 5F 61
City Hgts. SE1 ... 3B 82
CITY OF LONDON ... 5K 71
City of Westminster College
... 7F 69
City Pav. EC1 ... 3E 70
City Rd. N1 ... 5E 60
City Twr. EC2 ... 4J 71
City University ... 7E 60
City University Saddlers
Sports Cen., The ... 1F 71
City Wlk. SE1 ... 6A 82
City Wlk. Apartments
EC1 ... 7F 61
(off Seward St.)
Clabon M. SW1 ... 7J 77
Clack St. SE16 ... 5K 83
Clandon Ho. SE1 ... 5F 81
Clanricarde Gdns.
W2 ... 1K 75
Clapham Rd. SW9 ... 7B 90
Clare Ct. W11 ... 1F 75
WC1 ... 7K 59
Claredale Ho. E2 ... 5G 63
Claredale St. E2 ... 5F 63
Clare Gdns. W11 ... 6F 65
Clare Ho. SE1 ... 3D 92
Clare La. N1 ... 1H 61
Clare Mkt. WC2 ... 6B 70
Claremont Cl. N1 ... 5D 60
Claremont Ct. W2 ... 5B 66
W9 ... 5G 55
Claremont Rd. W9 ... 5F 55
Claremont Sq. N1 ... 5C 60
Claremont Vs. SE5 ... 7K 91
Clarence Ct. W6 ... 2A 84
Clarence Gdns. NW1 ... 7D 58
Clarence Ga. Gdns.
NW1 ... 2K 67
Clarence House ... 4F 79
Clarence Ho. SE17 ... 5H 91
Clarence M. SE16 ... 3K 83
Clarence Rd. NW6 ... 1G 55
Clarence Ter. NW1 ... 1K 67
Clarendon Cl. E9 ... 1K 63
W2 ... 7G 67
Clarendon Ct. NW2 ... 1A 54
Clarendon Cross W11 ... 1F 75
Clarendon Flats W1 ... 6B 68
Clarendon Gdns. W9 ... 2D 66
Clarendon Gro. NW1 ... 6G 59
Clarendon Ho. NW1 ... 5F 59
W2 ... 7G 67
Clarendon M. W2 ... 7G 67
Clarendon Pl. W2 ... 7G 67
Clarendon Rd. W11 ... 7E 64
Clarendon St. SW1 ... 4D 88
Clarendon Ter. W9 ... 1D 66
Clarendon Wlk. W11 ... 6E 64
Clare St. E2 ... 4H 63
Clareville Ct. SW7 ... 2D 86
Clareville Gro. SW7 ... 2D 86
Clareville Gro. M.
SW7 ... 2D 86
Clareville St. SW7 ... 2D 86
Clarewood Ct. W1 ... 4J 67
Clarges M. W1 ... 2C 78
Clarges St. W1 ... 2D 78
Clarion Ho. SW1 ... 3F 89
W1 ... 6G 69
Clarissa St. E8 ... 2C 62
Clarke's M. W1 ... 3B 68
Clark Ho. SW10 ... 7C 86
Clarkson Row NW1 ... 5E 58
Clarkson St. E2 ... 6G 63
Clark's Pl. EC2 ... 5A 72
Clark St. E1 ... 4H 73
Classic Mans. E9 ... 1H 63
Clavering Av. SW13 ... 5A 84
Claverton St. SW1 ... 4F 89
Clave St. E1 ... 3J 83
Claxton Gro. W6 ... 4D 84
Claybrook Rd. W6 ... 5D 84
Clay Ct. *SE1 ... 6A 82*
(off Long La.)
Claydon SE17 ... 1G 91
Claylands Pl. SW8 ... 7C 90
Claylands Rd. SW8 ... 6B 90
Clay St. W1 ... 4K 67
Clayton Cres. N1 ... 3K 59
Clayton Ho. E9 ... 1J 63
SW13 ... 7A 84
Clayton St. SE11 ... 5C 90
Clearbrook Way E1 ... 5K 73
Clearwater Ter. W11 ... 4D 74
Clearwell Dr. W9 ... 2A 66
Cleaver Ho. NW3 ... 1J 57
Cleaver Sq. SE11 ... 4D 90
Cleaver St. SE11 ... 3D 90
Cleeve Ho. E2 ... 7B 62
Cleeve Workshops
E2 ... 7B 62
Clegg Ho. SE16 ... 6K 83
Clegg St. E1 ... 2H 83
Cleland Ho. E2 ... 4K 63
Clem Attlee Ct. SW6 ... 6H 85
Clem Attlee Pde.
SW6 ... 6H 85
Clement Cl. NW6 ... 1B 54
Clement Ho. W10 ... 3B 64
Clement's Inn WC2 ... 6B 70
Clement's Inn Pas.
WC2 ... 6B 70
Clements La. EC4 ... 7K 71
Clement's Rd. SE16 ... 7F 83
Clemson Ho. E8 ... 3D 62
Clennam St. SE1 ... 4H 81
Clenston M. W1 ... 5J 67
Cleopatra's Needle ... 2A 80
Clere Pl. EC2 ... 1K 71
Clere St. EC2 ... 1K 71
CLERKENWELL ... 2D 70
Clerkenwell Cl. EC1 ... 1D 70
(not continuous)
Clerkenwell Grn. EC1 ... 2D 70
Clerkenwell Rd. EC1 ... 2C 70
Clermont Rd. E9 ... 2J 63
Cleve Ho. NW6 ... 1A 56
Cleveland Gdns. W2 ... 6C 66
Cleveland Gro. E1 ... 2J 73
Cleveland Mans. W9 ... 1K 65
Cleveland M. W1 ... 3E 68
Cleveland Pl. SW1 ... 2F 79
Cleveland Rd. N1 ... 1K 61
Cleveland Row SW1 ... 3E 78
Cleveland Sq. W2 ... 6C 66
Cleveland St. W1 ... 2D 68
Cleveland Ter. W2 ... 6C 66
Cleveland Way E1 ... 2J 73
Cleve Rd. NW6 ... 1K 55
Clichy Est. E1 ... 4K 73
Clichy Ho. E1 ... 4K 73
Clifford Ct. W2 ... 4A 66
Clifford Gdns. NW10 ... 5A 54
Clifford Haigh Ho.
SW6 ... 7C 84
Clifford Ho. W14 ... 2G 85
Clifford Rd. N1 ... 2A 62
Clifford's Inn Pas.
EC4 ... 6C 70
Clifford St. W1 ... 1E 78
Clifton Ct. NW8 ... 1E 66
SE15 ... 7H 93
Clifton Cres. SE15 ... 7H 93
Clifton Gdns. W9 ... 2C 66
Clifton Ga. SW10 ... 5C 86
Clifton Hill NW8 ... 4B 56
Clifton Ho. E2 ... 1C 72
Clifton Pl. SE16 ... 4K 83
SW10 ... 5C 86
W2 ... 6F 67
Clifton Rd. W9 ... 1D 66
Clifton St. EC2 ... 2A 72
Clifton Vs. W9 ... 3B 66
Climsland Ho. SE1 ... 2D 80
Clinger Ct. N1 ... 3A 62
Clink Exhibition, The ... 2J 81
Clink St. SE1 ... 2H 81
Clink Wharf SE1 ... 2J 81
Clipper Cl. SE16 ... 4K 83
Clipstone M. W1 ... 3E 68
Clipstone St. W1 ... 3D 68
Clive Ct. W9 ... 1D 66
Cliveden Ho. SW1 ... 1A 88
Cliveden Pl. SW1 ... 1A 88
Cloak La. EC4 ... 7H 71
Clock Mus., The ... 5H 71
Clock Pl. SE1 ... 1F 91
Clock Twr. M. N1 ... 3H 61
Cloisters, The ... 6J 79
Cloisters, The E1 ... 3C 72
Cloth Ct. EC1 ... 4F 71
Cloth Fair EC1 ... 4F 71
Clothier St. E1 ... 5B 72
Cloth St. EC1 ... 3G 71
Cloudesley Mans. N1 ... 3C 60
Cloudesley Pl. N1 ... 3C 60
Cloudesley Rd. N1 ... 2C 60
(not continuous)
Cloudesley Sq. N1 ... 2C 60
Cloudesley St. N1 ... 3D 60
Clovelly Ho. W2 ... 5C 66
Clovelly Way E1 ... 5K 73
Clover M. SW3 ... 5K 87
Cloysters Grn. E1 ... 2E 82
Club Row E1 ... 1C 72
E2 ... 1C 72
Clunbury St. N1 ... 5K 61
Clunie Ho. SW1 ... 6K 77
Cluny Est. SE1 ... 6A 82
Cluny M. SW5 ... 2J 85
Cluny Pl. SE1 ... 6A 82
Cluse Ct. N1 ... 4G 61
(not continuous)
Clyde Ct. NW1 ... 4H 59
Clyde Flats SW6 ... 7G 85
Clydesdale Ho. W11 ... 5H 65
Clydesdale Rd. W11 ... 5G 65
Coach & Horses Yd.
W1 ... 7D 68
Coach Ho. M. SE1 ... 6A 82
Coalport Ho. SE11 ... 1C 90
Coate St. E2 ... 5F 63
Cobalt Sq. SW8 ... 5A 90
Cobbett St. SW8 ... 7B 90
Cobbold Ct. SW1 ... 1G 89
Cobb's Ct. EC4 ... 6F 71
Cobb's Hall SW6 ... 6C 84
Cobb St. E1 ... 4C 72
Cobden Bldgs. WC1 ... 6A 60
Cobden Ho. E2 ... 6F 63
NW1 ... 4E 58
Cobham M. NW1 ... 1G 59
Cobourg Rd. SE5 ... 5C 92
Cobourg St. NW1 ... 7F 59
Coburg Cl. SW1 ... 1F 89
Coburg Dwellings E1 ... 6K 73
Cochrane Cl. NW8 ... 5F 57
Cochrane M. NW8 ... 5F 57
Cochrane St. NW8 ... 5F 57
Cochrane Theatre ... 4K 69
Cockburn Ho. SW1 ... 4H 89
Cock Hill E1 ... 4B 72
Cock La. EC1 ... 4E 70
Cockpit Steps SW1 ... 5H 79
Cockpit Theatre ... 2G 67
Cockpit Yd. WC1 ... 3B 70
Cockspur Ct. SW1 ... 2H 79
Cockspur St. SW1 ... 2H 79
Code St. E1 ... 2D 72
Codling Cl. E1 ... 2F 83
Codrington Ct. E1 ... 2G 73
Codrington M. W11 ... 6F 65
Coin St. SE1 ... 2C 80
(not continuous)
Coke St. E1 ... 5E 72
Colas M. NW6 ... 2K 55
Colbeck M. SW7 ... 2B 86
Colchester St. E1 ... 5D 72
Coldbath Sq. EC1 ... 1C 70
Colebert Av. E1 ... 1J 73
Colebert Ho. E1 ... 1K 73
Colebrook Ct. SW3 ... 2H 87
Colebrooke Pl. N1 ... 3F 61
Colebrooke Row N1 ... 5E 60
Coleby Path SE5 ... 7K 91
Colechurch Ho. SE1 ... 4E 92
Colegrove Rd. SE15 ... 6D 92
Coleherne Ct. SW5 ... 4B 86
Coleherne Mans.
SW5 ... 3B 86
Coleherne M. SW10 ... 4A 86
Coleherne Rd. SW10 ... 4A 86
Cole Ho. SE1 ... 5D 80
Coleman Flds. N1 ... 2H 61
Coleman Rd. SE5 ... 7A 92
Coleman St. EC2 ... 5J 71
Coleman St. Bldgs.
EC2 ... 5J 71
Coleridge Ct. SW1 ... 1G 89
W14 ... 7D 74
Coleridge Gdns.
NW6 ... 1C 56
SW10 ... 7B 86
Coleridge Ho. SE17 ... 3H 91
SW1 ... 4E 88
Coleridge Sq. SW10 ... 7C 86
Coleshill Flats SW1 ... 2B 88
Cole St. SE1 ... 5H 81
Colet Ct. W6 ... 2D 84
Colet Gdns. W14 ... 2D 84
Colet Ho. SE17 ... 4F 91
Coley St. WC1 ... 2B 70
Colin Winter Ho. E1 ... 1K 73
Coliseum Theatre ... 1J 79
Collard Pl. NW1 ... 1C 58
College Ct. SW3 ... 4K 87
W6 ... 3B 84
College Cres. NW3 ... 1E 56
College Cross N1 ... 1D 60
College E. E1 ... 4D 72
College Gro. NW1 ... 2G 59
College Hill EC4 ... 7H 71
College Mans. NW6 ... 2F 55
College M. N1 ... 1D 60
(not continuous)
SW1 ... 6J 79
College of Arms ... 7G 71
College Pde. NW6 ... 2F 55
College Pl. NW1 ... 2F 59
SW10 ... 7C 86
College Rd. NW10 ... 4A 54
College St. EC4 ... 7H 71
Collett Rd. SE16 ... 7F 83
Collier St. N1 ... 5A 60
Collingham Gdns.
SW5 ... 2B 86
Collingham Pl. SW5 ... 2A 86
Collingham Rd. SW5 ... 1B 86
Collingwood Ho. E1 ... 2H 73
SE16 ... 5G 83
(off Cherry Gdn. St.)
SW1 ... 4G 89
W1 ... 3E 68
Collingwood St. E1 ... 1H 73
Collinson Ct. SE1 ... 5G 81
Collinson Ho. SE15 ... 7E 92
Collinson St. SE1 ... 5G 81
Collinson Wlk. SE1 ... 5G 81
Collin's Yd. N1 ... 3E 60
Colnbrook St. SE1 ... 7E 80
Colne Ho. NW8 ... 2F 67
Colombo St. SE1 ... 3E 80
Colombo Street Sports &
Community Cen. ... 3E 80
Colonnade WC1 ... 2J 69
Colonnades, The W2 ... 5B 66
Colonnade Wlk. SW1 ... 2C 88
Colosseum Ter. NW1 ... 7D 58
Colour Ct. SW1 ... 3F 79
Colstead Ho. E1 ... 6H 73
Columbia Point SE16 ... 6K 83
Columbia Rd. E2 ... 6C 62
Columbia Road Flower Market
(Sundays only) ... *6D 62*
(off Columbia Rd.)
Columbus Ct. SE16 ... 3K 83
Colverson Ho. E1 ... 4J 73
Colville Est. N1 ... 3A 62
Colville Est. W. E2 ... 7D 62
Colville Gdns. W11 ... 6H 65
(not continuous)
Colville Ho. *E2 ... 4J 63*
(off Waterloo Gdns.)
Colville Ho's. W11 ... 5G 65
Colville M. W11 ... 6H 65
Colville Pl. W1 ... 4F 69
Colville Rd. W11 ... 6H 65
Colville Sq. W11 ... 6G 65
Colville Ter. W11 ... 6G 65
Colwith Rd. W6 ... 6B 84
Colworth Gro. SE17 ... 2H 91
Colwyn Ho. SE1 ... 7C 80
Colyer Cl. N1 ... 4B 60
Combe, The NW1 ... 7D 58
Combe Ho. W2 ... 4J 65
Comber Gro. SE5 ... 7H 91
Comber Ho. SE5 ... 7H 91
Comedy Store ... 1G 79
Comedy Theatre ... 1G 79
Comeragh M. W14 ... 4F 85
Comeragh Rd. W14 ... 4F 85
Comfort St. SE15 ... 6A 92
Commercial Rd. E1 ... 5E 72
Commercial St. E1 ... 2C 72
Commercial Way
SE15 ... 7D 92
Commodity Quay E1 ... 1D 82
Commonwealth Av.
W12 ... 7A 64
(not continuous)
Commonwealth
Conference Cen. ... 3F 79
Commonwealth Institute
... 6H 75
Compass Ct. SE1 ... 3C 82
Compter Pas. EC2 ... 6H 71
Compton Cl. NW1 ... 7D 58
SE15 ... 7E 92
Compton Pas. EC1 ... 1F 71
Compton Pl. WC1 ... 1J 69
Compton Rd. NW10 ... 7C 54
Compton St. EC1 ... 1E 70
Comus Ho. SE17 ... 2A 92
Comus Pl. SE17 ... 2A 92
Conant Ho. SE11 ... 5E 90
Conant M. E1 ... 7E 72
Concert Hall App.
SE1 ... 3B 80
Concorde Way SE16 ... 2K 93
Conduit Ct. WC2 ... 7J 69
Conduit M. W2 ... 6E 66
Conduit Pas. W2 ... 6E 66
Conduit Pl. W2 ... 6E 66
Conduit St. W1 ... 7D 68
Coney Way SW8 ... 6B 90
Congreve St. SE17 ... 1A 92
Coningham Ct. SW10 ... 7D 86
Conisbrough NW1 ... 3E 58
Coniston NW1 ... 6E 58
Coniston Ct. W2 ... 6H 67
Conistone Way N7 ... 1K 59
Coniston Ho. SE5 ... 7G 91
Conlan St. W10 ... 1E 64
Connaught Cl. W2 ... 6H 67
Connaught Ct. W2 ... 6J 67
Connaught Ho. W1 ... 1C 78
Connaught M. SE11 ... 1D 90
Connaught Pl. W2 ... 7J 67
Connaught Sq. W2 ... 6J 67
Connaught St. W2 ... 6G 67
Conrad Ho. SW8 ... 7J 89
Consort Ct. W8 ... 6A 76
Consort Ho. W2 ... 1B 76
Consort Lodge NW8 ... 3J 57
Cons St. SE1 ... 4D 80
Constable Ct. SE16 ... 3H 93
Constable Ho. NW3 ... 1K 57
Constance Allen Ho.
W10 ... 6D 64
Constantine Ct. E1 ... 6F 73
Constitution Hill SW1 ... 4C 78
Content St. SE17 ... 2J 91
Convent Gdns. W11 ... 6G 65
Conway Ho. SW3 ... 4K 87
Conway M. W1 ... 2E 68
Conway St. W1 ... 2E 68
(not continuous)
Conybeare NW3 ... 1H 57
Cook Ct. SE16 ... 3K 83
Cookham Ho. E2 ... 1C 72
Cook's Rd. SE17 ... 5E 90
Coomassie Rd. W9 ... 1G 65
Coombs St. N1 ... 5F 61
Coomer M. SW6 ... 6H 85
Coomer Pl. SW6 ... 6H 85
Coomer Rd. SW6 ... 6H 85
Cooperage, The SE1 ... 3C 82
Cooper Cl. SE1 ... 5D 80
Cooper Ho. NW8 ... 2E 66
Coopers Cl. E1 ... 2K 73
Coopers La. NW1 ... 4H 59
(not continuous)
Coopers Lodge SE1 ... 4C 82
Cooper's Rd. SE1 ... 4D 92
Coopers Row EC3 ... 7C 72
Cope Ho. EC1 ... 7H 61
Copeland Ho. SE11 ... 7B 80
Copenhagen Ho. N1 ... 3B 60
Copenhagen St. N1 ... 3K 59
Cope Pl. W8 ... 7J 75
Copford Wlk. N1 ... 2G 61
Copley Cl. SE17 ... 6F 91
Copperfield Ho. SE1 ... 5E 82
W1 ... 3B 68
W11 ... 2D 74
Copperfield St. SE1 ... 4F 81
Copper Row SE1 ... 3C 82
Copperworks, The
N1 ... 5K 59
Copthall Av. EC2 ... 5K 71
(not continuous)
Copthall Bldgs. EC2 ... 5K 71
Copthall Cl. EC2 ... 5J 71
Coptic St. WC1 ... 4J 69
Coral St. SE1 ... 5D 80
Coram Ho. WC1 ... 1J 69
Coram St. WC1 ... 2J 69
Corbet Ct. EC3 ... 6K 71
Corbet Ho. N1 ... 4C 60
SE5 ... 7G 91
Corbet Pl. E1 ... 3C 72
Corbett Ho. SW10 ... 5C 86
Corbetts La. SE16 ... 2J 93
(not continuous)
Corbetts Pas. SE16 ... 2J 93
Corbetts Wharf SE16 ... 4G 83
Corbiere Ho. N1 ... 2K 61
Corbridge Cres. E2 ... 4G 63
Cordelia Ho. N1 ... 4B 62
Cordwainers Ct. E9 ... 1H 63
Corelli Ct. SW5 ... 2J 85
Corfe Ho. SW8 ... 7A 90
Corfield St. E2 ... 7H 63
Coriander Ct. SE1 ... 4D 82
Cork Sq. E1 ... 2G 83
Cork St. W1 ... 1E 78
Cork St. M. W1 ... 1E 78
Corlett St. NW1 ... 3G 67
Cormorant Lodge *E1 ... 2E 82*
(off Thomas More St.)
Cornell Bldg. E1 ... 5E 72
Corner Ho. St. WC2 ... 2J 79
Cornhill EC3 ... 6K 71
Cornick Ho. SE16 ... 7H 83
Cornish Ho. SE17 ... 6E 90
Cornwall Av. E2 ... 7J 63
Cornwall Cres. W11 ... 7E 64
Cornwall Gdns. SW7 ... 7B 76
Cornwall Gdns. Wlk.
SW7 ... 7B 76
Cornwall Ho. SW7 ... 7B 76
Cornwallis Ho. *SE16 ... 5G 83*
(off Cherry Gdn. St.)
Cornwall Mans.
SW10 ... 7D 86
W8 ... 5B 76
W14 ... 6C 74
Cornwall M. Sth.
SW7 ... 7C 76
Cornwall M. W. SW7 ... 7B 76
Cornwall Rd. SE1 ... 2C 80
Cornwall Sq. SE11 ... 3E 90
Cornwall St. E1 ... 7H 73
Cornwall Ter. NW1 ... 2K 67

Cornwall Ter. M.
NW1 2K 67
Cornwood Dr. E1 5J 73
Coronation Ct. W10 4A 64
Coroners' Court 3G 59
Coronet Cinema 2J 75
Coronet St. N1 7A 62
Corporation Row EC1 1D 70
Corsham St. N1 7K 61
Coryton Path W9 1H 65
Cosgrove Ho. E2 3F 63
Cosmo Pl. WC1 3K 69
Cosser St. SE1 6C 80
Cosway Mans. NW1 3H 67
Cosway St. NW1 3H 67
Cotes Ho. NW8 2G 67
Cotham St. SE17 2H 91
Cotleigh Rd. NW6 1J 55
Cotman Ho. NW8 4G 57
Cotswold Ct. EC1 1G 71
Cottage Cl. E1 2K 73
Cottage Grn. SE5 7K 91
Cottage Pl. SW3 6G 77
Cottesloe Ho. NW8 1G 67
Cottesloe M. SE1 6D 80
Cottesloe Theatre 2C 80
(in National Theatre)
Cottesmore Ct. W8 6B 76
Cottesmore Gdns.
W8 6B 76
Cottingham Rd. SW8 7B 90
Cottington St. SE11 3D 90
Cottle Way SE16 5H 83
Cottons Cen. SE1 2A 82
Cotton's Gdns. E2 6B 62
Cottons La. SE1 2K 81
Coulson St. SW3 3J 87
Coulter Rd. W6 7A 74
Councillor St. SE5 7G 91
Counter Ct. SE1 3J 81
Counters Ct. W14 6F 75
Counter St. SE1 3A 82
County Hall Apartments
SE1 5A 80
County Hall (Former)
4A 80
County St. SE1 7H 81
Courtauld Ho. E2 3F 63
Courtauld Institute Galleries
7A 70
Court Cl. NW8 1E 56
(not continuous)
Courtenay Sq. SE11 4C 90
Courtenay St. SE11 3C 90
Courtfield Gdns.
SW5 2A 86
Courtfield Ho. EC1 3C 70
Courtfield M. SW5 2B 86
Courtfield Rd. SW7 2C 86
Courthope Ho. SE16 7K 83
Courtnell St. W2 5J 65
Courtney Ho. W14 6F 75
Court St. E1 3G 73
Courtville Ho. W10 7F 55
Courtyard, The EC3 6J 71
(in Royal Exchange)
N1 1B 60
NW1 1B 58
SW3 5F 87
Courtyard Theatre, The
King's Cross 5K 59
Cousin La. EC4 1J 81
COVENT GARDEN 7K 69
Covent Garden 7K 69
Covent Gdn. WC2 7K 69
Coventry Cl. NW6 4K 55
Coventry Rd. E1 2H 73
E2 1H 73
Coventry St. W1 1G 79
Coverdale Rd. NW2 1D 54
W12 3A 74
Coverley Cl. E1 3F 73
Coverley Point SE11 2A 90
Cowcross St. EC1 3E 70
Cowdenbeath Path
N1 2A 60
Cowley St. SW1 7J 79
Cowling Cl. W11 2E 74
Cowper Ho. SE17 3H 91
SW1 4H 89
Cowper's Ct. EC3 6K 71
Cowper St. EC2 1K 71
Cowper Ter. W10 4C 64
Cox Ho. W6 5E 84
Cox's Ct. E1 4C 72
Coxson Way SE1 5C 82
Crabtree Cl. E2 5C 62
Crabtree La. SW6 7B 84
(not continuous)
Crace St. NW1 6G 59
Crafts Council & Gallery
5D 60
Cragie Ho. SE1 2D 92
Craig's Ct. SW1 2J 79
Craik Ct. NW6 5H 55
Crail Row SE17 2K 91
Cramer St. W1 4B 68
Crammond Cl. W6 6E 84
Crampton St. SE17 2G 91
Cranbourn All. WC2 7H 69
Cranbourne NW1 1G 59
Cranbourne Pas.
SE16 5G 83
Cranbourn Ho. SE16 5G 83
Cranbourn St. WC2 7H 69
Cranbrook NW1 3F 59
Cranbrook Est. E2 5K 63
Crane Ct. EC4 6D 70
Cranfield Ct. W1 4H 67
Cranfield Ho. WC1 3J 69
Cranfield Row SE1 6D 80
Cranleigh W11 2G 75
Cranleigh Ho's. NW1 5F 59
Cranleigh St. NW1 5F 59
Cranley Gdns. SW7 3D 86
Cranley M. SW7 3D 86
Cranley Pl. SW7 2E 86
Cranmer Ct. SW3 2H 87
Cranmer Ho. SW9 7C 90
Cranmer Rd. SW9 7D 90
Cranston Est. N1 4K 61
Cranswick Rd. SE16 3H 93
Cranwood Ct. EC1 7K 61
Cranwood St. EC1 7K 61
Craven Hill W2 7D 66
Craven Hill Gdns.
W2 7C 66
(not continuous)
Craven Hill M. W2 7D 66
Craven Lodge W2 7D 66
Craven Pas. WC2 2J 79
Craven Rd. W2 7D 66
Craven St. WC2 2J 79
Craven Ter. W2 7D 66
Crawford Bldgs. W1 4H 67
Crawford Mans. W1 4H 67
Crawford M. W1 4J 67
Crawford Pas. EC1 2C 70
Crawford Pl. W1 5H 67
Crawford St. W1 4H 67
Crayford Ho. SE1 5K 81
Cray Ho. NW8 3F 67
Crayle Ho. EC1 1E 70
Creasy Est. SE1 7A 82
Credenhill Ho. SE15 7G 93
Crediton Rd. NW10 3C 54
Credon Rd. SE16 3H 93
Creechurch La. EC3 6B 72
(not continuous)
Creechurch Pl. EC3 6B 72
Creed Ct. EC4 6F 71
Creed La. EC4 6F 71
Creek Ho. W14 6F 75
Crefeld Cl. W6 6E 84
Creighton Rd. NW6 4D 54
Cremer Bus. Cen. E2 5C 62
Cremer St. E2 5C 62
Cremorne Est. SW10 6F 87
(not continuous)
Cremorne Rd. SW10 7D 86
Crescent EC3 7C 72
Crescent Ho. EC1 2G 71
Crescent Mans. W11 7F 65
Crescent Pl. SW3 1G 87
Crescent Row EC1 2G 71
Crescent St. N1 1B 60
Cresswell Gdns.
SW5 3C 86
Cresswell Pl. SW10 3C 86
Cressy Ct. E1 3K 73
Cressy Ho's. E1 3K 73
Cressy Pl. E1 3K 73
Cresta Ho. NW3 1E 56
Crestfield St. WC1 6K 59
Crewdson Rd. SW9 7C 90
Cricketers Ct. SE11 2E 90
Crimscott St. SE1 7B 82
Crimsworth Rd. SW8 7H 89
Crinan St. N1 4K 59
Cringle St. SW8 7E 88
Cripplegate St. EC2 3H 71
Crispe Ho. N1 3B 60
Crispin Pl. E1 3C 72
Crispin St. E1 4C 72
Crisp Rd. W6 4A 84
Criterion Ct. E8 1D 62
Criterion Theatre 1G 79
Crofters Way NW1 2G 59
Croft Ho. W10 7F 55
Crofton Ho. SW3 6G 87
Crofts Ho. E2 4F 63
Crofts St. E1 1E 82
Cromer St. WC1 7J 59
Crompton Ct. SW3 1G 87
Crompton Ho. SE1 7H 81
W2 2E 66
Crompton St. W2 2E 66
Cromwell Cl. E1 2F 83
Cromwell Cres. SW5 1J 85
Cromwell Gdns. SW7 1F 87
Cromwell Gro. W6 6B 74
Cromwell Highwalk
EC2 3H 71
Cromwell Lodge E1 2J 73
Cromwell Mans.
SW5 1K 85
Cromwell M. SW7 1F 87
Cromwell Pl. EC2 3H 71
SW7 1F 87
Cromwell Rd. SW5 1K 85
SW7 1E 86
Cromwell Twr. EC2 3H 71
Crondall Ct. N1 5A 62
Crondall St. N1 5K 61
Crone Ct. NW6 5H 55
Cronin St. SE15 7C 92
Crooked Billet Yd.
N1 6B 62
Cropley Ct. N1 4J 61
(not continuous)
Cropley St. N1 4J 61
Cropthorne Ct. W9 7D 56
Crosby Ct. SE1 4J 81
Crosby Row SE1 5J 81
Crosby Sq. EC3 6A 72
Crossbow Ho. N1 3A 62
Crossfield Ct. W10 5D 64
Crossfield Ho. W11 1E 74
Cross Keys Cl. W1 4B 68
Cross Keys Sq. EC1 4G 71
Cross La. EC3 1A 82
(not continuous)
Crosslet St. SE17 1K 91
Crossmount Ho. SE5 7G 91
Cross St. N1 2E 60
Crosswall EC3 7C 72
Croston St. E8 2F 63
Crowder St. E1 7G 73
Crowland Ho. NW8 3C 56
Crown Ct. EC2 6H 71
NW8 7H 57
WC2 6K 69
Crowndale Ct. NW1 4G 59
Crowndale Rd. NW1 4F 59
Crown Lodge SW3 2H 87
Crown Office Row
EC4 7C 70
Crown Pas. SW1 3F 79
Crown Pl. EC2 3A 72
(not continuous)
SE16 4H 93
Crown Reach SW1 4H 89
Crown St. SE5 7H 91
Crowther Cl. SW6 6H 85
Crowthorne Rd. W10 6C 64
Croxley Rd. W9 7H 55
Croydon Ho. SE1 4D 80
Crozier Ho. SW8 7A 90
Crucifix La. SE1 4A 82
Cruden Ho. SE17 6F 91
Cruden St. N1 3F 61
Cruikshank Ho. NW8 4G 57
Cruikshank St. WC1 6C 60
Crutched Friars EC3 7B 72
Crystal Wharf N1 5F 61
Cube Ho. SE16 7C 82
Cubitt St. WC1 7B 60
Cubitt's Yd. WC2 7K 69
Cuddington SE17 1G 91
Cudworth St. E1 1H 73
Cuffley Ho. W10 3A 64
Cuff Point E2 6C 62
Culford Gdns. SW3 2K 87
Culford Mans. SW3 2K 87
Culford Rd. N1 1A 62
Culham Ho. E2 7C 62
W2 4J 65
Culling Rd. SE16 6J 83
Culloden Cl. SE16 4F 93
Cullum St. EC3 7A 72
Cullum Welch Ct. N1 6K 61
Cullum Welch Ho.
EC1 2G 71
Culmore Rd. SE15 7H 93
Culpepper Ct. SE11 1C 90
Culross Bldgs. NW1 5J 59
Culross Ho. W10 6D 64
Culross St. W1 1A 78
Culverhouse WC1 4A 70
Culworth Ho. NW8 4G 57
Culworth St. NW8 5G 57
Cumberland Ct. SW1 3D 88
W1 6K 67
Cumberland Cres.
W14 1F 85
(not continuous)
Cumberland Gdns.
WC1 6C 60
Cumberland Ga. W1 7J 67
Cumberland Ho. W8 5B 76
Cumberland Mans.
W1 5J 67
Cumberland Mkt.
NW1 6D 58
Cumberland M. SE11 4D 90
Cumberland Pl. NW1 6C 58
Cumberland St. SW1 3D 88
Cumberland Ter.
NW1 5C 58
Cumberland Ter. M.
NW1 5C 58
(not continuous)
Cuming Mus. 2G 91
Cumming St. N1 5B 60
Cunard Pl. EC3 6B 72
Cundy St. SW1 2B 88
Cunningham Ct. W9 2D 66
Cunningham Ho. SE5 7J 91
Cunningham Pl. NW8 1E 66
Cureton St. SW1 2H 89
Curlew St. SE1 4C 82
Curran Ho. SW3 2G 87
Cursitor St. EC4 5C 70
Curtain Pl. EC2 1B 72
Curtain Rd. EC2 7B 62
Curtis Ho. SE17 3J 91
Curtis St. SE1 1C 92
Curtis Way SE1 1C 92
Curzon Cinema
Mayfair 3C 78
Soho 7H 69
Curzon Ga. W1 3B 78
Curzon Sq. W1 3B 78
Curzon St. W1 3B 78
Custance Ho. N1 5J 61
Custance St. N1 6J 61
Custom Ho. Wlk. EC3 1A 82
Cut, The SE1 4D 80
Cuthbert Harrowing Ho.
EC1 2G 71
Cuthbert Ho. W2 3E 66
Cuthbert St. W2 2E 66
Cutlers Gdns. EC2 4B 72
Cutler St. E1 5B 72
Cuxton Ho. SE17 3B 92
Cygnet Ho. SW3 4H 87
Cygnet St. E1 1D 72
Cynthia St. N1 5B 60
Cyntra Pl. E8 1H 63
Cypress Ho. SE16 5K 83
(off Woodland Cres.)
Cypress Pl. W1 2F 69
Cyprus Pl. E2 5K 63
Cyprus St. E2 5J 63
(not continuous)
Cyrus Ho. EC1 1F 71
Cyrus St. EC1 1F 71

D

Dabbs La. EC1 2D 70
Dacre Ho. SW3 6F 87
Dacre St. SW1 6G 79
Dagmar Gdns. NW10 5C 54
Dagmar Pas. N1 2F 61
Dagmar Ter. N1 2F 61
Dagobert Ho. E1 4K 73
Dain Ct. W8 1K 85
Dainton Ho. W2 4J 65
Dalehead NW1 5E 58
Dale Ho. N1 3A 62
(off New Era Est.)
NW8 3C 56
Dale Rd. SE17 6F 91
Dale Row W11 6F 65
Dalgarno Gdns. W10 3A 64
Dalgarno Way W10 2A 64
Dali Universe 4A 80
Dalkeith Ct. SW1 2H 89
Dallington Sq. EC1 1F 71
(off Dallington St.)
Dallington St. EC1 1F 71
DALSTON 1C 62
Dalton Ho. SW1 3C 88
Damer Ter. SW10 7D 86
Dame St. N1 4G 61
Damien Ct. E1 5H 73
Damien St. E1 5H 73
Damory Ho. SE16 1H 93
Danbury St. N1 4F 61
Danby Ho. E9 1G 63
W10 7F 55
Dandridge Ho. E1 3C 72
Danes Ct. NW8 3J 57
Danesfield SE5 5A 92
Danes Ho. W10 3A 64
Dane St. WC1 4A 70
Daniel Gdns. SE15 7C 92
Daniell Ho. N1 4K 61
Dan Leno Wlk. SW6 7A 86
Dansey Pl. W1 7G 69
Danson Rd. SE17 4F 91
Dante Pl. SE11 2F 91
Dante Rd. SE11 1E 90
Danube Ct. SE15 7D 92
Danube St. SW3 3H 87
Danvers Ho. E1 6F 73
Danvers St. SW3 6F 87
Da Palma Ct. SW6 6J 85
Daplyn St. E1 3E 72
D'Arblay St. W1 6F 69
Darcy Ho. E8 2G 63
Darent Ho. NW8 3F 67
Darfield NW1 3E 58
Darfield Way W10 6C 64
Dark Ho. Wlk. EC3 1K 81
Darley Ho. SE11 4A 90
Darling Row E1 2H 73
Darlington Ho. SW8 7H 89
Darnay Ho. SE16 6E 82
Darnley Ter. W11 2D 74
Dartford Ho. SE1 2D 92
Dartford St. SE17 5H 91
Dartington NW1 3F 59
Dartington Ho. W2 3A 66
Dartle Ct. SE16 5F 83
Dartmouth Cl. W11 5H 65
Dartmouth St. SW1 5G 79
Dartrey Twr. SW10 7D 86
Dartrey Wlk. SW10 7D 86
Dart St. W10 6F 55
Darvell Ho. SE17 4K 91
Darwen Pl. E2 3G 63
Darwin Ct. NW1 2B 58
SE17 2K 91
(off Barlow St.)
Darwin Ho. SW1 5E 88
Darwin St. SE17 1K 91
(not continuous)
Daryngton Ho. SE1 5J 81
SW8 7J 89
Datchet Ho. NW1 6D 58
Datchworth Ho. N1 1E 60
Date St. SE17 4H 91
Dauncey Ho. SE1 5E 80
Davenant St. E1 4F 73
Davenport Ho. SE11 7C 80
Daventry St. NW1 3G 67
Daver Ct. SW3 4H 87
Davey's Ct. WC2 7J 69
Davey St. SE15 6D 92
Davidge Ho. SE1 5D 80
Davidge St. SE1 5E 80
David Ho. SW8 7J 89
David Lloyd Leisure
Fulham Broadway
7K 85
South Kensington
1B 86
David M. W1 3A 68
Davidson Gdns. SW8 7J 89
Davies M. W1 7C 68
Davies St. W1 6C 68
Da Vinci Ct. SE16 3G 93
Davis Ho. W12 1A 74
Dawes Ho. SE17 2J 91
Dawes Rd. SW6 7F 85
Dawes St. SE17 3K 91
Dawson Ho. E2 7J 63
Dawson Pl. W2 7J 65
Dawson St. E2 5D 62
Day Ho. SE5 7G 91
Daynor Ho. NW6 2K 55
Deacon Ho. SE11 2B 90
Deacon M. N1 1K 61
Deacon Way SE17 1G 91
Deal Ho. SE15 5K 93
SE17 4B 92
Deal Porters Wlk.
SE16 3K 83
Deal Porters Way
SE16 6K 83
Deal St. E1 3E 72
Deal Wlk. SW9 7C 90
Dean Abbott Ho.
SW1 1G 89
Dean Bradley St.
SW1 7J 79
Dean Ct. SW8 7J 89
Deancross St. E1 6J 73
Deanery M. W1 2B 78
Deanery St. W1 2B 78
Dean Farrar St. SW1 6H 79
Dean Ho. E1 6J 73
Dean Ryle St. SW1 1J 89
Dean's Bldgs. SE17 2J 91
Dean's Ct. EC4 6F 71
Dean's M. W1 5D 68
Dean Stanley St.
SW1 7J 79
Dean St. W1 5G 69
Dean's Yd. SW1 6H 79
Dean Trench St. SW1 7J 79
Deauville Ct. SE16 4K 83
Debdale Ho. E2 3F 63
De Beauvoir Ct. N1 1K 61
De Beauvoir Cres.
N1 2A 62
De Beauvoir Est. N1 2A 62
De Beauvoir Rd. N1 2A 62
De Beauvoir Sq. N1 1B 62
DE BEAUVOIR TOWN 2A 62
Debenham Ct. E8 3E 62
Debnams Rd. SE16 2J 93
Decima St. SE1 6A 82
Deerhurst Ho. SE15 6E 92
Defoe Ho. EC2 3G 71
Defoe Pl. EC2 3G 71
Delafield Ho. E1 6F 73
Delaford Rd. SE16 3H 93
Delaford St. SW6 7F 85
Delamere St. W2 3C 66
Delamere Ter. W2 3B 66
Delancey Pas. NW1 3D 58
Delancey St. NW1 3C 58
Delancey Studios
NW1 3D 58
Delarch Ho. SE1 5E 80
De Laune St. SE17 4E 90
Delaware Mans. W9 1A 66
Delaware Rd. W9 1A 66
Delfina Studio Trust 4A 82
Delhi St. N1 3K 59
Dellow Ho. E1 7H 73
Dellow St. E1 7H 73
Dell's M. SW1 2F 89
Delmerend Ho. SW3 3G 87
Delorme St. W6 6D 84
Delta Point E2 6E 62
Delta St. E2 6E 62
Delverton Ho. SE17 3F 91
Delverton Rd. SE17 4F 91
Den, The 4K 93
Denbigh Cl. W11 7H 65
Denbigh Ho. SW1 6K 77
W11 6H 65
Denbigh M. SW1 2E 88
Denbigh Pl. SW1 3E 88
Denbigh Rd. W11 7H 65
Denbigh St. SW1 2E 88
(not continuous)
Denbigh Ter. W11 7H 65
Denby Ct. SE11 1B 90
Dence Ho. E2 7E 62
Dengie Wlk. N1 2G 61
Denholme Rd. W9 6H 55
Denland Ho. SW8 7B 90
Denman Pl. W1 7G 69
Denman St. W1 1G 79
Denmark Gro. N1 4C 60
Denmark Pl. WC2 5H 69
Denmark Rd. NW6 5H 55
(not continuous)
Denmark St. WC2 6H 69
Denne Ter. E8 3D 62
Denning Cl. NW8 7D 56
Denning Point E1 5D 72
Denny Cres. SE11 3D 90
Denny St. SE11 3D 90
Densham Ho. NW8 5F 57
Denstone Ho. SE15 6E 92
Dent Ho. SE17 2A 92
Denton Ho. N1 1F 61
Denyer St. SW3 2H 87
Denys Ho. EC1 3C 70
Depot Rd. W12 7B 64
Depot St. SE5 6J 91
Deptford Bus. Pk.
SE15 5K 93
De Quincey Ho. SW1 4E 88
Derby Ga. SW1 4J 79
(not continuous)
Derby Ho. SE11 1C 90
Derby Lodge WC1 6A 60
Derby Rd. E9 2K 63
Derbyshire St. E2 7F 63
(not continuous)
Derby St. W1 3B 78
Dereham Pl. EC2 7B 62
Dericote St. E8 2G 63
Dering St. W1 6C 68
Dering Yd. W1 6D 68
Derrycombe Ho. W2 4J 65
Derry Ho. NW8 2F 67
Derry St. W8 5A 76
Derwent NW1 7E 58
Derwent Ct. SE16 4K 83
Derwent Ho. SW7 1D 86
Desborough Cl. W2 3B 66
Desborough Ho. W14 5H 85
Desborough St. W2 3A 66
Design Mus. 4D 82
Detling Ho. SE17 2A 92
De Vere Cotts. W8 6C 76
De Vere Gdns. W8 5C 76
Deverell St. SE1 7J 81
De Vere M. W8 6C 76
Devereux Ct. WC2 6C 70
Devizes St. N1 3K 61
Devonia Rd. N1 4F 61
Devon Mans. SE1 4C 82
(off Tooley St.)
Devonport W2 5G 67
Devonport Ho. W2 4J 65
Devonport Rd. W12 3A 74
(not continuous)
Devonport St. E1 6K 73
Devonshire Cl. W1 3C 68
Devonshire Ct. E1 7K 63
WC1 3K 69
Devonshire Gro.
SE15 6H 93
Devonshire Ho. SE1 6G 81
SW1 3H 89
Devonshire M. SW10 6E 86
Devonshire M. Nth.
W1 3C 68
Devonshire M. Sth.
W1 3C 68
Devonshire M. W.
W1 2B 68
Devonshire Pl. W1 2B 68
W8 7A 76
Devonshire Pl. M.
W1 3B 68
Devonshire Row EC2 4B 72
Devonshire Row M.
W1 2D 68
Devonshire Sq. EC2 5B 72
Devonshire St. W1 3B 68
Devonshire Ter. W2 6D 66
Devon St. SE15 6H 93
De Walden Ho. NW8 4G 57
De Walden St. W1 4B 68
Dewey Rd. N1 4C 60
Dewhurst Rd. W14 6C 74
Dewsbury Ter. NW1 2D 58
Dhonau Ho. SE1 1D 92
Diadem Ct. W1 6G 69
Dial Wlk., The W8 4B 76
Diamond St. SE15 7B 92
Diana, Princess of Wales
Memorial Walk 2B 76
Dibden St. N1 2F 61
Dibdin Ho. W9 4A 56

Dickens Est. SE1 5E 82
SE16 6E 82
Dickens House 2A 70
Dickens Ho. NW6 6J 55
NW8 1F 67
SE17 4F 91
WC1 1J 69
Dickens M. EC1 3E 70
Dickens Sq. SE1 6H 81
Dickinson Ct. EC1 2F 71
Dicksee Ho. NW8 2E 66
Dickson Ho. E1 5G 73
Dieppe Cl. W14 3G 85
Digby Mans. W6 4A 84
Digby St. E2 7K 63
Dighton Ct. SE5 6G 91
Dignum St. N1 4C 60
Dilke St. SW3 5K 87
Dilston Gro. SE16 1J 93
Dimes Pl. W6 2A 84
Dinerman Ct. NW8 2D 56
Dingley Pl. EC1 7H 61
Dingley Rd. EC1 6H 61
Dinmont Est. E2 4F 63
Dinmont Ho. E2 4G 63
Dinmont St. E2 4G 63
Dinmore Ho. E9 2J 63
Dinnington Ho. E1 1H 73
Dinton Ho. NW8 1G 67
Disbrowe Rd. W6 6F 85
Discovery Bus. Pk.
SE16 7E 82
Discovery Wlk. E1 2G 83
Disney Pl. SE1 4H 81
Disney St. SE1 4H 81
Diss St. E2 6C 62
Distaff La. EC4 7G 71
Distillery La. W6 4B 84
Distillery Rd. W6 4B 84
Distin St. SE11 2C 90
Dixon Ho. W10 6C 64
Dixon's All. SE16 5G 83
Dobree Av. NW10 1A 54
Dobson Cl. NW6 1E 56
Dobson Ho. SE5 7K 91
SE14 6K 93
Doby Ct. EC4 7H 71
Dock Cotts. E1 1K 83
Dockhead SE1 5D 82
Dockhead Wharf SE1 4D 82
Dockley Rd. SE16 7E 82
Dockley Rd. Ind. Est.
SE16 7E 82
Dock Offices SE16 6K 83
Dock St. E1 7E 72
Dodd Ho. SE16 2H 93
Doddington Gro.
SE17 5E 90
Doddington Pl. SE17 5E 90
Dodson St. SE1 5D 80
Dog & Duck Yd. WC1 3B 70
Dolben Ct. SW1 2H 89
Dolben St. SE1 3E 80
(not continuous)
Dolland Ho. SE11 4B 90
Dolland St. SE11 4B 90
Dolphin Cl. SE16 4K 83
Dolphin Sq. SW1 4F 89
Dombey Ho. SE1 5E 82
W11 2D 74
Dombey St. WC1 3A 70
(not continuous)
Domecq Ho. *EC1 1F 71*
(off Dallington St.)
Domingo St. EC1 1G 71
Dominion Ct. E8 1D 62
Dominion St. EC2 3K 71
Dominion Theatre 5H 69
Donaldson Rd. NW6 3H 55
Donato Dr. SE15 6A 92
Donegal Ho. E1 1H 73
Donegal St. N1 5B 60
Doneraile Ho. SW1 4C 88
Don Gratton Ho. E1 4F 73
Donkin Ho. SE16 2H 93
Donmar Warehouse Theatre
6J 69
Donnelly Ct. SW6 7F 85
Donne Pl. SW3 1H 87
Donnington Ct. NW1 1D 58
Donnington Mans.
NW10 2A 54
Donnington Rd.
NW10 2A 54
Donovan Ct. SW10 4E 86
Donovan Ho. E1 7J 73
Doon St. SE1 3C 80
Dora Ho. W11 1D 74
Dorando Cl. W12 7A 64
Dorchester Ct. N1 1B 62
SW1 7K 77
Doric Ho. E2 5K 63
Doric Way NW1 6G 59
Dorking Ho. SE1 6K 81
Dorman Way NW8 2E 56
Dormstone Ho. SE17 2A 92
Dorney NW3 1H 57
Dorrington St. EC1 3C 70
Dorrit Ho. W11 2D 74
Dorrit St. SE1 4H 81
Dorset Bldgs. EC4 6E 70
Dorset Cl. NW1 3J 67
Dorset Ct. N1 1B 62
Dorset Ho. NW1 2K 67
Dorset M. SW1 6C 78
Dorset Ri. EC4 6E 70
Dorset Rd. SW8 7K 89
Dorset Sq. NW1 2J 67
Dorset St. W1 4K 67
Dorset Wharf W6 7B 84
Dorton Cl. SE15 7B 92
Doughty Ct. E1 2H 83
Doughty Ho. SW10 6D 86
Doughty M. WC1 2A 70
Doughty St. WC1 1A 70
Douglas Ct. NW6 1K 55
Douglas Johnstone Ho.
SW6 6G 85
Douglas Pl. SW1 2G 89
Douglas Rd. NW6 2H 55
Douglas St. SW1 2G 89
Douglas Waite Ho.
NW6 1A 56
Doulton Ho. SE11 7B 80
Douro Pl. W8 6B 76
Douthwaite Sq. E1 2F 83
Dove Ct. EC2 6J 71
Dovehouse St. SW3 3F 87
Dove M. SW5 2C 86
Dover Ct. EC1 1E 70
Dover Flats SE1 2B 92
Dover Ho. SE15 5K 93
Dove Row E2 3E 62
Dover St. W1 1D 78
Dover Yd. W1 2E 78
Doves Yd. N1 3D 60
Doveton Ho. E1 1J 73
Doveton St. E1 1J 73
Dove Wlk. SW1 3A 88
Dovey Lodge N1 1D 60
Dowgate Hill EC4 7J 71
Dowland St. W10 6F 55
Dowlas St. SE5 7A 92
Dowler Ho. E1 6F 73
Downend Ct. SE15 6C 92
Downey Ho. E1 2K 73
Downfield Cl. W9 2A 66
Downham Ct. N1 1K 61
Downham Rd. N1 1J 61
Downing Ho. W10 5D 64
Downing St. SW1 4J 79
Down Pl. W6 2A 84
Down St. W1 3C 78
Down St. M. W1 3C 78
Dowrey St. N1 2C 60
Doyce St. SE1 4G 81
Doyle Gdns. NW10 4A 54
Doyle Ho. SW13 7A 84
D'Oyley St. SW1 1A 88
Draco St. SE17 5G 91
Dragon Rd. SE15 6A 92
Dragon Yd. WC1 5K 69
Drake Ct. SE1 5H 81
W12 5A 74
Drake Ho. E1 4J 73
SW1 5G 89
Drakeland Ho. W9 1H 65
Drakes Courtyard
NW6 1H 55
Drake St. WC1 4A 70
Draper Ho. SE1 1F 91
Draper Pl. N1 2F 61
Drapers Gdns. EC2 5K 71
Drappers Way SE16 1F 93
Draycott Av. SW3 1G 87
Draycott Cl. SE5 7J 91
(not continuous)
Draycott Pl. SW3 2J 87
Draycott Ter. SW3 2K 87
Drayford Cl. W9 1H 65
Drayson M. W8 5K 75
Drayton Gdns. SW10 3D 86
Dresden Ho. SE11 1B 90
Drewett Ho. E1 6F 73
Drill Hall Arts Cen. 3G 69
Drinkwater Ho. SE5 7J 91
Dr Johnson's House 5D 70
Dron Ho. E1 3J 73
Droop St. W10 7D 54
Drovers Pl. SE15 7H 93
Druid St. SE1 4B 82
Drummond Cres.
NW1 6G 59
Drummond Ga. SW1 3H 89
Drummond Ho. E2 4F 63
Drummond Rd. SE16 6G 83
Drummond St. NW1 1E 68
Drum St. E1 5D 72
Drury La. WC2 5K 69
Drury Lane Theatre Royal
6A 70
Dryburgh Ho. SW1 3C 88
Dryden Ct. SE11 2D 90
Dryden Mans. W14 5F 85
Dryden St. WC2 6K 69
Drysdale Ho. N1 6B 62
Drysdale Pl. N1 6B 62
Drysdale St. N1 7B 62
Dublin Av. E8 2F 63
Ducal St. E2 7D 62
Du Cane Cl. W12 6A 64
Du Cane Rd. W12 6A 64
Duchess M. W1 4D 68
Duchess of Bedford Ho.
W8 4J 75
Duchess of Bedford's Wlk.
W8 5H 75
Duchess St. W1 4D 68
Duchess Theatre 7A 70
Duchy St. SE1 2D 80
(not continuous)
Duck La. W1 6G 69
Dudley Ct. W1 6J 67
WC2 5J 69
Dudley Ho. W2 4E 66
Dudley Rd. NW6 4F 55
Dudley St. W2 4E 66
Dudmaston M. SW3 3F 87
Duffell Ho. SE11 4B 90
Dufferin Av. EC1 2J 71
Dufferin Ct. EC1 2J 71
Dufferin St. EC1 2H 71
Dufour's Pl. W1 6F 69
Dugard Way SE11 1E 90
Duke of Wellington Pl.
SW1 5B 78
Duke of York Column
(Memorial) 3G 79
Duke of Yorks Sq.
SW3 2K 87
Duke of York's Theatre
1J 79
Duke of York St.
SW1 2F 79
Dukes Ct. W2 7B 66
Duke's Ho. SW1 1H 89
Dukes La. W8 4K 75
Duke's La. Chambers
W8 4A 76
(off Dukes La.)
Duke's La. Mans. *W8 4A 76*
(off Dukes La.)
Duke's M. W1 5B 68
Duke's Pl. EC3 6B 72
Duke's Rd. WC1 7H 59
Duke St. SW1 2F 79
W1 5B 68
Duke St. Hill SE1 2K 81
Duke St. Mans. W1 6B 68
Duke's Yd. W1 7B 68
Dulford St. W11 7E 64
Dulverton NW1 3F 59
Dulverton Mans.
WC1 2B 70
Dumain Ct. SE11 2E 90
Dumpton Pl. NW1 1A 58
Dunbridge St. E2 1F 73
Duncan Ho. SW1 4F 89
Duncannon Ho. SW1 4H 89
Duncannon St. WC2 1J 79
Duncan Rd. E8 3G 63
Duncan St. N1 4E 60
Duncan Ter. N1 5E 60
(not continuous)
Dunch St. E1 6H 73
Dundalk Ho. E1 5J 73
Dundas Ho. E2 4J 63
Dundee Ct. E1 3G 83
SE1 6A 82
(off Long La.)
Dundee Ho. W9 6C 56
Dundee St. E1 3G 83
Dundonald Rd.
NW10 3C 54
Dunelm St. E1 5K 73
Dunloe Ct. E2 5D 62
Dunloe St. E2 5C 62
Dunlop Pl. SE16 7D 82
Dunmore Point E2 7C 62
Dunmore Rd. NW6 3E 54
Dunmow Ho. SE11 3B 90
Dunmow Wlk. N1 2G 61
Dunnico Ho. SE17 3A 92
Dunn's Pas. WC1 5K 69
Dunoon Ho. N1 3A 60
Dunraven St. W1 7K 67
Dunsany Rd. W14 7C 74
Dunstable M. W1 3B 68
Dunstan Ho's. E1 3K 73
Dunster Ct. EC3 7B 72
Dunster Gdns. NW6 1H 55
Dunsterville Way
SE1 5K 81
Dunston Rd. E8 3C 62
Dunston St. E8 2C 62
Dunton Rd. SE1 3C 92
Dunworth M. W11 5G 65
Duplex Ride SW1 5K 77
Durant St. E2 6E 62
Durban Ho. W12 1A 74
Durfey Pl. SE5 7K 91
Durham Ct. NW6 5K 55
(not continuous)
Durham Ho. NW8 7G 57
Durham Ho. St. WC2 1K 79
Durham Pl. SW3 4J 87
Durham St. SE11 4A 90
Durham Ter. W2 5A 66
Durham Yd. E2 6G 63
Durrels Ho. W14 1H 85
Durward Ho. W8 5B 76
Durward St. E1 3G 73
Durweston M. W1 3K 67
Durweston St. W1 4K 67
Dyer's Bldgs. EC1 4C 70
Dyne Rd. NW6 1F 55
Dynham Rd. NW6 1J 55
Dyott St. WC1 5H 69
Dysart St. EC2 2A 72

E

Eagle Cl. SE16 4J 93
Eagle Ct. EC1 3E 70
Eagle Ho. E1 2H 73
N1 4J 61
Eagle Pl. SW1 1F 79
SW7 3D 86
Eagle St. WC1 4A 70
Eagle Wharf Ct. SE1 3C 82
Eagle Wharf Rd. N1 4H 61
Eagle Works E. E1 2D 72
Eagle Works W. E1 2C 72
Eamont Ct. NW8 4H 57
Eamont St. NW8 4G 57
Eardley Cres. SW5 3K 85
Earle Ho. SW1 2H 89
Earlham St. WC2 6H 69
Earl Ho. NW1 2H 67
Earlom Ho. WC1 7C 60
EARL'S COURT 3K 85
Earls Court Exhibition Building
3J 85
Earl's Ct. Gdns. SW5 2A 86
Earls Ct. Rd. SW5 1K 85
W8 6J 75
Earl's Ct. Sq. SW5 3K 85
Earlsferry Way N1 1K 59
(not continuous)
Earlsmead Rd. NW10 6A 54
Earls Ter. W8 7H 75
Earlstoke St. EC1 6E 60
Earlston Gro. E9 3H 63
Earl St. EC2 3K 71
(not continuous)
Earls Wlk. W8 7J 75
Early M. NW1 2D 58
Earnshaw St. WC2 5H 69
Earsby St. W14 1F 85
(not continuous)
Easleys M. W1 5B 68
E. Arbour St. E1 5K 73
East Block SE1 4B 80
Eastbourne M. W2 5D 66
Eastbourne Ter. W2 5D 66
Eastcastle St. W1 5E 68
Eastcheap EC3 7A 72
Eastern Ho. E2 7G 63
E. Harding St. EC4 5D 70
E. India Ct. SE16 4J 83
Eastlake Ho. NW8 2F 67
East La. SE16 4E 82
(Chambers St.)
SE16 5E 82
(Scott Lidgett Cres.)
East Mt. St. E1 3H 73
(not continuous)
Easton St. WC1 1C 70
East Pas. EC1 3F 71
East Point SE1 3E 92
E. Poultry Av. EC1 4E 70
East Rd. N1 7J 61
SW3 4A 88
East Row W10 2E 64
Eastry Ho. SW8 7J 89
East Smithfield E1 1D 82
East St. SE17 3H 91
(not continuous)
E. Surrey Gro. SE15 7C 92
E. Tenter St. E1 6D 72
Eastwell Ho. SE1 6K 81
Eaton Cl. SW1 2A 88
Eaton Ga. SW1 1A 88
Eaton La. SW1 7D 78
Eaton Mans. SW1 2A 88
Eaton M. Nth. SW1 1A 88
Eaton M. Sth. SW1 1B 88
Eaton M. W. SW1 1B 88
Eaton Pl. SW1 7A 78
Eaton Row SW1 7C 78
Eaton Sq. SW1 1A 88
Eaton Ter. SW1 1A 88
Eaton Ter. M. SW1 1A 88
Ebbisham Dr. SW8 5A 90
Ebenezer Ho. SE11 2D 90
Ebenezer Mussel Ho.
E2 5J 63
Ebenezer St. N1 6J 61
Ebley Cl. SE15 5C 92
Ebony Ho. E2 7E 62
Ebor St. E1 1C 72
Ebury Bri. SW1 3C 88
Ebury Bri. Est. SW1 3C 88
Ebury Bri. Rd. SW1 4B 88
Ebury M. SW1 1B 88
Ebury M. E. SW1 1C 88
Ebury Sq. SW1 2B 88
Ebury St. SW1 2B 88
Ecclesbourne Rd. N1 1H 61
Eccleston Bri. SW1 1D 88
Eccleston M. SW1 7B 78
Eccleston Pl. SW1 2C 88
Eccleston Sq. SW1 2D 88
Eccleston Sq. M.
SW1 2E 88
Eccleston St. SW1 7B 78
Eckford St. N1 4C 60
Edbrooke Rd. W9 2J 65
Edenbridge Cl. SE16 4G 93
Eden Cl. W8 6K 75
Edenham Way W10 3G 65
Eden Ho. NW8 2G 67
Edgar Ho. SW8 7J 89
Edgar Wallace Cl.
SE15 7B 92
Edgcott Ho. W10 3A 64
Edge St. W8 2K 75
Edgeworth Ho. NW8 2C 56
Edgson Ho. SW1 3C 88
Edgware Rd. NW8 2E 66
Edinburgh Cl. E2 5J 63
Edinburgh Ga. SW1 4J 77
Edinburgh Ho. W9 6B 56
Edison Ho. SE1 1J 91
Edis St. NW1 2A 58
Editha Mans. SW10 6C 86
Edith Gro. SW10 6C 86
Edith Ho. W6 3A 84
Edith Neville Cotts.
NW1 6G 59
Edith Rd. W14 2E 84
Edith St. E2 4D 62
Edith Summerskill Ho.
SW6 7H 85
Edith Ter. SW10 7C 86
Edith Vs. W14 2G 85
Edith Yd. SW10 7D 86
Edmonton Ct. SE16 6K 83
Edmund Ho. SE17 4F 91
Edmund St. SE5 7J 91
Ednam Ho. SE15 6E 92
Edric Ho. SW1 1H 89
Edric Rd. SE14 7K 93
Edward VII Mans.
NW10 6C 54
Edward Bond Ho.
WC1 7K 59
(off Cromer St.)
Edward Dodd Ct. N1 6K 61
Edward Edward's Ho.
SE1 3E 80
Edwardes Pl. W8 7H 75
Edwardes Sq. W8 7H 75
Edward Ho. SE11 3B 90
W2 2E 66
Edward Kennedy Ho.
W10 2F 65
Edward M. NW1 6D 58
Edward Robinson Ho.
SE14 7K 93
Edwards M. W1 6A 68
Edward Sq. N1 3A 60
Edwin St. E1 1K 73
Effie Pl. SW6 7K 85
Effie Rd. SW6 7K 85
Egbert St. NW1 2A 58
Egerton Cres. SW3 1H 87
Egerton Gdns. NW10 3A 54
SW3 7G 77
Egerton Gdns. M.
SW3 7H 77
Egerton Pl. SW3 7H 77
Egerton Ter. SW3 7H 77
Eglington Ct. SE17 5G 91
Eglon M. NW1 1K 57
Elan Ct. E1 4G 73
Eland Ho. SW1 6E 78
Elba Pl. SE17 1H 91
Elbourn Ho. SW3 3G 87
Elcho St. SW11 7G 87
Elcot Av. SE15 7G 93
Elden Ho. SW3 1G 87
Elder St. E1 3C 72
(not continuous)
Elder Wlk. N1 2F 61
Eldon Ct. NW6 3J 55
Eldon Rd. W8 7B 76
Eldon St. EC2 4K 71
Eldridge Ct. SE16 7E 82
Eleanor Ct. E2 3E 62
Eleanor Ho. W6 4A 84
ELEPHANT & CASTLE
7F 81
Elephant & Castle
SE1 1F 91
Elephant & Castle Superbowl
1G 91
Elephant La. SE16 4J 83
Elephant Rd. SE17 1G 91
Elf Row E1 7K 73
Elgar Ct. W14 7E 74
Elgar Ho. NW6 1D 56
SW1 4D 88
Elgin Av. W9 2H 65
Elgin Ct. W9 1A 66
Elgin Cres. W11 1F 75
Elgin Est. W9 2J 65
Elgin Mans. W9 7A 56
Elgin M. W11 6F 65
Elgin M. Nth. W9 6B 56
Elgin M. Sth. W9 6B 56
Elgood Cl. W11 1E 74
Elgood Ho. NW8 5F 57
Elia M. N1 5E 60
Elias Pl. SW8 6C 90
Elia St. N1 5E 60
Elim Est. SE1 6A 82
Elim St. SE1 6K 81
(not continuous)
Eliot M. NW8 5C 56
Elizabeth Av. N1 2H 61
Elizabeth Bri. SW1 2C 88
Elizabeth Cl. W9 2D 66
Elizabeth Ct. NW1 1H 67
SW1 7H 79
SW10 6F 87
Elizabeth Fry M. E8 1H 63
Elizabeth Ho. SE11 2D 90
W6 3B 84
Elizabeth Newcomen Ho.
SE1 4J 81
Elizabeth St. SW1 1B 88
Elkington Point SE11 2C 90
Elkstone Rd. W10 3G 65
Ellaline Rd. W6 6C 84
Ellen St. E1 6F 73
Ellen Wilkinson Ho.
E2 6K 63
SW6 6G 85
Ellerslie Rd. W12 2A 74
Ellery Ho. SE17 2K 91
Ellington Ho. SE1 7H 81
Elliot Ho. W1 4H 67
Elliott's Pl. N1 3F 61
Elliott Sq. NW3 1H 57
Elliotts Row SE11 1E 90
Ellis Franklin Ct.
NW8 4C 56
Ellis Ho. SE17 3J 91
Ellis St. SW1 1K 87
Ellsworth St. E2 6H 63
Ellwood Ct. W9 2A 66
Elmbridge Wlk. E8 1F 63
Elm Ct. EC4 7C 70
W9 3K 65
Elmer Ho. *NW1 3G 67*
(off Penfold St.)
Elmfield Ho. NW8 4B 56
W9 2K 65
Elmfield Way W9 3J 65
Elm Friars Wlk. NW1 1H 59
Elm Ho. W10 1F 65
Elmington Est. SE5 7J 91
Elmore St. N1 1H 61
Elm Pk. Chambers
SW10 4E 86
Elm Pk. Gdns. SW10 4E 86
Elm Pk. Ho. SW10 4E 86
Elm Pk. La. SW3 4E 86
Elm Pk. Mans. SW10 5D 86
Elm Pk. Rd. SW3 5E 86
Elm Pl. SW7 3E 86
Elm Quay Ct. SW8 6G 89
Elms M. W2 7E 66
Elm St. WC1 2B 70
Elmton Ct. NW8 1E 66
Elm Tree Cl. NW8 6E 56
Elm Tree Ct. NW8 6E 56
Elm Tree Rd. NW8 6E 56
Elnathan M. W9 2B 66
Elsden M. E2 5K 63
Elsham Rd. W14 5E 74
Elsham Ter. W14 6E 74
Elsie La. Ct. W2 4K 65
Elsinore Ho. N1 3C 60
W6 4B 84
Elsted St. SE17 2K 91
Elstow Grange NW6 1C 54
Elsworthy Ct. NW3 1J 57
Elsworthy Ri. NW3 1H 57
Elsworthy Rd. NW3 2G 57
Elsworthy Ter. NW3 1H 57
Eluna Apartments E1 1H 83
Elvaston M. SW7 6D 76
Elvaston Pl. SW7 7C 76
Elver Gdns. E2 5F 63
Elverton St. SW1 1G 89
Elwin St. E2 6E 62
Elworth Ho. SW8 7B 90
Ely Cotts. SW8 7A 90
Ely Ct. EC1 4D 70
NW6 4J 55
Ely Ho. SE15 7F 93
Ely Pl. EC1 4D 70
Elystan Pl. SW3 3H 87
Elystan St. SW3 2G 87
Elystan Wlk. N1 3C 60
Emanuel Ho. SW1 7G 79
Embankment Gdns.
SW3 5K 87
Embankment Pl.
WC2 2K 79
Embassy Ct. NW8 5F 57
Embassy Ho. NW6 1A 56
Embassy Theatre
Central School of
Speech & Drama 1E 56
Emba St. SE16 5F 83
Emberton SE5 5A 92
Emberton Ct. EC1 7E 60
Emerald St. WC1 3A 70
Emerson St. SE1 2G 81
Emery Hill St. SW1 7F 79
Emery St. SE1 6D 80
Emily Ct. SE1 5G 81

Emily Ho. W10 ....1F 65
Emmanuel Ho. SE11 ...2C 90
Emma St. E2 ....4G 63
Emminster NW6 ....2A 56
Emperor's Ga. SW7 ...7B 76
Empire Cinema
Leicester Sq. 7H 69
Empire Ho. SW3 ....7G 77
Empress App. SW6 .....5J 85
Empress Pl. SW6 ......4J 85
Empress State Bldg.
SW6 ....4J 85
Empress St. SE17 .....5H 91
Enbrook St. W10 ....7F 55
Endell St. WC2 ....5J 69
Endsleigh Ct. WC1 .....1H 69
Endsleigh Gdns.
WC1 ....1G 69
Endsleigh Pl. WC1 .....1H 69
Endsleigh St. WC1 .....1G 69
Energize Fitness Club
..............3D 84
Enfield Cloisters N1 ....6A 62
Enfield Rd. N1 ....1B 62
Enford St. W1 ....3J 67
Engine Ct. SW1 ....3F 79
Englefield NW1 ....7E 58
Englefield Rd. N1 ......1B 62
English Grounds SE1 ...3A 82
Enid St. SE16 ....6D 82
Ennerdale NW1 ....6E 58
Ennismore Gdns.
SW7 ....5G 77
Ennismore Gdns. M.
SW7 ....6G 77
Ennismore M. SW7 ....6G 77
Ennismore St. SW7 ....6G 77
Ensbury Ho. SW8 ......7A 90
Ensign Ind. Cen. E1 ....1E 82
Ensign St. E1 ....7E 72
Ensor M. SW7 ....3E 86
Enterprise Ho. E9 ......1J 63
Enterprise Ind. Est.
SE16 ....4K 93
Epcot M. NW10 ....7D 54
Epirus M. SW6 ....7J 85
Epirus Rd. SW6 ....7H 85
Epworth St. EC2 ....2K 71
Equity Sq. E2 ....7D 62
Erasmus St. SW1 ....2H 89
Eresby Ho. SW7 ....5H 77
Eresby Pl. NW6 ....1J 55
Eric Fletcher Ct. N1 ....1H 61
Eric Wilkins Ho. SE1 ....4E 92
Erlich Cotts. E1 ....3J 73
Ernest Harriss Ho.
W9 ....1J 65
Eros 1G 79
Errington Rd. W9 ....1H 65
Errol St. EC1 ....2H 71
Erskine Ho. SW1 ....4E 88
Erskine M. NW3 ....1K 57
Erskine Rd. NW3 ....1K 57
Eskdale NW1 ....5E 58
Esmeralda Rd. SE1 .....2F 93
Esmond Ct. W8 ....6B 76
Esmond Rd. NW6 ....3H 55
Esporta Health & Fitness
Islington *3E 60*
(off Islington Grn.)
Esprit Ct. E1 ....4C 72
Essendine Mans. W9 ...7K 55
Essendine Rd. W9 ......1K 65
Essex Ct. EC4 ....6C 70
Essex Rd. N1 ....3F 61
Essex St. WC2 ....6C 70
Essex Vs. W8 ....5J 75
Estcourt Rd. SW6 ......7G 85
Estella Ho. W11 ....1D 74
Esterbrooke St. SW1 ...2G 89
Etal Ho. N1 ....1E 60
Etcetera Theatre 1D 58
Ethel St. SE17 ....2H 91
Ethnard Rd. SE15 ......6G 93
Eton Av. NW3 ....1E 56
Eugene Cotter Ho.
SE17 ....2K 91
Eugenia Rd. SE16 .....2K 93
Europa Pl. EC1 ....7G 61
Eustace Bldg. SW8 .....6C 88
Eustace Ho. SE11 ......1A 90
Eustace Rd. SW6 ....7J 85
Euston Cen. NW1 ......1E 68
(not continuous)
Euston Gro. NW1 ......7G 59
Euston Rd. NW1 ....2D 68
Euston Sq. NW1 ....7G 59
(not continuous)
Euston Sta. Colonnade
NW1 ....7G 59
Euston St. NW1 ....7F 59
Euston Twr. NW1 ......1E 68
EUSTON UNDERPASS
..............1F 69
Evangalist Ho. *EC4* *6E 70*
(off Black Friars La.)
Evans Ho. SW8 ....7H 89
W12 ....1A 74
Evedon Ho. *N1* *3A 62*
(off New Era Est.)
Evelina Mans. SE5 .....7J 91
Evelyn Ct. N1 ....5J 61
(not continuous)
Evelyn Denington Ct.
N1 ....1E 60
Evelyn Fox Ct. W10 ....4B 64
Evelyn Gdns. SW7 .....4D 86
Evelyn Ho. W8 ....5A 76
Evelyn Lowe Est.
SE16 ....7E 82
Evelyn Mans. SW1 .....7E 78
W14 ....5F 85
Evelyn Wlk. N1 ....5J 61
Evelyn Yd. W1 ....5G 69
Everard Ho. E1 ....6F 73
Everett Ho. SE17 ......3K 91
Evergreen Sq. E8 ......1C 62
Everilda St. N1 ....3B 60
Everington St. W6 .....5D 84
(not continuous)
Eversholt St. NW1 .....4F 59
Eversley Ho. E2 ....7E 62
Everton Bldgs. NW1 ....7E 58
Evesham Ho. E2 ....5J 63
NW8 ....3C 56
SW1 ....3D 88
Evesham St. W11 ......1C 74
Ewen Ho. N1 ....3A 60
Ewer St. SE1 ....3G 81
Ewhurst Cl. E1 ....4K 73
Exbury Ho. SW1 ....3G 89
Excel Ct. WC2 ....1H 79
Excelsior Ind. Est.
SE15 ....5K 93
Exchange Arc. EC2 .....3B 72
Exchange Bldg. E1 .....2C 72
Exchange Ct. WC2 .....1K 79
Exchange Ho. EC2 .....3B 72
SW1 ....2G 89
Exchange Pl. EC2 ......3A 72
Exchange Sq. EC2 ......3A 72
Exchange St. EC1 ......7G 61
Exeter Ct. NW6 ....5K 55
Exeter Ho. *N1* *3A 62*
(off New Era Est.)
SE15 ....6F 93
W2 ....5C 66
Exeter M. SW6 ....7J 85
Exeter St. WC2 ....7K 69
Exhibition Cl. W12 ....1A 74
Exhibition Rd. SW7 ....5F 77
Exmoor St. W10 ....2D 64
Exmouth Ho. EC1 ......1D 70
Exmouth Mkt. EC1 .....1C 70
Exmouth M. NW1 ......7F 59
Exmouth Pl. E8 ....1G 63
Exmouth St. E1 ....5K 73
Exonbury NW8 ....3B 56
Exon St. SE17 ....3A 92
Export Ho. SE1 ....5B 82
Express Newspapers
SE1 ....2E 80
Exton St. SE1 ....3C 80
Eynham Rd. W12 ......5A 64
Eynsford Ho. SE1 ......5J 81
SE15 ....5K 93
SE17 ....2A 92
Eyre Ct. NW8 ....4E 56
Eyre St. Hill EC1 ......2C 70
Ezra St. E2 ....6D 62

F

Fabian Rd. SW6 ....7H 85
Fairbank Est. N1 ....5K 61
Fairbriar Residence
SW7 ....1D 86
Fairburn Ho. W14 .....4H 85
Fairby Ho. SE1 ....1D 92
Fairchild Ho. E9 ......1K 63
N1 ....6A 62
Fairchild Pl. EC2 ......2B 72
Fairchild St. EC2 ......2B 72
Fairclough St. E1 ......6F 73
Fairfax Pl. NW6 ....1D 56
W14 ....7F 75
Fairfax Rd. NW6 ....1D 56
Fairfield E1 ....3K 73
NW1 ....3E 58
Fairford Ho. SE11 .....2D 90
Fairhazel Mans.
NW6 ....1C 56
Fairholme Rd. W14 ....4F 85
Fairholt St. SW7 ....6H 77
Fairstead Wlk. N1 .....2G 61
Fair St. SE1 ....4B 82
Fairway Ct. SE16 ......5K 83
Fakruddin St. E1 ......2F 73
Falcon WC1 ....3K 69
Falconberg Ct. W1 .....5H 69
Falconberg M. W1 .....5G 69
Falcon Cl. SE1 ....2F 81
Falcon Ct. EC4 ....6D 70
N1 ....5F 61
Falconet Ct. E1 ....3H 83
Falcon Highwalk EC2 ...4G 71
Falcon Ho. SW5 ....3B 86
Falcon Lodge W9 ......3K 65
Falcon Point SE1 ......1F 81
Falkirk Ho. W9 ....6B 56
Falkirk St. N1 ....5B 62
Falkland Ho. W8 ......7A 76
W14 ....3G 85
Fallodon Ho. W11 .....4H 65
Fallow Ct. SE16 ....4F 93
Falmouth Ho. SE11 ....3D 90
W2 ....7G 67
Falmouth Rd. SE1 .....7H 81
Falstaff Bldg. E1 ......7G 73
Falstaff Ct. SE11 ......2E 90
Falstaff Ho. N1 ....5A 62
Fane St. W14 ....5H 85
Fann St. EC1 ....2G 71
EC2 ....2G 71
(not continuous)
Fanshaw St. N1 ....6A 62
Faraday Ho. SE1 ......5H 81
W10 ....3F 65
Faraday Mans. W14 ....5F 85
Faraday Mus. 1E 78
Faraday Rd. W10 ......3E 64
Fareham St. W1 ....5G 69
Farjeon Ho. NW6 ......1E 56
Farleigh Ho. N1 ....1F 61
Farley Ct. NW1 ....2A 68
W14 ....6G 75
Farm Cl. SW6 ....7K 85
Farmer's Rd. SE5 ......7F 91
Farmer St. W8 ....2J 75
Farm La. SW6 ....6K 85
(not continuous)
Farm La. Trad. Est.
SW6 ....6J 85
Farm Pl. W8 ....2J 75
Farm St. W1 ....1C 78
Farnaby Ho. W10 ......7G 55
Farncombe St. SE16 ....5F 83
Farndale Ho. NW6 .....2A 56
Farnell M. SW5 ....3A 86
Farnham Ho. NW1 .....2H 67
SE1 ....4G 81
Farnham Pl. SE1 ......3F 81
Farnham Royal SE11 ...4B 90
Faroe Rd. W14 ....7D 74
Farrell Ho. E1 ....6K 73
Farriers Ho. EC1 ....2H 71
Farrier St. NW1 ....1D 58
Farrier Wlk. SW10 .....5C 86
Farringdon La. EC1 ....2D 70
Farringdon Rd. EC1 ....1C 70
Farringdon St. EC4 ....4E 70
Farrow La. SE14 ....7K 93
Farthing All. SE1 ......5E 82
Farthing Flds. E1 ......2H 83
Fashion & Textile Mus.
..............4B 82
Fashion St. E1 ....4C 72
Faulkners All. EC1 ....3E 70
Faunce Ho. SE17 ......5F 91
Faunce St. SE17 ......5E 90
Faversham Ho. NW1 ...3F 59
SE17 ....4A 92
Fawcett Ct. SW10 .....5C 86
Fawcett St. SW10 .....6B 86
Fawkham Ho. SE1 .....2D 92
Fazeley Ct. W9 ....3J 65
Featherstone St. EC1 ...1J 71
Felixstowe Rd.
NW10 ....6A 54
Felix St. E2 ....5H 63
Fellbrigg St. E1 ......2H 73
Fellmongers Path
SE1 ....5C 82
Fellows Ct. E2 ....4C 62
(not continuous)
Fellows Rd. NW3 ......1F 57
Felton Ho. N1 ....3K 61
Felton St. N1 ....3K 61
Fenchurch Av. EC3 ....6A 72
Fenchurch Bldgs.
EC3 ....6B 72
Fenchurch Ho. EC3 ....7C 72
Fenchurch Pl. EC3 .....7B 72
Fenchurch St. EC3 .....7A 72
Fen Ct. EC3 ....6A 72
Fendall St. SE1 ....7B 82
(not continuous)
Fenelon Pl. W14 ......2H 85
Fenham Rd. SE15 .....7F 93
Fennel Apartments
SE1 ....4C 82
Fenner Cl. SE16 ......1H 93
Fenner Ho. E1 ....2H 83
Fenning St. SE1 ......4A 82
Fentiman Rd. SW8 ....6K 89
Fenton St. E1 ....5H 73
Ferdinand Pl. NW1 ....1B 58
Ferdinand St. NW1 ....1B 58
Fermain Ct. E. N1 ....2B 62
Fermain Ct. Nth. N1 ...2B 62
Fermain Ct. W. N1 ....2A 62
Fermoy Ho. W9 ....2H 65
Fermoy Rd. W9 ....2G 65
Fern Cl. N1 ....4A 62
Ferndown NW1 ....1G 59
Fernhead Rd. W9 .....5H 55
Ferneigh Cl. W9 ......6H 55
Fernsbury St. WC1 ....7C 60
Fernshaw Cl. SW10 ...6C 86
Fernshaw Mans.
SW10 ....6C 86
Fernshaw Rd. SW10 ...6C 86
Fern Wlk. SE16 ....4F 93
Ferriby Cl. N1 ....1C 60
Ferrybridge Ho. SE11 ...7B 80
Festival Ct. E8 ....1D 62
Fetter La. EC4 ....6D 70
(not continuous)
Fettes Ho. NW8 ....5F 57
Field Ct. WC1 ....4B 70
Fieldgate Mans. E1 ....4F 73
(not continuous)
Fieldgate St. E1 ....4F 73
Field Ho. NW6 ....6D 54
Fielding Ct. WC2 ......6J 69
Fielding Ho. NW6 .....6K 55
Fielding Rd. W14 .....6D 74
Fielding St. SE17 .....5G 91
Field Rd. W6 ....4E 84
Fields Est. E8 ....1F 63
Field St. WC1 ....6A 60
Fife Ter. N1 ....4B 60
Fifth Av. W10 ....1E 64
Figure Ct. SW3 ....4K 87
Filmer Rd. SW6 ....7G 85
Filton Ct. SE14 ....7K 93
Finborough Ho.
SW10 ....5C 86
Finborough Rd.
SW10 ....4A 86
Finborough Theatre, The
..............5B 86
Finch La. EC3 ....6K 71
Finchley Pl. NW8 ......4E 56
Finchley Rd. NW3 .....1E 56
NW8 ....3E 56
Finch Lodge W9 ......3K 65
Fingest Ho. NW8 .....1G 67
Finnemore Ho. N1 ....2G 61
Finn Ho. N1 ....6K 61
Finnis St. E2 ....7H 63
FINSBURY 7D 60
Finsbury Av. EC2 .....4K 71
(not continuous)
Finsbury Av. Sq. EC2 ...3A 72
Finsbury Cir. EC2 .....4K 71
Finsbury Est. EC1 .....7E 60
Finsbury Leisure Cen.
..............1G 71
Finsbury Mkt. EC2 ....2A 72
(not continuous)
Finsbury Pavement
EC2 ....3K 71
Finsbury Sq. EC2 .....2K 71
Finsbury St. EC2 ......3J 71
Finstock Rd. W10 .....5C 64
Fiona Ct. NW6 ....4J 55
Fir Ho. W10 ....1E 64
Firle Ho. W10 ....3A 64
First Av. W10 ....1G 65
First St. SW3 ....1H 87
Firth Ho. E2 ....7E 62
Fir Tree Ho. SE14 .....7K 93
Fisher Ho. E1 ....7K 73
N1 ....3C 60
Fisher St. WC1 ....4A 70
Fisherton St. NW8 .....2E 66
Fishmongers Hall Wharf
EC4 ....1K 81
Fish St. Hill EC3 ......1K 81
Fish Wharf EC3 ....1K 81
Fitness First
America Sq. 7C 72
Bloomsbury 2J 69
Camden 3D 58
Chancery Lane *5D 70*
(off Thavies Inn)
Covent Garden 1J 79
Embankment 2K 79
Fetter La. 5D 70
Gracechurch St. ...7A 72
Gt. Marlborough St.
..............6E 68
Hammersmith 1B 84
High Holborn 4A 70
Islington 5E 60
Kilburn 3G 55
Kingly St. 7E 68
Old Street 1J 71
Paternoster Sq. 5F 71
Queen Victoria St.
..............7G 71
Fitrooms 6H 85
Fitzalan St. SE11 .....1B 90
Fitzgeorge Av. W14 ....2E 84
Fitzhardinge Ho. W1 ...5A 68
Fitzhardinge St. W1 ...5A 68
Fitzjames Av. W14 ....2F 85
Fitzmaurice Ho.
SE16 ....2H 93
Fitzmaurice Pl. W1 ....2D 78
FITZROVIA 3D 68
Fitzroy Ct. W1 ....2F 69
Fitzroy Ho. SE1 ....3D 92
Fitzroy M. W1 ....2E 68
Fitzroy Rd. NW1 ......2A 58
Fitzroy Sq. W1 ....2E 68
Fitzroy St. W1 ....2E 68
(not continuous)
Fitzroy Yd. NW1 ......2A 58
Fives Ct. SE11 ....7E 80
Flamstead Ho. *SW3* *3G 87*
(off Cale St.)
Flank St. E1 ....7E 72
Flatiron Yd. SE1 ......3H 81
Flaxley Ho. SW1 ......3C 88
Flaxman Ct. W1 ....6G 69
WC1 ....7H 59
Flaxman Ho. SE1 ......6E 80
Flaxman Ter. WC1 .....7H 59
Flecker Ho. SE5 ....7J 91
Fleet Bldg. EC4 ....5E 70
Fleetfield WC1 ....6K 59
Fleet Pl. EC4 ....5E 70
(not continuous)
Fleet Sq. WC1 ....7B 60
Fleet St. EC4 ....6C 70
Fleet St. Hill E1 ......2K 72
Fleetway WC1 ....6K 59
Fleming Cl. W9 ....2J 65
Fleming Ct. W2 ....3E 66
Fleming Ho. SE16 .....5E 82
Fleming Lodge W9 ....3K 65
Fleming Rd. SE17 .....5F 91
Flemming Cl. SW10 ...5D 86
Fletcher Bldgs. WC2 ...6K 69
Fletcher Ho. *SE15* *7K 93*
(off Clifton Way)
Fletcher St. E1 ....7F 73
Fleur-de-Lis St. E1 ....2B 72
Flinders Ho. E1 ....3H 83
Flinton St. SE17 ......3B 92
Flint St. SE17 ....2K 91
Flitcroft St. WC2 ......6H 69
Flitton Ho. N1 ....1E 60
Flockton St. SE16 .....5E 82
Flood St. SW3 ....4H 87
Flood Wlk. SW3 ....5H 87
Floral St. WC2 ....7J 69
Florence Ct. N1 ....1E 60
W9 ....7D 56
Florence Ho. SE16 ....4G 93
W11 ....1D 74
Florence Nightingale Mus.
..............5A 80
Florence St. N1 ....1E 60
Florey Lodge *W9* *3K 65*
(off Admiral Wlk.)
Florida St. E2 ....7E 62
Florin Ct. EC1 ....3G 71
SE1 ....5C 82
Flower & Dean Wlk.
E1 ....4D 72
Flower Wlk., The
SW7 ....5C 76
Foley Ho. E1 ....6J 73
Foley St. W1 ....4E 68
Folgate St. E1 ....3B 72
(not continuous)
Foliot Ho. N1 ....4A 60
Folkstone Ho. SE17 ....3B 92
Follett Ho. SW10 ......7E 86
Follingham Ct. N1 .....6B 62
Folly M. W11 ....5G 65
Fontenoy Ho. SE11 ....2E 90
Fonthill Ho. SW1 ......3D 88
W14 ....6F 75
Forber Ho. E2 ....7J 63
Forbes St. E1 ....6F 73
Fordham St. E1 ....5F 73
Fordie Ho. SW1 ....7K 77
Fordingley Rd. W9 .....7H 55
Ford Sq. E1 ....4H 73
Foreland Ho. W11 .....7E 64
Forest Cl. NW6 ....1E 54
Fore St. EC2 ....4H 71
Fore St. Av. EC2 ......4J 71
Formosa St. W9 ....2B 66
Forset Ct. W2 ....5H 67
Forset St. W1 ....5H 67
Forston St. N1 ....4H 61
Forsyte Ho. SW3 ......4H 87
Forsyth Gdns. SE17 ...5F 91
Forsyth Ho. E9 ....1K 63
SW1 ....3F 89
Fortescue Av. E8 ......1H 63
Fort Rd. SE1 ....2D 92
Fort St. E1 ....4B 72
Fortune Ct. E8 ....1D 62
Fortune Ho. EC1 ......2H 71
SE11 ....2C 90
Fortune St. EC1 ....2H 71
Fortune Theatre 6K 69
Forum Magnum Sq.
SE1 ....4A 80
Fosbrooke Ho. SW8 ...7J 89
Fosbury M. W2 ....1B 76
Foscote Ct. W9 ....3K 65
Foscote M. W9 ....2K 65
Foss Ho. NW8 ....4B 56
Fossil Ct. *SE1* *6A 82*
(off Long La.)
Foster Ct. NW1 ....1E 58
Foster La. EC2 ....5G 71
Foubert's Pl. W1 ......6E 68
Foulis Ter. SW7 ....3F 87
Founders Ct. EC2 .....5J 71
Founders Ho. SW1 ....3G 89
Foundling Ct. WC1 ....1J 69
Foundling Mus., The ...1K 69
Foundry M. NW1 ......1F 69
Foundry Pl. E1 ....3J 73
Fountain Ct. EC4 ......7C 70
SW1 ....2C 88
Fountain Grn. Sq.
SE16 ....5F 83
Fountain Ho. NW6 .....1F 55
SE16 ....5F 83
W1 ....2A 78
Fountain Sq. SW1 .....1D 88
Fount St. SW8 ....7H 89
Fournier St. E1 ....3C 72
Fourscore Mans. E8 ....1F 63
Fourth Av. W10 ....1E 64
Fowey Cl. E1 ....2G 83
Fowey Ho. SE11 ....3D 90
Fowler Rd. N1 ....2F 61
Fox & Knot St. EC1 ....3F 71
Fox Cl. E1 ....1K 73
Foxcote SE5 ....4B 92
Foxcroft WC1 ....5B 60
Foxfield NW1 ....3D 58
Foxley Rd. SW9 ....7D 90
Frampton NW1 ....1G 59
Frampton Ho. NW8 .....2F 67
Frampton Pk. Est. E9 ...1K 63
Frampton Pk. Rd. E9 ...1J 63
Frampton St. NW8 .....2F 67
Francis Ct. EC1 ....3E 70
Francis Ho. N1 ....3A 62
SW10 ....7B 86
Francis St. SW1 ....1E 88
Francis Wlk. N1 ....2A 60
Frank Beswick Ho.
SW6 ....6H 85
Frank Ho. SW8 ....7J 89
Frankland Cl. SE16 ....7H 83
Frankland Rd. SW7 ....7E 76
Franklin Ho. E1 ....3H 83
Franklin Sq. W14 ......4H 85
Franklin's Row SW3 ...3K 87
Frank Soskice Ho.
SW6 ....6H 85
Frank Whymark Ho.
SE16 ....5J 83
Frazier St. SE1 ....5C 80
Frean St. SE16 ....6E 82
Frearson Ho. WC1 .....6B 60
Freda Corbet Cl.
SE15 ....7E 92
Frederick Charrington Ho.
E1 ....1J 73
Frederick Cl. W2 ......7J 67
Frederick Ct. *SW3* *2K 87*
(off Duke of York Sq.)
Frederick Dobson Ho.
W11 ....1E 74
Frederick Rd. SE17 ....5F 91
Frederick's Pl. EC2 ....6J 71
Frederick's Row EC1 ...6E 60
Frederick St. WC1 .....7A 60
Frederick Ter. E8 ......1C 62
Frederic M. SW1 ......5K 77
Freeling Ho. NW8 ......2E 56
Freeling St. N1 ....1A 60
(Carnoustie Dr.)
N1 ....1K 59
(Pembroke St.)
Freemantle St. SE17 ...3A 92
Free Trade Wharf E1 ...7K 73
Fremantle Ho. E1 ......2G 73
Fremont St. E9 ....2J 63
(not continuous)
French Ordinary Ct.
EC3 ....7B 72
French Pl. E1 ....1B 72
Frensham St. SE15 ....6F 93
Freshfield Av. E8 ......1C 62
Freshwater Ct. *W1* *4H 67*
(off Crawford St.)
Freston Rd. W10 ......7C 64
W11 ....1D 74
Frewell Ho. EC1 ....3C 70
Friars Cl. SE1 ....2F 81
Friar St. EC4 ....6F 71
Friary Ct. SW1 ....3F 79
Friary Est. SE15 ....5F 93
(not continuous)
Friary Rd. SE15 ....6F 93
Friday St. EC4 ....7G 71
Friendship Ho. SE1 ....5F 81
Friend St. EC1 ....6E 60
Frinstead Ho. W10 .....7C 64
Frith Ho. NW8 ....2F 67
Frith St. W1 ....6G 69
Frithville Ct. W12 ......3A 74
Frithville Gdns. W12 ...2A 74
Frobisher Ct. W12 .....5A 74
Frobisher Cres. EC2 ...3H 71
Frobisher Ho. E1 ......2H 83
SW1 ....5G 89
Frome St. N1 ....4G 61
Frostic Wlk. E1 ....4D 72
Fruiterers Pas. *EC4* *1H 81*
(off Queen St. Pl.)
Frying Pan All. E1 .....4C 72
Fulbourne St. E1 ......3G 73
Fulcher Ho. N1 ....3A 62
Fulford St. SE16 ....5H 83
FULHAM BROADWAY ...7K 85
Fulham B'way. SW6 ....7K 85
Fulham B'way. Shop. Cen.
SW6 ....7K 85
Fulham Pal. Rd. SW6 ...6D 84
W6 ....3B 84

Fulham Pools 6F 85
Fulham Rd. SW3 3F 87
SW6 7J 85
(Fulham High St.)
SW6 7K 85
(King's Rd.)
SW10 6C 86
Fuller Cl. E2 1E 72
Fullwood's M. N1 6K 61
Fulmer Ho. NW8 2H 67
Fulneck E1 3K 73
Fulton M. W2 7C 66
Fulwood Pl. WC1 4B 70
Funland 1G 79
(in Trocadero Cen.)
Furley Ho. SE15 7F 93
Furley Rd. SE15 7F 93
Furness Ho. SW1 3D 88
Furnival Mans. W1 4E 68
Furnival St. EC4 5C 70
Fursecroft W1 5J 67
Fusion Health & Leisure Cen. 1F 91
Fye Foot La. EC4 7G 71
Fynes St. SW1 1G 89

G

Gabriel Ho. N1 3E 60
SE11 1A 90
Gabriels Wharf SE1 2D 80
Gaddesden Ho. EC1 7K 61
Gadebridge Ho. SW3 3G 87
(off Cale St.)
Gadsden Ho. W10 2F 65
Gage Brown Ho.
W10 6D 64
(off Bridge Cl.)
Gage St. WC1 3K 69
Gainford Ho. E2 6G 63
Gainford St. N1 2C 60
Gainsborough Ct.
SE16 3H 93
W12 4A 74
Gainsborough Ho.
SW1 2H 89
Gainsborough Mans.
W14 5F 85
Gainsborough Studios E.
N1 3J 61
Gainsborough Studios Nth.
N1 3J 61
Gainsborough Studios Sth.
N1 3J 61
Gainsborough Studios W.
N1 3J 61
Gainsford St. SE1 3C 82
Gairloch Ho. NW1 1G 59
Gaitskell Ho. SE17 5A 92
Galaxy Ho. EC2 1K 71
(off Leonard St.)
Galen Pl. WC1 4K 69
Gales Gdns. E2 7H 63
Galleon Cl. SE16 4K 83
Gallery Ct. SE1 5K 81
SW10 6C 86
(off Gunter Gro.)
Galleywall Rd. SE16 1G 93
Galleywall Rd. Trad. Est.
SE16 2H 93
Galleywood Ho. W10 3A 64
Galsworthy Ho. W11 6F 65
Galton St. W10 7E 54
Galway Cl. SE16 4H 93
Galway Ho. EC1 7H 61
Galway St. EC1 7H 61
Gambia St. SE1 3F 81
Gambier Ho. EC1 7H 61
Gandolfi St. SE15 6A 92
Ganton St. W1 7E 68
Garbett Ho. SE17 5E 90
Garbutt Pl. W1 4B 68
Garden Ct. EC4 7C 70
NW8 6E 56
W11 1F 75
Garden Ho. SW7 7B 76
Garden Ho., The W6 6D 84
Garden M. W2 1K 75
Garden Pl. E8 3D 62
Garden Rd. NW8 6D 56
Garden Row SE1 7E 80
Garden Ter. SW1 3G 89
SW7 5H 77
Garden Wlk. EC2 1A 72
Gardner Ct. EC1 2E 70
Gardners La. EC4 7G 71
Gard St. EC1 6F 61
Garfield Ct. NW6 1D 54
Garland Ct. SE17 2H 91
Garlands Ho. NW8 4C 56
Garlick Hill EC4 7H 71
Garnault M. EC1 7D 60
Garnault Pl. EC1 7D 60
Garner St. E2 5F 63
Garnet Ho. E1 2J 83
Garnet St. E1 1J 83
Garnies Cl. SE15 7C 92
Garraway Ct. SW13 7A 84
Garrett Ho. SE1 4E 80
W12 6A 64
Garrett St. EC1 1H 71
Garrick Ct. E8 1D 62
(off Jacaranda Gro.)
Garrick Ho. W1 3C 78
Garrick St. WC2 7J 69
Garrick Theatre 1J 79
Garrick Yd. WC2 7J 69
Garsdale Ter. W14 3H 85
Garson Ho. W2 7E 66
Garston Ho. N1 1E 60
Garter Way SE16 5K 83
Garway Rd. W2 6A 66
Gascoigne Pl. E2 7C 62
(not continuous)
Gascony Av. NW6 1J 55
Gaskin St. N1 2E 60
Gaspar Cl. SW5 1B 86
Gaspar M. SW5 1B 86
Gasson Ho. SE14 6K 93
Gastein Rd. W6 5D 84
Gastigny Ho. EC1 7H 61
Gataker Ho. SE16 6H 83
Gataker St. SE16 6H 83
Gate Cinema 2J 75
Gateforth St. NW8 2G 67
Gate Hill Ct. W11 2H 75
Gate Ho. N1 1K 61
(off Ufton Rd.)
Gatehouse Sq. SE1 2H 81
Gate Lodge W9 3K 65
Gate M. SW7 5H 77
Gatesborough St.
EC2 1A 72
Gates Ct. SE17 4G 91
Gatesden WC1 7K 59
Gate St. WC2 5A 70
Gate Theatre, The 2J 75
Gateway SE17 5H 91
Gateway Arc. N1 4E 60
Gateways, The SW3 2H 87
Gatliff Cl. SW1 4C 88
Gatliff Rd. SW1 4C 88
(not continuous)
Gattis Wharf N1 4K 59
Gaugin Ct. SE16 3G 93
Gaumont Ter. W12 4A 74
Gaunt St. SE1 6G 81
Gavel St. SE17 1K 91
Gawber St. E2 6J 63
Gaydon Ho. W2 3A 66
Gayfere St. SW1 7J 79
Gayhurst SE17 5K 91
Gayhurst Ho. NW8 1G 67
Gayhurst Rd. E8 1E 62
Gaymead NW8 3B 56
Gaysley Ho. SE11 2C 90
Gaywood St. SE1 7E 80
Gaza St. SE17 4E 90
Gedling Pl. SE1 6D 82
Gees Ct. W1 6B 68
Gee St. EC1 1G 71
Geffrye Ct. N1 5B 62
Geffrye Est. N1 5B 62
Geffrye Mus. 5B 62
Geffrye St. E2 4C 62
Geldart Rd. SE15 7G 93
Gemini Ct. E1 1E 82
Geoffrey Ho. SE1 6K 81
George Ct. WC2 1K 79
George Eliot Ho.
SW1 2F 89
George Elliston Ho.
SE1 4E 92
George Eyre Ho.
NW8 5F 57
George Gillett Ct.
EC1 1H 71
George Inn Yd. SE1 3J 81
George Lindgren Ho.
SW6 7H 85
George Loveless Ho.
E2 6D 62
George Lowe Ct. W2 3A 66
George Mathers Rd.
SE11 1E 90
George M. NW1 7F 59
George Padmore Ho.
E8 2F 63
George Peabody Ct.
NW1 3G 67
George Row SE16 5E 82
George's Sq. SW6 5H 85
George St. W1 5J 67
George Tingle Ho.
SE1 6D 82
George Walter Ct.
SE16 2K 93
George Yd. EC3 6K 71
W1 7B 68
Georgiana St. NW1 2E 58
Georgian Ct. E9 2K 63
Georgina Gdns. E2 6D 62
Geraldine St. SE11 7E 80
Gerald M. SW1 1B 88
Gerald Rd. SW1 1B 88
Gerards Cl. SE16 4J 93
Gerrard Pl. W1 7H 69
Gerrard Rd. N1 4E 60
Gerrard St. W1 7G 69
Gerridge Ct. SE1 6D 80
(off Gerridge St.)
Gerridge St. SE1 6D 80
Gertrude St. SW10 6D 86
Gervase St. SE15 7H 93
Gibbings Ho. SE1 5F 81
Gibbon Ho. NW8 2F 67
Gibbon's Rents SE1 3A 82
Gibbs Grn. W14 3G 85
(not continuous)
Gibbs Grn. Cl. W14 3H 85
Gibraltar Wlk. E2 7D 62
Gibson Cl. E1 1K 73
Gibson Rd. SE11 2B 90
Gibson Sq. N1 2D 60
Gielgud Theatre 7G 69
Gifford Ho. SW1 4E 88
Gifford St. N1 1K 59
Gilbert Bri. EC2 4H 71
(off Gilbert Ho.)
Gilbert Collection 7A 70
Gilbert Ho. E2 6K 63
(off Usk St.)
EC2 4H 71
SW1 4D 88
SW8 7J 89
SW13 7A 84
Gilbert Pl. WC1 4J 69
Gilbert Rd. SE11 2D 90
Gilbert Sheldon Ho.
W2 3F 67
Gilbert St. W1 6B 68
Gilbeys Yd. NW1 1B 58
Gildea St. W1 4D 68
Giles Ho. SE16 6E 82
W11 6J 65
Gillam Ho. SE16 2J 93
Gillfoot NW1 5E 58
Gillies Ho. NW6 1E 56
Gillingham M. SW1 1E 88
Gillingham Row SW1 1E 88
Gillingham St. SW1 2D 88
Gillison Wlk. SE16 6F 83
Gillman Ho. E2 4F 63
Gillray Ho. SW10 6E 86
Gilpin Cl. W2 3E 66
Gilray Ho. W2 7E 66
Gilston Rd. SW10 4D 86
Giltspur St. EC1 5F 71
Ginger Apartments
SE1 4D 82
Girdler's Rd. W14 1D 84
Girling Ho. N1 3A 62
Gironde Rd. SW6 7H 85
Girton Vs. W10 5D 64
Gisburn Ho. SE15 6F 93
Gissing Wlk. N1 1D 60
Gladstone Ct. SW1 2H 89
Gladstone St. SE1 7E 80
Gladwin Ho. NW1 5F 59
Glamis Pl. E1 7K 73
Glamis Rd. E1 1K 83
Glasgow Ho. W9 5B 56
Glasgow Ter. SW1 4E 88
Glass Art Gallery, The 5A 82
Glasshill St. SE1 4F 81
Glass Ho., The SE1 5A 82
Glasshouse Flds. E1 7K 73
(not continuous)
Glasshouse St. W1 1F 79
Glasshouse Wlk.
SE11 3K 89
Glasshouse Yd. EC1 2G 71
Glass St. E2 1H 73
Glassworks Studios
E2 6B 62
Glastonbury Ct. SE14 7K 93
Glastonbury Ho. SW1 3C 88
Glastonbury Pl. E1 6J 73
Glazbury Rd. W14 2F 85
Glebe Ho. SE16 7H 83
Glebe Pl. SW3 5G 87
Glebe Rd. E8 1C 62
Gledhow Gdns. SW5 2C 86
Gledstanes Rd. W14 4F 85
Glenallan Ho. W14 2G 85
Glencoe Mans. SW9 7C 90
Glendower Pl. SW7 1E 86
Gleneagles Cl. SE16 4G 93
Glenfinlas Way SE5 7F 91
Glengall Pas. NW6 2J 55
Glengall Rd. NW6 2H 55
SE15 5D 92
Glengall Ter. SE15 5D 92
Glenridding NW1 5F 59
Glenrose Ct. SE1 6A 82
(off Long La.)
Glenroy St. W12 5A 64
Glenshaw Mans.
SW9 7C 90
Glenthorne Rd. W6 1A 84
Glentworth St. NW1 2K 67
Gliddon Rd. W14 2E 84
Globe, The SE1 5J 81
Globe Rd. E1 7K 63
E2 5J 63
Globe St. SE1 6J 81
Globe Ter. E2 6K 63
GLOBE TOWN 6K 63
Globe Town Mkt. E2 6K 63
Globe Yd. W1 6C 68
Gloucester W14 2G 85
Gloucester Arc. SW7 1C 86
Gloucester Av. NW1 1A 58
Gloucester Ct. EC3 1B 82
Gloucester Cres.
NW1 2C 58
Gloucester Gdns. W2 5C 66
Gloucester Ga. NW1 4C 58
(not continuous)
Gloucester Ga. M.
NW1 4C 58
Gloucester Ho. NW6 5K 55
SW9 7D 90
Gloucester M. W2 6D 66
Gloucester M. W. W2 6C 66
Gloucester Pk. Apartments
SW7 1C 86
Gloucester Pl. NW1 1J 67
W1 3K 67
Gloucester Pl. M.
W1 4K 67
Gloucester Rd. SW7 6C 76
Gloucester Sq. E2 3E 62
W2 6F 67
Gloucester St. SW1 4E 88
Gloucester Ter. W2 5B 66
Gloucester Wlk. W8 4K 75
Gloucester Way EC1 7D 60
Glynde M. SW3 7H 77
Glynde Reach WC1 7K 59
Glyn St. SE11 4A 90
Goater's All. SW6 7H 85
Godfree Ct. SE1 4J 81
(off Long La.)
Godfrey Ho. EC1 7J 61
Godfrey St. SW3 3H 87
Goding St. SE11 3K 89
Godliman St. EC4 6G 71
Godstone Ho. SE1 6K 81
Godwin Cl. N1 4H 61
Godwin Ct. NW1 4F 59
Godwin Ho. E2 4D 62
NW6 4A 56
(not continuous)
Golborne Gdns. W10 2G 65
Golborne Ho. W10 2F 65
Golborne M. W10 3F 65
Golborne Rd. W10 3F 65
Goldbeaters Ho. W1 6H 69
(off Manette St.)
Golden Cross M.
W11 5G 65
Golden Hinde 2J 81
Golden Jubilee Bridges, The 3A 80
Golden La. EC1 1G 71
Golden La. Est. EC1 1G 71
Golden Lane Leisure Cen. 2G 71
Golden Sq. W1 7F 69
Goldhawk M. W12 5A 74
Goldhawk Rd. W6 5A 74
Goldhurst Ter. NW6 1A 56
Golding St. E1 6F 73
Golding Ter. E1 5F 73
Goldington Bldgs.
NW1 3G 59
Goldington Cres.
NW1 4G 59
Goldington St. NW1 4G 59
Goldman Cl. E2 1E 72
Goldney Rd. W9 2J 65
Goldsmith Ct. WC2 5K 69
Goldsmith's Pl. NW6 3A 56
Goldsmith's Row E2 5E 62
Goldsmith's Sq. E2 4F 63
Goldsmith St. EC2 5H 71
Goldsworthy Gdns.
SE16 2K 93
Goldthorpe NW1 3E 58
Gomm Rd. SE16 7J 83
Gooch Ho. EC1 3C 70
Goodge Pl. W1 4F 69
Goodge St. W1 4F 69
Goodman's Ct. E1 7C 72
Goodman's Stile E1 5E 72
Goodmans Yd. E1 7C 72
Goodrich Ct. W10 6C 64
Goodrich Ho. E2 4K 63
Goodson St. N1 4C 60
Goods Way NW1 4J 59
Goodwin Cl. SE16 7D 82
Goodwins Ct. WC2 7J 69
Goodwood Ct. W1 3D 68
Goodyear Pl. SE5 6H 91
Goodyer Ho. SW1 3G 89
Gophir La. EC4 7J 71
Gopsall St. N1 3K 61
Gordon Ct. W12 6A 64
Gordon Ho. E1 7K 73
SW1 7F 79
Gordon Mans. W14 6C 74
WC1 2G 69
Gordon Pl. W8 4K 75
Gordon Sq. WC1 1G 69
Gordon St. WC1 1G 69
Gorefield Ho. NW6 4K 55
Gorefield Pl. NW6 4J 55
Gore Rd. E9 2K 63
Gore St. SW7 6D 76
Gorham Pl. W11 1E 74
Goring St. EC3 5B 72
Gorleston St. W14 1F 85
(not continuous)
Gorsuch Pl. E2 6C 62
Gorsuch St. E2 6C 62
Gosfield St. W1 3E 68
Goslett Yd. WC2 6H 69
Gosling Ho. E1 7J 73
Gosset St. E2 6D 62
Goswell Pl. EC1 7F 61
Goswell Rd. EC1 5E 60
Gothic Ct. SE5 7G 91
Gough Ho. N1 2F 61
Gough Sq. EC4 5D 70
Gough St. WC1 1B 70
Gouldman Ho. E1 2J 73
Goulston St. E1 5C 72
Govan St. E2 3F 63
Gowan Ho. E2 7D 62
Gower Ct. WC1 1G 69
Gower Ho. SE17 3H 91
Gower M. WC1 4H 69
Gower M. Mans.
WC1 3H 69
Gower Pl. WC1 1F 69
Gower St. WC1 1F 69
Gower's Wlk. E1 5E 72
Gracechurch St. EC3 7K 71
Gracehill E1 3K 73
Grace Ho. SE11 5B 90
Graces All. E1 7E 72
Graces M. NW8 5D 56
Graduate Pl. SE1 6A 82
Grafton M. W1 2E 68
Grafton Pl. NW1 7H 59
Grafton St. W1 1D 78
Grafton Way W1 2E 68
WC1 2E 68
Graham Ct. SE14 5K 93
Graham St. N1 5F 61
Graham Ter. SW1 2A 88
Grampians, The W6 5C 74
Granary Rd. E1 2G 73
Granary St. NW1 3G 59
Granby Pl. SE1 5C 80
Granby St. E2 1D 72
(not continuous)
Granby Ter. NW1 5E 58
Grand Av. EC1 3F 71
(not continuous)
Grand Junc. Wharf
N1 5G 61
Grand Union W2 4F 67
Grand Union Cen.
W10 1D 64
Grand Union Cl. W9 3H 65
Grand Union Cres. E8 2F 63
Grand Union Wlk.
NW1 1D 58
Grand Vitesse Ind. Cen.
SE1 3F 81
Grange, The SE1 6C 82
W14 2G 85
Grange Ct. WC2 6B 70
Grange Ho. SE1 7C 82
Grange Pl. NW6 1J 55
Grange Rd. SE1 7B 82
Grange St. N1 3K 61
Grange Wlk. SE1 6B 82
Grange Wlk. M. SE1 7B 82
Grange Way NW6 1J 55
Grange Yd. SE1 7C 82
Gransden Av. E8 1H 63
Grantbridge St. N1 4F 61
Grantham Ct. SE16 4K 83
Grantham Ho. SE15 6F 93
Grantham Pl. W1 3C 78
Grantley Ho. SE14 5K 93
Grantley St. E1 7K 63
Grant Mus. of Zoology &
Comparative Anatomy 2G 69
(off Gower St.)
Grants Quay Wharf
EC3 1K 81
Grant St. N1 4C 60
Grantully Rd. W9 7A 56
Granville Ct. N1 2K 61
Granville Mans. W12 4B 74
Granville Pl. W1 6A 68
Granville Rd. NW6 5J 55
(not continuous)
Granville Sq. SE15 7B 92
WC1 7B 60
Granville St. WC1 7B 60
Grape St. WC2 5J 69
Graphite Sq. SE11 3A 90
Grasmere NW1 7D 58
Grasmere Point SE15 7J 93
Gratton Rd. W14 7E 74
Gravel La. E1 5C 72
Gray Ho. SE17 3H 91
Grayling Sq. E2 6F 63
Gray's Inn 3B 70
Gray's Inn Bldgs. EC1 2C 70
(off Rosebery Av.)
Gray's Inn Pl. WC1 4B 70
Gray's Inn Rd. WC1 6K 59
Gray's Inn Sq. WC1 3C 70
Grayson Ho. EC1 7H 61
Gray St. SE1 5D 80
Gray's Yd. W1 5B 68
Gt. Arthur Ho. EC1 2G 71
Gt. Bell All. EC2 5J 71
Gt. Castle St. W1 5D 68
Gt. Central St. NW1 3J 67
Gt. Chapel St. W1 5G 69
Great Chu. La. W6 3D 84
Great Coll. St. SW1 6J 79
Great Cft. WC1 7K 59
Gt. Cumberland M.
W1 6J 67
Gt. Cumberland Pl.
W1 5J 67
Gt. Dover St. SE1 5H 81
Gt. Eastern St. EC2 7A 62
Gt. Eastern Wlk. EC2 4B 72
Gt. Eastern Wharf
SW11 7H 87
Gt. George St. SW1 5H 79
Gt. Guildford Bus. Sq.
SE1 3G 81
Gt. Guildford St. SE1 2G 81
Great Hall 4K 87
Gt. James St. WC1 3A 70
Gt. Marlborough St.
W1 6E 68
Gt. Maze Pond SE1 4K 81
Gt. Newport St. WC2 7J 69
Gt. New St. EC4 5D 70
Greatorex Ho. E1 3E 72
Greatorex St. E1 3E 72
Gt. Ormond St. WC1 3K 69
Gt. Percy St. WC1 6B 60
Gt. Peter St. SW1 7G 79
Gt. Portland St. W1 2D 68
Gt. Pulteney St. W1 7F 69
Gt. Queen St. WC2 6K 69
Gt. Russell St. WC1 5H 69
Gt. St Helen's EC3 5A 72
Gt. St Thomas Apostle
EC4 7H 71
Gt. Scotland Yd. SW1 3J 79
Gt. Smith St. SW1 6H 79
Gt. Suffolk St. SE1 3F 81
Gt. Sutton St. EC1 2F 71
Gt. Swan All. EC2 5J 71
(not continuous)
Gt. Titchfield St. W1 2D 68
Great Twr. St. EC3 7A 72
Gt. Trinity La. EC4 7H 71
Great Turnstile WC1 4B 70
Gt. Turnstile Ho. WC1 4B 70
Gt. Western Rd. W9 2H 65
W11 3H 65
Gt. Winchester St.
EC2 5K 71
Gt. Windmill St. W1 7G 69
Great Yd. SE1 4B 82
Greaves Twr. SW10 7D 86
Greek Ct. W1 6H 69
Greek St. W1 6H 69
Green Arbour Ct. EC1 5E 70
Greenaway Ho. NW8 2C 56
WC1 7C 60
Green Bank E1 3G 83
Greenberry St. NW8 5G 57
Greencoat Mans.
SW1 7F 79
Greencoat Pl. SW1 1F 89
Greencoat Row SW1 7F 79
Greencourt Ho. E1 2K 73
Greencroft Gdns.
NW6 1A 56
Green Dragon Ct. SE1 3J 81
Green Dragon Ho.
WC2 5K 69
Green Dragon Yd. E1 4E 72
Greene Ho. SE1 7J 81
Greenfield Rd. E1 4F 73
Greenham Cl. SE1 5C 80
Greenham Ho. E9 2J 63
Greenheath Bus. Cen.
E2 1H 73
Greenhill's Rents EC1 3E 70
Green Hundred Rd.
SE15 6F 93
Greenland Pl. NW1 2D 58
Greenland Rd. NW1 2D 58
Greenland St. NW1 2D 58
Greenman St. N1 1G 61
Green Pk. 3D 78
Green's Ct. W1 7G 69
W11 3G 75
Green St. W1 7K 67
Green Ter. EC1 7D 60
Green Wlk. SE1 7A 82
Greenwell St. W1 2D 68
Greenwich Ct. E1 5H 73
Greenwood Theatre 4K 81
Green Yd. WC1 1B 70
Green Yd., The EC3 6A 72
Greet Ho. SE1 5D 80
Greet St. SE1 3D 80
Gregory Pl. W8 4A 76
Greig Ter. SE17 5F 91
Grendon Ho. E9 1J 63
N1 5A 60
Grendon St. NW8 1G 67
Grenfell Ho. SE5 7G 91
Grenfell Rd. W11 7D 64
Grenfell Twr. W11 7D 64
Grenfell Wlk. W11 7D 64

Grenier Apartments
SE15 . . . . .7H 93
Grenville Ho. SW1 . . . . .5G 89
Grenville M. SW7 . . . . . .1C 86
Grenville Pl. SW7 . . . . . .7C 76
Grenville St. WC1 . . . . .2K 69
Gresham St. EC2 . . . . . .5G 71
Gresse St. W1 . . . . .4G 69
Gretton Ho. E2 . . . . .6J 63
Greville Hall NW6 . . . . .4B 56
Greville Ho. SW1 . . . . . .6K 77
Greville M. NW6 . . . . . .3A 56
Greville Pl. NW6 . . . . . .4B 56
Greville Rd. NW6 . . . . . .4A 56
Greville St. EC1 . . . . . . .4C 70
(not continuous)
Greycoat Gdns. SW1 . . .7G 79
Greycoat Pl. SW1 . . . . . .7G 79
Greycoat St. SW1 . . . . . .7G 79
Grey Eagle St. E1 . . . . . .3C 72
Greyfriars Pas. EC1 . . . . .5F 71
Greyhound Ct. WC2 . . . .7B 70
Greyhound Mans. W6 . . .5E 84
Greyhound Rd. NW10 . . .6A 54
W6 . . . . .6C 84
W14 . . . . .5F 85
Grey Ho. W12 . . . . .1A 74
Greystoke Ho. SE15 . . . .6F 93
Greystoke Pl. EC4 . . . . .5C 70
Griffin Ho. *N1* *3A 62*
(off New Era Est.)
W6 . . . . .2D 84
Griggs Ct. SE1 . . . . .7B 82
Grigg's Pl. SE1 . . . . . . .7B 82
Grimaldi Ho. N1 . . . . . . .4A 60
Grimsby St. E2 . . . . .2D 72
Grimsel Path SE5 . . . . . .7F 91
Grimthorpe Ho. EC1 . . . .1E 70
Grindall Ho. E1 . . . . . . .2H 73
Grindal St. SE1 . . . . . . .5C 80
Grisedale NW1 . . . . .6E 58
Grittleton Rd. W9 . . . . . .1J 65
Grocer's Hall Ct. EC2 . . .6J 71
Grocer's Hall Gdns.
EC2 . . . . .6J 71
Groombridge Ho.
SE17 . . . . .3B 92
Groombridge Rd. E9 . . .1K 63
Groome Ho. SE11 . . . . . .2B 90
Groom Pl. SW1 . . . . . . .6B 78
Grosvenor Cotts.
SW1 . . . . .1A 88
Grosvenor Ct. NW6 . . . .2D 54
SE5 . . . . .6H 91
Grosvenor Ct. Mans.
W2 . . . . .6J 67
Grosvenor Cres. SW1 . . .5B 78
Grosvenor Cres. M.
SW1 . . . . .5A 78
Grosvenor Est. SW1 . . . .1H 89
Grosvenor Gdns.
SW1 . . . . .6C 78
Grosvenor Gdns. M. E.
SW1 . . . . .6D 78
Grosvenor Gdns. M. Nth.
SW1 . . . . .7C 78
Grosvenor Gdns. M. Sth.
SW1 . . . . .7D 78
Grosvenor Ga. W1 . . . . .1A 78
Grosvenor Hill W1 . . . . .7C 68
Grosvenor Hill Ct. W1 . . .7C 68
Grosvenor Pk. SE5 . . . . .6G 91
Grosvenor Pl. SW1 . . . . .4B 78
Grosvenor Rd. SW1 . . . .5C 88
Grosvenor Sq. W1 . . . . .7B 68
Grosvenor St. W1 . . . . . .7C 68
Grosvenor Studios
SW1 . . . . .1A 88
Grosvenor Ter. SE5 . . . . .7F 91
Grotto Ct. SE1 . . . . .4G 81
Grotto Pas. W1 . . . . . . .3B 68
Grove Cotts. SW3 . . . . . .5H 87
Grove Ct. NW8 . . . . .6E 56
SW10 . . . . .4D 86
Grove Dwellings E1 . . . .3J 73
Grove End Gdns.
NW8 . . . . .5E 56
Grove End Ho. NW8 . . . .7E 56
Grove End Rd. NW8 . . . .5E 56
Grove Gdns. NW8 . . . . . .7H 57
Grove Hall Ct. NW8 . . . .6D 56
Grove Ho. SW3 . . . . . . .5H 87
Groveland Ct. EC4 . . . . .6H 71
Grove Mans. W6 . . . . . .5A 74
Grove M. W6 . . . . .6A 74
Grove Pas. E2 . . . . .4G 63
Grover Ho. SE11 . . . . . .4B 90
Guards Memorial 3H 79
Guards' Mus. 5F 79
Guildhall
City 5H 71
Westminster 5J 79
Guildhall Art Gallery 5J 71
Guildhall Bldgs. EC2 . . .5J 71
Guildhall Library 5H 71
Guildhall Offices EC2 . . .5H 71
Guildhall Yd. EC2 . . . . .5H 71
Guildhouse St. SW1 . . . .1E 88
Guilford Pl. WC1 . . . . . .2A 70
Guilford St. WC1 . . . . . .2J 69
Guinea Ct. E1 . . . . .7E 72
Guinness Ct. E1 . . . . . . .6C 72
EC1 . . . . .7H 61
NW8 . . . . .3H 57
SE1 . . . . .4A 82
SW3 . . . . .2J 87
Guinness Sq. SE1 . . . . . .7A 82
Guinness Trust SW3 . . . .2J 87
Guinness Trust Bldgs.
SE11 . . . . .3E 90
W6 . . . . .3B 84
Gulliver's Ho. EC1 . . . . .2G 71
Gulston Wlk. SW3 . . . . .2K 87
Gun Ho. E1 . . . . .3J 83
Gunpowder Sq. EC4 . . . .5D 70
(not continuous)
Gun St. E1 . . . . .4C 72
Gunter Gro. SW10 . . . . .6C 86
Gunter Hall Studios
SW10 . . . . .6C 86
Gunterstone Rd. W14 . . .2E 84
Gunthorpe St. E1 . . . . . .4D 72
Gun Wharf E1 . . . . .3J 83
Gurney Ho. E2 . . . . .4F 63
Guthrie Ct. SE1 . . . . . . .5D 80
Guthrie St. SW3 . . . . . . .3G 87
Gutter La. EC2 . . . . . . .5H 71
Guy St. SE1 . . . . .4K 81
Gwendwr Rd. W14 . . . . .3F 85
Gwilym Maries Ho.
E2 . . . . .6G 63
Gwynne Ho. E1 . . . . .4G 73
SW1 . . . . .3A 88
WC1 . . . . .1C 60
Gwynne Pl. WC1 . . . . . .7B 60

H

Haarlem Rd. W14 . . . . . .7C 74
Haberdasher Est. N1 . . . .6K 61
Haberdasher Pl. N1 . . . .6K 61
Haberdasher St. N1 . . . .6K 61
Habington Ho. SE5 . . . . .7J 91
Hackford Rd. SW9 . . . . .7C 90
Hackney City Farm 4E 62
Hackney Rd. E2 . . . . . . .7C 62
Haddon Hall St. SE1 . . . .7K 81
Hadfield Ho. E1 . . . . . . .6F 73
Hadleigh Cl. E1 . . . . . . .1J 73
Hadleigh Ho. E1 . . . . . . .1J 73
Hadleigh St. E2 . . . . . . .1K 73
Hadlow Ho. SE17 . . . . . .3B 92
Hadrian Est. E2 . . . . . . .5F 63
Hadstock Ho. NW1 . . . . .6H 59
HAGGERSTON 5C 62
Haggerston Rd. E8 . . . . .1C 62
Haggerston Studios
E8 . . . . .2B 62
Hague St. E2 . . . . .7F 63
Haig Ho. E2 . . . . .5E 62
Haines St. SW8 . . . . . . .7F 89
Hainton Cl. E1 . . . . .6H 73
Halcomb St. N1 . . . . . . .3A 62
Halcrow St. E1 . . . . .4H 73
Halcyon Wharf E1 . . . . . .3F 83
Haldane Rd. SW6 . . . . . .7H 85
Hale Ho. SW1 . . . . .3H 89
Hales Prior N1 . . . . .5A 60
Half Moon Ct. EC1 . . . . .4G 71
Half Moon Cres. N1 . . . .4B 60
(not continuous)
Half Moon Pas. E1 . . . . .6D 72
(not continuous)
Half Moon St. W1 . . . . . .2D 78
Halford Rd. SW6 . . . . . . .6J 85
Haliwell Ho. NW6 . . . . . .3A 56
Halkett Ho. E2 . . . . .3J 63
Halkin Arc. SW1 . . . . . . .6K 77
Halkin M. SW1 . . . . .6A 78
Halkin Pl. SW1 . . . . .6A 78
Halkin St. SW1 . . . . .5B 78
Hallam Ct. W1 . . . . .3D 68
Hallam Ho. SW1 . . . . . . .4F 89
Hallam M. W1 . . . . .3D 68
Hallam St. W1 . . . . .2D 68
Halley Ho. E2 . . . . .4F 63
Hallfield Est. W2 . . . . . .5C 66
(not continuous)
Hall Ga. NW8 . . . . .6E 56
Halliford St. N1 . . . . . . .1H 61
Halling Ho. SE1 . . . . . . .5K 81
Hall Pl. W2 . . . . .2E 66
(not continuous)
Hall Rd. NW8 . . . . .7D 56
Hall St. EC1 . . . . .6F 61
Hall Twr. W2 . . . . .3F 67
Halpin Pl. SE17 . . . . . . .2K 91
Halsey M. SW3 . . . . .1J 87
Halsey St. SW3 . . . . .1J 87
Halstead Ct. N1 . . . . . . .5K 61
Halstow Rd. NW10 . . . . .7C 54
Halton Cross St. N1 . . . .2F 61
Halton Ho. N1 . . . . .1F 61
Halton Mans. N1 . . . . . .1F 61
Halton Pl. N1 . . . . .2G 61
Halton Rd. N1 . . . . .1F 61
Hambledon SE17 . . . . . .5K 91
Hambley Ho. SE16 . . . . .2G 93
Hamilton Bldgs. EC2 . . . .2B 72
Hamilton Cl. NW8 . . . . . .7E 56
Hamilton Ct. W9 . . . . . . .6C 56
Hamilton Gdns. NW8 . . .6D 56
Hamilton Hall NW8 . . . .5C 56
Hamilton Ho. NW8 . . . . .6E 56
W8 . . . . .4A 76
Hamilton Lodge E1 . . . . .2J 73
Hamilton M. W1 . . . . . . .4C 78
Hamilton Pl. W1 . . . . . . .3B 78
Hamilton Sq. SE1 . . . . . .4K 81
Hamilton Ter. NW8 . . . . .5B 56
Hamlet Ct. SE11 . . . . . . .3E 90
Hamlet Way SE1 . . . . . . .5K 81
Hammerfield Ho.
SW3 . . . . .3H 87
Hammersley Ho.
SE14 . . . . .7K 93
HAMMERSMITH 2B 84
Hammersmith Bri.
W6 . . . . .5A 84
Hammersmith Bri. Rd.
W6 . . . . .4A 84
HAMMERSMITH BROADWAY
. . . . .2B 84
Hammersmith B'way.
W6 . . . . .2B 84
Hammersmith Fitness &
Squash Cen. 3C 84
HAMMERSMITH FLYOVER
. . . . .3A 84
Hammersmith Flyover
W6 . . . . .3A 84
Hammersmith Gro.
W6 . . . . .5A 74
Hammersmith Ind. Est.
W6 . . . . .5B 84
Hammersmith Rd.
W6 . . . . .2C 84
W14 . . . . .2C 84
Hammett St. EC3 . . . . . .7C 72
Hammond Lodge *W9* . . .*3K 65*
(off Admiral Wlk.)
Hamond Sq. N1 . . . . . . .4A 62
Hampden Cl. NW1 . . . . .5H 59
Hampden Gurney St.
W1 . . . . .6J 67
Hampstead Lodge
NW1 . . . . .3G 67
Hampstead Rd. NW1 . . . .4E 58
Hampstead Theatre 1E 56
Hampton Cl. NW6 . . . . . .7J 55
Hampton St. SE17 . . . . . .2F 91
Hamston Ho. W8 . . . . . .6B 76
Ham Yd. W1 . . . . .7G 69
Hanbury Ho. E1 . . . . . . .3E 72
SW8 . . . . .6K 89
Hanbury M. N1 . . . . . . .3H 61
Hanbury St. E1 . . . . . . .3C 72
Hand Ct. WC1 . . . . .4B 70
Handel Bus. Cen.
SW8 . . . . .5K 89
Handel House Mus. . . .*7C 68*
(off Brook St.)
Handel Mans. SW13 . . . .7A 84
WC1 . . . . .1K 69
Handel St. WC1 . . . . . . .1J 69
Handforth Rd. SW9 . . . . .7C 90
Handley Rd. E9 . . . . . . .1K 63
Hanging Sword All.
EC4 . . . . .6D 70
Hankey Ho. SE1 . . . . . . .5K 81
Hankey Pl. SE1 . . . . . . .5K 81
Hannah Mary Way
SE1 . . . . .2F 93
Hannell Rd. SW6 . . . . . .7E 84
Hannibal Rd. E1 . . . . . . .3K 73
Hanover Flats W1 . . . . .7B 68
(not continuous)
Hanover Gdns. SE11 . . .6C 90
Hanover Ga. NW1 . . . . . .7H 57
Hanover Ga. Mans.
NW1 . . . . .1H 67
Hanover Ho. NW8 . . . . .5G 57
Hanover Pl. WC2 . . . . . .6K 69
Hanover Rd. NW10 . . . . .1A 54
Hanover Sq. W1 . . . . . . .6D 68
Hanover Steps W2 . . . . .6H 67
Hanover St. W1 . . . . . . .6D 68
Hanover Ter. NW1 . . . . .7J 57
Hanover Ter. M.
NW1 . . . . .7H 57
Hanover Yd. N1 . . . . . . .4F 61
Hansard M. W14 . . . . . .4D 74
Hans Ct. SW3 . . . . .6J 77
Hans Cres. SW1 . . . . . . .6J 77
Hanson St. W1 . . . . .3E 68
Hans Pl. SW1 . . . . .6K 77
Hans Rd. SW3 . . . . .6J 77
Hans St. SW1 . . . . .7K 77
Hanway Pl. W1 . . . . . . .5G 69
Hanway St. W1 . . . . . . .5G 69
Hanwell Ho. W2 . . . . . . .4J 65
Hanworth Ho. SE5 . . . . .7E 90
(not continuous)
Harad's Pl. E1 . . . . .1F 83
Harben Rd. NW6 . . . . . .1D 56
Harbet Rd. W2 . . . . .4F 67
Harbledown Ho. SE1 . . . .5J 81
Harcourt Bldgs. EC4 . . . .7C 70
Harcourt Ho. W1 . . . . . .5C 68
Harcourt St. W1 . . . . . . .4H 67
Harcourt Ter. SW10 . . . .4B 86
Harding Cl. SE17 . . . . . .5G 91
Hardinge La. E1 . . . . . . .6K 73
(not continuous)
Hardinge Rd. NW10 . . . .3A 54
Hardinge St. E1 . . . . . . .6K 73
(not continuous)
Harding Ho. SW13 . . . . .6A 84
Hardwicke M. WC1 . . . . .7B 60
Hardwick Ho. NW8 . . . . .1H 67
Hardwick St. EC1 . . . . . .7D 60
Hardwidge St. SE1 . . . . .4A 82
Hare Ct. EC4 . . . . .6C 70
Hare Marsh E2 . . . . .1E 72
Hare Pl. EC4 . . . . .6D 70
Hare Row E2 . . . . .4H 63
Hare Wlk. N1 . . . . .5B 62
(not continuous)
Harewood Av. NW1 . . . .2H 67
Harewood Pl. W1 . . . . . .6D 68
Harewood Row NW1 . . . .3H 67
Harfleur Ct. SE11 . . . . . .2E 90
Harford Ho. SE5 . . . . . . .6H 91
W11 . . . . .4H 65
Harkness Ho. E1 . . . . . .6F 73
Harlequin Ct. E1 . . . . . . .1E 82
Harleyford Ct. SE11 . . . .5A 90
Harleyford Rd. SE11 . . . .5A 90
Harleyford St. SE11 . . . .6C 90
Harley Gdns. SW10 . . . .4D 86
Harley Ho. NW1 . . . . . . .2B 68
Harley Pl. W1 . . . . .4C 68
Harley Rd. NW3 . . . . . . .1F 57
Harley St. W1 . . . . .2C 68
Harlowe Cl. E8 . . . . .2F 63
Harlowe Ho. E8 . . . . . . .2C 62
Harlynwood SE5 . . . . . . .7G 91
Harman Cl. SE1 . . . . . . .4E 92
Harmont Ho. W1 . . . . . .4C 68
Harmood Gro. NW1 . . . .1C 58
Harmood St. NW1 . . . . . .1C 58
Harmsworth M. SE11 . . .7E 80
Harmsworth St. SE17 . . .4E 90
Harold Ct. SE16 . . . . . . .5K 83
Harold Est. SE1 . . . . . . .7B 82
Harold Laski Ho. EC1 . . .7F 61
Harold Maddison Ho.
SE17 . . . . .3F 91
Harold Pl. SE11 . . . . . . .4C 90
Harold Wilson Ho.
SW6 . . . . .6H 85
Harp All. EC4 . . . . .5E 70
Harper Rd. SE1 . . . . . . .6G 81
Harp La. EC3 . . . . .1A 82
Harpley Sq. E1 . . . . .7K 63
Harpur M. WC1 . . . . . . .3A 70
Harpur St. WC1 . . . . . . .3A 70
Harriet Cl. E8 . . . . .2E 62
Harriet Ho. SW6 . . . . . . .7B 86
Harriet St. SW1 . . . . . . .5K 77
Harriet Wlk. SW1 . . . . . .5K 77
Harrington Ct. SW7 . . . . .1F 87
W10 . . . . .6G 55
Harrington Gdns.
SW7 . . . . .2B 86
Harrington Ho. NW1 . . . .6E 58
Harrington Rd. SW7 . . . .1E 86
Harrington Sq. NW1 . . . .4E 58
Harrington St. NW1 . . . . .5E 58
(not continuous)
Harriott Ho. E1 . . . . . . .4K 73
Harris Bldgs. E1 . . . . . . .6F 73
Harrison Ho. SE17 . . . . .3J 91
Harrisons Ct. SE14 . . . . .5K 93
Harrison St. WC1 . . . . . .7K 59
Harris St. SE5 . . . . .7K 91
Harrods 6J 77
Harrowby St. W1 . . . . . .5H 67
Harrow Club Sports Cen.
. . . . .7C 64
Harrow Lodge NW8 . . . .1E 66
Harrow Pl. E1 . . . . .5B 72
Harrow Rd. NW10 . . . . . .6A 54
W2 . . . . .4B 66
(not continuous)
W9 . . . . .2H 65
W10 . . . . .1D 64
Harrow Rd. Bri. W2 . . . .3D 66
Harrow St. NW1 . . . . . . .3H 67
Harry Hinkins Ho.
SE17 . . . . .4H 91
Harry Lambourn Ho.
SE15 . . . . .7H 93
Hartington Ho. SW1 . . . .3H 89
Hartington Rd. SW8 . . . .7J 89
Hartismere Rd. SW6 . . . .7H 85
Hartland NW1 . . . . .3F 59
Hartland Rd. NW1 . . . . .1C 58
NW6 . . . . .4G 55
Hartley Ho. SE1 . . . . . . .1D 92
Hartley St. E2 . . . . .6K 63
(not continuous)
Hartop Point SW6 . . . . . .7F 85
Hartshorn All. EC3 . . . . .6B 72
Hart St. EC3 . . . . .7B 72
Harvard Ho. SE17 . . . . . .5E 90
Harvey Ho. E1 . . . . .2G 73
N1 . . . . .3K 61
SW1 . . . . .4H 89
Harvey Lodge W9 . . . . . .3K 65
Harvey's Bldgs.
WC2 . . . . .1K 79
Harvey St. N1 . . . . .3K 61
Harvington Wlk. E8 . . . .1F 63
Harvist Rd. NW6 . . . . . .6D 54
Harwood Ct. N1 . . . . . . .3K 61
Harwood Rd. SW6 . . . . .7K 85
Hasker St. SW3 . . . . . . .1H 87
Hassard St. E2 . . . . .5D 62
Hastings Cl. SE15 . . . . .7E 92
Hastings Ho. W12 . . . . .7A 64
WC1 . . . . .7J 59
Hastings St. WC1 . . . . . .7J 59
Hat & Mitre Ct. EC1 . . . .2F 71
Hatcham Rd. SE15 . . . . .6J 93
Hatchers M. SE1 . . . . . .5B 82
Hatfield Cl. SE14 . . . . . .7K 93
Hatfield Ho. EC1 . . . . . .2G 71
Hatfields SE1 . . . . .2D 80
Hathaway Ho. N1 . . . . . .6A 62
Hatherley Ct. W2 . . . . . .6A 66
Hatherley Gro. W2 . . . . .5A 66
Hatherley St. SW1 . . . . .2F 89
Hatteraick St. SE16 . . . .4K 83
Hatton Gdn. EC1 . . . . . .3D 70
Hatton Pl. EC1 . . . . .3D 70
Hatton Row NW8 . . . . . .2F 67
Hatton St. NW8 . . . . . . .2F 67
Hatton Wall EC1 . . . . . . .3D 70
Haunch of Venison Yd.
W1 . . . . .6C 68
Havelock St. N1 . . . . . . .2K 59
Haven M. N1 . . . . .1D 60
Havenpool NW8 . . . . . . .3B 56
Haven St. NW1 . . . . . . .1D 58
Havering St. E1 . . . . . . .6K 73
Haverstock Pl. N1 . . . . .6G 61
Haverstock St. N1 . . . . .5F 61
Havil St. SE5 . . . . .7A 92
Havisham Ho. SE16 . . . .5E 82
Hawes St. N1 . . . . .1F 61
Hawkins Ho. SW1 . . . . . .5F 89
Hawkshead NW1 . . . . . . .6E 58
Hawksmoor M. E1 . . . . . .7G 73
Hawksmoor Pl. E2 . . . . .1F 72
Hawksmoor St. W6 . . . . .6D 84
Hawkstone Rd. SE16 . . . .1K 93
Hawkwell Wlk. N1 . . . . .2H 61
Hawley Cres. NW1 . . . . .1D 58
Hawley M. NW1 . . . . . . .1C 58
Hawley Rd. NW1 . . . . . .1C 58
(not continuous)
Hawley St. NW1 . . . . . . .1C 58
Hawthorne Ho. SW1 . . . .4F 89
Hawthorn Wlk. W10 . . . .1E 64
Hawtrey Rd. NW3 . . . . . .1G 57
Hayden Piper Ho.
SW3 . . . . .5J 87
Hayden's Pl. W11 . . . . . .5G 65
Haydon St. EC3 . . . . . . .7C 72
Haydon Wlk. E1 . . . . . . .7D 72
Hayes Pl. NW1 . . . . .2H 67
Hayfield Pas. E1 . . . . . . .2K 73
Hayfield Yd. E1 . . . . .2K 73
Hay Hill W1 . . . . .1D 78
Hayles Bldgs. SE11 . . . . .1F 91
Hayles St. SE11 . . . . . . .1E 90
Haymans Point SE11 . . . .3A 90
Hayman St. N1 . . . . .1F 61
Haymarket SW1 . . . . . . .1G 79
Haymarket Arc. SW1 . . . .1G 79
Haymarket Ct. *E8* *1D 62*
(off Jacaranda Gro.)
Haymarket Theatre Royal
. . . . .2H 79
Haymerle Ho. SE15 . . . . .6E 92
Haymerle Rd. SE15 . . . . .6E 92
Hayne Ho. W11 . . . . . . .2E 74
Hayne St. EC1 . . . . .3F 71
Hay's Galleria SE1 . . . . .2A 82
Hays La. SE1 . . . . .3A 82
Hay's M. W1 . . . . .1C 78
Hay St. E2 . . . . .3F 63
Hayward Gallery 3B 80
Hayward Ho. N1 . . . . . . .4C 60
Hayward's Pl. EC1 . . . . .2E 70
Hazelmere Rd. NW6 . . . .2H 55
Hazel Rd. NW10 . . . . . . .6A 54
(not continuous)
Hazel Way SE1 . . . . .1C 92
Hazlewood Cres.
W10 . . . . .2F 65
Hazlewood Twr. W10 . . . .2F 65
Hazlitt M. W14 . . . . .7E 74
Hazlitt Rd. W14 . . . . . . .7E 74
Headbourne Ho. SE1 . . . .6K 81
Headfort Pl. SW1 . . . . . .5B 78
Headlam St. E1 . . . . . . .2H 73
Head's M. W11 . . . . .6J 65
Healey Ho. SW9 . . . . . . .7D 90
Hearn's Bldgs. SE17 . . . .2K 91
Hearn St. EC2 . . . . .2B 72
Heathcock Ct. *WC2* *1K 79*
(off Exchange Ct.)
Heathcote St. WC1 . . . . .1A 70
Heather Wlk. W10 . . . . .1F 65
Heathfield St. W11 . . . . .1E 74
Heathpool Ct. E1 . . . . . .2G 73
Heaton Ho. SW10 . . . . . .5D 86
Hebden Ct. E2 . . . . .3C 62
Heber Mans. W14 . . . . . .5F 85
Hebron Rd. W6 . . . . .7A 74
Heckfield Pl. SW6 . . . . . .7J 85
Hector Ho. E2 . . . . .5G 63
Heddon St. W1 . . . . .7E 68
(not continuous)
Hedgegate Ct. W11 . . . .5H 65
Hedger St. SE11 . . . . . . .1E 90
Hedingham Cl. N1 . . . . .1G 61
Hedsor Ho. E2 . . . . .1C 72
Heidegger Cres.
SW13 . . . . .7A 84
Heiron St. SE17 . . . . . . .6F 91
Heldar Ct. SE1 . . . . .5K 81
Helena Pl. E9 . . . . .3H 63
Helen Gladstone Ho.
SE1 . . . . .4E 80
Helen Ho. E2 . . . . .5G 63
Helen Peele Cotts.
SE16 . . . . .6J 83
Helen's Pl. E2 . . . . .6J 63
Helen Taylor Ho.
SE16 . . . . .7E 82
Helix Ct. W11 . . . . .3D 74
Hellings St. E1 . . . . .3F 83
Helmet Row EC1 . . . . . .7H 61
Helmsdale Ho. NW6 . . . .5A 56
Helmsley Pl. E8 . . . . . . .1G 63
Helmsley St. E8 . . . . . . .1H 63
Helsby Ct. NW8 . . . . . . .1E 66
Helston NW1 . . . . .4F 59
Helston Ho. SE11 . . . . . .3D 90
Hemans St. SW8 . . . . . .7H 89
Hemans St. Est. SW8 . . .7H 89
Hemingford Rd. N1 . . . .3B 60
Hemming St. E1 . . . . . . .2F 73
Hemp Wlk. SE17 . . . . . .1K 91
Hemstal Rd. NW6 . . . . . .1J 55
Hemsworth Ct. N1 . . . . .4A 62
Hemsworth St. N1 . . . . .4A 62
Hemus Pl. SW3 . . . . . . .4H 87
Hen & Chicken Ct.
EC4 . . . . .6C 70
Henderson Ct. SE14 . . . .5K 93
Henderson Dr. NW8 . . . .1E 66
Hendre Ho. SE1 . . . . . . .2B 92
Hendre Rd. SE1 . . . . . . .2B 92
Heneage La. EC3 . . . . . .6B 72
Heneage Pl. EC3 . . . . . .6B 72
Heneage St. E1 . . . . . . .3D 72
Henley Cl. SE16 . . . . . . .4J 83
Henley Dr. SE1 . . . . .1D 92
Henley Ho. E2 . . . . .1D 72
Henley Prior N1 . . . . . . .5A 60
Henley Rd. NW10 . . . . . .2B 54
Henniker M. SW3 . . . . . .5E 86
Henrietta Ho. W6 . . . . . .4A 84
Henrietta M. WC1 . . . . . .1K 69
Henrietta Pl. W1 . . . . . .6C 68
Henrietta St. WC2 . . . . .7K 69
Henriques St. E1 . . . . . .5F 73
Henry Dickens Ct.
W11 . . . . .1D 74
Henry Ho. SE1 . . . . .3D 80
SW8 . . . . .7K 89
Henry Wise Ho. SW1 . . . .2F 89
Henshaw St. SE17 . . . . . .1J 91
Henslow Ho. SE15 . . . . .7E 92
Henstridge Pl. NW8 . . . .4G 57
Hepworth Ct. N1 . . . . . .2E 60
Herald's Pl. SE11 . . . . . .1E 90
Herald St. E2 . . . . .1H 73
Herbal Hill EC1 . . . . . . .2D 70
Herbal Hill Gdns.
EC1 . . . . .2D 70
Herbal Pl. EC1 . . . . .2D 70
Herbert Cres. SW1 . . . . .6K 77
Herbert Gdns. NW10 . . . .4A 54
Herbert Ho. E1 . . . . .5C 72
Herbert Morrison Ho.
SW6 . . . . .6G 85
Herbrand Est. WC1 . . . . .1J 69
Herbrand St. WC1 . . . . . .1J 69
Hercules Rd. SE1 . . . . . .7B 80
Hereford Bldgs. SW3 . . . .5F 87
Hereford Ho. NW6 . . . . .5J 55
SW3 . . . . .6H 77
SW10 . . . . .7B 86
Hereford M. W2 . . . . . . .6K 65
Hereford Retreat
SE15 . . . . .7E 92
Hereford Rd. W2 . . . . . .5K 65
Hereford Sq. SW7 . . . . . .2D 86
Hereford St. E2 . . . . . . .1E 72
Her Majesty's Theatre
. . . . .2G 79
Hermes Cl. W9 . . . . .2J 65
Hermes St. N1 . . . . .5C 60
Hermitage Ct. E1 . . . . . .3F 83
Hermitage Rooms 7B 70
Hermitage St. W2 . . . . . .4E 66
Hermitage Vs. SW6 . . . . .5J 85
Hermitage Wall E1 . . . . .3F 83
Hermitage Waterside
E1 . . . . .2E 82
Hermit Pl. NW6 . . . . . . .3A 56
Hermit St. EC1 . . . . .6E 60
Heron Ho. NW8 . . . . . . .5G 57
Heron Pl. W1 . . . . .5B 68
Herrick St. SW1 . . . . . . .2H 89
Herries St. W10 . . . . . . .5F 55
Hertford Pl. W1 . . . . . . .2E 68
Hertford Rd. N1 . . . . . . .2B 62
(not continuous)
Hertford St. W1 . . . . . . .3C 78

Hesketh Pl. W11 1E 74
Hesper M. SW5 3A 86
Hessel St. E1 6G 73
Hester Rd. SW11 7G 87
Hestia Ho. SE1 5A 82
Hethpool Ho. W2 2E 66
Hever Ho. SE15 5K 93
Heversham Ho. SE15 6J 93
Hewer St. W10 3D 64
Hewett St. EC2 2B 72
Heyford Av. SW8 7K 89
Heyford Ter. SW8 7K 89
Heygate St. SE17 2G 91
Hickes Ho. NW6 1E 56
Hickleton NW1 3E 58
Hickling Ho. SE16 7H 83
Hide Pl. SW1 2G 89
Hide Twr. SW1 2G 89
Higgins Ho. N1 3A 62
Highbridge Ct. SE14 7K 93
High Holborn WC1 5J 69
Highlever Rd. W10 3A 64
Highstone Mans. NW1 1E 58
High Timber St. EC4 7G 71
Highway, The E1 1F 83
Highworth St. NW1 3H 67
Hilary Cl. SW6 7A 86
Hilborough Ct. E8 1D 62
Hildyard Rd. SW6 5K 85
Hiley Rd. NW10 6A 54
Hilgrove Rd. NW6 1D 56
Hillary Ct. W12 5A 74
Hillbeck Cl. SE15 6J 93 (not continuous)
Hillcrest W11 1G 75
Hillersden Ho. SW1 3C 88
Hillery Cl. SE17 2K 91
Hill Farm Rd. W10 3B 64
Hillgate Pl. W8 2J 75
Hillgate St. W8 2J 75
Hilliard Ho. E1 2H 83
Hilliards Ct. E1 2H 83
Hillingdon St. SE17 6E 90
Hillman Dr. W10 2B 64
Hill Rd. NW8 6D 56
Hillsborough Ct. NW6 3A 56
Hillside Cl. NW8 4B 56
Hillsleigh Rd. W8 2H 75
Hills Pl. W1 6E 68
Hill St. W1 2B 78
Hilltop Ct. NW8 1D 56
Hill Vw. NW3 2J 57
Hill-Wood Ho. NW1 5F 59
Hinchinbrook Ho. NW6 3A 56
Hind Ct. EC4 6D 70
Hinde Ho. W1 5B 68
Hinde M. W1 5B 68
Hinde St. W1 5B 68
Hindmarsh Cl. E1 7F 73
Hindon Ct. SW1 1E 88
Hinstock NW6 2A 56
Hippodrome M. W11 1E 74
Hippodrome Pl. W11 1E 74
Hithe Gro. SE16 7K 83
HMS Belfast 2B 82
Hoadly Ho. SE1 3G 81
Hobart Pl. SW1 6C 78
Hobbs Ct. SE1 4D 82
Hobbs Pl. N1 3A 62
Hobbs Pl. Est. N1 4A 62
Hobson's Pl. E1 3E 72
Hobury St. SW10 6D 86
Hocker St. E2 7C 62
Hockliffe Ho. W10 3A 64
Hockney Ct. SE16 3H 93
Hodnet Gro. SE16 1K 93
Hoffman Sq. N1 6K 61
Hofland Rd. W14 6D 74
Hogan M. W2 3E 66
Hogarth Ct. E1 5F 73
EC3 7B 72
NW1 1F 59
Hogarth Ho. SW1 2H 89
Hogarth Pl. SW5 2A 86
Hogarth Rd. SW5 2A 86
Hogshead Pas. E1 1H 83
Holbeck Row SE15 7F 93
Holbein Ho. SW1 3A 88
Holbein M. SW1 3A 88
Holbein Pl. SW1 2A 88
HOLBORN 4A 70
Holborn EC1 4C 70
Holborn Cir. EC1 4D 70
Holborn Pl. WC1 4A 70
Holborn Viaduct EC4 4D 70
Holcroft Ct. W1 3E 68
Holcroft Rd. E9 1K 63
Holden Ho. N1 3G 61
Holford Ho. SE16 2G 93
WC1 6B 60
Holford M. WC1 6C 60
Holford Pl. WC1 6B 60
Holford St. WC1 6C 60
Holford Yd. WC1 5C 60
Holland Gdns. W14 6F 75
Holland Gro. SW9 7D 90
Holland Ho. NW10 5A 54
HOLLAND PARK 3G 75
Holland Pk. 4G 75
Holland Pk. W11 3F 75
Holland Pk. Av. W11 4D 74
Holland Pk. Ct. W14 4F 75
Holland Pk. Gdns. W14 3E 74
Holland Pk. Mans. W11 3F 75
Holland Pk. M. W11 3F 75
Holland Pk. Rd. W14 7G 75
HOLLAND PARK RDBT. 4D 74
Holland Pk. Ter. W11 3F 75
Holland Pk. Theatre (Open Air) *5H 75* *(in Holland Pk.)*
Holland Pas. N1 2G 61
Holland Pl. W8 4A 76
Holland Pl. Chambers W8 4A 76
Holland Ri. Ho. SW9 7B 90
Holland Rd. W14 4D 74
Holland St. SE1 2F 81
W8 5K 75
Holland Vs. Rd. W14 4E 74
Holland Wlk. W8 3H 75
Hollen St. W1 5G 69
Holles St. W1 5D 68
Hollisfield WC1 7K 59
Hollybush Gdns. E2 6H 63
Hollybush Ho. E2 6H 63
Hollybush Pl. E2 6H 63
Holly Ho. W10 1E 64
Holly M. SW10 4D 86
Holly St. E8 1D 62
Hollywood Ct. SW10 5C 86
Hollywood M. SW10 5C 86
Hollywood Rd. SW10 5C 86
Holman Ho. E2 6K 63
Holman Hunt Ho. W6 4E 84
Holmbrook NW1 5F 59
Holmead Rd. SW6 7B 86
Holmefield Ho. W10 2F 65
Holmesdale Ho. NW6 2K 55
Holmes Pl. SW10 5D 86
Holmes Place Health Club
Barbican 3G 71 *(off Aldersgate St.)*
Hammersmith 2C 84
St Luke's 2J 71
Holmes Ter. SE1 4C 80
Holocaust Memorial Garden, The 4K 77
Holst Ct. SE1 6C 80
Holst Mans. SW13 6A 84
Holsworthy Sq. WC1 2B 70
Holyoak Rd. SE11 2E 90
Holyport Rd. SW6 7C 84
Holyrood St. SE1 3A 82
Holywell Cen. EC2 1A 72
Holywell Cl. SE16 3H 93
Holywell La. EC2 1B 72
Holywell Row EC2 2A 72
Homefield St. N1 5A 62
Homer Row W1 4H 67
Homer St. W1 4H 67
Homestead Rd. SW6 7G 85
Honduras St. EC1 1G 71
Honey La. EC2 6H 71
Honey La. Ho. SW10 5B 86
Honiton Rd. NW6 4G 55
Hood Ct. EC4 6D 70
Hood Ho. SW1 4G 89
Hooper's Ct. SW3 5J 77
Hooper Sq. E1 6E 72
Hooper St. E1 6E 72
Hope Ct. NW10 6D 54
Hopefield Av. NW6 4F 55
Hope Sq. EC2 4A 72
Hopetown St. E1 4D 72
Hopewell St. SE5 7K 91
Hopewell Yd. SE5 7K 91
Hope Wharf SE16 4J 83
Hop Gdns. WC2 1J 79
Hopgood St. W12 3B 74
Hopkinsons Pl. NW1 2A 58
Hopkins St. W1 6F 69
Hopton's Gdns. SE1 2F 81
Hopton St. SE1 1E 80
Hopwood Rd. SE17 5K 91
Hopwood Wlk. E8 1F 63
Horatio Ct. SE16 3K 83
Horatio Ho. E2 5D 62
W6 3C 84
Horatio St. E2 5D 62
Horbury Cres. W11 1J 75
Horbury M. W11 1H 75
Hordle Prom. E. SE15 7D 92
Hordle Prom. Sth. SE15 7C 92
Hormead Rd. W9 2G 65
Hornbeam Cl. SE11 1C 90
Hornby Cl. NW3 1F 57
Hornby Ho. SE11 5C 90
Horner Ho. N1 3B 62
Hornshay St. SE15 6K 93
Hornton Ct. W8 5K 75
Hornton Pl. W8 5K 75
Hornton St. W8 4K 75
Horse & Dolphin Yd. W1 7H 69
Horseferry Rd. SW1 7G 79
Horseferry Rd. Est. SW1 7G 79
Horseguards Av. SW1 3J 79
Horse Guards Parade 3H 79
Horse Guards Rd. SW1 3H 79
Horselydown La. SE1 4C 82
Horselydown Mans. SE1 4C 82
Horsemongers M. SE1 5H 81
Horse Ride SW1 4E 78
Horseshoe Ct. EC1 1F 71
Horseshoe Wharf SE1 2J 81
Horse Yd. N1 2F 61
Horsfield Ho. N1 1G 61
Horsley St. SE17 5J 91
Horsman Ho. SE5 6G 91
Horsman St. SE5 6H 91
Hortensia Ho. SW10 7C 86
Hortensia Rd. SW10 6C 86
Horton Ho. SE15 6K 93
SW8 7A 90
W6 4E 84
Horwood Ho. E2 7H 63
NW8 1H 67
Hosier La. EC1 4E 70
Hothfield Pl. SE16 7K 83
Hotspur St. SE11 3C 90
Houghton St. WC2 6B 70 (not continuous)
Houndsditch EC3 5B 72
Houseman Way SE5 7K 91
Houses of Parliament 6K 79
Hove St. SE15 7J 93
Howard Bldg. SW8 6C 88
Howard Ho. SW1 4F 89
W1 2D 68
Howell Wlk. SE1 2F 91
Howick Pl. SW1 7F 79
Howie St. SW11 7G 87
Howland Est. SE16 6J 83
Howland M. E. W1 3F 69
Howland St. W1 3E 68
Howley Pl. W2 3D 66
How's St. E2 4C 62
HOXTON 5J 61
Hoxton Hall Theatre 5B 62
Hoxton Mkt. N1 7A 62
Hoxton Sq. N1 7A 62
Hoxton St. N1 3A 62
Hoyland Cl. SE15 7G 93
HQS Wellington 1C 80
Hub, The 5K 57
Huberd Ho. SE1 6K 81
Hubert Ho. NW8 2G 67
Hucknall Ct. NW8 1E 66
Huddleston Cl. E2 5H 63
Hudson Bldg. E1 3E 72
Hudson Ho. SW10 7C 86
W11 6F 65
Hudson's Pl. SW1 1E 88
Huggin Ct. EC4 7H 71
Huggin Hill EC4 7H 71
Hugh Astor Ct. SE1 6F 81
Hugh Cubitt Ho. N1 5B 60
Hugh Dalton Av. SW6 6G 85
Hughenden Ho. NW8 1G 67
Hughes Ho. E2 7J 63
SE17 2F 91
Hughes Mans. E1 2F 73
Hugh Gaitskell Cl. SW6 6G 85
Hugh M. SW1 2D 88
Hugh Platt Ho. E2 5H 63
Hugh St. SW1 2D 88
Hugo Ho. SW1 6K 77
Huguenot Pl. E1 3D 72
Hullbridge M. N1 2J 61
Hull St. EC1 7G 61
Hulme Pl. SE1 5H 81
Humber Dr. W10 2C 64
Humbolt Rd. W6 6E 84
Hume Ct. N1 1F 61
Hume Ho. W11 3D 74
Humphrey St. SE1 3C 92
Hungerford Ho. SW1 5F 89
Hungerford La. WC2 2J 79 (not continuous)
Hungerford St. E1 6H 73
Hunsdon Rd. SE14 6K 93
Hunslett St. E2 5K 63
Hunstanton Ho. NW1 3H 67
Hunt Cl. W11 2D 74
Hunter Cl. SE1 7K 81
Hunter Ho. SE1 5F 81
SW5 4K 85
SW8 7H 89
WC1 1J 69
Hunterian Mus., The 6B 70
Hunter Lodge W9 3K 65
Hunter St. WC1 1K 69
Huntingdon St. N1 1A 60
Huntley St. WC1 2F 69
Hunton St. E1 2E 72
Hunt's Ct. WC2 1H 79
Huntsman St. SE17 2K 91
Huntsworth M. NW1 1J 67
Hurdwick Pl. *NW1 4E 58* *(off Hampstead Rd.)*
Hurley Ho. SE11 2E 90
Huron University 6F 77
Hurst Ho. WC1 5B 60
Hurstway Rd. W11 7D 64
Hurstway Wlk. W11 7D 64
Huson Cl. NW3 1G 57
Hutchinson Ho. NW3 1J 57
SE14 7K 93
Hutton St. EC4 6E 70
Huxley Ho. NW8 2F 67
Huxley St. W10 7E 54
Hyde Pk. 1H 77
Hyde Pk. Barracks 5H 77
HYDE PARK CORNER 4B 78
Hyde Pk. Cnr. W1 4B 78
Hyde Pk. Cres. W2 6G 67
Hyde Pk. Gdns. W2 7F 67
Hyde Pk. Gdns. M. W2 7F 67 (not continuous)
Hyde Pk. Ga. SW7 5C 76 (not continuous)
Hyde Pk. Ga. M. SW7 5D 76
Hyde Pk. Mans. NW1 4G 67 (not continuous)
Hyde Pk. Pl. W2 7H 67
Hyde Pk. Sq. W2 6G 67
Hyde Pk. Sq. M. W2 6G 67
Hyde Pk. St. W2 6G 67
Hyde Pk. Towers W2 1C 76
Hyde Rd. N1 3A 62
Hydra Bldg., The EC1 7D 60
Hyndman St. SE15 6G 93
Hyson Rd. SE16 3H 93
Hythe Ho. SE16 4K 83
W6 1B 84

I

Ian Bowater Ct. N1 6K 61
Ibberton Ho. SW8 7A 90
W14 7F 75
Ibbott St. E1 1K 73
ICA Cinema *3H 79* *(off Carlton Ho. Ter.)*
ICA Theatre *2H 79* *(off Carlton Ho. Ter.)*
Ice Wharf Marina N1 4K 59
Icknield Ho. SW3 3H 87
Icon Apartments SE1 6A 82
Idol La. EC3 1A 82
Iffley Rd. W6 6A 74
Ifield Rd. SW10 5B 86
Ightham Ho. SE17 2A 92
Ikon Ho. E1 7K 73
Ilbert St. W10 7D 54
Ilchester Gdns. W2 7A 66
Ilchester Mans. W8 6J 75
Ilchester Pl. W14 6G 75
Ilderton Rd. SE16 3H 93
Ilderton Wharf SE15 5K 93
Ilfracombe Flats *SE1 4H 81* *(off Marshalsea Rd.)*
Iliffe St. SE17 3F 91
Iliffe Yd. SE17 3F 91
IMAX National Film Theatre 3C 80
Imber St. N1 3J 61
Imperial College of Science, Technology & Medicine 6E 76
Imperial Coll. Rd. SW7 7D 76
Imperial Ct. NW8 4H 57
SE11 4C 90
Imperial Pde. EC4 6E 70
Imperial War Mus. 7D 80
India Pl. WC2 7A 70
India St. EC3 6C 72
Indus Ct. SE15 7D 92
Infirmary Ct. SW3 5K 87
Ingelow Ho. W8 4A 76
Ingestre Pl. W1 6F 69
Inglebert St. EC1 6C 60
Inglefield Sq. E1 2H 83
Ingoldisthorpe Gro. SE15 5D 92
Ingram Cl. SE11 1B 90
Ingrebourne Ho. NW8 3F 67
Inigo Pl. WC2 7J 69
Inkerman Ter. W8 7K 75
Inner Circ. NW1 7A 58
Inner Ct. SW3 6G 87
Inner Temple La. EC4 6C 70
Innis Ho. SE17 3A 92
Innis St. SE15 7B 92
Inns of Court & City Yeomanry Mus. 4B 70
Institute of Archaeology 1G 69
Institute of Classical Studies 1G 69
Institute of Contemporary Arts 3H 79
International Ho. E1 1D 82
Inver Ct. W2 6B 66
Invergarry Ho. NW6 5A 56
Inverness Gdns. W8 3A 76
Inverness M. W2 7B 66
Inverness Pl. W2 7B 66
Inverness St. NW1 2C 58
Inverness Ter. W2 6B 66
Invicta Plaza SE1 2E 80
Inville Rd. SE17 4K 91
Inville Wlk. SE17 4K 91
Inwood Ct. NW1 1F 59
Inworth Wlk. N1 2G 61
Ion Ct. E2 5E 62
Ion Sq. E2 5E 62
Ipsden Bldgs. SE1 4D 80
Ireland Yd. EC4 6F 71
Iron Bri. Ho. NW1 1K 57
Ironmonger La. EC2 6H 71
Ironmonger Pas. EC1 7H 61
Ironmonger Row EC1 7H 61
Ironmonger Row Baths 7G 61
Ironside Cl. SE16 4K 83
Irving Ho. SE17 4E 90
Irving Mans. W14 5F 85
Irving Rd. W14 6D 74
Irving St. WC2 1H 79
Irwell Est. SE16 5J 83
Irwin Gdns. NW10 3A 54
Isaac Way SE1 4H 81
Isabella Ho. SE11 3E 90
W6 4A 84
Isabella St. SE1 3E 80
Isambard Pl. SE16 3K 83
Isis Ho. NW8 2F 67
Isleden Ho. N1 2G 61
ISLINGTON 3E 60
Islington Grn. N1 3E 60
Islington High St. N1 5D 60 (not continuous)
Islington Mus. 1E 60
Islington Pk. St. N1 1D 60
Islington Pl. N1 3C 60
Ivatt Pl. W14 4H 85
Iveagh Ct. E1 6C 72
Iveagh Ho. SW10 7D 86
Iver Ho. *N1 3A 62* *(off New Era Est.)*
Iverna Ct. W8 6K 75
Iverna Gdns. W8 6K 75
Ives St. SW3 1H 87
Ivimey St. E2 6F 63
Ivor Ct. NW1 1J 67
Ivories, The N1 1G 61
Ivor Pl. NW1 2J 67
Ivor St. NW1 1E 58
Ivory Ho. E1 2D 82
Ivybridge La. WC2 1K 79
Ivychurch La. SE17 3C 92
Ivy Ct. SE16 4F 93
Ivy Lodge W11 2J 75
Ivy St. N1 4A 62
Ixworth Pl. SW3 3G 87

J

Jacana Ct. E1 1D 82
Jacaranda Gro. E8 1D 62
Jackman Ho. E1 3H 83
Jackman St. E8 3G 63
Jackson Cl. E9 1K 63
Jacks Pl. E1 3C 72
Jacob Mans. E1 5G 73
Jacob St. SE1 4D 82
Jacob's Well M. W1 5B 68
Jacotts Ho. W10 2A 64
Jacqueline Ho. NW1 2K 57
Jago Wlk. SE5 7J 91
Jamaica Rd. SE1 5D 82
SE16 6F 83
Jamaica St. E1 5K 73
James Anderson Ct. E2 4B 62
James Brine Ho. E2 6D 62
James Campbell Ho. E2 5J 63
James Collins Cl. W9 2G 65
James Ct. N1 2H 61
James Docherty Ho. E2 5H 63
James Hammett Ho. E2 6D 62
James Hill Ho. W10 1F 65
James Ho. *SW8 7K 89* *(off Wheatsheaf La.)*
James Middleton Ho. E2 6H 63
Jameson Ct. E2 5J 63
Jameson Ho. SE11 3A 90
Jameson St. W8 2K 75
James Stewart Ho. NW6 1H 55
James St. W1 5B 68
WC2 6K 69
James Stroud Ho. SE17 4H 91
Jamestown Rd. NW1 2C 58
Jane Austen Ho. SW1 4E 88
Jane St. E1 6H 73
Janeway Pl. SE16 5G 83
Janeway St. SE16 5F 83
Jarman Ho. E1 4J 73
SE16 1K 93
Jarrow Rd. SE16 2J 93
Jasmin Lodge SE16 4G 93
Jason Ct. W1 5B 68
Jasper Wlk. N1 6J 61
Java Wharf SE1 4D 82
Jay M. SW7 5D 76
Jean Darling Ho. SW10 6E 86
Jean Pardies Ho. E1 4J 73
Jeffrey's Pl. NW1 1E 58
Jeffrey's St. NW1 1D 58
Jeger Av. E2 3C 62
Jellicoe Ho. E2 5E 62
NW1 2D 68
Jenkinson Ho. E2 6K 63
Jenner Ho. WC1 1K 69
Jennifer Ho. SE11 2D 90
Jenningsbury Ho. *SW3 3H 87* *(off Cale St.)*
Jephson Ho. SE17 5E 90
Jerdan Pl. SW6 7J 85
Jeremy Bentham Ho. E2 6F 63
Jermyn St. SW1 2E 78
Jermyn Street Theatre 1F 79
Jerome Cres. NW8 1G 67
Jerome Ho. NW1 3H 67
SW7 1E 86
Jerome St. E1 3C 72
Jerrold St. N1 5B 62
Jersey St. E2 7H 63
Jerusalem Pas. EC1 2E 70
Jervis Ct. W1 6D 68
Jervis Rd. SW6 6H 85
Jerwood Space Art Gallery 4G 81
Jessel Ho. SW1 1H 89
WC1 7J 59
Jessel Mans. W14 5F 85
Jessie Duffett Ho. SE5 7G 91
Jesson Ho. SE17 2J 91
Jessop Ct. N1 5F 61
Jevons Ho. NW8 1E 56
Jewel House *1C 82* *(in The Tower of London)*
Jewel Tower 6J 79
Jewish Mus.
Camden Town 3D 58
Jewry St. EC3 6C 72
Jim Griffiths Ho. SW6 6G 85
Joanna Ho. W6 3A 84
Joan St. SE1 3E 80
Jocelin Ho. N1 3B 60
Jockey's Flds. WC1 3B 70
Johanna St. SE1 5C 80
John Adam St. WC2 1K 79
John Aird Ct. W2 3D 66 (not continuous)
John Barker Ct. NW6 1D 54
John Carpenter St. EC4 7E 70
John Cartwright Ho. E2 6G 63
John Fearon Wlk. *W10 6F 55* *(off Dart St.)*
John Felton Rd. SE16 5E 82
John Fielden Ho. E2 6G 63
John Fisher St. E1 7E 72
John Horner M. N1 4G 61
John Islip St. SW1 3H 89
John Kennedy Ho. SE16 1K 93
John Knight Lodge SW6 7K 85
John McKenna Wlk. SE16 6F 83
John Maurice Cl. SE17 1J 91
John Orwell Sports Cen. 3G 83
John Parry Ct. N1 4B 62
John Penry Ho. SE1 4E 92
John Prince's St. W1 5D 68
John Pritchard Ho. E1 2F 73
John Ratcliffe Ho. NW6 7J 55
John Rennie Wlk. E1 2H 83
John Roll Way SE16 6F 83
John Ruskin St. SE5 7E 90
John's M. WC1 2B 70
John Smith Av. SW6 7G 85
Johnson Cl. E8 2E 62
Johnson Ho. E2 7F 63
NW1 5F 59
NW3 1J 57
SW1 2B 88
Johnson Lodge W9 3K 65
Johnson Mans. W14 5F 85
Johnson's Ct. EC4 6D 70
Johnson's Pl. SW1 4E 88
Johnson St. E1 7K 73
John's Pl. E1 5H 73
John Strachey Ho. SW6 6H 85
John St. WC1 2B 70

John Trundle Ct. EC2 . . .3G **71**
John Trundle Highwalk EC2 . . . . .3G **71**
John Wesley Highwalk EC2 . . . . .4G **71**
John Wheatley Ho. SW6 . . . . .6H **85**
John Williams Cl. SE14 . . . . .6K **93**
Joiner St. SE1 . . . . .3K **81**
Joiners Yd. N1 . . . . . . .5K **59**
Jonathan St. SE11 . . . .3A **90**
Jones St. W1 . . . . .1C **78**
Jonson Ho. SE1 . . . . . .7K **81**
Jordan Ho. N1 . . . . .2K **61**
Jordans Ho. NW8 . . . . . .1F **67**
Joscoyne Ho. E1 . . . . . .5H **73**
Joseph Conrad Ho. SW1 . . . . .2F **89**
Joseph Priestley Ho. *E2 . . . . .6G 63* *(off Canrobert St.)*
Joseph Trotter Cl. EC1 . . . . .7D **60**
Joubert Mans. SW3 . . . .3H **87**
Jowett St. SE15 . . . . . . .7D **92**
Jowitt Ho. E2 . . . . .6K **63**
Jubilee Bldgs. NW8 . . . .3E **56**
Jubilee Hall Sports Cen. 7K **69**
Jubilee Ho. SE11 . . . . . .2D **90**
WC1 . . . . .1A **70**
Jubilee Mans. E1 . . . . . .5J **73**
Jubilee Mkt. *WC2 . . . . . .7K 69* *(off Covent Gdn.)*
Jubilee Pl. SW3 . . . . . . .3H **87**
Jubilee Sports Cen. & Baths 7G **55**
Jubilee St. E1 . . . . .5J **73**
Jubilee Walkway SE1 . . .1F **81**
Jubilee Yd. SE1 . . . . . . .4C **82**
Judd St. WC1 . . . . .6J **59**
Juer St. SW11 . . . . .7H **87**
Juliet Ho. N1 . . . . .5A **62**
Julius Nyerere Cl. N1 . . . . .3A **60**
Junction Av. NW10 . . . . .1B **64**
Junction M. W2 . . . . . . .5G **67**
Junction Pl. W2 . . . . . . .5G **67**
Juniper Ct. W8 . . . . .7A **76**
Juniper Cres. NW1 . . . . .1B **58**
Juniper Ho. W10 . . . . . .1E **64**
Juniper St. E1 . . . . .7J **73**
Jurston Ct. SE1 . . . . . . .5D **80**
Justice Wlk. SW3 . . . . . .6G **87**
Juxon Ho. EC4 . . . . .6F **71**
Juxon St. SE11 . . . . .1B **90**

K

Katherine Cl. SE16 . . . . .3K **83**
Katherine Ho. W10 . . . . .2E **64**
Katherine Sq. W11 . . . . .2E **74**
Kay St. E2 . . . . .4F **63**
Kean Ho. SE17 . . . . .5E **90**
Kean St. WC2 . . . . .6A **70**
Keats Cl. SE1 . . . . .2C **92**
Keats Ho. E2 . . . . .6J **63**
SE5 . . . . .7H **91**
SW1 . . . . .5F **89**
Keats Pl. EC2 . . . . .4J **71**
Keble Pl. SW13 . . . . . . .6A **84**
Kedleston Wlk. E2 . . . . .6H **63**
Keeley St. WC2 . . . . . . .6A **70**
Keeling Ho. E2 . . . . .5G **63**
Keeton's Rd. SE16 . . . . .6G **83** (not continuous)
Keir Hardie Ho. W6 . . . .5C **84**
Keith Ho. NW6 . . . . . . .6A **56**
SW8 . . . . .7J **89**
Kelfield Ct. W10 . . . . . .5D **64**
Kelfield Gdns. W10 . . . . .5B **64**
Kelfield M. W10 . . . . . . .5C **64**
Kellet Ho's. *WC1 . . . . . .7K 59* *(off Tankerton St.)*
Kellett Ho. N1 . . . . .3A **62**
Kellow Ho. SE1 . . . . .4J **81**
Kell St. SE1 . . . . .6F **81**
Kelly M. W9 . . . . .2H **65**
Kelsey St. E2 . . . . .1G **73**
Kelso Pl. W8 . . . . .6A **76**
Kelvin Ct. W11 . . . . .1J **75**
Kember St. N1 . . . . .1A **60**
Kemble St. WC2 . . . . . . .6A **70**
Kempe Ho. SE1 . . . . .7K **81**
Kempe Rd. NW6 . . . . . . .5C **54**
Kemp Ho. E2 . . . . .4K **63**
W1 . . . . .7G **69**
Kemps Ct. W1 . . . . .6G **69**
Kempsford Gdns. SW5 . . . . .4K **85**
Kempsford Rd. SE11 . . . .2D **90** (not continuous)
Kempton Ct. E1 . . . . . . .3G **73**
Kempton Ho. N1 . . . . . . .3A **62**
Kemsing Ho. SE1 . . . . . .5K **81**
Kenbrook Ho. W14 . . . . .6H **75**
Kenchester Cl. SW8 . . . .7K **89**
Kendal NW1 . . . . .6D **58**
Kendal Cl. SW9 . . . . . . .7E **90**
Kendal Ho. E9 . . . . .1J **63**
N1 . . . . .4B **60**
Kendall Pl. W1 . . . . .4A **68**
Kendal Steps W2 . . . . . .6H **67**
Kendal St. W2 . . . . .6H **67**
Kender St. SE14 . . . . . . .7K **93**
Kendrick M. SW7 . . . . . .1E **86**
Kendrick Pl. SW7 . . . . . .2E **86**
Kenilworth Rd. NW6 . . . .2H **55**
Kenley Wlk. W11 . . . . . .2E **74**
Kennedy Ho. SE11 . . . . .3A **90**
Kennedy Wlk. SE17 . . . .2K **91**
Kennet Ct. W9 . . . . .3J **65**
Kenneth Campbell Ho. NW8 . . . . .1F **67**
Kenneth Ct. SE11 . . . . . .1D **90**
Kennet Ho. NW8 . . . . . . .2F **67**
Kenneth Younger Ho. SW6 . . . . .6H **85**
Kennet Rd. W9 . . . . .1H **65**
Kennet St. E1 . . . . .2F **83**
Kennett Wharf La. EC4 . . . . .1H **81**
Kenning Ho. N1 . . . . . . .2A **62**
Kenning St. SE16 . . . . . .4K **83**
Kennings Way SE11 . . . .3D **90**
KENNINGTON 5D **90**
Kennington Grn. SE11 . . . . .4C **90**
Kennington Gro. SE11 . . . . .5B **90**
Kennington La. SE11 . . .4A **90**
KENNINGTON OVAL . . .6C **90**
Kennington Oval SE11 . . . . .5B **90**
Kennington Pal. Ct. SE11 . . . . .3C **90**
Kennington Pk. Gdns. SE11 . . . . .5E **90**
Kennington Pk. Ho. SE11 . . . . .4D **90**
Kennington Pk. Pl. SE11 . . . . .5D **90**
Kennington Pk. Rd. SE11 . . . . .7C **90**
Kennington Rd. SE1 . . . .6C **80**
SE11 . . . . .7C **80**
Kenrick Pl. W1 . . . . .3A **68**
KENSAL GREEN 6A **54**
Kensal Ho. W10 . . . . . . .2D **64**
KENSAL RISE 5C **54**
Kensal Rd. W10 . . . . . . .1D **64**
KENSAL TOWN 2F **65**
Kensal Wharf W10 . . . . .1D **64**
KENSINGTON 5A **76**
Kensington Arc. W8 . . . .5A **76**
Kensington Cen. W14 . . .1E **84** (not continuous)
Kensington Chu. Ct. W8 . . . . .5A **76**
Kensington Chu. St. W8 . . . . .2K **75**
Kensington Chu. Wlk. W8 . . . . .4A **76** (not continuous)
Kensington Ct. W8 . . . . .5B **76**
Kensington Ct. Gdns. W8 . . . . .6B **76**
Kensington Ct. M. W8 . . . . .6B **76**
Kensington Ct. Pl. W8 . . . . .6B **76**
Kensington Gdns. 2C **76**
Kensington Gdns. Sq. W2 . . . . .6A **66** (not continuous)
Kensington Ga. W8 . . . .6C **76**
Kensington Gore SW7 . . . . .5D **76**
Kensington Hall Gdns. W14 . . . . .3G **85**
Kensington Hgts. W8 . . .3J **75**
Kensington High St. W8 . . . . .6J **75**
W14 . . . . .1G **85**
Kensington Ho. W8 . . . .5B **76**
W14 . . . . .5D **74**
Kensington Mall W8 . . . .2K **75**
Kensington Mans. SW5 . . . . .3K **85** (not continuous)
Kensington Palace 3B **76**
Kensington Pal. Gdns. W8 . . . . .2A **76**
Kensington Pk. Gdns. W11 . . . . .1G **75**
Kensington Pk. M. W11 . . . . .6G **65**
Kensington Pk. Rd. W11 . . . . .6G **65**
Kensington Pl. W8 . . . .3J **75**
Kensington Rd. SW7 . . .5B **76**
W8 . . . . .5B **76**
Kensington Sports Cen. 7D **64**
Kensington Sq. W8 . . . .5A **76**
Kensington Village W14 . . . . .2H **85**
Kensington W. W14 . . . .1E **84**
Kensworth Ho. EC1 . . . .7K **61**
Kent Ct. E2 . . . . .4D **62**
Kent Ho. SE1 . . . . .4D **92**
SW1 . . . . .4G **89**
W8 . . . . .5B **76**
W11 . . . . .2G **75**
Kentish Bldgs. SE1 . . . . .3J **81**
Kentish Town Rd. NW1 . . . . .2D **58**
Kentmere Ho. SE15 . . . .6J **93**
Kenton Ct. W14 . . . . . . .7G **75**
Kenton Ho. E1 . . . . .1K **73**
Kenton St. WC1 . . . . . . .1J **69**
Kent Pk. Ind. Est. SE15 . . . . .5G **93**
Kent Pas. NW1 . . . . . . .1J **67**
Kent St. E2 . . . . .4D **62**
Kent Ter. NW1 . . . . .7H **57**
Kent Yd. SW7 . . . . .5H **77**
Kenway Rd. SW5 . . . . . .2A **86**
Ken Wilson Ho. E2 . . . . .4F **63**
Kenwrick Ho. N1 . . . . . .3B **60**
Kenyon Mans. W14 . . . .5F **85**
Keppel Ho. SW3 . . . . . .2G **87**
Keppel Row SE1 . . . . . . .3G **81**
Keppel St. WC1 . . . . . . .3H **69**
Kerbela St. E2 . . . . .1E **72**
Kerrier Ho. SW10 . . . . . .7D **86**
Kerrington Ct. W10 . . . .2E **64**
W12 . . . . .4B **74**
Kerry Ho. E1 . . . . .5J **73**
Keslake Mans. NW10 . . .5C **54**
Keslake Rd. NW6 . . . . . .5C **54**
Keston Ho. SE17 . . . . . .3B **92**
Kestrel Ho. EC1 . . . . . . .6G **61**
Ketton Ho. W10 . . . . . . .2A **64**
Kevan Ho. SE5 . . . . .7G **91**
Keybridge Ho. SW8 . . . .6K **89**
Key Cl. E1 . . . . .2H **73**
Keyes Ho. SW1 . . . . . . .4G **89**
Keyham Ho. W2 . . . . . . .4J **65**
Key Ho. SE11 . . . . .5C **90**
Keyse Rd. SE1 . . . . .7C **82**
Keystone Cres. N1 . . . . .5K **59**
Keyworth Pl. SE1 . . . . . .6F **81**
Keyworth St. SE1 . . . . . .6F **81**
Kibworth St. SW8 . . . . . .7A **90**
Kiffen St. EC2 . . . . .1K **71**
KILBURN 4G **55**
Kilburn Bri. NW6 . . . . . .3K **55**
Kilburn Ga. NW6 . . . . . .4A **56**
Kilburn High Rd. NW6 . . . . .1H **55**
Kilburn Ho. NW6 . . . . . .5H **55**
Kilburn La. W9 . . . . .5F **55**
W10 . . . . .6D **54**
Kilburn Pk. Rd. NW6 . . . .7J **55**
Kilburn Pl. NW6 . . . . . . .3K **55**
Kilburn Priory NW6 . . . .3A **56**
Kilburn Sq. NW6 . . . . . . .2J **55**
Kilburn Va. NW6 . . . . . .3A **56**
Kilburn Va. Est. NW6 . . .2K **55**
Kildare Ct. W2 . . . . .5K **65**
Kildare Gdns. W2 . . . . . .5K **65**
Kildare Ter. W2 . . . . . . .5K **65**
Killick St. N1 . . . . .4A **60**
Kilmarsh Rd. W6 . . . . . .1A **84**
Kilmuir Ho. SW1 . . . . . .2B **88**
Kilner Ho. SE11 . . . . . . .5C **90**
Kilravock St. W10 . . . . .7E **54**
Kimber Ct. *SE1 . . . . . . .6A 82* *(off Long La.)*
Kimberley Rd. NW6 . . . .2F **55**
Kimble Ho. NW8 . . . . . . .1H **67**
Kimbolton Ct. SW3 . . . .2G **87**
Kimbolton Row SW3 . . . .2G **87**
Kinburn St. SE16 . . . . . .4K **83**
Kincaid Rd. SE15 . . . . . .7G **93**
Kincardine Gdns. W9 . . .2J **65**
Kinder Ho. N1 . . . . .4K **61**
Kindersley Ho. E1 . . . . .6F **73**
Kinder St. E1 . . . . .6G **73**
King & Queen St. SE17 . . . . .3H **91**
King Charles I Island *WC2 . . . . .2J 79* *(off Trafalgar Sq.)*
King Charles Ct. SE17 . . .5E **90**
King Charles Ho. SW6 . . . . .7B **86**
King Charles St. SW1 . . .4H **79**
King Charles Ter. E1 . . . .1H **83**
King David La. E1 . . . . . .7J **73**
King Edward III M. SE16 . . . . .5H **83**
King Edward Bldg. EC1 . . . . .5F **71**
King Edward Mans. E8 . . . . .3H **63**
King Edwards Mans. SW6 . . . . .7J **85**
King Edward's Rd. E9 . . .2H **63**
King Edward St. EC1 . . . .5G **71**
King Edward Wlk. SE1 . . . . .6D **80**
Kingfisher Ct. SE1 . . . . .5H **81**
Kingfisher Ho. W14 . . . .6G **75**
King George IV Ct. *SE17 . . . . .3J 91* *(off Dawes St.)*
King George VI Memorial 3G **79**
Kingham Cl. W11 . . . . . .4D **74**
King Henry's Reach W6 . . . . .5B **84**
King Henry's Rd. NW3 . . . . .1F **57**
King Henry's Stairs E1 . . . . .3H **83**
King Henry Ter. E1 . . . . .1H **83**
Kinghorn St. EC1 . . . . . .3F **71**
King James Ct. SE1 . . . .5F **81**
King James St. SE1 . . . .5F **81**
King John Ct. EC2 . . . . .1B **72**
Kinglake Est. SE17 . . . . .3B **92**
Kinglake St. SE17 . . . . .4A **92** (not continuous)
Kingly Ct. W1 . . . . .7F **69**
Kingly St. W1 . . . . .6E **68**
Kings Arms Ct. E1 . . . . .4E **72**
Kings Arms Yd. EC2 . . . .5J **71**
King's Bench St. SE1 . . .4F **81**
King's Bench Wlk. EC4 . . . . .7D **70**
Kingsbridge Rd. W10 . . .5B **64**
Kings Coll. Ct. NW3 . . . .1H **57**
King's College London
Chelsea Campus . . .4F 87 *(off Chelsea Sq.)*
(St Thomas' Campus)
Lambeth Pal. Rd. 7K **79**
St Thomas' House 6A **80**
Strand Campus 7B **70**
Waterloo Campus 3C **80**
King's Coll. Rd. NW3 . . .1G **57**
Kingscote St. EC4 . . . . . .7E **70**
Kings Ct. N7 . . . . .1A **60**
NW8 . . . . .3J **57**
SE1 . . . . .4G **81**
Kings Ct. Nth. SW3 . . . .4G **87**
Kings Ct. Sth. SW3 . . . .5G **87**
KING'S CROSS 6J **59**
King's Cross Bri. N1 . . .6K **59**
King's Cross Rd. WC1 . . .6A **60**
Kingsdale Gdns. W11 . . .3D **74**
Kingsdown Cl. SE16 . . . .4H **93**
W10 . . . . .6D **64**
King's Gdns. NW6 . . . . . .1K **55**
Kingsgate Mans. WC1 . . . . .4A **70**
Kingsgate Pde. SW1 . . . .7F **79**
Kingsgate Pl. NW6 . . . . .1J **55**
Kingsgate Rd. NW6 . . . . .1J **55**
King's Gro. SE15 . . . . . .7H **93**
Kings Head Theatre 2E **60**
King's Head Yd. SE1 . . . .3J **81**
Kingshill SE17 . . . . .2H **91**
Kingshold Rd. E9 . . . . . .1K **63**
Kings Ho. SW8 . . . . .7K **89**
SW10 . . . . .6E 86 *(off Park Wlk.)*
King's Ho. Studios SW10 . . . . .6E **86**
Kingsland NW8 . . . . .3H **57**
Kingsland Rd. E2 . . . . . .6B **62**
E8 . . . . .2B **62**
Kingsley Flats SE1 . . . . .1A **92**
Kingsley Ho. SW3 . . . . . .6F **87**
Kingsley Mans. W14 . . . .5F **85**
Kingsley M. E1 . . . . .1H **83**
W8 . . . . .7B **76**
Kingsley Rd. NW6 . . . . .2H **55**
Kings Mall W6 . . . . .2A **84**
Kings Mans. SW3 . . . . . .6G **87**
King's M. WC1 . . . . .2B **70**
Kingsmill NW8 . . . . .4F **57**
Kingsmill Ho. *SW3 . . . . .3H 87* *(off Cale St.)*
Kingsmill Ter. NW8 . . . .4F **57**
Kingsnorth Ho. W10 . . . .6D **64**
Kings Pde. NW10 . . . . . .3B **54**
King's Pl. SE1 . . . . .5G **81**
King Sq. EC1 . . . . .7G **61**
Kings Reach Twr. SE1 . . .2D **80**
King's Rd. SW3 . . . . . . .6E **86**
SW6 . . . . .7B **86**
SW10 . . . . .7D **86**
King's Scholars' Pas. SW1 . . . . .7E **78**
King Stairs Cl. SE16 . . . .4H **83**
King's Ter. NW1 . . . . . .3E **58**
Kingston Ho. NW6 . . . . .1F **55**
Kingston Ho. E. SW7 . . . .5G **77**
Kingston Ho. Nth. SW7 . . . . .5G **77**
Kingston Ho. Sth. SW7 . . . . .5G **77**
Kingstown St. NW1 . . . .2A **58** (not continuous)
King St. EC2 . . . . .6H **71**
SW1 . . . . .3F **79**
W6 . . . . .2A **84**
WC2 . . . . .7J **69**
Kings Wlk. Shop. Cen. SW3 . . . . .3J **87**
Kingsway WC2 . . . . .5A **70**
Kingsway Mans. WC1 . . . .4A **70**
Kingsway Pl. EC1 . . . . . .1D **70**
Kings Wharf E8 . . . . . . .2B **62**
Kingswood E2 . . . . .5J **63**
Kingswood Av. NW6 . . . .3E **54**
Kingswood Cl. SW8 . . . .7K **89**
Kingswood Ct. NW6 . . . .1K **55**
Kington Ho. NW6 . . . . . .3B **56**
Kingward Ho. E1 . . . . . .3E **72**
King William St. EC4 . . .6K **71**
Kingwood Rd. SW6 . . . .7E **84**
Kinnerton Pl. Nth. SW1 . . . . .5K **77**
Kinnerton Pl. Sth. SW1 . . . . .5K **77**
Kinnerton St. SW1 . . . . .5A **78**
Kinnerton Yd. SW1 . . . . .5K **77**
Kinnoul Rd. W6 . . . . . . .5E **84**
Kinsham Ho. E2 . . . . . . .1F **73**
Kintore Way SE1 . . . . . .1C **92**
Kipling Est. SE1 . . . . . . .5K **81**
Kipling Ho. SE5 . . . . . . .7H **91**
Kipling St. SE1 . . . . .5K **81**
Kirby Est. SE16 . . . . . . .6H **83**
Kirby Gro. SE1 . . . . .4A **82**
Kirby St. EC1 . . . . .3D **70**
Kirkeby Ho. EC1 . . . . . .3C **70**
Kirkman Pl. W1 . . . . . . .4G **69**
Kirkstall Ho. SW1 . . . . .3C **88**
Kirkstone NW1 . . . . . . .6E **58**
Kirk St. WC1 . . . . .2B **70**
Kirkwall Pl. E2 . . . . . . .6K **63**
Kirtling St. SW8 . . . . . .7E **88**
Kirton Gdns. E2 . . . . . . .7D **62**
Kirwyn Way SE5 . . . . . .7F **91**
Kite Pl. E2 . . . . .6F **63**
Kitson Rd. SE5 . . . . . . .7J **91**
Kittiwake Ct. *SE1 . . . . .5H 81* *(off Gt. Dover St.)*
Kleine Wharf N1 . . . . . .3B **62**
Knaresborough Pl. SW5 . . . . .1A **86**
Knighten St. E1 . . . . . . .3G **83**
Knight Ho. SE17 . . . . . .2A **92**
Knightrider Ct. EC4 . . . .7G **71**
Knightrider St. EC4 . . . .7F **71**
Knights Arc. SW1 . . . . . .5J **77**
KNIGHTSBRIDGE 5H **77**
Knightsbridge SW1 . . . .5H **77**
SW7 . . . . .5H **77**
Knightsbridge Ct. SW1 . . . . .5K **77**
Knightsbridge Grn. SW1 . . . . .5J **77** (not continuous)
Knight's Ho. SW10 . . . . .7C **86**
Knight's Wlk. SE11 . . . . .2E **90** (not continuous)
Knivet Rd. SW6 . . . . . . .6J **85**
Knoll Ho. NW8 . . . . . . .4C **56**
Knolly's Ho. WC1 . . . . . .1J **69**
Knot Ho. SE1 . . . . .3C **82**
Knottisford St. E2 . . . . .6K **63**
Knowlden Ho. E1 . . . . . .7J **73**
Knox St. W1 . . . . .3J **67**
Knoyle Ho. W14 . . . . . . .6E **74**
Kotree Way SE1 . . . . . . .2F **93**
Kramer M. SW5 . . . . . . .4K **85**
Krupnik Pl. EC2 . . . . . . .1B **72**
Kylestrome Ho. SW1 . . . .2B **88**
Kynance M. SW7 . . . . . .7B **76**
Kynance Pl. SW7 . . . . . .7C **76**

L

Laburnum Ct. E2 . . . . . .3C **62**
SE16 . . . . .5K **83**
Laburnum St. E2 . . . . . .3C **62**
Lacine Ct. SE16 . . . . . . .4K **83**
Lackington St. EC2 . . . . .3K **71**
Lackland Ho. SE1 . . . . . .3D **92**
Lacland Ho. SW10 . . . . .7E **86**
Lacon Ho. WC1 . . . . . . .3A **70**
Ladbroke Cres. W11 . . . .6F **65**
Ladbroke Gdns. W11 . . . .7G **65**
Ladbroke Gro. W10 . . . . .1D **64**
W11 . . . . .5F **65**
Ladbroke Gro. Ho. W11 . . . . .1G **75**
Ladbroke M. W11 . . . . . .3F **75**
Ladbroke Rd. W11 . . . . . .2F **75**
Ladbroke Sq. W11 . . . . . .1G **75**
Ladbroke Ter. W11 . . . . .1H **75**
Ladbroke Wlk. W11 . . . . .2H **75**
Lady Margaret Ho. SE17 . . . . .5J **91**
Lady May Ho. SE5 . . . . .7G **91**
Lady Micos Almshouses E1 . . . . .5K **73**
LA Fitness
Aldgate 7D **72**
Bayswater 7A **66**
Bloomsbury 3A **70**
Leadenhall 6B **72**
Marylebone 3J **67**
Novello 7A **70**
Piccadilly 2G **79**
St Pauls 4G **71**
South Kensington 1G **87**
Victoria 6E **78**
Lafone St. SE1 . . . . .4C **82**
Lagonier Ho. EC1 . . . . . .7H **61**
Laird Ho. SE5 . . . . .7G **91**
Lake Ho. SE1 . . . . .5G **81**
Lakeside Rd. W14 . . . . .6C **74**
Lakeside Ter. EC2 . . . . .3H **71**
Lake Vw. Ct. SW1 . . . . .6D **78**
Laleham Ho. E2 . . . . . . .1C **72**
Lamberhurst Ho. SE15 . . . . .6K **93**
Lambert Jones M. EC2 . . . . .3G **71**
Lambert St. N1 . . . . .1C **60**
LAMBETH 7A **80**
Lambeth Bri. SE1 . . . . . .1K **89**
SW1 . . . . .1K **89**
Lambeth High St. SE1 . . . . .2A **90**
Lambeth Hill EC4 . . . . . .7G **71**
Lambeth Palace 7A **80**
Lambeth Pal. Rd. SE1 . . . . .7A **80**
Lambeth Rd. SE1 . . . . . .1A **90**
Lambeth Towers SE11 . . . . .7C **80**
Lambeth Wlk. SE11 . . . .7C **80** (not continuous)
Lamb La. E8 . . . . .1G **63**
Lambourne Gro. SE16 . . . . .3K **93**
Lambourne Ho. NW8 . . .3F **67**
Lamb's Bldgs. EC1 . . . . .2J **71**
Lamb's Conduit Pas. WC1 . . . . .3A **70**
Lamb's Conduit St. WC1 . . . . .2A **70** (not continuous)
Lambs Health & Fitness 2H **71**
Lamb's M. N1 . . . . .3E **60**
Lamb's Pas. EC1 . . . . . .3J **71**
Lamb St. E1 . . . . .3C **72**
Lambton Pl. W11 . . . . . .7H **65**
Lamb Wlk. SE1 . . . . .5A **82**
LAMDA 3D **84**
LAMDA Theatre 1J **85**
Lamlash St. SE11 . . . . . .1E **90**
Lamont Rd. SW10 . . . . . .6D **86**
Lamont Rd. Pas. SW10 . . . . .6E **86**
Lampern Sq. E2 . . . . . . .6F **63**
Lampeter Sq. W6 . . . . . .6E **84**
Lamplighter Cl. E1 . . . . .2J **73**
Lamp Office Ct. WC1 . . .2A **70**
Lanark Ho. SE1 . . . . . . .4E **92**
Lanark Mans. W9 . . . . . .1D **66**
W12 . . . . .5B **74**
Lanark M. W9 . . . . .7C **56**
Lanark Pl. W9 . . . . .1D **66**
Lanark Rd. W9 . . . . .5B **56**
Lancashire Ct. W1 . . . . .7C **68**
Lancaster Cl. N1 . . . . . . .1B **62**
W2 . . . . .1A **76**
Lancaster Ct. SW6 . . . . .7H **85**
W2 . . . . .7D **66**
Lancaster Ga. W2 . . . . . .1C **76**
Lancaster House 4F **79**
Lancaster Lodge W11 . . .5F **65**
Lancaster M. W2 . . . . . .7D **66**
Lancaster Pl. WC2 . . . . .7A **70**
Lancaster Rd. W11 . . . . .6E **64**
Lancaster St. SE1 . . . . . .5E **80**
Lancaster Ter. W2 . . . . .7E **66**
Lancaster Wlk. W2 . . . . .1D **76**
Lancefield Ct. W10 . . . . .5F **55**
Lancefield St. W10 . . . . .6G **55**
Lancelot Pl. SW7 . . . . . .5J **77**
Lancer Sq. W8 . . . . .4A **76**
Lanchester Ct. W2 . . . . .6J **67**
Lancing St. NW1 . . . . . .7G **59**
Lancresse Ct. N1 . . . . . .2A **62**
Landale Ho. SE16 . . . . . .6K **83**
Landmann Ho. SE16 . . . .2H **93**
Landmark Ho. W6 . . . . . .3A **84**
Landon Pl. SW1 . . . . . . .6J **77**
Landor Ho. W2 . . . . .4J **65**
Landrake NW1 . . . . .3F **59**
Landseer Ho. NW8 . . . . .1F **67**
SW1 . . . . .2H **89**
Landulph Ho. SE11 . . . . .3D **90**
Landward Ct. W1 . . . . . .5H **67**
Lane, The NW8 . . . . . . .4C **56**
Lanesborough Ct. *N1 . . .6A 62* *(off Fanshaw St.)*
Lanesborough Pl. SW1 . . . . .4B **78**
Laney Ho. EC1 . . . . .3C **70**
Lanfrey Pl. W14 . . . . . . .4G **85**
Langdale NW1 . . . . .6E **58**
Langdale Cl. SE17 . . . . .5G **91**
Langdale Ho. SW1 . . . . .4E **88**
Langdale St. E1 . . . . . . .6G **73**
Langdon Ct. EC1 . . . . . .5F **61**
Langdon Way SE1 . . . . . .2F **93**
Langford Cl. NW8 . . . . .4D **56**
Langford Ct. NW8 . . . . .4D **56**
Langford Pl. NW8 . . . . .4D **56**
Langham Mans. SW5 . . . .4A **86**
Langham Pl. W1 . . . . . .4D **68**
Langham St. W1 . . . . . .4D **68**
Langhorne Ct. NW8 . . . .2E **56**
Lang Ho. SW8 . . . . .7J **89**
Langland Ho. SE5 . . . . .7K **91**
Langler Rd. NW10 . . . . .5B **54**
Langley Ct. WC2 . . . . . .7J **69**

Langley Ho. W2 3K 65
Langley La. SW8 5K 89
Langley Mans. SW8 5A 90
Langley St. WC2 6J 69
Langmore Ho. E1 6F 73
Lang St. E1 1J 73
Langthorn Ct. EC2 5K 71
Langthorne St. SW6 7C 84
Langton Cl. WC1 1B 70
Langton Ho. SE11 1B 90
Langton Rd. SW9 7F 91
Langton St. SW10 6D 86
Langtry Pl. SW6 5K 85
Langtry Rd. NW8 3A 56
Langtry Wlk. NW8 2B 56
Lanhill Rd. W9 1J 65
Lannoy Point SW6 7F 85
Lansdowne Ct. W11 1F 75
Lansdowne Cres. W11 1F 75
Lansdowne Dr. E8 1F 63
Lansdowne Ho. W11 2G 75
Lansdowne M. W11 3G 75
Lansdowne Pl. SE1 6K 81
Lansdowne Ri. W11 1F 75
Lansdowne Rd. W11 1F 75
Lansdowne Row W1 2D 78
Lansdowne Ter. WC1 2K 69
Lansdowne Wlk. W11 2F 75
Lant Ho. SE1 5G 81
Lant St. SE1 4G 81
Lapford Cl. W9 1H 65
Lapwing Ct. *SE1* *5H 81*
(off Swan St.)
Lapworth Ct. W2 3B 66
Larch Ct. SE1 5A 82
W9 3J 65
Larch Ho. SE16 4K 83
W10 1E 64
Larcom St. SE17 2G 91
Larissa St. SE17 3K 91
Lark Row E2 3J 63
Larnach Rd. W6 6C 84
Lascelles Ho. NW1 2H 67
Latham Ct. SW5 2J 85
Latimer Ho. W11 1H 75
Latimer Ind. Est. W10 5A 64
Latimer Pl. W10 5B 64
Latimer Rd. W10 4A 64
(not continuous)
Latona Rd. SE15 6E 92
Latvia Ct. SE17 4H 91
Latymer Ct. W6 2D 84
Lauderdale Mans. W9 7A 56
(not continuous)
Lauderdale Pde. W9 7A 56
Lauderdale Pl. EC2 3G 71
Lauderdale Rd. W9 7A 56
Lauderdale Twr. EC2 3G 71
Laud St. SE11 3A 90
Laugan Wlk. SE17 3H 91
Launcelot St. SE1 5C 80
Launceston Pl. W8 6C 76
Laundry La. N1 1G 61
Laundry Rd. W6 6E 84
Laurence Pountney Hill EC4 7J 71
Laurence Pountney La. EC4 1J 81
Laurie Ho. SE1 7F 81
W8 3J 75
Lauriston Ho. E9 1K 63
Lauriston Rd. E9 1K 63
Lavender Cl. SW3 6F 87
Lavender Gro. E8 1D 62
Lavendon Ho. NW8 1H 67
Laverton M. SW5 2B 86
Laverton Pl. SW5 2B 86
Lavina Gro. N1 4A 60
Lavington St. SE1 3F 81
Lawes Ho. W10 6G 55
Lawford Rd. N1 1A 62
Lawfords Wharf NW1 1E 58
Lawn La. SW8 5K 89
Lawrence Ho. SW1 2H 89
Lawrence La. EC2 6H 71
Lawrence Mans. SW3 6G 87
Lawrence Pl. N1 2K 59
Lawrence St. SW3 6G 87
Lawson Ho. W12 7A 64
Law St. SE1 6K 81
Laxfield Ct. E8 3F 63
Laxford Ho. SW1 2B 88
Laxley Cl. SE5 7F 91
Laxton Pl. NW1 1D 68
Layard Rd. SE16 1H 93
Layard Sq. SE16 1H 93
Laystall Ct. WC1 2C 70
Laystall St. EC1 2C 70
Layton's Bldgs. SE1 4J 81
Lazenby Ct. WC2 7J 69
Leadenhall Mkt. EC3 6A 72
Leadenhall Pl. EC3 6A 72
Leadenhall St. EC3 6A 72
Lea Ho. NW8 2G 67
Leake Ct. SE1 5B 80
Leake St. SE1 4B 80
(not continuous)
Leamington Ho. W11 4H 65
Leamington Rd. Vs. W11 4H 65
Leamore St. W6 2A 84
Leary Ho. SE11 4B 90
Leatherdale St. E1 1K 73
(Harpley Sq.)
E1 7C 63
(Portelet Rd.)
Leather La. EC1 3C 70
(not continuous)
Leathermarket, The SE1 5A 82
Leathermarket Ct. SE1 5A 82
Leathermarket St. SE1 5A 82
Leather Rd. SE16 2K 93
Leather St. E1 7K 73
Lebus Ho. NW8 5G 57
Lecky St. SW7 3E 86
Le Cordon Bleu London Culinary Arts Institute *4B 68*
(off Marylebone La.)
Ledam Ho. EC1 3C 70
Ledbury Ho. W11 6H 65
Ledbury M. Nth. W11 6J 65
Ledbury M. W. W11 7J 65
Ledbury Rd. W11 5H 65
Ledbury St. SE15 7F 93
Leeds Ct. EC1 1E 70
Lee Ho. EC2 4H 71
Leeke St. WC1 6A 60
Lees Ct. W1 7A 68
Lees Ho. SE17 4K 91
Lees Pl. W1 7A 68
Lee St. E8 2C 62
Leeve Ho. W10 7G 55
Leeward Ct. E1 2F 83
Leeward Ho. *N1* *3A 62*
(off New Era Est.)
Leff Ho. NW6 1F 55
Lefroy Ho. SE1 5G 81
Leicester Ct. W9 3J 65
WC2 7H 69
Leicester Flds. WC2 1H 79
Leicester Pl. WC2 7H 69
Leicester Sq. WC2 1H 79
Leicester St. WC2 7H 69
Leigh Gdns. NW10 5A 54
Leigh Pl. EC1 3C 70
Leigh St. WC1 1J 69
Leighton Gdns. NW10 4A 54
Leighton Ho. SW1 2H 89
Leighton House Art Gallery & Mus. 6H 75
Leighton Mans. W14 5F 85
Leinster Gdns. W2 6C 66
Leinster M. W2 1C 76
Leinster Pl. W2 6C 66
Leinster Sq. W2 6K 65
(not continuous)
Leinster Ter. W2 7C 66
Leitch Ho. NW8 1E 56
Leith Mans. W9 7A 56
Leith Yd. NW6 2J 55
Lelitia Cl. E8 3E 62
Leman Pas. E1 6E 72
Leman St. E1 6D 72
Le Moal Ho. E1 4K 73
Lena Gdns. W6 7B 74
Len Freeman Pl. SW6 6G 85
Lenham Ho. SE1 6K 81
Lennox Gdns. SW1 7J 77
Lennox Gdns. M. SW1 7J 77
Lenthall Ho. SW1 4F 89
Lenthall Rd. E8 1D 62
Len Williams Ct. NW6 5K 55
Leonard Ct. W8 6J 75
WC1 1H 69
Leonard St. EC2 1K 71
Leonora Ho. W9 1C 66
Leontine Cl. SE15 7F 93
Leopards Ct. EC1 3C 70
Leopold Bldgs. E2 6C 62
Leopold M. E9 2J 63
Leopold Wlk. SE11 4A 90
Leo St. SE15 7H 93
Leo Yd. EC1 2F 71
Leroy St. SE1 7A 82
Lerry Cl. W14 5H 85
Lesley Ct. SW1 7G 79
Leslie Ho. SW8 7J 89
Leslie Prince Ct. SE5 7J 91
Letchmore Ho. W10 2A 64
Letterstone Rd. SW6 7G 85
Leverett St. SW3 1H 87
Leverington Pl. N1 7A 62
Leverstock Ho. SW3 3H 87
Lever St. EC1 7F 61
Levita Ho. NW1 6H 59
(not continuous)
Lewes Ho. SE1 4B 82
SE15 6F 93
Lewis Ct. SE16 3H 93
Lewisham Lions Cen. 4K 93
Lewisham St. SW1 5H 79
Lewis Silkin Ho. SE15 5K 93
Lexham Gdns. W8 1K 85
Lexham Gdns. M. W8 7B 76
Lexham Ho. W8 1A 86
Lexham M. W8 1K 85
Lexham Wlk. W8 7B 76
Lexington Apartments EC1 1J 71
Lexington St. W1 6F 69
Leybourne Ho. SE15 6K 93
Leybourne Rd. NW1 1D 58
Leybourne St. NW1 1C 58
Leyden St. E1 4C 72
Leysdown Ho. SE17 3B 92
Liberty Ho. E1 7E 72
Library Mans. W12 4A 74
Library Pl. E1 7H 73
Library St. SE1 5E 80
Lickey Ho. W14 5H 85
Liddell Gdns. NW10 4A 54
Lidlington Pl. NW1 5F 59
Light Horse Ct. SW3 4A 88
Ligonier St. E2 1C 72
Lilac Pl. SE11 2A 90
Lilestone Ho. NW8 1F 67
Lilestone St. NW8 1G 67
Lilley Cl. E1 3F 83
Lillie Mans. SW6 6G 85
Lillie Rd. SW6 6D 84
Lillie Road Fitness Cen. 6D 84
Lillie Yd. SW6 5K 85
Lillington Gdns. Est. SW1 2F 89
Lily Cl. W14 2D 84
(not continuous)
Lily Pl. EC1 3D 70
Limeburner La. EC4 6E 70
Lime Cl. E1 2F 83
Lime Gro. W12 4A 74
Limerston St. SW10 5D 86
Limes, The W2 1K 75
Limes Ct. NW6 1E 54
Lime St. EC3 7A 72
Lime St. Pas. EC3 7A 72
Linacre Ct. W6 3D 84
Linale Ho. N1 5J 61
Lincoln Ho. SE5 7D 90
SW3 5J 77
Lincoln M. NW6 2G 55
Lincolns Inn Flds. WC2 5A 70
Lincoln's Inn Hall 5B 70
Lincoln St. SW3 2J 87
Linden Av. NW10 5C 54
Linden Ct. W12 3A 74
Linden Gdns. W2 1K 75
Linden M. W2 1K 75
Lindley Est. SE15 7F 93
Lindley Ho. E1 3J 73
SE15 7E 92
Lindley St. E1 3J 73
Lindsay Ho. SW7 6C 76
Lindsay Sq. SW1 3H 89
Lindsey M. N1 1H 61
Lindsey St. EC1 3F 71
Linfield WC1 7A 60
Linford Ho. E2 2F 63
Lingfield Ho. SE1 5F 81
Linhope St. NW1 1J 67
Link Ho. W10 6D 64
Link Rd. E1 7E 72
Links Yd. E1 3D 72
Linkwood Wlk. NW1 1H 59
Linley Sambourne House 5J 75
Linnell Ho. E1 3C 72
Linsey St. SE16 1E 92
(not continuous)
Linslade Ho. E2 3F 63
NW8 1H 67
Linstead Hall SW7 6F 77
Lintaine Cl. W6 6F 85
Linton Ct. NW1 1F 59
Linton St. N1 3H 61
(not continuous)
Lion Ct. E1 7K 73
N1 3A 60
SE1 3B 82
Lionel Ho. W10 3E 64
Lionel Mans. W14 7C 74
Lionel M. W10 3E 64
Lion Mills E2 5F 63
Lisgar Ter. W14 1G 85
Liskeard Ho. SE11 3D 90
Lisle St. WC2 7H 69
Lisson Grn. Est. NW8 1G 67
LISSON GROVE 3H 67
Lisson Gro. NW1 1G 67
NW8 7F 57
Lisson Ho. NW1 3G 67
Lisson St. NW1 3G 67
Lister Ho. E1 3F 73
Lister Lodge W9 3K 65
Listowel Cl. SW9 7D 90
Litchfield St. WC2 7H 69
Lit. Albany St. NW1 7D 58
(Albany St.)
NW1 1D 68
(Longford St.)
Little Angel Theatre 2F 61
Lit. Argyll St. W1 6E 68
Lit. Boltons, The SW5 3B 86
SW10 3B 86
Littlebourne Ho. SE17 3B 92
Little Britain EC1 4F 71
Lit. Chelsea Ho. SW10 6D 86
Lit. Chester St. SW1 6C 78
Little Cloisters SW1 6J 79
Little Coll. La. EC4 7J 71
Little Coll. St. SW1 6J 79
Lit. Dean's Yd. SW1 6J 79
Lit. Dorrit Ct. SE1 4H 81
Lit. Edward St. NW1 6D 58
Lit. Essex St. WC2 7C 70
Lit. George St. SW1 5J 79
Lit. London Ct. SE1 5D 82
Lit. Marlborough St. W1 6E 68
Lit. Newport St. WC2 7H 69
Lit. New St. EC4 5D 70
Lit. Portland St. W1 5D 68
Lit. Russell St. WC1 4J 69
Lit. St James's St. SW1 3E 78
Little Sanctuary SW1 5J 79
Lit. Smith St. SW1 6H 79
Lit. Somerset St. E1 6C 72
Lit. Titchfield St. W1 4E 68
Littleton Ho. SW1 4E 88
Lit. Trinity La. EC4 7H 71
Little Turnstile WC1 4A 70
Livermere Ct. E8 2D 62
Livermere Rd. E8 2C 62
Liverpool Gro. SE17 4H 91
Liverpool Rd. N1 1D 60
Liverpool St. EC2 4A 72
Livesey Mus. for Children 6G 93
Livesey Pl. SE15 5F 93
Livingstone Ho. SE5 7G 91
Livingstone Lodge W9 3K 65
Livingstone Mans. W14 5F 85
Livingwell Sports Club
Greville Rd. *4A 56*
(within Regents Plaza)
Livonia St. W1 6F 69
Lizard St. EC1 7H 61
Lizmans Ter. W8 7K 75
Llewellyn St. SE16 5F 83
Lloyd Baker St. WC1 7B 60
(not continuous)
Lloyd's Av. EC3 6B 72
Lloyds' Building 6A 72
Lloyd Sq. WC1 6C 60
Lloyd's Row EC1 7D 60
Lloyd St. WC1 6C 60
Lloyds Wharf SE1 4D 82
Loanda Cl. E8 2C 62
Lochaline St. W6 5B 84
Lochmore Ho. SW1 2B 88
Lockbridge Ct. W9 3J 65
Locksfields SE17 2K 91
Lockwood Ho. SE11 6C 90
Lockwood Sq. SE16 7G 83
Lockyer Est. SE1 4K 81
(not continuous)
Lockyer Ho. SW8 7H 89
Lockyer St. SE1 5K 81
Loddiges Ho. E9 1J 63
Loddon Ho. NW8 2F 67
Lodge Rd. NW8 1F 67
Loftie St. SE16 5F 83
Lofting Ho. N1 1D 60
Lofting Rd. N1 1B 60
Loftus Road 2A 74
Loftus Rd. W12 3A 74
Loftus Vs. W12 3A 74
Logan M. W8 1J 85
Logan Pl. W8 1J 85
Lohmann Ho. SE11 5C 90
Lolesworth Cl. E1 4D 72
Lollard St. SE11 1B 90
(not continuous)
Loman St. SE1 4F 81
Lomas St. E1 3F 73
Lombard Ct. EC3 7K 71
Lombard La. EC4 6D 70
Lombard St. EC3 6K 71
Lombardy Pl. W2 1A 76
Lomond Gro. SE5 7J 91
Loncroft Rd. SE5 5B 92
Londinium Twr. E1 7D 72
London Apollo 3B 84
London Aquarium 4A 80
London Bri. EC4 2K 81
SE1 2K 81
London Bri. St. SE1 3K 81
London Bri. Wlk. SE1 2K 81
London Business School 1J 67
London Canal Mus. 4K 59
London City College 3C 80
London Coliseum *1J 79*
(off St Martin's La.)
London College of Fashion, The
Hackney 1H 63
St Luke's 2G 71
London Dungeon 3K 81
London Eye 4A 80
London Flds. E. Side E8 1G 63
London Flds. W. Side E8 1F 63
London Fire Brigade Mus. 4G 81
London Fruit Exchange E1 4C 72
London Guildhall University
Coke St. 5F 73
London Ho. NW8 4H 57
WC1 1A 70
London La. E8 1H 63
London Metropolitan University
Goulston St. 5C 72
Jewry St. 6C 72
Manningtree St. 5E 72
Minories 7C 72
Moorgate 4K 71
London M. W2 6F 67
London Palladium 6E 68
London Rd. SE1 6E 80
London School of Economics & Political Science, The 6B 70
London South Bank University
London Rd. 6F 81
New Kent Rd. 7H 81
London South Bank University Sports Cen. 6F 81
London Stock Exchange 5F 71
London St. EC3 7B 72
W2 5E 66
London Telecom Tower, The 3E 68
London Television Cen., The 2C 80
London Ter. E2 5E 62
London Transport Mus. 7K 69
London Underwriting Cen. EC3 7B 72
London Wall EC2 4H 71
London Wall Bldgs. EC2 4K 71
London Wharf E2 3G 63
London Wildlife Trust 3H 59
London Zoo 4A 58
Long Acre WC2 7J 69
Longfellow Way SE1 2D 92
Longfield Est. SE1 1D 92
Longford Ho. E1 5J 73
Longford St. NW1 1D 68
Longhope Cl. SE15 6B 92
Longhurst Ho. W10 6G 55
Longland Ct. SE1 3E 92
Longlands Ct. W11 7H 65
Long La. EC1 4F 71
SE1 5J 81
Longleat Ho. SW1 3G 89
Longley St. SE1 2E 92
Longman Ho. E2 5K 63
E8 3D 62
Longmoore St. SW1 2E 88
Longmore Gdns. Est. SW1 2F 89
Longridge Ho. SE1 7H 81
Longridge Rd. SW5 2J 85
Long's Ct. WC2 1H 79
Longshott Ct. SW5 2J 85
Longstone Ct. *SE1* *5H 81*
(off Gt. Dover St.)
Long St. E2 6C 62
Longville Rd. SE11 1E 90
Long Wlk. SE1 6B 82
Long Yd. WC1 2A 70
Lonsdale Ho. W11 6H 65
Lonsdale M. W11 6H 65
Lonsdale Pl. N1 1D 60
Lonsdale Rd. NW6 4G 55
W11 6G 65
Lonsdale Sq. N1 1D 60
Lonsdale Yd. W11 1J 75
Lorden Wlk. E2 7E 62
Lord Hills Bri. W2 4B 66
Lord Hills Rd. W2 3B 66
Lord North St. SW1 7J 79
Lord Roberts M. SW6 7A 86
Lord's Cricket Ground 7F 57
Lordship Pl. SW3 6G 87
Lords Vw. NW8 7F 57
Lorenzo St. WC1 6A 60
Loris Rd. W6 6B 74
Lorne Cl. NW8 7H 57
Lorne Gdns. W11 4D 74
Lorrimore Rd. SE17 6F 91
Lorrimore Sq. SE17 5F 91
Lorton Ho. NW6 3K 55
Lothbury EC2 5J 71
Lothrop St. W10 6E 54
Lots Rd. SW10 7C 86
Loudoun Rd. NW8 1D 56
Loughborough St. SE11 3B 90
Louisa Gdns. E1 2K 73
Louisa St. E1 2K 73
Louise De Marillac Ho. E1 4J 73
Lovat La. EC3 7A 72
(not continuous)
Lovegrove St. SE1 4F 93
Lovelace Ho. E8 2D 62
Love La. EC2 5H 71
Lovelinch Cl. SE15 6K 93
Lovell Ho. E8 2E 62
Lovers' Wlk. W1 2A 78
Lowder Ho. E1 2H 83
Lowell Ho. SE5 7H 91
Lwr. Addison Gdns. W14 5E 74
Lwr. Belgrave St. SW1 7C 78
Lwr. Clarendon Wlk. W11 6E 64
Lwr. Grosvenor Pl. SW1 6D 78
Lwr. James St. W1 7F 69
Lwr. John St. W1 7F 69
Lower Mall W6 3A 84
Lower Marsh SE1 5C 80
Lwr. Merton Ri. NW3 1G 57
Lower Rd. SE1 4C 80
SE16 5J 83
(not continuous)
Lwr. Robert St. WC2 1K 79
Lwr. Sloane St. SW1 2A 88
Lwr. Thames St. EC3 1K 81
Lowerwood Ct. W11 6F 65
Lowndes Cl. SW1 7B 78
Lowndes Ct. SW1 6K 77
W1 6E 68
Lowndes Lodge SW1 6K 77
Lowndes Pl. SW1 7A 78
Lowndes Sq. SW1 5K 77
Lowndes St. SW1 6K 77
Lowood Ho. E1 7J 73
Lowood St. E1 7H 73
Lowry Ct. SE16 3H 93
Lowther Gdns. SW7 6F 77
Lowther Ho. E8 2C 62
SW1 4F 89
Loxham St. WC1 7K 59
LSO St Lukes 1H 71
Lucan Ho. N1 3K 61
Lucan Pl. SW3 2G 87
Lucas Ho. SW10 7B 86
Lucerne M. W8 2K 75
Lucey Rd. SE16 7E 82
Lucey Way SE16 7E 82
Lucy Brown Ho. SE1 3H 81
Ludgate B'way. EC4 6E 70
Ludgate Cir. EC4 6E 70
Ludgate Hill EC4 6E 70
Ludgate Sq. EC4 6F 71
Ludlow St. EC1 1G 71
Ludwell Ho. W14 6E 74
Luke Ho. E1 6G 73
Luke St. EC2 1A 72
Lukin St. E1 6K 73
Lullingstone Ho. SE15 6K 93
Lulworth NW1 1G 59
SE17 3J 91
Lulworth Ct. N1 1B 62
Lulworth Ho. SW8 7A 90
Lumley Ct. WC2 1K 79
Lumley Flats SW1 3A 88
Lumley St. W1 6B 68
Lumsdon NW8 3B 56
Luna Ho. SE16 4F 83
Luntley Pl. E1 4E 72
Lupino Ct. SE11 1B 90
Lupin Point SE1 5D 82
Lupus St. SW1 5D 88
Lurgan Av. W6 5D 84
Luscombe Way SW8 7J 89
Luton St. NW8 2F 67
Lutyens Ho. SW1 4E 88
Luxborough Ho. W1 3A 68
Luxborough St. W1 2A 68
Luxborough Twr. W1 3A 68
Luxemburg Gdns. W6 1C 84
Luxford St. SE16 2K 93
Lyall M. SW1 7A 78
Lyall M. W. SW1 7A 78
Lyall St. SW1 7A 78
Lyceum Theatre 7A 70
Lydford NW1 3F 59
Lydford Rd. W9 1H 65
Lygon Ho. E2 6D 62
Lygon Pl. SW1 7C 78
Lyly Ho. SE1 7K 81
Lyme St. NW1 1E 58
Lyme Ter. NW1 1E 58
Lympstone Gdns. SE15 7F 93
Lynbrook Gro. SE15 7B 92

Lyndhurst Ct. NW8 3E 56
Lynne Ct. NW6 1A 56
Lynn Ho. SE15 6G 93
Lynton Est. SE1 2E 92
Lynton Ho. W2 6C 66
Lynton Mans. SE1 6C 80
Lynton Rd. NW6 3H 55
SE1 2D 92
Lyon Ho. NW8 2G 67
Lyons Pl. NW8 2E 66
Lyon St. N1 1A 60
Lyons Wlk. W14 1E 84
Lyric Ct. E8 1D 62 (off Holly St.)
Lyric Theatre
Hammersmith 2A 84
Westminster 7G 69
Lysander Ho. E2 5G 63
Lysia Ct. SW6 7B 84
Lysia St. SW6 7C 84
Lytham St. SE17 4J 91
Lyttelton Cl. NW3 1G 57
Lyttelton Theatre 2C 80 (in National Theatre)

M

Mabledon Ct. WC1 7H 59
Mabledon Pl. WC1 7H 59
Mablethorpe Rd. SW6 7E 84
McAuley Cl. SE1 6C 80
Macauley Ho. W10 3E 64
Macbeth Ho. N1 4A 62
Macbeth St. W6 3A 84
Macclesfield Ho. EC1 7G 61
Macclesfield Rd. EC1 6G 61
Macclesfield St. W1 7H 69
McCoid Way SE1 5G 81
Mace Cl. E1 2G 83
Mace St. E2 5K 63
Macfarland Gro. SE15 7B 92
Macfarlane Rd. W12 3A 74
Macfarren Pl. NW1 2B 68
Macfarron Ho. W10 6F 55
McGlashon Ho. E1 2E 72
McGregor Ct. N1 6B 62
McGregor Rd. W11 4G 65
McIndoe Ct. N1 2J 61
Macintosh Ho. W1 3B 68
McIntosh Ho. SE16 2K 93
Mackennal St. NW8 5H 57
Macklin St. WC2 5K 69
Mackonochie Ho. EC1 3C 70
Mack's Rd. SE16 1F 93
Mackworth Ho. NW1 6E 58
Mackworth St. NW1 6E 58
McLaren Ho. SE1 5E 80
McLeod's M. SW7 7B 76
Macleod St. SE17 4H 91
Maclise Ho. SW1 2J 89
Maclise Rd. W14 7E 74
Macmillan Ho. NW8 7H 57
Macnamara Ho. SW10 7E 86
Macready Ho. W1 4H 67
Macroom Ho. W9 6H 55
Macroom Rd. W9 6H 55
Mac's Pl. EC4 5D 70
Madame Tussaud's 2A 68
Maddocks Ho. E1 7H 73
Maddock Way SE17 6F 91
Maddox St. W1 7D 68
Madison, The SE1 4J 81
Madrigal La. SE5 7F 91
Madron St. SE17 3B 92
Magazine Ga. W2 2H 77
Magdalen Pas. E1 7D 72
Magdalen St. SE1 3A 82
Magee St. SE11 5C 90
Magnin Cl. E8 2F 63
Magnolia Lodge W8 7A 76
Magpie All. EC4 6D 70
Magri Wlk. E1 4J 73
Maguire St. SE1 4D 82
Maida Av. W2 3D 66
MAIDA HILL 2H 65
MAIDA VALE 7A 56
Maida Va. W9 4A 56
Maiden La. NW1 1H 59
SE1 3H 81
WC2 1K 79
Maidstone Bldgs. M. SE1 3H 81
Mail Coach Yd. E2 6B 62
Maismore St. SE15 6F 93
Maitland Ct. W2 7E 66
Maitland Ho. E2 4J 63 (off Waterloo Gdns.)
SW1 5E 88
Major Rd. SE16 6F 83
Makins St. SW3 2H 87
Malam Ct. SE11 2C 90
Malcolm Ho. N1 5A 62
Malcolm Pl. E2 1J 73
Malcolm Rd. E1 1J 73
Malcolmson Ho. SW1 4G 89
Maldon Cl. N1 2G 61
Malet Pl. WC1 2G 69
Malet St. WC1 2G 69
Mall, The SW1 4F 79
Mallard Cl. NW6 3K 55
Mallard Ho. NW8 5G 57
Mall Chambers W8 2K 75
Mall Galleries 2H 79
Mall Gallery WC2 6J 69 (in Thomas Neal's Shop. Mall)
Mallon Gdns. E1 4D 72
Mallord St. SW3 5F 87
Mallory Bldgs. EC1 2F 71
Mallory St. NW8 1H 67
Mallow St. EC1 1J 71
Mall Rd. W6 3A 84
Mall Vs. W6 3A 84
Malmesbury E2 5J 63
Malmsey Ho. SE11 3B 90
Malta St. EC1 1F 71
Maltby St. SE1 5C 82
Maltings Pl. SE1 5B 82
Malton M. W10 5E 64
Malton Rd. W10 5E 64
Maltravers St. WC2 7B 70
Malt St. SE1 5E 92
Malvern Cl. W10 4G 65
Malvern Ct. SW7 1F 87
Malvern M. NW6 6J 55
Malvern Pl. NW6 6H 55
Malvern Rd. E8 1E 62
NW6 5H 55 (not continuous)
Malvern Ter. N1 2C 60
Manbre Rd. W6 5B 84
Manchester Dr. W10 2E 64
Manchester Ho. SE17 3H 91
Manchester M. W1 4A 68
Manchester Sq. W1 5B 68
Manchester St. W1 4A 68
Manciple St. SE1 5J 81
Mandela Cl. W12 1A 74
Mandela Ho. E2 7F 62
Mandela St. NW1 2F 59
SW9 7C 90 (not continuous)
Mandela Way SE1 1A 92
Manderley W14 6G 75
Mandeville Ho. SE1 3D 92
Mandeville Pl. W1 5B 68
Manette St. W1 6H 69
Manitoba Ct. SE16 5K 83
Manley Ho. SE11 3C 90
Manley St. NW1 2A 58
Manneby Prior N1 5B 60
Manningford Cl. EC1 6E 60
Manning Ho. W11 6F 65
Manningtree St. E1 5E 72
Manny Shinwell Ho. SW6 6H 85
Manor Ct. SW3 4H 87
Manor Est. SE16 2G 93
Manor Gro. SE15 6J 93
Manor Ho. NW1 3H 67
Manor Ho. Ct. W9 2C 66
Manor Ho. Dr. NW6 1C 54
Manor M. NW6 4K 55
Manor Pl. SE17 4F 91
Manresa Rd. SW3 4G 87
Mansell St. E1 6D 72
Mansfield Ct. E2 3D 62
Mansfield Ho. N1 3A 62 (off New Era Est.)
Mansfield M. W1 4C 68
Mansfield St. W1 4C 68
Mansford St. E2 5F 63
Mansion House 6J 71
Mansion Ho. Pl. EC4 6J 71
Mansion Ho. St. EC4 6J 71
Mansions, The SW5 3A 86
Manson M. SW7 2D 86
Manson Pl. SW7 2E 86
Manston NW1 1F 59
Manston Ho. W14 7F 75
Mantus Cl. E1 1K 73
Mantus Rd. E1 1J 73
Mapesbury Rd. NW2 1E 54
Mapes Ho. NW6 1F 55
Mape St. E2 1G 73 (not continuous)
Mapledene Est. E8 1E 62
Mapledene Rd. E8 1D 62
Maple Lodge W8 7A 76
Maple M. NW6 4A 56
Maple Pl. W1 2F 69
Maples Pl. E1 3H 73
Maple St. E2 5F 63
W1 3E 68
Maple Wlk. W10 1D 64
Marathon Ho. NW1 3J 67
Marban Rd. W9 6G 55
Marble Arch 7K 67
MARBLE ARCH 7J 67
Marble Arch W1 7J 67
Marble Arch Apartments W1 5J 67
Marble Ho. W9 2J 65
Marble Quay E1 2E 82
Marbles Ho. SE5 5H 91
Marchant Ct. SE1 3D 92
Marchant Ho. N1 3A 62 (off New Era Est.)
Marchbank Rd. W14 4J 85
Marchmont St. WC1 1J 69
Marcia Rd. SE1 2B 92
Marco Polo Ho. SW8 7C 88
Marco Rd. W6 7A 74
Marden Sq. SE16 7G 83
Mardyke Ho. SE17 1K 91
Mare St. E2 4H 63
E8 1H 63
Margaret Ct. W1 5E 68
Margaret Herbison Ho. SW6 6H 85
Margaret Ho. W6 4A 84
Margaret Ingram Cl. SW6 6G 85
Margaret St. W1 5D 68
Margaretta Ter. SW3 5G 87
Margaret White Ho. NW1 6G 59
Margery St. WC1 7C 60
Margravine Gdns. W6 3D 84
Margravine Rd. W6 4C 84
Maria Cl. SE1 1F 93
Marian Pl. E2 4G 63
Marian St. E2 4G 63
Maria Ter. E1 3K 73
Marie Lloyd Ho. N1 5J 61
Marigold All. SE1 1E 80
Marigold St. SE16 5G 83
Marine St. SE16 6E 82
Marion Ho. NW1 2K 57
Marjorie M. E1 6K 73
Market Ct. W1 5E 68
Market Entrance SW8 7F 89
Market La. W12 5A 74
Market M. W1 3C 78
Market Pl. SE16 1F 93 (not continuous)
W1 5E 68
Market St. E1 3C 72
Market Yd. M. SE1 6B 82
Markham Pl. SW3 3J 87
Markham Sq. SW3 3J 87
Markham St. SW3 3H 87
Mark Ho. E2 5K 63
Markland Ho. W10 7C 64
Mark La. EC3 7B 72
Mark Sq. EC2 1A 72
Markstone Ho. SE1 5E 80
Mark St. EC2 1A 72
Markyate Ho. W10 2A 64
Marland Ho. SW1 6K 77
Marlborough W9 6C 56
Marlborough Av. E8 3E 62 (not continuous)
Marlborough Cl. SE17 2F 91
Marlborough Ct. W1 6E 68
W8 1J 85
Marlborough Flats SW3 1H 87
Marlborough Ga. Ho. W2 7E 66
Marlborough Gro. SE1 4E 92
Marlborough Hill NW8 2E 56
Marlborough House 3F 79
Marlborough Ho. NW1 1D 68
Marlborough Lodge NW8 5C 56
Marlborough Pl. NW8 5C 56
Marlborough Rd. SW1 3F 79
Marlborough St. SW3 2G 87
Marlbury NW8 3B 56
Marley Ho. W11 1D 74
Marloes Rd. W8 7A 76
Marlowe Ct. SW3 2H 87
Marlowes, The NW8 3E 56
Marlow Ho. E2 7C 62
SE1 6C 82
W2 6B 66 (off Hallfield Est.)
Marlow Workshops E2 7C 62
Marne St. W10 6E 54
Marnock Ho. SE17 3J 91
Marqueen Ct. W8 4A 76 (off Kensington Chu. St.)
Marrick Ho. NW6 3B 56
Marryat Ho. SW1 4E 88
Marshall Ho. N1 4K 61
NW6 4H 55
SE1 7B 82
SE17 3J 91
Marshall's Pl. SE16 7D 82
Marshall St. W1 6F 69
Marshalsea Rd. SE1 4H 81
Marsham Ct. SW1 1H 89
Marsham St. SW1 7H 79
Marsh Cen., The E1 5D 72
Marsh Ho. SW1 4H 89
Marshwood Ho. NW6 3K 55
Marsland Cl. SE17 4F 91
Marsom Ho. N1 5J 61
Marston Cl. NW6 1D 56
Marsworth Ho. E2 3E 62
Martara M. SE17 4G 91
Martello St. E8 1G 63
Martello Ter. E8 1G 63
Martha Ct. E2 4H 63
Martha's Bldgs. EC1 1J 71
Martha St. E1 6H 73
Martineau Est. E1 7J 73 (off Cable St.)
Martineau Ho. SW1 4E 88
Martin Ho. SE1 7H 81
SW8 7J 89
Martin La. EC4 7K 71 (not continuous)
Martlett Ct. WC2 6K 69
Marvell Ho. SE5 7J 91
Marville Rd. SW6 7G 85
Mary Bayly Ho. W11 2E 74
Mary Flux Ct. SW5 3A 86
Mary Grn. NW8 2B 56
Mary Ho. W6 3A 84
Marylands Rd. W9 2K 65
Maryland Wlk. N1 2G 61
MARYLEBONE 3B 68
Marylebone Cricket Club 6F 57
MARYLEBONE FLYOVER 4G 67
Marylebone Fly-Over W2 4F 67
Marylebone High St. W1 3B 68
Marylebone La. W1 4B 68
Marylebone M. W1 4C 68
Marylebone Pas. W1 5F 69
Marylebone Rd. NW1 3H 67
Marylebone St. W1 4B 68
Marylee Way SE11 2B 90
Mary Macarthur Ho. E2 6K 63
W6 5E 84
Maryon Ho. NW6 1D 56
Mary Pl. W11 1E 74
Marys Ct. NW1 1H 67
Mary Seacole Cl. E8 2C 62
Mary Smith Ct. SW5 2K 85
Marysmith Ho. SW1 3H 89
Mary St. N1 3H 61
Mary Ter. NW1 3D 58
Marzell Ho. W14 4G 85
Masbro' Rd. W14 7D 74
Masefield Ho. NW6 6J 55
Mason Cl. SE16 3F 93
Mason Ho. E9 1K 63
SE1 2F 93
Mason's Arms M. W1 6D 68
Mason's Av. EC2 5J 71
Masons Pl. EC1 6F 61
Mason St. SE17 2K 91
Masons Yd. EC1 6F 61
SW1 2F 79
Massinger St. SE17 2A 92
Massingham St. E1 1K 73
Masterman Ho. SE5 7J 91
Masters Dr. SE16 4G 93
Masters Lodge E1 6K 73
Matheson Lang Ho. SE1 5C 80
Matheson Rd. W14 2G 85
Mathews Yd. WC2 6J 69
Mathieson Ct. SE1 5F 81
Mathison Ho. SW10 7C 86
Matilda Ho. E1 2E 82
Matilda St. N1 3B 60
Matisse Ct. EC1 1J 71
Matlock Ct. NW8 4C 56
W11 1J 75
Maton Ho. SW6 7G 85
Matson Ho. SE16 7H 83
Matthew Cl. W10 2C 64
Matthew Parker St. SW1 5H 79
Maude Ho. E2 5E 62
Maudlins Grn. E1 2E 82
Maunsel St. SW1 1G 89
Mavor Ho. N1 3B 60
Mawbey Ho. SE1 4D 92
Mawbey Pl. SE1 4D 92
Mawbey Rd. SE1 4D 92
Mawbey St. SW8 7J 89
Mawdley Ho. SE1 5D 80
Mawson Ct. N1 3K 61
Mawson Ho. EC1 3C 70
Maxilla Wlk. W10 6D 64
Maxwell Rd. SW6 7A 86
Maybury Ct. W1 4B 68
Maydew Ho. SE16 1J 93
MAYFAIR 1C 78
Mayfair M. NW1 1K 57
Mayfair Pl. W1 2D 78
Mayfield Ho. E2 5H 63
Mayfield Rd. E8 1C 62
Mayflower St. SE16 5J 83
Mayford NW1 4F 59 (not continuous)
Maygood St. N1 4C 60
Maylands Ho. SW3 2H 87
Maylie Ho. SE16 5G 83
Maynard Cl. SW6 7B 86
Maynards Quay E1 1J 83
Mayo Ho. E1 4J 73
Mays Ct. WC2 1J 79
May St. W14 4H 85 (North End Rd.)
W14 4G 85 (Vereker Rd.)
Mazenod Av. NW6 1K 55
MCC Cricket Mus. & Tours 7E 56
Meadcroft Rd. SE11 6E 90 (not continuous)
SE17 6E 90
Mead Ho. W11 2G 75
Meadowbank NW3 1J 57
Meadowbank Cl. SW6 7B 84
Meadow Ct. N1 4A 62
Meadow M. SW8 6A 90
Meadow Pl. SW8 7K 89
Meadow Rd. SW8 7A 90
Meadow Row SE1 7G 81
Mead Row SE1 6C 80
Meakin Est. SE1 6A 82
Meard St. W1 6G 69 (not continuous)
Mecca Bingo
Camden 2D 58
Fulham Broadway 7J 85
Hackney 5D 62
Islington 1G 61
Kilburn 1J 55
Mecklenburgh Pl. WC1 1A 70
Mecklenburgh Sq. WC1 1A 70
Mecklenburgh St. WC1 1A 70
Medburn St. NW1 4G 59
Medway Ct. WC1 7J 59
Medway Ho. NW8 2G 67
SE1 5K 81
Medway St. SW1 7G 79
Meeting Ho. All. E1 2H 83
Meeting Ho. La. SE15 7H 93
Melbourne Ct. W9 1D 66
Melbourne Ho. W8 3J 75
Melbourne Mans. W14 5E 84
Melbourne Pl. WC2 7B 70
Melbourne Ter. SW6 7A 86
Melbury Ct. W8 6H 75
Melbury Dr. SE5 7A 92
Melbury Ho. SW8 7A 90
Melbury Rd. W14 6G 75
Melbury Ter. NW1 2H 67
Melchester W11 5H 65
Melcombe Ct. NW1 3J 67
Melcombe Ho. SW8 7A 90
Melcombe Pl. NW1 3J 67
Melcombe Regis Ct. W1 4B 68 (off Weymouth St.)
Melcombe St. NW1 2K 67
Melford Ct. SE1 6B 82
Melina Pl. NW8 7E 56
Melior Pl. SE1 4A 82
Melior St. SE1 4A 82
Mellish Ho. E1 5G 73
Melon Pl. W8 4K 75
Melrose Gdns. W6 6A 74
Melrose Ho. NW6 6K 55
SW1 3C 88
Melrose Ter. W6 5B 74
Melton Ct. SW7 2F 87
Melton St. NW1 7F 59
Melville Pl. N1 1G 61
Melwood Ho. E1 6H 73
Memel Ct. EC1 2G 71
Memel St. EC1 2G 71
Menard Ct. EC1 7H 61
Mendham Ho. SE1 6A 82
Mendip Ct. SE14 6K 93
Mendip Ho's. E2 6K 63
Mendora Rd. SW6 7F 85
Menier Chocolate Factory (Theatre and Art Gallery) 3H 81
Menotti St. E2 1F 73
Mentmore Ter. E8 1H 63
Mentone Mans. SW10 7B 86
Mepham St. SE1 3C 80
Mercer Bldg. EC2 1B 72
Mercer Ho. SW1 3C 88
Merceron Ho's. E2 6J 63
Merceron St. E1 2H 73
Mercers Pl. W6 1B 84
Mercer St. WC2 6J 69
Merchant Ct. E1 2K 83
Meredith St. EC1 7E 60
Mereworth Ho. SE15 5K 93
Meriden Ct. SW3 4G 87
Meriden Ho. N1 3B 62 (off Wilmer Gdns.)
Meridian Ct. SE16 4E 82 (off Bermondsey Wall W.)
Merlins Ct. WC1 7C 60
Merlin St. WC1 7C 60
Mermaid Ct. E8 1C 62
SE1 4J 81
Merrick Sq. SE1 6J 81
Merrington Rd. SW6 5K 85
Merritt's Bldgs. EC2 2A 72
Merrivale NW1 3F 59
Merrow St. SE17 5H 91
Merrow Wlk. SE17 3K 91
Merthyr Ter. SW13 6A 84
Mertoun Ter. W1 4J 67
Messina Av. NW6 1J 55
Messiter Ho. N1 3B 60
Methley St. SE11 4D 90
Methwold Rd. W10 3C 64
Metro Central Hgts. SE1 7G 81
Metropolis SE11 7F 81
Metropolitan Bus. Cen. N1 1B 62
Metropolitan Sta. Bldgs. W6 2B 84 (off Beadon Rd.)
Metropolitan Wharf E1 2K 83
Mews, The N1 2H 61
Mews St. E1 2E 82
Mexborough NW1 3E 58
Meymott St. SE1 3E 80
Meynell Cres. E9 1K 63
Meynell Gdns. E9 1K 63
Miah Ter. E1 3F 83
Micawber Ct. N1 6H 61
Micawber Ho. SE16 5F 83
Micawber St. N1 6H 61
Michael Cliffe Ho. EC1 7D 60
Michael Faraday Ho. SE17 4A 92
Michael Stewart Ho. SW6 6H 85
Michelangelo Ct. SE16 3G 93
Michelson Ho. SE11 2B 90
Mickledore NW1 5F 59
Micklethwaite Rd. SW6 6K 85
Mickleton Ho. W2 4J 65
Middle Dartrey Wlk. SW10 7D 86 (off Dartrey Wlk.)
Middlefield NW8 2E 56
Middle Row W10 2E 64
Middlesex CC Club 6F 57
Middlesex Pas. EC1 4F 71
Middlesex St. E1 4B 72
Middle St. EC1 3G 71
Middle Temple La. EC4 6C 70
Middleton Ho. E8 1D 62
SE1 7J 81
SW1 2H 89
Middleton Pl. W1 4E 68
Middleton Rd. E8 1C 62
Middleton St. E2 6G 63
Middle Yd. SE1 2A 82
Midford Pl. W1 2F 69
Midhope Ho. WC1 7K 59
Midhope St. WC1 7K 59
Midland Rd. NW1 5H 59
Midway Ho. EC1 6F 61
Milborne Gro. SW10 4D 86
Milcote St. SE1 5E 80
Mile End Rd. E1 3J 73
Miles Bldgs. NW1 3G 67
Miles Ct. E1 6G 73
Miles Pl. NW1 3F 67 (off Broadley St.)
Miles St. SW8 6J 89 (not continuous)
Miles St. Bus. Est. SW8 6J 89
Milford La. WC2 7C 70
Milk St. EC2 6H 71
Milk Yd. E1 1J 83
Millais Ho. SW1 2J 89
Millbank SW1 7J 79
Millbank Ct. SW1 1J 89
Millbank Twr. SW1 2J 89
Millbrook Ho. SE15 6F 93
Millbrook Pl. NW1 4E 58 (off Hampstead Rd.)
Millender Wlk. SE16 2K 93
Millennium Arena 7B 88
Millennium Bridge 1F 81
Millennium Bri. Ho. EC4 7G 71
Millennium Pl. E2 5H 63
Millennium Sq. SE1 4D 82
Miller St. NW1 4E 58 (not continuous)
Millers Way W6 5B 74
Millers Wharf Ho. E1 3E 82
Miller Wlk. SE1 3D 80
Milliners Ho. SE1 5B 82
Millman Ct. WC1 2A 70
Millman M. WC1 2A 70
Millman Pl. WC1 2A 70
Millman St. WC1 2A 70
Mill Pond Cl. SW8 7H 89
Millpond Est. SE16 5G 83
Mill Row N1 3B 62
Mills Ct. EC2 1A 72
Millstream Ho. SE16 5H 83

Millstream Rd. SE1 . . .5C 82
Mill St. SE1 . . .5D 82
W1 . . .7E 68
Millwall FC . . .4K 93
Millwood St. W10 . . .4E 64
Mill Yd. E1 . . .7E 72
Milman Rd. NW6 . . .4D 54
Milman's Ho. SW10 . . .6E 86
Milman's St. SW10 . . .6E 86
Milner Ct. SE15 . . .7D 92
Milner Pl. N1 . . .2D 60
Milner Sq. N1 . . .1D 60
Milner St. SW3 . . .1J 87
Milroy Wlk. SE1 . . .2E 80
Milson Rd. W14 . . .6D 74
Milton Cl. SE1 . . .2C 92
Milton Ct. EC2 . . .3J 71
Milton Ct. Wlk. EC2 . . .3J 71
Milton Ho. E2 . . .6J 63
SE5 . . .7J 91
Milton Mans. W14 . . .5F 85
Milton St. EC2 . . .3J 71
Milverton Rd. NW6 . . .1B 54
Milverton St. SE11 . . .4D 90
Milward St. E1 . . .4H 73
Mina Rd. SE17 . . .4B 92
Mincing La. EC3 . . .7A 72
Minera M. SW1 . . .1B 88
Minerva Cl. SW9 . . .7D 90
Minerva St. E2 . . .5G 63
Minerva Wlk. EC1 . . .5F 71
Minford Gdns. W14 . . .5C 74
Minford Ho. W14 . . .5C 74
Miniver Pl. EC4 . . .7H 71
Minnow St. SE17 . . .2B 92
Minnow Wlk. SE17 . . .2B 92
Minories EC3 . . .6C 72
Minster Ct. EC3 . . .7B 72
Minster Pavement
EC3 . . .7B 72
Mintern St. N1 . . .4K 61
Minton Ho. SE11 . . .1C 90
Mint St. SE1 . . .4G 81
Mirabel Rd. SW6 . . .7H 85
Miranda Cl. E1 . . .4J 73
Miranda Ho. N1 . . .5A 62
Missenden SE17 . . .4K 91
Missenden Ho. NW8 . . .1G 67
Mitali Pas. E1 . . .6E 72
Mitchell Ho. N1 . . .1E 60
Mitchell St. EC1 . . .1G 71
(not continuous)
Mitford Bldgs. SW6 . . .7J 85
Mitre Bri. Ind. Pk.
W10 . . .2A 64
(not continuous)
Mitre Ct. EC2 . . .6H 71
Mitre Ho. SW3 . . .3J 87
Mitre Rd. SE1 . . .4D 80
Mitre Sq. EC3 . . .6B 72
Mitre St. EC3 . . .6B 72
Mitre Way W10 . . .3A 64
Mitre Yd. SW3 . . .1H 87
Moatfield NW6 . . .1E 54
Moatlands Ho. WC1 . . .7K 59
Moberly Sports &
Education Cen. 6D 54
(off Chamberlayne Rd.)
Mobil Ct. WC2 . . .6B 70
Mocatta Ho. E1 . . .2G 73
Model Bldgs. WC1 . . .7B 60
Modern Ct. EC4 . . .5E 70
Modling Ho. E2 . . .5K 63
Mole Ho. NW8 . . .2F 67
Molesworth Ho. SE17 . . .6E 90
Molton Ho. N1 . . .3B 60
Molyneux St. W1 . . .4H 67
Monarch Ho. W8 . . .6J 75
Monck St. SW1 . . .7H 79
Monckton Ct. W14 . . .6G 75
Moncorvo Cl. SW7 . . .5G 77
Monet Ct. SE16 . . .3G 93
Moneyer Ho. N1 . . .6J 61
Monica Shaw Ct.
NW1 . . .5H 59
(not continuous)
Monkton St. SE11 . . .1D 90
Monkwell Sq. EC2 . . .4H 71
Monmouth Pl. W2 . . .6A 66
Monmouth Rd. W2 . . .6K 65
Monmouth St. WC2 . . .6J 69
Monnow Rd. SE1 . . .3E 92
Monroe Ho. NW8 . . .7H 57
Monson Rd. SE14 . . .7K 93
Montagu Ct. W1 . . .4K 67
Montague Cl. SE1 . . .2J 81
Montague Ho. *N1* . . .*3A 62*
(off New Era Est.)
Montague Pl. WC1 . . .3H 69
Montague Sq. SE15 . . .7K 93
Montague St. EC1 . . .4G 71
WC1 . . .3J 69
Montagu Mans. W1 . . .3K 67
Montagu M. Nth. W1 . . .4K 67
Montagu M. Sth. W1 . . .5K 67
Montagu M. W. W1 . . .5K 67
Montagu Pl. W1 . . .4J 67
Montagu Row W1 . . .4K 67
Montagu Sq. W1 . . .4K 67
Montagu St. W1 . . .5K 67
Montaigne Cl. SW1 . . .2H 89
Montclare St. E2 . . .1C 72
Monteagle Ct. N1 . . .4B 62
Montford Pl. SE11 . . .4C 90
Montfort Ho. E2 . . .6J 63
Montgomery Ho. W2 . . .4E 66
Montgomery Lodge
E1 . . .2J 73
Monthope Rd. E1 . . .4D 72
Montpelier M. SW7 . . .6H 77
Montpelier Pl. E1 . . .6J 73
SW7 . . .6H 77
Montpelier Sq. SW7 . . .5H 77
Montpelier St. SW7 . . .6H 77
Montpelier Ter. SW7 . . .5H 77
Montpelier Wlk. SW7 . . .6H 77
Montreal Pl. WC2 . . .7A 70
Montrose Av. NW6 . . .4F 55
Montrose Ct. SW7 . . .5F 77
Montrose Ho. SW1 . . .5B 78
Montrose Pl. SW1 . . .5B 78
Monument, The . . .7K 71
Monument St. EC3 . . .7K 71
Monza St. E1 . . .2J 83
Moodkee St. SE16 . . .6J 83
Moon St. N1 . . .2E 60
Moore Ct. N1 . . .3E 60
Moore Ho. E1 . . .7K 73
E2 . . .7J 63
Moore Pk. Ct. SW6 . . .7B 86
Moore Pk. Rd. SW6 . . .7A 86
Moore St. SW3 . . .1J 87
Moorfields EC2 . . .4J 71
Moorfields Highwalk
EC2 . . .4J 71
(not continuous)
Moorgate EC2 . . .5J 71
Moorgate Pl. EC2 . . .5J 71
Moorgreen Ho. EC1 . . .6E 60
Moorhouse Rd. W2 . . .5J 65
Moor La. EC2 . . .4J 71
(not continuous)
Moor Pl. EC2 . . .4J 71
Moor St. W1 . . .6H 69
Moran Ho. E1 . . .3H 83
Mora St. EC1 . . .7H 61
Moravian Cl. SW10 . . .6E 86
Moravian Pl. SW10 . . .6F 87
Moravian St. E2 . . .6J 63
Mordern Ho. NW1 . . .2H 67
Morecambe Cl. E1 . . .3K 73
Morecambe St. SE17 . . .2H 91
More Cl. W14 . . .2D 84
Moreland St. EC1 . . .6F 61
More London Pl. SE1 . . .3A 82
More London Riverside
SE1 . . .3B 82
More's Gdn. SW3 . . .6F 87
Moreton Cl. SW1 . . .3F 89
Moreton Ho. SE16 . . .6H 83
Moreton Pl. SW1 . . .3F 89
Moreton St. SW1 . . .3F 89
Moreton Ter. SW1 . . .3F 89
Moreton Ter. M. Nth.
SW1 . . .3F 89
Moreton Ter. M. Sth.
SW1 . . .3F 89
Morgan Ho. SW1 . . .2F 89
Morgan Rd. W10 . . .3G 65
Morland Ho. NW1 . . .5F 59
NW6 . . .3J 55
SW1 . . .1J 89
W11 . . .6E 64
Morland M. N1 . . .1D 60
Morley St. SE1 . . .6D 80
Mornington Av. W14 . . .2G 85
Mornington Av. Mans.
W14 . . .2H 85
Mornington Ct. NW1 . . .4E 58
Mornington Cres.
NW1 . . .4E 58
Mornington Pl. NW1 . . .4E 58
Mornington Sports &
Leisure Cen. *2D 58*
(off Stanmore Pl.)
Mornington St. NW1 . . .4D 58
Mornington Ter. NW1 . . .3D 58
Morocco St. SE1 . . .5A 82
Morocco Wharf *E1* . . .*3G 83*
(off Wapping High St.)
Morpeth Gro. E9 . . .2K 63
Morpeth Mans. SW1 . . .1E 88
Morpeth Rd. E9 . . .3K 63
Morpeth St. E2 . . .6K 63
Morpeth Ter. SW1 . . .7E 78
Morrel Ct. E2 . . .4F 63
Morrells Yd. SE11 . . .3D 90
Morris Ho. E2 . . .7J 63
NW8 . . .2G 67
Morrison Bldgs. Nth.
E1 . . .5E 72
Morriss Ho. SE16 . . .5G 83
Morris St. E1 . . .6H 73
Morshead Mans. W9 . . .7K 55
Morshead Rd. W9 . . .7K 55
Mortain Ho. SE16 . . .2G 93
Mortimer Ct. NW8 . . .5D 56
Mortimer Cres. NW6 . . .3A 56
Mortimer Est. NW6 . . .3A 56
Mortimer Ho. W11 . . .2D 74
W14 . . .2F 85
Mortimer Mkt. WC1 . . .2F 69
Mortimer Pl. NW6 . . .3A 56
Mortimer Rd. N1 . . .1B 62
(not continuous)
NW10 . . .6A 54
Mortimer Sq. W11 . . .1D 74
Mortimer St. W1 . . .5D 68
Morton Ho. SE17 . . .5F 91
Morton M. SW5 . . .2A 86
Morton Pl. SE1 . . .7C 80
Morton Rd. N1 . . .1H 61
Morwell St. WC1 . . .4G 69
Moscow Mans. SW5 . . .1K 85
Moscow Pl. W2 . . .7A 66
Moscow Rd. W2 . . .7K 65
Mosedale NW1 . . .7E 58
Mosque Ter. *E1* . . .*4F 73*
(off Fieldgate St.)
Mosque Twr. *E1* . . .*4E 72*
(off Fieldgate St.)
Moss Cl. E1 . . .4F 73
Mossington Gdns.
SE16 . . .2J 93
Mossop St. SW3 . . .1H 87
Mostyn Gdns. NW10 . . .6C 54
Motcomb St. SW1 . . .6A 78
Motley Av. EC2 . . .1A 72
Moules Ct. SE5 . . .7G 91
Moulins Rd. E9 . . .1K 63
Moulsford Ho. W2 . . .4K 65
Mounsey Ho. W10 . . .6F 55
Mount, The W8 . . .3J 75
Mountain Ho. SE11 . . .2B 90
Mountbatten Ct.
SE16 . . .3K 83
Mt. Carmel Chambers
W8 . . .4K 75
Mountfort Cres. N1 . . .1C 60
Mountfort Ter. N1 . . .1C 60
Mountjoy Cl. *EC2* . . .*4H 71*
(off Thomas More Highwalk)
Mountjoy Ho. EC2 . . .4H 71
Mount Mills EC1 . . .7F 61
Mt. Pleasant WC1 . . .2C 70
Mt. Pleasant Rd.
NW10 . . .1A 54
Mount Row W1 . . .1C 78
Mount St. W1 . . .1A 78
Mount St. M. W1 . . .1C 78
Mount Ter. E1 . . .4G 73
Mowbray Rd. NW6 . . .1G 55
Mowlem St. E2 . . .4H 63
Mowll St. SW9 . . .7C 90
Moxon St. W1 . . .4A 68
Moye Cl. E2 . . .4F 63
Moylan Rd. W6 . . .6F 85
Moyle Ho. SW1 . . .4F 89
Mozart St. W10 . . .7G 55
Mozart Ter. SW1 . . .2B 88
Muirfield Cl. SE16 . . .4H 93
Mulberry Cl. SW3 . . .6F 87
Mulberry Ct. EC1 . . .7F 61
SW3 . . .5F 87
Mulberry Ho. E2 . . .6J 63
Mulberry Housing
Co-operative SE1 . . .2D 80
Mulberry Rd. E8 . . .1C 62
Mulberry St. E1 . . .5E 72
Mulberry Wlk. SW3 . . .5F 87
Mulgrave Rd. SW6 . . .5G 85
Mullen Twr. WC1 . . .2C 70
Mullet Gdns. E2 . . .6F 63
Mulletsfield WC1 . . .7K 59
Mulready Ho. SW1 . . .2J 89
Mulready St. NW8 . . .2G 67
Multon Ho. E9 . . .1J 63
Mulvaney Way SE1 . . .5K 81
(not continuous)
Munday Ho. SE1 . . .7J 81
Munden St. W14 . . .1E 84
Mund St. W14 . . .4H 85
Mundy Ho. W10 . . .6F 55
Mundy St. N1 . . .6A 62
Munro Ho. SE1 . . .5C 80
Munro M. W10 . . .4F 65
(not continuous)
Munro Ter. SW10 . . .7E 86
Munster M. SW6 . . .7E 84
Munster Rd. SW6 . . .7E 84
Munster Sq. NW1 . . .7D 58
Munton Rd. SE17 . . .1H 91
Murchison Ho. W10 . . .3E 64
Murdoch Ho. SE16 . . .6K 83
Murdock St. SE15 . . .6G 93
Muriel St. N1 . . .4B 60
(not continuous)
Murphy Ho. SE1 . . .6F 81
(Borough Rd.)
SE1 . . .5K 81
(Long La.)
Murphy St. SE1 . . .5C 80
Murray Gro. N1 . . .5H 61
Murray St. NW1 . . .1G 59
Musard Rd. W6 . . .5F 85
Musbury St. E1 . . .5J 73
Muscal W6 . . .5E 84
Muscott Ho. E2 . . .3E 62
Muscovy St. EC3 . . .1B 82
Museum Chambers
WC1 . . .4J 69
Museum Ho. E2 . . .6J 63
Museum La. SW7 . . .7F 77
Mus. of Brands,
Packaging and Advertising
. . .*6H 65*
(off Colville M.)
Mus. of Classical Archaeology
. . .*1G 69*
(off Gower Pl.)
Mus. of Garden History
. . .7A 80
Mus. of London . . .4G 71
Mus. of the Order of St John
. . .2E 70
Museum Pas. E2 . . .6J 63
Museum St. WC1 . . .4J 69
Mutrix Rd. NW6 . . .2K 55
Myddelton Pas. EC1 . . .6D 60
Myddelton Sq. EC1 . . .6D 60
Myddelton St. EC1 . . .7D 60
Myddleton Ho. N1 . . .5C 60
Myers Ho. SE5 . . .7G 91
Myers La. SE14 . . .5K 93
Myles Ct. SE16 . . .5J 83
Mylne St. EC1 . . .6C 60
Myrdle Ct. E1 . . .5F 73
Myrdle St. E1 . . .4F 73
Myrtle Wlk. N1 . . .5A 62
Mytton Ho. SW8 . . .7A 90

N

N1 Shop. Cen. N1 . . .4D 60
Nags Head Ct. EC1 . . .2H 71
Nainby Ho. SE11 . . .2C 90
Nalton Ho. NW6 . . .1D 56
Nantes Pas. E1 . . .3C 72
Nant St. E2 . . .6H 63
Naoroji St. WC1 . . .7C 60
Napier Cl. W14 . . .6G 75
Napier Ct. N1 . . .4J 61
Napier Gro. N1 . . .4H 61
Napier Ho. SE17 . . .6F 91
Napier Pl. W14 . . .7G 75
Napier Rd. W14 . . .7G 75
Napier Ter. N1 . . .1E 60
Nascot St. W12 . . .5A 64
Nashe Ho. SE1 . . .7J 81
Nash Ho. NW1 . . .4C 58
SW1 . . .4D 88
Nash St. NW1 . . .6D 58
Nassau St. W1 . . .4E 68
Nathan Ho. SE11 . . .2D 90
Nathaniel Cl. E1 . . .4D 72
National Army Mus. . . .5K 87
National Film Theatre, The
. . .2B 80
National Gallery . . .1H 79
National Portrait Gallery
. . .1H 79
National Ter. SE16 . . .4G 83
National Theatre . . .2B 80
Natural History Mus.
Knightbridge . . .7E 76
Nautilus Bldg., The
EC1 . . .6D 60
Navarre St. E2 . . .1C 72
Naylor Ho. SE17 . . .2K 91
W10 . . .6F 55
Naylor Rd. SE15 . . .7G 93
Nazrul St. E2 . . .6C 62
Neal St. WC2 . . .6J 69
Neal's Yd. WC2 . . .6J 69
Neate Ho. SW1 . . .4F 89
Neate St. SE5 . . .6A 92
(not continuous)
Neathouse Pl. SW1 . . .1E 88
Nebraska St. SE1 . . .5J 81
Neckinger SE16 . . .6D 82
Neckinger Est. SE16 . . .6D 82
Neckinger St. SE1 . . .5D 82
Needham Ho. SE11 . . .2C 90
Needham Rd. W11 . . .6J 65
Needleman St. SE16 . . .5K 83
Nella Rd. W6 . . .6C 84
Nelldale Rd. SE16 . . .1H 93
Nell Gwynn Ho. SW3 . . .2H 87
Nelson Cl. NW6 . . .6J 55
Nelson Ct. SE1 . . .4F 81
SE16 . . .3K 83
Nelson Gdns. E2 . . .6F 63
Nelson Ho. SW1 . . .5F 89
Nelson Pas. EC1 . . .6H 61
Nelson Pl. N1 . . .5F 61
Nelson's Column . . .2H 79
Nelson Sq. SE1 . . .4E 80
Nelson St. E1 . . .5G 73
Nelsons Yd. NW1 . . .4E 58
Nelson Ter. N1 . . .5F 61
Neptune Ho. SE16 . . .6K 83
Neptune St. SE16 . . .6J 83
Nesham Ho. N1 . . .3A 62
Nesham St. E1 . . .2E 82
Ness St. SE16 . . .6E 82
Nestor Ho. E2 . . .5G 63
Netherton Gro. SW10 . . .6D 86
Netherwood Pl. W14 . . .6C 74
Netherwood Rd. W14 . . .6C 74
Netley St. NW1 . . .7E 58
Nettlecombe NW1 . . .1G 59
Nettleden Ho. SW3 . . .2H 87
Nettleton Ct. EC2 . . .4G 71
Nevern Pl. SW5 . . .2K 85
Nevern Rd. SW5 . . .2J 85
Nevern Sq. SW5 . . .2J 85
Nevill Ct. EC4 . . .5D 70
SW10 . . .7D 86
Neville Cl. NW1 . . .5H 59
NW6 . . .5H 55
Neville Ct. NW8 . . .5E 56
Neville Rd. NW6 . . .5H 55
Neville St. SW7 . . .3E 86
Neville Ter. SW7 . . .3E 86
Nevitt Ho. N1 . . .5K 61
Newall Ho. SE1 . . .6H 81
New Ambassadors Theatre
. . .6H 69
Newark St. E1 . . .4G 73
(not continuous)
New Bentham Ct. N1 . . .1H 61
Newbery Ho. N1 . . .1G 61
Newbold Cotts. E1 . . .5J 73
Newbolt Ho. SE17 . . .3J 91
New Bond St. W1 . . .6C 68
New Bri. St. EC4 . . .6E 70
New Broad St. EC2 . . .4K 71
Newburgh St. W1 . . .6E 68
New Burlington M.
W1 . . .7E 68
New Burlington Pl.
W1 . . .7E 68
New Burlington St.
W1 . . .7E 68
Newburn Ho. SE11 . . .3B 90
Newburn St. SE11 . . .4B 90
Newbury Ho. W2 . . .6B 66
Newbury St. EC1 . . .3G 71
Newby NW1 . . .7E 58
New Caledonian Mkt.
SE1 . . .6B 82
Newcastle Cl. EC4 . . .5E 70
Newcastle Ct. EC4 . . .7H 71
Newcastle Ho. W1 . . .3A 68
Newcastle Pl. W2 . . .3F 67
Newcastle Row EC1 . . .2D 70
New Cavendish St.
W1 . . .4B 68
New Change EC4 . . .6G 71
New Charles St. EC1 . . .6F 61
New Church Rd. SE5 . . .7H 91
(not continuous)
New College M. N1 . . .1D 60
Newcombe St. W8 . . .2K 75
Newcomen St. SE1 . . .4J 81
New Compton St.
WC2 . . .6H 69
New Concordia Wharf
SE1 . . .4D 82
New Ct. EC4 . . .7C 70
Newcourt Ho. E2 . . .7H 63
Newcourt St. NW8 . . .5G 57
New Covent Garden Market
. . .7G 89
New Coventry St. W1 . . .1H 79
New Crane Pl. E1 . . .2J 83
New Crane Wharf E1 . . .2J 83
New Cross Rd. SE14 . . .7J 93
Newent Cl. SE15 . . .7A 92
New Era Est. N1 . . .3A 62
New Era Ho. *N1* . . .*3A 62*
(off New Era Est.)
New Fetter La. EC4 . . .5D 70
Newgate St. EC1 . . .5F 71
New Globe Wlk. SE1 . . .2G 81
New Goulston St. E1 . . .5C 72
Newham's Row SE1 . . .5B 82
NEWINGTON . . .7G 81
Newington Butts SE1 . . .1F 91
SE11 . . .2F 91
Newington C'way.
SE1 . . .7F 81
Newington Ct. Bus. Cen.
SE1 . . .6G 81
Newington Ind. Est.
SE17 . . .2G 91
New Inn B'way. EC2 . . .1B 72
New Inn Pas. WC2 . . .6B 70
New Inn Sq. EC2 . . .1B 72
New Inn St. EC2 . . .1B 72
New Inn Yd. EC2 . . .1B 72
New Jubilee Wharf E1 . . .2J 83
New Kent Rd. SE1 . . .7G 81
Newland Ct. EC1 . . .1J 71
Newland Ho. SE14 . . .6K 93
Newlands NW1 . . .6E 58
Newlands Quay E1 . . .1J 83
New London St. EC3 . . .7B 72
New London Theatre . . .5K 69
Newlyn NW1 . . .3F 59
Newman Pas. W1 . . .4F 69
Newman's Ct. EC3 . . .6K 71
Newman's Row WC2 . . .4B 70
Newman St. W1 . . .4F 69
Newman Yd. W1 . . .5G 69
Newnham Ter. SE1 . . .6C 80
New Nth. Pl. EC2 . . .1A 72
New Nth. Rd. N1 . . .1G 61
New North St. WC1 . . .3A 70
New Oxford St. WC1 . . .5H 69
New Pl. Sq. SE16 . . .6G 83
New Players Theatre . . .2K 79
Newport Ct. WC2 . . .7H 69
Newport Pl. WC2 . . .7H 69
Newport St. SE11 . . .2A 90
New Priory Ct. NW6 . . .1K 55
Newquay Ho. SE11 . . .3C 90
New Quebec St. W1 . . .6K 67
New Ride SW1 . . .5F 77
SW7 . . .5F 77
New River Head EC1 . . .6D 60
New River Wlk. N1 . . .1G 61
New Rd. E1 . . .4G 73
New Row WC2 . . .7J 69
New Spring Gdns. Wlk.
SE11 . . .4K 89
New Sq. WC2 . . .5C 70
New Sq. Pas. WC2 . . .5C 70
Newstead Ho. *N1* . . .*4D 60*
(off Tolpuddle St.)
New St. EC2 . . .4B 72
New St. Sq. EC4 . . .5D 70
Newton Ct. W8 . . .4K 75
Newton Ho. E1 . . .7G 73
NW8 . . .2B 56
Newton Mans. W14 . . .5F 85
Newton Rd. W2 . . .6K 65
Newton St. WC2 . . .5K 69
New Twr. Bldgs. E1 . . .3H 83
New Turnstile WC1 . . .4A 70
New Union St. EC2 . . .4J 71
New Wharf Rd. N1 . . .4K 59
Next Generation Club
Carlton . . .4K 65
Niagra Cl. N1 . . .4H 61
Niagra Ct. SE16 . . .6K 83
Nicholas La. EC4 . . .7K 71
(not continuous)
Nicholas Pas. EC4 . . .7K 71
Nicholas Rd. E1 . . .1K 73
Nicholl St. E2 . . .3E 62
Nichols Ct. E2 . . .5C 62
Nicholson Ho. SE17 . . .3J 91
Nicholson St. SE1 . . .3E 80
Nickleby Ho. SE16 . . .5E 82
W11 . . .2D 74
Nigel Ho. EC1 . . .3C 70
Nightingale Ho. E1 . . .2E 82
E2 . . .3B 62
W12 . . .5A 64
Nightingale Lodge
W9 . . .*3K 65*
(off Admiral Wlk.)
Nightingale M. SE11 . . .1E 90
Nightingale Pl. SW10 . . .6D 86
(not continuous)
Nile St. N1 . . .6J 61
Nile Ter. SE15 . . .4C 92
NINE ELMS . . .7F 89
Nine Elms La. SW8 . . .7F 89
Nipponzan Myohoji
Peace Pagoda . . .7K 87
Nirvana Apartments
N1 . . .*3E 60*
(off Islington Grn.)
Niton St. SW6 . . .7C 84
Noble Ct. E1 . . .7F 73
Noble St. EC2 . . .5G 71
Noel Coward Ho.
SW1 . . .2F 89
Noel Coward Theatre . . .7J 69
Noel Rd. N1 . . .4E 60
Noel St. W1 . . .6F 69
Noko W10 . . .6D 54
Norburn St. W10 . . .4E 64
Norden Ho. E2 . . .7H 63
Norfolk Cres. W2 . . .5G 67
Norfolk Ho. EC4 . . .7G 71
SW1 . . .1H 89
Norfolk M. W10 . . .4F 65
Norfolk Pl. W2 . . .5F 67
(not continuous)
Norfolk Rd. NW8 . . .3F 57
Norfolk Row SE1 . . .1A 90
(not continuous)
Norfolk Sq. W2 . . .6F 67
Norfolk Sq. M. W2 . . .6F 67
Norfolk Ter. W6 . . .4E 84
Norland Ho. W11 . . .3D 74
Norland Pl. W11 . . .3F 75
Norland Rd. W11 . . .3D 74
Norland Sq. W11 . . .3F 75
Norland Sq. Mans.
W11 . . .3E 74
Norman Butler Ho.
W10 . . .2E 64
Normand Gdns. W14 . . .5F 85
Normand Mans. W14 . . .5F 85
Normand M. W14 . . .5F 85
Normand Rd. W14 . . .5G 85
Norman Ho. SW8 . . .7J 89
Norman St. EC1 . . .7G 61
Norris Ho. E9 . . .2K 63
N1 . . .3A 62
Norris St. SW1 . . .1G 79
Northampton Rd. EC1 . . .1D 70
Northampton Row
EC1 . . .1D 70
Northampton Sq. EC1 . . .7E 60
Northampton St. N1 . . .1G 61
Nth. Audley St. W1 . . .6A 68
North Av. NW10 . . .7A 54
Northaw Ho. W10 . . .2A 64
North Bank NW8 . . .7G 57
North Block SE1 . . .4B 80

Nth. Branch Av. NW10 7B 54
Northburgh St. EC1 2F 71
Nth. Carriage Dr. W2 7G 67
Northchurch SE17 3K 91
(not continuous)
Northchurch Ho. E2 3F 63
Northchurch Rd. N1 1J 61
(not continuous)
Northchurch Ter. N1 1A 62
North Ct. SW1 7J 79
W1 3F 69
North Cres. WC1 3G 69
Northdown St. N1 4K 59
North End Cres. W14 2G 85
North End Ho. W14 2F 85
North End Pde. W14 2F 85
North End Rd. SW6 5H 85
W14 1F 85
Northesk Ho. E1 2G 73
Northfield Ho. SE15 6F 93
Northfleet Ho. SE1 4J 81
Northflock St. SE16 4E 82
Nth. Flower Wlk. W2 1D 76
North Ga. NW8 5G 57
Nth. Gower St. NW1 7F 59
Northiam WC1 7K 59
Northiam St. E9 3H 63
Northington St. WC1 2B 70
NORTH KENSINGTON 4C 64
North M. WC1 2B 70
Nth. Pole Rd. W10 4A 64
Northport St. N1 3K 61
North Ride W2 7G 67
North Ri. W2 6H 67
North Row W1 7K 67
Nth. Row Bldgs. W1 7A 68
Nth. Tenter St. E1 6D 72
North Ter. SW3 7G 77
WC2 2H 79
Northumberland All. EC3 6B 72
(not continuous)
Northumberland Av. WC2 2J 79
Northumberland Ho. SW1 2J 79
Northumberland Pl. W2 5J 65
Northumberland St. WC2 2J 79
Nth. Western Commercial Cen. NW1 1J 59
Northwest Pl. N1 4D 60
Nth. Wharf Rd. W2 4E 66
Northwick Cl. NW8 1E 66
Northwick Ho. NW8 1D 66
Northwick Ter. NW8 1E 66
Norton Folgate E1 3B 72
Norton Folgate Ho. E1 3C 72
Norton Ho. E1 6G 73
SW1 7H 79
Norwich St. EC4 5C 70
Notley St. SE5 7J 91
Notting Barn Rd. W10 2C 64
Nottingdale Sq. W11 2E 74
Nottingham Ct. WC2 6J 69
Nottingham Ho. WC2 6J 69
Nottingham Pl. W1 2A 68
Nottingham St. W1 3A 68
Nottingham Ter. NW1 2A 68
NOTTING HILL 1G 75
Notting Hill Ga. W11 2H 75
Nottingwood Ho. W11 7E 64
Nuffield Lodge W9 3K 65
Nugent Ter. NW8 5D 56
Nun Ct. EC2 5J 71
Nursery La. E2 3C 62
W10 4A 64
Nursery Row SE17 2J 91
Nutbourne St. W10 6E 54
Nutcroft Rd. SE15 7G 93
Nutford Pl. W1 5H 67
Nuttall St. N1 4B 62
Nutt St. SE15 7D 92
Nye Bevan Ho. SW6 7G 85

O

Oak Ct. SE15 7D 92
Oakden St. SE11 1D 90
Oakeford Ho. W14 7F 75
Oakey La. SE1 6C 80
Oakfield St. SW10 5C 86
Oakham Ho. W10 2A 64
Oak Ho. W10 1E 64
Oakington Rd. W9 1K 65
Oakley Cres. EC1 5F 61
Oakley Gdns. SW3 5H 87
Oakley Ho. SW1 1K 87
Oakley Pl. SE1 4C 92
Oakley Rd. N1 1K 61
Oakley Sq. NW1 4F 59
Oakley St. SW3 5G 87
Oakley Studios SW3 5G 87
Oakley Wlk. W6 5D 84
Oakley Yd. E2 1D 72
Oak Lodge W8 7A 76
Oaks, The NW6 1D 54
Oakshott Ct. NW1 5G 59
(not continuous)
Oak Tree Ho. W9 1K 65
Oak Tree Rd. NW8 7F 57
Oakwood Ct. W14 6G 75
Oakwood La. W14 6G 75
Oakwood Mans. W14 6G 75
Oakworth Rd. W10 3B 64
Oasis Sports Cen. 5J 69
Oat La. EC2 5H 71
Oatwell Ho. SW3 3H 87
Oberon Ho. N1 4A 62
Observatory Gdns. W8 4K 75
Observatory Rd. SW7 7E 76
Occupation Rd. SE17 3G 91
Ockbrook E1 3K 73
Octagon, The SW10 7C 86
Octagon Arc. EC2 4A 72
Octagon Ct. SE16 3K 83
Octavia Ho. SW1 7G 79
W10 2E 64
Octavia M. W10 1G 65
Odeon Cinema
Camden Town 2D 58
Covent Garden 6H 69
Kensington 6J 75
Leicester Square 1H 79
Marble March 6K 67
Panton St. 1H 79
Swiss Cottage 1E 56
Tottenham Court Rd. 4G 69
West End 1H 79
Whiteleys 6B 66
Odette Duval Ho. E1 4K 73
Odhams Wlk. WC2 6J 69
O'Donnell Ct. WC1 1K 69
Odontological Mus., The 5B 70
(within The Royal College of Surgeons)
Offham Ho. SE17 2A 92
Offley Rd. SW9 7C 90
Offord Rd. N1 1A 60
Offord St. N1 1B 60
Ogle St. W1 3E 68
O'Gorman Ho. SW10 7D 86
Okehampton Rd. NW10 3B 54
Olaf Ct. W8 4K 75
Olaf St. W11 1D 74
Old Bailey EC4 6F 71
Old Bailey (Central Criminal Court) 5F 71
Old Barge Ho. All. SE1 1D 80
Old Barracks W8 4B 76
Old Barrack Yd. SW1 5A 78
(not continuous)
Old Bethnal Grn. Rd. E2 6F 63
Old Billingsgate Mkt. EC3 1A 82
Old Billingsgate Wlk. EC3 1A 82
Old Bond St. W1 1E 78
Old Brewer's Yd. WC2 6J 69
Old Broad St. EC2 6K 71
Old Brompton Rd. SW5 4K 85
SW7 2E 86
Old Bldgs. WC2 5C 70
Old Burlington St. W1 7E 68
Oldbury Ho. W2 3A 66
Oldbury Pl. W1 2B 68
Old Canal M. SE15 4D 92
Old Castle St. E1 5C 72
Old Cavendish St. W1 5C 68
Old Change Ct. EC4 6G 71
Old Chelsea M. SW3 6G 87
Old Church St. SW3 3F 87
Old Compton St. W1 7G 69
Old Ct. Ho. W8 5A 76
Old Ct. Pl. W8 4A 76
Old Curiosity Shop 5B 70
Old Fish St. Hill EC4 7G 71
Old Fleet La. EC4 5E 70
Old Ford Rd. E2 6J 63
Old Gloucester St. WC1 3K 69
Old Jamaica Rd. SE16 6E 82
Old Jewry EC2 6J 71
Old Kent Rd. SE1 1A 92
SE15 5F 93
Old Manor Ct. NW8 4D 56
Old Manor Yd. SW5 2A 86
Old Market Sq. E2 6C 62
Old Marylebone Rd. W1 4H 67
Old Mitre Ct. EC4 6D 70
Old Montague St. E1 4E 72
Old Nichol St. E2 1C 72
Old North St. WC1 3A 70
Old Nursery Ct. E2 5D 62
Old Palace Yd. SW1 6J 79
Old Paradise St. SE11 1A 90
Old Pk. La. W1 3B 78
Old Pye St. SW1 6G 79
Old Pye St. Est. SW1 7G 79
Old Quebec St. W1 6K 67
Old Queen St. SW1 5H 79
Old Red Lion Theatre 5D 60
Old Royal Free Pl. N1 3D 60
Old Royal Free Sq. N1 3D 60
Old Seacoal La. EC4 6E 70
Old Sth. Lambeth Rd. SW8 7K 89
Old Spitalfields Market 3C 72
Old Sq. WC2 5C 70
OLD STREET 7J 61
Old St. EC1 2G 71
Old Theatre Ct. SE1 2H 81
Old Vic Theatre, The 4D 80
O'Leary Sq. E1 3J 73
Oliphant St. W10 7D 54
Olive Blythe Ho. W10 2E 64
Olive Ct. N1 3D 60
Oliver Ho. SE16 5E 82
SW8 7J 89
Olivers Wharf E1 3G 83
Olivers Yd. EC1 1K 71
Olive Tree Ho. SE15 6K 93
Olive Waite Ho. NW6 1A 56
Olivier Theatre 2C 80
(in National Theatre)
Olmar St. SE1 5E 92
Olney Ho. NW8 1H 67
Olney Rd. SE17 6F 91
(not continuous)
Olympia 7F 75
Olympia M. W2 1B 76
Olympia Way W14 7F 75
O'Meara St. SE1 3H 81
Omega Ho. SW10 7D 86
Omega Pl. N1 5K 59
O'Neill Ho. NW8 5G 57
One Owen St. EC1 5E 60
Ongar Rd. SW6 5J 85
Onslow Cl. W10 6G 55
Onslow Ct. SW10 4D 86
Onslow Cres. SW7 2F 87
Onslow Gdns. SW7 2E 86
Onslow M. E. SW7 2E 86
Onslow M. W. SW7 2E 86
Onslow Sq. SW7 1F 87
Onslow St. EC1 2D 70
Ontario St. SE1 6F 81
Opal M. NW6 2H 55
Opal St. SE11 2E 90
Operating Theatre Mus. 3K 81
Ophelia Ho. W6 3C 84
Opie Ho. NW8 4G 57
Oppidans Rd. NW3 1J 57
Orange Pl. SE16 7K 83
Orangery Gallery, The 5G 75
Orange St. WC2 1H 79
Orange Tree Ct. SE5 7A 92
Orange Yd. W1 6H 69
Oratory La. SW3 3F 87
Orbain Rd. SW6 7F 85
Orb St. SE17 2J 91
Orchard Cl. N1 1H 61
W10 3F 65
Orchard Ho. SE16 6K 83
SW6 7F 85
W1 5A 68
Orchard M. N1 1K 61
Orchardson Ho. NW8 2E 66
Orchardson St. NW8 2E 66
Orchard Sq. W14 4G 85
Orchard St. W1 6A 68
Orchard Studios W6 1C 84
Orde Hall St. WC1 2A 70
Ordnance Hill NW8 3F 57
Ordnance M. NW8 4F 57
Oriel Dr. SW13 6A 84
Orient St. SE11 1E 90
Orient Wharf E1 3G 83
Orion Bus. Cen. SE14 4K 93
Orion Ho. E1 2H 73
Orkney Ho. N1 3A 60
Orme Ct. W2 1B 76
Orme Ct. M. W2 1B 76
Orme Ho. E8 2D 62
Orme La. W2 1A 76
Orme Sq. W2 1A 76
Ormond Cl. WC1 3K 69
Ormonde Ct. NW8 3J 57
Ormonde Ga. SW3 4K 87
Ormonde Pl. SW1 2B 88
Ormonde Ter. NW8 3J 57
Ormond M. WC1 2K 69
Ormond Yd. SW1 2F 79
Ormrod Ct. W11 6F 65
Ormsby St. E2 4C 62
Ormside St. SE15 6J 93
Orpen Ho. SW5 2K 85
Orsett M. W2 5B 66
(not continuous)
Orsett St. SE11 3B 90
Orsett Ter. W2 5B 66
Orsman Rd. N1 3A 62
Orton St. E1 3E 82
Orwell Ct. E8 3F 63
Osbert St. SW1 2G 89
Osborn Cl. E8 2E 62
Osborn St. E1 4D 72
Oscar Faber Pl. N1 1B 62
Osier Ct. E1 2K 73
Osier St. E1 2K 73
Oslo Ct. NW8 5G 57
Osmani School Sports Cen. 2F 73
Osman Rd. W6 6B 74
Osnaburgh St. NW1 2D 68
(Euston Rd.)
NW1 7D 58
(Robert St.)
Osnaburgh Ter. NW1 1D 68
Osprey Ct. E1 1E 82
Ospringe Ho. SE1 4D 80
Osram Ct. W6 7B 74
Osric Path N1 5A 62
Ossington Bldgs. W1 3A 68
Ossington Cl. W2 1K 75
Ossington St. W2 1A 76
Ossory Rd. SE1 4E 92
Ossulston St. NW1 5G 59
Ostend Pl. SE1 1G 91
Osten M. SW7 7B 76
Oswald Bldg. SW8 6C 88
Oswell Ho. E1 2H 83
Oswin St. SE11 1F 91
Otford Ho. SE1 5K 81
SE15 5K 93
Othello Cl. SE11 3E 90
Other Cinema, The 7G 69
(off Rupert St.)
Otterburn Ho. SE5 7G 91
Otto St. SE17 6E 90
Outer Circ. NW1 5H 57
Outram Pl. N1 2K 59
Outwich St. EC3 5B 72
Oval, The E2 4G 63
Oval Cricket Ground, The 5B 90
Oval House Theatre 6C 90
Oval Mans. SE11 5B 90
Oval Pl. SW8 7A 90
Oval Rd. NW1 1C 58
Oval Way SE11 4B 90
Oversley Ho. W2 3K 65
Overstone Rd. W6 7A 74
Overy Ho. SE1 5E 80
Ovington Ct. SW3 7H 77
Ovington Gdns. SW3 7H 77
Ovington M. SW3 7H 77
Ovington Sq. SW3 7H 77
Ovington St. SW3 7H 77
Owen Mans. W14 5F 85
Owen's Row EC1 6E 60
Owen St. EC1 5E 60
Owgan Cl. SE5 7K 91
Oxendon St. SW1 1G 79
Oxenholme NW1 5F 59
Oxford & Cambridge Mans. NW1 4H 67
Oxford Cir. W1 6E 68
Oxford Cir. Av. W1 6E 68
Oxford Ct. EC4 7J 71
W9 3J 65
Oxford Dr. SE1 3A 82
Oxford Gdns. W10 6B 64
Oxford Ga. W6 1D 84
Oxford Rd. NW6 5K 55
Oxford Sq. W2 6H 67
Oxford St. W1 6K 67
Oxley Cl. SE1 3D 92
Oxo Tower Wharf SE1 1D 80
Oystergate Wlk. EC4 1J 81
Oyster Row E1 6J 73

P

Pace Pl. E1 6H 73
Pacific Wharf SE16 3K 83
Packenham Ho. E2 6D 62
Packington Sq. N1 3G 61
Packington St. N1 2F 61
Padbury SE17 4B 92
Padbury Ct. E2 7D 62
Padbury Ho. NW8 1H 67
PADDINGTON 6E 66
Paddington Bowling & Sports Club 1A 66
Paddington Grn. W2 3F 67
Paddington St. W1 3A 68
Paddington Wlk. W2 4E 66
Pageantmaster Ct. EC4 6E 70
Page St. SW1 1H 89
Page's Wlk. SE1 1A 92
Paget Ho. E2 4J 63
Paget St. EC1 6E 60
Pagham Ho. W10 2A 64
Painswick Ct. SE15 7C 92
Painters M. SE16 1F 93
Pakeman Ho. SE1 4F 81
Pakenham St. WC1 7B 60
Palace Av. W8 4B 76
Palace Bingo 1G 91
Palace Ct. W2 7A 66
(not continuous)
Palace Gdns. M. W8 2K 75
Palace Gdns. Ter. W8 2K 75
Palace Ga. W8 5C 76
Palace Grn. W8 3A 76
Palace Mans. W14 1F 85
Palace M. SW1 2B 88
SW6 7H 85
Palace Pl. SW1 6E 78
Palace Pl. Mans. W8 5B 76
Palace St. SW1 6E 78
Palace Theatre Soho 6H 69
Palace Wharf W6 7B 84
Palamon Ct. SE1 3D 92
Palestra Ho. SE1 3E 80
Palfrey Pl. SW8 7B 90
Palgrave Gdns. NW1 1H 67
Palgrave Ho. SE5 7G 91
Palissy St. E2 7C 62
(not continuous)
Palladium Ct. E8 1D 62
Pallant Ho. SE1 7K 81
Palliser Ct. W14 3E 84
Palliser Rd. W14 3E 84
Pall Mall SW1 3F 79
Pall Mall E. SW1 2H 79
Pall Mall Pl. SW1 3F 79
Palm Ct. SE15 7D 92
Palmerston Ho. SE1 5C 80
W8 3J 75
Palmerston Mans. W14 6F 85
Palmerston Rd. NW6 1H 55
(not continuous)
Palmer St. SW1 6G 79
(not continuous)
Palm Tree Ho. SE14 7K 93
Palyn Ho. EC1 7H 61
Pamela Ho. E8 2D 62
Pancras La. EC4 6H 71
Pancras Rd. NW1 4G 59
Pangbourne NW1 7E 58
Pangbourne Av. W10 3B 64
Panton St. SW1 1G 79
Paper Bldgs. EC4 7D 70
Parade, The SW11 7K 87
Paradise Row E2 6H 63
Paradise St. SE16 5H 83
Paradise Wlk. SW3 5J 87
Paragon M. SE1 1K 91
Paramount Bldg. EC1 1E 70
Paramount Ct. WC1 2F 69
Pardoner Ho. SE1 6K 81
Pardoner St. SE1 6K 81
(not continuous)
Pardon St. EC1 1F 71
Parfett St. E1 4F 73
(not continuous)
Parfrey St. W6 5B 84
Paris Gdn. SE1 2E 80
Paris Ho. E2 5G 63
Park App. SE16 7H 83
Park Bus. Cen. NW6 7K 55
Park Cl. E9 2K 63
SW1 5J 77
W14 6H 75
Park Cres. W1 2C 68
Park Cres. M. E. W1 2D 68
Park Cres. M. W. W1 2C 68
Parker M. WC2 5K 69
Parkers Row SE1 5D 82
Parker St. WC2 5K 69
Parkfield St. N1 4D 60
Parkgate N1 2K 61
Parkgate Rd. SW11 7H 87
Park Ho. E9 1J 63
Parkhouse St. SE5 7K 91
Parkinson Ho. E9 1J 63
SW1 2F 89
Parkland Ct. W11 4E 74
Park La. W1 7K 67
Park Lodge NW8 1F 57
W14 7H 75
Park Lorne NW8 7H 57
Park Mans. NW8 5G 57
SW1 5J 77
SW8 5K 89
Park M. W10 5F 55
Park Pl. N1 2K 61
SW1 3E 78
Park Pl. Vs. W2 3D 66
Park Rd. NW1 7H 57
NW8 7H 57
Parkside SW1 4K 77
Parkside Est. E9 2K 63
Park Sq. E. NW1 1C 68
Park Sq. M. NW1 2C 68
Park Sq. W. NW1 1C 68
Park Steps W2 7H 67
Park St. SE1 2G 81
W1 7A 68
Park Towers W1 3C 78
Park Vw. Apartments SE16 7H 83
Park Vw. Est. E2 5K 63
Park Village E. NW1 3C 58
Park Village W. NW1 4C 58
Parkville Rd. SW6 7G 85
Park Wlk. SW10 5D 86
Parkway NW1 3C 58
Park W. W2 5H 67
Park W. Pl. W2 5H 67
Parkwood NW8 3J 57
Parliament Ct. E1 4B 72
Parliament Sq. SW1 5J 79
Parliament St. SW1 4J 79
Parliament Vw. SE1 1A 90
Parmiter Ind. Est. E2 4H 63
Parmiter St. E2 4H 63
Parmoor Ct. EC1 1G 71
Parnell Ho. WC1 4H 69
Parr Ct. N1 4J 61
Parr St. N1 4J 61
Parry Ho. E1 3H 83
Parry Rd. W10 6F 55
Parry St. SW8 5K 89
Parsons Ho. W2 2E 66
Parsons Lodge NW6 1A 56
Partridge Ct. EC1 1E 70
Pascall Ho. SE17 5G 91
Pascal St. SW8 7H 89
Pasley Cl. SE17 4G 91
Passfield Hall WC1 1H 69
Passfields W14 4G 85
Passing All. EC1 2F 71
Passmore House E2 3C 62
Passmore St. SW1 3A 88
Pastor St. SE11 1F 91
(not continuous)
Paternoster La. EC4 6F 71
Paternoster Row EC4 6G 71
Paternoster Sq. EC4 6F 71
Paterson Ct. EC1 7J 61
Pater St. W8 7J 75
Paton St. EC1 7G 61
Patrick Coman Ho. EC1 7E 60
Patriot Sq. E2 5H 63
Pat Shaw Ho. E1 1K 73
Patterdale NW1 7D 58
Patterdale Rd. SE15 7J 93
Pattern Ho. EC1 1E 70
Pattison Ho. E1 5K 73
SE1 4H 81
Paul Daisley Ct. NW6 1E 54
Paul Ho. W10 2E 64
Pauline Ho. E1 3F 73
Paul St. EC2 2K 71
Paul's Wlk. EC4 7F 71
Paultons Ho. SW3 5F 87
Paultons Sq. SW3 5F 87
Paultons St. SW3 6F 87
Pavan Ct. E2 7K 63
Paveley Dr. SW11 7G 87
Paveley Ho. N1 5A 60
Paveley St. NW8 7G 57
Pavilion NW8 7F 57
Pavilion, The SW8 7H 89
Pavilion Ct. NW6 6J 55
Pavilion Pde. W12 5A 64
Pavilion Rd. SW1 5K 77
Pavilion St. SW1 7K 77
Pavilion Ter. W12 5A 64
Paxton Ter. SW1 5D 88
Paymal Ho. E1 4K 73
Payne Ho. N1 3B 60
Paynes Wlk. W6 6E 84
Peabody Av. SW1 3C 88
Peabody Bldgs. E1 7E 72
EC1 2H 71
SW3 6G 87
Peabody Cl. SW1 5D 88
Peabody Ct. EC1 2H 71
Peabody Est. E1 7K 73
E2 5G 63
EC1 2H 71
(Dufferin St., not continuous)
EC1 2D 70
(Farringdon La.)
N1 2G 61
SE1 3D 80
(Duchy St.)
SE1 4H 81
(Marshalsea Rd.)
SE1 3G 81
(Southwark St.)
SW1 1F 89
SW3 5H 87
SW6 5H 85
W6 4B 84
W10 3B 64
Peabody Sq. SE1 5E 80
(not continuous)
Peabody Ter. EC1 2D 70
Peabody Twr. EC1 2H 71
Peabody Trust SE17 2J 91
Peabody Yd. N1 2G 61
Peach Rd. W10 6D 54
Peacock St. SE17 2F 91
Peacock Theatre 6A 70
Peacock Yd. SE17 2F 91
Pearce Ho. SW1 2H 89
Pear Ct. SE15 7C 92
Pearl St. E1 2H 83
Pearman St. SE1 6D 80

Pear Pl. SE1 ....4C 80
Pearse St. SE15 ....6B 92
Pearson St. E2 ....4C 62
Pear Tree Cl. E2 ....3C 62
Pear Tree Ct. EC1 ....2D 70
Peartree La. E1 ....1K 83
Pear Tree St. EC1 ....1F 71
Peary Pl. E2 ....6K 63
Peckham Gro. SE15 ....7B 92
Peckham Hill St.
SE15 ....7E 92
Peckham Pk. Rd.
SE15 ....7E 92
Pecks Yd. E1 ....3C 72
Pedley St. E1 ....2D 72
Pedworth Gdns. SE16 ....2J 93
Peebles Ho. NW6 ....5K 55
Peel Gro. E2 ....5J 63
Peel Pas. W8 ....3J 75
Peel Pct. NW6 ....5J 55
Peel St. W8 ....3J 75
Peerless St. EC1 ....7J 61
Pegasus Pl. SE11 ....5C 90
Peldon Wlk. N1 ....2F 61
Pelham Ct. SW3 ....2G 87
Pelham Cres. SW7 ....2G 87
Pelham Ho. W14 ....2G 85
Pelham Pl. SW7 ....1G 87
Pelham St. SW7 ....1F 87
Pelican Pas. E1 ....1J 73
Pelican Wharf E1 ....2K 83
Pelier St. SE17 ....5H 91
Pella Ho. SE11 ....3B 90
Pellant Rd. SW6 ....6F 85
Pellew Ho. E1 ....2H 73
Pelter St. E2 ....6C 62
(not continuous)
Pember Rd. NW10 ....7C 54
Pemberton Ct. E1 ....7K 63
Pemberton Pl. E8 ....1H 63
Pemberton Row EC4 ....5D 70
Pembridge Cres.
W11 ....7J 65
Pembridge Gdns. W2 ....1J 75
Pembridge M. W11 ....7J 65
Pembridge Pl. W2 ....7K 65
Pembridge Rd. W11 ....1J 75
Pembridge Sq. W2 ....1K 75
Pembridge Studios
W11 ....7J 65
Pembridge Vs. W2 ....6K 65
W11 ....1J 75
Pembroke W14 ....2H 85
Pembroke Av. N1 ....2K 59
Pembroke Cl. SW1 ....5B 78
Pembroke Cotts. W8 ....7J 75
Pembroke Ct. W8 ....7J 75
Pembroke Gdns. W8 ....1H 85
Pembroke Gdns. Cl.
W8 ....7H 75
Pembroke Ho. SW1 ....7A 78
W2 ....6B 66
Pembroke M. W8 ....7J 75
Pembroke Pl. W8 ....7J 75
Pembroke Rd. W8 ....1H 85
Pembroke Sq. W8 ....7J 75
Pembroke St. N1 ....1K 59
(not continuous)
Pembroke Studios
W8 ....7H 75
Pembroke Ter. NW8 ....3E 56
Pembroke Vs. W8 ....1J 85
Pembroke Wlk. W8 ....1J 85
Pemell Cl. E1 ....1K 73
Pemell Ho. E1 ....1K 73
Penally Pl. N1 ....2K 61
Penang Ho. E1 ....2H 83
Penang St. E1 ....2H 83
Penarth Cen. SE15 ....5J 93
Penarth St. SE15 ....5J 93
Pencombe M. W11 ....7H 65
Pencraig Way SE15 ....6G 93
Pendley Ho. E2 ....3F 63
Pendrell Ho. WC2 ....6H 69
Penfield Lodge W9 ....3K 65
Penfold Pl. NW1 ....3G 67
Penfold St. NW1 ....3G 67
NW8 ....2F 67
Penhurst Pl. SE1 ....7B 80
Peninsula Apartments
W2 ....4G 67
(off Praed St.)
Peninsula Hgts. SE1 ....3K 89
Penley Ct. WC2 ....7B 70
Penmayne Ho. SE11 ....3D 90
Pennack Rd. SE15 ....6D 92
Pennant M. W8 ....1A 86
Pennard Mans. W12 ....5A 74
Pennard Rd. W12 ....4A 74
Pennethorne Cl. E9 ....3J 63
Pennethorne Rd.
SE15 ....7G 93
Penn Ho. NW8 ....2G 67
Pennington St. E1 ....1F 83
Penn St. N1 ....3K 61
Pennyford Ct. NW8 ....1E 66
Pennymoor Wlk. W9 ....1H 65
Penrose Gro. SE17 ....4G 91
Penrose Ho. SE17 ....4G 91
(not continuous)
Penrose St. SE17 ....4G 91
Penryn Ho. SE11 ....3E 90
Penryn St. NW1 ....4G 59
Penry St. SE1 ....2B 92
Penshurst Ho. SE15 ....5K 93
Pentagram Yd. W11 ....6J 65
Penton Gro. N1 ....5C 60
Penton Ho. N1 ....5C 60
Penton Pl. SE17 ....2F 91
Penton Ri. WC1 ....6B 60
Penton St. N1 ....4C 60
PENTONVILLE 5A 60
Pentonville Rd. N1 ....6K 59
Pentridge St. SE15 ....7C 92
Penywern Rd. SW5 ....3K 85
Penzance Ho. SE11 ....3D 90
Penzance Pl. W11 ....2E 74
Penzance St. W11 ....2E 74
Peony Ct. SW3 ....5D 86
Peperfield WC1 ....7A 60
Pepler Ho. W10 ....2E 64
Pepler M. SE5 ....4C 92
Peploe Rd. NW6 ....4D 54
Pepper St. SE1 ....4G 81
Pepys Ho. E2 ....6K 63
Pepys St. EC3 ....7B 72
Percival David Foundation of
Chinese Art 2H 69
Percival St. EC1 ....1E 70
Percy Cir. WC1 ....6B 60
Percy M. W1 ....4G 69
Percy Pas. W1 ....4G 69
Percy St. W1 ....4G 69
Percy Yd. WC1 ....6B 60
Peregrine Ho. EC1 ....6F 61
Perham Rd. W14 ....4F 85
Perkin's Rents SW1 ....7G 79
Perkins Sq. SE1 ....2H 81
Perrin Ho. NW6 ....6J 55
Perronet Ho. SE1 ....7F 81
Perryn Rd. SE16 ....6G 83
Perry's Pl. W1 ....5G 69
Perseverance Pl.
SW9 ....7D 90
Perseverance Works
E2 ....6B 62
Perth Ho. N1 ....1A 60
Peter Best Ho. E1 ....5G 73
Peterborough Ct.
EC4 ....6D 70
Peter Butler Ho. SE1 ....4E 82
Peterchurch Ho.
SE15 ....6G 93
Peter Ho. SW8 ....7J 89
Peterley Bus. Cen.
E2 ....4H 63
Peter Pan Statue 2E 76
Peters Ct. W2 ....5B 66
Petersham Ho. SW7 ....1E 86
Petersham La. SW7 ....6C 76
Petersham M. SW7 ....7C 76
Petersham Pl. SW7 ....7C 76
Peter's Hill EC4 ....7G 71
Peter's La. EC1 ....3F 71
(not continuous)
Peter St. W1 ....7G 69
Petherton Ct. NW10 ....3C 54
Petiver Cl. E9 ....1K 63
Petley Rd. W6 ....6B 84
Peto Pl. NW1 ....1D 68
Petrie Mus. of
Egyptian Archaeology
.......2G 69
Petticoat La. E1 ....4B 72
Petticoat Lane Market
.......4B 72
(off Middlesex St.)
Petticoat Sq. E1 ....5C 72
Petticoat Twr. E1 ....5C 72
Petty France SW1 ....6F 79
Petty Wales EC3 ....1B 82
Petyt Pl. SW3 ....6G 87
Petyward SW3 ....2H 87
Peveril Ho. SE1 ....7K 81
Pheasantry Ho. SW3 ....3H 87
Phelp St. SE17 ....5J 91
Phene St. SW3 ....5H 87
Philadelphia Ct.
SW10 ....7D 86
Philbeach Gdns. SW5 ....3J 85
Philchurch Pl. E1 ....6F 73
Philia Ho. NW1 ....1E 58
Philip Ct. W2 ....3E 66
Philip Ho. NW6 ....3A 56
Philip Mole Ho. W9 ....1J 65
Phillimore Ct. W8 ....5K 75
Phillimore Gdns.
NW10 ....2A 54
W8 ....5J 75
Phillimore Gdns. Cl.
W8 ....6J 75
Phillimore Pl. W8 ....5J 75
Phillimore Ter. W8 ....6K 75
Phillimore Wlk. W8 ....6J 75
Phillipp St. N1 ....3A 62
Philpot La. EC3 ....7A 72
Philpot St. E1 ....4G 73
Phipps Ho. W12 ....7A 64
Phipp St. EC2 ....1A 72
Phoenix Cl. E8 ....2C 62
Phoenix Ct. E1 ....1H 73
NW1 ....5H 59
Phoenix Lodge Mans.
W6 ....1B 84
Phoenix Pl. WC1 ....1B 70
Phoenix Rd. NW1 ....6G 59
Phoenix St. WC2 ....6H 69
Phoenix Theatre 6H 69
Phoenix Wharf E1 ....3H 83
Phoenix Wharf Rd.
SE1 ....5D 82
Phoenix Yd. WC1 ....7B 60
Photographers' Gallery
.......7J 69
(off Gt. Newport St.)
Physic Pl. SW3 ....5J 87
Piazza, The WC2 ....7K 69
(not continuous)
Piccadilly W1 ....4C 78
Piccadilly Arc. SW1 ....2E 78
Piccadilly Circus 1G 79
Piccadilly Cir. W1 ....1G 79
Piccadilly Pl. W1 ....1F 79
Piccadilly Theatre 7F 69
Pickard St. EC1 ....6F 61
Pickering Cl. E9 ....1K 63
Pickering Ho. W2 ....6C 66
Pickering M. W2 ....5B 66
Pickering Pl. SW1 ....3F 79
Pickering St. N1 ....2F 61
Pickfords Wharf N1 ....5G 61
SE1 ....2J 81
Pickwick Ho. SE16 ....5E 82
W11 ....2D 74
Pickwick St. SE1 ....5G 81
Picton Pl. W1 ....6B 68
Picton St. SE5 ....7J 91
Pied Bull Yard *N1 ....3E 60*
(off Theberton St.)
WC1 ....4J 69
Pier Head E1 ....3G 83
(not continuous)
Pierhead Wharf E1 ....3G 83
Pier Ho. SW3 ....6H 87
Pierrepont Arc. N1 ....4E 60
Pierrepont Row N1 ....4E 60
Pietra Lara Bldg. EC1 ....1G 71
Piggott Ho. E2 ....4K 63
Pikemans Ct. SW5 ....2J 85
Pilgrimage St. SE1 ....5J 81
Pilgrim Ho. SE1 ....7K 81
Pilgrim St. EC4 ....6E 70
Pilton Pl. SE17 ....3H 91
Pilton Pl. Est. SE17 ....3H 91
PIMLICO 4E 88
Pimlico Ho. SW1 ....3C 88
Pimlico Rd. SW1 ....3A 88
Pimlico Wlk. N1 ....6A 62
Pinchin & Johnsons Yd.
E1 ....7F 73
Pinchin St. E1 ....7F 73
Pincombe Ho. SE17 ....3J 91
Pindar St. EC2 ....3A 72
Pindock M. W9 ....2B 66
Pineapple Ct. SW1 ....6F 79
Pine Ho. SE16 ....4K 83
W10 ....1E 64
Pinehurst Ct. W11 ....6H 65
Pine M. NW10 ....4C 54
Pine St. EC1 ....1C 70
Pine Tree Ho. SE14 ....7K 93
Pinner Ct. NW8 ....1E 66
Pinners Pas. *EC2 ....5A 72*
(off Austin Friars)
Pioneer Ho. WC1 ....6A 60
Pioneer Way W12 ....6A 64
Pippin Ho. W10 ....7C 64
Pitfield Est. N1 ....6A 62
Pitfield St. N1 ....3A 62
Pitman St. SE5 ....7G 91
(not continuous)
Pitt's Head M. W1 ....3B 78
Pitt St. W8 ....4K 75
Place, The 7H 59
Plaisterers Highwalk
EC2 ....4G 71
Planetree Ct. W6 ....1D 84
Plantain Pl. SE1 ....4J 81
Plantation Pl. EC3 ....7A 72
Platina St. EC2 ....1K 71
Platt St. NW1 ....4G 59
Playfair Mans. W14 ....6F 85
Playfair St. W6 ....4B 84
Playhouse Ct. *SE1 ....4G 81*
(off Southwark Bri. Rd.)
Playhouse Theatre 2K 79
Playhouse Yd. EC4 ....6E 70
Plaza Pde. NW6 ....4A 56
Plaza Shop. Cen., The
W1 ....5F 69
Pleasant Pl. N1 ....1F 61
Pleasant Row NW1 ....3D 58
Plender Pl. NW1 ....3F 59
Plender St. NW1 ....3E 58
Pleydell Ct. EC4 ....6D 70
Pleydell Est. EC1 ....7H 61
Pleydell St. EC4 ....6D 70
Plough Ct. EC3 ....7K 71
Ploughmans Cl. NW1 ....2G 59
Plough Pl. EC4 ....5D 70
Plough St. E1 ....5D 72
Plough Yd. EC2 ....2B 72
Plover Ho. SW9 ....7C 90
Plowden Bldgs. *EC4 ....7C 70*
(off Middle Temple La.)
Plumber's Row E1 ....4E 72
Plumtree Ct. EC4 ....5E 70
Plympton Av. NW6 ....1G 55
Plympton Pl. NW8 ....2G 67
Plympton Rd. NW6 ....1G 55
Plympton St. NW8 ....2G 67
Pocock St. SE1 ....4E 80
Point, The W2 ....4E 66
Point West SW7 ....1B 86
Poland St. W1 ....5F 69
Polesworth Ho. W2 ....3K 65
Pollard Ho. N1 ....5A 60
Pollard Row E2 ....6F 63
Pollard St. E2 ....6F 63
Pollen St. W1 ....6E 68
Pollitt Dr. NW8 ....1F 67
Pollock Ho. W10 ....1E 64
Pollock's Toy Mus. 3F 69
Polperro Ho. W2 ....4K 65
Polperro M. SE11 ....1E 90
Polychrome Ct. SE1 ....5E 80
Polygon, The NW8 ....2F 57
Polygon Rd. NW1 ....5G 59
Pomell Way E1 ....5D 72
Pomeroy Ho. E2 ....5K 63
W11 ....6E 64
Pomeroy St. SE15 ....7K 93
Pond Ho. SW3 ....2G 87
Pond Pl. SW3 ....2G 87
Ponler St. E1 ....6G 73
Ponsonby Ho. E2 ....4J 63
(not continuous)
Ponsonby Pl. SW1 ....3H 89
Ponsonby Ter. SW1 ....3H 89
Ponton Rd. SW8 ....6H 89
Pont St. SW1 ....7J 77
Pont St. M. SW1 ....7J 77
Pontypool Pl. SE1 ....4E 80
Poole Ct. N1 ....1B 62
Poole Ho. SE11 ....1B 90
Pooles Bldgs. WC1 ....2C 70
Pooles La. SW10 ....7C 86
Poole St. N1 ....3J 61
Pool Ho. NW8 ....3F 67
Poonah St. E1 ....6K 73
Pope Ho. SE5 ....7J 91
SE16 ....2G 93
Pope's Head All. EC3 ....6K 71
Pope St. SE1 ....5B 82
Popham Rd. N1 ....2G 61
Popham St. N1 ....2F 61
(not continuous)
Poplar Gro. W6 ....5B 74
Poplar Ho. SE16 ....5K 83
Poplar M. W12 ....3A 74
Poplar Pl. W2 ....7A 66
Poppins Ct. EC4 ....6E 70
Porchester Ct. W2 ....7B 66
Porchester Gdns. W2 ....7B 66
Porchester Gdns. M.
W2 ....6B 66
Porchester Ga. W2 ....1B 76
(not continuous)
Porchester Ho. E1 ....5G 73
Porchester Leisure Cen.
.......5A 66
Porchester M. W2 ....5B 66
Porchester Pl. W2 ....6H 67
Porchester Rd. W2 ....5B 66
Porchester Sq. W2 ....5B 66
Porchester Ter. W2 ....6C 66
Porchester Ter. Nth.
W2 ....5B 66
Porchester Wlk. W2 ....5B 66
Porlock St. SE1 ....4K 81
Portcullis Ho. SW1 ....5J 79
Portelet Ct. N1 ....2A 62
Portelet Rd. E1 ....7K 63
Porten Ho's. W14 ....7E 74
Porten Rd. W14 ....7E 74
Porters Lodge, The
SW10 ....7C 86
(off Coleridge Gdns.)
Porter St. SE1 ....2H 81
W1 ....3K 67
Porters Wlk. E1 ....1H 83
Porteus Rd. W2 ....3D 66
Portgate Cl. W9 ....1H 65
Portia Ct. SE11 ....3E 90
Porticos, The SW3 ....6E 86
Portishead Ho. W2 ....4J 65
Portland Ct. N1 ....1B 62
SE1 ....6J 81
Portland Ho. SW1 ....7E 78
Portland M. W1 ....6F 69
Portland Pl. W1 ....2C 68
Portland Rd. W11 ....7E 64
Portland Sq. E1 ....2G 83
Portland St. SE17 ....3J 91
Portland Wlk. SE17 ....5K 91
Portman Cl. W1 ....5K 67
Portman Ga. NW1 ....2H 67
Portman Mans. W1 ....3K 67
Portman M. Sth. W1 ....6A 68
Portman Pl. E2 ....7K 63
Portman Sq. W1 ....5A 68
Portman St. W1 ....6A 68
Portman Towers W1 ....5K 67
Portnall Ho. W9 ....7G 55
Portnall Rd. W9 ....5G 55
Portobello Ct. Est.
W11 ....6H 65
Portobello M. W11 ....1J 75
Portobello Rd. W10 ....2E 64
W11 ....5G 65
Portobello Road Market
.......3E 64
Portpool La. EC1 ....3C 70
Portsea Hall W2 ....6J 67
Portsea M. W2 ....6H 67
Portsea Pl. W2 ....6H 67
Portsmouth St. WC2 ....6A 70
Portsoken St. E1 ....7C 72
Portugal St. WC2 ....6A 70
Pory Ho. SE11 ....2B 90
Postern, The EC2 ....4H 71
Post Office Ct. EC3 ....6K 71
Post Office Way SW8 ....7G 89
Potier St. SE1 ....7K 81
Potter Cl. SE15 ....7B 92
Potters Flds. SE1 ....3B 82
Pottery La. W11 ....2F 75
Pottery St. SE16 ....5G 83
Pott St. E2 ....7H 63
Poultry EC2 ....6J 71
Povey Ho. SE17 ....2A 92
Powell Ho. *W2 ....7E 66*
(off Gloucester Ter.)
W2 ....5B 66
(Gloucester Ter.)
Powis Ct. W11 ....5H 65
Powis Gdns. W11 ....5H 65
Powis M. W11 ....5H 65
Powis Pl. WC1 ....2K 69
Powis Sq. W11 ....5H 65
(not continuous)
Powis Ter. W11 ....5H 65
Pownall Rd. E8 ....3D 62
Poynter Ho. NW8 ....1E 66
W11 ....2D 74
Poyser St. E2 ....5H 63
Praed M. W2 ....5F 67
Praed St. W2 ....6E 66
Pratt M. NW1 ....3E 58
Pratt St. NW1 ....3E 58
Pratt Wlk. SE11 ....1B 90
Preachers Ct. EC1 ....2F 71
Prebend St. N1 ....3G 61
Precinct, The N1 ....3G 61
Premier Cnr. W9 ....5G 55
Premier Ho. N1 ....1E 60
Prescot St. E1 ....7D 72
Prescott Ho. SE17 ....6F 91
President Dr. E1 ....2G 83
President Ho. EC1 ....7F 61
President Quay E1 ....2D 82
President St. EC1 ....6G 61
Press Ct. SE1 ....3E 92
Preston Cl. SE1 ....1A 92
Preston Ho. SE1 ....1A 92
(Preston Cl.)
SE1 ....6C 82
(Stanworth St.)
Prestwood Ho. SE16 ....6G 83
Prestwood St. N1 ....5H 61
Priam Ho. E2 ....5H 63
Price Ho. N1 ....3G 61
Price's St. SE1 ....3F 81
Price's Yd. N1 ....3B 60
Prideaux Ho. WC1 ....6B 60
Prideaux Pl. WC1 ....6B 60
Priestley Ho. EC1 ....1G 71
Priest's Ct. EC2 ....5G 71
Prima Rd. SW9 ....7C 90
PRIMROSE HILL 2A 58
Primrose Hill EC4 ....6D 70
Primrose Hill Ct.
NW3 ....1J 57
Primrose Hill Rd.
NW3 ....1J 57
Primrose Hill Studios
NW1 ....2A 58
Primrose M. NW1 ....1K 57
Primrose Sq. E9 ....1K 63
Primrose St. EC2 ....3A 72
Prince Albert Ct.
NW8 ....3J 57
Prince Albert Rd.
NW1 ....6G 57
NW8 ....6G 57
Prince Charles Cinema
.......7H 69
Prince Consort Rd.
SW7 ....6D 76
Princedale Rd. W11 ....2E 74
Prince Edward Mans.
W2 ....7K 65
Prince Edward Theatre
.......6H 69
Princelet St. E1 ....3D 72
Prince of Orange Ct.
SE16 ....7K 83
Prince of Wales Pas.
NW1 ....7E 58
Prince of Wales Ter.
W8 ....5B 76
Prince of Wales Theatre
.......1G 79
Prince Regent Ct.
NW8 ....4H 57
Prince Regent M.
NW1 ....7E 58
Princes Arc. SW1 ....2F 79
Princes Cir. WC2 ....5J 69
Prince's Ct. SW3 ....6J 77
Princes Ct. Bus. Cen.
E1 ....1H 83
Prince's Gdns. SW7 ....6F 77
Prince's Ga. SW7 ....5F 77
(not continuous)
Prince's Ga. Ct. SW7 ....5F 77
Prince's Ga. M. SW7 ....6F 77
Princes Ho. W11 ....1H 75
Princes M. W2 ....7A 66
W6 ....3A 84
Princes Pl. SW1 ....2F 79
W11 ....2E 74
Princess Alice Ho.
W10 ....2B 64
Princess Ct. W1 ....4J 67
W2 ....7B 66
Princess Louise Cl.
W2 ....3F 67
Princess Mary Ho.
SW1 ....2H 89
Princess of Wales
Memorial Fountain
.......4F 77
Princes Sq. W2 ....7K 65
(not continuous)
Princess Rd. NW1 ....2A 58
NW6 ....5J 55
Princess St. SE1 ....7F 81
Princes St. EC2 ....6J 71
W1 ....6D 68
Prince's Twr. SE16 ....4J 83
Prince's Yd. W11 ....3F 75
Princethorpe Ho. W2 ....3A 66
Princeton St. WC1 ....4A 70
Printers Inn Ct. EC4 ....5C 70
Printer St. EC4 ....5D 70
Printing Ho. Yd. E2 ....7B 62
Printwork Apartments
SE1 ....6A 82
(off Long La.)
Prioress St. SE1 ....7K 81
Priory Ct. EC4 ....6F 71
Priory Grn. Est. N1 ....4B 60
Priory Ho. E1 ....3C 72
EC1 ....1E 70
SW1 ....3G 89
Priory Mans. SW10 ....4D 86
Priory Pk. Rd. NW6 ....2H 55
Priory Rd. NW6 ....2A 56
Priory Ter. NW6 ....2A 56
Priory Wlk. SW10 ....4D 86
Pritchard Ho. E2 ....4G 63
Pritchard's Rd. E2 ....3F 63
Priter Rd. SE16 ....7F 83
Priter Way SE16 ....7F 83
Probyn Ho. SW1 ....1H 89
Procter Ho. SE1 ....3E 92
SE5 ....7K 91
Procter St. WC1 ....4A 70
Prospect Ho. N1 ....5C 60
SE1 ....7E 80
W10 ....6D 64
Prospect Pl. E1 ....2J 83
(not continuous)
Prospect St. SE16 ....5H 83
Prospect Wharf E1 ....1K 83
Prothero Rd. SW6 ....7F 85
Proud Ho. E1 ....5G 73
Provence St. N1 ....4G 61
Providence Ct. W1 ....7B 68
Providence Pl. N1 ....3E 60
Providence Row N1 ....5A 60
Providence Row Cl.
E2 ....7H 63
Providence Sq. SE1 ....4E 82
Providence Twr.
SE16 ....4E 82
Providence Yd. E2 ....6E 62
Provost Est. N1 ....6J 61
Provost St. N1 ....5J 61
Prowse Pl. NW1 ....1E 58
Prudent Pas. EC2 ....6H 71
Prusom's Island E1 ....2J 83
Prusom St. E1 ....2H 83
Pudding La. EC3 ....1K 81
Puddle Dock EC4 ....7F 71
(not continuous)
Pugin Ct. N1 ....1D 60
Pulham Ho. SW8 ....7A 90
Pullen's Bldgs.
SE17 ....3F 91
Pulteney Ter. N1 ....3B 60
(not continuous)
Pulton Pl. SW6 ....7J 85
Puma Ct. E1 ....3C 72
Pump Ct. EC4 ....6C 70
Pump Ho. Cl. SE16 ....5K 83
Pump House Gallery, The
.......7A 88
Pump Ho. M. E1 ....7E 72
Pump La. SE14 ....7K 93
Punderson's Gdns.
E2 ....6H 63
Purbeck Ho. SW8 ....7A 90
Purbrook Est. SE1 ....5B 82
Purbrook St. SE1 ....6B 82

Purcell Cres. SW6 ... 7D 84
(not continuous)
Purcell Ho. SW10 ... 6E 86
Purcell Mans. W14 ... 6F 85
Purcell Room ... 2B 80
Purcell St. N1 ... 4A 62
Purchese St. NW1 ... 4G 59
Purday Ho. W10 ... 7F 55
Purley Pl. N1 ... 1E 60
Purves Rd. NW10 ... 6A 54
Puteaux Ho. E2 ... 5K 63
Pynfolds SE16 ... 5H 83

Q

Quad Ct. SE1 ... 6B 82
Quadrangle, The
SW10 ... 7E 84
W2 ... 5G 67
W12 ... 6A 64
Quadrangle Cl. SE1 ... 1A 92
Quadrant, The W10 ... 7D 54
Quadrant Arc. W1 ... 1F 79
Quadrant Bus. Cen.
NW6 ... 2F 55
Quadrant Ho. SE1 ... 3E 80
Quain Mans. W14 ... 6F 85
Quaker Ct. E1 ... 2C 72
EC1 ... 1H 71
Quaker St. E1 ... 2C 72
Quality Ct. WC2 ... 5C 70
Quastel Ho. SE1 ... 5J 81
Quayside Cotts. E1 ... 2E 82
Quayside Ho. W10 ... 1E 64
Quebec M. W1 ... 6K 67
Quebec Wharf E8 ... 2B 62
Quedgeley Ct. SE15 ... 6C 92
Queen Alexandra Mans.
WC1 ... 6J 59
Queen Anne M. W1 ... 4D 68
Queen Anne's Ga.
SW1 ... 5G 79
Queen Anne St. W1 ... 5C 68
Queen Anne's Wlk.
WC1 ... 2K 69
Queen Anne Ter. E1 ... 1H 83
Queenbridge Sports & Community Cen. ... 1D 62
Queen Caroline St.
W6 ... 2B 84
(not continuous)
Queen Catherine Ho.
SW6 ... 7B 86
Queen Elizabeth Bldgs.
EC4 ... 7C 70
Queen Elizabeth Hall ... 2A 80
Queen Elizabeth II Conference Cen. ... 5H 79
Queen Elizabeth St.
SE1 ... 4B 82
Queenhithe EC4 ... 7H 71
Queen Isabella Way
EC1 ... 5F 71
Queen Margaret Flats
E2 ... 6H 63
Queen Marys Bldgs.
SW1 ... 1F 89
Queen Mother Sports Cen., The ... 1E 88
Queensberry M. W.
SW7 ... 1E 86
Queensberry Pl. SW7 ... 1E 86
Queensberry Way
SW7 ... 1E 86
Queensborough M.
W2 ... 7C 66
Queensborough Pas.
W2 ... 7C 66
Queensborough Studios
W2 ... 7C 66
Queensborough Ter.
W2 ... 7B 66
Queensbridge Ct. E2 ... 4D 62
Queensbridge Rd. E2 ... 2D 62
E8 ... 2D 62
Queensbury St. N1 ... 1H 61
Queen's Chapel of the Savoy, The ... 7A 70
Queen's Club Gdns.
W14 ... 5F 85
Queen's Club, The (Tennis Courts) ... 4F 85
Queens Club Ter.
W14 ... 5G 85
(off Normand Rd.)
Queens Ct. NW8 ... 4E 56
W2 ... 1B 76
Queensdale Cres.
W11 ... 2D 74
(not continuous)
Queensdale Pl. W11 ... 3E 74
Queensdale Rd. W11 ... 3D 74
Queensdale Wlk.
W11 ... 3E 74
Queen's Elm Pde.
SW3 ... 3F 87
(off Old Church St.)
Queen's Elm Sq.
SW3 ... 4F 87
Queen's Gallery ... 5D 78
Queen's Gdns. W2 ... 7C 66
Queen's Ga. SW7 ... 5D 76
Queen's Ga. Gdns.
SW7 ... 7C 76
Queen's Ga. M. SW7 ... 5D 76
Queen's Ga. Pl. SW7 ... 7D 76
Queensgate Pl. NW6 ... 1J 55
Queen's Ga. Pl. M.
SW7 ... 7D 76
Queen's Ga. Ter.
SW7 ... 6C 76
Queen's Gro. NW8 ... 3E 56
Queen's Gro. Studios
NW8 ... 3E 56
Queen's Head Pas.
EC4 ... 5G 71
Queen's Head St. N1 ... 3F 61
Queen's Head Yd.
SE1 ... 3J 81
Queens Ho. SE17 ... 5J 91
SW8 ... 7K 89
W2 ... 7B 66
Queen's Ice Bowl ... 1B 76
Queen's Mans. W6 ... 1C 84
Queensmead NW8 ... 2F 57
Queen's M. W2 ... 7A 66
(not continuous)
Queensmill Rd. SW6 ... 7C 84
Queens Pk. Ct. W10 ... 7D 54
Queen's Pk. Rangers FC ... 2A 74
Queens Pk. School Sports Cen. ... 2C 54
Queen Sq. WC1 ... 2K 69
Queen Sq. Pl. WC1 ... 2K 69
Queen's Quay EC4 ... 7H 71
Queen's Row SE17 ... 5J 91
Queens Ter. E1 ... 2J 73
NW8 ... 3E 56
Queen's Theatre Westminster ... 7G 69
Queenstown Rd.
SW8 ... 6C 88
Queen St. EC4 ... 7H 71
(not continuous)
W1 ... 2C 78
Queen St. Pl. EC4 ... 1H 81
Queen's Wlk. SW1 ... 2E 78
Queen's Wlk., The
SE1 ... 1D 80
(Oxo Tower Wharf)
SE1 ... 2K 81
(Tooley St.)
SE1 ... 2B 80
(Waterloo Rd.)
Queensway W2 ... 5B 66
Queens Wharf W6 ... 4A 84
Queen's Yd. WC1 ... 2F 69
Queen Victoria Memorial ... 5E 78
Queen Victoria St.
EC4 ... 7E 70
Queen Victoria Ter.
E1 ... 1H 83
Quendon Ho. W10 ... 2A 64
Quenington Ct. SE15 ... 6C 92
Quentin Ho. SE1 ... 5D 80
(not continuous)
Quest, The W11 ... 1F 75
Quex M. NW6 ... 2K 55
Quex Rd. NW6 ... 2K 55
Quick St. N1 ... 5F 61
Quick St. M. N1 ... 5E 60
Quickswood NW3 ... 1H 57
Quilp St. SE1 ... 4G 81
(not continuous)
Quilter Ho. W10 ... 6G 55
Quilter St. E2 ... 6E 62
Quinton Ho. SW8 ... 7J 89

R

Rabbit Row W8 ... 2K 75
Raceway, The (Go-Kart Track) ... 3J 59
Rackstraw Ho. NW3 ... 1J 57
Racton Rd. SW6 ... 6J 85
RADA ... 3G 69
Radcliffe Ho. SE16 ... 2G 93
Radcliffe Rd. SE1 ... 6B 82
Radcot St. SE11 ... 4D 90
Raddington Rd. W10 ... 4F 65
Radisson Ct. *SE1 ... 6A 82*
(off Long La.)
Radius Apartments
N1 ... 5K 59
Radlett Pl. NW8 ... 3G 57
Radley Ho. NW1 ... 1J 67
Radley M. W8 ... 7K 75
Radnor Ho. EC1 ... 7H 61
Radnor Lodge W2 ... 6F 67
Radnor M. W2 ... 6F 67
Radnor Pl. W2 ... 6G 67
Radnor Rd. NW6 ... 3E 54
SE15 ... 7E 92
Radnor St. EC1 ... 7H 61
Radnor Ter. W14 ... 1G 85
Radnor Wlk. SW3 ... 4H 87
Radstock St. SW11 ... 7G 87
(not continuous)
Radway Ho. W2 ... 3K 65
Railway App. SE1 ... 3K 81
Railway Arches E2 ... 4C 62
E8 ... 1H 63
W12 ... 4A 74
Railway Av. SE16 ... 4K 83
(not continuous)
Railway Cotts. W6 ... 5B 74
Railway M. W11 ... 5F 65
Railway St. N1 ... 5K 59
Rainbow St. SE5 ... 7A 92
Raine St. E1 ... 2H 83
Rainham Ho. NW1 ... 3F 59
Rainham Rd. NW10 ... 7B 54
Rainsford St. W2 ... 5G 67
Rainville Rd. W6 ... 6B 84
Raleigh Ct. SE16 ... 3K 83
W12 ... 5A 74
Raleigh Ho. SW1 ... 5G 89
Raleigh M. N1 ... 3F 61
Raleigh St. N1 ... 3F 61
Ralph Brook Ct. N1 ... 6K 61
Ralph Ct. W2 ... 5B 66
Ralston St. SW3 ... 4J 87
Ramar Ho. E1 ... 3E 72
Ramillies Pl. W1 ... 6E 68
Ramillies St. W1 ... 6E 68
Rampart St. E1 ... 6G 73
Rampayne St. SW1 ... 3G 89
Ramsay Ho. NW8 ... 4G 57
Ramsay M. SW3 ... 5G 87
Ramsey St. E2 ... 1F 73
Ramsfort Ho. SE16 ... 2G 93
Randall Rd. SE11 ... 3A 90
Randall Row SE11 ... 2A 90
Randell's Rd. N1 ... 2K 59
Randolph Av. W9 ... 5A 56
Randolph Cres. W9 ... 2C 66
Randolph Gdns. NW6 ... 5A 56
Randolph M. W9 ... 2D 66
Randolph Rd. W9 ... 2C 66
Randolph St. NW1 ... 1F 59
Ranelagh Bri. W2 ... 4B 66
Ranelagh Cotts. SW1 ... 3B 88
Ranelagh Gro. SW1 ... 3B 88
Ranelagh Ho. SW3 ... 3J 87
Ranelagh Rd. SW1 ... 4F 89
Rangoon St. EC3 ... 6C 72
Rankine Ho. SE1 ... 7G 81
Rannoch Rd. W6 ... 5B 84
Ransome's Dock Bus. Cen.
SW11 ... 7H 87
Ranston St. NW1 ... 3G 67
Raphael Ct. SE16 ... 3H 93
Raphael St. SW7 ... 5J 77
Rapley Ho. E2 ... 7E 62
Raquel Ct. SE1 ... 4A 82
Rashleigh Ho. WC1 ... 7J 59
Ratcliffe Ct. *SE1 ... 5H 81*
(off Gt. Dover St.)
Rathbone Ho. NW6 ... 3J 55
Rathbone Pl. W1 ... 4G 69
Rathbone St. W1 ... 4F 69
Raven Row E1 ... 3H 73
(not continuous)
Ravensbourne Ho.
NW8 ... 3G 67
Ravenscar NW1 ... 3E 58
Ravenscroft St. E2 ... 5D 62
Ravensdon St. SE11 ... 4D 90
Ravenstone SE17 ... 4B 92
Ravensworth Rd.
NW10 ... 6A 54
Ravent Rd. SE11 ... 2B 90
Raven Wharf SE1 ... 4C 82
Ravey St. EC2 ... 1A 72
Rawlings St. SW3 ... 1J 87
Rawreth Wlk. N1 ... 2H 61
Rawstorne Pl. EC1 ... 6E 60
Rawstorne St. EC1 ... 6E 60
(not continuous)
Rayburne Ct. W14 ... 6E 74
Ray Gunter Ho. SE17 ... 4F 91
Ray Ho. N1 ... 3K 61
W10 ... 5D 64
(off Cambridge Gdns.)
Raymede Towers
W10 ... 3D 64
Raymond Bldgs. WC1 ... 3B 70
Raymouth Rd. SE16 ... 1H 93
Rayne Ho. W9 ... 1A 66
Rayner Ct. W12 ... 5B 74
Raynham W2 ... 5H 67
Raynham Ho. E1 ... 1K 73
Raynor Pl. N1 ... 2H 61
Ray St. EC1 ... 2D 70
Ray St. Bri. EC1 ... 2D 70
Reachview Cl. NW1 ... 1F 59
Read Ho. SE11 ... 5C 90
Reading Ho. SE15 ... 6F 93
W2 ... 6C 66
Reapers Cl. NW1 ... 2G 59
Reardon Ho. E1 ... 2H 83
Reardon Path E1 ... 3H 83
(not continuous)
Reardon St. E1 ... 2H 83
Reaston St. SE14 ... 7K 93
Record St. SE15 ... 5J 93
Rector St. N1 ... 3G 61
Rectory Chambers
SW3 ... 5G 87
Reculver Ho. SE15 ... 5K 93
Reculver Rd. SE16 ... 3K 93
Red Anchor Cl. SW3 ... 6F 87
Redan Pl. W2 ... 6A 66
Redan St. W14 ... 6D 74
Redbourn Ho. W10 ... 2A 64
Redburn St. SW3 ... 5J 87
Redcar St. SE5 ... 7G 91
Redcastle Cl. E1 ... 7J 73
Redchurch St. E2 ... 1C 72
Redcliffe Cl. SW5 ... 4A 86
Redcliffe Gdns.
SW10 ... 4B 86
Redcliffe M. SW10 ... 4B 86
Redcliffe Pl. SW10 ... 6C 86
Redcliffe Rd. SW10 ... 4C 86
Redcliffe Sq. SW10 ... 4B 86
Redcliffe St. SW10 ... 5B 86
Redclyf Ho. E1 ... 1K 73
Red Cow La. EC1 ... 1G 71
Redcross Way SE1 ... 4H 81
Reddins Rd. SE15 ... 6E 92
Rede Pl. W2 ... 6K 65
Redesdale St. SW3 ... 5H 87
Redfield La. SW5 ... 1K 85
Redfield M. SW5 ... 1K 85
Redford Ho. W10 ... 6G 55
Redford Wlk. N1 ... 2F 61
Redgrave Ter. E2 ... 7F 63
Redhill St. NW1 ... 5D 58
Redington Ho. N1 ... 4B 60
Red Lion Cl. SE17 ... 5J 91
Red Lion Ct. EC4 ... 6D 70
SE1 ... 2H 81
Red Lion Row SE17 ... 5H 91
Red Lion Sq. WC1 ... 4A 70
Red Lion St. WC1 ... 3A 70
Red Lion Yd. W1 ... 2C 78
Redlynch Ct. W14 ... 5F 75
Redman Ho. EC1 ... 3C 70
SE1 ... 5H 81
Redman's Rd. E1 ... 3J 73
Redmead La. E1 ... 3E 82
Redmill Ho. E1 ... 2H 73
Redmond Ho. N1 ... 3B 60
Red Pl. W1 ... 7A 68
Redrup Ho. SE14 ... 6K 93
Redruth Rd. E9 ... 2K 63
Redshank Ho. SE1 ... 3D 92
Redvers St. N1 ... 6B 62
Redwing Ct. SE1 ... 5H 81
Redwood Ct. NW6 ... 1E 54
Redwood Mans. W8 ... 7A 76
Reece M. SW7 ... 1E 86
Reedworth St. SE11 ... 2D 90
Rees St. N1 ... 3H 61
Reeves Ho. SE1 ... 5C 80
Reeves M. W1 ... 1A 78
Reflection Ho. E2 ... 1E 72
Regal Cl. E1 ... 3F 73
Regal Ct. NW6 ... 5H 55
Regal La. NW1 ... 3B 58
Regan Way N1 ... 4A 62
Regency Ho. NW1 ... 1D 68
SW1 ... 1H 89
Regency Lodge NW3 ... 1E 56
Regency Pde. NW3 ... 1E 56
Regency Pl. SW1 ... 1H 89
Regency St. SW1 ... 1H 89
Regency Ter. SW7 ... 3E 86
Regent Ct. NW8 ... 7G 57
W8 ... 6A 76
Regent Ho. W14 ... 1E 84
Regent Pl. W1 ... 7F 69
Regent's Bri. Gdns.
SW8 ... 7K 89
Regents College ... 1A 68
Regents Ct. E8 ... 3D 62
Regents M. NW8 ... 4D 56
REGENT'S PARK ... 7D 58
Regent's Pk. ... 5K 57
Regent's Pk. Barracks ... 5C 58
Regents Pk. Est.
NW1 ... 6E 58
Regent's Pk. Gdns. M.
NW1 ... 2K 57
Regents Pk. Golf & Tennis School ... 4J 57
Regent's Pk. Ho.
NW8 ... 7H 57
Regent's Pk. Open Air Theatre ... 7A 58
Regent's Pk. Rd.
NW1 ... 1K 57
(not continuous)
Regent's Pk. Ter.
NW1 ... 2C 58
Regents Plaza NW6 ... 4A 56
Regent Sq. WC1 ... 7K 59
Regent's Row E8 ... 3E 62
Regent St. NW10 ... 7D 54
SW1 ... 1G 79
W1 ... 5D 68
Regents Wharf E2 ... 3G 63
N1 ... 4A 60
Regina Point SE16 ... 6K 83
Regis Ct. NW1 ... 3J 67
Regis Ho. W1 ... 3B 68
Regnart Bldgs. NW1 ... 7F 59
Relay Rd. W12 ... 1B 74
Reliance Sq. EC2 ... 1B 72
Relton M. SW7 ... 6H 77
Rembrandt Cl. SW1 ... 3A 88
Rembrandt Ct. SE16 ... 3H 93
Remington St. N1 ... 5F 61
Remnant St. WC2 ... 5A 70
Remsted Ho. NW6 ... 3A 56
Remus Bldg., The
EC1 ... 7D 60
Rendle Ho. W10 ... 2E 64
Renforth St. SE16 ... 5K 83
Renfrew Ho. NW6 ... 5A 56
Renfrew Rd. SE11 ... 1E 90
Rennie Cotts. E1 ... 1K 73
Rennie Ct. SE1 ... 2E 80
Rennie Est. SE16 ... 2H 93
Rennie Ho. SE1 ... 7G 81
Rennie St. SE1 ... 2E 80
(not continuous)
Renoir Cinema Brunswick Square ... 2K 69
Renoir Ct. SE16 ... 3H 93
Rephidim St. SE1 ... 7A 82
Repton Ho. SW1 ... 2F 89
Reston Pl. SW7 ... 5C 76
Restormel Ho. SE11 ... 2D 90
Retford St. N1 ... 5B 62
Reunion Row E1 ... 1H 83
Reverdy Rd. SE1 ... 2E 92
Rewell St. SW6 ... 7C 86
Rex Pl. W1 ... 1B 78
Reynolds Ho. E2 ... 4K 63
NW8 ... 5F 57
SW1 ... 2H 89
Rheidol M. N1 ... 4G 61
Rheidol Ter. N1 ... 4F 61
Rhoda St. E2 ... 1D 72
Rhodes Ho. N1 ... 6J 61
Ribblesdale Ho.
NW6 ... 2K 55
Riceyman Ho. WC1 ... 7C 60
Richard Anderson Ct.
SE14 ... 7K 93
Richard Burbidge Mans.
SW13 ... 6A 84
Richard Ho. SE16 ... 2K 93
Richard Neale Ho. E1 ... 7H 73
Richardson Cl. E8 ... 2C 62
Richardson's M. W1 ... 2E 68
Richard's Pl. SW3 ... 1H 87
Richard St. E1 ... 5G 73
Richbell WC1 ... 3A 70
Richbell Pl. WC1 ... 3A 70
Richborne Ter. SW8 ... 7A 90
Richborough Ho.
SE15 ... 6K 93
Richbourne Ct. *W1 ... 5H 67*
(off Harrowby St.)
Richford Ga. W6 ... 6A 74
Richford St. W6 ... 5A 74
Rich Ind. Est. SE1 ... 7B 82
SE15 ... 6H 93
Rich La. SW5 ... 4A 86
Richmond American University in London, The ... 6B 76
Richmond Av. N1 ... 2B 60
Richmond Bldgs. W1 ... 6G 69
Richmond College The American Institute University in London ... 5A 76
Richmond Cotts. W14 ... 1F 85
Richmond Ct. SW1 ... 5K 77
W14 ... 1E 84
Richmond Cres. N1 ... 2B 60
Richmond Gro. N1 ... 1E 60
(not continuous)
Richmond Ho. NW1 ... 5D 58
SE17 ... 3J 91
Richmond Mans.
SW5 ... 3A 86
Richmond M. W1 ... 6G 69
Richmond Rd. E8 ... 1C 62
Richmond Ter. SW1 ... 4J 79
Richmond Way W12 ... 4D 74
W14 ... 5D 74
Rickett St. SW6 ... 5K 85
Rickman Ho. E1 ... 7K 63
Rickman St. E1 ... 7K 63
Riddell Ct. SE5 ... 3C 92
Ridgewell Cl. N1 ... 2H 61
Ridgmount Gdns.
WC1 ... 2G 69
Ridgmount Pl. WC1 ... 3G 69
Ridgmount St. WC1 ... 3G 69
Riding Ho. St. W1 ... 4D 68
Rifle Ct. SE11 ... 5D 90
Riga M. E1 ... 5E 72
Riley Ho. SW10 ... 7E 86
Riley Rd. SE1 ... 6B 82
Riley St. SW10 ... 6E 86
Rill Ho. SE5 ... 7K 91
Rima Ho. SW3 ... 5E 86
Ring, The W2 ... 1F 77
(not continuous)
Ring Ho. E1 ... 7J 73
Ring Rd. W12 ... 1A 74
Ringsfield Ho. SE17 ... 4H 91
Ripley Ho. SW1 ... 5E 88
Ripplevale Gro. N1 ... 1B 60
Risborough SE17 ... 1G 91
Risborough Ho. NW8 ... 1H 67
Risborough St. SE1 ... 4F 81
Risdon Ho. SE16 ... 5K 83
Risdon St. SE16 ... 5J 83
Risinghill St. N1 ... 4C 60
Rising Sun Ct. EC1 ... 4F 71
Rita Rd. SW8 ... 6K 89
Ritchie Ho. SE16 ... 6J 83
Ritchie St. N1 ... 4D 60
Ritson Ho. N1 ... 3A 60
Riven Ct. W2 ... 6B 66
River Ct. SE1 ... 1E 80
Riverfleet WC1 ... 6K 59
Riverford Ho. W2 ... 4J 65
River Lodge SW1 ... 5F 89
River Pl. N1 ... 1G 61
Riverside SW11 ... 7H 87
WC1 ... 6K 59
Riverside Ct. SW8 ... 5H 89
Riverside Ho. N1 ... 1G 61
Riverside Mans. E1 ... 2J 83
Riverside Studios ... 4A 84
Riverside Workshops
SE1 ... 2H 81
River St. EC1 ... 6C 60
River Ter. W6 ... 4A 84
WC2 ... 1A 80
Riverton Cl. W9 ... 7H 55
Riverview Gdns.
SW13 ... 5A 84
River Vw. Hgts. SE16 ... 4E 82
Rivet Ho. SE1 ... 3D 92
Rivington Pl. EC2 ... 7B 62
Rivington St. EC2 ... 7A 62
Rivington Wlk. E8 ... 2F 63
Robert Adam St. W1 ... 5A 68
Roberta St. E2 ... 6E 62
Robert Bell Ho. SE16 ... 1E 92
Robert Cl. W9 ... 2D 66
Robert Dashwood Way
SE17 ... 2G 91
Robert Gentry Ho.
W14 ... 4F 85
Robert Jones Ho.
SE16 ... 1E 92
Robert Morton Ho.
NW8 ... 2D 56
Roberts Ct. N1 ... 3F 61
Roberts M. SW1 ... 7A 78
Roberts Pl. EC1 ... 1D 70
Robert St. NW1 ... 7D 58
WC2 ... 1K 79
Robert Sutton Ho. E1 ... 6J 73
Robin Ct. SE16 ... 1E 92
Robin Hood Ct. *EC4 ... 5D 70*
(off Shoe La.)
Robin Ho. NW8 ... 5G 57
Robin Howard Dance Theatre ... 7H 59
Robinson Ct. N1 ... 2F 61
Robinson Ho. W10 ... 6C 64
Robinson Rd. E2 ... 5J 63
Robinson St. SW3 ... 5J 87
Roby Ho. EC1 ... 1G 71
Rochelle St. E2 ... 7C 62
(not continuous)
Rochemont Wlk. E8 ... 3E 62
Rochester Ct. E2 ... 1G 73
NW1 ... 1F 59
Rochester Ho. SE1 ... 5J 81
SE15 ... 6K 93
Rochester Pl. NW1 ... 1E 58
Rochester Row SW1 ... 1F 89
Rochester Sq. NW1 ... 1F 59
Rochester St. SW1 ... 7G 79
Rochester Wlk. SE1 ... 3J 81
Rochford Wlk. E8 ... 1F 63
Rock Circus ... *1G 79*
(in Trocadero Cen.)
Rock Gro. Way SE16 ... 1F 93
(not continuous)
Rockingham St. SE1 ... 7G 81
Rockley Ct. W14 ... 5C 74
Rockley Rd. W14 ... 4C 74
Rockwood Pl. W12 ... 4B 74
Rocliffe St. N1 ... 5F 61
Rocque Ho. SW6 ... 7G 85
Rodborough Ct. W9 ... 2J 65
Roderick Ho. SE16 ... 1J 93
Rodin Ct. N1 ... 3E 60
Roding Ho. N1 ... 3C 60
Roding M. E1 ... 2F 83
Rodmarton St. W1 ... 4K 67
Rodmell WC1 ... 7K 59
Rodney Ct. W9 ... 1D 66
Rodney Ho. N1 ... 5B 60
SW1 ... 4F 89
W11 ... 7J 65
Rodney Pl. SE17 ... 1H 91
Rodney Rd. SE17 ... 1H 91
(not continuous)
Rodney St. N1 ... 4B 60
Roger Dowley Ct. E2 ... 4J 63
Rogers Est. E2 ... 7K 63
Rogers Ho. SW1 ... 1H 89
Roger St. WC1 ... 2B 70
Rohere Ho. EC1 ... 6G 61
Rokeby Ho. WC1 ... 2A 70
Roland Gdns. SW7 ... 3D 86

Roland Ho. SW7 . . . . . .3D 86
Roland M. E1 . . . . .3K 73
Roland Way SE17 . . . . . .4K 91
SW7 . . . . .3D 86
Rollins St. SE15 . . . . . .5K 93
Rolls Bldgs. EC4 . . . . . .5D 70
Rolls Pas. EC4 . . . . . . .5C 70
Rolls Rd. SE1 . . . . .3D 92
Roman Ho. EC2 . . . . . . .4H 71
Roman Rd. E2 . . . . .7J 63
Roman Way SE15 . . . . . .7J 93
Romer Ho. W10 . . . . . . .6F 55
Romford St. E1 . . . . .4F 73
Romilly Ho. W11 . . . . . .1E 74
Romilly St. W1 . . . . .7H 69
Romney Cl. SE14 . . . . . .7K 93
Romney Ct. W12 . . . . . .4B 74
Romney M. W1 . . . . .3A 68
Romney St. SW1 . . . . . .7H 79
Ronald Buckingham Ct. SE16 . . . . .4K 83
Ronald St. E1 . . . . .6K 73
Rood La. EC3 . . . . .7A 72
Roof Ter. Apartments, The EC1 . . . . .2F 71 (off Gt. Sutton St.)
Roosevelt Memorial . . .7B 68
Rootes Dr. W10 . . . . . . .3C 64
Ropemaker St. EC2 . . . .3J 71
Roper La. SE1 . . . . .5B 82
Ropers Orchard SW3 . . .6G 87
Rope Wlk. Gdns. E1 . . . .5F 73
Ropewalk M. E8 . . . . . . .1E 62
Ropley St. E2 . . . . .5E 62
Rosalind Ho. N1 . . . . . . .5B 62
Rosaline Rd. SW6 . . . . .7F 85
Rosaline Ter. SW6 . . . . .7F 85
Rosary Gdns. SW7 . . . . .2C 86
Rosaville Rd. SW6 . . . . .7G 85
Roscoe St. EC1 . . . . . . .2H 71 (not continuous)
Roscoe St. Est. EC1 . . . .2H 71
Rose All. EC2 . . . . .4B 72
SE1 . . . . .2H 81
Rose & Crown Ct. EC2 . . . . .5G 71
Rose & Crown Yd. SW1 . . . . .2F 79
Rosebank SW6 . . . . .7B 84
Rosebank Wlk. NW1 . . . .1H 59
Roseberry St. SE16 . . . .2G 93
Rosebery Av. EC1 . . . . . .2C 70
Rosebery Ct. EC1 . . . . . .1C 70
W1 . . . . .2C 78
Rosebery Ho. E2 . . . . . .4K 63
Rosebery Sq. EC1 . . . . . .2C 70
Rose Ct. E1 . . . . .4C 72
N1 . . . . .3E 60
Rosedene NW6 . . . . .2C 54 (not continuous)
Rosedew Rd. W6 . . . . . .6C 84
Roseford Ct. W12 . . . . . .5C 74
Rosehart M. W11 . . . . . .6J 65
Rosemary Branch Theatre 2K 61
Rosemary Ho. N1 . . . . . .3K 61
Rosemary Rd. SE15 . . . .7D 92
Rosemary St. N1 . . . . . .2J 61
Rosemoor St. SW3 . . . . .2J 87
Rose Sq. SW7 . . . . .2F 87
Rose St. EC4 . . . . .5F 71
WC2 . . . . .7J 69 (not continuous)
Rosetta Cl. SW8 . . . . . . .7K 89
Rosewood Ho. SW8 . . . .5A 90
Roslin Ho. E1 . . . . .7K 73
Rosmead Rd. W11 . . . . .7F 65
Rosoman Pl. EC1 . . . . . .1D 70
Rosoman St. EC1 . . . . . .7D 60
Rosscourt Mans. SW1 . . . . .6D 78
Rossendale Way NW1 . . . . .1F 59
Rossetti Ct. WC1 . . . . . .3G 69
Rossetti Gdn. Mans. SW3 . . . . .5J 87
Rossetti Ho. SW1 . . . . . .2H 89
Rossetti M. NW8 . . . . . .3F 57
Rossetti Rd. SE16 . . . . .3G 93
Rossetti Studios SW3 . . . . .5H 87
Ross Ho. E1 . . . . .3H 83
Rossmore Cl. NW1 . . . . .2H 67
Rossmore Ct. NW1 . . . . .1J 67
Rossmore Rd. NW1 . . . .2H 67
Rotary St. SE1 . . . . .6E 80
Rothay NW1 . . . . .6D 58
Rotheley Ho. E9 . . . . . . .1K 63
Rotherfield Ct. *N1* . . . . . .*1J 61* (off Rotherfield St., not continuous)
Rotherfield St. N1 . . . . .1G 61
Rotherham Wlk. SE1 . . .3E 80
ROTHERHITHE 5J 83
Rotherhithe Bus. Est. SE16 . . . . .2J 93
Rotherhithe New Rd. SE16 . . . . .4F 93
Rotherhithe Old Rd. SE16 . . . . .1K 93
Rotherhithe St. SE16 . . .4J 83
Rotherhithe Tunnel SE16 . . . . .2K 83
Rotherwick Ho. E1 . . . . .1E 82
Rothery St. N1 . . . . .2F 61
Rothesay Ct. SE11 . . . . .6C 90
Rothley Ct. NW8 . . . . . . .1E 66
Rothsay St. SE1 . . . . . . .6A 82
Rothwell St. NW1 . . . . . .2K 57
Rotten Row SW1 . . . . . . .4J 77
SW7 . . . . .4F 77
Rouel Rd. SE16 . . . . . . .6E 82 (Dockley Rd.)
SE16 . . . . .1E 92 (Southwark Pk. Rd.)
Roundhouse, The 1A 58
Roupell St. SE1 . . . . . . .3D 80
Rousden St. NW1 . . . . . .1E 58
Rover Ho. N1 . . . . .3B 62
Rowallan Rd. SW6 . . . . .7E 84
Rowan Ct. SE15 . . . . . . .7C 92
Rowan Ho. *SE16* . . . .*5K 83* (off Woodland Cres.)
Rowan Lodge W8 . . . . . .7A 76
Rowan Rd. W6 . . . . .2C 84
Rowan Ter. W6 . . . . .1C 84
Rowan Wlk. W10 . . . . . .1E 64
Rowcross St. SE1 . . . . . .3C 92
Rowdon Av. NW10 . . . . .1A 54
Rowington Cl. W2 . . . . .3A 66
Rowland Hill Ho. SE1 . . .4E 80
Rowley Way NW8 . . . . . .2B 56
Roxburghe Mans. W8 . . .5B 76
Roxby Pl. SW6 . . . . .5K 85
Royal Academy of Arts (Burlington House) 1E 78
Royal Academy of Music Mus. 2B 68
Royal Air Force Memorial 3K 79
Royal Albert Hall 5E 76
Royal Arc. W1 . . . . .1E 78
Royal Av. SW3 . . . . .3J 87
Royal Av. Ho. SW3 . . . . .3J 87
Royal Belgrave Ho. SW1 . . . . .2D 88
Royal Ceremonial Dress Collection, The 3A 76
Royal College of Art . . .5D 76
Royal College of Music 6E 76
Royal College of Obstetricians & Gynaecologists 1J 67
Royal College of Physicians 1C 68
Royal College of Surgeons 5B 70
Royal Coll. St. NW1 . . . .1E 58
Royal Ct. EC3 . . . . .6K 71
Royal Courts of Justice 6B 70
Royal Court Theatre . . .2A 88
Royal Cres. W11 . . . . . .4D 74
Royal Cres. M. W11 . . . .3D 74
Royal Exchange 6K 71
Royal Exchange Av. EC3 . . . . .6K 71
Royal Exchange Bldgs. EC3 . . . . .6K 71
Royal Festival Hall 3B 80
Royal Fusiliers Mus. . . . *1C 82* (in The Tower of London)
Royal Geographical Society . . . .*5E 76* (off Kensington Gore)
Royal Hospital Chelsea Mus. 4A 88
Royal Hospital Rd. SW3 . . . . .6J 87
Royal Mews, The 6D 78
Royal M. SW1 . . . . .6D 78
Royal Mint Ct. EC3 . . . . .1D 82
Royal Mint Pl. E1 . . . . . .7D 72
Royal Mint St. E1 . . . . . .7D 72
Royal Oak Ct. N1 . . . . . .6A 62
Royal Oak Yd. SE1 . . . . .5A 82
Royal Opera Arc. SW1 . . . . .2G 79
Royal Opera House 6K 69
Royal Pde. SW6 . . . . . . .7E 84
Royal Rd. SE17 . . . . . . .5E 90
Royal St. SE1 . . . . .6B 80
Royal Twr. Lodge E1 . . .1E 82
Royalty Mans. W1 . . . . . .6G 69
Royalty M. W1 . . . . .6G 69
Royalty Studios W11 . . . .6F 65
Royal Westminster Lodge SW1 . . . . .1G 89
Royle Bldg. N1 . . . . .4G 61
Royston Ct. *W8* . . . .*2K 75* (off Kensington Chu. St.)
Royston Ho. SE15 . . . . .6G 93
Royston St. E2 . . . . .5K 63
Rozel Ct. N1 . . . . .2A 62
Ruby St. SE15 . . . . .5G 93
Ruby Triangle SE15 . . . .5G 93
Rudbeck Ho. SE15 . . . . .7E 92
Rudge Ho. SE16 . . . . . . .6F 83
Rudgwick Ter. NW8 . . . .3H 57
Rudolf Pl. SW8 . . . . . . .6K 89
Rudolph Rd. NW6 . . . . .5K 55
Rufford St. N1 . . . . .2K 59
Rufus Ho. SE1 . . . . .6C 82
Rufus St. N1 . . . . .7A 62
Rugby Mans. W14 . . . . .1F 85
Rugby St. WC1 . . . . . . .2A 70
Rumball Ho. SE5 . . . . . .7A 92
Rumbold Rd. SW6 . . . . .7B 86
Rum Cl. E1 . . . . .1J 83
Rumford Ho. SE1 . . . . . .7G 81
Runacres Ct. SE17 . . . . .4G 91
Runcorn Pl. W11 . . . . . .7E 64
Rupack St. SE16 . . . . . .5J 83
Rupert Ct. W1 . . . . .7G 69
Rupert Ho. SE11 . . . . . .2D 90
SW5 . . . . .2J 85
Rupert Rd. NW6 . . . . . . .5H 55
Rupert St. W1 . . . . .7G 69
Rushmead E2 . . . . .7G 63
Rushmore Ho. W14 . . . . .7F 75
Rushton St. N1 . . . . . . .4K 61
Rushworth St. SE1 . . . . .4F 81
Ruskin Ho. SW1 . . . . . . .2H 89
Ruskin Mans. W14 . . . . .6F 85
Russell Ct. SW1 . . . . . . .3F 79
WC1 . . . . .2J 69
Russell Gdns. W14 . . . . .6E 74
Russell Gdns. M. W14 . . . . .5E 74
Russell Ho. SW1 . . . . . .3E 88
Russell Lodge SE1 . . . . .6J 81
Russell Mans. WC1 . . . .3K 69
Russell Rd. W14 . . . . . . .6F 75
Russell Sq. WC1 . . . . . . .2J 69
Russell Sq. Mans. WC1 . . . . .3K 69
Russell St. WC2 . . . . . . .7K 69
Russell's Wharf Flats W10 . . . . .1G 65
Russia La. E2 . . . . .4J 63
Russia Row EC2 . . . . . . .6H 71
Ruston M. W11 . . . . .6E 64
Rust Sq. SE5 . . . . .7J 91
Rutherford Ho. E1 . . . . .2G 73
Rutherford St. SW1 . . . .1G 89
Ruth Ho. W10 . . . . .1E 64
Rutland Ct. SW7 . . . . . .5H 77
Rutland Gdns. SW7 . . . .5H 77
Rutland Gdns. M. SW7 . . . . .5H 77
Rutland Ga. SW7 . . . . . .5H 77
Rutland Ga. M. SW7 . . .5G 77
Rutland Gro. W6 . . . . . .3A 84
Rutland Ho. W8 . . . . . . .7A 76
Rutland M. NW8 . . . . . . .3B 56
Rutland M. E. SW7 . . . . .6H 77
Rutland M. Sth. SW7 . . .6G 77
Rutland M. W. SW7 . . . .6G 77
Rutland Pl. EC1 . . . . . . .3F 71
Rutland Rd. E9 . . . . .2K 63
Rutland St. SW7 . . . . . .6H 77
Rutley Cl. SE17 . . . . . . .5E 90
Rydal Water NW1 . . . . . .7E 58
Ryder Ct. SW1 . . . . .2F 79
Ryder Dr. SE16 . . . . . . .4G 93
Ryder Ho. E1 . . . . .1K 73
Ryder's Ter. NW8 . . . . . .4C 56
Ryder St. SW1 . . . . .2F 79
Ryder Yd. SW1 . . . . .2F 79
Rydon St. N1 . . . . .2H 61
Rye Ho. SE16 . . . . .4K 83
SW1 . . . . .3C 88
Rylston Rd. SW6 . . . . . .6G 85
Rysbrack St. SW3 . . . . .6J 77

S

Saatchi Gallery 2K 87
Sable St. N1 . . . . .1F 61
Sackville St. W1 . . . . . .1F 79
Saddle Yd. W1 . . . . .2C 78
Sadler Ho. EC1 . . . . . . .6E 60
Sadler's Wells Theatre 6D 60
Saffron Hill EC1 . . . . . .3D 70
Saffron St. EC1 . . . . . . .3D 70
Saffron Wharf SE1 . . . . .4D 82
Sage St. E1 . . . . .7J 73
Sage Way WC1 . . . . . . .7A 60
Sail St. SE11 . . . . .1B 90
Sainsbury Wing . . . . . .*1H 79* (in National Gallery)
St Agnes Cl. E9 . . . . . . .2J 63
St Agnes Pl. SE11 . . . . .6D 90
St Agnes Well EC1 . . . . .1K 71
St Albans Ct. EC2 . . . . .5H 71
St Alban's Gro. W8 . . . . .6B 76
St Albans Mans. W8 . . . .6B 76
St Alban's Pl. N1 . . . . . .3E 60
St Alban's St. SW1 . . . . .1G 79 (not continuous)
St Albans Studios W8 . . . . .6B 76
St Albans Ter. W6 . . . . . .5E 84
St Alphage Gdn. EC2 . . .4H 71
St Alphage Highwalk EC2 . . . . .4H 71
St Alphage Ho. EC2 . . . .4J 71
St Andrews Chambers W1 . . . . .4F 69
St Andrews Cl. SE16 . . .4H 93
St Andrew's Hill EC4 . . . .7F 71 (not continuous)
St Andrews Mans. W1 . . . . .4A 68
W14 . . . . .5F 85
St Andrew's Pl. NW1 . . .1D 68
St Andrew's Rd. W14 . . .5F 85
St Andrews Sq. W11 . . . .6E 64
St Andrew St. EC1 . . . . .4D 70
St Andrew's Wharf SE1 . . . . .4D 82
St Anne's Ct. NW6 . . . . .3F 55
W1 . . . . .6G 69
St Anne's Flats NW1 . . .6G 59
St Ann's Ho. WC1 . . . . . .7C 60
St Ann's La. SW1 . . . . . .7H 79
St Ann's Rd. W11 . . . . . .1D 74
St Ann's St. SW1 . . . . . .6H 79
St Ann's Ter. NW8 . . . . .4F 57
St Ann's Vs. W11 . . . . . .3D 74
St Anselm's Pl. W1 . . . . .7C 68
St Anthony's Cl. E1 . . . . .2E 82
St Anthony's Flats NW1 . . . . .5G 59
St Aubins Ct. N1 . . . . . . .2K 61
St Augustine's Ct. SE1 . . . . .3G 93
St Augustine's Ho. NW1 . . . . .6G 59
St Augustine's Mans. SW1 . . . . .2F 89
St Augustine's Rd. NW1 . . . . .1G 59
St Barnabas St. SW1 . . .3B 88
St Bartholomew's Hospital Mus. 4F 71
St Benet's Pl. EC3 . . . . .7K 71
St Botolph Row EC3 . . . .6C 72
St Botolph St. EC3 . . . . .6C 72
St Brelades Ct. N1 . . . . .2K 61
St Bride's Av. EC4 . . . . .6E 70
St Bride's Crypt Mus. 6E 70
St Bride's Pas. EC4 . . . . .6E 70
St Bride St. EC4 . . . . . . .5E 70
St Catherines M. SW3 . . . . .1J 87
St Chad's Pl. WC1 . . . . .6K 59
St Chad's St. WC1 . . . . .6K 59 (not continuous)
St Charles Pl. W10 . . . . .4E 64
St Charles Sq. W10 . . . .3D 64
St Christopher's Ho. NW1 . . . . .5G 59
St Christopher's Pl. W1 . . . . .5B 68
St Clare St. EC3 . . . . . . .6C 72
St Clements Ct. EC4 . . . .7K 71
SE14 . . . . .5K 93
W11 . . . . .1D 74
St Clements Ho. *E1* . . . .*4C 72* (off Leyden St.)
St Clement's La. WC2 . . . . .6B 70
St Clements Mans. SW6 . . . . .6D 84
St Columb's Ho. W10 . . .4F 65
St Cross St. EC1 . . . . . . .3D 70
St Davids Cl. SE16 . . . . .4H 93
St Dunstan's All. EC3 . . .1A 82
St Dunstan's Ct. EC4 . . .6D 70
St Dunstans Hill EC3 . . .1A 82
St Dunstan's La. EC3 . . .1A 82
St Dunstan's Rd. W6 . . .4C 84
St Edmund's Cl. NW8 . . .3J 57
St Edmund's Ct. NW8 . . .3J 57
St Edmunds Sq. SW13 . . . . .6A 84
St Edmund's Ter. NW8 . . . . .3H 57
St Ermin's Hill SW1 . . . .6G 79
St Ervan's Rd. W10 . . . .3F 65
St Eugene Ct. NW6 . . . .3F 55
St Francis' Ho. NW1 . . . .5G 59
St George's Bldgs. SE1 . . . . .7E 80
St George's Cathedral 6D 58
St George's Cir. SE1 . . . .6E 80
St Georges Ct. EC4 . . . . .5E 70
SW1 . . . . .3E 88
SW7 . . . . .1G 87
W8 . . . . .6C 76
St George's Dr. SW1 . . .2D 88
St George's Flds. W2 . . .6H 67
St George's Ho. NW1 . . .5G 59
St George's La. EC3 . . . .7K 71
St George's Mans. SW1 . . . . .3H 89
St George's M. NW1 . . .1K 57
SE1 . . . . .6D 80
St George's RC Cathedral 6D 80
St George's Rd. SE1 . . .6D 80
St George's Sq. SW1 . . .3G 89
St George's Sq. M. SW1 . . . . .4G 89
St George's Ter. NW1 . . .2K 57
SE15 . . . . .7D 92
St George St. W1 . . . . . .6D 68
St George's Way SE15 . . . . .6A 92
St George's Wharf SE1 . . . . .4D 82
St George Wharf SW8 . . .5J 89
St Giles Cir. W1 . . . . . . .5H 69
St Giles Court 5J 69
St Giles High St. WC2 . . . . .5H 69
St Giles Pas. WC2 . . . . .6H 69
St Giles Ter. EC2 . . . . . .4H 71
St Helena Ho. WC1 . . . .7C 60
St Helena Rd. SE16 . . . .2K 93
St Helena St. WC1 . . . . .7C 60
St Helen's Gdns. W10 . . . . .4C 64
St Helen's Pl. EC3 . . . . .5A 72
St Helier Ct. N1 . . . . . . .2A 62
St Hilda's Cl. NW6 . . . . .1D 54
St Hilda's Wharf E1 . . . .2J 83
St James App. EC2 . . . . .2A 72
St James Ct. E2 . . . . . . .7F 63
SW1 . . . . .6F 79
St James Ind. M. SE1 . . . . .4F 93
St James Mans. SE1 . . .6C 80
St James Residences W1 . . . . .7G 69
ST JAMES'S 3F 79
St James's SW1 . . . . . . .2F 79
St James's Av. E2 . . . . . .4K 63
St James's Chambers SW1 . . . . .2F 79
St James's Cl. NW8 . . . .3J 57
St James's Gdns. W11 . . . . .2E 74 (not continuous)
St James's Mkt. SW1 . . .1G 79
St James's Palace 4F 79
St James's Pk. 4G 79
St James's Pas. EC3 . . .6B 72
St James's Pl. SW1 . . . .3E 78
St James's Rd. SE1 . . . .3F 93
SE16 . . . . .6F 83
St James's Sq. SW1 . . . .2F 79
St James's St. SW1 . . . .2E 78
St James's Ter. NW8 . . .4J 57
St James's Ter. M. NW8 . . . . .3J 57
St James St. W6 . . . . . .4A 84
St James's Wlk. EC1 . . .1E 70
St John's Cl. SW6 . . . . . .7J 85
St John's Ct. E1 . . . . . . .3G 83
W6 . . . . .1A 84
St John's Est. N1 . . . . . .5K 61
SE1 . . . . .4C 82
St John's Gdns. W11 . . .1F 75
St John's Gate 2E 70
St Johns Ho. SE17 . . . . .5J 91
St John's La. EC1 . . . . .2E 70
St John's Lodge NW3 . . .1G 57
St John's M. W11 . . . . . .6J 65
St John's Path EC1 . . . . .2E 70
St John's Pl. EC1 . . . . . .2E 70
St John's Sq. EC1 . . . . . .2E 70
St John's Ter. W10 . . . . .1D 64
St John St. EC1 . . . . . . .5D 60
St John's Vs. W8 . . . . . .7B 76
ST JOHN'S WOOD 5F 57
St John's Wood Ct. NW8 . . . . .7F 57
St John's Wood High St. NW8 . . . . .4F 57
St John's Wood Pk. NW8 . . . . .2E 56
St John's Wood Rd. NW8 . . . . .1E 66
St John's Wood Ter. NW8 . . . . .4F 57
St Josephs Almshouses W6 . . . . .1D 84
St Joseph's Cl. W10 . . . .4F 65
St Joseph's Cotts. SW3 . . . . .2J 87
St Joseph's Flats NW1 . . . . .6G 59
St Joseph's Ho. W6 . . . .1D 84
St Jude's Rd. E2 . . . . . . .5H 63
St Julian's Rd. NW6 . . . .1H 55
St Katharine Docks 1D 82
St Katharine's Pct. NW1 . . . . .4C 58
St Katharine's Way E1 . . . . .2D 82 (not continuous)
St Katharine's Yacht Haven 1D 82
St Katherine's Row EC3 . . . . .7B 72
St Katherines Wlk. W11 . . . . .2D 74
St Laurence Cl. NW6 . . .3D 54
St Lawrence Ct. N1 . . . .2K 61
St Lawrence Ho. SE1 . . .6B 82
St Lawrence Ter. W10 . . . . .3E 64
St Leonard M. N1 . . . . . .4A 62
St Leonard's Ct. N1 . . . .6K 61
St Leonard's Ter. SW3 . . . . .4J 87
St Loo Av. SW3 . . . . . . .5H 87
St Loo Ct. SW3 . . . . . . .5H 87
ST LUKE'S 1H 71
St Luke's Cl. EC1 . . . . . .1H 71
St Lukes Ct. W11 . . . . . .5H 65
St Luke's Est. EC1 . . . . .7J 61
St Luke's M. W11 . . . . . .5G 65
St Luke's Rd. W11 . . . . .4G 65
St Luke's St. SW3 . . . . . .3G 87
St Luke's Yd. W9 . . . . . .5G 55 (not continuous)
St Margarets Cl. EC2 . . .5J 71
St Margarets Ct. SE1 . . .3J 81
St Margaret's La. W8 . . .7A 76
St Margaret's Rd. NW10 . . . . .6A 54
St Margaret St. SW1 . . .5J 79
St Marks Cl. NW8 . . . . . .5D 56
St Mark's Cres. NW1 . . .2B 58
St Mark's Gro. SW10 . . .7B 86
St Marks Ho. SE17 . . . . .5J 91
St Mark's Pl. W11 . . . . . .6F 65
St Mark's Rd. W10 . . . . .3C 64
St Mark's Sq. NW1 . . . . .3A 58
St Mark St. E1 . . . . .6D 72
St Martin-in-the-Fields Church 1J 79
St Martin's Almshouses NW1 . . . . .2E 58
St Martin's Cl. NW1 . . . .2E 58
St Martins Ct. EC4 . . . . .5G 71
N1 . . . . .2B 62
WC2 . . . . .7J 69
St Martin's La. WC2 . . . .7J 69
St Martin's le-Grand EC1 . . . . .5G 71
St Martin's Pl. WC2 . . . .1J 79
St Martin's St. WC2 . . . .1H 79 (not continuous)
St Martin's Theatre 7J 69
St Mary Abbot's Ct. W14 . . . . .7G 75
St Mary Abbot's Pl. W8 . . . . .7H 75
St Mary Abbot's Ter. W14 . . . . .7G 75
St Mary at Hill EC3 . . . .1A 82
St Mary Axe EC3 . . . . . .6A 72
St Marychurch St. SE16 . . . . .4J 83
St Mary Graces Ct. E1 . . . . .7D 72
St Mary le-Park Ct. SW11 . . . . .7H 87
St Mary Newington Cl. SE17 . . . . .3B 92
St Mary's Est. SE16 . . . .5J 83
St Mary's Flats NW1 . . .6G 59
St Mary's Gdns. SE11 . . .1D 90
St Mary's Ga. W8 . . . . . .7A 76
St Mary's Ho. N1 . . . . . .2F 61
St Mary's Mans. W2 . . . .3E 66
St Mary's M. NW6 . . . . .1A 56
St Mary's Path *E1* . . . . . .*5E 72* (off Adler St.)
N1 . . . . .2E 60
St Mary's Pl. W8 . . . . . .7A 76
St Mary's Sq. W2 . . . . . .3E 66
St Mary's Ter. W2 . . . . . .3D 66
St Mary's Twr. EC1 . . . . .2H 71
St Mary's Wlk. SE11 . . . .1D 90
St Matthews Ct. SE1 . . . .7G 81
St Matthews Ho. SE17 . . . . .5J 91
St Matthew's Lodge NW1 . . . . .4F 59
St Matthew's Row E2 . . .7E 62
St Matthew St. SW1 . . . .7G 79
St Michael's All. EC3 . . .6K 71
St Michael's Ct. SE1 . . . .5H 81
St Michael's Flats NW1 . . . . .5G 59
St Michael's Gdns. W10 . . . . .4E 64
St Michaels M. SW1 . . . .2A 88
St Michael's St. W2 . . . .5F 67
St Mildred's Ct. EC2 . . . .6J 71
St Nicholas' Flats NW1 . . . . .5G 59
St Olaf Ho. SE1 . . . . . . .2K 81
St Olaf's Rd. SW6 . . . . .7F 85
St Olaf Stairs SE1 . . . . .2K 81
St Olave's Ct. EC2 . . . . .6J 71
St Olave's Est. SE1 . . . .4B 82
St Olave's Gdns. SE11 . . . . .1C 90
St Olaves Ho. SE11 . . . .1C 90
St Olave's Mans. SE11 . . . . .1C 90
St Olave's Ter. SE1 . . . .4B 82
St Olav's Sq. SE16 . . . . .5J 83
St Oswald's Pl. SE11 . . .3A 90
St Oswalds Studios SW6 . . . . .5J 85
St Oswulf St. SW1 . . . . .2H 89
St Owen Ho. SE1 . . . . . .6B 82
ST PANCRAS 7J 59
St Pancras Commercial Cen. NW1 . . . . .2F 59
St Pancras Way NW1 . . .1E 58
St Paul's All. *EC4* . . . . . .*6F 71* (off St Paul's Chyd.)

St Paul's Bldgs. EC1 1F 71 (off Dallington St.)
St Paul's Cathedral 6G 71
St Paul's Chyd. EC4 6F 71 (not continuous)
St Paul's Cres. NW1 1H 59
St Paul's M. NW1 1H 59
St Paul's Studios W14 3E 84
St Pauls Ter. SE17 5F 91
St Paul St. N1 3G 61 (not continuous)
St Pauls Vw. Apartments EC1 7C 60
St Peter's All. EC3 6K 71
St Peter's Av. E2 5F 63
St Petersburgh M. W2 7A 66
St Petersburgh Pl. W2 7A 66
St Peter's Cen. E1 2H 83 (off Reardon St.)
St Peter's Chu. Ct. N1 4F 61
St Peter's Cl. E2 5F 63
St Peters Ho. SE17 5J 91
WC1 7K 59
St Peters Pl. W9 2A 66
St Peter's Sq. E2 5F 63
St Peter's St. N1 3F 61
St Peter's St. M. N1 4F 61
St Peter's Way N1 1B 62
St Philip Ho. WC1 7C 60
St Philip's Way N1 3H 61
St Quintin Av. W10 4B 64
St Quintin Gdns. W10 4B 64
St Richard's Ho. NW1 6G 59
St Saviour's Est. SE1 6C 82
St Saviour's Wharf SE1 4D 82 (Mill St.)
SE1 4D 82 (off Shad Thames)
St Stephen's Av. W12 5A 74
St Stephen's Cl. NW8 3H 57
St Stephen's Cres. W2 5K 65
St Stephen's Gdns. W2 5J 65 (not continuous)
St Stephens Ho. SE17 5J 91
St Stephen's M. W2 4K 65
St Stephen's Row EC4 6J 71
St Stephen's Ter. SW8 7A 90
St Stephen's Wlk. SW7 1C 86
St Swithins La. EC4 7J 71
St Thomas Ct. NW1 1F 59
St Thomas Ho. E1 5K 73
St Thomas's Pl. E9 1J 63
St Thomas's Sq. E9 1H 63
St Thomas St. SE1 3J 81
St Thomas's Way SW6 7G 85
St Vincent De Paul Ho. E1 4J 73
St Vincent Ho. SE1 6C 82
St Vincent St. W1 4B 68
Salamanca Pl. SE1 2A 90
Salamanca Sq. SE1 2A 90
Salamanca St. SE1 2K 89
SE11 2K 89
Salem Rd. W2 7B 66
Sale Pl. W2 4G 67
Sale St. E2 1F 73
Salisbury Cl. SE17 2J 91
Salisbury Ct. EC4 6E 70
SE16 7F 83
Salisbury Ho. EC2 4K 71
N1 2E 60
SW1 3H 89
SW9 7D 90
Salisbury M. SW6 7G 85
Salisbury Pas. SW6 7G 85
Salisbury Pavement SW6 7G 85
Salisbury Pl. W1 3K 67
Salisbury Sq. EC4 6D 70
Salisbury St. NW8 2F 67
Salter Rd. SE16 3K 83
Salters Ct. EC4 6H 71
Salter's Hall Ct. EC4 7J 71
Salters Rd. W10 2C 64
Saltram Cres. W9 6H 55
Saltwood Gro. SE17 4J 91
Saltwood Ho. SE15 6K 93
Salusbury Rd. NW6 2F 55
Sambrook Ho. E1 4J 73
SE11 2C 90
Samford Ho. N1 3C 60
Samford St. NW8 2G 67
Sampson Ho. SE1 2E 80
Sampson St. E1 3F 83
Samuel Cl. E8 2D 62
Samuel Ct. N1 7A 62
Samuel Ho. E8 3C 62
Samuel Jones Ind. Est. SE15 7B 92
Samuel Lewis Trust Dwellings SW3 2G 87
SW6 7K 85
W14 1G 85
Samuel Richardson Ho. W14 2G 85
Samuel's Cl. W6 1B 84
Samuel St. SE15 7C 92
Sancroft Ho. SE11 3B 90
Sancroft St. SE11 3B 90
Sanctuary, The SW1 6H 79
Sanctuary St. SE1 5H 81
Sandalwood Mans. W8 7A 76
Sandbourne NW8 3A 56
W11 5J 65
Sandby Ho. NW6 3J 55
Sandell St. SE1 4C 80
Sanderling Lodge E1 1D 82
Sanders Ho. WC1 6C 60
Sandfield WC1 7K 59
Sandford Row SE17 3J 91
Sandford St. SW6 7B 86
Sandgate St. SE15 5G 93
Sandgate Trad. Est. SE15 5G 93
Sandhills, The SW10 5D 86
Sandhurst Ho. E1 4J 73
Sandland St. WC1 4B 70
Sandpiper Ct. E1 1E 82 (off Thomas More St.)
Sandringham Ct. W1 6F 69
W9 7D 56
Sandringham Flats WC2 7H 69
Sandringham Ho. W14 1E 84
Sandwich Ho. SE16 4K 83
WC1 7J 59
Sandwich St. WC1 7J 59
Sandys Row E1 4B 72
Sankey Ho. E2 4K 63
Sans Wlk. EC1 1D 70
Santley Ho. SE1 5D 80
Saperton Wlk. SE11 1B 90
Sapperton Ct. EC1 1G 71
Sapperton Ho. W2 4J 65
Sapphire Ct. E1 7E 72
Saracens Head Yd. EC3 6C 72
Sarah Ho. E1 5G 73
Sarah St. N1 6B 62
Sarah Swift Ho. SE1 4K 81
Sara La. Ct. N1 4B 62
Sardinia St. WC2 6A 70
Sarnesfield Ho. SE15 6G 93
Sarratt Ho. W10 3A 64
Satchwell Rd. E2 7E 62
Satchwell St. E2 7E 62
Saul Ct. SE15 6C 92
Saunders St. SE11 1C 90
Savage Gdns. EC3 7B 72 (not continuous)
Savannah Cl. SE15 7C 92
Savile Row W1 7E 68
Savona Ho. SW8 7E 88
Savona St. SW8 7E 88
Savoy Bldgs. WC2 1A 80
Savoy Ct. SW5 1K 85
WC2 1A 80
Savoy Hill WC2 1A 80
Savoy Pl. WC2 1K 79
Savoy Row WC2 7A 70
Savoy Steps WC2 1A 80
Savoy St. WC2 7A 70
Savoy Theatre 1K 79
Savoy Way WC2 1A 80
Sawyer St. SE1 4G 81
Saxon Hall W2 1A 76
Saxon Ho. E1 4D 72
Scafell NW1 6E 58
Scala St. W1 3F 69
Scampston M. W10 5D 64
Scandrett St. E1 3G 83
Scarborough St. E1 6D 72
Scarsdale Pl. W8 6A 76
Scarsdale Studios W8 7K 75
Scarsdale Vs. W8 7K 75
Scawfell St. E2 5D 62
Sceptre Ct. EC3 1D 82
Sceptre Ho. E1 1J 73
Sceptre Rd. E2 7J 63
Schafer Ho. NW1 1E 68
Schiller International University 3C 80
Schomberg Ho. SW1 1H 89
School App. E2 6B 62
School Ho. SE1 1A 92
Schooner Cl. SE16 4K 83
Science Mus. 7E 76
Sclater St. E1 1C 72
Scoop, The 3B 82
Scoresby St. SE1 3E 80
Scorton Ho. N1 4B 62
SCOTCH HOUSE 5J 77
Scotia Ct. SE16 5K 83
Scotland Pl. SW1 3J 79
Scotson Ho. SE11 2C 90
Scotswood St. EC1 1D 70
Scott Ellis Gdns. NW8 7E 56
Scott Ho. N1 2J 61
NW8 2G 67
Scott Lidgett Cres. SE16 5E 82
Scotts Ct. W12 5A 74
Scott's Rd. W12 5A 74
Scott's Sufferance Wharf SE1 5D 82
Scott St. E1 2G 73
Scott's Yd. EC4 7J 71
Scovell Cres. SE1 5G 81
Scovell Rd. SE1 5G 81
Screen on Baker Street (Cinema) 3K 67
Screen on the Green Cinema 3E 60
Scriven Ct. E8 2D 62
Scriven St. E8 2D 62
Scrope Ho. EC1 3C 70
Scrubs La. NW10 3A 64
W10 3A 64
Scrutton St. EC2 2A 72
Seabright St. E2 7G 63
Seaford Ho. SE16 4K 83
Seaford St. WC1 7K 59
Seaforth Pl. SW1 6F 79
Seagrave Cl. E1 4K 73
Seagrave Lodge SW6 5K 85
Seagrave Rd. SW6 5K 85
Seal Ho. SE1 6K 81
Searles Rd. SE1 1K 91
Searson Ho. SE17 2F 91
Sears St. SE5 7J 91
Seaton Cl. SE11 3D 90
Sebastian Ho. N1 5A 62
Sebastian St. EC1 7F 61
Sebbon St. N1 1F 61
Sebright Ho. E2 4F 63
Sebright Pas. E2 5F 63
Secker St. SE1 3C 80
Second Av. W10 1F 65
Sedan Way SE17 3A 92
Sedding St. SW1 1A 88
Sedding Studios SW1 1A 88
Seddon Highwalk EC2 3G 71 (off Seddon Ho.)
Seddon Ho. EC2 3G 71
Seddon St. WC1 7B 60
Sedgmoor Pl. SE5 7B 92
Sedlescombe Rd. SW6 6H 85
Sedley Ho. SE11 3C 90
Sedley Pl. W1 6C 68
Seething La. EC3 7B 72
Sekforde St. EC1 2E 70
Selbourne Ho. SE1 6J 81
Selby Ho. W10 6F 55
Selby Sq. W10 6F 55
Selby St. E1 2F 73
Seldon Ho. SW1 4E 88
SW8 7E 88
Selfridges 6B 68
Selina Ho. NW8 1F 67
Selma Ho. W12 6A 64
Selwood Pl. SW7 3E 86
Selwood Ter. SW7 3E 86
Semley Ho. SW1 2C 88
Semley Pl. SW1 2B 88
Senior St. W2 3A 66
Seraph Ct. EC1 6G 61
Serjeants Inn EC4 6D 70
Serlby Ct. W14 6G 75 (off Somerset Sq.)
Serle St. WC2 5B 70
Sermon La. EC4 6G 71
Serpentine, The 3G 77
Serpentine Gallery 4E 76
Serpentine Rd. W2 3G 77
Setchell Rd. SE1 1C 92
Setchell Way SE1 1C 92
Seth St. SE16 5K 83
Settles St. E1 4F 73
Seven Dials WC2 6J 69
Seven Dials Ct. WC2 6J 69
Seven Islands Leisure Cen. 7J 83
Seven Stars Yd. E1 3D 72 (off Brick La.)
Severn Av. W10 6F 55
Seville Ho. E1 3F 83 (off Hellings St.)
Seville M. N1 1A 62
Seville St. SW1 5K 77
Sevington St. W9 2A 66
Sewardstone Rd. E2 4J 63
Seward St. EC1 1F 71
Seymour Ho. NW1 6H 59
WC1 1J 69
Seymour Leisure Cen. 4J 67
Seymour M. W1 5A 68
Seymour Pl. W1 4J 67
Seymour St. W1 6J 67
W2 6J 67
Seymour Wlk. SW10 5C 86
Shackleton Ct. W12 5A 74
Shackleton Ho. E1 2J 83
Shacklewell St. E2 1D 72
Shad Thames SE1 3C 82
SHADWELL 1H 83
Shadwell Gdns. E1 7J 73
Shadwell Pierhead E1 1K 83
Shadwell Pl. E1 7J 73
Shaftesbury Av. W1 7G 69
WC1 5J 69
WC2 5J 69
Shaftesbury Cen. W10 2C 64
Shaftesbury Ct. N1 5J 61
Shaftesbury M. SE1 6J 81
W8 7K 75
Shaftesbury Pl. EC2 4G 71 (off London Wall)
W14 2H 85
Shaftesbury St. N1 5H 61 (not continuous)
Shaftesbury Theatre 5J 69
Shaftesbury Vs. W8 6K 75
Shafto M. SW1 7K 77
Shafts Ct. EC3 6A 72
Shahjalal Ho. E2 4F 63
Shakespeare's Globe & Exhibition 1G 81
Shakespeare Twr. EC2 3G 71
Shalcomb St. SW10 6D 86
Shalfleet Dr. W10 7C 64
Shalford Ct. N1 4E 60
Shalford Ho. SE1 6K 81
Shand St. SE1 4A 82
Shan Ho. WC1 2A 70
Shannon Ct. SE15 7C 92
Shannon Pl. NW8 4H 57
Shap St. E2 4C 62
Shard's Sq. SE15 6F 93
Sharnbrook Ho. W14 5J 85
Sharon Gdns. E9 2J 63
Sharpleshall St. NW1 1K 57
Sharpness Ct. SE15 6C 92
Sharratt St. SE15 5K 93
Sharsted St. SE17 4E 90
Sharwood WC1 5B 60
Shaver's Pl. SW1 1G 79
Shawfield St. SW3 4H 87
Shaw Theatre 6H 59
Shearwater Ct. E1 1E 82 (off Star Pl.)
Sheba Pl. E1 2D 72
Sheen Gro. N1 2C 60
Sheep La. E8 3G 63
Sheffield St. WC2 6A 70
Sheffield Ter. W8 4J 75
Sheldon Ct. SW8 7J 89
Sheldon Ho. N1 2B 62
Sheldon Pl. E2 5F 63 (not continuous)
Sheldon Sq. W2 4D 66
Sheldrake Pl. W8 4H 75
Shelley Ct. SW3 5K 87
Shelley Ho. E2 7J 63
SE17 3H 91
SW1 5E 88
Shelton St. WC2 6J 69 (not continuous)
Shene Ho. EC1 3C 70
Shenfield St. N1 5B 62 (not continuous)
Shepherdess Pl. N1 6H 61
Shepherdess Wlk. N1 4H 61
Shepherd Mkt. W1 3C 78
SHEPHERD'S BUSH 4B 74
Shepherds Bush Empire Theatre 4B 74
Shepherd's Bush Grn. W12 4B 74
Shepherd's Bush Mkt. W12 4A 74 (not continuous)
Shepherd's Bush Pl. W12 4C 74
Shepherd's Bush Rd. W6 5B 74
Shepherds Cl. W1 7A 68
Shepherds Ct. W12 4C 74
Shepherds Pl. W1 7A 68
Shepherd St. W1 3C 78
Sheppard Dr. SE16 3G 93
Sheppard Ho. E2 5F 63
Shepperton Rd. N1 2H 61
Shepton Ho's. E2 6K 63
Sherard Ho. E9 1J 63
Sheraton Ho. SW1 5D 88
Sheraton St. W1 6G 69
Sherborne Ho. SW1 3D 88
SW8 7A 90
Sherborne La. EC4 7J 71
Sherborne St. N1 2J 61
Sherbourne Ct. SW5 1A 86
Sherbrooke Ho. E2 4J 63
Sherbrooke Rd. SW6 7F 85
Sherbrooke Ter. SW6 7F 85
Shere Ho. SE1 6J 81
Sheridan Bldgs. WC2 6K 69
Sheridan Ct. NW6 1D 56
SW5 2A 86
Sheridan Ho. E1 6J 73
SE11 2D 90
Sheridan St. E1 6H 73
Sheringham NW8 2F 57
Sheringham Ho. NW1 3G 67
Sherlock Ct. NW8 2E 56
Sherlock Holmes Mus. 2K 67
Sherlock M. W1 3A 68
Sherren Ho. E1 2K 73
Sherston Ct. SE1 1F 91
WC1 7C 60
Sherwin Ho. SE11 5C 90
Sherwood NW6 1F 55
Sherwood Ct. W1 4J 67
Sherwood Gdns. SE16 4F 93
Sherwood St. W1 7F 69
Shillibeer Pl. W1 4H 67
Shillingford St. N1 2F 61
Shillingstone Ho. W14 7F 75
Shinfield St. W12 6A 64
Ship & Mermaid Row SE1 4K 81
Shiplake Ho. E2 7C 62
Ship Tavern Pas. EC3 7A 72
Shipton Ho. E2 5D 62
Shipton St. E2 6D 62
Shipwright Yd. SE1 3A 82
Shirland M. W9 7H 55
Shirland Rd. W9 7G 55
Shirley Ho. SE5 7K 91
Shoe La. EC4 5D 70
Shore Bus. Cen. E9 1J 63
SHOREDITCH 6A 62
Shoreditch Ct. E8 1D 62
Shoreditch High St. E1 7B 62
Shoreditch Ho. N1 7K 61
Shore M. E9 1J 63
Shore Pl. E9 1J 63
Shore Rd. E9 1J 63
Shorncliffe Rd. SE1 3C 92
Shorrold's Rd. SW6 7H 85
Shorter St. E1 7C 72
Shortlands W6 2C 84
Shorts Gdns. WC2 6J 69
Short St. SE1 4D 80
Shottsford W2 5J 65
Shouldham St. W1 4H 67
Shrewsbury Ct. EC1 2H 71
Shrewsbury Ho. SW3 6G 87
SW8 5B 90
Shrewsbury M. W2 4J 65
Shrewsbury Rd. W2 5J 65
Shrewsbury St. W10 2B 64
Shropshire Pl. WC1 2F 69
Shroton St. NW1 3G 67
Shrubbery Cl. N1 3H 61
Shrubland Rd. E8 2D 62
Shurland Gdns. SE15 7D 92
Shuters Sq. W14 4G 85
Shuttle St. E1 2E 72
Sicilian Av. WC1 4K 69
Siddons La. NW1 2K 67
Sidford Ho. SE1 7C 80
Sidford Pl. SE1 7B 80
Sidmouth Ho. SE15 7F 93
W1 5H 67
Sidmouth Pde. NW2 1A 54
Sidmouth Rd. NW2 1A 54
Sidmouth St. WC1 7K 59
Sidney Boyd Ct. NW6 1K 55
Sidney Est. E1 5J 73 (Bromhead St.)
E1 4J 73 (Lindley St.)
Sidney Godley (VC) Ho. E2 6K 63
Sidney Gro. EC1 6E 60
Sidney Ho. E2 5K 63
Sidney Sq. E1 4J 73
Sidney St. E1 3H 73 (not continuous)
Sidney Webb Ho. SE1 6K 81
Sidworth St. E8 1H 63
Siege Ho. E1 5H 73
Signal Ho. E8 1H 63
Signmakers Yd. NW1 3D 58
Silbury St. N1 6J 61
Silchester Rd. W10 6D 64
Silesia Bldgs. E8 1H 63
Silex St. SE1 5F 81
Silk Ct. E2 6F 63
Silk St. EC2 3H 71
Sillitoe Ho. N1 3K 61
Silsoe Ho. NW1 5D 58
Silverdale NW1 6E 58
Silverdale Ct. EC1 1F 71
Silver Pl. W1 7F 69
Silver Rd. W12 1C 74
Silverthorn NW8 3B 56
Silverthorne Loft SE17 6H 91
Silverton Rd. W6 7C 84
Silvester Ho. E1 5H 73
E2 7J 63
W11 5G 65
Silvester St. SE1 5J 81
Silwood Est. SE16 2K 93
Silwood St. SE16 2K 93
Simla Ho. SE1 5K 81
Simmonds Ct. SW5 2A 86
Simms Rd. SE1 2E 92
Simon Cl. W11 7H 65
Simon Ct. W9 7J 55
Simpson Ho. NW8 7G 57
SE11 4B 90
Sinclair Gdns. W14 5D 74
Sinclair Ho. WC1 7J 59
Sinclair Mans. W12 5D 74
Sinclair Rd. W14 5D 74
Singer St. EC2 7K 61
Sirdar Rd. W11 1D 74
Sirinham Point SW8 6B 90
Sir John Kirk Cl. SE5 7G 91
Sir John Soane's Mus. 5A 70
Sir Nicholas Garrow Ho. W10 1F 65
Sir Oswald Stoll Foundation, The SW6 7A 86
Sir Oswald Stoll Mans. SW6 7A 86
Sise La. EC4 6J 71
Sissinghurst Ho. SE15 6K 93
Sister Mabel's Way SE15 7E 92
Sivill Ho. E2 6D 62
Six Bridges Ind. Est. SE1 4F 93
Sixth Av. W10 6E 54
Skelwith Rd. W6 6B 84
Skenfrith Ho. SE15 6G 93
Sketchley Gdns. SE16 3K 93
Skinner Pl. SW1 2A 88
Skinners La. EC4 7H 71
Skinner St. EC1 7D 60
Skipwith Ho. EC1 3C 70
Skipworth Rd. E9 2K 63
Skylark Ct. SE1 5H 81
Skyline Ct. SE1 7C 82
Skyline Plaza Bldg. E1 5F 73
Slade Wlk. SE17 6F 91
Slaidburn St. SW10 6D 86
Slaney Ct. NW10 1A 54
Sleaford Ind. Est. SW8 7F 89
Sleaford St. SW8 7E 88
Sleigh Ho. E2 6K 63
Sligo Ho. E1 2K 73
Slingsby Pl. WC2 7J 69
Slippers Pl. SE16 6H 83
Sloane Av. SW3 2G 87
Sloane Av. Mans. SW3 2J 87
Sloane Ct. E. SW3 3A 88
Sloane Ct. W. SW3 3A 88
Sloane Gdns. SW1 2A 88
Sloane Ga. Mans. SW1 1A 88
Sloane Sq. SW1 2K 87
Sloane St. SW1 5K 77
Sloane Ter. SW1 1K 87
Sloane Ter. Mans. SW1 1A 88
Sloman Ho. W10 6F 55
Sly St. E1 6G 73
Smallbrook M. W2 6E 66
Smart's Pl. WC2 5K 69
Smeaton Ct. SE1 7G 81
Smeaton St. E1 2G 83
Smithfield (Central Markets) 4E 70
Smithfield St. EC1 4E 70
Smith's Ct. W1 7G 69
Smith Sq. SW1 7J 79
Smith St. SW3 3J 87
Smith Ter. SW3 4J 87
Smithy St. E1 3J 73
Smokehouse Yd. EC1 3F 71
Smyrk's Rd. SE17 4B 92
Smyrna Rd. NW6 1K 55
Snarsgate St. W10 4A 64
Snowden St. EC2 3A 72
Snowdon Aviary 3K 57
Snow Hill EC1 4E 70
Snow Hill Ct. EC1 5F 71 (not continuous)
Snowman Ho. NW6 2B 56
Snowsfields SE1 4K 81
Soane Ct. NW1 1F 59
SOHO 6G 69
Soho Sq. W1 5G 69
Soho St. W1 5G 69
Soho Theatre & Writers Cen. 6G 69
Solander Gdns. E1 7H 73 (Cable St.)
E1 7J 73 (Highway, The)
Solarium Ct. SE1 1D 92
Soley M. WC1 6C 60
Somer Ct. SW6 6J 85
Somerford St. E1 2G 73
Somers Cl. NW1 4G 59
Somers Cres. W2 6G 67
Somerset Ct. NW1 5G 59

Somerset House . . . 7A 70
Somerset Sq. W14 . . . 6F 75
SOMERS TOWN . . . 5G 59
Somers Town Community Sports Cen. . . . 5G 59
Somerton Ho. WC1 . . . 7H 59
Somerville Av. SW13 . . . 6A 84
Sondes St. SE17 . . . 5J 91
Sonning Ho. E2 . . . 7D 62
Sophia Ho. W6 . . . 4A 84
Sopwith Way SW8 . . . 6C 88
Sotheran Cl. E8 . . . 2F 63
Sotherby Lodge E2 . . . 4K 63
Souldern Rd. W14 . . . 7D 74
Southacre W2 . . . 6G 67
Sth. Africa Rd. W12 . . . 1A 74
Southall Pl. SE1 . . . 5J 81
Southam Ho. W10 . . . 2F 65
Southampton Bldgs. WC2 . . . 4C 70
Southampton Pl. WC1 . . . 4K 69
Southampton Row WC1 . . . 3K 69
Southampton St. WC2 . . . 7K 69
Southampton Way SE5 . . . 7K 91
Southam St. W10 . . . 2F 65
Sth. Audley St. W1 . . . 1B 78
South Av. NW10 . . . 1A 64
South Bank . . . 2B 80
Sth. Bank Bus. Cen. SW8 . . . 6H 89
South Block SE1 . . . 5A 80
Sth. Bolton Gdns. SW5 . . . 3B 86
Southborough Ho. SE17 . . . 3A 92
Southborough Rd. E9 . . . 2K 63
Sth. Branch Av. NW10 . . . 1B 64
Southbury NW8 . . . 2D 56
Sth. Carriage Dr. SW1 . . . 5F 77
SW7 . . . 5F 77
South City Ct. SE15 . . . 7B 92
Southcombe St. W14 . . . 1E 84
Southcott Ho. W9 . . . 2D 66
Southcott M. NW8 . . . 5G 57
South Cres. WC1 . . . 4G 69
Sth. Eaton Pl. SW1 . . . 1B 88
Sth. Edwardes Sq. W8 . . . 7H 75
South End W8 . . . 6B 76
South End Row W8 . . . 6B 76
Southern Row W10 . . . 2E 64
Southern St. N1 . . . 4A 60
Southernwood Retail Pk. SE1 . . . 3C 92
Southerton Rd. W6 . . . 7A 74
Southey Ho. SE17 . . . 3H 91
Southgate Ct. N1 . . . 1K 61
Southgate Gro. N1 . . . 1K 61
Southgate Rd. N1 . . . 2K 61
Sth. Island Pl. SW9 . . . 7B 90
SOUTH KENSINGTON . . . 1F 87
Sth. Kensington Sta. Arc. SW7 . . . 1F 87
SOUTH LAMBETH . . . 7K 89
Sth. Lambeth Pl. SW8 . . . 5K 89
Sth. Lambeth Rd. SW8 . . . 6K 89
South Lodge NW8 . . . 6E 56
SW7 . . . 5H 77
Sth. Molton La. W1 . . . 6C 68
Sth. Molton St. W1 . . . 6C 68
South Pde. SW3 . . . 3F 87
South Pl. EC2 . . . 4K 71
South Pl. M. EC2 . . . 4K 71
South Ri. W2 . . . 7H 67
South Sq. WC1 . . . 4C 70
South St. W1 . . . 2B 78
Sth. Tenter St. E1 . . . 7D 72
South Ter. SW7 . . . 1G 87
SOUTHWARK . . . 3F 81
Southwark Bri. SE1 . . . 1H 81
Southwark Bri. Bus. Cen. *SE1 . . . 3H 81*
(off Southwark Bri. Rd.)
Southwark Bri. Office Village SE1 . . . 2H 81
Southwark Bri. Rd. SE1 . . . 6F 81
Southwark Cathedral . . . 2J 81
Southwark Pk. Est. SE16 . . . 1H 93
Southwark Pk. Rd. SE16 . . . 1D 92
Southwark Pk. Sports Cen. Track . . . 1K 93
Southwark Pk. Sports Complex . . . 1K 93
Southwark Playhouse . . . 3G 81
Southwark St. SE1 . . . 2E 80
Southway Cl. W12 . . . 5A 74
Southwell Gdns. SW7 . . . 1C 86
Southwell Ho. SE16 . . . 2G 93
Sth. Wharf Rd. W2 . . . 5E 66
Southwick M. W2 . . . 5F 67
Southwick Pl. W2 . . . 6G 67
Southwick St. W2 . . . 5G 67
Southwick Yd. W2 . . . 6G 67
Southwold Mans. W9 . . . 7K 55
Southwood Ct. EC1 . . . 6E 60
Southwood Ho. W11 . . . 7E 64
Southwood Smith Ho. E2 . . . 6G 63
Southwood Smith St. N1 . . . 3D 60
Sovereign Cl. E1 . . . 1H 83
Sovereign Ct. W8 . . . 6A 76
Sovereign Ho. E1 . . . 2H 73
Sovereign M. E2 . . . 4C 62
Spafield St. EC1 . . . 1C 70
Spa Grn. Est. EC1 . . . 6E 60
Spanish Pl. W1 . . . 5B 68
Sparkes Cotts. SW1 . . . 2A 88
Spa Rd. SE16 . . . 7C 82
Sparrick's Row SE1 . . . 4K 81
Sparrow Ho. E1 . . . 2K 73
Speakers' Corner . . . 7K 67
Spear M. SW5 . . . 2K 85
Spectrum Pl. SE17 . . . 5J 91
Speed Highwalk EC2 . . . 3H 71
Speed Ho. EC2 . . . 3J 71
Speedy Pl. WC1 . . . 7J 59
Speke's Monument . . . 2D 76
Speldhurst Rd. E9 . . . 1K 63
Spellbrook Wlk. N1 . . . 2H 61
Spelman Ho. E1 . . . 4E 72
Spelman St. E1 . . . 3E 72
(not continuous)
Spencer Ct. NW8 . . . 5C 56
Spencer House . . . 3E 78
Spencer Mans. W14 . . . 5F 85
Spencer M. W6 . . . 5E 84
Spencer Pl. N1 . . . 1E 60
Spencer St. EC1 . . . 7E 60
Spenlow Ho. SE16 . . . 5F 83
Spenser St. SW1 . . . 6F 79
Spens Ho. WC1 . . . 2A 70
Spice Ct. E1 . . . 2F 83
Spice Quay Hgts. SE1 . . . 3D 82
Spire Ho. W2 . . . 7D 66
Spirit Quay E1 . . . 2F 83
SPITALFIELDS . . . 3C 72
Spital Sq. E1 . . . 3B 72
Spital St. E1 . . . 3E 72
Spital Yd. E1 . . . 3B 72
Splendour Wlk. SE16 . . . 4J 93
Spode Ho. SE11 . . . 7C 80
Sportsman Pl. E2 . . . 3E 62
Spriggs Ho. N1 . . . 1F 61
Sprimont Pl. SW3 . . . 3J 87
Springall St. SE15 . . . 7H 93
Springalls Wharf SE16 . . . 4E 82
Springbank Wlk. NW1 . . . 1H 59
Springfield La. NW6 . . . 3A 56
Springfield Rd. NW8 . . . 3C 56
Springfield Wlk. NW6 . . . 3A 56
Spring Gdns. SW1 . . . 2H 79
(not continuous)
Spring Ho. WC1 . . . 7C 60
Spring M. W1 . . . 3K 67
Spring St. W2 . . . 6E 66
Spring Va. Ter. W14 . . . 7D 74
Spring Wlk. E1 . . . 3F 73
Springwater WC1 . . . 3A 70
Spruce Ho. SE16 . . . 5K 83
Spurgeon St. SE1 . . . 7J 81
Spur Rd. SE1 . . . 4C 80
SW1 . . . 5E 78
Square, The W6 . . . 4B 84
Squire Gdns. NW8 . . . 7E 56
Squirries St. E2 . . . 6F 63
Stables Lodge *E8 . . . 1H 63*
(off Mare St.)
Stables Market, The . . . 1C 58
Stables Way SE11 . . . 3C 90
Stable Wlk. N1 . . . 4K 59
Stable Way W10 . . . 6B 64
Stable Yd. SW1 . . . 4E 78
Stable Yd. Rd. SW1 . . . 3E 78
(not continuous)
Stacey St. WC2 . . . 6H 69
Stack Ho. SW1 . . . 2B 88
Stackhouse St. SW3 . . . 6J 77
Stacy Path SE5 . . . 7A 92
Stadium St. SW10 . . . 7D 86
Stafford Cl. NW6 . . . 7J 55
Stafford Ct. W8 . . . 6J 75
Stafford Cripps Ho. E2 . . . 7K 63
SW6 . . . 6H 85
Stafford Ho. SE1 . . . 3D 92
Stafford Mans. SW1 . . . 6E 78
W14 . . . 7C 74
Stafford Pl. SW1 . . . 6E 78
Stafford Rd. NW6 . . . 6J 55
Stafford St. W1 . . . 2E 78
Stafford Ter. W8 . . . 6J 75
Staff St. EC1 . . . 7K 61
Stainer St. SE1 . . . 3K 81
Staining La. EC2 . . . 5H 71
Stainsbury St. E2 . . . 5K 63
Stalbridge Flats W1 . . . 6B 68
Stalbridge Ho. NW1 . . . 5E 58
Stalbridge St. NW1 . . . 3H 67
Stalham St. SE16 . . . 7H 83
Stamford Bridge . . . 7A 86
Stamford Bri. Studios *SW6 . . . 7B 86*
(off Wandon Rd.)
Stamford Bldgs. *SW8 . . . 7K 89*
(off Meadow Pl.)
Stamford Cotts. SW6 . . . 7B 86
Stamford Ga. SW6 . . . 7B 86
Stamford St. SE1 . . . 3C 80
Stamp Pl. E2 . . . 6C 62
Standard Pl. EC2 . . . 7B 62
Stanesgate Ho. SE15 . . . 7F 93
Stanfield Ho. NW8 . . . 1F 67
Stanford Ct. SW7 . . . 7B 76
Stanford Pl. SE17 . . . 2A 92
Stanford Rd. W8 . . . 6B 76
Stanford St. SW1 . . . 2G 89
Stangate SE1 . . . 6B 80
Stanhope Gdns. SW7 . . . 1D 86
Stanhope Ga. W1 . . . 3B 78
Stanhope M. E. SW7 . . . 1D 86
Stanhope M. Sth. SW7 . . . 2D 86
Stanhope M. W. SW7 . . . 1D 86
Stanhope Pde. NW1 . . . 6E 58
Stanhope Pl. W2 . . . 6J 67
Stanhope Row W1 . . . 3C 78
Stanhope St. NW1 . . . 5E 58
Stanhope Ter. W2 . . . 7F 67
Stanier Cl. W14 . . . 4H 85
Stanlake M. W12 . . . 3A 74
Stanlake Rd. W12 . . . 2A 74
Stanlake Vs. W12 . . . 3A 74
Stanley Bri. Studios SW6 . . . 7B 86
Stanley Cl. SW8 . . . 6A 90
Stanley Cohen Ho. EC1 . . . 2G 71
Stanley Cres. W11 . . . 7G 65
Stanley Gdns. W11 . . . 7G 65
Stanley Gdns. M. W11 . . . 7H 65
Stanley Ho. SW10 . . . 7C 86
Stanley Mans. SW10 . . . 5D 86
Stanley M. SW10 . . . 7C 86
Stanley Studios *SW10 . . . 5D 86*
(off Fulham Rd.)
Stanmore Pl. NW1 . . . 2D 58
Stanmore St. N1 . . . 2A 60
Stannard Cotts. E1 . . . 1K 73
Stannary Pl. SE11 . . . 4D 90
Stannary St. SE11 . . . 5D 90
Stansbury Ho. W10 . . . 6F 55
Stansbury Sq. W10 . . . 6F 55
Stansfield Ho. SE1 . . . 2D 92
Stanswood Gdns. SE5 . . . 7B 92
Stanway Ct. N1 . . . 5B 62
(not continuous)
Stanway St. N1 . . . 4B 62
Stanwick Rd. W14 . . . 2G 85
Stanworth St. SE1 . . . 5C 82
Staple Inn WC1 . . . 4C 70
Staple Inn Bldgs. WC1 . . . 4C 70
Staple St. SE1 . . . 5K 81
Stapleton Ho. E2 . . . 6G 63
Star All. EC3 . . . 7B 72
Starcross St. NW1 . . . 7F 59
Starling Ho. NW8 . . . 4G 57
Star Pl. E1 . . . 1D 82
Star Rd. W14 . . . 5G 85
Star St. W2 . . . 5F 67
Star Yd. WC2 . . . 5C 70
Station App. NW1 . . . 2K 67
Station App. Rd. SE1 . . . 5C 80
Station Arc. W1 . . . 2D 68
Stationer's Hall Ct. EC4 . . . 6F 71
Station Ter. NW10 . . . 5B 54
Staunton Ho. SE17 . . . 2A 92
Staveley NW1 . . . 6E 58
Staverton Rd. NW2 . . . 1A 54
Stavordale Lodge W14 . . . 6H 75
Stayner's Rd. E1 . . . 1K 73
Steadman Ct. EC1 . . . 1H 71
Stead St. SE17 . . . 2J 91
Stean St. E8 . . . 2C 62
Stebbing Ho. W11 . . . 2D 74
Stedham Pl. WC1 . . . 5J 69
Steedman St. SE17 . . . 2G 91
Steel's La. E1 . . . 6K 73
Steelyard Pas. EC4 . . . 1J 81
Steeple Ct. E1 . . . 1H 73
Steeple Wlk. N1 . . . 2H 61
Stelfox Ho. WC1 . . . 6B 60
Stephan Cl. E8 . . . 2F 63
Stephen M. W1 . . . 4G 69
Stephenson Ho. SE1 . . . 6G 81
Stephenson Way NW1 . . . 1F 69
Stephen St. W1 . . . 4G 69
Stepney City Apartments E1 . . . 4K 73
Stepney Grn. E1 . . . 3K 73
Stepney Way E1 . . . 4G 73
Sterling St. SW7 . . . 6H 77
Sterndale Rd. W14 . . . 7C 74
Sterne St. W12 . . . 4C 74
Sterry St. SE1 . . . 5J 81
Stevedore St. E1 . . . 2G 83
Stevenson Cres. SE16 . . . 3G 93
Stevenson Ho. NW8 . . . 2C 56
Stevens St. SE1 . . . 6B 82
Steward St. E1 . . . 4B 72
Stewart's Gro. SW3 . . . 3F 87
Stewart's Rd. SW8 . . . 7E 88
Stew La. EC4 . . . 7G 71
Stifford Ho. E1 . . . 4K 73
Stillington St. SW1 . . . 1F 89
Stirling Ct. EC1 . . . 1E 70
Stockbeck NW1 . . . 5F 59
Stockholm Ho. E1 . . . 7F 73
Stockholm Rd. SE16 . . . 4K 93
Stockholm Way E1 . . . 2E 82
Stockleigh Hall NW8 . . . 4H 57
Stockton Ct. SW1 . . . 7G 79
Stockton Ho. E2 . . . 6G 63
Stoddart Ho. SW8 . . . 6B 90
Stone Bldgs. WC2 . . . 4B 70
Stonecutter St. EC4 . . . 5E 70
Stonefield St. N1 . . . 2D 60
Stone Hall W8 . . . 7A 76
Stone Hall Gdns. W8 . . . 7A 76
Stone Hall Pl. W8 . . . 7A 76
Stonehouse NW1 . . . 3F 59
Stone Ho. Ct. EC3 . . . 5B 72
Stonehouse Ho. W2 . . . 4J 65
Stoneleigh Pl. W11 . . . 1D 74
Stoneleigh St. W11 . . . 1D 74
Stonemason Ct. SE1 . . . 5G 81
Stones End St. SE1 . . . 5G 81
Stoney La. E1 . . . 5B 72
Stoney St. SE1 . . . 2J 81
Stonor Rd. W14 . . . 2G 85
Stopford Rd. SE17 . . . 4F 91
Stopher Ho. SE1 . . . 5F 81
Store St. WC1 . . . 4G 69
Storey Ct. NW8 . . . 7E 56
Storey's Ga. SW1 . . . 5H 79
Stork's Rd. SE16 . . . 7F 83
Storrington WC1 . . . 7K 59
Story St. N1 . . . 1A 60
Stothard Ho. E1 . . . 1K 73
Stothard St. E1 . . . 1J 73
Stoughton Cl. SE11 . . . 2B 90
Stourcliffe Cl. W1 . . . 5J 67
Stourcliffe St. W1 . . . 6J 67
Stourhead Ho. SW1 . . . 3G 89
Strale Ho. N1 . . . 3A 62
Strand WC2 . . . 2J 79
Strand La. WC2 . . . 7B 70
Strand Theatre . . . 7A 70
Strang Ho. N1 . . . 3G 61
Strang Print Room . . . 1G 69
Strangways Ter. W14 . . . 6G 75
Stranraer Way N1 . . . 1K 59
Stratford Pl. W1 . . . 6C 68
Stratford Rd. W8 . . . 1K 85
Stratford Studios W8 . . . 7K 75
Stratford Vs. NW1 . . . 1F 59
Strathearn Ho. W2 . . . 7G 67
Strathearn Pl. W2 . . . 7G 67
Strathmore Ct. NW8 . . . 6G 57
Strathmore Gdns. W8 . . . 2K 75
Strathnairn St. SE1 . . . 2F 93
Stratton Ct. N1 . . . 1B 62
Stratton St. W1 . . . 2D 78
Streatham St. WC1 . . . 5J 69
Streatley Rd. NW6 . . . 1G 55
Strickland Ho. E2 . . . 7D 62
Stringer Ho. N1 . . . 3B 62
Strode Rd. SW6 . . . 7D 84
Strome Ho. NW6 . . . 5A 56
Strood Ho. SE1 . . . 5K 81
Strouts Pl. E2 . . . 6C 62
Strutton Ct. SW1 . . . 7G 79
Strutton Ground SW1 . . . 6G 79
Strype St. E1 . . . 4C 72
Stuart Ho. W14 . . . 1E 84
Stuart Mill Ho. N1 . . . 5A 60
Stuart Rd. NW6 . . . 7J 55
Stuart Twr. W9 . . . 7D 56
Stubbs Dr. SE16 . . . 3G 93
Stubbs Ho. E2 . . . 6K 63
SW1 . . . 2H 89
Stucley Pl. NW1 . . . 1D 58
Studd St. N1 . . . 2E 60
Studholme St. SE15 . . . 7G 93
Studio Pl. SW1 . . . 5K 77
Studios, The W8 . . . 3K 75
Studland SE17 . . . 3J 91
Stukeley St. WC2 . . . 5K 69
Stunell Ho. SE14 . . . 6K 93
Sturdee Ho. E2 . . . 5E 62
Sturgeon Rd. SE17 . . . 4G 91
Sturge St. SE1 . . . 4G 81
Sturminster Ho. SW8 . . . 7A 90
Sturt St. N1 . . . 5H 61
Stutfield St. E1 . . . 6F 73
Styles Ho. SE1 . . . 3E 80
Stylus Ho. E1 . . . 6K 73
Sudeley St. N1 . . . 5F 61
Sudrey St. SE1 . . . 5G 81
Suffield Ho. SE17 . . . 3F 91
Suffolk La. EC4 . . . 7J 71
Suffolk Pl. SW1 . . . 2H 79
Suffolk St. SW1 . . . 1H 79
Sugar Bakers Ct. EC3 . . . 6B 72
Sugar Loaf Wlk. E2 . . . 6J 63
Sugar Quay EC3 . . . 1B 82
Sugar Quay Wlk. EC3 . . . 1B 82
Sugden St. SE5 . . . 6J 91
Sulgrave Gdns. W6 . . . 5B 74
Sulgrave Rd. W6 . . . 5B 74
Sulkin Ho. E2 . . . 6K 63
Sullivan Ct. SW5 . . . 1K 85
Sullivan Ho. SE11 . . . 2B 90
SW1 . . . 5D 88
Sullivan Rd. SE11 . . . 1D 90
Sultan St. SE5 . . . 7G 91
Summercourt Rd. E1 . . . 5K 73
Summerfield Av. NW6 . . . 4F 55
Summers St. EC1 . . . 2C 70
Sumner Bldgs. SE1 . . . 2G 81
Sumner Pl. SW7 . . . 2E 86
Sumner Pl. M. SW7 . . . 2F 87
Sumner Rd. SE15 . . . 6D 92
Sumner St. SE1 . . . 2F 81
Sunbeam Cres. W10 . . . 2B 64
Sunbury Ho. E2 . . . 7C 62
Sunbury Workshops E2 . . . 7C 62
Sun Ct. EC3 . . . 6K 71
Sunderland Ho. W2 . . . 4J 65
Sunderland Ter. W2 . . . 5A 66
Sundridge Ho. E9 . . . 1K 63
Sunlight Sq. E2 . . . 7H 63
Sunningdale Cl. SE16 . . . 4G 93
Sunningdale Gdns. W8 . . . 7K 75
Sun Pas. SE16 . . . 6E 82
Sun Rd. W14 . . . 4G 85
Sun St. EC2 . . . 3A 72
EC2 . . . 3K 71
Sun St. Pas. EC2 . . . 4A 72
Sun Wlk. E1 . . . 1D 82
Surma Cl. E1 . . . 2G 73
Surrendale Pl. W9 . . . 2K 65
Surrey Canal Rd. SE14 . . . 5K 93
SE15 . . . 5K 93
Surrey County Cricket Club . . . 5B 90
Surrey Gro. SE17 . . . 4A 92
Surrey Quays Rd. SE16 . . . 6K 83
Surrey Quays Shop. Cen. SE16 . . . 7K 83
Surrey Row SE1 . . . 4E 80
Surrey Sq. SE17 . . . 3A 92
Surrey Steps WC2 . . . 7B 70
Surrey St. WC2 . . . 7B 70
Surrey Ter. SE17 . . . 3B 92
Sussex Ct. W2 . . . 6E 66
Sussex Gdns. W2 . . . 7E 66
Sussex Lodge W2 . . . 6F 67
Sussex Mans. SW7 . . . 2E 86
WC2 . . . 7K 69
Sussex M. E. W2 . . . 6F 67
Sussex M. W. W2 . . . 7F 67
Sussex Pl. NW1 . . . 1J 67
W2 . . . 6F 67
W6 . . . 3B 84
Sussex Sq. W2 . . . 7F 67
Sussex St. SW1 . . . 4D 88
Sutherland Av. W9 . . . 2K 65
Sutherland Ct. W9 . . . 2K 65
Sutherland Ho. W8 . . . 7A 76
Sutherland Pl. W2 . . . 5J 65
Sutherland Row SW1 . . . 3D 88
Sutherland Sq. SE17 . . . 4G 91
Sutherland St. SW1 . . . 3C 88
Sutherland Wlk. SE17 . . . 4H 91
Sutton Est. EC1 . . . 7K 61
W10 . . . 3A 64
Sutton Est., The N1 . . . 1E 60
SW3 . . . 3H 87
Sutton La. EC1 . . . 2F 71
Sutton Row W1 . . . 5H 69
Sutton St. E1 . . . 7J 73
Sutton's Way EC1 . . . 2H 71
Sutton Wlk. SE1 . . . 3B 80
Sutton Way W10 . . . 3A 64
Swain St. NW8 . . . 1G 67
Swallow Ct. SE1 . . . 5H 81
W9 . . . 3K 65
Swallowfield *NW1 . . . 7D 58*
(off Munster Sq.)
Swallow Ho. NW8 . . . 4G 57
Swallow Pas. W1 . . . 6D 68
Swallow Pl. W1 . . . 6D 68
Swallow St. W1 . . . 1F 79
Swanage Ct. N1 . . . 1B 62
Swanage Ho. SW8 . . . 7A 90
Swanbourne SE17 . . . 2G 91
Swanbourne Ho. NW8 . . . 1G 67
Swan Ct. E1 . . . 1E 82
SW3 . . . 4H 87
SW6 . . . 7J 85
Swanfield St. E2 . . . 7C 62
Swan La. EC4 . . . 1J 81
Swanley Ho. SE17 . . . 3B 92
Swan Mead SE1 . . . 7A 82
Swan Pas. E1 . . . 7E 72
Swan Rd. SE16 . . . 4K 83
Swanscombe Ho. W11 . . . 2D 74
Swanscombe Rd. W11 . . . 2D 74
Swan St. SE1 . . . 6H 81
Swan Wlk. SW3 . . . 5J 87
Swedeland Ct. E1 . . . 4B 72
Swedenborg Gdns. E1 . . . 7F 73
Swedenborg Pl. E1 . . . 7G 73
Sweeney Cres. SE1 . . . 5D 82
Swift Lodge W9 . . . 2K 65
Swinbrook Rd. W10 . . . 3F 65
Swinburne Ho. E2 . . . 7J 63
Swindon St. W12 . . . 2A 74
Swingfield Ho. E9 . . . 2J 63
Swinley Ho. NW1 . . . 6D 58
Swinton Pl. WC1 . . . 6A 60
Swinton St. WC1 . . . 6A 60
Swiss Cen. W1 . . . 1H 79
SWISS COTTAGE . . . 1E 56
Swiss Cottage Sports Cen. . . . 1F 57
Swiss Ct. WC2 . . . 1H 79
Swiss Re Tower . . . 5B 72
Swiss Ter. NW6 . . . 1E 56
Sybil Thorndike Casson Ho. SW5 . . . 4K 85
Sycamore Ct. NW6 . . . 2K 55
Sycamore Gdns. W6 . . . 5A 74
Sycamore Ho. W6 . . . 5A 74
Sycamore Lodge *W8 . . . 7A 76*
(off Stone Hall Pl.)
Sycamore St. EC1 . . . 2G 71
Sycamore Wlk. W10 . . . 1E 64
Sydney Cl. SW3 . . . 2F 87
Sydney M. SW3 . . . 2F 87
Sydney Pl. SW7 . . . 2F 87
Sydney St. SW3 . . . 2G 87
Sylvan Gro. SE15 . . . 6H 93
Sylvan Ter. SE15 . . . 7H 93
Sylvia Ct. N1 . . . 5K 61
Symes M. NW1 . . . 4E 58
Symington Ho. SE1 . . . 7J 81
Symister M. N1 . . . 7A 62
Symons St. SW3 . . . 2K 87
Symphony M. W10 . . . 6F 55

T

Tabard Gdn. Est. SE1 . . . 6J 81
Tabard Ho. SE1 . . . 6K 81
Tabard St. SE1 . . . 4J 81
Tabernacle St. EC2 . . . 2K 71
Tabor Rd. W6 . . . 7A 74
Tachbrook Est. SW1 . . . 4G 89
Tachbrook M. SW1 . . . 1E 88
Tachbrook St. SW1 . . . 2F 89
(not continuous)
Tadema Ho. NW8 . . . 2F 67
Tadema Rd. SW10 . . . 7D 86
Tadmor St. W12 . . . 3C 74
Tadworth Ho. SE1 . . . 5E 80
Tailor Ho. WC1 . . . 2K 69
Tailworth St. E1 . . . 4E 72
Tait Ho. SE1 . . . 3D 80
Talbot Ct. EC3 . . . 7K 71
Talbot Gro. Ho. W11 . . . 6E 64
Talbot Rd. W2 . . . 5J 65
W11 . . . 6G 65
(not continuous)
Talbot Sq. W2 . . . 6F 67
Talbot Wlk. W11 . . . 6E 64
Talbot Yd. SE1 . . . 3J 81
Talgarth Mans. W14 . . . 3E 84
Talgarth Rd. W6 . . . 3C 84
W14 . . . 3D 84
Tallis St. EC4 . . . 7D 70
Tamar Ho. SE11 . . . 3D 90
Tamarind Ct. SE1 . . . 4D 82
W8 . . . 7A 76
Tamarind Yd. E1 . . . 2F 83
Tamplin Ho. W10 . . . 6G 55
Tamworth St. SW6 . . . 5J 85
Tangerine Ho. SE1 . . . 5K 81
Tangmere WC1 . . . 7A 60
Tankerton Ho's. *WC1 . . . 7K 59*
(off Tankerton St.)
Tankerton St. WC1 . . . 7K 59
Tanner Ho. SE1 . . . 5B 82
Tanneries, The E1 . . . 2K 73
Tanner St. SE1 . . . 5B 82
(not continuous)
Tanswell St. SE1 . . . 5C 80
Tapley Ho. SE1 . . . 5E 82
Taplow SE17 . . . 3K 91
Taplow Ho. E2 . . . 7C 62
Taplow St. N1 . . . 5H 61
Tapp St. E1 . . . 1G 73
Tarbert Wlk. E1 . . . 7J 73
Tarling Ho. E1 . . . 6H 73
Tarling St. E1 . . . 6H 73
Tarling St. Est. E1 . . . 6J 73
Tarnbrook Ct. SW1 . . . 2A 88
Tarns, The NW1 . . . 6E 58
Tarn St. SE1 . . . 7G 81
Tarplett Ho. SE14 . . . 6K 93

Tarranbrae NW6 1E 54
Tarrant Ho. E2 6J 63
W14 6E 74
Tarrant Pl. W1 4J 67
Tarver Rd. SE17 4F 91
Tasman Ho. E1 2H 83
Tasso Rd. W6 5E 84
Tasso Yd. W6 6E 84
Tate Britain 2J 89
Tate Modern 2F 81
Tatham Pl. NW8 4F 57
Tatsfield Ho. SE1 6K 81
Tatum St. SE17 2K 91
Taunton Ho. W2 6C 66
Taunton M. NW1 2J 67
Taunton Pl. NW1 1J 67
Tavern Ct. SE1 7H 81
Taverners Cl. W11 3E 74
Tavistock Ct. WC1 1H 69
WC2 *7K 69*
(off Covent Gdn.)
Tavistock Cres. W11 4G 65
(not continuous)
Tavistock Ho. WC1 1H 69
Tavistock M. W11 5G 65
Tavistock Pl. WC1 1J 69
Tavistock Rd. W11 5G 65
(not continuous)
Tavistock Sq. WC1 1H 69
Tavistock St. WC2 7K 69
(not continuous)
Taviton St. WC1 1G 69
Tavy Cl. SE11 3D 90
(not continuous)
Tay Bldgs. SE1 6A 82
Tayler Ct. NW8 2E 56
Tayport Cl. N1 1K 59
Teal Ct. E1 1E 82
Teale St. E2 4F 63
Tea Trade Wharf SE1 4D 82
Ted Roberts Ho. E2 5H 63
Tedworth Gdns. SW3 4J 87
Tedworth Sq. SW3 4J 87
Teesdale Cl. E2 5F 63
Teesdale St. E2 5G 63
Teesdale Yd. E2 5G 63
Telegraph St. EC2 5J 71
Telephone Pl. SW6 5H 85
Telfer Ho. EC1 7G 61
Telford Ho. SE1 6G 81
W10 3E 64
Telford Rd. W10 3E 64
Telfords Yd. E1 1F 83
Telford Ter. SW1 5E 88
Temeraire St. SE16 4K 83
Templar Ct. NW8 7E 56
Temple Av. EC4 7D 70
Temple Bar 6C 70
Temple Bar Gate 6F 71
Temple Chambers
EC4 7D 70
Templecombe Rd. E9 2J 63
Temple Ct. SW8 7J 89
Temple Dwellings *E2* *6G 63*
(off Temple St.)
Temple Gdns. EC4 7C 70
Temple La. EC4 6D 70
Temple of Mithras (remains)
6J 71
Temple Pl. WC2 7B 70
Temple St. E2 5G 63
Templeton Pl. SW5 2K 85
Temple W. M. SE11 7E 80
Temple Yd. E2 5G 63
Tempus Wharf SE16 4E 82
Tenby Ho. W2 6C 66
Tenby Mans. W1 3B 68
Tench St. E1 2G 83
Tenda Rd. SE16 2G 93
Tenison Ct. W1 7E 68
Tenison Way SE1 3B 80
Tenniel Cl. W2 7B 66
Tennis St. SE1 4J 81
Tennyson Ho. SE17 3H 91
Tennyson Mans.
SW3 6G 87
W14 5F 85
Tennyson Rd. NW6 2G 55
Tenterden Ho. SE17 4A 92
Tenterden St. W1 6D 68
Tenter Ground E1 4C 72
Tenter Pas. E1 6D 72
Tent St. E1 1G 73
Terling Ho. W10 3A 64
Terling Wlk. N1 2G 61
Terminus Pl. SW1 7D 78
Terrace, The E2 6J 63
EC4 7C 70
NW6 2J 55
Terrace Av. NW10 7A 54
Terrace Rd. E9 1K 63
Terraces, The NW8 4E 56
Terrace Wlk. SW11 7J 87
Terretts Pl. N1 1E 60
Terrick St. W12 6A 64
Territorial Ho. SE11 2D 90
Testerton Rd. W11 7D 64
Testerton Wlk. W11 7D 64
Tetbury Pl. N1 3E 60
Tetcott Rd. SW10 7C 86
(not continuous)
Thackeray Ct. SW3 3J 87
W14 7E 74
Thackeray Ho. WC1 1J 69
Thackeray St. W8 6B 76
Thamesbrook SW3 4G 87
Thames Ct. SE15 7C 92
Thames Exchange Bldg.
EC4 7H 71
Thames Hgts. SE1 4C 82
Thames Ho. EC4 7H 71
SW1 1J 89
Thames Reach W6 6B 84
Thames Wlk. SW11 7G 87
Thames Wharf Studios
W6 6B 84
Thanet Ho. WC1 7J 59
Thanet St. WC1 7J 59
Thavie's Inn EC4 5D 70
Thaxted Ct. N1 5J 61
Thaxted Ho. SE16 1J 93
Thaxton Rd. W14 5H 85
Thayer St. W1 4B 68
The ....
Names prefixed with 'The' for example 'The Angel Cen.' are indexed under the main name such as 'Angel Cen., The'
Theatro Technis 3F 59
Theberton St. N1 2D 60
Theed St. SE1 3D 80
Theobald's Rd. WC1 4A 70
Theobald St. SE1 7J 81
Theseus Wlk. N1 5F 61
Thessaly Ho. SW8 7E 88
Thessaly Rd. SW8 7E 88
(not continuous)
Thetford Ho. SE1 6C 82
Third Av. W10 6E 54
Thirleby Rd. SW1 7F 79
Thirlmere NW1 6D 58
Thirza Ho. E1 6K 73
Thistle Gro. SW10 3D 86
Thomas Burt Ho. E2 6G 63
Thomas Darby Ct.
W11 6E 64
Thomas Doyle St.
SE1 6F 81
Thomas Hollywood Ho.
E2 5J 63
Thomas More Highwalk
EC2 4G 71
Thomas More Ho.
EC2 4G 71
Thomas More Sq. E1 1E 82
Thomas More St. E1 1E 82
Thomas Neal's Cen.
WC2 6J 69
Thomas Pl. W8 7A 76
Thompson Ho. SE14 6K 93
W10 2E 64
Thompson's Av. SE5 7G 91
Thomson Ho. SE17 2A 92
SW1 4H 89
Thorburn Ho. SW1 5K 77
Thorburn Sq. SE1 2E 92
Thoresby St. N1 6H 61
Thornaby Ho. E2 6G 63
Thornbill Ho. SE15 7E 92
Thornbury Ct. W11 7J 65
Thorncroft St. SW8 7J 89
Thorndike Cl. SW10 7C 86
Thorndike Ho. SW1 3G 89
Thorndike St. SW1 2G 89
Thorne Ho. E2 6K 63
Thornewill Ho. E1 7K 73
Thorney Ct. W8 5C 76
Thorney Cres. SW11 7F 87
Thorney St. SW1 1J 89
Thornfield Rd. W12 4A 74
Thorngate Rd. W9 1K 65
Thornhaugh M. WC1 2H 69
Thornhaugh St. WC1 2H 69
Thornhill Bri. Wharf
N1 3A 60
Thornhill Cres. N1 1B 60
Thornhill Gro. N1 1B 60
Thornhill Ho's. N1 1C 60
Thornhill Rd. N1 1C 60
Thornhill Sq. N1 1B 60
Thornton Ho. SE17 2A 92
Thornton Pl. W1 3K 67
Thorold Ho. SE1 4G 81
Thorparch Rd. SW8 7H 89
Thorpe Cl. W10 5F 65
Thorpe Ho. N1 3B 60
Thrale St. SE1 3H 81
Thrasher Cl. E8 2C 62
Thrawl St. E1 4D 72
Threadneedle St.
EC2 6J 71
Three Barrels Wlk.
EC4 1H 81
Three Colt Cnr. E2 2E 72
Three Colts La. E2 1G 73
Three Cranes Wlk.
EC4 1H 81
Three Cups Yd. WC1 4B 70
Three Kings Yd. W1 7C 68
Three Oak La. SE1 4C 82
Three Quays EC3 1B 82
Three Quays Wlk.
EC3 1B 82
Threshers Pl. W11 7E 64
Throgmorton Av. EC2 5K 71
(not continuous)
Throgmorton St. EC2 5K 71
Thrush St. SE17 3F 91
Thurland Ho. SE16 2G 93
Thurland Rd. SE16 6E 82
Thurloe Cl. SW7 1G 87
Thurloe Ct. SW3 2G 87
Thurloe Pl. SW7 1F 87
Thurloe Pl. M. SW7 1F 87
Thurloe Sq. SW7 1F 87
Thurloe St. SW7 1F 87
Thurlow St. SE17 3K 91
(not continuous)
Thurlow Wlk. SE17 3A 92
(not continuous)
Thurnscoe NW1 3E 58
Thurso Ho. NW6 5A 56
Thurstan Dwellings
WC2 5A 70
Thurtle Rd. E2 3D 62
Tibberton Sq. N1 1G 61
Tiber Gdns. N1 3K 59
Tickford Ho. NW8 7G 57
Tideway Ind. Est.
SW8 6F 89
Tideway Wlk. SW8 6F 89
Tiger Ho. WC1 7H 59
Tilbury Cl. SE15 7D 92
Tilbury Ho. SE14 5K 93
Tilehurst NW1 7D 58
Tileyard Rd. N7 1J 59
Tilleard Ho. W10 6F 55
Tillet Way E2 6E 62
Tillman St. E1 6H 73
Tilloch St. N1 1A 60
Tilney Ct. EC1 1H 71
Tilney St. W1 2B 78
Tilson Cl. SE15 7A 92
Tilton St. SW6 6F 85
Timberland Cl. SE15 7E 92
Timberland Rd. E1 6H 73
Timber St. EC1 1G 71
Tinsley Rd. E1 3K 73
Tintangel Ct. EC1 1E 70
Tintern Ho. NW1 5D 58
SW1 2C 88
Tinworth St. SE11 3K 89
Tisbury Ct. W1 7G 69
Tisdall Ho. SE17 2K 91
Tisdall Pl. SE17 2K 91
Tissington Ct. SE16 2K 93
Titchborne Row W2 6G 67
Titchfield Rd. NW8 3J 57
Tite St. SW3 4J 87
Titmuss St. W12 5A 74
Tiverton Rd. NW10 3C 54
Tiverton St. SE1 7G 81
Tobacco Dock E1 1H 83
Tobacco Quay E1 1G 83
Tobin Cl. NW3 1H 57
Todber Ho. W14 6E 74
Tokenhouse Yd. EC2 5J 71
Tolchurch W11 5H 65
Tolhurst Dr. W10 6F 55
Tollard Ho. W14 7G 75
Tollbridge Cl. W10 1F 65
Tollet St. E1 1K 73
Tollgate Gdns. NW6 4A 56
Tollgate Ho. NW6 4A 56
Tolmers Sq. NW1 1F 69
(not continuous)
Tolpaide Ho. SE11 2C 90
Tolpuddle St. N1 4C 60
Tom Blau Gallery *4C 82*
(off Queen Elizabeth St.)
Tomkyns Ho. SE11 2C 90
Tomline Ho. SE1 3G 81
Tomlinson Cl. E2 7D 62
Tompion Ho. EC1 1F 71
Tompion St. EC1 7F 61
(not continuous)
Tomson Ho. SE1 6C 82
Tom Williams Ho.
SW6 6G 85
Tonbridge Ho's. WC1 7J 59
Tonbridge St. WC1 6J 59
Tonbridge Wlk. WC1 6J 59
Toneborough NW8 3B 56
Took's Ct. EC4 5C 70
Tooley St. SE1 2K 81
Topham St. EC1 1C 70
Torbay Ct. NW1 1D 58
Torbay Mans. NW6 1G 55
Torbay Rd. NW6 1G 55
Torbay St. NW1 1D 58
Tor Ct. W8 4K 75
Tor Gdns. W8 4J 75
Tornay Ho. E9 1K 63
N1 4A 60
Torquay St. W2 4A 66
Torrens St. EC1 5E 60
Torridon Ho. NW6 5A 56
Torrington Pl. E1 2F 83
WC1 3G 69
Torrington Sq. WC1 2H 69
Tortington Ho. SE15 7F 93
Tothill Ho. SW1 1H 89
Tothill St. SW1 5G 79
Tottenhall NW1 1B 58
Tottenham Ct. Rd. W1 2F 69
Tottenham M. W1 3F 69
Tottenham St. W1 4F 69
Toulmin St. SE1 5G 81
Toulon St. SE5 7G 91
Toulouse Ct. SE16 3H 93
Tounson Ct. SW1 2H 89
Tourist Info. Cen.
City of London 6G 71
Hammersmith 2B 84
King's Cross 6J 59
Leicester Sq. 1H 79
Regent St. 2G 79
Southwark 2H 81
Waterloo International
Terminal 4B 80
Tournay Rd. SW6 7H 85
Toussaint Wlk. SE16 6F 83
Tovy Ho. SE1 4E 92
Tower 42 5A 72
Tower Bri. SE1 3C 82
Tower Bri. App. E1 2C 82
Tower Bri. Bus. Complex
SE16 7G 83
Tower Bri. Bus. Sq.
SE16 1G 93
Tower Bridge Experience
2C 82
Tower Bri. Plaza SE1 3C 82
Tower Bri. Rd. SE1 7A 82
Tower Bri. Sq. SE1 4C 82
Tower Bri. Wharf E1 3E 82
Tower Bldgs. E1 3H 83
Tower Ct. N1 1G 61
NW8 4H 57
WC2 6J 69
Towergate SE1 1A 92
TOWER HILL 1C 82
Tower Hill EC3 1B 82
Tower Hill Ter. EC3 1B 82
Tower Ho. E1 4F 73
Tower Mill Rd. SE15 7A 92
Tower of London, The
1C 82
Tower of London
Vis. Cen., The 1B 82
Tower Pl. EC3 1B 82
Tower Pl. E. EC3 1B 82
Tower Pl. W. EC3 1B 82
Tower Royal EC4 7J 71
Tower St. WC2 6H 69
Tower Wlk. *SE1* *1A 92*
(off Aberdour St.)
Townley St. SE17 3J 91
(not continuous)
Townsend Ho. SE1 2F 93
Townsend St. SE17 2K 91
Townshend Ct. NW8 4H 57
Townshend Est. NW8 4G 57
Townshend Rd. NW8 3G 57
(not continuous)
Toynbee St. E1 4C 72
Toynbee Studios 5D 72
Tradescant Ho. E9 1J 63
Tradescant Rd. SW8 7K 89
Tradewinds Ct. E1 2F 83
Trafalgar Av. SE15 4D 92
Trafalgar Chambers
SW3 3F 87
Trafalgar Ct. E1 2K 83
Trafalgar Gdns. W8 6B 76
Trafalgar Ho. SE17 3J 91
Trafalgar Point N1 1K 61
Trafalgar Square 2H 79
Trafalgar Sq. WC2 2H 79
Trafalgar St. SE17 3J 91
Trafalgar Studios 2J 79
Trafford Ho. N1 5K 61
Trahorn Cl. E1 2G 73
Traitors' Gate 2C 82
Tralee Ct. SE16 3G 93
Transept St. NW1 4H 67
Tranton Rd. SE16 6F 83
Trappes Ho. SE16 2G 93
Treadgold Ho. W11 7D 64
Treadgold St. W11 7D 64
Treadway St. E2 5G 63
Treasury Pas. SW1 4J 79
Treaty St. N1 3A 60
Trebeck St. W1 2C 78
Trebovir Rd. SW5 3K 85
Trederwen Rd. E8 2F 63
Tregunter Rd. SW10 5B 86
Trelawney Ho. SE1 4G 81
Trellick Twr. W10 2G 65
Trematon Ho. SE11 3D 90
Trenchold St. SW8 6J 89
Tresco Ho. SE11 3C 90
Tresham Cres. NW8 1G 67
Tressell Cl. N1 1F 61
Tress Pl. SE1 2E 80
Trevanion Rd. W14 3F 85
Trevelyan Gdns.
NW10 3A 54
Trevelyan Ho. E2 7K 63
SE5 7F 91
Treveris St. SE1 3F 81
Treverton St. W10 2D 64
Treverton Towers
W10 3D 64
Treves Ho. E1 2F 73
Trevithick Ho. SE16 2H 93
Trevor Pl. SW7 5H 77
Trevor Sq. SW7 6H 77
Trevor St. SW7 5H 77
Trevor Wlk. SW7 5J 77
(not continuous)
Trevose Ho. SE11 3B 90
Triangle, The E8 2H 63
EC1 1F 71
Triangle Est. *SE11* *4C 90*
(off Kennington Rd.)
Triangle Rd. E8 2G 63
Tricycle Cinema 1H 55
Tricycle Theatre 1H 55
Trident Pl. SW3 5F 87
Trig La. EC4 7G 71
Trigon Rd. SW8 7B 90
Trimdon NW1 3F 59
Trinity Chu. Rd.
SW13 6A 84
Trinity Chu. Sq. SE1 5H 81
Trinity Ct. N1 2A 62
SE1 6H 81
W2 5C 66
WC1 1B 70
Trinity Grn. E1 3J 73
Trinity Ho. SE1 6H 81
Trinity M. E1 3J 73
W10 5D 64
Trinity Pl. EC3 1C 82
Trinity Sq. EC3 1B 82
Trinity St. SE1 5H 81
(not continuous)
Trinity Twr. E1 1E 82
Trio Pl. SE1 5H 81
Triton Sq. NW1 1E 68
Trocadero Cen. 1G 79
Trocette Mans. SE1 6A 82
Trojan Ct. NW6 1F 55
Troon Cl. SE16 3H 93
Tropical Ct. W10 6D 54
Trothy Rd. SE1 1F 93
Trotwood Ho. SE16 5G 83
Troutbeck NW1 7D 58
Troy Ct. W8 6J 75
Trump St. EC2 6H 71
Trundle St. SE1 4G 81
Truro Ho. W2 4J 65
Trussley Rd. W6 7A 74
Tryon Cres. E9 2J 63
Tryon St. SW3 3J 87
Tudor Gro. E9 1J 63
Tudor Ho. E9 1J 63
W14 1D 84
Tudor Rd. E9 2H 63
Tudor St. EC4 7D 70
Tufton Ct. SW1 7J 79
Tufton St. SW1 6H 79
Tullis Ho. E9 1K 63
Tunbridge Ho. EC1 6E 60
Tunis Rd. W12 2A 74
Tunnel App. SE16 5J 83
Tunnel Rd. SE16 4J 83
Tupman Ho. SE16 5E 82
Turin St. E2 7E 62
Turk's Head Yd. EC1 3E 70
Turk's Row SW3 3K 87
Turnagain La. EC4 5E 70
Turnberry Cl. SE16 4H 93
Turnbull Ho. N1 3F 61
Turner Ct. SE16 5K 83
Turner Ho. NW8 4G 57
SW1 2H 89
Turner's All. EC3 7A 72
Turner St. E1 4G 73
Turneville Rd. W14 5G 85
Turnmill St. EC1 2E 70
Turnour Ho. E1 6G 73
Turnpike Ho. EC1 7F 61
Turnstone Ho. *E1* *1E 82*
(off Star Pl.)
Turpentine La. SW1 3D 88
Turpin Cl. E1 7K 73
Turquand St. SE17 2H 91
Turville Ho. NW8 1G 67
Turville St. E2 1D 72
Tuscan Ho. E2 6K 63
Tustin Est. SE15 7J 93
Tuttle Ho. SW1 4G 89
Tweezer's All. WC2 7C 70
Twine Ct. E1 7J 73
Twyford Pl. WC2 5A 70
Twyford St. N1 2A 60
Twynholm Mans.
SW6 7E 84
Tyburn Tree (site of) 7J 67
Tyburn Way W1 7K 67
Tyers Est. SE1 4A 82
Tyers Ga. SE1 5A 82
Tyers St. SE11 4A 90
Tyers Ter. SE11 4A 90
Tyler Cl. E2 4C 62
Tyler's Ct. W1 6G 69
Tylney Ho. E1 5H 73
Tyndale La. N1 1E 60
Tyndale Mans. N1 1E 60
Tyndale Ter. N1 1E 60
Tyne St. E1 5D 72
Tyrrell Ho. SW1 5F 89
Tysoe St. EC1 7D 60
Tyssen St. N1 4B 62
Tytherton E2 5J 63

U

Udall St. SW1 2F 89
Udimore Ho. W10 3A 64
Ufford St. SE1 4D 80
Ufton Gro. N1 1K 61
Ufton Rd. N1 1K 61
(not continuous)
Ullswater Ho. SE15 6J 93
Ulster Pl. NW1 2C 68
Ulster Ter. NW1 2C 68
Umberston St. E1 5G 73
Underhill Pas. NW1 2D 58
Underhill St. NW1 3D 58
Undershaft EC3 6A 72
Underwood Ho. W6 6A 74
Underwood Rd. E1 2E 72
Underwood Row N1 6H 61
Underwood St. N1 6H 61
Unicorn Theatre 3B 82
Union Canal Wlk.
W10 1A 64
Union Ct. EC2 5A 72
W9 3J 65
Union Sq. N1 3H 61
Union St. SE1 3E 80
Union Theatre 3F 81
Union Wlk. E2 6B 62
Union Wharf N1 3H 61
(Arlington Av.)
N1 5G 61
(Wenlock Rd.)
Union Yd. W1 6D 68
Unit Workshops E1 5E 72
Unity M. NW1 4G 59
Unity Wharf SE1 4D 82
University College London
Department of Geological
Sciences Collection
2G 69
University of London
Institute of
Latin American Studies
1H 69
School of Oriental &
African Studies 2H 69
Senate House 3H 69
University of Westminster
Marylebone Campus
3A 68
School of Languages
1E 68
University of Westminster and
Library
Holborn 4A 70
University of Westminster
(Cavendish Campus)
Bolsover St. 3D 68
Hanson St. 3E 68
University of Westminster
(Regent Campus)
Lit. Titchfield St. 4E 68
Regent St. 5D 68
Wells St. 4E 68
University St. WC1 2F 69
Unwin Cl. SE15 6E 92
Unwin Mans. W14 5G 85
Unwin Rd. SW7 6E 76
Upbrook M. W2 6D 66
Upcerne Rd. SW10 7C 86
Upnall Ho. SE15 6K 93
Upnor Way SE17 3B 92
Up. Addison Gdns.
W14 4E 74
Up. Belgrave St. SW1 6B 78
Up. Berenger Wlk.
SW10 *7E 86*
(off Berenger Wlk.)
Up. Berkeley St. W1 6J 67
Up. Blantyre Wlk.
SW10 *7E 86*
(off Blantyre Wlk.)
Up. Brook St. W1 1A 78
Up. Camelford Wlk.
W11 6E 64
Up. Cheyne Row
SW3 6G 87
Up. Clarendon Wlk.
W11 6E 64
Up. Dartrey Wlk.
SW10 *7D 86*
(off Whistler Wlk.)
Up. Dengie Wlk. *N1* *2G 61*
(off Baddow Wlk.)
Upper Feilde W1 7A 68
Up. Grosvenor St. W1 1A 78
Upper Ground SE1 2C 80
Up. Hawkwell Wlk.
N1 *2H 61*
(off Baddow Wlk.)
Up. James St. W1 7F 69
Up. John St. W1 7F 69
Upper Lodge W8 3B 76
Upper Marsh SE1 6B 80
Up. Montagu St. W1 3J 67

Up. Phillimore Gdns. W8 . . . 5J 75
Up. Rawreth Wlk. *N1* . . . *2H 61* *(off Basire St.)*
Up. St Martin's La. WC2 . . . 7J 69
Upper St. N1 . . . 1E 60
Up. Tachbrook St. SW1 . . . 1E 88
Up. Talbot Wlk. W11 . . . 6E 64
Up. Thames St. EC4 . . . 7F 71
Up. Whistler Wlk. *SW10* . . . *7D 86* *(off Worlds End Est.)*
Up. Wimpole St. W1 . . . 3B 68
Up. Woburn Pl. WC1 . . . 7H 59
Upwey Ho. N1 . . . 3A 62
Urlwin St. SE5 . . . 6G 91
Usborne M. SW8 . . . 7B 90
Usk St. E2 . . . 6K 63
Utopia Village NW1 . . . 2A 58
Uverdale Rd. SW10 . . . 7D 86
Uxbridge Rd. W12 . . . 3A 74
Uxbridge St. W8 . . . 2J 75

V

Vale, The SW3 . . . 5E 86
Vale Cl. W9 . . . 7C 56
Vale Ct. W9 . . . 7D 56
Valentine Pl. SE1 . . . 5E 80
Valentine Row SE1 . . . 5E 80
Vale Royal N7 . . . 1J 59
Vale Royal Ho. WC2 . . . 7H 69
Vallance Rd. E1 . . . 2F 73
E2 . . . 7F 63
Valois Ho. SE1 . . . 6C 82
Vanbrugh Ct. SE11 . . . 2D 90
Vanburgh Ho. E1 . . . 3C 72
Vancouver Ho. E1 . . . 3H 83
Vanderbilt Vs. W12 . . . 4C 74
Vandon Ct. SW1 . . . 6F 79
Vandon Pas. SW1 . . . 6F 79
Vandon St. SW1 . . . 6F 79
Vandy St. EC2 . . . 2A 72
Vane St. SW1 . . . 1F 89
Vange Ho. W10 . . . 3A 64
Vanston Pl. SW6 . . . 7J 85
Vantage Pl. W8 . . . 7K 75
Vantrey Ho. SE11 . . . 2C 90
Varcoe Rd. SE16 . . . 4H 93
Varden St. E1 . . . 5G 73
Varley Ho. NW6 . . . 3J 55
Varna Rd. SW6 . . . 7F 85
Varndell St. NW1 . . . 6E 58
Varnishers Yd. N1 . . . 5K 59
Vassall Rd. SW9 . . . 7E 90
Vat Ho. SW8 . . . 7K 89
Vauban Est. SE16 . . . 7D 82
Vauban St. SE16 . . . 7D 82
Vaudeville Theatre . . . 1K 79
Vaughan Est. E2 . . . 6C 62
Vaughan Ho. SE1 . . . 4E 80
Vaughan Way E1 . . . 1E 82
VAUXHALL . . . 4K 89
Vauxhall Bri. SW1 . . . 3J 89
Vauxhall Bri. Rd. SW1 . . . 7E 78
VAUXHALL CROSS . . . 4K 89
Vauxhall Distribution Pk. SW8 . . . 6G 89
Vauxhall Gro. SW8 . . . 5K 89
Vauxhall St. SE11 . . . 3B 90
Vauxhall Wlk. SE11 . . . 3A 90
Vawdrey Cl. E1 . . . 2J 73
Venables St. NW8 . . . 2F 67
Venice Ct. NW8 . . . 1F 67
SE5 . . . 7H 91
Venn Ho. N1 . . . 3B 60
Venture Ho. *W10* . . . *6D 64* *(off Bridge Cl.)*
Verdi Ho. W10 . . . 5F 55
Vere Ct. W2 . . . 5A 66
Vereker Rd. W14 . . . 4F 85
Vere St. W1 . . . 6C 68
Verity Cl. W11 . . . 6E 64
Verney Ho. NW8 . . . 1G 67
Verney Rd. SE16 . . . 5F 93
Verney Way SE16 . . . 4G 93
Vernon Ho. SE11 . . . 4B 90
WC1 . . . 4K 69
Vernon Mans. W14 . . . 5G 85
Vernon M. W14 . . . 2F 85
Vernon Pl. WC1 . . . 4K 69
Vernon Ri. WC1 . . . 6B 60
Vernon Sq. WC1 . . . 6B 60
Vernon St. W14 . . . 2E 84
Vernon Yd. W11 . . . 7G 65
Verona Ct. SE14 . . . 5K 93
Verulam Bldgs. WC1 . . . 3B 70
Verulam Ho. W6 . . . 5A 74
Verulam St. WC1 . . . 3C 70
Verwood Ho. SW8 . . . 7B 90
Vesage Ct. EC1 . . . 4D 70
Vesta Ct. SE1 . . . 5A 82
Vestry Ct. SW1 . . . 7H 79
Vestry St. N1 . . . 6J 61
Viaduct Bldgs. EC1 . . . 4D 70
Viaduct Pl. E2 . . . 7G 63
Viaduct St. E2 . . . 7G 63
Vibart Wlk. N1 . . . 2K 59
Vicarage Ct. W8 . . . 4A 76
Vicarage Gdns. W8 . . . 3K 75
Vicarage Ga. W8 . . . 3A 76 (not continuous)
Vicar's Cl. E9 . . . 3J 63
Viceroy Ct. NW8 . . . 4H 57
Vickery Ct. EC1 . . . 1H 71
Victor Cazalet Ho. *N1* . . . *2E 60* *(off Gaskin St.)*
Victoria & Albert Mus. . . . 7F 77
Victoria Arc. SW1 . . . 7D 78
Victoria Av. EC2 . . . 4B 72
Victoria Bldgs. E8 . . . 3H 63
Victoria Chambers EC2 . . . 1A 72
Victoria Colonnade WC1 . . . 4K 69
Victoria Cotts. E1 . . . 3E 72
Victoria Ct. SE1 . . . 2B 92
Victoria Emb. EC4 . . . 5K 79
SW1 . . . 5K 79
WC2 . . . 5K 79
Victoria Gdns. W11 . . . 2J 75
Victoria Gro. W8 . . . 6C 76
Victoria Gro. M. W2 . . . 1K 75
Victoria Ho. SW1 . . . 3C 88 (Ebury Bri. Rd.)
SW1 . . . 1F 89 (Francis St.)
SW8 . . . 7K 89
Victoria Mans. SW8 . . . 7K 89
W14 . . . 5G 85
Victoria M. NW6 . . . 2J 55
Victoria Palace Theatre . . . 7E 78
Victoria Pk. Ct. E9 . . . 1K 63
Victoria Pk. Rd. E9 . . . 3H 63
Victoria Pk. Sq. E2 . . . 6J 63
Victoria Pas. NW8 . . . 1E 66
Victoria Pl. Shop. Cen. SW1 . . . 1D 88
Victoria Ri. NW6 . . . 1D 56
Victoria Rd. NW6 . . . 4G 55
W8 . . . 5C 76
Victoria Sq. SW1 . . . 6D 78
Victoria St. SW1 . . . 7D 78
Victoria Yd. E1 . . . 6F 73
Victor Wharf *SE1* . . . *2J 81* *(off Clink St.)*
Victory Ct. W9 . . . 2J 65
Victory Pl. SE17 . . . 1H 91
Vigo St. W1 . . . 1E 78
Viking Ct. SW6 . . . 6K 85
Villa St. SE17 . . . 4K 91
Villiers St. WC2 . . . 1J 79
Vince Ct. N1 . . . 7K 61
Vincent Ct. W1 . . . 5J 67
Vincent Ho. SW1 . . . 1H 89 (Regency St.)
SW1 . . . 2G 89 (Vincent Sq.)
Vincent Sq. SW1 . . . 1G 89
Vincent Sq. Mans. *SW1* . . . *1F 89* *(off Walcott St.)*
Vincent St. SW1 . . . 1G 89
Vincent Ter. N1 . . . 4E 60
Vince St. EC1 . . . 7K 61
Vine Cotts. E1 . . . 5J 73
Vine Ct. E1 . . . 4F 73
Vinegar St. E1 . . . 2G 83
Vinegar Yd. SE1 . . . 4A 82
Vine Hill EC1 . . . 2C 70
Vine La. SE1 . . . 3B 82
Vine Sq. W14 . . . 4H 85
Vine St. EC3 . . . 6C 72
W1 . . . 1F 79
Vine St. Bri. EC1 . . . 2D 70
Vine Yd. SE1 . . . 4H 81
Vineyard M. EC1 . . . 1C 70
Vineyard Wlk. EC1 . . . 1C 70
Vinopolis . . . 2H 81
Vinson Ho. N1 . . . 5K 61
Vintners Ct. EC4 . . . 7H 71
Vintner's Pl. EC4 . . . 7H 71
Violet Hill NW8 . . . 5C 56
Violet Hill Ho. NW8 . . . 5C 56 (not continuous)
Violet St. E2 . . . 1H 73
Virgil Pl. W1 . . . 4J 67
Virgil St. SE1 . . . 6B 80
Virginia Ct. WC1 . . . 1H 69
Virginia Rd. E2 . . . 7C 62
Virginia St. E1 . . . 1F 83
Visage NW3 . . . 1F 57
Viscount Ct. W2 . . . 6K 65
Viscount St. EC1 . . . 2G 71
Vittoria Ho. N1 . . . 3B 60
Vixen M. E8 . . . 1C 62
Vogans Mill SE1 . . . 4D 82
Vogler Ho. E1 . . . 7J 73
Vollasky Ho. E1 . . . 3E 72
Voss St. E2 . . . 7F 63
Voyager Bus. Est. SE16 . . . 6E 82
Vue Cinema
Fulham Broadway . . . 7K 85
Islington . . . 4D 60
Leicester Square . . . 7H 69
Shepherds Bush . . . 4C 74
Vyner St. E2 . . . 3H 63

W

W12 W12 . . . 4C 74
Wadding St. SE17 . . . 2J 91
Wade Ho. SE1 . . . 5E 82
Wadeson St. E2 . . . 4H 63
Wadham Gdns. NW3 . . . 2G 57
Wagner St. SE15 . . . 7J 93
Wainwright Ho. E1 . . . 2J 83
Waite St. SE15 . . . 5C 92
Waithman St. EC4 . . . 6E 70
Wakefield M. WC1 . . . 7K 59
Wakefield St. WC1 . . . 7K 59
Wakelin Ho. N1 . . . 1E 60
Wakeman Ho. NW10 . . . 6C 54
Wakeman Rd. NW10 . . . 7B 54
Wakley St. EC1 . . . 6E 60
Walberswick St. SW8 . . . 7K 89
Walbrook EC4 . . . 7J 71 (not continuous)
Walbrook Ct. N1 . . . 4A 62
Walbrook Wharf EC4 . . . 1H 81
Walburgh St. E1 . . . 6G 73
Walcorde Av. SE17 . . . 2H 91
Walcot Gdns. SE11 . . . 1C 90
Walcot Sq. SE11 . . . 1D 90
Walcott St. SW1 . . . 1F 89
Walden Ho. SW1 . . . 2B 88
Walden St. E1 . . . 5G 73 (not continuous)
Waldron M. SW3 . . . 5F 87
Waleran Flats SE1 . . . 1A 92
Wales Cl. SE15 . . . 7H 93
Walford Ho. E1 . . . 6G 73
Walham Grn. Ct. SW6 . . . 7A 86
Walham Gro. SW6 . . . 7J 85
Walham Yd. SW6 . . . 7J 85
Walker Ho. NW1 . . . 5G 59
Walker's Ct. W1 . . . 7G 69
Walkinshaw Ct. N1 . . . 1H 61
Wallace Collection . . . 5A 68
Wallace Ct. NW1 . . . 4H 67
Wallgrave Rd. SW5 . . . 1A 86
Wallingford Av. W10 . . . 4C 64
Wallis All. SE1 . . . 4H 81
Wallside EC2 . . . 4H 71
Walmer Ho. W10 . . . 6D 64
Walmer Pl. W1 . . . 3J 67
Walmer Rd. W10 . . . 6B 64
W11 . . . 7E 64
Walmer St. W1 . . . 3J 67
Walnut Ct. *W8* . . . *7A 76* *(off St Mary's Ga.)*
Walnut Tree Ho. SW10 . . . 5B 86
Walnut Tree Wlk. SE11 . . . 1C 90
Walpole Ct. W14 . . . 7D 74
Walpole Ho. SE1 . . . 5C 80
Walpole M. NW8 . . . 3E 56
Walpole St. SW3 . . . 3J 87
Walsham Ho. SE17 . . . 3J 91
Walsingham NW8 . . . 2F 57
Walsingham Mans. SW6 . . . 7B 86
Walston Ho. SW1 . . . 3G 89
Walter Ho. *SW10* . . . *7E 86* *(off Riley St.)*
Walter Langley Ct. *SE16* . . . *4K 83* *(off Brunel Rd.)*
Walters Cl. SE17 . . . 2H 91
Walters Ho. SE17 . . . 6E 90
Walter St. E2 . . . 7K 63
Walterton Rd. W9 . . . 2H 65
Waltham Ho. NW8 . . . 2C 56
Walton Cl. SW8 . . . 7K 89
Walton Ho. E2 . . . 1C 72
SW3 . . . 7J 77
Walton Pl. SW3 . . . 6J 77
Walton St. SW3 . . . 1H 87
Walton Vs. N1 . . . 1B 62
WALWORTH . . . 3H 91
Walworth Pl. SE17 . . . 4H 91
Walworth Rd. SE17 . . . 1G 91
Wandle Ho. NW8 . . . 3G 67
Wandon Rd. SW6 . . . 7B 86 (not continuous)
Wandsdown Pl. SW6 . . . 7A 86
Wandsworth Rd. SW8 . . . 7J 89
Wansey St. SE17 . . . 2G 91
WAPPING . . . 2H 83
Wapping Dock St. E1 . . . 3H 83
Wapping High St. E1 . . . 3E 82
Wapping La. E1 . . . 1H 83
Wapping Wall E1 . . . 2J 83
Warbeck Rd. W12 . . . 3A 74
Warburton Ho. E8 . . . 2G 63
Warburton Rd. E8 . . . 2H 63
Warburton St. E8 . . . 2G 63
Wardalls Gro. SE14 . . . 7K 93
Wardens Gro. SE1 . . . 3G 81
Wardour M. W1 . . . 6F 69
Wardour St. W1 . . . 5F 69
Ward Point SE11 . . . 2C 90
Wardrobe Pl. EC4 . . . 6F 71
Wardrobe Ter. EC4 . . . 7F 71
Wareham Ct. N1 . . . 1B 62
Wareham Ho. SW8 . . . 7A 90
Warfield Rd. NW10 . . . 7C 54
Warfield Yd. NW10 . . . 7C 54
Wargrave Ho. E2 . . . 7C 62
Warham St. SE5 . . . 7F 91
Warley St. E2 . . . 6K 63
Warlock Rd. W9 . . . 1H 65
Warmsworth NW1 . . . 2E 58
Warndon St. SE16 . . . 2K 93
Warneford St. E9 . . . 2H 63
Warner Ho. NW8 . . . 6C 56
Warner Pl. E2 . . . 5F 63
Warner St. EC1 . . . 2C 70
Warner Yd. EC1 . . . 2C 70
Warnford Ct. EC2 . . . 5K 71
Warnham WC1 . . . 7A 60
Warren Ct. NW1 . . . 1E 68
Warren Ho. W14 . . . 1H 85
Warren M. W1 . . . 2E 68
Warren St. W1 . . . 2E 68
Warrington Cres. W9 . . . 2C 66
Warrington Gdns. W9 . . . 2C 66
Warwick W14 . . . 2H 85
Warwick Av. W2 . . . 3C 66
W9 . . . 2B 66
Warwick Bldg. SW8 . . . 6C 88
Warwick Chambers W8 . . . 6J 75
Warwick Cl. W8 . . . 7H 75
Warwick Ct. EC4 . . . 6F 71
WC1 . . . 4B 70
Warwick Cres. W2 . . . 3C 66
Warwick Est. W2 . . . 4B 66
Warwick Gdns. W14 . . . 7H 75
Warwick Ho. St. SW1 . . . 2H 79
Warwick La. EC4 . . . 5F 71
Warwick Mans SW5 . . . 1J 85
Warwick Pas. EC4 . . . 6F 71
Warwick Pl. W9 . . . 3C 66
Warwick Pl. Nth. SW1 . . . 2E 88
Warwick Rd. W14 . . . 7G 75
Warwick Row SW1 . . . 6D 78
Warwick Sq. EC4 . . . 5F 71
SW1 . . . 3E 88 (not continuous)
Warwick Sq. M. SW1 . . . 2E 88
Warwick St. W1 . . . 7F 69
Warwick Way SW1 . . . 3C 88
Warwick Yd. EC1 . . . 2H 71
Washington Ho. SW3 . . . 5J 77
Watercress Pl. N1 . . . 1B 62
Waterden Ct. W11 . . . 3E 74
Waterford Ho. W11 . . . 7G 65
Waterford Rd. SW6 . . . 7A 86 (not continuous)
Water Gdns., The W2 . . . 5H 67
Watergate EC4 . . . 7E 70
Watergate Wlk. WC2 . . . 2K 79
Waterhead NW1 . . . 6E 58
Waterhouse Cl. W6 . . . 3D 84
Waterhouse Sq. EC1 . . . 4C 70
Water La. EC3 . . . 1B 82
NW1 . . . 1D 58
SE14 . . . 7K 93
Waterloo Bri. SE1 . . . 1A 80
Waterloo Gdns. E2 . . . 4J 63
N1 . . . 1E 60
Waterloo Pas. NW6 . . . 1H 55
Waterloo Pl. SW1 . . . 2G 79
Waterloo Rd. SE1 . . . 2B 80
Waterloo Ter. N1 . . . 1E 60
Waterman's Wlk. EC4 . . . 1J 81
Waterman Way E1 . . . 2G 83
Waterside N1 . . . 5G 61
W2 . . . 4E 66
Waterside Cl. SE16 . . . 5F 83
Waterside Pl. NW1 . . . 2B 58
Waterside Point SW11 . . . 7H 87
Waterson St. E2 . . . 6B 62
Water St. WC2 . . . 7C 70
Water Twr. Pl. N1 . . . 3E 60
Watling Ct. EC4 . . . 6H 71
Watling St. EC4 . . . 6G 71
SE15 . . . 6B 92
Watney Mkt. E1 . . . 6H 73
Watney St. E1 . . . 6H 73
Watson's M. W1 . . . 4H 67
Watts Ho. W10 . . . 3E 64
Watts St. E1 . . . 2H 83
Wavel Ct. E1 . . . 2J 83
Wavel M. NW6 . . . 1A 56
Waveney Cl. E1 . . . 2F 83
Waverley Ct. NW6 . . . 1E 54
Waverley Pl. NW8 . . . 4E 56
Waverton St. W1 . . . 2B 78
Waylett Ho. SE11 . . . 4C 90
Waynflete Ho. SE1 . . . 3G 81
Waynflete Sq. W10 . . . 6C 64
Weald Cl. SE16 . . . 3G 93
Wear Pl. E2 . . . 7G 63 (not continuous)
Weatherbury W2 . . . 5J 65
Weavers La. SE1 . . . 3B 82
Weavers Ter. SW6 . . . 6K 85
Weaver St. E1 . . . 2E 72
Weavers Way NW1 . . . 2G 59
Webb Cl. W10 . . . 2B 64
Webber Row SE1 . . . 6D 80
Webber St. SE1 . . . 4D 80
Webb Ho. SW8 . . . 7H 89
Webb St. SE1 . . . 7A 82
Webster Rd. SE16 . . . 7F 83
Wedderburn Ho. SW1 . . . 3A 88
Wedgewood Ho. SW1 . . . 4D 88
Wedgewood M. W1 . . . 6H 69
Wedgwood Ho. E2 . . . 7K 63
SE11 . . . 7C 80
Wedlake St. W10 . . . 1F 65
Weighhouse St. W1 . . . 7B 68
Weir's Pas. NW1 . . . 6H 59
Welbeck Ct. W14 . . . 1G 85
Welbeck Ho. W1 . . . 5C 68
Welbeck St. W1 . . . 4B 68
Welbeck Way W1 . . . 5C 68
Welford Ct. NW1 . . . 1D 58
W9 . . . 3J 65
Welland M. E1 . . . 2F 83
Wellclose Sq. E1 . . . 7F 73 (not continuous)
Wellclose St. E1 . . . 1F 83
Wellcome Collection . . . 1G 69
Wellcome Mus., The . . . *5B 70* *(within The Royal College of Surgeons)*
Well Ct. EC4 . . . 6H 71 (not continuous)
Weller Ct. W11 . . . 2G 75
Weller Ho. SE16 . . . 5E 82
Weller St. SE1 . . . 4G 81
Wellesley Ct. W9 . . . 6C 56
Wellesley Ho. NW1 . . . 7G 59
SW1 . . . 3C 88
Wellesley Mans. W14 . . . 3G 85
Wellesley Pl. NW1 . . . 7G 59
Wellesley St. E1 . . . 4K 73
Wellesley Ter. N1 . . . 6H 61
Welling Sq. N1 . . . 2A 60
Wellington Arch . . . 4B 78
Wellington Bldgs. SW1 . . . 4B 88
Wellington Cl. W11 . . . 6J 65
Wellington Ct. NW8 . . . 4E 56
SW1 . . . 5J 77
Wellington Ho. SE17 . . . 5H 91
Wellington Mans. W14 . . . 5G 85
Wellington Monument . . . 4B 78
Wellington Mus. . . . 4B 78
Wellington Pl. NW8 . . . 6F 57
Wellington Rd. NW8 . . . 4F 57
NW10 . . . 7D 54
Wellington Row E2 . . . 6D 62
Wellington Sq. SW3 . . . 3J 87
Wellington St. WC2 . . . 7K 69
Wellington Ter. E1 . . . 2G 83
W2 . . . 1A 76
Wells Ct. NW6 . . . 4K 55
Wells Ho. EC1 . . . 6D 60
SE16 . . . 6K 83
W10 . . . 2E 64
Wells M. W1 . . . 4F 69
Wells Ri. NW8 . . . 3J 57
Wells Rd. W12 . . . 5A 74
Wells Sq. WC1 . . . 7A 60
Wells St. W1 . . . 4E 68
Well St. E9 . . . 1K 63
Wells Way SE5 . . . 6A 92
SW7 . . . 6E 76
Welsford St. SE1 . . . 3E 92 (not continuous)
Welsh Ho. E1 . . . 2H 83
Welshpool Ho. E8 . . . 2F 63
Welshpool St. E8 . . . 2F 63 (not continuous)
Welstead Ho. E1 . . . 6G 73
Welton Ho. E1 . . . 4K 73
Welwyn St. E2 . . . 6K 63
Wendle Ct. SW8 . . . 6J 89
Wendover SE17 . . . 3A 92 (not continuous)
Wendover Ct. W1 . . . 4A 68
Wendover Ho. W1 . . . 4A 68
Wenham Ho. SW8 . . . 7E 88
Wenlake Ho. EC1 . . . 1G 71
Wenlock Barn Est. N1 . . . 5J 61
Wenlock Ct. N1 . . . 5K 61
Wenlock Rd. N1 . . . 5G 61
Wenlock St. N1 . . . 5H 61
Wentworth Ct. W6 . . . 6E 84
Wentworth Dwellings E1 . . . 5C 72
Wentworth St. E1 . . . 5C 72
Werrington St. NW1 . . . 5F 59
Wesley Cl. SE17 . . . 2F 91
Wesley Ct. SE16 . . . 7G 83
Wesley's House, Chapel & Mus. of Methodism . . . 2K 71
Wesley Sq. W11 . . . 6E 64
Wesley St. W1 . . . 4B 68
Wessex Ho. SE1 . . . 3D 92
Wessex St. E2 . . . 7K 63
Wesson Mead SE5 . . . 7H 91
W. Arbour St. E1 . . . 5K 73
West Block SE1 . . . 5A 80
Westbourne Bri. W2 . . . 4C 66
Westbourne Ct. W2 . . . 5C 66
Westbourne Cres. W2 . . . 7E 66
Westbourne Cres. M. W2 . . . 7E 66
Westbourne Gdns. W2 . . . 5A 66
WESTBOURNE GREEN . . . 5H 65
Westbourne Gro. W11 . . . 7G 65
Westbourne Gro. M. W11 . . . 6J 65
Westbourne Gro. Ter. W2 . . . 5A 66
Westbourne Ho. SW1 . . . 3C 88
Westbourne Pk. Pas. W2 . . . 3K 65 (not continuous)
Westbourne Pk. Rd. W2 . . . 4K 65
W11 . . . 6F 65
Westbourne Pk. Vs. W2 . . . 4K 65
Westbourne St. W2 . . . 7E 66
Westbourne Ter. W2 . . . 5C 66
Westbourne Ter. M. W2 . . . 5C 66
Westbourne Ter. Rd. W2 . . . 4C 66
Westbourne Ter. Rd. Bri. W2 . . . 3C 66
WEST BROMPTON . . . 4A 86
Westbrook Ho. E2 . . . 6J 63
Westbury Ho. W11 . . . 4J 65
W. Carriage Dr. W2 . . . 1G 77 (not continuous)
W. Central St. WC1 . . . 5J 69
West Cen. Av. NW10 . . . 7A 54
Westcliffe Apartments W2 . . . 4F 67
Westcott Rd. SE17 . . . 5E 90
W. Cromwell Rd. W14 . . . 3G 85
W. Cross Route W10 . . . 7C 64
W. Eaton Pl. SW1 . . . 1A 88
W. Eaton Pl. M. SW1 . . . 1A 88
West End Ct. NW6 . . . 1A 56
West End La. NW6 . . . 1K 55 (not continuous)
West End Quay W2 . . . 4F 67
Westerham NW1 . . . 3E 58
Westerham Ho. SE1 . . . 6K 81
Western Ct. NW6 . . . 5H 55
Western M. W9 . . . 2H 65
Western Pl. SE16 . . . 4K 83
Westfield Cl. SW10 . . . 7C 86
Westfield Ct. NW10 . . . 6D 54
Westfield Ho. *SW10* . . . *7E 86* *(off Cremorne Est.)*
West Gdn. Pl. W2 . . . 6H 67
West Gdns. E1 . . . 1H 83
Westgate Cen., The E8 . . . 2G 63
Westgate M. W10 . . . 1E 64
Westgate St. E8 . . . 2G 63
Westgate Ter. SW10 . . . 4B 86
W. Halkin St. SW1 . . . 6A 78
W. Harding St. EC4 . . . 5D 70
Westhill Ct. W11 . . . 7H 65
Westhope Ho. E2 . . . 1F 73
W. Kensington Ct. W14 . . . 3G 85
W. Kensington Mans. W14 . . . 4G 85
WEST KILBURN . . . 7G 55
Westlake SE16 . . . 2K 93
Westland Pl. N1 . . . 6J 61
West La. SE16 . . . 5G 83
W. London Crematorium NW10 . . . 1A 64
Westmacott Ho. NW8 . . . 2F 67
West Mall W8 . . . 2K 75
West M. SW1 . . . 2E 88
WESTMINSTER . . . 5J 79
Westminster Abbey . . . 6J 79
Westminster Abbey Chapter House . . . 6H 79
Westminster Abbey Mus. . . . 6J 79
Westminster Abbey Pyx Chamber . . . 6H 79
Westminster Bri. SW1 . . . 5K 79
Westminster Bri. Rd. SE1 . . . 5A 80
Westminster Bus. Sq. SE11 . . . 5A 90
Westminster Children's Sports Cen., The . . . 3E 66
Westminster Ct. NW8 . . . 2E 66
Westminster Gdns. SW1 . . . 1J 89
Westminster Hall . . . 5J 79

Westminster Mans. SW1 7H 79
Westminster Pal. Gdns. SW1 7G 79
Westminster RC Cathedral 7E 78
Westmoreland Pl. SW1 4D 88
Westmoreland Rd. SE17 5H 91 (not continuous)
Westmoreland St. W1 4B 68
Westmoreland Ter. SW1 3D 88
Westmoreland Wlk. SE17 5J 91 (not continuous)
Westonbirt Ct. SE15 6C 92
W. One Ho. W1 4E 68
W. One Shop. Cen. W1 6B 68
Weston Ho. E9 2J 63
NW6 1F 55
Weston Ri. WC1 5B 60
Weston St. SE1 3K 81 (not continuous)
Weston Wlk. E8 1H 63
West Point SE1 3E 92
W. Poultry Av. EC1 4E 70
West Ri. W2 7H 67
West Rd. SE1 4B 80
SW3 4K 87
West Row W10 1E 64
Westside Ct. W9 1K 65
West Smithfield EC1 4E 70
West Sq. SE11 7E 80
West St. E2 5H 63
WC2 6H 69
W. Tenter St. E1 6D 72
Westview Cl. W10 5B 64
W. Warwick Pl. SW1 2E 88
Westway W2 3J 65
W9 3J 65
W10 5F 65
W12 6A 64
Westway Lodge W9 3K 65
Westway Sports Cen. 6C 64
Westwick Gdns. W14 5C 74
Westwood Ho. W12 3B 74
Wetherby Gdns. SW5 2C 86
Wetherby Mans. SW5 3A 86
Wetherby M. SW5 3A 86
Wetherby Pl. SW7 2C 86
Wevco Wharf SE15 5G 93
Wexford Ho. E1 4J 73
Weybridge Ct. SE16 4G 93
Weyhill Rd. E1 5F 73
Wey Ho. NW8 2F 67
Weymouth Ct. E2 4D 62
Weymouth Ho. SW8 7A 90
Weymouth M. W1 3C 68
Weymouth St. W1 4B 68
Weymouth Ter. E2 4D 62
Whalebone Ct. EC2 5J 71
Wharf, The EC3 2B 82
Wharfdale Rd. N1 4K 59
Wharfedale Ho. NW6 2A 56
Wharfedale St. SW10 4A 86
Wharfedale Yard N1 4K 59
Wharf Pl. E2 3F 63
Wharf Rd. N1 5G 61 (Baldwin Ter.)
N1 3H 59 (Camley St.)
Wharton Cotts. WC1 7C 60
Wharton Ho. SE1 6C 82
Wharton St. WC1 7B 60
Wheatfield Ho. W9 7K 55
Wheatley St. W1 4B 68
Wheatsheaf La. SW6 7B 84
SW8 7J 89
Wheatstone Ho. W10 3E 64
Wheatstone Rd. W10 3F 65
Wheeler Gdns. N1 2K 59
Wheler Ho. E1 2C 72
Wheler St. E1 2C 72
Whetstone Pk. WC2 5A 70
Whidborne Bldgs. WC1 7K 59
Whidborne St. WC1 7K 59 (not continuous)
Whiskin St. EC1 7E 60
Whistler Twr. SW10 7E 86
Whistler Wlk. SW10 7D 86
Whiston Ho. N1 1F 61
Whiston Rd. E2 4C 62
Whitacre M. SE11 4D 90
Whitby Ho. NW8 3C 56
Whitby St. E1 1C 72 (not continuous)
Whitchurch Ho. W10 6D 64
Whitchurch Rd. W11 7D 64
Whitcomb Ct. WC2 1H 79
Whitcomb St. WC2 1H 79
Whitebeam Cl. SW9 7B 90
White Bear Yd. EC1 2C 70
WHITECHAPEL 4E 72
Whitechapel Art Gallery 4D 72
Whitechapel High St. E1 5D 72
Whitechapel Rd. E1 5E 72
Whitechapel Sports Cen. 3G 73
White Church La. E1 5E 72
White Church Pas. E1 5E 72
WHITE CITY 6A 64
White City Cl. W12 1A 74
White City Rd. W12 7A 64
White Conduit St. N1 4D 60
Whitecross Pl. EC2 3K 71
Whitecross St. EC1 1H 71
Whitefriars St. EC4 6D 70
Whitehall SW1 2J 79
Whitehall Ct. SW1 3J 79 (not continuous)
Whitehall Gdns. SW1 3J 79
Whitehall Pl. SW1 3J 79
White Hart Ct. EC2 4A 72
White Hart St. EC4 5F 71
SE11 3D 90
White Hart Yd. SE1 3J 81
Whitehaven St. NW8 2G 67
Whiteheads Gro. SW3 3H 87
White Heather Ho. *WC1 7K 59*
(off Cromer St.)
White Horse All. EC1 3E 70
Whitehorse M. SE1 6D 80
White Horse St. W1 3D 78
White Horse Yd. EC2 5J 71
White Ho., The NW1 1D 68
White Kennett St. E1 5B 72
Whitelands Ho. SW3 3J 87
Whiteleys Cen. (Shop. Cen.) W2 6B 66
White Lion Ct. EC3 6A 72
SE15 6K 93
White Lion Hill EC4 7F 71
White Lion St. N1 5C 60
White Lyon Ct. EC2 3G 71
White Post St. SE15 7K 93
White's Grounds SE1 5B 82
White's Grounds Est. SE1 4B 82
White's Row E1 4C 72
Whitethorn Ho. E1 2J 83
White Tower *1C 82*
(in The Tower of London)
Whitfield Ho. NW8 2G 67
Whitfield Pl. W1 2E 68
Whitfield St. W1 2E 68
Whitgift Ho. SE11 1A 90
Whitgift St. SE11 1A 90
Whitley Ho. SW1 5F 89
Whitman Ho. E2 7J 63
Whitmore Est. N1 3B 62
Whitmore Gdns. NW10 4A 54
Whitmore Ho. N1 3B 62
Whitmore Rd. N1 3A 62
Whitstable Ho. W10 6D 64
Whittaker St. SW1 2A 88
Whittaker Way SE1 2F 93
Whittington Av. EC3 6A 72
Whittlesey St. SE1 3D 80
Whitton NW3 1J 57
Whitworth Ho. SE1 7H 81
Wicker St. E1 6G 73
Wickfield Ho. SE16 5F 83
Wickford Ho. E1 1J 73
Wickford St. E1 1J 73
Wickham Cl. E1 4K 73
Wickham Ho. *N1 3A 62*
(off New Era Est.)
Wickham St. SE11 3A 90
Wicklow St. WC1 6A 60
Wicksteed Ho. SE1 7H 81
Wickway Ct. SE15 6C 92
Widegate St. E1 4B 72
Widford Ho. N1 5E 60
Widley Rd. W9 7K 55
Wigmore Hall 5C 68
Wigmore Pl. W1 5C 68
Wigmore St. W1 6A 68
Wigton Pl. SE11 4D 90
Wilbraham Ho. SW8 7J 89
Wilbraham Mans. *SW1 1A 88*
(off Wilbraham Pl.)
Wilbraham Pl. SW1 1K 87
Wilby M. W11 2H 75
Wilcox Cl. SW8 7K 89 (not continuous)
Wilcox Pl. SW1 7F 79
Wilcox Rd. SW8 7J 89
Wild Ct. WC2 6A 70 (not continuous)
Wilde Cl. E8 2E 62
Wilde Ho. *W2 7E 66*
(off Gloucester Ter.)
Wild's Rents SE1 6A 82
Wild St. WC2 6K 69
Wilfred St. SW1 6E 78
Wilkes St. E1 3D 72
Wilkie Ho. SW1 3H 89
Wilkins Ho. SW1 5D 88
Wilkinson Ho. N1 5K 61
Wilkinson St. SW8 7A 90
Wilks Pl. N1 5B 62
Willesden La. NW6 1E 54
Willesden Sports Stadium 2A 54
William IV St. WC2 1J 79
William Caslon Ho. E2 5H 63
William Channing Ho. E2 6G 63
William Cobbett Ho. W8 6A 76
William Dromey Ct. NW6 1G 55
William Dunbar Ho. NW6 5H 55
William Ellis Way SE16 7F 83
William Fenn Ho. E2 5E 62
William Gibbs Ct. SW1 7G 79
William Henry Wlk. SW8 6G 89
William Hunt Mans. SW13 6A 84
William M. SW1 5K 77
William Morris Ho. W6 5D 84
William Rathbone Ho. E2 6G 63
William Rd. NW1 7E 58
William Rushbrooke Ho. SE16 1E 92
William Saville Ho. NW6 5H 55
William's Bldgs. E2 1J 73
Williams Cl. SW6 7F 85
Williams Ho. E9 2H 63
SW1 2H 89
Williamson Ct. SE17 4G 91
William St. SW1 5K 77
Willoughby Highwalk EC2 4J 71
Willoughby Ho. E1 3G 83
EC2 4J 71
Willoughby St. WC1 4J 69
Willowbrook Est. SE15 7E 92
Willow Brook Rd. SE15 6D 92
Willow Ct. EC2 1A 72
NW6 1E 54
W9 3K 65
Willow Ho. W10 1D 64
Willow Pl. SW1 1F 89
Willow St. EC2 1A 72
Willow Wlk. SE1 1B 92
Willow Way W11 1D 74
Willsbridge Ct. SE15 6C 92
Wilman Gro. E8 1F 63
Wilmcote Ho. W2 3A 66
Wilmer Gdns. N1 3A 62 (not continuous)
Wilmington Sq. WC1 7C 60 (not continuous)
Wilmington St. WC1 7C 60
Wilmot Pl. NW1 1E 58
Wilmot St. E2 1G 73
Wilsham St. W11 2D 74
Wilson Gro. SE16 5G 83
Wilson's Rd. W6 3D 84
Wilson St. EC2 4K 71
Wilton Ct. E1 5H 73
Wilton Cres. SW1 5A 78
Wilton M. SW1 6B 78
Wilton Pl. SW1 5A 78
Wilton Rd. SW1 7D 78
Wilton Row SW1 5A 78
Wilton Sq. N1 2J 61
Wilton St. SW1 6C 78
Wilton Ter. SW1 6A 78
Wilton Vs. N1 3J 61
Wiltshire Cl. SW3 2J 87
Wiltshire Row N1 3J 61
Wimbolt St. E2 6E 62
Wimborne Ho. NW1 2H 67
SW8 7B 90
Wimbourne Ct. N1 4J 61
Wimbourne St. N1 4J 61
Wimpole M. W1 3C 68
Wimpole St. W1 3C 68
Winchelsea Ho. SE16 4K 83
Winchester Av. NW6 2F 55
Winchester Cl. SE17 2F 91
Winchester Ct. W8 4K 75
Winchester Ho. SW3 6F 87
SW9 7D 90
W2 6C 66
Winchester Rd. NW3 1F 57
Winchester Sq. SE1 2J 81
Winchester St. SW1 3D 88
Winchester Wlk. SE1 2J 81
Winchester Wharf SE1 2J 81
Winch Ho. SW10 7D 86
Winchilsea Ho. NW8 7E 56
Winckworth Ct. N1 7K 61
Wincott St. SE11 1D 90
Windermere NW1 7D 58
Windermere Av. NW6 3F 55
Windermere Point SE15 7J 93
Winding, The W2 4F 67
Windmill WC1 3A 70
Windmill Cl. SE1 1F 93
Windmill Row SE11 4C 90
Windmill St. W1 4G 69 (not continuous)
Windmill Wlk. SE1 3D 80
Windrose Cl. SE16 4K 83
Windrush Ho. NW8 2F 67
Windsor Cen., The N1 2F 61
Windsor Ct. SW3 3H 87
W2 7A 66
W10 6C 64
(off Bramley Rd.)
Windsor Gdns. W9 2J 65
Windsor Ho. E2 6K 63
N1 4H 61
NW1 6D 58
Windsor Pl. SW1 1F 89
Windsor St. N1 2F 61
Windsor Ter. N1 6H 61
Windsor Way W14 1D 84
Windspoint Dr. SE15 6G 93
Wine Cl. E1 1J 83 (not continuous)
Wine Office Ct. EC4 5D 70
Wingfield Ho. E2 7C 62
NW6 4A 56
Wingrad Ho. E1 4J 73
Wingrave SE17 1J 91 (not continuous)
Wingrave Rd. W6 6B 84
Wingreen NW8 2B 56
Winicotte Ho. W2 3F 67
Winkley St. E2 5G 63
Winkworth Cotts. E1 1K 73
Winnett St. W1 7G 69
Winnington Ho. SE5 7G 91
W10 2E 64
Winsham Ho. NW1 6H 59
Winsland M. W2 5E 66
Winsland St. W2 5E 66
Winsley St. W1 5E 68
Winslow SE17 4A 92
Winslow Rd. W6 5B 84
Winston Ho. WC1 1H 69
Winterbourne Ho. W11 1E 74
Winterleys NW6 5H 55
Winter Lodge SE16 4F 93
Winterton Ho. E1 6J 73
Winterton Pl. SW10 5D 86
Winthrop Ho. W12 7A 64
Winthrop St. E1 3G 73
Wireworks Ct. SE1 5G 81
Wisden Ho. SW8 6B 90
Wisley Ho. SW1 3G 89
Wistow Ho. E2 3E 62
Witan St. E2 7H 63
Withers Pl. EC1 1H 71
Withy Ho. E1 2K 73
Witley Ct. WC1 2J 69
Woburn Ct. SE16 3H 93
Woburn Mans. *WC1 3G 69*
(off Torrington Pl.)
Woburn M. WC1 1H 69
Woburn Pl. WC1 1H 69
Woburn Sq. WC1 2H 69
Woburn Wlk. WC1 7H 59
Wodeham Gdns. E1 3F 73
Wolcot Ho. NW1 5F 59
Wolfe Ho. W12 7A 64
Wollaston Cl. SE1 1G 91
Wollaton Ho. N1 4D 60
Wollett Ct. NW1 1F 59
Wolseley St. SE1 5D 82
Wolsey Ct. NW6 1D 56
Wolsey St. E1 4J 73
Wolverley St. E2 7G 63
Wolverton SE17 3K 91
Wolverton Gdns. W6 1C 84
Wontner Cl. N1 1G 61
Woodbridge St. EC1 1E 70 (not continuous)
Woodchester Sq. W2 3A 66
Woodchurch Rd. NW6 1K 55
Wood Cl. E2 1E 72
Woodfall St. SW3 4J 87
Woodfield Pl. W9 2H 65
Woodfield Rd. W9 3H 65
Woodford Ct. W12 4C 74
Woodger Rd. W12 5B 74
Woodhall NW1 7E 58
Woodland Cres. SE16 5K 83
Woodlands Ct. NW10 3C 54
Wood La. W12 5A 64
Woodlawn Rd. SW6 7C 84
Woodman's M. W12 4A 64
Wood's Bldgs. E1 3G 73
Woodseer St. E1 3D 72
Woodsford SE17 3J 91
Woodsford Sq. W14 4F 75
Woods M. W1 7K 67
Woods Pl. SE1 7B 82
Woodstock Ct. SE11 3B 90
Woodstock Gro. W12 4D 74
Woodstock M. W1 4B 68
Woodstock St. W1 6C 68
Wood St. EC2 6H 71 (not continuous)
Woodville Ho. SE1 6C 82
Woodville Rd. NW6 4H 55
Wooler St. SE17 4J 91
Woolf M. WC1 1H 69
Woollon Ho. E1 5J 73
Woolstaplers Way SE16 7E 82
Woolstone Ho. E2 3E 62
Wooster Pl. SE1 1K 91
Wootton St. SE1 4D 80
Worcester Ct. W9 3J 65
Worcester Ho. SE11 7C 80
SW9 7D 90
W2 6C 66
Wordsworth Ho. NW6 6J 55
Wordsworth Mans. *W14 5G 85*
(off Queens Club Gdns.)
Wordsworth Rd. SE1 2D 92
Worfield St. SW11 7H 87
Worgan St. SE11 3A 90
Worlds End Est. SW10 7E 86
World's End Pas. SW10 7E 86
World's End Pl. SW10 7D 86
Worlidge St. W6 3A 84
Wormwood St. EC2 5A 72
Wornington Rd. W10 2E 64 (not continuous)
Wornum Ho. W10 5G 55
Woronzow Rd. NW8 3F 57
Worship St. EC2 2K 71
Worth Gro. SE17 4J 91
Worthington Ho. EC1 6D 60
Wrayburn Ho. SE16 5F 83
Wren Ho. SW1 4G 89
Wrenn Ho. SW13 6A 84
Wren St. WC1 1B 70
Wrentham Av. NW10 4C 54
Wrestlers Ct. EC3 5A 72
Wrigglesworth St. SE14 7K 93
Wright's La. W8 5K 75
Wrotham Ho. SE1 6K 81
Wrotham Rd. NW1 1F 59
Wyatt Dr. SW13 7A 84
Wyatt Ho. NW8 2E 66
Wybert St. NW1 1E 68
Wyclif Ct. EC1 7E 60
Wyclif St. EC1 7E 60
Wycombe Ho. NW8 1G 67
Wycombe Sq. W8 3J 75
Wykeham Ho. SE1 3G 81
Wyllen Cl. E1 2J 73
Wymering Mans. W9 7K 55 (not continuous)
Wymering Rd. W9 7K 55
Wymondham Ct. NW8 2F 57
Wyndham Deedes Ho. E2 5F 63
Wyndham Est. SE5 7H 91
Wyndham Ho. SW1 2A 88
Wyndham M. W1 4J 67
Wyndham Pl. W1 4J 67
Wyndham Rd. SE5 7F 91
Wyndhams Ct. E8 1C 62
Wyndham's Theatre 7J 69
Wyndham St. W1 3J 67
Wyndham Yd. W1 4J 67
Wynford Ho. N1 4B 60
Wynford Rd. N1 4A 60
Wynnstay Gdns. W8 6K 75
Wynyard Ho. SE11 3B 90
Wynyard Ter. SE11 3B 90
Wynyatt St. EC1 7E 60
Wytham Ho. NW8 2F 67
Wythburn Ct. W1 5J 67
Wythburn Pl. W1 6J 67
Wyvil Rd. SW8 7J 89

Y

Yalding Rd. SE16 7E 82
Yard, The *N1 5K 59*
(off Caledonian Rd.)
Yardley St. WC1 7C 60 (not continuous)
Yarmouth Pl. W1 3C 78
Yarrell Mans. W14 5G 85
Yarrow Ho. W10 3B 64
Yates Ho. E2 6F 63
Yatton Ho. W10 3B 64
Yeadon Ho. W10 3B 64
Yearby Ho. W10 2B 64
Yeate St. N1 1J 61
Yeldham Ho. W6 4C 84
Yeldham Rd. W6 4C 84
Yeldham Vs. W6 3C 84
Yeoman Ct. SE1 4D 92
Yeoman's Row SW3 7H 77
Yeoman's Yd. E1 7D 72
Yeovil Ho. W10 2A 64
Yew Ho. *SE16 5K 83*
(off Woodland Cres.)
York Av. SE17 3H 91
York Bri. NW1 1A 68
York Bldgs. WC2 1K 79
York Ga. NW1 2A 68
York Ho. SE1 7B 80
SW3 3K 87
W1 3J 67
W8 4A 76
York Ho. Pl. W8 4A 76
Yorkley Ho. W10 2A 64
York Mans. SW5 3A 86
W1 3A 68
York Pas. W8 4A 76
York Pl. WC2 1K 79
York Pl. Mans. W1 3K 67
York Rd. SE1 4B 80
Yorkshire Grey Yd. WC1 4A 70
York St. W1 4J 67
York St. Chambers W1 3J 67
York Ter. E. NW1 2B 68
York Ter. W. NW1 2A 68
Yorkton St. E2 5E 62
York Way N1 2K 59
York Way Ct. N1 3K 59
Young Ct. NW6 1E 54
Youngs Bldgs. EC1 1H 71
Young St. W8 5A 76
Young Vic Theatre, The 4D 80
Yoxall Ho. W10 2A 64

Z

Zampa Rd. SE16 4J 93
Zander Ct. E2 6F 63
Zenobia Mans. W14 5G 85
Zetland Ho. W8 6A 76
Zion Ho. E1 5J 73
Zoar St. SE1 2G 81

HOSPITALS and HOSPICES covered by this atlas.

N.B. Where Hospitals and Hospices are not named on the map, the reference given is for the road in which they are situated.

ABBEY CHURCHILL LONDON, THE 6D **80**
22 Barkham Terrace
LONDON
SE1 7PW
Tel: 020 7928 5633

CHARING CROSS HOSPITAL 5C **84**
Fulham Palace Road
LONDON
W6 8RF
Tel: 020 8846 1234

CHELSEA & WESTMINSTER HOSPITAL 6D **86**
369 Fulham Road
LONDON
SW10 9NH
Tel: 020 8746 8000

CROMWELL HOSPITAL, THE 1A **86**
162-174 Cromwell Road
LONDON
SW5 0TU
Tel: 020 7460 2000

EASTMAN DENTAL HOSPITAL & DENTAL INSTITUTE, THE 1A **70**
256 Gray's Inn Road
LONDON
WC1X 8LD
Tel: 020 7915 1000

ELIZABETH GARRETT ANDERSON & OBSTETRIC HOSPITAL, THE 2F **69**
Huntley Street
LONDON
WC1E 6DH
Tel: 0845 1555 000

EVELINA CHILDREN'S HOSPITAL 6A **80**
St Thomas' Hospital
Lambeth Palace Road
LONDON
SE1 7EH
Tel: 020 7188 7188

GORDON HOSPITAL 2G **89**
Bloomburg Street
LONDON
SW1V 2RH
Tel: 020 8746 8733

GREAT ORMOND STREET HOSPITAL FOR CHILDREN 2K **69**
Great Ormond Street
LONDON
WC1N 3JH
Tel: 020 7405 9200

GUY'S HOSPITAL 3K **81**
St Thomas Street
LONDON
SE1 9RT
Tel: 020 7188 7188

GUY'S NUFFIELD HOUSE 4J **81**
Newcomen Street
LONDON
SE1 1YR
Tel: 020 7188 5292

HARLEY STREET CLINIC 3C **68**
35 Weymouth Street
LONDON
W1G 8BJ
Tel: 020 7935 7700

HEART HOSPITAL, THE 4B **68**
16-18 Westmoreland Street
LONDON
W1G 8PH
Tel: 020 7573 8888

HOSPITAL FOR TROPICAL DISEASES 2F **69**
Mortimer Market,
Capper Street
LONDON
WC1E 6AU
Tel: 020 7387 9300

HOSPITAL OF ST JOHN & ST ELIZABETH 5E **56**
60 Grove End Road
LONDON
NW8 9NH
Tel: 020 7806 4000

KING EDWARD VII'S HOSPITAL SISTER AGNES 3B **68**
5-10 Beaumont Street
LONDON
W1G 6AA
Tel: 020 7486 4411

LATIMER DAY HOSPITAL 3E **68**
40 Hanson Street
LONDON
W1W 6UL
Tel: 020 7612 1645

LISTER HOSPITAL, THE 4C **88**
Chelsea Bridge Road
LONDON
SW1W 8RH
Tel: 020 7730 3417

LONDON BRIDGE HOSPITAL 2K **81**
27 Tooley Street
LONDON
SE1 2PR
Tel: 020 7407 3100

LONDON CHEST HOSPITAL 4K **63**
Bonner Road
LONDON
E2 9JX
Tel: 020 7377 7000

LONDON CLINIC, THE 2B **68**
20 Devonshire Place
LONDON
W1G 6BW
Tel: 020 7935 4444

LONDON INDEPENDENT BMI HOSPITAL, THE 3K **73**
1 Beaumont Square
LONDON
E1 4NL
Tel: 020 7780 2400

LONDON WELBECK HOSPITAL 4C **68**
27 Welbeck Street
LONDON
W1G 8EN
Tel: 020 7224 2242

MIDDLESEX HOSPITAL, THE 4F **69**
Mortimer Street
LONDON
W1T 3AA
Tel: 020 7636 8333

MILDMAY MISSION HOSPITAL (HOSPICE) 7C **62**
Hackney Road
LONDON
E2 7NA
Tel: 020 7613 6300

MOORFIELDS EYE HOSPITAL 7J **61**
162 City Road
LONDON
EC1V 2PD
Tel: 020 7253 3411

NATIONAL HOSPITAL FOR NEUROLOGY & NEUROSURGERY, THE 2K **69**
Queen Square
LONDON
WC1N 3BG
Tel: 020 7837 3611

NHS WALK-IN CENTRE (CHARING CROSS) 4C **84**
Charing Cross Hospital
Fulham Palace Road
LONDON
W6 8RF
Tel: 020 8846 1234

NHS WALK-IN CENTRE (LIVERPOOL STREET) 3B **72**
Exchange Arcade
Bishopsgate
LONDON
EC2M 3WA
Tel: 0845 880 1242

NHS WALK-IN CENTRE (SOHO) 6G **69**
1 Frith Street
LONDON
W1D 3HZ
Tel: 020 7534 6500

NHS WALK-IN CENTRE (WHITECHAPEL) 4G **73**
The Royal London Hospital
174 Whitechapel Road
LONDON
E1 1BZ
Tel: 020 7943 1333

NIGHTINGALE CAPIO DAY HOSPITAL 3H **67**
1b Harewood Row
LONDON
NW1 6SE
Tel: 020 7725 9940

NIGHTINGALE CAPIO HOSPITAL (ENFORD STREET) 3J **67**
23-24 Enford Street
LONDON
W1H 1DG
Tel: 020 7723 3635

NIGHTINGALE CAPIO HOSPITAL (LISSON GROVE) 3H **67**
11-19 Lisson Grove
LONDON
NW1 6SH
Tel: 020 7535 7700

NIGHTINGALE CAPIO HOSPITAL (RADNOR WALK) 4H **87**
1-5 Radnor Walk
LONDON
SW3 4BP
Tel: 020 7349 3900

PEMBRIDGE PALLIATIVE CARE CENTRE, THE 3C **64**
St Charles Hospital
Exmoor Street
LONDON
W10 6DZ
Tel: 020 8962 4410 / 4411

PORTLAND HOSPITAL FOR WOMEN & CHILDREN, THE 2D **68**
205-209 Great Portland Street
LONDON
W1W 5AH
Tel: 020 7580 4400

PRINCESS GRACE HOSPITAL (OUTPATIENTS), THE 3B **68**
30 Devonshire Street
LONDON
W1G 6PU
Tel: 020 7908 3602

PRINCESS GRACE HOSPITAL, THE 3A **68**
42-52 Nottingham Place
LONDON
W1U 5NY
Tel: 020 7486 1234

PRINCESS LOUISE DAY HOSPITAL 4C **64**
St. Quintin Avenue
LONDON
W10 6DL
Tel: 020 8969 0133

ROYAL BROMPTON HOSPITAL 3G **87**
Sydney Street
LONDON
SW3 6NP
Tel: 020 7352 8121

ROYAL BROMPTON HOSPITAL (FULHAM WING) 3F **87**
Fulham Road
LONDON
SW3 6HP
Tel: 020 7352 8121

ROYAL LONDON HOMOEOPATHIC HOSPITAL, THE 3K **69**
Great Ormond Street
LONDON
WC1N 3HR
Tel: 0845 1555 000

ROYAL LONDON HOSPITAL, THE 4G **73**
Whitechapel Road
LONDON
E1 1BB
Tel: 020 7377 7000

ROYAL MARSDEN HOSPITAL (FULHAM), THE 3F **87**
Fulham Road
LONDON
SW3 6JJ
Tel: 020 7352 8171

ROYAL NATIONAL ORTHOPAEDIC HOSPITAL (CENTRAL LONDON OUTPATIENT DEPT.) 2D **68**
45-51 Bolsover Street
LONDON
W1W 5AQ
Tel: 020 7387 5070

ROYAL NATIONAL THROAT, NOSE & EAR HOSPITAL 6A **60**
330 Gray's Inn Road
LONDON
WC1X 8DA
Tel: 020 7915 1300

ST BARTHOLOMEW'S HOSPITAL 4F **71**
West Smithfield
LONDON
EC1A 7BE
Tel: 020 7377 7000

ST CHARLES HOSPITAL 3C **64**
Exmoor Street
LONDON
W10 6DZ
Tel: 020 8969 2488

ST JOHN'S HOSPICE 5E **56**
Hospital of St John & St Elizabeth
60 Grove End Road
LONDON
NW8 9NH
Tel: 020 7806 4040

ST JOSEPH'S HOSPICE 2H **63**
Mare Street
LONDON
E8 4SA
Tel: 020 8525 6000

ST LUKE'S HOSPITAL FOR THE CLERGY 2E **68**
14 Fitzroy Square
LONDON
W1T 6AH
Tel: 020 7388 4954

ST MARY'S HOSPITAL 5F **67**
Praed Street
LONDON
W2 1NY
Tel: 020 7725 6666

ST PANCRAS HOSPITAL 3G **59**
4 St Pancras Way
LONDON
NW1 0PE
Tel: 020 7530 3500

ST THOMAS' HOSPITAL 6A **80**
Lambeth Palace Road
LONDON
SE1 7EH
Tel: 020 7188 7188

UNIVERSITY COLLEGE HOSPITAL 1F **69**
235 Euston Road
LONDON
NW1 2BU
Tel: 0845 1555000

WELLINGTON HOSPITAL, THE 6F **57**
8a Wellington Place
LONDON
NW8 9LE
Tel: 020 7586 5959

WESTERN EYE HOSPITAL 3J **67**
171 Marylebone Road
LONDON
NW1 5QH
Tel: 020 7886 6666

RAIL, DOCKLANDS LIGHT RAILWAY, RIVERBUS AND LONDON UNDERGROUND STATIONS

with their map square reference

A

Aldgate (Tube) 6C 72
Aldgate East (Tube) 5D 72
Angel (Tube) 4D 60

B

Baker Street (Tube) 2K 67
Bank (Tube & DLR) 6J 71
Bankside Pier (Riverbus) 1G 81
Barbican (Rail & Tube) 3G 71
Barons Court (Tube) 3E 84
Bayswater (Tube) 7B 66
Bermondsey (Tube) 6F 83
Bethnal Green (Rail) 1G 73
Bethnal Green (Tube) 7J 63
Blackfriars (Rail & Tube) 7E 70
Blackfriars Millennium Pier (Riverbus) 7D 70
Bond Street (Tube) 6C 68
Borough (Tube) 5H 81
Brondesbury Park (Rail) 2E 54

C

Cadogan Pier (Riverbus) 6H 87
Caledonian Road & Barnsbury (Rail) 1A 60
Cambridge Heath (Rail) 5H 63
Camden Road (Rail) 1E 58
Camden Town (Tube) 2D 58
Canada Water (Tube) 6K 83
Cannon Street (Rail & Tube) 7J 71
Chancery Lane (Tube) 4C 70
Charing Cross (Rail & Tube) 2J 79
City Thameslink (Rail) 5E 70
Covent Garden (Tube) 6K 69

E

Earl's Court (Tube) 3K 85
Edgware Road (Tube) 4G 67
Elephant & Castle (Rail & Tube) 1G 91
Embankment (Tube) 2K 79
Embankment Pier (Riverbus) 2K 79
Essex Road (Rail) 1G 61
Euston (Rail & Tube) 7G 59
Euston Square (Tube) 1F 69

F

Farringdon (Rail & Tube) 3E 70
Fenchurch Street (Rail) 7B 72
Festival Pier (Riverbus) 2A 80
Fulham Broadway (Tube) 7K 85

G

Gloucester Road (Tube) 1C 86
Goldhawk Road (Tube) 5A 74
Goodge Street (Tube) 3G 69
Great Portland Street (Tube) 2D 68
Green Park (Tube) 2D 78

H

Hammersmith (Tube) 2B 84
High Street Kensington (Tube) 5A 76
Holborn (Tube) 4A 70
Holland Park (Tube) 3G 75
Hyde Park Corner (Tube) 4B 78

K

Kennington (Tube) 3E 90
Kensal Green (Rail & Tube) 6A 54
Kensal Rise (Rail) 5C 54
Kensington Olympia (Rail & Tube) 7F 75
Kilburn High Road (Rail) 3K 55
Kilburn Park (Tube) 4K 55
King's Cross (Rail & Tube) 5J 59
King's Cross St Pancras (Tube) 6J 59
Knightsbridge (Tube) 5K 77

L

Ladbroke Grove (Tube) 5F 65
Lambeth North (Tube) 6C 80
Lancaster Gate (Tube) 7E 66
Latimer Road (Tube) 7D 64
Leicester Square (Tube) 7H 69
Liverpool Street (Rail & Tube) 4A 72
London Bridge (Rail & Tube) 3K 81
London Bridge City Pier (Riverbus) 2A 82
London Fields (Rail) 1H 63

M

Maida Vale (Tube) 6B 56
Mansion House (Tube) 7H 71
Marble Arch (Tube) 6K 67
Marylebone (Rail & Tube) 2J 67
Millbank Millennium Pier (Riverbus) 2K 89
Monument (Tube) 7K 71
Moorgate (Rail & Tube) 4J 71
Mornington Crescent (Tube) 4E 58

N

Notting Hill Gate (Tube) 2J 75

O

Old Street (Rail & Tube) 1J 71
Oval (Tube) 6C 90
Oxford Circus (Tube) 5E 68

P

Paddington (Rail & Tube) 5E 66
Piccadilly Circus (Tube) 1G 79
Pimlico (Tube) 3G 89

Q

Queen's Park (Rail & Tube) 5G 55
Queensway (Tube) 1B 76

R

Regent's Park (Tube) 2C 68
Rotherhithe (Tube) 4K 83
Royal Oak (Tube) 4B 66
Russell Square (Tube) 2J 69

S

St James's Park (Tube) 6G 7
St John's Wood (Tube) 4E 5
St Katharine's Pier (Riverbus) 2D 8
St Pancras International (Rail) 6J 5
St Paul's (Tube) 5G 7
Savoy Pier (Riverbus) 1A 8
Shadwell (Tube & DLR) 7H 7
Shepherd's Bush (Rail & Tube) 4C 7
Shepherd's Bush (Tube) 3A 7
Sloane Square (Tube) 2A 8
South Bermondsey (Rail) 3J 9
South Hampstead (Rail) 1D 5
South Kensington (Tube) 1F 8
Southwark (Tube) 3E 8
Stepney Green (Tube) 2K 7
Surrey Quays (Tube) 1K 9
Swiss Cottage (Tube) 1E 5

T

Temple (Tube) 7B 7
Tottenham Court Road (Tube) 5H 6
Tower Gateway (DLR) 7C 7
Tower Hill (Tube) 7C 7
Tower Millennium Pier (Riverbus) 2B 8

V

Vauxhall (Rail & Tube) 4K 8
Victoria (Rail & Tube) 7D 7
Victoria Coach (Bus) 2D 88

W

Wapping (Tube) 3J 83
Warren Street (Tube) 1F 69
Warwick Avenue (Tube) 2C 66
Waterloo (Rail & Tube) 4C 80
Waterloo East (Rail) 4C 80
Waterloo International (Rail) 4B 80
Waterloo Millennium Pier (Riverbus) 4A 80
Westbourne Park (Tube) 3H 65
West Brompton (Rail & Tube) 4K 85
West Kensington (Tube) 3G 85
Westminster (Tube) 5K 79
Westminster Millennium Pier (Riverbus) 4K 79
Whitechapel (Tube) 3G 73
White City (Tube) 1B 74
Wood Lane (Tube) 1B 74